FUNDAMENTALS OF PARALEGALISM

FUNDAMENTALS OF PARALEGALISM

Second Edition

Thomas E. Eimermann

Coordinator of Legal Studies
Illinois State University

LITTLE, BROWN AND COMPANY

Boston   Toronto

Library of Congress Catalog Card No. 86-81465

ISBN 0-316-23119-3

Sixth Printing

Second Edition

MV PA

Published simultaneously in Canada
by Little, Brown & Company (Canada) Limited

Printed in the United States of America

To my parents

Summary of Contents

Contents

Table of Illustrations

Forms

Exhibits

Preface

This text for introductory paralegal and legal assistant courses discusses the role played by the legal assistant in the American legal system and provides materials designed to develop basic paralegal skills. It discusses the legal facts and concepts that a paralegal needs to understand and then describes what paralegals do and how they do it. The presentation does not assume any previous legal knowledge and carefully defines the legal terms introduced.

Part I introduces the paralegal profession, exploring the historical development of the paralegal movement, the variety of tasks that paralegals perform, and the advantages and disadvantages of pursuing a paralegal career. Part II discusses the larger legal environment within which paralegals function: the organization of the court system; sources of the law; basic substantive legal concepts; civil, criminal, and administrative procedures; and the organization and operation of law offices. Part III focuses on the basic skills that paralegals exercise in their jobs: interviewing and investigation, legal research, legal writing, and advocacy roles in legal proceedings. In Part IV the book discusses the paralegal's professional responsibilities, including the various legal and ethical requirements that affect paralegals.

Those who are familiar with the first edition of Fundamentals of Paralegalism will note that information has been reorganized and updated and a considerable amount of new material has been added, including chapters on law office administration and an introduction to substantive legal concepts in the areas of tort, contract, property, corporate, criminal, administrative, and constitutional law. References to how modern computer technology has affected the practice of law have also been added to several chapters. I have attempted to retain the simplicity of language and ease of reading that helped to make the first edition so popular.

Naturally, I owe a great deal of thanks to the many students, educators, paralegals, and attorneys who contributed ideas for both the original edition and this revision. Especially deserving of recognition are Marge Dover, John Gurdak, Amy Inlander, James Knecht, Suzanne Little, Fred Moore, Harry Poling, Jack Porter, Charles Reynard, Sandra Sabanske, Barbara Schmidt, and Tom Smith. I am also indebted to Au-

drey Meurer and Michelle Chaparro for their assistance in proofreading and indexing and to Rosemary Winfield for her superb work as copy-editor. Finally, a special thanks goes to my wife Kathy, my son Tim, and my daughter Jill for their understanding and support.

November 1986   Thomas Eimermann

Acknowledgments

I am grateful to copyright holders for permission to reprint excerpts from the following items:

American Bar Association, excerpts from various copyrighted materials. All rights reserved. Reprinted with permission.

American Jurisprudence, Proof of Facts, vol. 7, pp. 595-596. Copyright © 1960. Reprinted with permission of The Lawyers Co-operative Publishing Co.

American Jurisprudence 2d, vol. 49. Copyright © 1970. Reprinted with permission of the Lawyers Co-operative Publishing Co.

American Jurisprudence Trials, vol. 12, pp. 287-288. Copyright © 1966. Reprinted with permission of The Lawyers Co-operative Publishing Co.

American Law Reports, 3d series, vol. 40. Copyright © 1971. Quick Index. Copyright © 1973. Reprinted with permission of The Lawyers Co-operative Publishing Co.

Benjamin, Alfred, The Helping Interview, 3d ed. Copyright © 1981 by Houghton Mifflin Company. Used by permission.

Binder, D., and P. Berman, Fact Investigation. Copyright © 1984. Reprinted with permission of the West Publishing Company.

Corpus Juris Secundum, vol. A. Copyright © 1959. Vols. 51C, 52A. Copyright © 1969. Reprinted with permission of the West Publishing Company.

Eighth Decennial Digest, vol. 28. Copyright © 1978. Reprinted with permission of the West Publishing Company.

General Digest, index. Copyright © 1978. Reprinted with permission of the West Publishing Company.

Illinois Civil Practice Forms, vol. 7, pp. 298-299. Copyright © 1975. Reprinted with permission of Callaghan & Co., 3201 Old Glenview Road, Wilmette, IL 60091.

Illinois Law and Practice, Landlord and Tenant Volume. Copyright © 1956. Reprinted with permission of the West Publishing Company.

Index to Legal Periodicals. Copyright © 1976, 1977, 1978 by The H. W. Wilson Company. Material reproduced by permission of the publisher.

Llewellyn, Karl, The Common Law Tradition 522-529. Copyright ©
    1960. Reprinted with permission of Little, Brown and Company.
National Association of Legal Assistants, Code of Ethics and Professional
    Responsibility. Copyright © 1977. Published with permission of the
    National Association of Legal Assistants, Inc., 1420 South Utica,
    Tulsa, OK 74104.
———, Model Standards and Guidelines for Utilization of Legal Assis-
    tants. Copyright © 1977, 1985. Published with permission of the Na-
    tional Association of Legal Assistants, Inc., 1420 South Utica, Tulsa,
    OK 74104.
National Federation of Paralegal Associations, Affirmation of Responsi-
    bility. Copyright © 1977. Reprinted with permission of the National
    Federation of Paralegal Associations, Inc.
Nichols Cyclopedia of Legal Forms Annotated, vol. 5B. Copyright ©
    1985. Vol. 9B, copyright © 1983.
Northeastern Reporter, 2d series, vol. 280, pp. 208-209. Copyright ©
    1972. Reprinted with permission of the West Publishing Company.
Shepard's North Eastern Reporter Citations, vol. 2, p. 1583. Copyright
    © 1974. Reprinted with permission of Shepard's Citations, Inc.
Shepard's United States Citations, 1975 supp. to 1970 edition, p. 75.
    Copyright © 1975. Reprinted with permission of Shepard's Citations,
    Inc.
Smith-Hurd Annotated, tit. 38, p. 426. Copyright © 1972. Reprinted
    with permission of the West Publishing Company.
United States Code Annotated, tit. 15, p. 399, index vol., p. 41. Copy-
    right © 1975. Reprinted with permission of the West Publishing Com-
    pany.

FUNDAMENTALS
OF
PARALEGALISM

PART I
Introduction to the Profession

THE PARALEGAL MOVEMENT was born in the late 1960s, established its legitimacy in the early 1970s, and underwent tremendous growth in the late 1970s. The phenomenal growth rate has not only carried over into this decade but is expected to continue well into the next. Today, there is little doubt about the viability of the movement and the important role that paralegals will play in the future delivery of legal services in the United States.

Chapter 1 explores the historical development of the paralegal movement, the qualifications and training required of paralegals, the tasks that paralegals perform, and the advantages and disadvantages of a paralegal career. More detailed coverage of paralegal tasks and skills is contained in Part III, while an analysis of legal and ethical restrictions is contained in Part IV.

Chapter 1
Paralegalism: What's in a Name?

PARALEGAL, LEGAL ASSISTANT, lay assistant, legal technician, document clerk, lay advocate, and law clerk: All these labels have been used at one time or another to identify an individual who lacks membership in the bar but nevertheless carries out a variety of important legal tasks. The prefix *para* carries the meanings of "near" or "beside" and "similar to" or "subordinate to." The derivation of the word therefore suggests that a paralegal is one who works near or beside a lawyer or one who is subordinate to a lawyer. Paralegals are similar to lawyers in that both have knowledge of the law and have developed skills required to work with legal problems. Because paralegals are not licensed to practice law, there are many situations in which they must work beside or under the direction of a lawyer who is licensed to practice.

Paralegals are thus individuals with specialized legal training who perform such functions as gathering and analyzing facts relevant to legal disputes, performing legal research, drafting legal documents, preparing witnesses and evidence for presentation at legal proceedings, and even representing clients in some types of administrative hearings. A well-trained paralegal working under the supervision of an attorney can do just about anything except give legal advice to clients and represent clients in most types of judicial proceedings.

In 1971 the American Bar Association's Standing Committee on Ethics and Responsibility adopted *legal assistant* as the preferred designation for a person performing paralegal functions,[1] and the Special Committee on Lay Assistants for Lawyers became the Special Committee on Legal Assistants. It was not until 1986, however, that the ABA agreed on a formal definition of what a legal assistant was.[2] Seeking to limit the application of the term to "those persons who have achieved the education and experience required for the job"[3] and who performed work that

---

1. ABA Informal Opinion 1185 (1971).
2. ABA Standing Committee on Legal Assistants, Position Paper on the Question of Legal Assistant Licensure or Certification (Dec. 10, 1985). This position paper was approved by the ABA board of governors at its February 1986 meeting.
3. Id. at 4.

3

commonly was done by lawyers, the board of governors accepted the Standing Committee's definition that:

> A legal assistant is a person, qualified through education, training, or work experience, who is employed or retained by a lawyer, law office, governmental agency, or other entity in a capacity or function which involves the performance, under the ultimate direction and supervision of an attorney, of specifically-delegated substantive legal work, which work, for the most part, requires a sufficient knowledge of legal concepts that, absent such assistant, the attorney would perform the task.[4]

A. HISTORICAL DEVELOPMENT AND RECOGNITION

1. Early Forms of Practice

At the time the United States was founded a general distrust of lawyers led to an attempt to get along without them.[5] Many of the old justice of the peace systems did not require that judges have legal training. As the nation evolved, it soon became apparent that lawyers did serve an essential function, and they rapidly dominated both the legal and the political systems.

Before the twentieth century legal education in the United States was haphazard, and access to the profession was widely obtainable. Lawyers learned the law by serving an apprenticeship or clerkship with a practicing attorney and simply reading the law. Permission to practice was obtained by presenting themselves to a local judge for examination. Without any set standards the admission criteria differed widely, and personal influence was an inevitable factor. Since judges usually abided by the decisions of their colleagues, the standards for admission were determined by the most lenient judge in the state.[6]

These attorneys operated almost totally on their own. Most were sole practitioners, and they did not even use secretaries. The apprentice law clerks assisted in the longhand preparation of legal documents, but most contributed little else to the attorney's practice.[7] Indeed, rather than being paid for their contributions, many had to pay the attorney for the privilege of occupying a desk in his office.[8]

---

4. Id. at 4.
5. 1 A. Chroust, The Rise of the Legal Profession in America 27 (1965). See also J. Hurst, The Growth of American Law 251 (1950).
6. Hurst, supra note 3, at 276.
7. P. Hamlin, Legal Education in Colonial New York 35 (1939).
8. J. Beale, The History of Legal Education, in 1 Law: A Century of Progress 1835-1935 at 105 (1937).

2. Development of the Need for Paralegals

The introduction of the typewriter and the telephone, along with the movement toward partnership arrangements, led most attorneys to hire lay assistants for such clerical duties as answering the telephone, typing letters and documents, and keeping the account books. After the development of law schools replaced the old apprenticeship or clerkship arrangement, some attorneys used law school students as research clerks. Most attorneys, however, resisted delegating any of their legal tasks.

At the same time, several major professional groups had begun to make extensive use of paraprofessionals. This movement was led by medical doctors who, even prior to the Civil War, had begun using nurses as paraprofessionals. The doctors learned that by delegating such tasks as taking temperatures and giving injections they had more time to devote to what they considered to be the more challenging and rewarding aspects of their profession. As the sophistication of the medical sciences grew, so too did the diversity of paraprofessionals. Today the field is populated by such positions as registered nurses, licensed practical nurses, and nurses' aides; by physical therapists, occupational therapists, and inhalation therapists; and by radiologic technologists, laboratory technicians, operating room technicians, and medical records technicians. According to one estimate there are now approximately eleven paramedical personnel for every doctor in this country.[9] Other professionals who have made extensive use of paraprofessionals include dentists, architects, teachers, and law enforcement personnel.

The fact that the average medical doctor's income was more than twice that of the average lawyer was one factor that eventually led attorneys to seriously consider increased use of paraprofessionals,[10] and by the 1960s articles in professional journals began to advocate the need for broader delegation to lay personnel and even "the creation of a subprofessional class comparable to medical technicians."[11]

The American Bar Association's Special Committee of Legal Assistants commissioned Kline Strong of the University of Utah Law Research Institute to study the economics of using paralegals. Strong studied 104 law firms of four partners or less. He analyzed typical legal tasks in terms of tasks performed by a lawyer, tasks performed by a paralegal, and tasks performed by a secretary. He then calculated how

---

9. W. Statsky, Introduction to Paralegalism 18 (2d ed. 1982).
10. In an address to an Illinois Institute for Continuing Legal Education Workshop on October 20, 1973, Kline Strong (a prominent leader in the paralegal movement) made direct reference to this income differential as an incentive for making more extensive use of paralegals.
11. McCalpin, A Revolution in the Law Practice?, 15 Clev.-Mar. L. Rev. 203 (1966). See also Baker, Use Nonlawyers, 5 L. Office Econ. & Mgmt. 434 (1965); Williams, The Use of Nonlegal Personnel in a Law Office, 6 Prac. Law. 13 (1960).

much money would be saved by using a paralegal as opposed to the lawyer and secretary alone. Figuring an hourly rate at $3.00 per hour for secretaries, $5.00 per hour for paralegals, and $40.00 per hour for lawyers, Strong concluded that the firm using a paralegal could form a corporation for a client for $127.50, while it would cost the nonparalegal firm $253.50 in billable time. If the firm charged a flat $300 fee for the act of forming a corporation, it could increase its profit from $46.50 to $172.50, while leaving the attorney with 3.5 extra hours to spend on other cases. The secret, says Strong, is to have each procedure completed by the least expensive persons competent to handle that procedure. Even if the attorney were to save just one hour a day through utilization of a paralegal, he would be freeing himself to earn another $9,600 per year at the billable rate of $40.00 per hour. Spread over a twenty-five year period, that one hour of paralegal assistance could increase an attorney's income by $240,000.[12]

3. American Bar Association Recognition and Encouragement

While both governmental agencies and private law firms had been having lay personnel perform some paralegal functions, the established bar did not really begin to give much attention to the paralegal situation until the late 1960s. In 1967 the American Bar Association (ABA) issued a significant formal ethics opinion that clarified the legitimacy of delegating legal work to nonlawyers.[13] When the association's revised Code of Professional Responsibility and Canons of Judicial Ethics was promulgated in 1969, Ethical Consideration 3-6 favorably supported the extensive use of paralegals. In August 1968 the ABA's House of Delegates adopted Report Number 3 of the association's Special Committee on Availability of Legal Services. That report contained the following recommendation:

> Recognizing that freeing a lawyer from tedious and routine detail thus conserving his time and energy for truly legal problems will enable him to render his professional services to more people, thereby making legal services more fully available to the public, this Committee recommends:
>
> 1. That the legal profession recognize that there are many tasks in serving a client's needs which can be performed by a trained, non-lawyer assistant working under the direction and supervision of a lawyer;
> 2. That the profession encourage the training and employment of such employees; and

---

12. ABA Special Committee on Legal Assistants, Liberating the Lawyer: The Utilization of Legal Assistants by Law Firms in the United States 43 (1971).
13. ABA Opinion 316 (1967).

3. That there be created a special committee of this Association to consider:

   (a) The kinds of tasks which may be competently performed by a nonlawyer working under the direction and supervision of a lawyer;

   (b) The nature of the training which may be required is provided to develop competence and proficiency in the performance of such tasks;

   (c) The role, if any, to be played by the legal profession and the bar in providing such training;

   (d) The desirability of recognizing competence and proficiency in such assistants as by academic recognition or other suitable means; and

   (e) All appropriate methods for developing, encouraging, and increasing the training and utilization of nonlawyer assistants to better enable lawyers to discharge their professional responsibilities.[14]

The association then formed the Special Committee on Lay Assistants for Lawyers to carry out recommendation number three.

In 1971 this special ABA committee (renamed the Special Committee on Legal Assistants) released preliminary drafts of reports reviewing the use of paraprofessionals in other professions, reporting the results of research done on paralegal usage, and suggesting guidelines for the training of paralegals.[15] This special committee was awarded the status of a standing committee in 1975. Since that time it has actively sought to encourage the continued growth in the use of paralegals by granting approval status to educational programs that meet the ABA's criteria and publishing materials designed to help practitioners make efficient use of paralegals.[16]

In 1972 the National Paralegal Institute was founded under an Office of Economic Opportunity (OEO) grant with the charge of supporting and promoting the use of paralegals in public sectors of the law (especially in legal services offices). It was designed to assist in the development of training programs and materials and in ensuring that the certification process would not needlessly cripple paralegal use in the public sector.[17]

4. Growth in Use of Paralegals

The attention that the ABA gave to the use of lay legal assistants corresponded to a major increase in paralegal usage throughout the

14. ABA Special Committee, supra note 10, at v.
15. ABA Special Committee on Legal Assistants, Training for Legal Assistants (1971), Proposed Curriculum for Training of Law Office Personnel (1971), Liberating the Lawyer (1971), The Paraprofessional in Medicine, Dentistry, and Architecture (1971).
16. See Working with Legal Assistants (P. Ulrich and R. Mucklestone ed. 1980, 1981) and Legal Assistant Update (C. Farren and R. Larson ed. 1980, 1981, 1983, 1984).
17. Frey, A Short Review of the Paralegal Movement, 7 Clearinghouse Rev. 466 (1973).

entire profession. In a 1983 survey of randomly selected ABA members, 54 percent of the respondents stated that their firms employed parale-gals.[18] While Strong's study demonstrated that using paralegals was profitable for small firms as well as large, the large firms have made the greatest use of them. According to figures compiled in the 1985 National Law Journal survey of the country's 250 largest law firms, the Houston based firm of Vinson and Elkins is the largest employer of paralegals among private law firms. This firm employed 149 paralegals to support its 391 attorneys; three other firms in the survey employed more than 100 paralegals. Among firms with ninety to 100 lawyers the number of paralegals employed ranged from five to thirty-six, with twenty being the median. Only one firm reported not using paralegals at all.[19] Large firms adapt to the use of paralegals rapidly because they tended to be more specialized and to do a higher volume of business than smaller firms. They also are likely to have more efficient management systems and to have made delegation (to junior associates) a common practice.

Government agencies also have been quick to adapt to the use of paralegals. Since these agencies operate within fixed budgets and cannot simply pass the cost of their services on to clients, paralegals present a way for them to stretch limited resources. The Justice Department has used paralegals since 1964, calling them legal research analysts rather than legal assistants. The Federal Trade Commission, the Equal Employ-ment Opportunity Commission, the National Labor Relations Board, and the Environmental Protection Agency all use paralegal investigators. The Department of Health and Human Services' Bureau of Hearings and Appeals began to use lay employees to prepare and present disabil-ity cases,[20] and the Interstate Commerce Commission has revised its rules to delegate to paralegals the task of processing applications.[21]

The legal services programs funded by the Office of Economic Opportunity also make widespread use of paralegals to stretch its limited resources. One survey conducted in the early 1970s showed that 45 percent of the agency's offices employed paralegals. While most used only one or two, a few had as many as twenty.[22] By 1977 the Legal Services corporation (successor to the old OEO program) employed ap-proximately 1,300 paralegals, and approximately 60 percent of their programs used paralegals in administrative hearings.[23]

---

18. Law Poll, 69 A.B.A.J. 1626 (1983).
19. Annual Survey of the Nation's Largest Law Firms, Natl. L.J., Sept. 30, 1985, special section.
20. Frey, supra note 15, at 464.
21. Interstate Commerce Commission, Revision of Application Procedures, Ex Parte No. 55 (Sub no. 25) (1977).
22. Bar Association of Metropolitan St. Louis, Sample Feasibility Survey Questionnaire Results of Survey 463 (1968). This survey was related to the proposed establishment of a legal assistant training program at Meramac Community College.
23. C. Day-Jermany, Status Report on Paralegal Training and Career Development 2, 18 (1977).

State administrative agencies also use paralegals in their operations, roughly paralleling those at the federal level. Even some state
legislatures use paralegals on their committee staffs. In Illinois, for example, the Joint Committee on Administrative Rules created the position of a rules analyst for a nonlawyer to assist in research of proposed
rulemaking and existing agency rules and regulations.[24]

In addition to law offices and governmental agencies, banks, insurance companies, and other private corporations use paralegals. Banks
are most likely to employ them in their trust departments, while insurance companies frequently employ paralegals in claims work as well as in
their corporate law departments. Paralegals are also hired by trade associations and lobbying groups.

Indeed, the paralegal profession has grown so rapidly and in such
diverse directions that it is difficult to determine its true size. The United
States Department of Labor's Bureau of Labor Statistics estimated the
number of paralegal jobs at 28,000 in 1978 and projected that by 1990
the number of paralegal positions would increase to 66,000.[25] However,
by 1983 some writers estimated that there were already 80,000 paralegals.[26] Then in late 1985 Department of Labor statisticians rated the
paralegal profession as the fastest growing in the nation and predicted a
98 percent increase to a projected level of 104,000 jobs by 1995.[27]

5. Paralegal Organizations

As the number of paralegals has grown, paralegals have formed
associations to advance their professional interests. Two major national
organizations emerged in the mid-1970s in response to these needs representing differing viewpoints on some issues.

The National Federation of Paralegal Associations (NFPA) was
formed in June of 1974 as a federation of eight existing local paralegal
groups. The national umbrella organization was formed to improve
communication among local associations and to speak on issues of common concern. In fact, hearings held before the Senate Committee on the
Judiciary's Subcommittee on Representation of Citizens' Interests were
the impetus for forming the NFPA. The associations needed a representative speaking for their interests before the committee because these
hearings were held to determine whether the federal government should
regulate paralegals.[28] By 1985 the NFPA was an association of thirty-
four local affiliates representing over 8,200 paralegals. From its adminis-

---

24. Quoted from official announcement of the Joint Committee on Administrative Rules
of the Illinois General Assembly, Oct. 1, 1978.
25. Hussey, The Paralegal Profession: Here to Stay, 2 Legal Assistant Today 19 (1984).
26. Gilhool, Working Together: Professional and Paraprofessional, Trial 54 (1978); Simon, Paralegals: The Hottest Job Market, Natl. L.J., July 4, 1983, at 1.
27. Where the Jobs Will Be, U.S. News & World Rep. 45 (Dec. 23, 1985).
28. NFPA/NALA Focus: Two Perspectives, 3 Legal Assistant Update 81, 84 (1983).

trative offices in Chicago it publishes a bimonthly newsletter entitled the
National Paralegal Reporter.

In contrast to the federated structure of the NFPA, the National
Association of Legal Assistants is a direct membership organization with
approximately 3,500 paralegal members. They have local affiliate
groups, but membership in those groups is independent of membership
at the national level. The NALA was formed in 1975 as an outgrowth of
the Legal Assistant Section of the National Association of Legal Secretaries. It maintains administrative offices in Tulsa, Oklahoma, and
publishes both a bimonthly newsletter for its members and a bimonthly
magazine called Facts and Findings.

In 1985 another group, Professional Legal Assistants, Inc., was
formed in Raleigh, North Carolina, by some former members of NALA.
It publishes the PLA Newsletter. It is too early to know whether this third
group will be able to recruit a substantial membership or have much
influence on the profession.

These organizations all seek to promote the paralegal profession
and to monitor activities of bar associations and legislatures that might
affect their members' interests. NFPA and NALA have developed a formal set of ethical guidelines that their members are pledged to follow.[29]
PLA takes the position that a special code is not necessary because the
sections of the ABA Model Rules of Professional Practice that relate to
paralegals provide sufficient guidance for their members. PLA is establishing a foundation to provide loans and scholarships for paralegal education. The major philosophical difference between NFPA and NALA
centers on their positions regarding certification and the nature of the
relationship between paralegals and bar associations.[30]

While there are some drawbacks in not having a single organization
that can speak for the entire paralegal profession, the existence of competing organizations demonstrates the diversity of the profession.

6. Associate Membership in Bar Associations

Associate membership status in the American Bar Association and
in state and local bar associations is another form of recognition of the
growth and importance of paralegals. The ABA is currently discussing a
proposal that would offer paralegals the opportunity to become associate
members. Several state bar associations either have already adopted or
are considering such plans. The National Association of Legal Assistants
generally favors such plans because they are perceived as helping to
develop a "team approach," strengthening CLE programs, and increas-

---

29. See Chapter 11 for a discussion of the content and the role of these guidelines.
30. The certification controversy and the issue of associate membership in bar associations
    is discussed below and on pages 15-22 of this chapter. The association's ethical codes
    are discussed in Chapter 11.

ing the professional image of the paralegal. In responding to the ABA proposal on this subject, the National Federation of Paralegal Associations has expressed concern over the manner in which eligibility is defined, the lack of guaranteed access to sections, and the use of the associate membership fees. Some concern has also been expressed that associate bar membership could reduce the membership in paralegal organizations.

B.   ACCESS TO THE PROFESSION

At the present time there are no formal requirements that must be met before an individual can become a paralegal. In the final analysis one must simply convince an employer that he or she is capable of doing the job. No state or federal law licenses paralegals or restricts who can be hired for such positions. As the profession has developed, however, various certification and accreditation systems have been considered by bar associations, paralegal organizations, and state legislatures. This section examines present access into the profession, as well as efforts to limit access through certification and other forms of regulation.

1. Basic Qualifications

A paralegal must, of course, have a great deal of specific knowledge about what the law requires from both a substantive and procedural perspective. The specific knowledge required will vary depending on the specialized areas of law involved, and the knowledge is usually acquired through a combination of formal education and on-the-job training. In order to absorb this legal information and then to effectively carry out the duties of a paralegal, the individual must possess certain basic intellectual and personality traits.

Since the law is complex and often ambiguous, the individual must be reasonably intelligent. More specifically the paralegal must have an analytic and logical mind that is able to recognize and evaluate relevant facts and legal concepts. Paralegals must then be able to effectively communicate their conclusions in both written and verbal form. It is particularly important that they be able to write in clear, concise, well-written prose.

A number of personality traits are also important for success in this field. At times the paralegal will have to work closely with attorneys, clients, and members of the public. They must be congenial and diplomatic and present a good professional image. At other times, however, paralegals must work long solitary hours in law libraries and back rooms drafting, organizing, or digesting legal documents. These activities require patience, persistence, and the ability to work with a minimum of

supervision. Paralegals should be able to function well in stressful conditions because they live in a world of deadlines and often have conflicting demands placed on their time by attorneys.

Perhaps the most important characteristics of success in the paralegal field are ingenuity and good judgment. The best paralegals are individuals who are innovative and resourceful. Once the nature of the problem is understood, these individuals are capable of developing their own solutions. Because they exercise good judgment, they know when to proceed independently and when to bring matters to the attention of their supervising attorneys.

2. Education and Training

Prior to 1970 there were no formal educational programs for paralegals, and all learned their trade exclusively through some sort of on-the-job training. Many lawyers had simply begun to give their secretaries a variety of paralegal tasks along with their own instructions as to how it was to be done. Occasionally someone with a special skill, such as accounting, would be brought in to help process tax returns.

Formal paralegal education can probably be traced most directly to a series of short courses for paralegals that began in 1968 at the University of Denver College of Law. In 1969 the Law School and the College of Human Services at Columbia University ran an experimental program to train paralegals for newly created jobs with legal services offices in New York City.[31] Antioch School of Law was the first law school to closely integrate a comprehensive paralegal curriculum with the regular juris doctor program. With few exceptions, though, law schools have not become directly involved in paralegal education.

Meramac Community College of St. Louis was the first of a large number of junior and community colleges to offer a paralegal education program when it began a series of night classes in September 1969. Today, the junior colleges dominate (in terms of numbers) the delivery system for paralegal education.

Most of the junior college programs attempt to follow closely the recommendations and accreditation standards of the American Bar Association. Within the standard two-year perod the student is expected to combine general education courses in areas such as English, history, and the social sciences with a legal education component. The legal education portion is generally divided into general courses that introduce the student to law and the operation of the legal system and specialized courses that teach specific paralegal skills. The ABA originally required a combination of forty-five semester hours in general education and in-

---

31. Statsky, Professionals: Expanding the Legal Service Delivery Team, 24 J. Legal Educ. 397 (1972).

troductory law courses along with fifteen semester hours of legal specialty courses. However, that was later reduced to thirty and fifteen hours respectively.

Some bachelor degree-granting colleges and universities have also developed formal paralegal programs. Some of these have been incorporated into the regular four-year degree program. In these types of programs, a student merely substitutes a major in legal studies (or some similar title for the paralegal courses) for a traditional major in English, political science, or business.

At other universities paralegal programs have been assigned to extension or continuing education divisions and are segregated from the institution's regular degree programs. Sometimes they simply offer a series of short noncredit courses for working professionals, and at other times they offer special certificate programs at either the graduate or the undergraduate level.[32] Such programs are usually three to four months in duration and concentrate on a specialized area of legal training.

Still another educational delivery system is represented by the private business school. In 1970 the Institute for Paralegal Training opened in Philadelphia. Formed by three practicing attorneys expressly for providing paralegal training, the institute developed three-month specialty courses at the postbachelor level. Several other private institutions have since followed suit.

In 1972, in response to the development of special educational programs for paralegals, the American Bar Association's House of Delegates directed the Special Committee on Legal Assistants to concentrate its efforts on the development of standards for accreditation of formal education programs directed to the training of legal paraprofessionals. Pursuant to that directive the committee held a special conference of interested parties in May of 1973 on the campus of the University of Denver School of Law. In August of 1973 the House of Delegates formally adopted a set of standards for granting approval to educational programs and gave the responsibility for administering those standards to the Standing Committee on Legal Assistants.

As the number of programs seeking ABA approval grew, it consumed so much of the Committee's time and budget that the ABA began to look for ways to reduce the organization's role in the approval process. After holding public hearings on this issue in June of 1982, the Committee recommended a plan to create a special Advisory Commission that would assist the Standing Committee in administering the approval guidelines. The actual approval was still granted by the ABA, but several other groups were brought in to share the workload and some of the costs. This eleven-member Advisory Commission is appointed by the

---

32. A certificate program gives a certificate of completion rather than awarding a degree. It should not be confused with certification. See page 15.

president of the ABA, but three members must be legal assistant educators, two must be paralegals, one must be a legal administrator, and one must be a nonlegal educator from a postsecondary institution.

The growth in paralegal programs has been phenomenal. From those humble beginnings in 1968, 1969, and 1970 the number of programs in the United States grew to thirty-one in 1973,[33] 125 in 1976, over 250 in 1980, and to over 360 in 1985.[34] As of 1985, however, only eighty of these programs carried full or provisional approval by the ABA. For both philosophical and economic reasons, many schools have never sought ABA approval even though they may be in substantial compliance with the guidelines. Although graduation from an ABA accredited law school is a prerequisite to taking the bar examination in most states, graduation from an approved paralegal program is not a formal prerequisite for employment as a legal assistant. Nevertheless, some employers may choose to use graduation from an approved program as one of the criteria considered in their selection process.

A key issue in paralegal education today is the extent to which programs should train specialists versus generalists. By concentrating on a single specialty area, an educational institution can produce a "marketable" paralegal in a shorter period of time. Furthermore, the graduate of a specialist program will require less on-the-job training after graduation and therefore will be more productive in less time. However, that graduate's opportunities will most likely be limited to a smaller number of potential job openings. A graduate of a generalist program, on the other hand, will probably require more initial on-the-job training, but that individual will have a wider range of positions to choose from and will be better prepared to shift from one field to another later in his or her career. Another problem with the specialist approach is that students must choose the program they enter at a time when they may not have had enough exposure to the law to be able to make an intelligent choice.

Another key curriculum issue relates to the proper mixture of substantive legal theory versus "hands-on" practical experience in drafting and processing legal documents. Studying legal theory gives students a general understanding of basic legal principles and develops basic intellectual skills. However, in order to be useful to an employer, graduates also must have practical experience in drafting and processing the types of legal documents they will be expected to handle on the job. Internships can be particularly helpful in providing these hands-on experiences.

No matter how specialized the program and no matter how much

---

33. Haemmel, Paralegals/Legal Assistants — A Report of the Advances of the New Professional, 11 Am. Bus. L.J. 112 (1973).

34. Based on annual listings prepared by the ABA Standing Committee on Legal Assistants.

hands-on work is involved, graduates of paralegal programs still will need some in-house training because every law office has its own operating procedures. While some employers seeks individuals with the most specialized training in order to minimize the extent to which they must supplement it internally, other employers seek out the best "raw talent" they can find and are willing to subsidize more in-house training.

3. Licensing and Certification

As indicated earlier in this chapter, the term *paralegal* is somewhat vague and rather inclusive. Some people look on this vagueness as positive because it allows a great deal of variety and growth within the profession. Others feel that it has created an "identity crisis" and is detracting from the status and prestige of the profession.[35] Many who share this latter view support some type of formal certification or licensing of paralegals.

Certification refers to the formal recognition by a nongovernmental organization that an individual has met some predetermined set of qualifications. That set of qualifications typically includes educational requirements and passage of an examination. Only those who meet these criteria are allowed to claim the title that goes with the designated status (such as certified public accountant or chartered life underwriter), but a person without such certification is not legally restricted from working in that occupational area. The advantage of certification is that potential employers or clients know that the individual has met certain standards and therefore presumably are more likely to employ this individual rather than someone who is not certified.

Licensing refers to the process by which government agencies establish standards (or adopt those of other groups) and then prohibit those who have not met these standards from working in that occupational field. Thus, a lawyer who has not been admitted to the bar is prohibited from practicing law because he or she is not licensed. Because the states, rather than the federal government, usually undertake the licensing of professional groups, the standards often differ among states. That variation often creates problems for people who move out of the state in which they have been licensed or who live in a metropolitan area that encompasses more than one state.

In evaluating the various arguments presented in this section, bear in mind the differences between these two forms of regulation, and be aware that many people within the profession support certification but oppose licensing.

Both certification and licensure are frequently justified on a con-

---

35. See Brittain, Will the Real Legal Assistant Please Stand Up!, 2(3) Legal Assistant Today 14 (1985).

sumer protection basis. The public is supposedly protected because individuals who have been properly certified or licensed are in fact qualified to perform those services. Statutes that govern the unauthorized practice of law, however, prohibit paralegals from soliciting legal work from the public, so it is attorneys, rather than the public, who choose among individuals claiming to be qualified paralegals. The public relies on the judgment of attorneys who are licensed.

Although conceding that neither certification nor licensure is necessary to protect the public interest, many people believe that either certification or licensing is needed to help lawyers select qualified paralegals. Helping the attorneys in this way is thought to provide an indirect benefit to the general public as well. They argue that many attorneys either do not have time to carefully screen paralegals or do not know what they should be looking for. One advocate of licensing has argued that if paralegals are not licensed, an incompetent or unethical one could get his or her supervising attorney disbarred and then go to another law firm and do it all over again.[36] Opponents counter that attorneys are sufficiently well qualified to determine the competence of prospective paralegals and they are in the best position to do so. Since attorneys are responsible for reviewing the paralegal's work, it is argued that they are in a better position to assess competency than either a state licensing board or some national organization administering a certification program. It is further argued that if the attorney employer properly checks a paralegal's references, he or she will not hire a paralegal who previously exhibited incompetent or unethical behavior.

In 1985 a special study committee of the National Federation of Paralegal Associations concluded that

> Regulation is appropriate only when the public has no other way of differentiating between competent and incompetent practitioners. Although we all decry the unqualified practitioner, there is clear indication the public is not being victimized by legal assistants. It certainly does not appear that implementation of a full-scale regulatory process is warranted, given the small percentage of paralegals who work outside the law firm or corporate setting.[37]

Certification and the more extreme licensure are also viewed as methods for improving the prestige, level of compensation, and mobility of those within the affected group. As one advocate of licensing put it,

> Every time an employer hires an individual who calls himself a legal assistant and who, in turn, does not function effectively as a legal assistant because he/she lacks the necessary skills and competencies,

---

36. Deering, Legal Assistant Licensure, Has the Time Come?, AAFPE Newsletter 5 (1985).
37. Dick, Certification Report, 10 Natl. Paralegal Rep. 7 (1985).

> the profession loses ground. The image of the profession is tarnished and employers will continue to question the basic integrity of the profession as a whole. The problems created for the qualified legal assistant include a loss of professional image, underutilization, loss of status, lower salary and a reduction in available jobs.[38]

While conceding that it may add prestige, opponents dispute the contention that certification will increase a paralegal's compensation or mobility. Since compensation reflects both the value of that individual's contribution to the employer and the current conditions of the employment market, they argue that certification is unlikely to result in significant changes to either one. It is further asserted that unlike a field such as nursing, mobility is limited by one's degree of specialization and variations in the law from one state to the next. Neither of these factors would be improved by certification or licensing.

Among those who favor certification or licensing, there often is disagreement regarding the nature of the standards to be implemented. Is a formal educational requirement necessary, and will it needlessly screen out the poor and representatives of minority groups? Should a baccalaureate degree be required? How much specialized paralegal education is necessary, and what type of accreditation should be required of the program that provides that education? Should on-the-job training be applied toward certification or licensing, and if so what kind of reasonable standards can be used to assess the quality of that training?

Critics have long argued that arbitrary measures of training and experience are overemphasized and that real competence to do the job is not measured. Although standardized examinations can be used to test knowledge of basic legal principles and procedures, there is disagreement over what types of knowledge are essential. At the present time lawyers are expected to be qualified as generalists, and bar examinations are designed to test all major fields of legal knowledge. Should paralegals be required to be generalists also? Many of the existing educational programs for paralegals produce narrow specialists. Should a paralegal whose work is solely in the area of real estate be expected to know about forming corporations? While standardized exams may test legal knowledge, many argue that they cannot test basic competencies. Before a test of competencies can be developed, however, these competencies must be identified. Paralegal educators and other interested parties are currently focusing much attention on this problem but have reached no consensus either as to what comprises these competencies or how they can be measured by a standardized examination.

Finally, there is the issue of the appropriate certifying agent. Should a state agency control a formal licensing procedure? If

---

38. Brittain, supra note 33, at 34.

certification is to be voluntary, what, if any, should be the role of the bar associations? Which of several possible competing paralegal groups should be considered the official certifying agency?

At the conclusion of a 1971 report to the ABA House of Delegates, the Special Committee on Legal Assistants stated, "On the basis of the study of lay personnel in other professions, it appears essential that the organized bar take an active role in development and control of the licensing and certification standards of all lay employees for the legal profession."[39] In February 1972 the House of Delegates adopted a resolution instructing its Special Committee on Legal Assistants to develop "standards for ascertaining the proficiency of legal paraprofessionals."[40]

Since the ABA had given a great deal of attention to the role of paraprofessionals in the medical professions, the use of some type of certification or licensing arrangement seemed to be a logical next step. However, after the committee began to study the matter more thoroughly and after they held a series of public hearings on the issue during the winter of 1974-1975, its outlook on the matter began to change. The majority of the approximately fifty organizations that participated in the hearings were against the ABA's attempting to establish standards for certification at that time.

When the Special Committee on Legal Assistants released its report on the certification question, it concluded that:

1. The occupation of legal assistant is in a dynamic stage of development and will unlikely undergo further changes.
2. The numerous associations of legal assistants, which have been created throughout the country, further reflect the dynamic characteristics of this occupation. However, there is no organization as yet that can be identified as fully representative of and qualified to speak for legal assistants.
3. In addition to the investigations that have been and are being undertaken, there is need for a broadly based, national study to analyze the roles and functions, and the means by which the competencies may be measured.
4. Whether or not certification may in the future be considered to be an appropriate means to identify qualified legal assistants, it is premature to initiate such a program at this stage of development and before the competencies required to perform the roles and functions of legal assistants have been adequately defined.
5. If certification of legal assistants should eventually be undertaken,
   (a) the goal of such a program should be primarily to provide the general public with legal services, more widely available, more efficiently offered, and at lower cost, and
   (b) the operation of such a program should be national in scope and under the supervision of a board that includes lawyers, legal assistants, educators, and members of the general public.

---

39. ABA Special Committee on Legal Assistants, Certification of Legal Assistants 7 (1975).
40. Id. at 8.

6. It is appropriate that the legal profession, through the American Bar Association, continue to exercise the initiative and some control in considering issues related to the possible future certification of legal assistants, and in exercising this initiative and control seek the joint cooperation of appropriate and representative national associations of legal assistants, state and local bar associations, educators, and the general public.[41]

Although the ABA initially decided that it was premature to certify paralegals, the Oregon State Bar Association did not. Between 1974 and 1979 approximately twenty paralegals received certification under this program.[42] The Oregon certification program involved (1) an educational requirement (associate degree and completion of approved paralegal training program); (2) a work experience requirement (equivalent of two years of practical experience as a paralegal); and (3) satisfactory completion of a comprehensive examination covering general skills (such as interviewing, investigation, and legal research) and substantive areas of Oregon law. However, the program was discontinued in January 1980.[43]

At about the same time, the two major paralegal organizations took contrasting positions regarding certification. The National Federation of Paralegal Associations opposed certification attempts as unnecessary and possibly even counterproductive to the new profession. The National Association of Legal Assistants, on the other hand, viewed certification as a means of increasing the status of the profession and immediately began to develop a certification program of its own. NALA's program resulted from extensive study of certification programs administered by a variety of professional associations including the Institute for Legal Executives and the National Association of Legal Secretaries. To be a certified legal assistant (CLA), one must pass a nationally standardized examination and complete five units of continuing legal assistant education every five years. In order to take the examination, the paralegal must meet one of the following requirements:

1. Graduation from an ABA-approved legal assistant course or graduation from a legal assistant training course at a school that is institutionally accredited, plus one year's experience as a legal assistant;
2. Graduation from a legal assistant course neither approved by the ABA nor at an institutionally accredited school, plus two years' experience as a legal assistant; or
3. A bachelor's degree in any field plus one year's experience as a legal assistant.

---

41. Id. at 28.
42. Fuller, Oregon State Bar Certification Program, Outlook 3 (May 1979).
43. NFPA Professional Development Committee, 1982 Analysis of State Bar Activities in the Paralegal Profession, 3 Legal Assistant Update 60 (1983).

Prior to 1986 one could also sit for the examination if one

1. Had successfully completed the professional legal secretary examination and had five years' law related experience under the supervision of a member of the bar; or
2. Had seven years' law related experience under the supervision of a member of the bar.

Since the exam was first administered in November 1976 through July 1985, 1,761 legal assistants have participated in the program, and 1,200 of them have been granted the CLA status. Although forty-five states, the District of Columbia, and the Virgin Islands are represented, the largest number of CLA's was found in Florida (297) and Texas (214). By comparison, California had 93, Michigan 36, Illinois and New York 12, and Pennsylvania 6.[44]

The examination is a combination of true/false, multiple choice, matching, and essay questions that cover basic grammar and writing skills; various ethical issues; common office procedures; legal terminology and standard bibliographic resources; analytical skills; and a general overview of several substantive areas of legal knowledge. All applicants are tested on a general overview of the legal system and then choose four of nine possible specialty areas to be tested in (real estate, estate planning and probate, litigation, bankruptcy, contracts, tax, corporate, administrative, and criminal).

NALA has also introduced a specialty certification program that involves successful completion of a four-hour examination from a selected specialty area. At the present time they offer exams in civil litigation, probate and estate planning, corporate and business law, and criminal law and procedure. As of May 1985, forty-six people had taken these advanced exams. The association is planning to expand the number of areas in which specialty certification would be offered.

It is difficult to say what the effect of NALA's certification program has been. A survey of CLAs that was conducted by the organization in 1984 showed that 63 percent thought that they were given greater responsibilities and 65 percent attributed a salary increase to having received CLA status.[45]

In 1983 NFPA established a certification committee and instructed it to "actively study and seek input on the subject of certification."[46] After

---

44. December 5, 1985, letter from Marge Dover, executive director of the National Association of Legal Assistants.
45. Summary of Surveys of CLAs, 1985-86 Technical Manual for the National Association of Legal Assistants Inc., Certified Legal Assistant Examination and Program, app. A (1985).
46. Dick, supra note 37, at 7.

conducting a survey of its members and holding open hearings on the topic in February 1985, the committee concluded that although "certification was rarely an issue with employers who had a true understanding of the paralegal profession," paralegals could increase their credibility "by raising the caliber of individuals holding themselves out as paralegals."[47] It was felt that the best way to accomplish this objective was to establish uniform standards for practitioners and that paralegals should participate in setting these standards. NFPA has not, as of this writing, either made plans to develop its own certification program or to endorse the CLA program sponsored by NALA.

In December 1985 the Standing Committee on Legal Assistants released a position paper on licensing and certification in which it rejected any attempts to license legal assistants or to certify for minimum competencies.[48] The committee concluded that "licensure would be of no benefit to the legal assistant profession, the legal profession, or the general public."[49] In rejecting the concept of voluntary certification of minimal competencies, the committee noted that lawyers had not expressed a need for such programs and that to the extent that they desired assistance in establishing the competencies of potential employees, it was "readily available from the graduation certificates or degrees offered by ABA approved educational programs . . . or by favorable references from prior employers."[50] The committee report did appear to signal approval for the development of a voluntary certification program for legal assistants that focused on advanced competencies in specialized fields if it were to be national in scope and administered by a broadly based group that included lawyers, legal assistants, educators, and members of the general public. However, it also made clear that it did not view the ABA as an appropriate entity to initiate or sponsor such a program.

As of the time that this chapter was written, no states had chosen to license paralegals. Although bar associations do not appear to be particularly interested in operating certification programs for paralegals, some associations are involved in the process of drafting guidelines for lawyers regarding uses of paralegals.[51] Because some guidelines being considered by state bar associations include criteria that lawyers are to use in assessing a paralegal's qualifications, they raise the same issues as those involved in formal certification.

---

47. Id.
48. ABA Standing Committee on Legal Assistants, Position Paper on the Question of Legal Assistant Licensure or Certification (Dec. 10, 1985). This position paper was approved by the ABA board of governors at its February 1986 meeting.
49. Id. at 5.
50. Id. at 6.
51. NFPA Professional Development Committee, supra note 43, at 61.

Proposals pending in several states appear to be patterned after the
~~following section of the National Association of Legal Assistants' Model~~
Standards and Guidelines for Utilization of Legal Assistants:

> A legal assistant should meet certain minimum qualifications. The
> following standards may be used to determine an individual's
> qualifications as a legal assistant:
>
> 1. Successful completion of the Certified Legal Assistant (CLA) ex-
>   amination of the National Association of Legal Assistants, Inc.;
> 2. Graduation from an ABA approved program of study for legal
>   assistants;
> 3. Graduation from a course of study for legal assistants which is
>   institutionally accredited but not ABA approved, and which re-
>   quires not less than the equivalent of 60 semester hours of class-
>   room study;
> 4. Graduation from a course of study for legal assistants, other than
>   those set forth in (2) and (3) above, plus not less than six months
>   of in-house training as a legal assistant;
> 5. A baccalaureate degree in any field, plus not less than six months
>   in-house training as a legal assistant;
> 6. A minimum of three years of law-related experience under the
>   supervision of an attorney, including at least six months of in-
>   house training as a legal assistant; or
> 7. Two years of in-house training as a legal assistant.[52]

Thus they indirectly involve recognition of both the NALA certification
process and other minimum requirements.

C. THE NATURE OF THE WORK

Earlier in this chapter it was said that when working under the
supervision of an attorney, paralegals could do just about anything related to the practice of law except give legal advice to clients and represent clients in most types of judicial proceedings. This section provides a
general overview of the activities commonly performed by paralegals
involved in different areas of practice. Subsequent chapters teach general paralegal skills in interviewing, factual investigation, legal research,
and document drafting, but this text is not designed to provide detailed
instruction for individual specialty areas.

1. Litigation

Litigation is the area in which the greatest number of paralegals
work, and it is a procedural specialty rather than a substantive one.

---

52. National Association of Legal Assistants, Model Standards and Guidelines for Utilization of Legal Assistants 5 (annot. ed. 1985).

Litigation is the term that is used to identify a dispute that has taken the form of a lawsuit. In other words, either a civil or criminal complaint has been filed in court. Whether the dispute involves an act of negligence, the violation of a provision of a real estate contract, or a violation of the criminal code, many of the same procedural steps must be followed to resolve the dispute within the court system.

After discussing a case with the paralegal, attorneys will frequently have that paralegal prepare a preliminary draft of the pleadings that must be filed with the court. These pleadings include such documents as the plaintiff's formal complaint and the various responses available to the defendant (including cross-complaints, answers, and demurrers).[53] The paralegal is responsible for selecting the appropriate general clauses, and then integrating those standardized clauses with references to the specific facts of the case at hand.

Some litigation paralegals become involved in various investigative functions. They may locate and interview witnesses. They may search through various types of public records to find relevant background information ranging from environmental impact statements and rate requests to police reports and OSHA studies. The job also frequently involves obtaining releases for medical records and then translating their contents into language that can be understood by laymen. Paralegals may also take photographs of an accident scene or locate expert witnesses who can testify about such things as design flaws in manufactured goods.

Investigation in lawsuits also involves discovery devices like interrogatives, depositions, and subpoenas.[54] The paralegal's role may involve drafting interrogatories, assembling questions to be used at depositions, and drafting requests for subpoenas. On the other side of the fence paralegals frequently assist clients draft the answers to interrogatories and help locate and assemble subpoenaed materials.

Having gathered this information, whether through their own investigative work or as a result of the formal discovery process, paralegals usually are responsible for analyzing, organizing, and reporting it to the attorneys working on the case. The paralegal abstracts, prepares digests, and indexes the various materials that have been compiled.[55] Without

---

53. These documents are explained and illustrated in Chapters 5 and 9.
54. Interrogatories are formal written questions sent by one party to the other side in order to obtain factual information; depositions involve the taking of a witness's sworn testimony out of court and prior to the actual trial; and subpoenas are court orders commanding persons to turn over certain documents or other materials they have in their possession. These devices are explained in Chapters 5 and 9.
55. Abstracting involves summarizing the content of the material in question, while a digest involves a systematic arrangement of summarized materials that is arranged by subject matter. Indexing involves the creation of an alphabetized list providing cross-references to the location of the information in question. These processes are explained in more detail in Chapter 9.

such indexes and digests, the attorneys litigating the case frequently
would be overwhelmed by the volume and complexity of the materials
and not be able to easily find the portions supporting their position.

In cases involving legal as well as factual issues, paralegals investigate these legal questions through traditional legal reference books and
modern computerized data bases. The results of this research are then
presented to the attorney in the form of an internal memorandum. In
situations where the issue is contested in court, the paralegal may assist
in the drafting of a memorandum to the judge or even a formal legal
brief. In addition to finding and analyzing relevant statutes, regulations,
and court cases, paralegals are also used to check citations and to Shepar-
dize cases.[56]

As the case proceeds to the trial stage, paralegals contact and help
prepare witnesses and prepare and organize exhibits. During the trial,
the paralegal takes notes and provides the attorney with the appropriate
exhibits and trial folders when needed.

If an appeal is taken, a paralegal usually files the notice of appeal
and orders copies of the record and a transcript of the trial. After these
materials have been received, the paralegal is usually assigned to abstract
and digest them. Additional legal research is frequently undertaken at
this time. These activities then culminate in the preparation of a preliminary draft of an appellate brief.

While criminal and civil litigation differ from each other, the
paralegal skills involved are similar in both areas. In all types of litigation
paralegals must develop some substantive knowledge of the field being
litigated. Most civil litigation involves the area of torts, but questions of
contracts, property, commercial transactions, antitrust, and domestic relations are also frequently involved. Many law firms doing litigation work
tend to specialize in a limited number of substantive areas, however,
thereby making it easier for paralegals to operate effectively.

2. Corporate Law

Corporate law involves the formation, acquisition, maintenance,
merger, and dissolution of corporate business entities, and paralegals
who work in this field spend most of their time drafting documents and
preparing reports for stockholders and governmental agencies. The documents include articles of incorporation, corporate bylaws, resolutions,
notices, waivers, stock options, shareholder agreements, and pension
plan agreements. Paralegals may also complete various tax forms, securities reports, and even environmental impact statements.

---

56. The term *Shepardizing* refers to the use of Shepard's Citations books to locate other
cases that have cited the case being examined. This technique is discussed in Chapter 8.

Investigative functions include researching the availability of corporate names and trademarks, calculating tax advantages in different states, and monitoring proposed legislation and administrative regulations that affect corporate clients.

If the corporation becomes involved in litigation, the paralegal might then undertake some or all of the tasks described in the previous section. However, in many firms and corporate legal departments, the matter would be transferred to a specialized litigation department or a separate firm where specialized litigation paralegals would become involved.

3. Estate Planning and Probate

In planning a client's estate, paralegals are frequently responsible for preparing an inventory of the client's assets and liabilities. They also may research and calculate the tax consequences of alternative estate plans. Once the attorney and client have agreed on a particular plan, the paralegal prepares preliminary drafts of the wills and trust agreements to be used.

Paralegals assist in implementing an estate plan by changing beneficiary designations on life insurance policies and pension plans, preparing gift tax returns when needed, and changing the registration of real estate, stocks, and bonds.

In probating an estate, paralegals usually inventory the assets and liabilities of the deceased, locate and correspond with heirs, and assemble copies of insurance policies, marriage certificates, and other important records. They also may be responsible for preparing income and inheritance tax forms and periodic reports required by the courts.

4. Real Estate

In real estate sales paralegals are primarily responsible for assembling all the appropriate sales, financing, and title documents required for such transactions. They examine public records to determine the legal description of the property being sold, who the legal owners are, the nature of any encumbrances on the property, the assessed valuation, and whether any taxes are due. In preparing settlement sheets, paralegals must calculate taxes owed and the various credits that are due to the buyer and the seller. They probably also will be called on to coordinate the closing date with the parties to the sale, the attorneys, and the financial institution's representative.

Other aspects of real estate practice involve drafting leases and preparing eviction notices. Paralegals working for title companies search local property records and prepare preliminary abstracts of titles.

5. Family Law

Another specialized area of practice involves family law or domestic relations. While disputes involving separation, divorce, child custody, and child support are the most common, paralegals in this field also deal with adoption and guardianship questions.

A major part of the paralegal's role in divorce-related matters is investigative in nature. Key information regarding incomes, bank accounts, and property ownership must be assembled and assessed. At times it is necessary to gather sensitive information about such things as the physical and mental treatment of spouses and children and sexual activities outside the marriage.

Paralegals also participate in drafting the initial pleadings, requests for interim relief, and discovery documents normally associated with these types of cases.

6. Government Positions

Paralegals who work for government agencies peform the same basic tasks as those who work for private law offices. Most paralegals working in the federal government are either in the Justice Department or in the Office of the General Counsel of the cabinet-level departments and regulatory agencies. Their duties closely resemble those described above in the litigation section. However, some specialized positions exist in which the paralegal focuses on such duties as responding to Freedom of Information Act requests or interviewing applicants for naturalization. The substantive expertise required for these government positions depends on the particular agencies involved and can range from tax law to civil rights.

What distinguishes many government positions from those in the private sector is that they are part of a formal civil service system that carries with it certain career expectations and due process protections. Also, the responsibilities are usually greater than private sector positions, and the salaries are frequently higher.

Since 1975 the Office of Personnel Management (formerly known as the U.S. Civil Service Commission) has used two general job classifications for paralegals. The Legal Clerk/Technician (GS-986) has a clerical or technical background and serves chiefly as a document custodian,[57] while the Paralegal Specialist (GS-950) performs a full range of paralegal tasks, including legal reseach and analysis, case preparation for litigation, adjudication of applications, and other duties "requiring discretion and independent judgment in the application of specialized knowledge

---

57. Essrick, Managing Litigation for the Federal Government, 1 Working with Legal Assistants 56, 57 (1980).

of particular laws, regulations, precedents, or agency practices based thereon."[58]

The Legal Clerk and Technician series starts at the GS-4 level, while the Paralegal Specialist series begins at GS-5.[59] In order to qualify for the Technician series at the GS-4 level one needs two years of general experience (defined as general office clerical experience that demonstrates the ability to perform clerical duties satisfactorily). However, every half year of formal education beyond high school can be substituted for six months of the general experience requirement. The GS-5 level in this series requires an additional one year of specialized experience (defined as clerical work involving legal regulations or legal files), but successful completion of a bachelor's degree that included or was supplemented by at least twelve semester hours of coursework in law or paralegal subjects fully meets these education and experience requirements. To start at the GS-5 level in the Paralegal Specialist series, one is required to have three years of general experience (defined as responsible experience that demonstrated the ability to explain, apply or interpret rules, regulations, procedures, policies, precedents, or other kinds of criteria). In this case successful completion of a bachelor's degree may be substituted for this general experience requirement. A GS-7 rating in the Paralegal Specialist series requires an additional one year of specialized experience, and a GS-9 requires two years of specialized training. The specialized experience must be clearly paralegal in nature, but completion of a J.D. can be substituted for up to two years of specialized experience, and a year's specialized paralegal or law curriculum can be substituted for one year of experience.

The Paralegal Specialist series begins only one step above that of the Technician, but the median rating for people in this series is a GS-10, and 6 percent of all federal paralegals rise to the GS-14 and GS-15 levels.[60] Technicians by contrast seldom go beyond the GS-7 level.[61]

Finally, it should be pointed out that many other federal employees do paralegal work but are not classified in these series. The Hearings and Appeals Positions series (GS-930) involves conducting formal and informal hearings and conducting appellate reviews of prior decisions. These positions start at the GS-9 level and require five years of paralegal experience. While a J.D. may be substituted for the five years, a law degree is not required, and a bachelor's degree can be substituted for three years.

---

58. Office of Personnel Management, Special Qualification Standards GS-950 1 (1985).
59. Federal salaries utilize a step system within each GS rating. A salary increase may be received if (1) the employee is raised a step within the same GS level, (2) the employee is raised to a higher GS level, or (3) Congress raises the pay for that level and step. As of January 1988 GS-4 steps ranged from $13,513 to $17,563, and GS-5 steps ranged from $15,118 to $19,564.
60. Perko, Paralegals in the Federal Government, 4 Legal Assistant Update 75, 77 (1984).
61. Id. at 76.

Examples of other positions involving paralegal work include Research Analysts at the Federal Trade Commission, Equal Employment Specialists at the EEOC, and Procurement Specialists at the Department of Defense.[62] There are also paralegal positions within the military.[63]

At the state level paralegal positions are most likely to be located in the attorney general's office, but additional positions may be found in places like the secretary of state's office or a pollution control agency. The people who occupy these positions most likely act as investigators, hearing officers, or general litigation paralegals. The positions are usually part of the civil service system but may in some cases be exempt. The qualifications are usually written so that one can qualify either through formal paralegal education or practical experience.

On the local level paralegals will most frequently be found operating out of the prosecuting attorney's or public defender's office. In New York City 90 percent of the postindictment preparation for felony cases is handled by paralegals, and in Oregon City paralegals handle almost all of the nonsupport work.[64] Paralegals are also frequently employed by the city attorney's office and may work with local human relations commissions or zoning review boards.

7. Other Specialty Areas

This section has described the most common types of paralegal positions, but this listing is by no means complete. There are many other specialty areas including welfare law, labor law, insurance law, collections, workers' compensation, environmental, civil rights, admiralty, and international law. While the substantive areas may differ, the paralegal's activities will be variations of the same basic functions: gathering basic facts, researching legal questions, drafting legal documents, and on occasion direct advocacy. The diversity of areas affords individuals an opportunity to find the specific combination of tasks and subject areas that provide the best match with their own skills and interests.

D. CAREER CONSIDERATIONS

People select occupations for many reasons. Salary levels, working hours, and the availability of positions are prime considerations, but there are a variety of less tangible psychological factors as well. This section explores some of the advantages and disadvantages of a paralegal career. What is the significance of the fact that many paralegals exit the

---

62. Id. at 77.
63. See Hall, The Air Force Legal Assistant, 2(1) Legal Assistant Today 13 (1984).
64. A. Fins, Opportunities in Paralegal Careers 52 (1985).

profession after about three years?[65] Are they leaving the profession because they are dissatisfied with what it has to offer them, or are they just leaving what they considered to be a transitional job designed to provide them with income until they go to law school?

In the late 1970s the Minnesota Satisfaction Questionnaire was completed by members of the National Association of Legal Assistants and the National Federation of Paralegal Associations.[66] Among other things this survey shows that 28 percent of paralegals said that they planned to leave the field[67] and that the satisfaction ratings increase with the number of years' experience in the profession.[68]

When these results were compared with the results of similar questionnaires sent to accountants, engineers, managers, nurses, nursing supervisors, social workers, teachers, and secretaries they found that the paralegals ranked sixth in terms of overall satisfaction.

1. Independence, Creativity, and Responsibility

Among the nine professional groups involved in the Minnesota study, paralegals ranked highest in satisfaction regarding having "the chance to work alone on the job" and third highest in having "the chance to try one's own methods of doing the job" and "the freedom to use one's own judgment."[69] This implies that many people who become paralegals value and receive satisfaction from the opportunities they have to work independently as well as to be creative and exercise responsibility. At the same time, however, the paralegals surveyed ranked next to the lowest with respect to having "the chance to do something that makes use of my abilities."[70] Furthermore, those with at least four years of college education were much more dissatisfied with the extent to which their abilities were being used in their jobs.[71]

While these findings are subject to different interpretations, they indicate that most paralegals value their independence, the opportunities they have to exercise their creativity, and the amount of responsibility they have and that many paralegals seek additional opportunities to go even further. These findings also may explain why many paralegals leave the profession to become attorneys. It certainly indicates that if attorneys wish to retain good paralegals they need to respond to these desires for challenging tasks.

---

65. Walen, Paralegal Paradox: Job Satisfaction, 12 At Issue 1 (1985).
66. A random sample of 397 was selected from among the approximately 4,000 names on the membership lists of the two associations. Of the 235 returned, 200 were considered suitable for processing. Larson and Templeton, Job Satisfaction of Legal Assistants, 1 Legal Assistant Update at 55 (1980).
67. Id. at 62.
68. Id. at 61.
69. Id. at 59.
70. Id. at 59.
71. Id. at 63.

In a case study analysis of the turnover problem, Barbara Cone found that of ten paralegals studied, the five who stayed in the profession did so because they found challenges and opportunities for growth in their jobs. On the other hand, the five who left to seek out alternative careers did so because they thought that those other careers provided better pay and more opportunities for advancement.[72]

2. Compensation

Discussions of paralegal salaries, like discussion of the salaries of many other occupational groups, present a variety of problems. One of the most basic is the difficulty of gathering accurate information. While it is relatively easy to find that on January 1, 1985, a federal employee beginning at step 1 on a GS-5 scale in the Paralegal Specialty series made $15,118, it is very difficult to determine how many paralegals currently work for the government and the average GS rating of these paralegals at any given time. It is next to impossible to determine the average salary for paralegals employed in private law offices. The best one can do is to rely on surveys that are conducted by law office consulting firms, paralegal associations, and paralegal schools. However, such surveys must rely on good faith reporting and incomplete responses.

Another problem with salary data is that most surveys report only monthly salaries and do not consider either the value of fringe benefits or year-end bonuses. Fringe benefits can range from medical insurance and paid vacations to parking subsidies. Year-end bonuses can range from $25 to $5,000.[73] In some offices paralegals receive overtime, while in others they do not. Variation among different areas of the country and between urban and rural areas makes reported average salaries of limited usefulness in seeking specific jobs. Finally, figures that are accurate at the time that this book is written will be out of date by the time you read it.

Despite these problems it is useful to provide some idea of the range of salaries being paid to selected paralegals. It already has been noted that based on 1985 data, paralegals starting in the federal government receive $14,390 a year. An experienced paralegal (on the GS-12 scale) has a range of $31,619 to $41,105, and the 6 percent who make it to the top can earn $67,940. Surveys conducted by several regional paralegal groups and reports from the placement offices of paralegal programs indicate that starting salaries in private law offices range from $8,000 to $25,000 with the average in the $16,000 to $18,000 range. After five years most of the reported salaries are in the mid-twenties, and

---

72. Cone, Those Who Stayed and Those Who Left: Case Studies of Legal Assistants, 4 Legal Assistant Update 1 (1984).
73. Weisberg, Compensation of Paralegals, 3 Legal Assistant Update 49, 57 (1983).

top salaries for those with ten years or more experience and supervisory responsibilities sometimes approach $40,000.

3. Opportunities for Advancement

Better pay usually goes hand-in-hand with advancement to new positions. A common complaint regarding paralegal positions has been that they are "dead-end jobs" with no room for advancement. On the Minnesota survey paralegals expressed the least satisfaction regarding "chances for advancement on this job."[74]

Partly in response to this perceived problem, some law firms have created senior legal assistant positions to provide increased status for more experienced paralegals. In addition, paralegals have proven to be strong contenders for administrative positions within law firms, thus making it possible to advance to supervisor of a paralegal section, personnel director, and even head administrator for a firm.

Those who have found that opportunities for advancement within a particular firm are too limited have either moved to other firms or used their paralegal knowledge and contacts to get middle-management positions in banks and with corporate clients on whose cases they have worked. Still another approach is to become a freelance paralegal or a paralegal consultant.[75] There are also opportunities to either teach or direct paralegal education programs.

4. Working Environment

Paralegal satisfaction ratings varied on the basis of the type of specialty involved as well as the size and type of employer.[76] Turnover also varies with the size of the firm.[77] These indicators suggest that working environment has a great deal to do with the amount of satisfaction derived from the profession. In general, those who work in the field of civil litigation in large law firms receive the least satisfaction from their work. Those who work in nontraditional areas like banks and government agencies are apparently the most satisfied.

Several factors help to explain why the level of paralegal satisfaction is lower in large litigation firms. In smaller firms handling less complex cases the paralegal is more likely to have the opportunity to meet the parties involved, take statements from witnesses, attend depositions, and even sit at the counsel's table during the trial. However, in larger

---

74. Id. at 59.
75. See Cone, supra note 72, at 1; Keogh, Profile: Ann Pestritto, 2(3) Legal Assistant Today 24 (1985); Templeton, Four Careers, 2(3) Legal Assistant Today 14 (1984).
76. Templeton, Legal Assistant Job Satisfaction: A Further Analysis, 2 Legal Assistant Update 37, 40-43 (1981).
77. Canillo, The Legal Assistant Career Ladder in a Private Firm, 2 Legal Assistant Update 3 (1981).

firms using several paralegals to handle complex cases, the clients are
~~frequently faceless corporate entities, and the paralegals may spend~~
months engaged in document indexing and retrieval for a very esoteric
antitrust case.

Another factor related to the work environment is the nature of the
relationships among co-workers. On the Minnesota satisfaction survey,
paralegals ranked the lowest of the professional groups studied with
respect to "the way my co-workers get along with each other."[78] In commenting on this finding, Tony Bosniak has written that "paralegals may
be fighting each other for work and rank more than helping each other
gain respect from others for the career they have chosen and for the kind
of work paralegals can do."[79] The larger the firm, the greater the likelihood of conflicting personalities.

Problems frequently arise from the lack of a clear, mutually understood definition of the paralegal's role within the organization. This
confusion involves not only the nature of the work assigned to paralegals
but also various personnel policies and the paralegal's role in the social
structure of the firm. Paralegals are treated like clerical personnel on
some matters and then like lawyers on others. They often see themselves
as getting the worst of both worlds. Lawyers frequently fail to give
paralegals the credit and status they deserve, while secretaries (who may
be jealous of the paralegal's position or may simply not understand it)
often fail to show the respect and cooperation the paralegal believes is
deserved. The situation is further aggravated when clients are also confused about the paralegal's functions and responsibilities. Combining
this ambiguous understanding of the paralegal's role with the competitive nature of many paralegals frequently leads to anxiety and insecurity.

While these working conditions frequently cause dissatisfaction
with some aspects of being a paralegal and probably are responsible for
some decisions to leave the field, the reader must be careful to keep them
in perspective. There are many enlightened law firms, corporate legal
departments, and government agencies that make productive use of
paralegals and provide pleasant working environments.

E. SUMMARY

Paralegals or legal assistants are individuals who lack membership
in the bar but nevertheless possess legal knowledge and skills and perform (under the supervision of a licensed attorney) a variety of legal
tasks. They gather and analyze facts, research legal questions, assist in

78. Templeton, supra note 73, at 59.
79. Bosniak, Trouble in Paradise: A Paradox for Paralegals, 2 Legal Assistant Update 13,
    19 (1981).

the preparation of legal documents, and perform administrative functions. They even can represent clients before some administrative tribunals. Indeed, about the only things they cannot do (provided they are working under the supervision of an attorney) are give legal advice and represent clients in formal judicial proceedings.

As the practice of law has grown in sophistication and specialization and as lawyers have moved from solo practices into larger firms, the potential for using paralegals has also grown. Taking a lesson from the medical profession, lawyers have begun to see the economic advantage of delegating some of their work to well-trained paraprofessionals.

In 1967 the American Bar Association issued a significant ethics opinion that clarified the legitimacy of delegating legal work to nonlawyers, and in 1968 it created a special committee to encourage the training and employment of paralegals.

Since then the paralegal profession has grown rapidly, and paralegals now are used in a wide variety of legal settings including law offices, government agencies, banks, insurance companies, and other private corporations. Paralegals have formed national professional associations to represent their interests, and the U.S. Department of Labor rates it as the fastest-growing occupational group in the country.

Paralegals must be intelligent and possess both an analytical mind and good communications skills. They must be able to assume responsibility and to act independently. Above all they must exercise good judgment. Most paralegals receive a combination of formal paralegal education and on-the-job training. During the 1970s a variety of educational institutions began to offer paralegal training programs. Today more than 350 such programs exist at the business school level, the junior college level, the baccalaureate level, and the postbaccalaureate level. Most of these programs are offered by established public and private colleges and universities, but some proprietary schools have been formed especially for the purpose of offering such programs.

Although the American Bar Association has established an approval system for paralegal training programs, it has not supported certification or licensing of paralegals. The National Association of Legal Assistants has established a voluntary certification program, and several state bar associations are considering adoption of guidelines covering the employment and use of paralegals.

The specific duties paralegals perform depend a great deal on the type of employer and the area of the law that is involved. Major areas of specialization for paralegals include litigation, corporate, estate planning and probate, real estate, and family law. Paralegals working for governmental agencies are usually part of a civil service system and are frequently given a wide range of responsibilities. While the information gathered, the documents drafted, and the law researched vary from one setting to the next, paralegals perform basic tasks common to all areas.

As is true of any occupation, a paralegal career has both advantages and disadvantages, and a person contemplating such a career should have a realistic knowledge of both. Many of the potential disadvantages can be eliminated or reduced by choosing a specialty area and the type of organization that is best suited for individual personality and skills. The profession can be an exciting and intellectually challenging way to tangibly affect fellow human beings.

KEY TERMS

apprentice	legal assistant
ABA approval	licensing
certification	NALA
certificate program	NFPA
civil service	paralegal
clerkship	paralegal specialist
GS level	

REVIEW QUESTIONS

1. What actions did the American Bar Association take to encourage the use of paralegals?

2. What other factors have led to the increased use of paralegals?

3. What are the major differences between the two major paralegal associations?

4. What qualifications are needed to be a good paralegal?

5. What types of educational institutions offer paralegal programs?

6. What positions have paralegal organizations and the bar associations taken on certification and licensure?

7. What are the primary duties of a paralegal working in litigation? In corporate law? In estate planning and probate? In real estate? In family law?

8. Who, other than private law firms, is likely to employ paralegals? What, if anything, is likely to be different about the nature of the job with those employers?

9. What are some of the advantages and disadvantages of a paralegal career?

DISCUSSION QUESTIONS

1. Read Hussey, Are Training Programs Doing the Job?, 2 Legal Assistant Today 16 (1985). Whose arguments do you find most con-

vincing and why? If you were an employer who was seeking a paralegal, what type of educational background would you consider most desirable? Why?

2.   What do you feel are the most compelling arguments in favor of certification of paralegals? What are the most compelling arguments against it? If you were developing a certification program, what standards would you adopt? If a test were to be used, what would be the nature of the material covered and the format of the test?

3.   Based on your own personality and interests, what type of paralegal position do you find most appealing? Why? What type of position do you find least appealing? Why?

PROJECTS

1.   Has the bar association in your state formally discussed certification of paralegals? (One way to do find this out is to search through back issues of the state bar journal.) If there have been any proposals or actions, what positions were taken?

2.   Is there a paralegal association in your city or state? What is its position on the certification issue?

3.   How many professions are licensed in your state? What types of requirements have been established in those areas?

4.   Has your state civil service system established any job classifications that are specifically geared to paralegals? How many classifications might be appropriate for a well-trained paralegal (even if the position may not formally require paralegal training or experience)?

PART II
The American Legal System

BEFORE STUDENTS LEARN how to perform specific paralegal tasks, they need to understand how the legal system operates. Part II of the text therefore provides essential information about fundamental legal concepts.

Chapter 2 covers the organization and structure of the American legal system. Chapter 3 discusses how one finds and interprets the law. Chapter 4 introduces substantive legal concepts in areas like torts, contracts, property, commercial transactions, criminal law, and constitutional law, and Chapter 5 presents an elementary overview of civil and criminal procedure. Chapter 6 concludes this part with a discussion of the organization and operation of various types of law offices.

Chapter 2
Organization and
Structure of the
American Legal System

THE AMERICAN LEGAL SYSTEM is a complex set of institutions that vary in structure and procedure. Each of the fifty states, along with the federal government, runs its own set of courts under its own set of rules. And while the laws of one state are often similar to the laws of another, each state can ultimately determine for itself what those laws will be.[1] Thus where one state may choose to legalize gambling, another may not; where one state may choose to allow no-fault divorces, another may not.

Some see this diversity as one of the great strengths of our political system. They argue that it encourages experimentation and innovation by allowing the residents of Georgia, for example, to establish rules of conduct that differ from those established by the residents of Nevada. Critics, on the other hand, point to the problems it creates for interstate business and travel — such as forcing large corporations and other out-of-state parties to utilize the services of local attorneys and making it difficult for an attorney (or a paralegal) to move a practice from one state to another.

A. FUNCTIONS OF LAW

Although the laws themselves sometimes differ, the development and enforcement of those laws are essential functions of all fifty states as well as the federal government. Indeed, the development and enforcement of the law are essential governmental functions in all developed societies.

While the form of the law may vary (constitutional, statutory, administrative, and so forth), the law itself defines the type of conduct that is either prohibited or required. The criminal code usually prohibits the

---

1. This is because the United States operates under a system of government known as federalism. The United States Constitution divides the power to make various types of laws between the national government and the states. Subject to the restraints imposed by the Constitution itself, the states are free to determine what many of their own laws will be.

unauthorized taking of property that belongs to someone else. Tax laws require that certain types of individuals or corporations give part of their income to the government. The laws can apply to the behavior of individuals, businesses, and even governments themselves. Thus municipalities may be prohibited from dumping raw sewage into lakes and rivers, and the police prohibited from conducting unreasonable searches and seizures.

In order to be considered laws, these rules of conduct must be promulgated and enforced by the appropriate governmental agencies. Only the United States Congress can make federal statutory law. Administrative agencies can promulgate regulations only when they are acting under a proper delegation of legislative authority. The principles of the common law must be applied through a judge sitting in a court of competent jurisdiction.[2]

These rules of conduct also carry with them certain sanctions that can be imposed on those who fail to follow the rules. When individuals violate a section of the criminal law they may be fined, sent to prison, or in some cases even suffer loss of life. Persons who violate sections of the civil law may be forced to pay various penalties or damage awards. Similarly, they may be forced to carry out the terms of a contract or even to return to work after having been out on a strike. Police who conduct illegal searches and seizures may be denied the right to use that evidence in court and may even be forced to pay damages to the injured party. Even presidents can be cited for contempt if they fail to turn over subpoenaed materials.

While there may be a great deal of debate over the wisdom and appropriateness of a particular law (as there is, for example, over mandatory seatbelt laws), there is general agreement that laws themselves are necessary. As the Task Force on Law and Law Enforcement reported to the National Commission on the Causes and Prevention of Violence,

> Human welfare demands, at a minimum, sufficient order to insure that such basic needs as food production, shelter and child rearing be satisfied, not in a state of constant chaos and conflict, but on a peaceful, orderly basis with a reasonable level of day-to-day security. . . . When a society becomes highly complex, mobile, and pluralistic; the beneficiary, yet also the victim, of extremely rapid technological change; and when at the same time, and partly as a result of these factors, the influence of traditional stabilizing institutions such as family, church, and community wanes, then that society of necessity becomes increasingly dependent on highly structured, formalistic

---

2. All courts have some restrictions on the types of cases they can entertain. Constitutions and legislatures assign certain types of cases to particular courts. If a case is within a particular court's jurisdiction, the court has the legal authority to hear that case. Jurisdiction can be based on the nature of the parties involved, the subject matter, or the location of the incident being litigated.

systems of law and government to maintain social order. . . . For better or worse, we are by necessity increasingly committed to our formal legal institutions as the paramount agency of social control.[3]

It has thus been increasingly left to the legal system to define and enforce the rules of the society. Some of these rules are heavily influenced by the religious and moral beliefs of various elements in the society (such as restrictions on abortions, pornography, and gambling), while others (such as traffic regulations) have no moral content at all. Nevertheless, they help to provide the type of order and predictability that are essential elements of our modern society.

B.   SOURCES OF LAW

Laws can come from several different sources: from federal, state, and local governments and from legislatures, administrators, and judges. Generally speaking, though, when people think of law they think first of the legislative enactments of their state legislatures. This is because we are usually more aware of the state's criminal code than we are of other forms of law. Even though we have probably never read it, we picture a ponderous statute book filled with "thou shalt nots."

Statutory law consists of the enactments of legislative bodies. These legislative bodies can be the United States Congress, a state legislature, or a village board. These enactments are then published in the form of statutes or ordinances. Since the wording of these statutes is occasionally ambiguous, the judges who apply them serve as the ultimate arbitrators of their meaning.

Administrative law is similar to statutory law in that it usually consists of fairly specific regulations that are written in a form similar to statutes. Whereas statutory law is made by the legislative branch, administrative law is made by the executive branch or by independent regulatory agencies. These agencies can promulgate regulations in limited areas under the appropriate grants of authority from the legislative branch. As in the case of statutes, the judge who applies the regulation becomes the ultimate arbitrator of its meaning.

A third type of law is referred to as the common law. Common law consists of various legal principles that have evolved through the years from analysis of specific court decisions. Ultimately, these principles can be traced back to early medieval England, though they have been modified through the years by various state courts. When a legal dispute

---

3. J. Campbell, J. Sahid, and D. Stang, Law and Order Reconsidered: Report of the Task Force on Law and Law Enforcement to the National Commission on the Causes and Prevention of Violence 3, 5 (1970).

involves a subject that is not adequately covered by the other types of law, the judge applies the principles of the common law. In other words, in the absence of pronouncements from the constitution or a legislative or administrative body, the judge looks to the decisions of other judges in similar circumstances.

Closely related to the concept of common law is equity. The English Chancery Court allowed judges a freer hand in reaching a just result in situations where the common law had become too rigid and technical. Judges today are allowed to use their equity powers to "do justice" where specific laws do not cover the situation. Equity powers are primarily utilized in cases involving property rights and include the powers of a judge to issue an injunction or to order specific performance.[4] They allow judges to take preventive or remedial action, when otherwise the law would limit their decisions to monetary awards after the damage has been done.

The final source of law is the state or federal constitution. The prescriptions laid out in the constitution (as they are interpreted by the judges) constitute the highest form of man-made law. In order to be valid, statutes and administrative regulations must not conflict with the principles laid down in the constitution of the United States or the state involved.

C. CRIMINAL LAW AND CIVIL LAW

Just as law can be classified on the basis of its source, it also can be divided into the general categories of criminal law and civil law. Both types consist of rules of conduct that have been established by the appropriate legal authorities, but they differ in how they are enforced (Table 2.1).

When an individual violates a part of the criminal law, society considers itself to be the offended party and takes an active role in the sanctioning process. Thus if Peter Jones burglarizes Sam Smith's home, the criminal law views that act as an offense against society itself rather than simply as a matter between Smith and Jones. When the case goes to court, it is listed as People v. Jones or State v. Jones. Government attorneys prosecute the accused party, and the victim is merely a witness. The criminal law seeks not to redress the losses of the victim but to maintain the vitality of the rule of conduct involved. If a court of law determines that a provision of the criminal law has been violated, it may impose two broad types of sanctions — loss of liberty and financial penalty. Most commonly, the loss of liberty involves spending a few days in the county

---

4. Specific performance requires that a party carry through on a contract that has not been fulfilled.

Table 2.1 Comparison of Criminal and Civil Cases

CHARACTERISTIC	CRIMINAL	CIVIL
Source of the law	Government	Government
Offended party	Society	Individual
Investigation and "prosecution" of violations	Government	Individual
Burden of proof	Beyond a reasonable doubt	Preponderance of the evidence
Sanctions used	Fines, imprisonment, death	Monetary damages, injunctions, specific performance, etc.
Beneficiary of sanctions	Society	Individual

jail to several years in a state penitentiary. It can, however, range all the way from unsupervised probation to the inflicting of the death penalty. While a negotiated settlement will occasionally contain some provisions for restitution, the fines that are assessed as part of the criminal process become the property of the state rather than the victim.

In civil cases, on the other hand, the government takes a much more passive role. It develops the basic rules of conduct and provides a judicial system for the application of those rules, but the aggrieved party prosecutes the case. Thus when one party defaults on the terms of a contract, the other party must hire a lawyer and initiate the legal process on an individual basis.

The individual plaintiff plays an active role, and those who triumph benefit directly from the outcome. Under the civil law the party who is found to be at fault can be required to directly compensate the victim for various types of injuries sustained. Even when the damages are punitive (designed to punish the wrongdoer) rather than compensatory, the plaintiff becomes the beneficiary rather than the government.[5] In addition to awarding damages, civil court judges can issue injunctions and dissolve marriages.

Due to the serious consequences of violating criminal laws, standards of proof applied are different from civil standards. On the criminal side, the prosecution is required to prove its case "beyond a reasonable doubt," while in civil actions the plaintiff need only meet the "preponderance of the evidence" standard. The "beyond a reasonable doubt" standard is usually explained to jurors as being the degree of doubt that causes a reasonable person to refrain from acting. "Preponderance of

---

5. The government can become a plaintiff in a civil suit. Under these circumstances the government plaintiff benefits in the same way a private plaintiff does.

the evidence," on the other hand, is usually understood to mean that the facts asserted are more likely to be true than not true. A study conducted by Rita James Simon and Linda Mahan showed that judges tend to equate "beyond a reasonable doubt" with a median probability of approximately 8.8 out of 10, while jurors averaged approximately 8.6 out of 10. "Preponderance of the evidence" was interpreted by the judges as a median probability of 5.4 out of 10, with 7.1 out of 10 being the median for jurors.[6] Clearly the criminal law requires a greater degree of proof before its sanctions could be applied.

It should be noted that a single act could become the basis for actions in both the criminal and civil courts. For example, the victim of a battery could sue the attacker for civil damages at the same time the state is prosecuting the attacker on a criminal charge. The driver of an automobile involved in a traffic accident may receive a traffic ticket from the police and at the same time be sued by someone else involved in the accident. In certain types of antitrust cases the government can choose between seeking criminal charges and civil damages.

D. TYPES OF COURTS

When used in its legal context, a *court* is a governmental institution that adjudicates certain types of controversies. While some administrative agencies also adjudicate controversies, the term is usually reserved for an entity that is part of the judicial branch.[7] At first glance, the judicial systems of this country present a confusing mixture of titles and functions. In large part this is because there are actually fifty-one different court systems (the federal system plus one for each state). Not only are their jurisdictions divided in different ways, but the same types of courts often have different names. The basic trial court, for example, is called the Court of Common Pleas in Pennsylvania, the District Court in Minnesota, the Circuit Court in Illinois, the Superior Court in California, and the Supreme Court in New York. Some systems have justices of the peace and/or magistrates, while others do not. Rather than attempt to provide a description of each of these fifty-one court systems, this book simply reviews some general patterns found in them and leaves it to the reader to search out the details of specific states.[8]

---

6. Simon and Mahan, Quantifying Burdens of Proof, 5 Law & Soc. Rev. 319 (1971).
7. The Tax Court and the Court of Military Appeals are examples of exceptions to this convention. See page 50.
8. Relatively simple explanations of most state court systems can be found in books and pamphlets published by the individual states. These organization manuals are usually available in the reference section of local libraries. Another source for such information is The American Bench or the Court Calendar section of the Martindale-Hubbell Law Directory.

The powers and limitations of specific courts are determined by the constitution and statutes governing the operation of the court in question. *Jurisdiction* refers to the types of controversies a particular court is authorized to handle. Courts of general jurisdiction are authorized to adjudicate all types of civil and criminal cases, while courts of limited jurisdiction are limited to a narrow range of cases on a specific subject (such as probate, domestic relations, or traffic). Courts with original jurisdiction are those in which actions are initiated and considered for the first time, while courts with appellate jurisdiction are authorized to review the actions of other courts. If a specific court is the only one authorized to adjudicate a particular type of case, it is said to have *exclusive jurisdiction,* whereas if more than one court is authorized to hear the same type of case it is called *concurrent jurisdiction.* Furthermore, jurisdiction can be defined in terms of the nature of the parties involved in the dispute (*in personam*) or in terms of the subject of the dispute (*in rem*).

There are several important distinctions between trial courts and appellate courts (see Table 2.2). The trial court is charged with the basic handling of a case. In its more glorious moments it receives evidence and arguments presented by opposing attorneys and then determines whether the plaintiff has proven the case or whether the defendant is guilty of a criminal offense. Most of the time, however, is spent in far less dramatic proceedings in which the court receives plea agreements and ratifies out-of-court settlements. The appellate court selectively reviews those decisions.

In order to understand the difference between the two, it is necessary to distinguish between questions of law and questions of fact. In most cases the meaning of the law is relatively clear, but the facts themselves are very much in dispute. Under the criminal codes of most states

Table 2.2 Comparison of Trial and Appellate Courts

CHARACTERISTIC	TRIAL COURTS	APPELLATE COURTS
Decision makers	One judge and sometimes a jury[a]	Majority vote of three or more judges
Presentation of arguments by attorneys	Yes	Yes
Testimony of witnesses and introduction of physical evidence	Yes	No
Determination of questions of fact	Yes	No
Interpretation of the law	Judge — yes Jury — no	Yes

[a] In most jurisdictions the juries' decisions must be unanimous. Although most juries consist of twelve people, some courts use six-person juries for some types of cases.

it clearly is a crime for someone other than a physician, pharmacist, or other authorized medical person to sell or distribute narcotic drugs. When someone is on trial for selling narcotics, the focus is usually on whether the accused did in fact sell narcotics — a question of fact rather than of interpretation of the law. The evidence usually consists of an undercover police agent testifying that the accused did indeed sell the agent a substance that laboratory reports identify as a narcotic.

While the primary focus of most trials is on factual issues, at times legal issues are involved as well. In the example cited above the defendant might admit to selling the drug but claim an entrapment defense. The entrapment doctrine prohibits law enforcement officers from instigating criminal acts by otherwise innocent persons in order to lure them into committing a crime. Even with the entrapment defense, the primary emphasis is still on determining the facts. The most important fact is the defendant's predisposition to commit the crime.[9] However, there are occasions where interpretation of the entrapment doctrine itself is unclear — then there is a legal question. When Charles Hampton was arrested by Federal Drug Enforcement Administration agents in 1974, he claimed an entrapment defense on the basis that government agents had supplied him with a drug, then later arrested him for selling the very same drug to another government agent. This contention presented a legal question as well as a factual one.[10]

During the course of a trial numerous legal issues may be raised involving the conduct of the trial itself. Should a particular piece of evidence be excluded because it was the product of an illegal search and seizure? Should plaintiff's attorney be able to pursue a certain line of questioning? Should the judge present a particular set of instructions to the jury? Has the defendant's trial been tainted by prejudicial publicity? Then, too, there is always the possibility of challenging the constitutionality of the statute itself. A doctor charged with performing an illegal abortion could argue that the law he is charged with violating is itself unconstitutional.

When legal issues are raised in the trial courts, they are ruled on by the presiding judge. The trial then goes ahead on the basis of the judge's ruling. If it is ruled that the testimony is not admissible, then the trial goes on without it. If the judge rules that the search was not illegal, then

---

9. Had the defendant ever committed such a criminal act or thought of committing such an act before? If the government merely provided the opportunity to commit the crime, it is not guilty of entrapment; but if it actually placed the idea of committing the crime in an otherwise innocent person's mind, then it is entrapment.

10. In Hampton v. United States, 425 U.S. 484 (1976), the United States Supreme Court resolved the issue against Hampton. The court ruled that as long as the defendant was predisposed to commit the crime, it was not entrapment.

the objects discovered in that search are admitted as evidence. On the basis of the evidence that has been allowed, the jury then resolves the factual questions. Was the defendant at the scene of the crime as two impartial witnesses have testified, or was he, as three of his friends testified, across town playing poker? Was the fact that the defendant was driving 55 miles per hour on a snow-packed road the proximate cause of the plaintiff's injuries? What is appropriate compensation for never being able to walk again? If it is a bench trial rather than a jury trial, the judge will decide the factual questions as well as the legal ones.

Once these issues have been settled by the trial court, the losing party can usually have an appellate court review its case. (Most states and the federal government provide for one appeal as a matter of right in most types of cases. Additional appeals are usually at the discretion of the higher court.) That appeals court will ordinarily limit itself to reviewing the legal issues. Once it has been determined at the trial court level that the defendant did fire the shot that killed the murder victim — or that the defendant's conduct was not the proximate cause of the plaintiff's injuries — those factual issues are settled and are not open to review on appeal.

If the appellate court determines that a significant legal error[11] was made in the way the trial was conducted, it will usually cancel the original outcome and direct that the trial be conducted over again. Thus the reversal of a criminal conviction does not necessarily mean that the defendant will go free. The government can retry the person without being in violation of the double jeopardy clause.[12] On the other hand, if a key piece of evidence has been ruled to be inadmissible, the government may choose not to retry the defendant because it may feel that its case is too weak without the excluded evidence.

A single judge presides over a trial court, but several judges act together in appellate courts. The decisions at the appellate level are based on a majority vote of the judges who are participating. Lower-level appellate judges usually work in rotating panels of three, while in the upper-level appellate courts all the judges jointly decide each case. There are no witnesses giving testimony in the appellate courts and no juries. The judges merely review the trial transcript and the written briefs from the lawyers. Sometimes they have oral arguments in which they listen to the verbal arguments of opposing attorneys and then have an opportunity to question them.

---

11. If the error is deemed to be minor and not to have affected the result, the court labels it as "harmless error" and allows the decision to stand.
12. Double jeopardy is a situation in which a person is tried more than once for the same offense. The fifth and fourteenth amendments to the Constitution prohibit various forms of double jeopardy.

E.   FEDERAL COURTS

The basic trial court in the federal judiciary is the district court. There are ninety-three district courts spread among the fifty states, the District of Columbia, and the territories of Guam, the North Mariana Islands, Puerto Rico, and the Virgin Islands. Each state has at least one district court, with the larger states having as many as four within their borders. (See Figure 2.1.)

The number of judges assigned to each district varies from one to twenty-seven depending on the case load of the district. These district court judges are assisted by magistrates and bankruptcy judges. The district court judges are appointed by the president (with the consent of the Senate) for life terms.[13] The magistrates, on the other hand, are selected by a majority of the active judges of each district court for full-time terms of eight years or part-time terms of four years, and they can be removed for cause. Bankruptcy judges are appointed for fourteen-year terms by the court of appeals for the circuit in which the district is located. The magistrates supervise court calendars, hear procedural motions, issue subpoenas, hear minor criminal offense cases, and conduct civil pretrial hearings. In some district courts the magistrates, with the consent of the parties involved, conduct trials and enter judgments in civil cases.[14] Bankruptcy judges handle most bankruptcy cases entirely on their own. In a limited number of cases they conduct the trial but then must submit their proposed findings of fact to the district judge, who in turn enters the final order or judgment.

The jurisdiction of the district courts is both *in rem* and *in personam*. The court has jurisdiction over alleged violations of the federal criminal code; civil cases involving the application or interpretation of federal law (such as the Constitution, acts of Congress, and United States treaties) in which claims for at least $10,000 are involved; civil cases irrespective of monetary value where Congress has so authorized (such as voting rights violations, naturalization cases); *habeas corpus* petitions;[15] cases affecting ambassadors, other public ministers, and consuls where Congress gave them concurrent jurisdiction with the Supreme Court; and admiralty and maritime matters. They have *in personam* jurisdiction in diversity of citizenship cases with at least $10,000 at stake.[16]

---

13. All federal constitutional judges are appointed for "good behavior." In reality this means they can serve until they either die, voluntarily retire, or are convicted in impeachment proceedings.
14. See Wharton-Thomas v. United States, No. 82-5555 (3d Cir. 1983), and Pace-Maker Diagnostic Clinic of America, Inc. v. Instromedix, Inc., 712 F.2d 1305 (9th Cir. 1983).
15. A claim of unlawful imprisonment (by either federal or state officials) based on alleged violation of federal constitutional rights.
16. A case in which the parties are residents of different states or a dispute between a United States citizen and either a foreign country or a citizen of a foreign country.

Figure 2.1 District and Appellate Court Boundaries

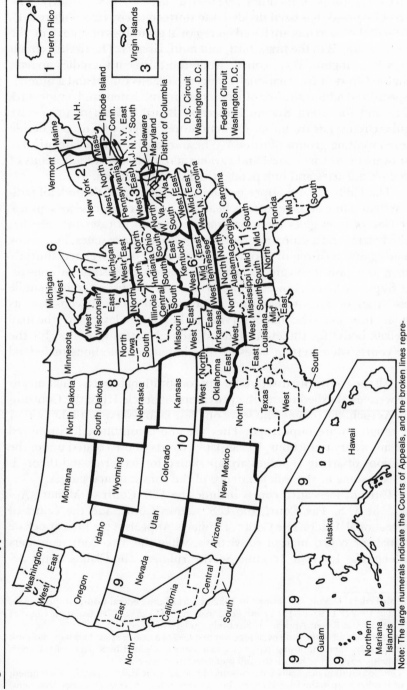

Note: The large numerals indicate the Courts of Appeals, and the broken lines represent jurisdiction boundaries of district courts.

Source: Administrative Office of the U.S. Courts.

The basic appellate court in the federal system is the United States Court of Appeals (sometimes referred to as the Circuit Court). The Court of Appeals has been divided into thirteen circuits (see Figure 2.1). Eleven of these circuits are based on regional groupings of states with the territories added to the first, third, and ninth circuits. The twelfth circuit covers Washington, D.C., courts, while the thirteenth handles appeals from the Court of International Trade, the Claims Court, and a number of specialized administrative offices including the Patent and Trademark Office and the Merit System Protection Board.[17] Each of the twelve regular circuits has from four to twenty-three judges who usually decide cases in rotating groups of three.[18] These courts have appellate jurisdiction over the district courts and various administrative adjudications of executive agencies and independent regulatory agencies.

The United States Supreme Court is at the top of the federal judicial system. Here all nine justices hear and decide every case as a group. The Constitution gives them original jurisdiction in cases between the United States and a state; in cases between two or more states; in cases by a state against a citizen of another state, an alien, or a foreign country;[19] and in any case involving foreign ambassadors, ministers, or consuls. The Supreme Court, however, prefers to have the district courts handle these types of cases whenever it is possible to do so. It considers its primary function to be that of serving as the court of last resort (the final appellate body) for the entire federal judicial system as well as for the state courts when certain cases involve important questions of federal law.

All the courts discussed so far are constitutional courts. That means they were established under the provisions of article III of the Constitution. As such, the judges who serve on these courts serve until they either die, resign, or are impeached. They are also constitutionally protected from any salary reductions. In legislative courts (those created under the provisions of article I) judges are appointed for set terms and theoretically lack some of the independence of the constitutional judges.

Current legislative courts include the U.S. Court of Military Appeals, the U.S. Tax Court, the U.S. Claims Court, and the Court of International Trade. The Court of Military Appeals is the final appellate tribunal for courts-martial convictions, while the Tax Court considers challenges to Internal Revenue Service rulings. The Claims Court de-

---

17. This Federal Circuit was formed in 1982 as part of the Federal Courts Improvement Act of 1982 (P.L. 97-164) as a consolidation of the old Court of Claims and the Court of Customs and Patent Appeals. It has twelve judges assigned to it.

18. Occasionally all of the justices sit together and decide a case *en banc*. This happens most frequently when the losing party in a case already decided by a panel of the court requests a rehearing before the full membership of the court.

19. The Constitution originally gave citizens of one state the right to sue the government of another state in the federal courts, but the eleventh amendment canceled that right.

Figure 2.2 Organization of the Federal Courts and Quasi-Judicial Administrative Agencies

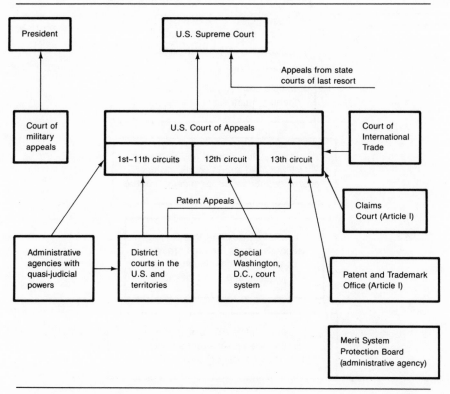

cides the validity of specific types of claims against the United States government, and the Court of International Trade (formally the Customs Court) reviews decisions and appraisals of imported merchandise made in collecting customs duties.

Figure 2.2 illustrates the organizational structure of the federal court system. The arrows indicate the avenues for appeals.

F.   STATE COURTS

While many important cases and significant constitutional issues are decided in the federal courts, most of the legal work in this country takes place in state courts. In fact, approximately 98 percent of the nation's judicial business occurs in the state courts.[20] An analysis of 1983

---

20. Cooke and Goodman, The State of the Nation's State Courts, Natl. L.J., March 19, 1984, at 23, col. 3.

Figure 2.3 Organization of State Court Systems

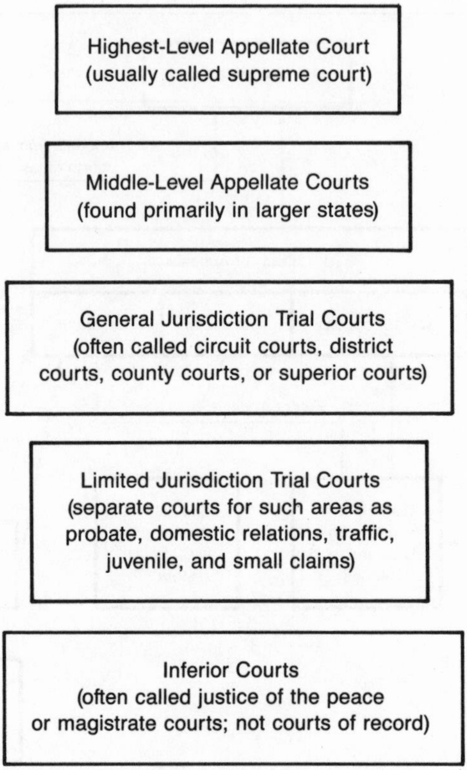

Highest-Level Appellate Court
(usually called supreme court)

Middle-Level Appellate Courts
(found primarily in larger states)

General Jurisdiction Trial Courts
(often called circuit courts, district
courts, county courts, or superior courts)

Limited Jurisdiction Trial Courts
(separate courts for such areas as
probate, domestic relations, traffic,
juvenile, and small claims)

Inferior Courts
(often called justice of the peace
or magistrate courts; not courts of record)

state court statistics showed that almost 82 million cases were filed in state courts that year, which is about one for every household in the country.[21] About 57 million were traffic cases, and 1 million were juvenile matters. Thus while paralegals may have some opportunities to work with federal courts, most will spend their time operating within their state court systems.

State court systems are often much more complex than the federal system. Rather than having one basic trial court with general jurisdiction, similar to federal district courts, many states have a confusing variety of specialized courts which often have overlapping jurisdiction. Figure 2.3 presents a simplified diagram of a pattern of court organization that is common in many states. Trial courts of limited jurisdiction cover areas like traffic offenses, misdemeanor criminal cases, small claims, juvenile, probate, domestic relations, and so forth. These courts are combined

---

21. Kelley, Record 82M Cases Flood State Courts, USA Today, Oct. 8, 1984, at 1A.

with a system of general jurisdiction trial courts that focus on felonies and large civil cases. They typically carry names like circuit courts, district courts, county courts, or superior courts.

Some states also maintain a system of inferior courts with names like justice of the peace court, city court, or magistrate court. These courts are not "courts of record," which means that no permanent record is kept of the testimony, lawyers' remarks, or judge's rulings. The absence of a record eliminates the possibility of an appeal and requires the losing party to initiate a complete new trial in a higher level trial court if it wishes to have the matter reconsidered.

States maintain either one or two levels of appellate courts. The larger states have generally gone to a two-tiered system like that in operation at the federal level. The intermediate level appellate courts usually sit in panels, while their courts of last resort sit *en banc*. On some matters appeals to the highest court are discretionary, while on others they are a matter of right. In a few states separate courts have been established to handle criminal versus civil appeals at the intermediate and/or highest level. Finally, as noted earlier in this chapter, even the name of the highest-level appellate court varies from state to state. While most states identify their court of last resort as the supreme court, in New York and Maryland it is called the court of appeals.

The trend in state court organization has been in the direction of what is called "court unification." The five basic elements of a unified court system are:

1. A consolidated court structure: the elimination of overlapping and conflicting jurisdictional boundaries of both subject matter and geography for trial courts;
2. Centralized management of the court system: a hierarchically organized management structure with primary responsibility vested in the chief justice of the state court of last resort;
3. Centralized rulemaking: rulemaking authority vested in the state's highest court and unencumbered by a legislative veto;
4. Unitary budgeting: a judicial budget prepared centrally at the state level without executive branch review and oversight; and
5. State financing of the courts: state funds used to finance the entire judicial system, with local fees and fines paid directly to the state treasury.[22]

Advocates of court unification argue that the above-listed features increases the independence and the efficiency of state courts. Some states

---

22. Tarr, Court Unification and Court Performance: A Preliminary Assessment, 64 Judicature 356, 358 (1981).

have selectively adopted some of the above reforms without implementing the entire package.

State courts have exclusive jurisdiction (that is, they are the only courts that have authority to hear that kind of case) over matters that do not fall within the purview or scope of the federal courts. In some areas, both the federal and state courts have authority to hear the same types of cases (concurrent jurisdiction). Whenever a federal law or a provision of the U.S. Constitution is involved, the federal courts have the right to the final say.

Judges for the state courts are selected in a variety of ways. Some are appointed by the state's chief executive and/or the state legislature. Others are selected in either partisan or nonpartisan elections. Still others use a modification of what has come to be known as the Missouri plan. These systems generally involve a special panel of lawyers and lay persons nominating a few candidates for the vacancy. The governor then appoints from among this select group. A year or two later the appointee goes before the electorate in a special retention election. In such an election the voters are asked simply whether Judge X should be retained.

G.   COURT PERSONNEL

The trial judge is, of course, the most powerful member of the courtroom team. Within the limits of the law, the judge decides whether a case is to be dismissed before it reaches the trial stage, the extent of pretrial discovery, and the amount of time the lawyers will have to prepare their cases. Once the trial is underway, the judge acts as the presiding officer, rules on objections, and determines when recesses will occur. If a jury is involved, the judge supervises their selection, removes them from the courtroom at key times to protect them from improper influences, and instructs them on the meaning of the law they are to apply. Where a jury is not involved, the judge also makes the substantive determination of guilt or innocence, liability or lack of liability, and so forth. In criminal cases the judge is also responsible for sentencing the convicted.

Lawyers are considered to be officers of the court. As such they are responsible for maintaining proper decorum in the courtroom and acting within the ethical restraints imposed on them by the courts and their profession.

Court clerks are responsible for keeping the court files in their proper condition and ensuring that the various motions filed by lawyers and the actions taken by judges are properly recorded. A head clerk of the courts is usually responsible for running the central records section

of the courthouse, while assistants are assigned to sit in on the actual courtroom proceedings.

The court reporter prepares a verbatim transcript of the courtroom proceedings. Most reporters use a stenotype machine rather than shorthand. Since it is expensive, a written transcript is prepared only if the case is being appealed.

Bailiffs are responsible for maintaining order in the courtroom. They are also responsible for watching over the jury during recesses or when the jury has been sequestered.[23]

Finally, sheriffs and marshals also serve as officers of the court when they serve summonses and other court documents, collect money as part of a court judgment, or otherwise assist in carrying out the court's orders.

H. SUMMARY

The development and enforcement of law is an essential governmental function in all developed societies. These laws regulate human conduct by imposing duties to do certain things and prohibiting other types of behavior. Under the federalist system of government in the United States, the states and the national government share the responsibility for formulating these laws.

The United States Constitution lays down fundamental legal principles and assigns powers to the various branches of government and the subunits (local governments). All law must be consistent with the dictates of the Constitution. Statutory law consists of the enactments of legislative bodies in the federal, state, and local governments. Administrative law is formulated by the executive branches and independent regulatory agencies. In situations where these laws do not resolve the conflict, the judge turns to the common law. In so doing the judge follows principles that are derived from previous decisions in related cases.

Whereas the civil law is designed to redress private wrongs, the criminal law is designed to punish those whose conduct offends society as a whole. In criminal law the state assumes the burden of prosecuting a case, while in the civil area the offended individual must pursue the matter personally. In both situations the state provides judicial apparatus for arbitrating the dispute. There are also major differences between civil and criminal cases with respect to the burden of proof required and the sanctions that are imposed.

---

23. When a jury is sequestered, the members sleep at a hotel and are kept isolated from the public and their families in order to prevent them from being exposed to prejudicial publicity, threats, or bribes or any other improper influences.

There is a basic difference between trial courts and appellate courts. The trial court not only makes the initial decision in a dispute but also develops the record that appellate courts review. The appellate courts do not take additional testimony about the facts of the dispute and will rarely substitute their own factual conclusions for those of the trial judge or jury. The appellate courts focus on reviewing the legal issues involved in a case. They examine the interpretation given to the law by the trial judge and procedures that were employed during the trial.

Compared to most state judiciaries the federal judicial system is relatively simple. The district court serves as a trial court of general jurisdiction (that is, it can hear cases involving a wide variety of criminal and civil matters). The court of appeals provides the first level of review, and then the Supreme Court sits as the court of last resort (the final appellate body). State court systems often have a variety of specialized courts at the trial level. Some have only one level of review, while others have a two-tiered system like the federal model.

While there is a great deal of variation among the federal judicial system and the states' systems, they also have much in common. This chapter has attempted to present the basic principles and procedures of these systems. The mastery of the materials is a prerequisite to the reader's future exploration of specific court systems and substantive areas of the law.

KEY TERMS

administrative law

appellate court

appellate jurisdiction

bankruptcy judge

civil law

common law

concurrent jurisdiction

constitutional court

constitutional law

court

court of record

criminal law

diversity of citizenship

en banc

entrapment

equity

exclusive jurisdiction

general jurisdiction

habeas corpus

inferior courts

injunction

in personam

in rem

jurisdiction

law

legislative court

limited jurisdiction

magistrate

ordinance

original jurisdiction

statutory law

trial court

REVIEW QUESTIONS

1.   What is the basic function of law in our society?

2.   Under what conditions does a judge apply the comon law?

3.   What are the primary differences between criminal law and civil law?

4.   What are the primary differences between trial courts and appellate courts?

5.   From what judicial bodies can you appeal directly to the United States Supreme Court?

6.   What are the methods used for selecting judges in the federal and state courts?

DISCUSSION QUESTIONS

1.   Do you believe that laws are in fact necessary? Many believe we have too much law today. Do you agree? If you do feel that we have too many laws, which ones should be eliminated? Do we need additional laws in some areas?

2.   What is the proper relationship between the law and morality? When, if ever, should laws be based on moral codes or used to enforce moral values?

3.   Should there be less variation in the law from one state to the next? Do the advantages of diversity really outweigh the disadvantages?

4.   How important is the method by which judges are selected? Which method do you think is best and why?

PROJECTS

1.   Read the United States Constitution and then make a list of the powers that are assigned to each of the following categories:
     a. Powers that are delegated to the federal government;
     b. Powers that neither the states nor the federal government can exercise; and
     c. Powers that states (but not the federal government) are specifically prohibited from exercising.

2.   Draw a diagram of your own state's court system. To what extent does your state system fit the criteria for a unified court system?

Chapter 3
Finding and Interpreting the Law

THE RESOLUTION OF A LEGAL conflict involves the application of general principles of law to the specific facts of the case at hand. But disagreements may arise regarding what principles should be applied or how they should be interpreted. Since the statutes and precedent cases are often ambiguous, lawyers and paralegals must learn the legal conventions for interpreting these materials. This chapter identifies where the law can be found and examines the legal reasoning process used to interpret it.

A. PUBLICATION OF PRIMARY SOURCE MATERIAL

1. Statutes

The United States is frequently referred to as a common law country because of its historical acceptance of English common law traditions, but most of the actual body of the common law has been superseded by legislative enactments. Today the law that governs most of our daily activities is statutory, and the law required in a given situation is usually found by reading the relevant ordinances and statutes. State and federal statutes are usually published in three primary forms: individual slip laws, periodic compilation of new laws passed within a certain time period, and unified codes. Paralegals need to be familiar with these publications.

When laws are first officially enacted, they are usually published individually as slip laws. Federal slip laws are available at libraries designated as official depositories and can be ordered directly from the United States Government Printing Office. State slip laws are usually available at larger libraries in the various states and from the state governments themselves.

At the end of a legislative term the federal and most state governments publish the laws passed during that term as one or more volumes in a continuing set. They are usually arranged in chronological order by

date of passage and are referred to as either statutes at large or sessions laws.

New federal statutes also appear in several other publications. West Publishing's U.S. Code Congressional and Administrative News and the Lawyers' Co-operative Publishing Company's Current Public Laws and Administrative Service both contain the full text of public laws along with information about the legislative history. These publications come out in pamphlet form on a monthly or semimonthly basis. United States Law Week is a weekly loose-leaf service that also includes the text of many of the more important laws passed during that particular week. Similar loose-leaf and pamphlet services exist in some states.

The publications discussed here are arranged chronologically by date of passage; however, codes[1] arrange the laws by subject matter. While the above publications contain only those laws passed during a particular time period, codes contain all public laws currently in force in a particular area. The United States Code is the official codification of federal statutes and is printed and distributed by the U.S. Government Printing Office. The United States Code Annotated and the United States Code Service (formally known as the Federal Code Annotated) are published by West and Lawyers' Co-operative respectively. In addition to the text of the laws themselves, these two annotated versions of the code have information about the legislative history and references to court decisions which have interpreted the statutes. Some state statutes are also published by West in an annotated form. Table 3.1 lists the most common publications and abbreviations.

Local ordinances are usually published as individual slip laws and then kept in a loose-leaf binder. They are usually found in local libraries and at the administrative offices of the governmental unit involved.

References to a specific statute, administrative regulation, or court case, should be followed by the appropriate citation so that others can easily locate and check the source. In the absence of special instructions from a court or publisher to the contrary, the Uniform System of Citation[2] is generally accepted as the guide for determining the proper format for citations.

Whenever possible, statutory citations should include the name of the statute and the section as it was originally enacted. Statutes currently in force are usually cited to the code. For example:

Administrative Procedure Act, 5 U.S.C. §552(b)(3) (1974)
Cannabis Control Act, Ill. Rev. Stat. ch. 56½, §701 (1973)

---

1. The formal names for these codes differ from one state to another. In addition to *codes*, they may be called *revised statutes, consolidated statutes,* or *compiled statutes.*
2. This booklet is published and distributed by the Harvard Law Review Association and is periodically updated through new editions.

Table 3.1 Common Publications Containing the Texts of Statutes

PUBLICATION	ABBRE-VIATION	COVERAGE
United States Code	U.S.C.	Codified federal statutes
United States Code Annotated	U.S.C.A.	Codified federal statutes with annotations
United States Code Service	U.S.C.S.	Codified federal statutes with annotations (same as F.C.A.)
Federal Code Annotated	F.C.A.	Codified federal statutes with annotations (same as U.S.C.S.)
United States Statutes at Large	Stat.	Federal statutes enacted at a particular time
U.S. Code Congressional and Administrative News	None[a]	Federal statutes enacted at a particular time
Current Public Laws and Administrative Service	None[a]	Federal statutes enacted at a particular time
United States Law Week	U.S.L.W.	Federal statutes enacted at a particular time
Alabama Code[b]	Ala. Code	Codified Alabama statutes
Arizona Revised Statutes Annotated[b]	Ariz. Rev. Stat. Ann.	Codified Arizona statutes with annotations
California Business and Professions Code[c]	Cal. Bus. & Prof. Code	Codified California statutes relating to business and the professions
New York Domestic Relations Law[c]	N.Y. Dom. Rel.	Codified New York statutes relating to domestic relations

[a] Because these publications are not used in formal citations, no abbreviation is given.
[b] These are typical of the format used in most states and are used to illustrate this pattern.
[c] A few states publish their laws in separate publications according to the subject.

The number 5 preceding the U.S.C. designation indicates that it is Title 5. The § symbol stands for section and *ch.* for chapter.

If the act does not appear in the code (either because it has been repealed or it was passed too recently to be included in the code), it is cited to the statutes at large (session laws) or simply to the public law number and its date of passage. For example:

Clayton Act §7, ch. 25, §7, 38 Stat. 631 (1914), Pub. L. No. 95-221, §1 (March 14, 1978)

When session laws are cited, the year of enactment is usually shown in parentheses. When codes are cited, the year of codification is usually given.

Local ordinances follow the same general format:

Portland, Ore., Police Code art. 30 (1953)

2. Administrative Regulations

Since legislatures often delegate considerable lawmaking authority to administrative agencies, it is frequently necessary to look beyond the statutes and to administrative regulations promulgated by these agencies. These materials are published in formats that resemble those used for statutes.

Federal administrative regulations and decisions are published in the Federal Register (Fed. Reg.). This publication is issued daily (except Sundays, Mondays, and the days following holidays). The Code of Federal Regulations (C.F.R.) is analogous to the United States Code in that it contains only those regulations that are of a general permanent nature and currently in force. It is organized on the basis of the same fifty titles as the United States Code.

Some states publish codes of regulations that correspond to the Code of Federal Regulations. In other states the regulations must be obtained from each individual agency. At both the state and federal levels some private publishers issue loose-leaf reporters that contain administrative regulations in specialized areas like taxes and labor law.

Citations for administrative regulations follow a form that is analogous to statutes, for example:

Atomic Energy Comm. Rules of Practice §2.701, 21 Fed. Reg. 805 (1956)
49 C.F.R. §6.1 (Supp. 1966)

Adjudicative decisions are cited in the following manner:

Electric Bond and Share Co., 11 S.E.C. 1146 (1942)

The abbreviation stands for the agency involved — in this case the Securities and Exchange Commission.

3. Constitutions

Since constitutions focus on the structure of the government itself, they usually have very little to say directly about specific legal problems. Instead, the constitution is more likely to be used when one is seeking to challenge an objectionable statute or the manner in which government agents conducted themselves (such as a fourth amendment challenge to an allegedly unreasonable search).

State and federal constitutions are usually included in the above-

mentioned compilations of statutes. The United States Constitution can be found in the United States Code, the United States Code Annotated, and the Federal Code Annotated. The Library of Congress also publishes a separate annotated edition of the constitution. A state statute compilation usually includes a copy of its state constitution, and a few even feature a copy of the U.S. Constitution with annotations to decisions in their own state courts.

Sections of constitutions are cited as follows:

U.S. Const. art. I, §8, cl. 3
U.S. Const. amend. XX, §3
Ill. Const. art. IV, §2(b)

4. Court Cases

Generally the decisions of trial courts are summarily recorded in the official case file and then stored at the local courthouse. While the decision is of great consequence to the parties involved, it usually has little significance for others.[3] The decisions of appellate courts, on the other hand, usually involve legal issues rather than factual issues and ordinarily are accompanied by a detailed justification for the court's decision. Since these decisions have precedent value,[4] it is important that they be made more readily available to the general legal community. In order to accomplish this, they are published in case reporters.

Case reporters, consisting of hundreds of volumes, are books that contain copies of the court's opinions. They are usually arranged in chronological order and divided into volumes according to the court that rendered the opinion. Thus, opinions of the United States District Courts are found in the Federal Supplement, while opinions from the United States Court of Appeals are in the Federal Reporter.

West Publishing Company is the major publisher of case reporters, and the West National Reporter System covers all appellate court decisions in the fifty states. The complete West system is briefly described in Table 3.2.

In addition to being reported by West, the decisions of selected courts are also recorded by the federal government, many states, and other private publishing houses. The federal government publishes United States Supreme Court cases in the United States Reports, while the Lawyers' Co-operative Publishing Company prints

---

3. There are occasions where trial courts (especially United States District Courts) will produce opinions involving significant legal issues. When these opinions are produced, they are published in the same manner as are the appellate court decisions.
4. The term *precedent* will be explained in more detail shortly. For now it means that the court's decision may be considered a factor in determining the intepretation of the law in another case.

Table 3.2 West Case Reporters

Name of Case Reporter	Abbreviation	Courts Covered
Supreme Court Reporter	S. Ct.	U.S. Supreme Court
Federal Reporter	F.	U.S. Circuit Courts, District
Federal Reporter, Second Series	F.2d	Courts prior to 1932, and some specialized federal courts such as Court of Claims and Customs and Patent Appeals
Federal Supplement	F. Supp.	U.S. District Courts since 1932 and some decisions of Customs Court and Court of Claims
Federal Rules Decisions	F.R.D.	U.S. District Court Opinions involving Federal Rules of Civil Procedure and Federal Rules of Criminal Procedure
Atlantic Reporter	A.	State courts in Conn., Dela.,
Atlantic Reporter, Second Series	A.2d	Maine, Md., N.H., N.J., Penn., R.I., Vt., and Dist. of Colum. Mun. Court of App.
North Eastern Reporter	N.E.	State courts in Ill., Ind., Mass.,
North Eastern Reporter, Second Series	N.E.2d	N.Y., and Ohio
North Western Reporter	N.W.	State court cases in Iowa, Mich.,
North Western Reporter, Second Series	N.W.2d	Minn., Neb., N.D., S.D., and Wis.
Pacific Reporter	P.	State court cases in Alaska, Ariz.,
Pacific Reporter, Second Series	P.2d	Calif., Colo., Hawaii, Idaho, Kan., Mont., Nev., N.M., Okla., Ore., Utah, Wash., and Wyo.
South Eastern Reporter	S.E.	State court cases in Ga., N.C.,
South Eastern Reporter, Second Series	S.E.2d	S.C., Va., and W.Va.
South Western Reporter	S.W.	State court cases in Ark., Ky.,
South Western Reporter, Second Series	S.W.2d	Mo., Tenn., and Texas; also has cases from Indian territories
Southern Reporter	So.	State court cases in Ala., Ga.,
Southern Reporter, Second Series	So. 2d	La., and Miss.
New York Supplement	N.Y.S.	State court cases from the state
New York Supplement, Second Series	N.Y.S.2d	of N.Y.
California Reporter	Cal. Rptr.	State court decisions from Calif.

Figure 3.1 Analysis of Case Citations

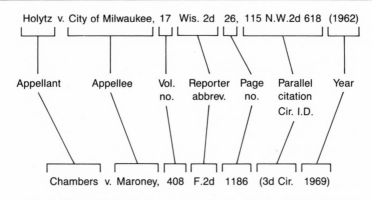

the United States Supreme Court Reports, Lawyers' Edition. Both, like West's Supreme Court Reporter, publish the complete opinions of the United States Supreme Court.[5] Several of the more commonly used case reporters are listed in Table 3.3.

Reporters are divided into official and unofficial categories. They are official when published at the direction of state or federal statutes. All others are unofficial. Since the opinions published in the unofficial reporters are the same as those in the official ones, either can be used. However, when citing the case in briefs or other legal documents, the official citation should be stated first. While states differ as to the precedent value of decisions that are published only in unofficial reporters, most lawyers routinely include such citations when presenting their cases.

Carefully examine Figure 3.1. Note that the citation begins with an abbreviated version of the names of the parties to the litigation. In the first case Janet Holytz, a minor, brought an appeal from a lower court decision that favored the City of Milwaukee. The party bringing the appeal (the appellant or petitioner) is usually listed first, and the opposing side (the appellee or respondent) is listed second.[6] In the second example, Frank Chambers is appealing a conviction for robbery by asking for a writ of habeas corpus against James F. Maroney, superintendent of the State Correctional Institution.[7] (The party responsible

---

5. United States Supreme Court opinions can also be found in a loose-leaf service entitled United States Law Week.
6. Some states follow the practice of listing the name of the original plaintiff first no matter which party brings the appeal.
7. The seeking of a writ of habeas corpus is a procedure in which the prisoner attempts to show the court that he is being held illegally by agents of the state. In instances such as this one it is a means of obtaining a federal court examination of the validity of a state criminal conviction.

Table 3.3 Commonly Used Case Reports Not Published by West

NAME OF CASE REPORTER	ABBRE-VIATION	COURTS COVERED
United States Supreme Court Reports	U.S.	U.S. Supreme Court
Lawyers' Edition, United States Supreme Court Reports	L. Ed.	U.S. Supreme Court
Lawyers' Edition, United States Supreme Court Reports, Second Series	L. Ed. 2d.	U.S. Supreme Court
Court of Claims	Ct. Cl.	U.S. Court of Claims
Court of Customs and Patent Appeals Reports	C.C.P.A.	Court of Customs and Patent Appeals Customs Court
Customs Court Reports	Cust. Ct.	Customs Court
Federal Communications Commission Reports[a]	F.C.C.	Federal Communications Commission Decisions
Illinois Reports[b]	Ill.	Illinois Supreme Court
Illinois Reports, Second Series	Ill. 2d	Illinois Supreme Court
Illinois Appellate Court Reports	Ill. App.	Illinois Appellate Court
Illinois Appellate Court Reports, Second Series	Ill. App. 2d	Illinois Appellate Court
Pennsylvania District and County Reports[b]	Pa. D.&C.	Pennsylvania District and County Courts
Pennsylvania District and County Reports, Second Series	Pa. D.&C.2d	Pennsylvania District and County Courts
Pennsylvania State Reports	Pa.	Pennsylvania Courts not covered in other Case Reporters
Pennsylvania Superior Court Reports	Pa. Super.	Pennsylvania Superior Court

[a] This is simply one of several similar reports related to different regulatory agencies. The abbreviation corresponds to the agency.

[b] These are used to illustrate the pattern found in states that publish their own court opinions. Other states have similar names for their reporters.

for bringing the case to the court in question is usually listed first. This may or may not be the party who originated the litigation at the trial level.)

This information is usually printed in prominent letters at the very beginning of the case. In determining the format for the first part of the citation, the major problem usually centers around which parts of the title should be omitted from the citation. As you can see above, the first

names and initials of individuals are omitted. Frank Chambers v. James F. Maroney becomes simply Chambers v. Maroney. Maroney's title as superintendent of the State Correctional Institution is also omitted. On the other hand, first names or initials that are part of corporate names are included (e.g., Williams v. D. L. Lewis & Co.). Common abbreviations such as *Co., Bd., Inc.* and *Natl.* can be used to shorten the title.

When there is more than one party on any side or when several cases have been consolidated, the citaton uses only the names of the first parties listed on each side or the first case listed. When the state is a party to a case in its own courts, it is usually listed as *People v.* or *State v.* On the other hand, if a state is a party to a suit in federal court, the listing would be *Illinois v.*

Questions about what names to use in the title often can be resolved by consulting the table of cases at the front of the case reporter or by referring to the top of subsequent pages to see how the editors of the reporter abbreviated the cases.

Look back to the two examples given near the beginning of this section and note the use of abbreviations for case reporters. Table 3.2 shows that *F.2d* stands for the Federal Reporter, Second Series, and that *N.W.2d* stands for North Western Reporter, Second Series. The *Wis. 2d* is similar to the *Ill. 2d* used in Table 3.3. The use of these abbreviations tells the reader that Holytz v. City of Milwaukee can be found in both the Wisconsin Reports, Second Series, and the North Western Reporter, Second Series. Chambers v. Maroney can be found in the Federal Reporter, Second Series.

The numbers immediately in front of the reporter abbreviation stand for the number of the volume in which the case is found. The numbers imediately after the reporter abbreviation stand for the page number on which the case begins. Thus it can be seen that Holytz v. City of Milwaukee can be found both on page 26 of volume 17 of Wisconsin Reports, Second Series, and on page 618 of volume 115 of the North Western Reporter, Second Series. When two such citations are given for the same case, they are referred to as parallel citations. Additional examples of parallel citations are:

Chambers v. Maroney, 399 U.S. 42, 90 S. Ct. 1975, 26 L. Ed. 2d 419 (1970)
McPherson v. Buick Motor Co., 217 N.Y. 282, 111 N.E. 1050 (Ct. App. 1916)

Following the identification of the volume and page of the reporters, the year in which the decision was rendered will appear in parentheses. *Holytz* was decided in 1962, and *Chambers* in 1969. In those cases where the identification of the court is not obvious from the type of reporter involved, there will be additional information about the court in parentheses. In the *Holytz* case a discerning reader can tell that the Wis-

consin Supreme Court made the decision because only Supreme Court decisions from that state are published in Wisconsin Reports. In the *Chambers* case one can tell it is a decision from a United States Court of Appeals because it appears in the Federal Reporter. Note that information on which circuit was involved is included in the parentheses with the year. Listed below are some of the common abbreviations used to indicate the appropriate courts:

(6th Cir. 1978)	Case was decided in the Sixth Circuit in 1978
(D.C. Cir. 1972)	Case was decided in the Washington, D.C., circuit in 1972
(D.C.R.I. 1969)	Case was decided in district court of Rhode Island in 1969
(N.D. Ill. 1971)	Case was decided in District Court for the Northern District of Illinois in 1971
(Cal. 1952)	Case was decided in the California Supreme Court in 1952
(Ill. App. 1946)	Case was decided in the Illinois appellate courts in 1946

Up to this point the citations given have been for the case itself, and therefore the key page number given is the page on which the case begins. Sometimes a writer will make reference to a specific part of the court decision where a particular quote appears or where an issue is discussed. In these instances a second page number will appear after the page number on which the case begins; for example, a quotation taken from page 1,189 of the Chambers v. Maroney decision would be cited as follows:

Chambers v. Maroney, 409 F.2d 1186, 1189 (3d Cir. 1969)

Sometimes citations will include information about prior or subsequent history of the case. For example:

Telex Corp. v. International Business Machines Corp., 367 F. Supp. 258 (N.D. Okla. 1973), 510 F.2d 894 (10th Cir. 1975), *cert. denied,* 423 U.S. 802 (1975)

This citation indicates that the case was first decided by the federal District Court for the Northern District of Oklahoma and can be found in volume 367 of the Federal Supplement beginning on page 258. The case was then appealed to the Tenth Circuit where the decision is reported in volume 510 of the Federal Reporter, Second Series. The United States Supreme Court's decision not to grant *certiorari* is reported on page 802 of volume 423 of the United States Supreme Court Reports.

B. PUBLICATION OF SECONDARY SOURCES

In addition to the case reporters and codes mentioned above, most law libraries contain a large number of resource books that help one to find and interpret the appropriate legal principles. These secondary source materials, as well as the various indexes and digests, are discussed in Chapter 8.

C. INTERPRETING THE LAW

A paralegal needs to be able to do much more than simply locate a statute or court case on the basis of a citation given by an attorney. To be truly valuable addition to the law office team, the paralegal must be able to read and properly interpret these materials. This is a difficult skill that often takes years of practice to master. One begins with a general understanding of how the legal reasoning process works.

1. Statutes

Court decisions are based on a specific set of facts and established legal rules that ostensibly apply to a relatively narrow set of similar circumstances. Statutes are generally written in a general format and are designed to apply to a comprehensive set of circumstances. While judges interpret legal rules in a specific factual context, legislatures formulate rules that are supposed to apply to a variety of future situations.

The formulation of such future-oriented rules is a difficult task, and statutes often are ambiguous. Sometimes the ambiguity results from sloppy draftsmanship, but more often it merely is the result of being applied to unanticipated circumstances. Sometimes the ambiguity has been written in purposely in order to provide a basis for compromise by glossing over conflicts among the legislators.

As an example, §1715 of Title 18 of the United States Code declares that

> Pistols, revolvers, and other firearms capable of being concealed on the person are non-mailable and shall not be deposited in or carried by the mails or delivered by any postmaster, letter carrier, or other person in the Postal Service. . . .
> Whoever knowingly deposits for mailing or delivery, or knowingly causes to be delivered by mail according to the direction thereon, or at any place to which it is directed to be delivered by the person to whom it is addressed, any pistol, revolver, or firearm declared non-mailable by this section, shall be fined not more than $1,000 or imprisoned not more than two years, or both.

To illustrate the ambiguity of statutes such as this, we see that no men-
tion is made of size. Thus, would a person who mailed a sawed-off
shotgun be in violation of this statute if the overall length of the weapon
was 22 inches? What if it was 12 inches in length — or 32 inches?
Section 31-1 of the Illinois Criminal Code declares that

> A person who knowingly resists or obstructs the performance by one
> known to the person to be a police officer of any authorized act
> within his official capacity commits a Class A misdemeanor.[8]

But is an unlawful arrest an authorized act? Is a person guilty of violating
this law if an attempt is made to keep a police officer from conducting an
illegal search of that person's house?
Or consider the meaning of the Mann Act. It declares that

> Whoever knowingly transports in interstate or foreign commerce,
> or in the District of Columbia or in any Territory or Possession of the
> United States, any woman or girl for the purpose of prostitution or
> debauchery, or for any other immoral purpose, or with the intent
> and purpose to induce, entice, or compel such woman or girl to
> become a prostitute or to give herself up to debauchery, or to engage
> in any other immoral practice. . . .
> Shall be fined not more than $5,000 or imprisoned not more than
> five years, or both.[9]

What constitutes "any other immoral practices"? Is it a violation of
this law for a man to transport his girlfriend from Sacramento, California, to Reno, Nevada, for the purpose of cohabiting with her? Is it a
violation of the act to transport a prostitute to another state so that she
can have a vacation (which does not involve any immoral behavior)? Is it
a violation to transport that same prostitute back to the state she left so
that she can voluntarily resume her work as a prostitute? Is it a violation
of the act for a man to transport a woman across state lines so that she
can perform a striptease number at a stag party?
These are just a few examples of the ambiguity that is often found
in statutes. When questions like these arise, the courts are assigned the
task of clarifying their meaning. They will, of course, look to *stare decisis*
and the manner in which other courts have interpreted the same words.
Often the situation is one that has not been addressed before, and the
court must strike out on its own. "In the interpretation of statutes," wrote
Chief Justice Hughes, "the function of the courts is easily stated. It is to
construe the language so as to give effect to the intent of Congress."[10] In

---

8. Ill. Rev. Stat., ch. 38, §31-1.
9. 18 U.S.C. §2421.
10. United States v. American Trucking Assns., 310 U.S. 534, 542 (1940).

seeking to determine this intent the courts use three main approaches: literalism, intrinsic analysis, and extrinsic analysis.

a. Literalism

Statutory interpretation usually begins with a literal reading of the statute itself. This literalistic approach assumes that

1. The words used reflect the true intentions of the legislature; and
2. The legislature intended that the words they used be interpreted in light of their common, ordinary meanings.

The following sections of the United States Supreme Court's opinion in Barrett v. United States illustrate the application of a literalistic approach. Petitioner Barrett, who had been convicted of violating part of the federal Gun Control Act of 1968, argued that the statute did not apply to his specific conduct (he was a Kentucky gun dealer who sold a gun, which had been previously shipped in from another state, to a Kentucky resident who was a convicted felon). Note the manner in which the court applies a literal interpretation of the words used in the act and how it focuses even on the tense of the verbs.

Barrett v. United States
423 U.S. 212 (1976)

MR. JUSTICE BLACKMUN delivered the opinion of the Court.

Petitioner Pearl Barrett has been convicted by a jury in the United States District Court for the Eastern District of Kentucky of a violation of 18 U.S.C. §922(h), a part of the Gun Control Act of 1968, Pub. L. 90-618, 82 Stat. 1213, amending the Omnibus Crime Control and Safe Streets Act of 1968, Pub. L. 90-351, 82 Stat. 197, enacted earlier the same year. The issue before us is whether §922(h) has application to a purchaser's intrastate acquisition of a firearm that previously, but independently of the purchaser's receipt, had been transported in interstate commerce from the manufacturer to a distributor and then from the distributor to the dealer. . . .

Petitioner was charged with a violation of §922(h). He pleaded not guilty. At the trial no evidence was presented to show that Barrett personally had participated in any way in the previous interstate movement of the firearm. The evidence was merely to the effect that he had purchased the revolver out of the local dealer's stock, and that the gun, having been manufactured and then warehoused in other States, had reached the dealer through interstate channels. At the close of the prosecution's case, Barrett moved for a directed verdict of acquittal on the ground that §922(h) was not applicable to his receipt of the firearm. The

motion was denied. The court instructed the jury that the statute's interstate requirement was satisfied if the firearm at some time in its past had traveled in interstate commerce. A verdict of guilty was returned. Petitioner received a sentence of three years, subject to the immediate parole eligibility provisions of 18 U.S.C. §4208(a)(2).

Petitioner concedes that Congress, under the Commerce Clause of the Constitution, has the power to regulate interstate trafficking in firearms. Brief for Petitioner 7. He states, however, that the issue before us concerns the scope of Congress' exercise of that power in this statute. He argues that, in its enactment of §922(h), Congress was interested in "the business of gun traffic," Brief for Petitioner 11; that the Act was meant "to deal with *businesses,* not individuals per se" (emphasis in original), id., at 14, that is, with mail-order houses, out-of-state sources, and the like; and that the Act was not intended to, and does not, reach an isolated intrastate receipt, such as Barrett's transaction, where the handgun was sold within Kentucky by a local merchant to a local resident with whom the merchant was acquainted, and where the transaction "has no apparent connection with interstate commerce," despite the weapon's manufacture and original distribution in States other than Kentucky. Id., at 6.

We feel, however, that the language of §922(h), the structure of the Act of which §922(h) is a part, and the manifest purpose of Congress are all adverse to petitioner's position.

Section 922(h) pointedly and simply provides that it is unlawful for four categories of persons, including a convicted felon, "to receive any firearm or ammunition which has been shipped or transported in interstate or foreign commerce." The quoted language is without ambiguity. It is directed unrestrictedly at the felon's receipt of any firearm that "has been" shipped in interstate commerce. It contains no limitation to a receipt which itself is part of the interstate movement. We therefore have no reason to differ with the Court of Appeals' majority's conclusion that the language "means exactly what it says." 504 F.2d, at 632.

It is to be noted, furthermore, that while the proscribed act, "to receive any firearm," is in the present tense, the interstate commerce reference is in the present perfect tense, denoting an act that has been completed. Thus, there is no warping or stretching of language when the statute is applied to a firearm that already has completed its interstate journey and has come to rest in the dealer's showcase at the time of its purchase and receipt by the felon. Congress knew the significance and meaning of the language it employed. It used the present perfect tense elsewhere in the same section, namely, in §922(h)(1) (a person who "has been convicted"), and in §922(h)(4) (a person who "has been adjudicated" or who "has been committed"), in contrast to its use of the present tense ("who is") in §§922(h)(1), (2), and (3). The statute's pattern is consistent and no unintended misuse of language or of tense is apparent.

Had Congress intended to confine §922(h) to direct interstate receipt, it would have so provided, just as it did in other sections of the Gun Control Act. See §922(a)(3) (declaring it unlawful for a nonlicensee to receive in the state where he resides a firearm purchased or obtained "by such a person outside that State"); §922(j) (prohibiting the receipt of a stolen firearm (moving as . . . interstate . . . commerce"); and §922(k) (prohibiting the receipt "in interstate . . . commerce" of a firearm the serial number of which has been removed). Statutes other than the Gun Control Act similarly utilize restrictive language when only direct interstate commerce is to be reached. . . .

The literal approach is not always as easy as it appears to be above. For example, does the phrase "every wife and mother" apply to all wives and all mothers or just to everyone who is both a wife and a mother? To deal with these types of ambiguities, the courts have developed several principles to guide their interpretation. The last antecedent doctrine declares that relative and qualifying words and phrases are applied to the words and phrases immediately preceding them and not to those that are more remote. The express mention/implied exclusion rule states that if some idea is not expressly stated, the legislature intended that it be excluded. The *ejusdem generis*[11] principle holds that when a series of specific enumerations is followed by a catchall phrase such as "and others," it is to be interpreted to be limited to matters that are like the ones specifically listed.

An interesting application of *ejusdem generis* appears in the following Supreme Court application of the Mann Act. Go back to page 70 and reread the words of the act itself. Then note the manner in which the opinions of Justices Day and McKenna differ in their application of the principle of *ejusdem generis* to a situation in which someone had transported a woman across state lines so that she could become his mistress.

Caminetti v. United States
242 U.S. 470 (1917)

MR. JUSTICE DAY delivered the opinion of the Court.

It is contended that the act of Congress is intended to reach only "commercialized vice," or the traffic in women for gain, and that the conduct for which the several petitioners were indicted and convicted, however reprehensible in morals, is not within the purview of the statute when properly construed in the light of its history and the purposes intended to be accomplished by its enactment. In none of the cases was it

---

11. This Latin phrase is translated as "of the same class."

charged or proved that the transportation was for gain or for the purpose of furnishing women for prostitution for hire, and it is insisted that,
such being the case, the acts charged and proved, upon which conviction
was had, do not come within the statute. . . .

In United States v. Bitty, 208 U.S. 393, it was held that the act of
Congress against the importation of alien women and girls for the purpose of prostitution "and any other immoral purpose" included the importation of an alien woman to live in concubinage with the person
importing her. In that case this court said:

> All will admit that full effect must be given to the intention of
> Congress as gathered from the words of the statute. There can be no
> doubt as to what class was aimed at by the clause forbidding the
> importation of alien women for purposes of "prostitution." It refers
> to women who, for hire or without hire, offer their bodies to indis-
> criminate intercourse with men. The lives and example of such per-
> sons are in hostility to "the idea of the family, as consisting in and
> springing from the union for life of one man and one woman in the
> holy estate of matrimony; the sure foundation of all that is stable and
> noble in our civilization; the best guaranty of that reverent morality
> which is the source of all beneficent progress in social and political
> improvement." Murphy v. Ramsey, 114 U.S. 15, 45. . . . Now the
> addition in the last statute of the words, "or for any other immoral
> purpose," after the word "prostitution," must have been made for
> some practical object. Those added words show beyond question that
> Congress had in view the protection of society against another class
> of alien women other than those who might be brought here merely
> for purposes of "prostitution." In forbidding the importation of alien
> women "for any other immoral purpose," Congress evidently
> thought that there were purposes in connection with the importa-
> tions of alien women which, as in the case of importations for pros-
> titution, were to be deemed immoral. It may be admitted that, in
> accordance with the familiar rule of *ejusdem generis,* the immoral
> purpose referred to by the words "any other immoral purpose" must
> be one of the same general class or kind as the particular purpose of
> "prostitution" specified in the same clause of the statute. 2 Lewis's
> Sutherland, Stat. Constr. §423, and authorities cited. But that rule
> cannot avail the accused in this case; for the immoral purpose
> charged in the indictment is of the same general class or kind as the
> one that controls in the importation of an alien woman for the pur-
> pose strictly of prostitution. The prostitute may, in the popular
> sense, be more degraded in character than the concubine, but the
> latter nonetheless must be held to lead an immoral life, if any regard
> whatever be had to the views that are almost universally held in this
> country as to the relations which may rightfully, from the standpoint
> of morality, exist between man and woman in the matter of sexual
> intercourse. . . .

MR. JUSTICE MCKENNA, dissenting.

The transportation which is made unlawful is of a woman or girl
"to become a prostitute or to give herself up to debauchery, or to engage

in any other immoral practice." Our present concern is with the words "any other immoral practice," which, it is asserted, have a special office. The words are clear enough as general descriptions; they fail in particular designation; they are class words, not specifications. Are they controlled by those which precede them? If not, they are broader in generalization and include those that precede them, making them unnecessary and confusing. To what conclusion would this lead us? "Immoral" is a very comprehensive word. It means a dereliction of morals. In such sense it covers every form of vice, every form of conduct that is contrary to good order. It will hardly be contended that in this sweeping sense it is used in the statute. But, if not used in such sense, to what is it limited and by what limited? If it be admitted that it is limited at all, that ends the imperative effect assigned to it in the opinion of the court. But not insisting quite on that, we ask again, By what is it limited? By its context, necessarily, and the purpose of the statute. . . .

In other words, it is vice as a business at which the law is directed, using interstate commerce as a facility to procure or distribute its victims. . . .

United States v. Bitty, 208 U.S. 393 is not in opposition. The statute passed upon was a prohibition against the importation of alien women or girls — a statute, therefore, of broader purpose than the one under review. Besides, the statute finally passed upon was an amendment to a prior statute, and the words construed were an addition to the prior statute, and necessarily, therefore, had an added effect. The first statute prohibited the importation of any alien woman or girl into the United States *for the purpose of prostitution* [italics mine]. The second statute repeated the words and added "*or for any other immoral purpose.*" Necessarily there was an enlargement of purpose, and besides, the act was directed against the importation of foreign corruption, and was construed accordingly. The case, therefore, does not contradict the rule; it is an example of it.

Principles like *ejusdem generis* and express mention/implied exclusion are guidelines that the court can either apply or not apply at its discretion. There are occasions on which judges openly reject the entire literalistic approach. Observe the manner in which judges choose to ignore the literal meaning of words in the statute when they conclude that such a reading would not in fact properly reflect the true intent of the legislature. The *Holy Trinity* case involves the application of a statute prohibiting importation of aliens for a specific job. United States v. Powell raises the question of what constitutes a concealable firearm.[12]

----

12. See the previous discussion of this statute on page 69.

The Church of the Holy Trinity v. United States
143 U.S. 457 (1892)

MR. JUSTICE BREWER delivered the opinion of the court.

Plaintiff in error is a corporation, duly organized and incorporated as a religious society, under the laws of the State of New York. E. Walpole Warren was prior to September, 1887, an alien residing in England. In that month the plaintiff in error made a contract with him, by which he was to remove to the city of New York and enter into its service as rector and pastor; and, in pursuance of such contract, Warren did so remove and enter upon such service. It is claimed by the United States that this contract on the part of the plaintiff in error was forbidden by chapter 164, 28 Stat. at L. 332, and an action was commenced to recover the penalty prescribed by that Act. The Circuit Court held that the contract was within the prohibition of the statute, and rendered judgment accordingly (36 Fed. Rep. 303); and the single question presented for our determination is whether it erred in that conclusion.

The first section describes the act forbidden, and is in these words:

> Be it enacted by the Senate and House of Representatives of the United States of America in Congress assembled, that from and after the passage of this Act it shall be unlawful for any person, company, partnership or corporation, in any manner whatsoever, to prepay the transportation, or in any way assist or encourage the importation or migration of any alien or aliens, any foreigner or foreigners, into the United States, its territories or the District of Columbia, under contract or agreement, parol or special, express or implied, made previous to the importation or migration of such alien or aliens, foreigner or foreigners, to perform labor or service of any kind in the United States, its territories or the District of Columbia.

It must be conceded that the act of the corporation is within the letter of this section, for the relation of rector to his church is one of service, and implies labor on the one side with compensation on the other. Not only are the general words "labor" and "service" both used, but also, as it were to guard against any narrow interpretation and emphasize a breadth of meaning, to them is added "of any kind"; and further, as noticed by the Circuit Judge in his opinion, the fifth section, which makes specific exceptions, among them professional actors, artists, lecturers, singers, and domestic servants, strengthens the idea that every other kind of labor and service was intended to be reached by the first section. While there is great force in this reasoning, we cannot think Congress intended to denounce with penalties a transaction like that in the present case. It is a familiar rule that a thing may be within the letter of the statute and yet not within the statute, because not within its spirit, nor within the intention of its makers.

United States v. Powell

423 U.S. 87 (1975)

MR. JUSTICE REHNQUIST delivered the opinion of the court.

Respondent was indicted on a single count of mailing a firearm capable of being concealed on the person (the sawed-off shotgun . . .), in violation of 18 U.S.C. §1715. At trial there was evidence that the weapon could be concealed on an average person. Respondent was convicted by a jury which was instructed that in order to return a guilty verdict it must find that she "knowingly caused to be delivered by mail a firearm capable of being concealed on the person." . . .

She contends that as a matter of statutory construction, particularly in light of the doctrine of *ejusdem generis,* the language "other firearms capable of being concealed on the person" simply does not extend to sawed-off shotguns. . . .

The thrust of respondent's argument is that the more general language of the statute ("firearms") should be limited by the more specific language ("pistols and revolvers") so that the phrase "other firearms capable of being concealed on the person" would be limited to "concealable weapons such as pistols and revolvers."

We reject this contention. The statute by its terms bans the mailing of "firearms capable of being concealed on the person," and we would be justified in narrowing the statute only if such a narrow reading was supported by evidence of congressional intent over and above the language of the statute.

In Gooch v. United States, 297 U.S. 124, 128 (1936), the Court said:

> The rule of *ejusdem generis,* while firmly established, is only an instrumentality for ascertaining the correct meaning of words when there is uncertainty. Ordinarily, it limits general terms which follow specific ones to matters similar to those specified; but it may not be used to defeat the obvious purpose of legislation. And, while penal statutes are narrowly construed, this does not require rejection of that sense of the words which best harmonizes with the context and the end in view.

b. Intrinsic Factors

If literalism is not followed by judges, they must rely on another method of determining the legislature's intent. Thus, when courts look beyond the literal meaning of the words themselves, they often focus on the context in which the disputed clause occurs. This intrinsic approach involves looking at the overall structure of the larger legislative package and asking the following questions: What was the title the legislature gave to the act? Are relevant subheadings provided? Is the same term used elsewhere in the statute or in related statutes? It is usually assumed

that the name chosen for the act is significant, that the clause is intended
to be read as part of a larger, more comprehensive regulatory scheme,
and that the legislature intended to be consistent in its approaches to the
problem. The following selections from the *Barrett* and the *Locken* cases
illustrate this type of contextual analysis. *Barrett* has been discussed before and deals with the interpretation of a federal gun control statute.
People v. Locken is a state case interpreting the obstruction of justice
statute presented on page 70.

Barrett v. United States
423 U.S. 212 (1976)

MR. JUSTICE BLACKMUN delivered the opinion of the Court. . . .

B. The very structure of the Gun Control Act demonstrates that
Congress did not intend merely to restrict interstate sales but sought
broadly to keep firearms away from the persons Congress classified as
potentially irresponsible and dangerous. These persons are comprehen-
sively barred by the Act from acquiring firearms by any means. Thus,
§922(d) prohibits a licensee from knowingly selling or otherwise disposing of any firearm (whether in an interstate or intrastate transaction, see
Huddleston v. United States, 415 U.S., at 833, to the same categories of
potentially irresponsible persons. If §922(h) were to be construed as
petitioner suggests, it would not complement §922(d), and a gap in the
statute's coverage would be created, for then, although the licensee is
prohibited from selling either interstate or intrastate to the designated
person, the vendee is not prohibited from receiving unless the transaction is itself interstate.

Similarly, §922(g) prohibits the same categories of potentially irresponsible persons from shipping or transporting any firearm in interstate commerce, or, see 18 U.S.C. §2(b), causing it to be shipped
interstate. Petitioner's proposed narrow construction of §922(h) would
reduce that section to a near redundancy with §922(g), since almost
every interstate shipment is likely to have been solicited or otherwise
caused by the direct recipient. That proposed narrow construction
would also create another anomaly: if a prohibited person seeks to buy
from his local dealer a firearm that is not currently in the dealer's stock,
and the dealer then orders it interstate, that person violates §922(h), but
under the suggested construction, he would not violate §922(h) if the
firearm were already on the dealer's shelf.

We note, too, that other sections of the Act clearly apply to and
regulate intrastate sales of a gun that has moved in intrastate commerce.
For example, the licensing provisions, §§922(a)(1) and 923(a), apply to
exclusively intrastate, as well as interstate, activity. Under §922(d), as
noted above, a licensee may not knowingly sell a firearm to any pro-

hibited person, even if the sale is intrastate. Huddleston v. United States, 415 U.S., at 833. Sections 922(c) and (a)(6), relating, respectively, to a physical presence at the place of purchase and to the giving of false information, apply to intrastate as well as to interstate transactions. So, too, do §922(b)(2) and (5).

Construing §922(h) as applicable to an intrastate retail sale that has been preceded by movement of the firearm in interstate commerce is thus consistent with the entire pattern of the Act. To confine §922(h) to direct interstate receipts would result in having the Gun Control Act cover every aspect of intrastate transactions in firearms except receipt. This, however, and obviously, is the most crucial of all. Congress surely did not intend to except from the direct prohibitions of the statute the very act it went to such pains to prevent indirectly, through complex provisions, in the other sections of the Act.

People v. Locken
59 Ill. 2d 459, 322 N.E.2d 51 (1974)

JUSTICE DAVIS.

Andy Locken, then age twenty, and his mother, Mrs. Erma Anderson, gave a party in honor of the Harper College wrestling team, of which Andy was a member, at their home at 907 Sigwalt Street, Arlington Heights. When one of the detectives, who was with the other peace officers, asked to be let into the house, the defendant, Andy Locken, asked if he had a warrant, and the officer replied, "We don't need any." The officer then tried to force his way into the Anderson/Locken home without a warrant and Andy Locken resisted his entrance. A scuffle ensued, and, after being sprayed with Mace, Andy was subdued, handcuffed, and placed under arrest. When Mrs. Anderson later called at the police station to inquire about her son, she was booked and placed under arrest.

The aggravated-assault charged against Andy Locken was withdrawn by the prosecution prior to trial, and the battery charge against him was disposed of in his favor, and Mrs. Anderson was acquitted on all charges. . . .

Section 31-1 of the Criminal Code (Ill. Rev. Stat. 1971, ch. 38, par. 31-1), under which Andy Locken was charged, provides:

> A person who knowingly resists or obstructs the performance by one known to the person to be a peace officer of any authorized act within his official capacity shall be fined not to exceed $500 or imprisoned in a penal institution other than the penitentiary not to exceed one year, or both.

As indicated by the Committee Comments upon §31-1, a complete understanding of §31-1 can be reached only by reading it in conjunction with §7-7:

> . . . Note that the offense covers only resistance or obstruction to "authorized" acts of the officer. *However, if the act resisted or obstructed is the making of an arrest, a private person is not authorized to resist such arrest with force even though he knows the arrest is unlawful* (§7-7).

(Emphasis added.) S.H.A., ch. 38, §31-1, Committee Comments at 735 (1970). Section 7-7 of the Criminal Code (Ill. Rev. Stat. 1971, ch. 38, par. 7-7) provides:

> (a) A person is not authorized to use force to resist an arrest which he knows is being made either by a police officer or by a private person summoned and directed by a peace officer to make the arrest, even if he believes that the arrest is unlawful and the arrest in fact is unlawful.

It appears that the legislature, by adopting §7-7, intended that the making of an unlawful arrest is to be considered an "authorized act" for purposes of §31-1. Consequently, resistance of even an unlawful arrest by a known officer is a violation of §31-1.

Just as the courts can decide not to follow literal interpretations, they can decide not to follow this type of intrinsic analysis. Returning to the *Caminetti* case, one can see how the dissenters used intrinsic analysis to support their conclusion that the Mann Act applied only to commercialized vice. The majority opinion, of course, rejects this approach in favor of a literal reading of the text itself.

Caminetti v. United States
242 U.S. 470 (1917)

MR. JUSTICE MCKENNA, dissenting.

For the context I must refer to the statute; of the purpose of the statute Congress itself has given us illumination. It devotes a section to the declaration that the "act shall be known and referred to as the 'White Slave Traffic Act.'" And its prominence gives it prevalence in the construction of the statute. It cannot be pushed aside or subordinated by indefinite words in other sentences, limited even there by the context. It is a peremptory rule of construction that all parts of a statute must be taken into account in ascertaining its meaning, and it cannot be said that §8 has no object. Even if it gives only a title to the act, it has especial weight. United States v. Union P.R. Co., 91 U.S. 72, 82. But it gives more

than a title; it makes distinctive the purpose of the statute. The designation "white slave traffic" has the sufficiency of an axiom. If apprehended, there is no uncertainty as to the conduct it describes. It is commercialized vice, immoralities having a mercenary purpose, and this is confirmed by other circumstances.

MR. JUSTICE DAY for the majority.

But it is contended that though the words are so plain that they cannot be misapprehended when given their usual and ordinary interpretation, and although the sections in which they appear do not in terms limit the offense defined and punished to acts of "commercialized vice," or the furnishing or procuring of transportation of women for debauchery, prostitution, or immoral practices for hire, such limited purpose is to be attributed to Congress and engrafted upon the act in view of the language of §8 and the report which accompanied the law upon its introduction into and subsequent passage by the House of Representatives.

In this connection, it may be observed that while the title of an act cannot overcome the meaning of plain and unambiguous words used in its body (United States v. Fisher, 2 Cranch, 358, 386; Goodlett v. Louisville & N.R. Co., 122 U.S. 391, 408; Patterson v. The Eudora, 190 U.S. 169, 172; Cornell v. Coyne, 192 U.S. 418, 430; Lapina v. Williams, 232 U.S. 78, 92), the title of this act embraces the regulation of interstate commerce "by prohibiting the transportation therein for immoral purposes of women and girls, and for other purposes." It is true that §8 of the act provides that it shall be known and referred to as the "White Slave Traffic Act," and the report accompanying the introduction of the same into the House of Representatives set forth the fact that a material portion of the legislation suggested was to meet conditions which had arisen in the past few years, and that the legislation was needed to put a stop to a villainous interstate and international traffic in women and girls. Still, the name given to an act by way of designation or description, or the report which accompanies it, cannot change the plain import of its words. If the words are plain, they give meaning to the act, and it is neither the duty nor the privilege of the courts to enter speculative fields in search of a different meaning.

c. Extrinsic Factors

In their search for legislative intent, courts will occasionally look beyond the literal meaning of the clause in question and beyond the statutory context in which that clause is located. In these cases they look for evidence of legislative intent that can be found outside of the statute itself. This type of analysis examines the act's legislative history.

The exact nature of the materials included in a legislative history will vary depending on the importance of the statute and the type of

legislative body involved. This section reviews the various types of documents that are usually available for federal legislation. Some types of similar documents also are available in state cases.

Statutes begin as bills. A legislator introduces a draft of what the proposed law should look like. Prior to passage there may be amendments that change various sections of the bill. The pattern that emerges from an examination of multiple bills and amendments can sometimes provide insight into the legislative intent of the final act. The court, for example, would probably not read the act as applying to a particular situation if the legislative history showed that an amendment to apply to that situation had been defeated.

Before bills are presented on the floor of the legislative body, they are usually sent to a committee. Committees often hold public hearings where interested parties can testify about the proposed law. The proceedings of these hearings are published, and the transcript becomes a part of the statute's legislative history. More important, the committee sometimes issues an official report discussing the nature of the proposed legislation and what they expect it to accomplish. This, too, becomes part of the history.

When the bill is debated on the floor of the legislative body, proponents and opponents often make statements about what they expect the bill to do or not to do. The transcripts of these debates become another source of information about legislative intent.

In determining legislative intent, courts may quote from any of these sources. Note the Supreme Court's use of legislative history in the *Holy Trinity* case.

The Church of the Holy Trinity v. United States
143 U.S. 457 (1892)

MR. JUSTICE BREWER delivered the opinion of the Court. . . .

Again, another guide to the meaning of a statute is found in the evil which it is designed to remedy; and for this the court properly looks at contemporaneous events, the situation as it existed, and as it was pressed upon the attention of the legislative body. United States v. Union Pac. R. Co., 91 U.S. 72, 79. The situation which called for this statute was briefly but fully stated by Mr. Justice Brown when, as district judge, he decided the case of United States v. Craig, 28 Fed. Rep. 795, 798:

> The motives and history of the Act are matters of common knowledge. It had become the practice for large capitalists in this country to contract with their agents abroad for the shipment of great numbers of an ignorant and servile class of foreign laborers, under contracts, by which the employer agreed, upon the one hand, to prepay their passage, while, upon the other hand, the laborers agreed to

work after their arrival for a certain time at a low rate of wages. The effect of this was to break down the labor market, and to reduce other laborers engaged in like occupations to the level of the assisted immigrant. The evil finally became so flagrant that an appeal was made to Congress for relief by the passage of the Act in question, the design of which was to raise the standard of foreign immigrants, and to discountenance the migration of those who had not sufficient means in their own hands, or those of their friends, to pay their passage.

It appears, also, from the petitions, and in the testimony presented before the committees of Congress, that it was this cheap unskilled labor which was making the trouble, and the influx of which Congress sought to prevent. It was never suggested that we had in this country a surplus of brain toilers, and, least of all, that the market for the services of Christian ministers was depressed by foreign competition. Those were matters to which the attention of Congress, or of the people, was not directed. So far, then, as the evil which was sought to be remedied interprets the statute, it also guides to an exclusion of this contract from the penalties of the Act.

A singular circumstance, throwing light upon the intent of Congress, is found in this extract from the report of the Senate Committee on Education and Labor, recommending the passage of the bill:

> The general facts and considerations which induce the committee to recommend the passage of this bill are set forth in the report of the Committee of the House. The committee report [sic] the bill back without amendment, although there are certain features thereof which might well be changed or modified, in the hope that the bill may not fail of passage during the present session. Especially would the committee have otherwise recommended amendments, substituting for the expression, "labor and service," whenever it occurs in the body of the bill, the words "manual labor" or "manual service," as sufficiently broad to accomplish the purposes of the bill, and that such amendments would remove objections which a sharp and perhaps unfriendly criticism may urge to the proposed legislation. The committee, however, believing that the bill in its present form will be construed as including only those whose labor or service is manual in character, and being very desirous that the bill become a law before the adjournment, have reported the bill without change.

(Page 6,059, Congressional Record, 48th Congress.) And referring back to the report of the Committee of the House, there appears this language:

> It seeks to restrain and prohibit the immigration or importation of laborers who would have never seen our shores but for the inducements and allurements of men whose only object is to obtain labor at the lowest possible rate, regardless of the social and material well-being of our own citizens and regardless of the evil consequences

which result to American laborers from such immigration. This class
of immigrants care nothing about our institutions, and in many instances never even heard of them; they are men whose passage is
paid by the importers; they come here under contract to labor for a
certain number of years; they are ignorant of our social condition,
and that they may remain so they are isolated and prevented from
coming into contact with Americans. They are generally from the
lowest social stratum, and live upon the coarsest food and in hovels
of a character before unknown to American workmen. They, as a
rule, do not become citizens, and are certainly not a desirable acquisition to the body politic. The inevitable tendency of their presence
among us is to degrade American labor, and to reduce it to the level
of the imported pauper labor.

(Page 5,359, Congressional Record, 48th Congress.)

We find, therefore, that the title of the Act, the evil which was
intended to be remedied, the circumstances surrounding the appeal to
Congress, the reports of the committee of each house, all concur in
affirming that the intent of Congress was simply to stay the influx of this
cheap unskilled labor.

Note also that there is often a great deal of ambiguity in the legislative history. It is not uncommon for both sides to quote sections of the
legislative history that favor their positions. This ambiguity is demonstrated in the *Powell* case.

United States v. Powell
423 U.S. 87 (1975)

MR. JUSTICE REHNQUIST delivered the opinion of the Court. . . .

The legislative history of this particular provision is sparse, but the
House report indicates that the purpose of the bill upon which §1715 is
based was to avoid having the Post Office serve as an instrumentality for
the violation of local laws which prohibited the purchase and possession
of weapons. H. R. Rep. No. 610, 69th Cong., 1st Sess. (1926). It would
seem that sawed-off shotguns would be even more likely to be prohibited
by local laws than would pistols and revolvers. A statement by the author
of the bill, Representative Miller of Washington, on the floor of the
House indicates that the purpose of the bill was to make it more difficult
for criminals to obtain concealable weapons. 66 Cong. Rec. 726 (1924).
To narrow the meaning of the language Congress used so as to limit it to
only those weapons which could be concealed as readily as pistols or
revolvers would not comport with that purpose. Cf. United States v.
Alpers, 338 U.S. 680, 682 (1950).

We therefore hold that a properly instructed jury could have found
the 22-inch sawed-off shotgun mailed by respondent to have been a

"[firearm] capable of being concealed on the person" within the meaning of 18 U.S.C. §1715. Having done so, we turn to the Court of Appeals' holding that this portion of the statute was unconstitutionally vague.

MR. JUSTICE STEWART in dissent.

The legislative history of the bill on which §1715 was based contains persuasive indications that it was not intended to apply to firearms larger than the largest pistols or revolvers. Representative Miller, the bill's author, made it clear that the legislative concern was not with the "shotgun, the rifle, or any firearm used in hunting or by the sportsman." 66 Cong. Rec. 727. As a supporter of the legislation stated: "The purpose . . . is to prevent the shipment of pistols and revolvers through the mails." 67 Cong. Rec. 12,041. The only reference to sawed-off shotguns came in a question posed by Representative McKeown: "Is there anything in this bill that will prevent the citizens of Oklahoma from buying sawed-off shotguns to defend themselves against these bank-robbing bandits?" Representative Blanton, an opponent of the bill, responded: "That may come next. Sometimes a revolver is more necessary than a sawed-off shotgun." 66 Cong. Rec. 729. In the absence of more concrete indicia of legislative intent, the pregnant silence that followed Representative Blanton's response can surely be taken as an indication that Congress intended the law to reach only weapons of the same general size as pistols and revolvers.

Sometimes the legislative history can include the failure of the legislative body to react to administrative or judicial interpretations. This aspect of the judicial reasoning process is well illustrated in the continuing controversy over the antitrust status of professional sports. In Federal Baseball Club v. National League[13] and Toolson v. New York Yankees, Inc.[14] the Supreme Court held that professional baseball was not covered by federal antitrust laws. The Court went on in other cases to rule that other professional sports (such as football, hockey, and boxing) were covered. Then in 1972 when the Court was forced to justify this inconsistency in the Curt Flood case,[15] the majority asserted that since Congress did not pass a specific law to include baseball, the Congress must have approved the Court's earlier position excluding it.

In addition to the legislative history materials discussed above, the courts may also consider interpretations that have been given by administrative agencies. Unless there is a clear reason to the contrary, the courts are expected to sustain the interpretations established by agencies set up to administer the law.

Finally, the courts will also consider the statute's relationship to the

---

13. 259 U.S. 200 (1922).
14. 346 U.S. 356 (1953).
15. Flood v. Kuhn, 407 U.S. 258 (1972).

common law. Except where there is a clear intent to the contrary, statutes are interpreted in a manner consistent with common law.

d. Conclusion

When courts are asked to interpret the meaning of statutes, they can use several techniques. They can use a dictionary and a grammar book to give a literal interpretation or they can study committee hearings and floor debates from the legislature. The following list summarizes the major principles of statutory interpretation:

1. Statutes should be interpreted to be consistent with the intent of the legislators who enacted them.
2. Statutes should be read literally and their words given meanings that were commonly used at the time the statutes were written.
   a. When modifying words and phrases are used, they should be assumed to modify the words and phrases to which they are closest.
   b. When a list of specific items is followed by a general catchall like "and others," it is to be interpreted as including only items that are of the same class or type as those specifically listed. (This rule is usually referred to by the Latin phrase *ejusdem generis*.)
   c. If something is not expressly mentioned, it should be assumed that the legislature did not want it included. (This rule is often referred to as *express mention/implied exclusion*.)
3. Individual parts of a statute should be interpreted so that they will be consistent with the other parts of the statute.
4. Unless the legislative intent is clearly to the contrary, statutes should be interpreted to be consistent with other statutes and with the common law.
5. Statutes should be interpreted to be consistent with committee reports, floor debates, and other aspects of the legislative history.

The legislative intent is not always clear and sometimes application of these principles can lead to contradictory results. Indeed, Table 3.4 demonstrates the way in which these principles can be set off against each other.

When the legal advocate is attempting to persuade a court to interpret case law in a way that will be favorable to the client, that advocate presents case precedents favorable to the client's interests and attempts to distinguish the case at hand from the fact situations of cases presented by the opposition. Likewise, when the legal advocate is attempting to persuade a court to interpret a statute in a way favorable to a particular client, that advocate urges the court to adopt the method of interpretation that favors the client. The paralegal, therefore, needs to develop the ability to work comfortably with each of the approaches (literalism, intrinsic factors, and extrinsic factors).

Table 3.4 Contrasting Canons of Construction

The following sets of thrusts and parries demonstrates the manner in which the canons of construction can be used on either side of an argument.

CANONS OF CONSTRUCTION	
THRUST	PARRY
1. A statute cannot go beyond its text.	1. To effect its purpose a statute may be implemented beyond its text.
2. Statutes in derogation of the common law will not be extended by construction.	2. Such acts will be liberally construed if their nature is remedial.
3. Statutes are to be read in the light of the common law and a statute affirming a common law rule is to be construed in accordance with the common law.	3. The common law gives way to a statute which is inconsistent with it. When a statute is designed as a revision of a whole body of law applicable to a given subject it supersedes the common law.
4. Where a foreign statute which has received construction has been adopted, previous construction is adopted too.	4. It may be rejected where there is conflict with the obvious meaning of the statute or where the foreign decisions are unsatisfactory in reasoning or where the foreign interpretation is not in harmony with the spirit or policy of the laws of the adopting state.
5. Where various states have already adopted the statute, the parent state is followed.	5. Where interpretations of other states are inharmonious, there is no such restraint.
6. Statutes *in pari materia* must be construed together.	6. A statute is not *in pari materia* if its scope and aim are distinct or where a legislative design to depart from the general purpose or policy of previous enactments may be apparent.
7. A statute imposing a new penalty or forfeiture, or a new liability or disability, or creating a new right of action will not be construed as having a retroactive effect.	7. Remedial statutes are to be liberally construed and if a retroactive interpretation will promote the ends of justice, they should receive such construction.
8. Where design has been distinctly stated no place is left for construction.	8. Courts have the power to inquire into real — as distinct from ostensible — purpose.
9. Definitions and rules of construction contained in an interpretation clause are part of the law and binding.	9. Definitions and rules of construction in a statute will not be extended beyond their necessary import nor allowed to defeat intention otherwise manifested.

Table 3.4 (*continued*)

CANONS OF CONSTRUCTION	
THRUST	PARRY
10. A statutory provision requiring liberal construction does not mean disregard of unequivocal requirements of the statute.	10. Where a rule of construction is provided within the statute itself, the rule should be applied.
11. Titles do not control meaning; preambles do not expand scope; section headings do not change language.	11. The title may be consulted as a guide when there is doubt or obscurity in the body; preambles may be consulted to determine rationale, and thus the true construction of terms; section headings may be looked upon as part of the statute itself.
12. If language is plain and unambiguous it must be given effect.	12. Not when literal interpretation would lead to absurd or mischievous consequences or thwart manifest purpose.
13. Words and phrases which have received judicial construction before enactment are to be understood according to that construction.	13. Not if the statute clearly requires them to have a different meaning.
14. After enactment, judicial decision upon interpretation of particular terms and phrases controls.	14. Practical construction by executive officers is strong evidence of true meaning.
15. Words are to be taken in their ordinary meaning unless they are technical terms or words of art.	15. Popular words may bear a technical meaning and technical words may have a popular signification and they should be construed to agree with evident intention or to make the statute operative.
16. Every word and clause must be given effect.	16. If inadvertently inserted or if repugnant to the rest of the statute, they may be rejected as surplusage.
17. The same language used repeatedly in the same connection is presumed to bear the same meaning throughout the statute.	17. This presumption will be disregarded where it is necessary to assign different meanings to make the statute consistent.
18. Words are to be interpreted according to the proper grammatical effect of their arrangement within the statute.	18. Rules of grammar will be disregarded where strict adherence would defeat purpose.

CANONS OF CONSTRUCTION

THRUST	PARRY
19. Exceptions not made cannot be read in.	19. The letter is only the "bark." Whatever is within the reason of the law is within the law itself.
20. Expression of one excludes another. [Quite typically: not "*the* other."]	20. The language may fairly comprehend many different cases where some only are expressly mentioned by way of example.
21. General terms are to receive a general construction.	21. They may be limited by specific terms with which they are associated or by the scope and purpose of the statute.
22. It is a general rule of construction that where general words follow an enumeration they are to be held as applying only to persons and things of the same general kind of class specifically mentioned (*ejusdem generis*).	22. General words must operate on something. Further, *ejusdem generis* is only an aid in getting the meaning and does not warrant confining the operations of a statute within narrower limits than were intended.
23. Qualifying or limiting words or clauses are to be referred to the next preceding antecedent.	23. Not when evident sense and meaning require a different construction.
24. Punctuation will govern when a statute is open to two constructions.	24. Punctuation marks will not control the plain and evident meaning of language.
25. It must be assumed that language has been chosen with due regard to grammatical propriety and is not interchangeable on mere conjecture.	25. "And" and "or" may be read interchangeably whenever the change is necessary to give the statute sense and effect.
26. There is a distinction between words of permission and mandatory words.	26. Words imparting permission may be read as mandatory and words imparting command may be read as permissive when such construction is made necessary by evident intention or by the rights of the public.
27. A proviso qualifies the provision immediately preceding.	27. It may clearly be intended to have a wider scope.
28. When the enacting clause is general, a proviso is construed strictly.	28. Not when it is necessary to extend the proviso to persons or cases which come within its equity.

SOURCE: Karl Llewellyn, The Common Law Tradition, app. C (1960).

2. Administrative Regulations

Administrative regulations have the same basic features as statutes. They are universalistic and future oriented. The fact that they were promulgated by an administrative agency rather than a legislative body does not affect interpretation of their meaning. Generally speaking, the approaches applied to statutes are also applied to regulations. The courts seek to find an interpretation that is internally and externally consistent and that is in the spirit of the statute that established and controls the agency in question.

3. Constitutions

Just as ambiguity can be found in statutes and administrative regulations, it can be found in constitutions. Indeed, the broader and more general the document the greater the likelihood that ambiguity will occur. Consider, for example, the following clauses contained in the United States Constitution:

> The Congress shall have Power to regulate *Commerce* with foreign Nations, and among the several States, and with the Indian Tribes (art. I, §8). The Congress shall have Power to make all Laws which shall be *necessary and proper* for carrying into Execution the foregoing Powers, and all other Powers vested by this Constitution in the Government of the United States, or in any Department or Officer thereof (art. I, §8).
>
> The *executive Power* shall be vested in a President of the United States of America (art. II, §1).
>
> The President, Vice-President, and all civil Officers of the United States, shall be removed from Office on Impeachment for, and Conviction of, Treason, Bribery, or other *high Crimes and Misdemeanors* (art. II, §4).
>
> Congress shall make *no law* respecting an *establishment of religion,* or prohibiting the *free exercise thereof*; or abridging the *freedom of speech,* or *of the press*; or the right of the people peaceably to assemble, and to petition the Government for a redress of grievances (amend. I).
>
> *Excessive* bail shall not be required, nor *excessive* fines imposed, nor *cruel and unusual* punishment inflicted (amend. VIII).
>
> No State shall make or enforce any law which shall abridge the *privileges or immunities* of citizens of the United States; nor shall any State deprive any person of life, liberty, or property, without *due process of law:* nor deny to any person within its jurisdiction the *equal protection of the laws* (amend. XIV).

The italicized words are not italicized in the Constitution itself but have been italicized here to draw attention to the ambiguity of various words and phrases.

Over the years the courts have been asked to interpret these and other parts of the Constitution. In approaching this task the courts generally use the same approaches discussed in the section on statutory construction. They attempt a literal reading of the words themselves, consider the relationship of the clause in question in conjunction with similar ones located elsewhere in the document, and go back to the minutes of the Constitutional Convention and to the legislative history of amendments.[16]

Once a court has formally interpreted the meaning of a particular clause of the Constitution, that court decision takes on precedent value and becomes the basis for a case law on the meaning of the Constitution. Therefore, rather than going back and starting again, succeeding courts follow the leads of previous courts, and gradually a series of cases develops that explains that "no law" as it is used in the first amendment really does not mean that the government cannot pass a law restricting obscene materials or punishing libelous statements. As the case law expands, one begins to understand when something is to be considered obscene and when it is not — or when a search is a reasonable search and when it is not.

It is important to realize that the courts (particularly the United States Supreme Court) have the greatest freedom in exercising discretion in the area of constitutional law. This is due not only to the great ambiguity involved but also to the view that the Constitution is a "living" document. The Supreme Court is thus legitimately able to change its interpretations to meet the needs of a changing society. As Oliver Wendell Holmes once declared: "[A] word is not a crystal, transparent and unchanged, it is the skin of a living thought and may vary greatly in color and content according to the circumstances and the time in which it is used."[17]

4. Court Cases

As demonstrated earlier in this chapter, when disagreements arise about the proper interpretation of statutes, administrative regulations, and constitutions, the courts clarify their meaning by applying established judicial criteria. In order to understand a particular statute or provision of the Constitution, one has to see how the courts have interpreted it. In order to do this, however, one also needs to know how to read and interpret court decisions.

---

16. James Madison took particularly extensive notes on the debates at the Philadelphia convention that created the United States Constitution. These notes and other important documents relating to the federal Constitution are available in several forms. One particularly good source is Max Farrand, ed., The Records of the Federal Convention of 1787 (1937). Records of state constitutional conventions will differ from state to state. In states such as Illinois, where the constitutions were revised fairly recently, the records are in general very good.

17. Towne v. Eisner, 245 U.S. 418, 425 (1918).

Let us begin by carefully examining a sample case. Chambers v. Maroney has been selected for use here because it illustrates the elements of a typical decision and, in conjunction with Texas v. White, shows the amount of flexibility that courts can exercise in determining the precedent value of a specific case.

a. The Sample Case

Chambers v. Maroney
399 U.S. 42 (1970)

MR. JUSTICE WHITE delivered the opinion of the Court.

Issue The principal question in this case concerns the admissibility of evidence seized from an automobile, in which petitioner was riding at the time of his arrest, after the automobile was taken to a police station and was there thoroughly searched without a warrant. The Court of Appeals for the Third Circuit found no violation of petitioner's Fourth Amendment rights. We affirm.

Judicial History

Disposition

I

Facts During the night of May 20, 1963, a Gulf service station in North Braddock, Pennsylvania, was robbed by two men, each of whom carried and displayed a gun. The robbers took the currency from the cash register; the service station attendant, one Stephen Kovacich, was directed to place the coins in his right-hand glove, which was then taken by the robbers. Two teen-agers, who had earlier noticed a blue compact station wagon circling the block in the vicinity of the Gulf station, then saw the station wagon speed away from a parking lot close to the Gulf station. About the same time, they learned that the Gulf station had been robbed. They reported to police, who arrived immediately, that four men were in the station wagon and one was wearing a green sweater. Kovacich told the police that one of the men who robbed him was wearing a green sweater and the other was wearing a trench coat. A description of the car and the two robbers was broadcast over the police radio. Within an hour, a light blue compact station wagon answering the description and carrying four men was stopped by the police about two miles from the Gulf station. Petitioner was one of the men in the station wagon. He was wearing a green sweater and there was a trench coat in the car. The

Facts

occupants were arrested and the car was driven to the police station. In the course of a thorough search of the car at the station, the police found concealed in a compartment under the dashboard two .38-caliber revolvers (one loaded with dumdum bullets), a right-hand glove containing small change, and certain cards bearing the name of Raymond Havicon, the attendant at a Boron service station in McKeesport, Pennsylvania, who had been robbed at gunpoint on May 13, 1963. In the course of a warrant-authorized search of petitioner's home the day after petitioner's arrest, police found and seized certain .38-caliber ammunition, including some dumdum bullets similar to those found in one of the guns taken from the station wagon.

Judicial History

Petitioner was indicted for both robberies. His first trial ended in a mistrial but he was convicted of both robberies at the second trial. Both Kovacich and Havicon identified petitioner as one of the robbers. The materials taken from the station wagon were introduced into evidence, Kovacich identifying his glove and Havicon the cards taken in the May 13 robbery. The bullets seized at petitioner's house were also introduced over objections of petitioner's counsel. Petitioner was sentenced to a term of four to eight years' imprisonment for the May 13 robbery and to a term of two to seven years' imprisonment for the May 20 robbery, the sentences to run consecutively. Petitioner did not take a direct appeal from these convictions. In 1965, petitioner sought a writ of habeas corpus in the state court, which denied the writ after a brief evidentiary hearing; the denial of the writ was affirmed on appeal in the Pennsylvania appellate courts. Habeas corpus proceedings were then commenced in the United States District Court for the Western District of Pennsylvania. An order to show cause was issued. Based on the State's response and the state court record, the petition for habeas corpus was denied without a hearing. The Court of Appeals for the Third Circuit affirmed, 408 F.2d 1186, and we granted *certiorari*, 396 U.S. 900 (1969).

II

Decision

We pass quickly to the claim that the search of the automobile was the fruit of an unlawful arrest. Both the courts below thought the arresting officers had probable cause to make the arrest. We agree. Having talked to the teen-age

observers and to the victim Kovacich, the police had ample cause to stop a light blue compact station wagon carrying four men to arrest the occupants, one of whom was wearing a green sweater and one of whom had a trench coat with him in the car.

Even so, the search that produced the incriminating evidence was made at the police station some time after the arrest and cannot be justified as a search incident to an arrest: "Once an accused is under arrest and in custody, then a search made at another place, without a warrant, is simply not incident to the arrest." Preston v. United States, 376 U.S. 364, 367. Dyke v. Taylor Implement Mfg. Co., 391 U.S. 216 (1968), is to the same effect; the reasons that have been thought sufficient to justify warrantless searches carried out in connection with an arrest no longer obtain when the accused is safely in custody at the station house.

Reasoning

There are, however, alternative grounds arguably justifying the search of the car in this case. In *Preston,* supra, the arrest was for vagrancy; it was apparent that the officers had no cause to believe that evidence of crime was concealed in the auto. In *Dyke,* supra, the Court expressly rejected the suggestion that there was probably cause to search the car, 391 U.S., at 221-222. Here the situation is different, for the police had probable cause to believe that the robbers, carrying guns and the fruits of the crime, had fled the scene in a light blue compact station wagon which would be carrying four men, one wearing a green sweater and another wearing a trench coat. As the state courts correctly held, there was probable cause to arrest the occupants of the station wagon that the officers stopped; just as obviously was there probable cause to search the car for guns and stolen money.

In terms of the circumstances justifying a warrantless search, the Court has long distinguished between an automobile and a home or office. In Carroll v. United States, 267 U.S. 132 (1925), the issue was the admissibility in evidence of contraband liquor seized in a warrantless search of a car on the highway. After surveying the law from the time of the adoption of the Fourth Amendment onward, the Court held that automobiles and other conveyances may be searched without a warrant in circumstances that would not justify the search without a warrant of a house or an office, provided that there is probable cause to believe that the car contains articles that the officers are entitled to seize. . . .

Neither *Carroll,* supra, nor other cases in this Court re-

quire or suggest that in every conceivable circumstance the search of an auto even with probable cause may be made without the extra protection for privacy that a warrant affords. But the circumstances that furnish probable cause to search a particular auto for particular articles are most often unforeseeable; moreover, the opportunity to search is fleeting since a car is readily movable. Where this is true, as in *Carroll* and the case before us now, if an effective search is to be made at any time, either the search must be made immediately without a warrant or the car itself must be seized and held without a warrant for whatever period is necessary to obtain a warrant for the search.

In enforcing the Fourth Amendment's prohibition against unreasonable searches and seizures, the Court has insisted upon probable cause as a minimum requirement for a reasonable search permitted by the Constitution. As a general rule, it has also required the judgment of a magistrate on the probable-cause issue and the issuance of a warrant before a search is made. Only in exigent circumstances will the judgment of the police as to probable cause serve as a sufficient authorization for a search. *Carroll,* supra, holds a search warrant unnecessary where there is *Reasoning* | probable cause to search an automobile stopped on the highway; the car is movable, the occupants are alerted, and the car's contents may never be found again if a warrant must be obtained. Hence an immediate search is constitutionally permissible.

Arguably, because of the preference for a magistrate's judgment, only the immobilization of the car should be permitted until a search warrant is obtained; arguably, only the "lesser" intrusion is permissible until the magistrate authorizes the "greater." But which is the "greater" and which the "lesser" intrusion is itself a debatable question and the answer may depend on a variety of circumstances. For constitutional purposes, we see no difference between on the one hand seizing and holding a car before presenting the probable cause issue to a magistrate and on the other hand carrying out an immediate search without a warrant. Given probable cause to search, either course is reasonable under the Fourth Amendment.

On the facts before us, the blue station wagon could have been searched on the spot when it was stopped since there was probable cause to search and it was a fleeting target for a search. The probable-cause factor still obtained at the station house and so did the mobility of the car unless

Reasoning

the Fourth Amendment permits a warrantless seizure of the car and the denial of its use to anyone until a warrant is secured. In that event there is little to choose in terms of practical consequences between an immediate search without a warrant and the car's immobilization until a warrant is obtained. [It was not unreasonable in this case to take the car to the station house. All occupants in the car were arrested in a dark parking lot in the middle of the night. A careful search at that point was impractical and perhaps not safe for the officers, and it would serve the owner's convenience and the safety of his car to have the vehicle and the keys together at the station house.] The same consequences may not follow where there is unforeseeable cause to search a house. Compare Vale v. Louisiana, ante, 399 U.S. 30. But as Carroll, supra, held, for the purpose of the Fourth Amendment there is a constitutional difference between houses and cars.

III

Decision

Neither of petitioner's remaining contentions warrants reversal of the judgment of the Court of Appeals. One of

Issue

them challenges the admissibility at trial of the .38-caliber ammunition seized in the course of a search of petitioner's

Reasoning

house. The circumstances relevant to this issue are somewhat confused, involving as they do questions of probable cause, a lost search warrant, and the Pennsylvania procedure for challenging the admissibility of evidence seized. Both the District Court and the Court of Appeals, however, after careful examination of the record, found that if there was error in admitting the ammunition, the error was harmless beyond a reasonable doubt. Having ourselves studied this record, we are not prepared to differ with the two courts below. See Harrington v. California, 395 U.S. 250 (1969).

Issue

The final claim is that petitioner was not afforded the effective assistance of counsel. The facts pertinent to this

Facts

claim are these: The Legal Aid Society of Allegheny County was appointed to represent petitioner prior to his first trial. A representative of the society conferred with petitioner, and a member of its staff, Mr. Middleman, appeared for petitioner at the first trial. There is no claim that petitioner was not then adequately represented by fully prepared counsel. The difficulty arises out of the second

Judicial History

trial. Apparently no one from the Legal Aid Society again conferred with petitioner until a few minutes before the second trial began. The attorney who then appeared to represent petitioner was not Mr. Middleman but Mr. Tamburo, another Legal Aid Society attorney. No charge is made that Mr. Tamburo was incompetent or inexperienced; rather the claim is that his appearance for petitioner was so belated that he could not have furnished effective legal assistance at the second trial. Without granting an evidentiary hearing, the District Court rejected petitioner's claim. The Court of Appeals dealt with the matter in an extensive opinion. After carefully examining the state court record, which it had before it, the court found ample grounds for holding that the appearance of a different attorney at the second trial had not resulted in prejudice to petitioner. The claim that Mr. Tamburo was unprepared

Reasoning

centered around his allegedly inadequate efforts to have the guns and ammunition excluded from evidence. But the Court of Appeals found harmless any error in the admission of the bullets and ruled that the guns and other materials seized from the car were admissible evidence. Hence the claim of prejudice from the substitution of counsel was without substantial basis. In this posture of the case we are not inclined to disturb the judgment of the Court of Appeals as to what the state record shows with respect to the adequacy of counsel. Unquestionably, the courts should make every effort to effect early appointments of counsel

Decision

in all cases. But we are not disposed to fashion a per se ruling requiring reversal of every conviction following tardy appointment of counsel or to hold that, whenever a habeas corpus petition alleges a belated appointment, an evidentiary hearing must be held to determine whether the defendant has been denied his constitutional right to counsel. The Court of Appeals reached the right result in denying a hearing in this case.

Disposition   Affirmed.

b. The Facts

Under the principle of standing, courts are not supposed to decide abstract issues or render advisory opinions. Rather, they are to decide cases that involve litigants who are personally affected by their decisions. As discussed later in this chapter, the development of legal rules is tied to the court's decisions in specific cases. It is therefore essential that a case analysis begin with a thorough understanding of the facts.

In approaching a civil case the paralegal should ask the following types of questions: Who was the original plaintiff (the person who first brought the matter to court)? Who was the original defendant? If the plaintiff claims to have been injured by the defendant's actions, in what manner is this injury alleged to have taken place? What is the nature of the injury? What is the plaintiff asking the court to do about it? In criminal cases, questions should include: Who is the defendant? What is the nature of the alleged criminal activity? What governmental unit is undertaking the prosecution? What methods were employed by the police in obtaining the evidence used against the defendant? Was the trial conducted in accordance with the requirements of the due process clause?[18]

In Chambers v. Maroney, the state prosecuted Chambers for robbery because two witnesses identified him and the police found incriminating evidence in searches of the car in which he was riding and in his home. The police stopped the automobile because it matched the description of one seen at the robbery and because two of its occupants matched descriptions of the robbers. After arresting Chambers and three other suspects in a dark parking lot in the middle of the night, the police drove the auto to the station. They searched it at the police station, without a search warrant, and found two revolvers and property belonging to a robbery victim in a concealed compartment under the dashboard. They also discovered and seized ammunition that fitted the confiscated revolvers when they conducted a warrant-authorized search of Chamber's home the next day.

The incriminating evidence from both searches was used against Chambers at his trial. At both of his trials Chambers was represented by lawyers from the Legal Aid Society but by different individuals each time, and he did not have the opportunity to confer with his attorney in the second trial until minutes before the trial began.

In analyzing the facts of a case, the paralegal must be sure to identify all the *relevant* facts; that is, the facts that are so essential to the court's decision that if they were to be changed the court's decision might also change. For example, the fact that Chambers was wearing a green sweater rather than a blue one would not ordinarily be important. In this case, however, it is important because his clothing matched that given in the description of the robber. The matching of the descriptions of the car and passengers establishes the probable cause used to justify the arrests and searches. On the other hand, there is nothing relevant about the description of the police who stopped them. Sometimes it is not clear whether or not a particular fact is essential to the decision. In this case, it

---

18. This listing of questions is intended to be illustrative rather than exhaustive. Additional questions may need to be raised in the context of a specific case.

is not altogether clear if it is important that the suspects were arrested in a dark parking lot at night.

c. The Judicial History

In addition to analyzing the facts that brought on the litigation in a specific case, the paralegal should analyze the manner in which other courts or administrative bodies have handled the same type of case. Since published opinions are usually the product of appellate courts, information normally is available about action taken by the trial court. If such a case was handled by a higher-level appellate court, there will also be information about how lower-level appellate courts disposed of the case.

In Chambers v. Maroney, the defendant's first trial ended in a mistrial, while his second ended with his conviction for two robberies because the trial judge allowed the state to introduce the evidence found in the automobile and in the house. In 1965 Chambers sought but was denied a writ of habeas corpus in the state court. The Pennsylvania appellate courts affirmed the lower court's decision. Then Chambers began habeas corpus proceedings in the United States District Court, but the district court denied the petition and the court of appeals affirmed. The U.S. Supreme Court then granted *certiorari*.[19]

d. The Issues

When a party takes a dispute to the courts, that party may be asking the court to resolve differences of opinion about the facts of the case and the meaning of the law.

These two types of disputes are called the *issues* of the case. The dispute that involves an event that is supposed to have taken place is an issue of fact. The dispute that involves the meaning or application of the law is an issue of law. Although the appellate courts usually accept the trial court's interpretation of the facts, there are occasions when appellate courts do make their own judgment concerning factual disputes.

Chambers raised several issues in his appeal: Did the police have probable cause to stop the auto and arrest the occupants? At the police station, did the police have a legal right to search the car that Chambers was riding in without obtaining a search warrant first? If the trial court had improperly allowed the evidence seized in his home to be admitted, would it have had a harmful effect on the outcome of the trial? Did the defendant receive adequate counsel?

e. The Decision

Court opinions are useful because they indicate how the court decided the issues raised in a given case. The process of resolving the issues

---

19. The granting of a writ of certiorari means the Supreme Court agrees to review a case.

of fact in a case is usually not important to anyone beyond the parties of
that case, but resolution of the legal issues can be quite significant for
many others faced with similar situations. Under the precedent system
used in United States courts, the legal interpretations of some courts can
be binding on the decisions of other courts, and where the interpretations are not binding they may nevertheless be quite persuasive. Because
lawyers who wish to advise a client on the legality of a particular action
need to determine the manner in which a previous decision might be
applied, the court decision should be analyzed at two different levels:
How was the issue settled in this particular case? What general principle
of law has been enunciated by the way in which the court resolved this
issue?

In the *Chambers* case we see that the court ruled that the police did
have probable cause to stop the automobile and arrest the occupants.
The court also ruled that the police had a legal right to search the car at
the station without first obtaining a search warrant. With respect to the
admission of the ammunition found in the search of Chambers's home,
the court concluded that even if there had been an error in admitting it,
the error was harmless.[20] Finally, the court ruled that Chambers was not
denied adequate assistance of counsel merely because he did not have an
opportunity to confer with his legal aid lawyer until a few minutes before
his second trial.

But what is the significance of the court's decision for future defendants? What general principles of law emerge that are likely to be applied to future cases? The answers to these questions are usually
presented in the form of a holding. The holding is a statement that the
law is to be interpreted in a certain way when a given set of facts exists. In
order to better understand the scope of the holding it is necessary to
explain the *ratio decidendi* and the *obiter dictum*. The *ratio decidendi* is a
decision on the legal issues of a specific case that the judge has proper
authority to decide. *Dictum* refers to comments the judge makes that are
not necessary to the resolution of the issues of the case and are in effect a
discussion of a hypothetical situation.

In the *Chambers* case the holding derived from the first issue is a
very narrow one: When police observe an automobile matching the description of one seen circling and then speeding away from the scene of a
robbery, and when police observe that the automobile contains two men
who are wearing clothing that fits the description of clothing being worn
by the robbers, then the police have probable cause to stop the automobile and arrest the occupants. Note that in stating the holding, the

---

20. Note the placement of the word *if*. The court is not in fact deciding that the evidence
was improperly admitted, but it is saying that it would not make any difference. If it
had been improperly admitted, the nature of the error was not great enough to affect
the trial's outcome.

right to stop and arrest is clearly tied to the fact that the automobile and its occupants fit the descriptions of the auto at the scene of the robbery and of the robbers themselves.

It is difficult to formulate a holding for the second issue. The court says that the police in the *Chambers* case did have the right to search the auto without a warrant at the police station. The question is whether the court means to give the police the right to search an auto back at the station any time they have probable cause to search it at the scene of the arrest, or if the power to search it (without a warrant) back at the station only applies in situations (like this one) in which the auto is stopped in a dark parking lot at night. Five years after this case, in Texas v. White,[21] the justices of the Supreme Court argued among themselves as to the holding in Chambers v. Maroney. In a *per curiam* opinion[22] the court declared: "In Chambers v. Maroney we held that police officers with probable cause to search an automobile on the scene where it was stopped could constitutionally do so later at the station house without first obtaining a warrant."[23] However, Justices Marshall and Brennan argued in dissent that the majority misstated the true holding of the *Chambers* case.

> Only by misstating the holding of Chambers v. Maroney, 399 U.S. 42 (1970), can the Court make that case appear dispositive of this one. The Court in its brief *per curiam* opinion today extends *Chambers* to a clearly distinguishable factual setting, without having afforded the opportunity for full briefing and oral argument. . . .
>
> *Chambers* did not hold, as the Court suggests, "that police officers with probable cause to search an automobile on the scene where it was stopped could constitutionally do so later at the station house without first obtaining a warrant." . . . *Chambers* simply held that to be the rule when it is reasonable to take the car to the station house in the first place. . . . The Court in *Chambers* went on to hold that once the car was legitimately at the station house a prompt search could be conducted. But in recognition of the need to justify the seizure and removal of the car to the station house, the Court added:
>
>> It was not unreasonable in this case to take the car to the station house. All occupants in the car were arrested in a dark parking lot in the middle of the night. A careful search at that point was impractical and perhaps not safe for the officers, and it would serve the owner's convenience and the safety of his car to have the vehicle and the keys together at the station house.
>
> Id., at 52 n.10.
>
> In this case, the arrest took place at 1:30 in the afternoon, and there is no indication that an immediate search would have been

---

21. 423 U.S. 67 (1975).
22. This is a decision of the court in which the author of the opinion is not identified. The form is usually used in short summary decisions.
23. 423 U.S. at 68.

either impractical or unsafe for the arresting officers. It may be, of
course, that respondent preferred to have his car brought to the
station house, but if his convenience was the concern of the police
they should have consulted with him. Surely a seizure cannot be
justified on the sole ground that a citizen might have consented to it
as a matter of convenience. Since, then, there was no apparent
justification for the warrantless removal of respondent's car, it is
clear that this is a different case from *Chambers*.[24]

It is wise for the paralegal to use the more narrow of two competing
holdings when analyzing a case but to remember that courts may adopt a
broader interpretation at a later date.

The court's response to the third issue presented in the *Chambers*
case is a narrow factual judgment concerning the lack of effect a possible
error may have had. It does not lend itself to any significant holding.

With regard to the fourth issue, the court holds that the mere fact
that an attorney is appointed minutes before a trial starts does not by
itself require an evidentiary hearing on the right to counsel issue.

f. The Reasoning

Most written court opinions devote considerable space to justifying
the court's decisions. In the reasoning sections the court usually follows
established patterns of legal reasoning and reviews the relevant provisions of the constitutions, statutes, and case law and then relates the
thought processes used to arrive at the court's judgment.

In the *Chambers* case the reasoning involves application of several
previous cases that interpreted the meaning of the fourth amendment
search and seizure clause. These patterns of reasoning will be presented
in greater detail later in this chapter.

g. The Disposition

After the appellate court has explicated the relevant facts, stated
and decided the issues, and justified its positions, it announces the actual
disposition of the case, the next steps in the legal process. These steps
usually consist of affirming (approving) or reversing (disapproving) the
judgment of the lower court. If the case is affirmed, the matter is considered settled, unless either the court that just decided the case changes its
mind and grants a motion to reconsider it or a higher-level appellate
court decides to review it. If the lower court decision is reversed, the
appellate court either sends the case back to the lower court to be done
over again or substitutes its own judgment for that of the lower court. If
it is sent back to the lower court, it is with the understanding that the
lower court must act in a way consistent with the principles of law the
higher court laid down in its decision. If the decision of an intermediate

---

24. Id. at 69.

appellate level court is then appealed to a still higher-level appellate court, the case is not sent back to the lower-level court until the higher court has reached its decision on the appeal.

In the *Chambers* case, the federal district court had denied Chambers's request for a writ of habeas corpus, and the appeals court had affirmed that denial. In the decision reprinted here the Supreme Court affirmed the decision of the court of appeals. In the final result, Chambers did not obtain his writ of habeas corpus and must remain in his Pennsylvania prison until the Pennsylvania authorities choose to release him.

If the Supreme Court had supported Chambers's position on the right to counsel issue, it probably would have ordered the district court to hold an evidentiary hearing on the quality of legal assistance that Chambers received. If the court had agreed with Chambers's assertion that the search of the automobile had been in violation of the fourth amendment, it would have required the Pennsylvania authorities either to grant him a new trial (at which the evidence seized in the search of the auto would not be admitted) or to release him from prison.

A case brief of Chambers v. Maroney is presented below. This case brief, which should not be confused with an appellate brief (which is discussed in Chapter 9), summarizes the various elements discussed in this section.

A Model Case Brief

Heading: Chambers v. Maroney, 399 U.S. 42 (1970)

Facts: Police stopped an automobile in which Chambers and three others were riding because the auto matched the description of one seen at a recent robbery and because two of the occupants matched descriptions of the robbers. Rather than searching the auto at night in a dark parking lot in a dangerous section of town, the police removed it to the police station where they then searched it without a warrant. This search revealed two revolvers and property belonging to the robbery victim. Police also found and seized ammunition that fit the revolvers when they conducted a warrant-authorized search of Chambers's home the next day. The incriminating evidence seized in both searches was used against Chambers at his trial. At both of his trials, Chambers was represented by lawyers from the Legal Aid Society, but by different individuals each time. He did not have an opportunity to confer with his attorney at the second trial until minutes before the trial began.

Judicial Chambers was prosecuted for robbery. After his initial trial
History: ended in a mistrial, he was convicted for two robberies. The
trial judge allowed the state to introduce the evidence
found in the automobile and in the house. After a Pennsylvania appellate court affirmed a lower state court's denial
of a writ of habeas corpus, Chambers commenced this
habeas corpus proceeding in the United States District
Court. The writ was denied, and the Court of Appeals
affirmed. The United States Supreme Court then granted
certiorari.

Specific 1. Did the police have probable cause to stop defendant's
Issues: automobile and arrest the occupants?   Yes
2. Did the police have a legal right to search defendant's
   automobile back at the station without having first obtained a search warrant?   Yes
3. If the admission of the ammunition found in the search
   of defendant's house was improper, was it a harmless
   error?   Yes
4. Was the defendant denied adequate assistance by counsel because he did not have an opportunity to confer
   with his second attorney until a few minutes before his
   second trial?   No

Holdings: 1. When police observe an automobile matching the description of one that was seen circling and then speeding
   away from the scene of a robbery, and when police observe that the automobile contains two men who are
   wearing clothing that fits the description of clothing being worn by the robbers, then there is probable cause
   for the police to stop the automobile and arrest the
   occupants.
2a. (Narrow interpretation) Police can remove an automobile to the police station and search it there without a
   warrant if they have probable cause to search it at the
   scene of the stop but cannot reasonably do so at night in
   a dangerous section of town.
2b. (Alternative broader interpretation) Police can search
   an automobile at the station house without a warrant
   any time they have probable cause to search it at the
   scene of the arrest.
3. The mere fact that an attorney was appointed minutes
   before the trial started does not by itself require an
   evidentiary hearing on the right to counsel issue.

Reasoning: 1. Based on information supplied by eyewitnesses, police had ample cause to stop the automobile.
   2. It was not unreasonable to search the auto at the police station because the officers had sufficient probable cause to have searched it at the scene.
      a. Preston v. United States and Dyke v. Taylor Implement Manufacturing Co. are not applicable here because in those cases the police lacked probable cause to believe that evidence of a crime was concealed in the auto.
      b. This situation is consistent with Carroll v. United States, in which police with probable cause could search the auto at the scene without a warrant.
      c. It was not practical for the police to search the vehicle at the scene of the arrest.
      d. The warrantless search at the police station was a lesser intrusion on the defendant than it would have been if they had immobilized the car until they could have gotten a warrant.
   3. The record indicates beyond a reasonable doubt that admitting the ammunition found in Chambers's house was a harmless error.
   4. While a late appointment of counsel might result in a poor defense in some cases, there is no reason to believe that it did in this particular case or that it would necessarily do so in all cases.

D.   THE ROLE OF PRECEDENT

The American legal system is built around the concept of *stare decisis*.[25] This concept says that once a court has established a legal principle, other courts should adhere to that same interpretation. It is applicable not only when the common law is applied but in situations involving statutory, administrative, and constitutional law as well. Once a court interprets a section of a statute, regulation, or constitution, that court's interpretation becomes a case precedent that has to be considered in any future applications of the same provision.

Stare decisis provides stability and continuity and allows people to act on the basis of a reasonable assurance that a legal obligation entered into one day will still be enforceable the next. It also ensures that legal rights are based on more than the idiosyncrasies of an individual judge.

---

25. A Latin term translated as "Let the decision stand."

The principle of *stare decisis* is applied through the use of a legal syllogism, for example:

> *Major Premise:* A landlord cannot withhold a tenant's security deposit for maintenance and repair expenses that result from ordinary wear and tear.
>
> *Minor Premise:* The dirt on the tenant's carpet was the result of ordinary wear and tear.
>
> *Conclusion:* The landlord cannot withhold the tenant's security deposit to cover the cost of having the carpet cleaned.

The major premise is supposed to be selected on the basis of *stare decisis*. In other words, once a judge has ruled that a landlord cannot withhold a tenant's security deposit for maintenance and repair expenses that result from ordinary wear and tear, other judges should not substitute a premise that would say that they could.

The key stages in the decision process are the selections of the major and minor premises. The choice of the major premise (the proper *stare decisis* rule) often involves the exercise of a great deal of judicial discretion. The minor premise represents a factual judgment. Once the major and minor premises have been explicated, application of the accepted rules of deductive logic produce the conclusion.

1. Mandatory and Persuasive Authority

The concept of legal authority is an integral part of the *stare decisis* system. As discussed in Chapter 2, there are fifty different state court systems plus a federal court system. Within each of these systems there are higher courts and lower courts, so not all court decisions carry equal weight.

Relevant precedent case decisions are either mandatory authority or persuasive authority. A decision is mandatory authority when it comes from a higher court in the state's own court system (or within the federal court system when it is a federal court deciding the case).[26] Figure 3.2 indicates the hierarchical nature of mandatory authority. Persuasive authority consists of the decisions of courts that do not constitute mandatory authority as well as the writings of legal scholars. Thus, persuasive authority may include decisions of other states, legal encyclopedias, or law review articles. The state statutes and constitution are of course mandatory authority for the courts of that state, and they are occasionally used as persuasive authority in other states.

---

26. When a federal court is deciding a case involving an interpretation of state law, it must follow the interpretations given by that state's own courts.

Figure 3.2 The Hierarchy of Precedents

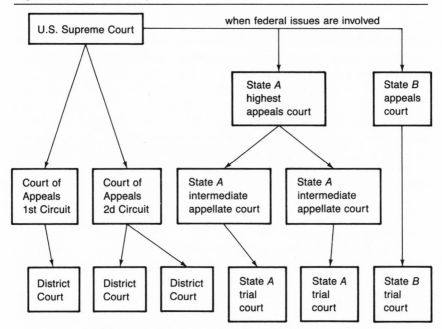

The decisions handed down by the various courts indicated are mandatory authority for the courts below them connected by an arrow. Thus a district court in the first circuit is required to follow the decisions of the court of appeals for the first circuit but can consider the decisions of the second circuit court of appeals as only advisory. Likewise the decisions of State A's highest appellate court are mandatory authority for State A but only persuasive authority for State B.

2. Overturning Precedent

While legal scholars have long extolled the values of *stare decisis,* they also have seen a need for the law to grow with society's changing needs so that courts do not repeat the mistakes of previous courts just because the other decision was rendered first.

In recognition of this need, the precedent system not only gives higher courts the right to reverse the decisions of lower courts but also gives courts the right to overrule their own previous decisions. Note how the Wisconsin Supreme Court overruled the common law doctrine of governmental immunity in the case of Holytz v. City of Milwaukee. The court emphasized the extent to which the doctrine of sovereign immunity was developed in a different era and is no longer appropriate.

Holytz v. City of Milwaukee
17 Wis. 2d 26, 115 N.W.2d 618 (1962)

GORDON, JUSTICE.

The order of the trial court sustaining the respondent's demurrer to the complaint presents an issue with respect to the tort liability of a municipal corporation. The trial court found that on the facts alleged in the complaint the city was entitled to invoke the defense of municipal tort immunity. The appellants urge that the city may not invoke such defense because (a) the drinking fountain and the water meter pit trap door were created and maintained by the city in its proprietary capacity, or (b) the meter contraption constituted a nuisance and at the time the injury occurred the relationship of governor to governed did not exist between Janet Holytz and the city of Milwaukee, or (c) the trap door was an "attractive nuisance" that was not created or maintained by the city in a governmental capacity.

Upon the facts of this case, we consider that the trial judge was correct in his conclusion that, based upon the past decisions of this court, no cause of action was asserted in the complaint. However, we are now prepared to disavow those rulings of this court which have created and preserved the doctrine of governmental immunity from tort claims. This makes it unnecessary that we rest this case on the elusive issues mentioned in the foregoing paragraph; the case turns exclusively on our abrogation of the principle of governmental immunity from tort claims. . . .

The rule of sovereign immunity developed in this country from an English doctrine and has been applied in the United States far beyond its original conception. The doctrine expanded to the point where the historical sovereignty of kings was relied upon to support a protective prerogative for municipalities. . . .

There are probably few tenets of American jurisprudence which have been so unanimously berated as the governmental immunity doctrine. This court and the highest courts of numerous other states have been unusually articulate in castigating the existing rule; text writers and law reviews have joined the chorus of denunciators. . . .

The immunization of municipalities from tort liability has been chipped away by a number of statutes in this state. Some examples are secs. 101.01 and 101.06, Wis. Stats. (safe place statute); sec. 345.05(1)(c) (2)(a), Wis. Stats. (motor vehicle accidents); sec. 270.58, Wis. Stats. (judgments against public officers); and sec. 81.15, Wis. Stats. (highway defects). . . .

The defendant argues that any change in the municipal immunity doctrine should be addressed to the legislature. We recognize that earlier decisions of this court contemplated precisely that. See Flamingo v.

Waukesha, 262 Wis. 219, 228, 55 N.W.2d 24 (1952) (concurring opinion); Britten v. Eau Claire, 260 Wis. 382, 386, 51 N.W.2d 30 (1951).

Not only have we previously expressed the view that any proposed change should be directed toward the legislature, but we also have expressed the view that the legislature's failure to enact a bill which had been introduced constituted ". . . an expression by the legislature that no change should be made. . . ." Schwenkhoff v. Farmers Mut. Automobile Ins. Co., 6 Wis. 2d 44, 47, 93 N.W.2d 867, 869 (1959).

We are satisfied that the governmental immunity doctrine has judicial origins. Upon careful consideration, we are now of the opinion that it is appropriate for this court to abolish this immunity notwithstanding the legislature's failure to adopt corrective enactments. . . .

On the other hand, courts sometimes choose not to overrule their prior decisions even when they admit that they are inconsistent in not doing so. Study the following sections from both the opinion of the court and a dissenting opinion in the most recent of several United States Supreme Court cases on the antitrust status of baseball.

Flood v. Kuhn
407 U.S. 258 (1972)

MR. JUSTICE BLACKMUN delivered the opinion of the Court. . . .

Accordingly, we adhere once again to *Federal Baseball* and *Toolson* and to their application to professional baseball. We adhere also to *International Boxing* and *Radovich* and to their respective applications to professional boxing and professional football. If there is any inconsistency or illogic in all this, it is an inconsistency and illogic of long standing that is to be remedied by the Congress and not by this Court. If we were to act otherwise, we would be withdrawing from the conclusion as to congressional intent made in *Toolson* and from the concerns as to retrospectively therein expressed. Under these circumstances, there is merit in consistency even though some might claim that beneath that consistency is a layer of inconsistency.[27] . . .

MR. JUSTICE MARSHALL, with whom MR. JUSTICE BRENNAN joins, dissenting.

We do not lightly overrule our prior constructions of federal statutes, but when our errors deny substantial federal rights, like the right to

---

27. Flood v. Kuhn, at 284.

compete freely and effectively to the best of one's ability as guaranteed by the antitrust laws, we must admit our error and correct it. We have done so before and we should do so again here. See, e.g., Blonder-Tongue Laboratories, Inc. v. University of Illinois Foundation, 402 U.S. 313 (1971); Boys Markets, Inc. v. Retail Clerks Union, 398 U.S. 235, 241 (1970).

To the extent that there is concern over any reliance interests that club owners may assert, they can be satisfied by making our decision prospective only. Baseball should be covered by the antitrust laws beginning with this case and henceforth, unless Congress decides otherwise.

Accordingly I would overrule *Federal Baseball Club* and *Toolson* and reverse the decision of the Court of Appeals.[28]

3. Sidestepping Precedent

Changes in the law are most likely to occur through a process of sidestepping existing precedents and selecting from among several alternate lines of precedents. Since the holding of any given case involves a particular set of facts, a judge can find that the facts of the case at hand differ from those of the precedent and therefore that the rule of law laid down in the precedent case does not apply.

When lawyers are presenting their cases, they attempt to stress how the facts of their cases are similar to those of favorable precedents and different from those of unfavorable precedents. In Texas v. White,[29] the state of Texas argued that Chambers v. Maroney[30] stood for the principle that whenever the police had the right to conduct a warrantless search of a suspect's automobile at the scene of the arrest, they also had the right to conduct such a warrantless search at the police station. White's lawyers, on the other hand, argued that Chambers v. Maroney stood for the principle that police could conduct a warrantless search of an automobile back at the station when conditions relating to the safety of the officers and the amount of available light made it impractical to conduct such a search on the scene. White's lawyers argued that since police could have safely searched White's car in the light, the *Chambers* case did not apply to White's situation.

Judge Cardozo's famous decision in MacPherson v. Buick Motor Co. demonstrates how the courts can utilize differing precedents. Note especially the way different factual situations are compared and how unfavorable precedents are dismissed.

---

28. Id. at 292-293.
29. 423 U.S. 67 (1975).
30. See page 92.

MacPherson v. Buick Motor Co.

217 N.Y. 282, 111 N.E. 1,050 (Ct. App. 1916)

CARDOZO, J.

The defendant is a manufacturer of automobiles. It sold an automobile to a retail dealer. The retail dealer resold to the plaintiff. While the plaintiff was in the car it suddenly collapsed. He was thrown out and injured. One of the wheels was made of defective wood, and its spokes crumbled into fragments. The wheel was not made by the defendant; it was bought from another manufacturer. There is evidence, however, that its defects could have been discovered by reasonable inspection, and that inspection was omitted. There is no claim that the defendant knew of the defect and willfully concealed it. The case, in other words, is not brought within the rule of Kuelling v. Lean Mfg. Co., 183 N.Y. 78, 75 N.E. 1,098, 2 L.R.A. (N.S.) 303, 111 Am. St. Rep. 691, 5 Ann. Cas. 124. The charge is one, not of fraud, but of negligence. The question to be determined is whether the defendant owed a duty of care and vigilance to anyone but the immediate purchaser.

The foundations of this branch of the law, at least in this state, were laid in Thomas v. Winchester, 6 N.Y. 397, 57 Am. Dec. 455. A poison was falsely labeled. The sale was made to a druggist, who in turn sold to a customer. The customer recovered damages from the seller who affixed the label. "The defendant's negligence," it was said, "put human life in imminent danger." A poison, falsely labeled, is likely to injure anyone who gets it. Because the danger is to be foreseen, there is a duty to avoid the injury. Cases were cited by way of illustration in which manufacturers were not subject to any duty irrespective of contract. The distinction was said to be that their conduct, though negligent, was not likely to result in injury to anyone except the purchaser. . . . Thomas v. Winchester became quickly a landmark of the law. In the application of its principle there may, at times, have been uncertainty or even error. There has never in this state been doubt or disavowal of the principle itself. The chief cases are well known, yet to recall some of them will be helpful. Loop v. Litchfield, 42 N.Y. 351, 1 Am. Rep. 513, is the earliest. It was the case of a defect in a small balance wheel used on a circular saw. The manufacturer pointed out the defect to the buyer, who wished a cheap article and was ready to assume the risk. The risk can hardly have been an imminent one, for the wheel lasted five years before it broke. In the meanwhile the buyer had made a lease of the machinery. It was held that the manufacturer was not answerable to the lessee. Loop v. Litchfield was followed in Losee v. Clute, 51 N.Y. 494, 10 Am. Rep. 638, the case of the explosion of a steam boiler. That decision has been criticized (Thompson on Negligence, 233; Shearman & Redfield on Negligence [6th Ed.] sec. 117); but it must be confined to its special facts. It was put

upon the ground that the risk of injury was too remote. The buyer in that case had not only accepted the boiler, but had tested it. The manufacturer knew that his own test was not the final one. The finality of the test has a bearing on the measure of diligence owing to persons other than the purchaser. Beven, Negligence (3d Ed.) pp. 50, 51, 54; Wharton, Negligence (2d Ed.) sec. 134.

These early cases suggest a narrow construction of the rule. Later cases, however, evince a more liberal spirit. First in importance is Devlin v. Smith, 89 N.Y. 470, 42 Am. Rep. 311. The defendant, a contractor, built a scaffold for a painter. The painter's servants were injured. The contractor was held liable. He knew that the scaffold, if improperly constructed, was a most dangerous trap. He knew that it was to be used by the workmen. He was building it for that very purpose. Building it for their use, he owed them a duty, irrespective of his contract with their master, to build it with care.

From Devlin v. Smith we pass over intermediate cases and turn to the latest case in this court in which Thomas v. Winchester was followed. That case is Statler v. Ray Mfg. Co., 195 N.Y. 478, 480, 88 N.E. 1,063. The defendant manufactured a large coffee urn. It was installed in a restaurant. When heated, the urn exploded and injured the plaintiff. We held that the manufacturer was liable. We said that the urn "was of such a character inherently that, when applied to the purposes for which it was designed, it was liable to become a source of great danger to many people if not carefully and properly constructed."

It may be that Devlin v. Smith and Statler v. Ray Mfg. Co. have extended the rule of Thomas v. Winchester. If so, this court is committed to the extension. The defendant argues that things imminently dangerous to life are poisons, explosives, deadly weapons — things whose normal function it is to injure or destroy. But whatever the rule in Thomas v. Winchester may once have been, it has no longer that restricted meaning. A scaffold (Devlin v. Smith, supra) is not inherently a destructive instrument. It becomes destructive only if imperfectly constructed. A large coffee urn (Statler v. Ray Mfg. Co., supra) may have within itself, if negligently made, the potency of a danger, yet no one thinks of it as an implement whose normal function is destruction. What is true of the coffee urn is equally true of bottles of aerated water. Torgesen v. Schultz, 192 N.Y. 156, 84 N.E. 956, 18 L.R.A. (N.S.) 726, 127 Am. St. Rep. 894. We have mentioned only cases in this court. But the rule has received a like extension in our courts of intermediate appeal. In Burke v. Ireland, 26 App. Div. 487, 59 N.Y. Supp. 369, in an opinion by Cullen, J., it was applied to a builder who constructed a defective building; in Kahner v. Otis Elevator Co., 96 App. Div. 169, 89 N.Y. Supp. 185, to the manufacturer of an elevator; in Davies v. Pelham Hod Elevating Co., 65 Hun, 573, 20 N.Y. Supp. 523, affirmed in this court without opinion, 146 N.Y. 363, 41 N.E. 88, to a contractor who furnished a defective rope with

knowledge of the purpose for which the rope was to be used. We are not required at this time either to approve or to disapprove the application of the rule that was made in these cases. It is enough that they help to characterize the trend of judicial thought.

Devlin v. Smith was decided in 1882. A year later a very similar case came before the Court of Appeal in England (Heaven v. Pender, 11 Q.B.D. 503). We find in the opinion of Brett, M.R., afterwards Lord Esher, the same conception of a duty, irrespective of contract, imposed upon the manufacturer by the law itself:

> Whenever one person supplies goods or machinery, or the like, for the purpose of their being used by another person under such circumstances that every one of ordinary sense would, if he thought, recognize at once that unless he used ordinary care and skill with regard to the condition of the thing supplied, or the mode of supplying it, there will be danger of injury to the person or property of him for whose use the thing is supplied, and who is to use it, a duty arises to use ordinary care and skill as the condition or manner of supplying such thing.

He then points out that for a neglect of such ordinary care or skill whereby injury happens, the appropriate remedy is an action for negligence. The right to enforce this liability is not to be confined to the immediate buyer. The right, he says, extends to the persons or class of persons for whose use the thing is supplied. It is enough that the goods "would in all probability be used at once . . . before a reasonable opportunity for discovering any defect which might exist," and that the thing supplied is of such a nature "that a neglect of ordinary care or skill as to its condition or the manner of supplying it would probably cause danger to the person or property of the person for whose use it was supplied, and who was about to use it." On the other hand, he would exclude a case "in which the goods are supplied under circumstances in which it would be a chance by whom they would be used or whether they would be used or not, or whether they would be used before there would probably be means of observing any defect," or where the goods are of such a nature that "a want of care or skill as to their condition or the manner of supplying them would not probably produce danger of injury to person or property." What was said by Lord Esher in that case did not command the full assent of his associates. His opinion has been criticized "as requiring every man to take affirmative precautions to protect his neighbors as well as to refrain from injuring them." Bohlen, Affirmative Obligations in the Law of Torts, 44 Am. Law Reg. (N.S.) 341. It may not be an accurate exposition of the law of England. Perhaps it may need some qualification even in our own state. Like most attempts at comprehensive definition, it may involve errors of inclusion and of exclusion. But its tests and standards, at least in their underlying principles, with whatever

qualification may be called for as they are applied to varying conditions, are the tests and standards of our law.

We hold, then, that the principle of Thomas v. Winchester is not limited to poisons, explosives, and things of like nature, to things which in their normal operation are implements of destruction. If the nature of a thing is such that it is reasonably certain to place life and limb in peril when negligently made, it is then a thing of danger. Its nature gives warning of the consequences to be expected. If to the element of danger there is added knowledge that the thing will be used by persons other than the purchaser, and used without new tests, then, irrespective of contract, the manufacturer of this thing of danger is under a duty to make it carefully. That is as far as we are required to go for the decision of this case. There must be knowledge of a danger, not merely possible, but probable. It is possible to use almost anything in a way that will make it dangerous if defective. That is not enough to charge the manufacturer with a duty independent of his contract. Whether a given thing is dangerous may be sometimes a question for the court and sometimes a question for the jury. There must also be knowledge that in the usual course of events the danger will be shared by others than the buyer. Such knowledge may often be inferred from the nature of the transaction. But it is possible that even knowledge of the danger and of the use will not always be enough. The proximity or remoteness of the relation is a factor to be considered. We are dealing now with the liability of the manufacturer of the finished product, who puts it on the market to be used without inspection by his customers. If he is negligent, where danger is to be foreseen, a liability will follow. . . .

From this survey of the decisions, there thus emerges a definition of the duty of a manufacturer which enables us to measure this defendant's liability. Beyond all question, the nature of an automobile gives warning of probable danger if its construction is defective. This automobile was designed to go fifty miles an hour. Unless its wheels were sound and strong, injury was almost certain. It was as much a thing of danger as a defective engine for a railroad. The defendant knew the danger. It knew also that the car would be used by persons other than the buyer. This was apparent from its size; there were seats for three persons. It was apparent also from the fact that the buyer was a dealer in cars, who bought to resell. The maker of this car supplied it for the use of purchasers from the dealer just as plainly as the contractor in Devlin v. Smith supplied the scaffold for use by the servants of the owner. The dealer was indeed the one person of whom it might be said with some approach to certainty that by him the car would not be used. Yet the defendant would have us say that he was the one person whom it was under a legal duty to protect. The law does not lead us to so inconsequent a conclusion. Precedents drawn from the days of travel by

stagecoach do not fit the conditions of travel today. The principle that the danger must be imminent does not change, but the things subject to the principle do change. They are whatever the needs of life in a developing civilization require them to be.

In reaching this conclusion, we do not ignore the decisions to the contrary in other jurisdictions. It was held in Cadillac Co. v. Johnson, 221 Fed. 801, 137 C.C.A. 279 L.R.A. 1,915E, 287, that an automobile is not within the rule of Thomas v. Winchester. There was, however, a vigorous dissent. Opposed to that decision is one of the Court of Appeals of Kentucky, Olds Motor Works v. Shaffer, 145 Ky. 616, 140 S.W. 1,047, 37 L.R.A. (N.S.) 560, Ann. Cas. 1913B, 689. The earlier cases are summarized by Judge Sanborn in Huset v. J. I. Case Threshing Machine Co., 120 Fed. 865, 57 C.C.A. 237, 61 L.R.A. 303. Some of them, at first sight inconsistent with our conclusion, may be reconciled upon the ground that the negligence was too remote, and that another cause had intervened. But even when they cannot be reconciled, the difference is rather in the application of the principle than in the principle itself. Judge Sanborn says, for example, that the contractor who builds a bridge, or the manufacturer who builds a car, cannot ordinarily foresee injury to other persons than the owner as the probable result. 120 Fed. 865, at page 867, 57 C.C.A. 237, at page 239, 61 L.R.A. 303. We take a different view. We think that injury to others is to be foreseen not merely as a possible, but as an almost inevitable, result. See the trenchant criticism in *Bohlen,* supra, at page 351. Indeed, Judge Sanborn concedes that his view is not to be reconciled with our decision in Devlin v. Smith, supra. The doctrine of that decision has now become the settled law of this state, and we have no desire to depart from it. . . .

We think the defendant was not absolved from a duty of inspection because it bought the wheels from a reputable manufacturer. It was not merely a dealer in automobiles. It was a manufacturer of automobiles. It was responsible for the finished product. It was not at liberty to put the finished product on the market without subjecting the component parts to ordinary and simple tests. Richmond & Danville R.R. Co. v. Elliott, 149 U.S. 266, 272. Under the charge of the trial judge nothing more was required of it. The obligation to inspect must vary with the nature of the thing to be inspected. The more probable the danger the greater the need of caution.

There is little analogy between this case and Carlson v. Phoenix Bridge Co., 132 N.Y. 273, 30 N.E. 750, where the defendant bought a tool for a servant's use. The making of tools was not the business in which the master was engaged. Reliance on the skill of the manufacturer was proper and almost inevitable. But that is not the defendant's situation. Both by its relation to the work and by the nature of its business, it is charged with a stricter duty.

Other rulings complained of have been considered, but no error has been found in them.

The judgment should be affirmed, with costs.

E.   SUMMARY

Statutes are published in the form of individual slip laws, statutes at large or sessions laws, and codes. In addition to providing the actual text of the legislation, annotated codes contain information about the legislative history and references to court decisions that have interpreted the legislation. The format of a legislative citation will depend on whether it is being cited by its public law number, its popular name, the statutes at large, or the code.

Where judicial decisions focus on the resolution of a particular conflict that has already occurred between specific parties, statutes ordinarily address future situations for general categories of people, business entities, governments, and so forth. For many reasons, these statutes often contain great ambiguity with respect to their application to a specific event.

In the process of applying the statute in a specific case, the courts must resolve at least part of the ambiguity. The court must decide what the statute means in the context of specific facts presented in the litigation. Whenever possible the court will look to previous court decisions that have interpreted that same statute. However, judges are sometimes asked to interpret statutes in situations where no other courts have done so or where appellate courts must review the interpretations of lower courts.

Under the fundamental principle of statutory interpretation, the judge should construe the language to be consistent with the intent of legislators who enacted the statute. This is done by giving ambiguous words their most common dictionary meaning. Judges also have developed principles like *ejusdem generis* and express mention/implied exclusion to guide them in using this literalistic approach. Sometimes, however, the courts will reject the outcome of such literal analysis and choose instead to focus on the context of the disputed section in the larger act. This intrinsic approach considers titles assigned to sections and consistency with other sections. At other times the court will look completely beyond the statutory text and use extrinsic analysis or what is commonly called the legislative history. Administrative interpretations and even the common law can be considered as part of this extrinsic analysis.

The interpretation of administrative regulations is similar to that of statutes. At the federal level the regulations are first published in the Federal Register and then in the Code of Federal Regulations. The

methods for publishing state regulations vary widely. Agency opinions and decisions are also published and interpreted like judicial cases.

The interpretation of constitutions also involves the use of literalism, and intrinsic and extrinsic analysis. The legislative history of a constitutional provision involves examination of the notes from the constitutional convention (where available) or the regular legislative hearings, committee reports, and debates that accompany the ratification of a constitutional amendment. Once a court has formally interpreted a constitutional provision, those cases take on precedent value and influence future interpretations of the same clause.

Court cases are found in books called case reporters published by the government (as in the case of United States Supreme Court Reports) or by a private publisher (as is the case with the Supreme Court Reporter). The paralegal must become familiar with these reporters, their official abbreviations, and the citation system that locates cases.

Most written opinions contain several distinct elements, usually beginning with an overview of the basic facts of the case. A judicial history section summarizes the actions of the various inferior courts. After reviewing this introductory material, the opinion then usually identifies the issues being decided, reports the court's decision, and provides a carefully reasoned legal justification for that decision. The manner in which these individual issues are answered will ultimately determine the final disposition of the case — it may be either affirmed or reversed. Often the reversals are sent back to the lower courts to be reconsidered in light of the legal principles that the appellate court has just decided.

The individual case holding is the basic unit of legal analysis in the precedent system. It is as important in the areas of constitutional and statutory law as it is in situations involving the common law. The principle of *stare decisis* holds that courts should decide cases in ways that will be consistent with previous court interpretations of the same legal principle and thus provide stability and continuity to human affairs.

Individual judges, however, often have much discretion in the selection and interpretation of the precedent to be applied. Conflicting precedents may be considered as either mandatory or persuasive authority. In addition, judges have the power to overrule precedent decisions of their own or inferior courts. Most of the time, however, judges choose to sidestep negative precedents by emphasizing the differences in the factual situations between the precedent case and the case being decided.

When analyzing the precedent value of any given case, the paralegal should remember this advice from William Zelermyer:

> Take one case for what it is — a decision given by certain men, at a certain time, in a certain place, on the basis of certain reasoning applied to certain questions arising out of certain happenings under certain circumstances. We cannot tell with certainty what the same or

other men would decide, at the same or another time, in the same or another place, on the basis of the same or other reasoning applied to the same or other questions arising out of other happenings under the same or other circumstances. One case does not provide an answer to a legal problem — it is but a clue to be used in the attempt to find an answer by the process of legal reasoning.[31]

KEY TERMS

affirmed

annotated codes

appellant

appellee

case reporter

citation

code

contextual analysis

disposition

ejusdem generis

express mention/implied exclusion

extrinsic analysis

holding

intrinsic analysis

issue

last antecedent doctrine

legislative history

legislative intent

literalism

mandatory authority

obiter dictum

parallel citation

persuasive authority

petitioner

precedent

ratio decidendi

remanded

respondent

reversed

sessions laws

sidestepping precedent

slip laws

stare decisis

statutes at large

syllogism

written opinion

REVIEW QUESTIONS

1. What is the difference in how statutes at large and codes are organized?

2. What is the official codification of federal statutes?

3. In what ways does the form of a statute differ from the form of a judicial decision?

4. What is the difference between the Federal Register and the Code of Federal Regulations?

---

31. W. Zelermyer, The Process of Legal Reasoning 112 (1963).

5. What are the differences between official case reporters and unofficial ones? Give an example or two of each.

6. Explain the meaning of each part of the following case citation: Pines v. Perssion, 14 Wis. 2d 590, 111 N.W.2d 409 (1961).

7. In which reporters would one find the following cases?

   93 S. Ct. 2071   551 P.2d 398
   18 F.R.D. 107   213 N.J. 652

8. If Robert Barrett sued the First National Bank of Congerville, what would be the name by which the case would be cited? Would the name change if the bank took the case to an appellate court after Barrett had won a victory in the trial court?

9. What do *ejusdem generis*, express mention/implied exclusion, and the last antecedent doctrine have in common?

10. Is a decision of the Fourth Circuit Court of Appeals mandatory authority for a federal district court in the Seventh Circuit? Is a decision of the Georgia Supreme Court persuasive authority for an appellate court in Minnesota?

DISCUSSION QUESTIONS

1. Why are statutes sometimes ambiguous? Could careful drafting remove all aspects of this ambiguity? Is it desirable to reduce the amount of ambiguity that usually occurs in drafting legislation?

2. What should be the criteria for rejecting a literalistic approach in favor of an intrinsic or extrinsic analysis?

3. While courts ordinarily abide by the principle of *stare decisis*, they can overturn or refuse to follow precedents when they think the law should be changed. Do you agree that judges should have such powers? What factors should a judge consider when determining whether a precedent should be followed?

4. In Flood v. Kuhn the majority opinion took the position that it was up to the legislative branch to overturn the principles established in the precedent cases. On the other hand, in both the dissenting opinion in *Flood* and in the Holytz v. City of Milwaukee opinion, the judges took the position that the court should change the law without waiting for legislative action. When should the courts require legislative action, and when should they take it on themselves to make the change?

5. What should be the role of persuasive authority? To what extent should the courts of Washington take into consideration the manner in which the courts of Alabama have resolved similar legal problems? Why should they give them any consideration at all?

6.   In Texas v. White the justices of the United States Supreme Court disagreed among themselves about the true nature of the court's holding in Chambers v. Maroney. Which group of justices do you think properly interpreted the original decision? Why do you take that position?

PROJECTS

1.   Locate and then read 15 U.S.C. §§1601-1611. Now answer the following questions: (a) Is the statute directed at a particular class or type of person (such as government officials, businesses with over twenty-five employees, and so on) or to the general public? (b) What behavior is being regulated (for example, are people required to file a tax return or prohibited from using a certain type of drug)? (c) Are there any special conditions that must occur before the statute becomes operative (for example, must the president declare a national emergency)? (d) Are there any specific exceptions or exclusions? (e) Is there a penalty for failure to comply? If so, what is it? Now locate 12 C.F.R. §§226.4, 226.6, and 226.8 and note the relationship of these sections to the statute.

2.   Read and then brief McBoyle v. United States, 283 U.S. 25 (1931). What principles of statutory construction were used in this case? Do you agree with their conclusion? Why or why not?

3.   Read and then brief Richardson v. Ramirez, 418 U.S. 24 (1974). What techniques of analysis are used to interpret the fourteenth amendment?

4.   Locate, read, and then brief Larsen v. General Motors Corporation, 391 F.2d 495 (8th Cir. 1968). What is the broadest, most expansive principle of law for which this case could properly be cited as precedent? What is the narrowest, most limited principle? Identify the types of authorities utilized in the reasoning. Which did the court choose to follow?

5.   Locate, read, and then brief Skinner v. Whitley, 281 N.C. 476, 189 S.E.2d 239 (1972). Now respond to the same questions listed in (1) above.

Chapter 4
Basic Legal Concepts

THIS CHAPTER INTRODUCES some common legal terms and concepts in several major areas of the law. There is no consensus as to what must be included and what can be left out of such an elementary overview. Nevertheless, the following materials represent one view of what constitutes a basic legal literacy for a beginning paralegal. Before proceeding with this chapter, it may be helpful to review the discussion in Chapter 2 on the differences between civil and criminal law.[1]

A. CRIMINAL LAW

A crime is an act that has been defined as a public wrong, that is prosecuted by the government, and that may carry a punishment of a fine or imprisonment. Certain acts were classified as crimes by the common law heritage, but today those common law crimes have been superseded by statutory ones. Nevertheless, those statutes incorporated many of the principles that were developed in the common law.

1. Classification of Crimes

Serious crimes like murder, rape, armed robbery, and aggravated assault are classified as felonies. Felonies generally involve a punishment that can include a year or more in a state prison. Misdemeanors include charges such as disorderly conduct and criminal damage to property. When incarceration is called for in such cases, it usually is for less than one year and is served in a county jail. Today the criminal law in most jurisdictions is entirely statutory in nature, and the legislature determines whether a given act is to be considered a felony or a misdemeanor.

The criminal codes of most states typically include crimes against persons (homicide, kidnapping, sex offenses, assault, and battery), crimes against property (theft, robbery, burglary, arson, and trespass), crimes against the public health or decency (drug laws, abortion, bribery,

---

1. See page 42.

and disorderly conduct), and crimes against the government itself (treason and official misconduct). The federal criminal law tends to focus on interstate activities.

Although the state criminal code usually can be divided neatly into felonies and misdemeanors, there are some other types of quasi-criminal law situations that are also included. Traffic laws are usually codified in a different part of the state's statutes and do not carry the same stigma as do violations of the criminal law. Nevertheless, the judicial proceedings used to enforce these traffic laws are criminal in nature. The state takes it on itself to prosecute offenders who in turn must be found guilty "beyond a reasonable doubt." Some juvenile proceedings are also criminal in nature. Local ordinances for matters like garbage disposal and barking dogs are additional examples of quasi-criminal proceedings.

2. Elements of a Crime

In order for a crime to take place, someone with a "guilty intent" (*mens rea*) must commit a "guilty act" (*actus rea*) that causes specified harmful results. The guilty act part of the formula consists of an action such as taking someone's life or property (such as homicide or theft) or making an improper physical contact with someone (such as battery or rape). The classification of what crime has been committed often depends on the results of the act. For example, if one person shoots another with an intent to kill that person, the actual damage done by the shooting (that is, did the victim live or die?) will determine whether the person has committed homicide or only attempted homicide.

The *mens rea* (the nature of a person's intent) is also a critical factor in the classification of most crimes. In order to commit a crime, one must have a "guilty mind." Although it is difficult to prove what was going on in someone's mind, the courts allow judges and juries to infer the defendant's state of mind from both statements and actions. Furthermore, the law assumes that people know the probable consequences of their acts. A person who strikes another may be presumed to have intended the infliction of harm in that such a result naturally flows from hitting another.

The intent is also important in distinguishing one crime from another. The same act and the same result can constitute different crimes based on the intent of the criminal. For example, murder, voluntary manslaughter, involuntary manslaughter, and reckless homicide all involve the taking of a human life. They differ primarily in terms of the intent of the person responsible for the killing. Compare the way in which these offenses are defined in the Illinois criminal code:

A person who kills an individual without lawful justification commits murder if, in performing the acts which cause the death:

(1) He either intends to kill or do great bodily harm to that individual or another, or knows that such acts will cause death to that individual or another; or

(2) He knows that such acts create a strong probability of death or great bodily harm to that individual or another; or

(3) He is attempting or committing a forcible felony other than voluntary manslaughter.[2] . . .

A person who kills an individual without lawful justification commits voluntary manslaughter if at the time of the killing he is acting under a sudden and intense passion resulting from serious provocation by:

(1) The individual killed, or

(2) Another whom the offender endeavors to kill, but he negligently or accidentally causes the death of the individual killed.[3] . . .

A person who kills an individual without lawful justification commits involuntary manslaughter if his acts whether lawful or unlawful which cause the death are such as are likely to cause death or great bodily harm to some individual, and he performs them recklessly. If the acts which cause the death consist of the driving of a motor vehicle, the person may be prosecuted for reckless homicide or if he is prosecuted for involuntary manslaughter, he may be found guilty of the included offense of reckless homicide.[4] . . .

In a similar fashion the misdemeanor of assault becomes the felony of aggravated assault when either the assailant uses a deadly weapon or the victim of the assault is a teacher or policeman.[5] This type of overlapping of charges often provides a basis for reaching compromise agreements through the plea bargaining process.[6]

3. Parties to the Crime

Under the common law a person who committed a criminal act was the perpetrator (or principal in the first degree). An abbettor (or principal in the second degree) was one who incited, counseled, or otherwise encouraged the perpetrator, and a person who received, comforted, or otherwise assisted someone known to be a perpetrator was considered an accessory. While many state statutes no longer use these specific categories, they still define criminal liability in terms that encompass the abettors and accessories as well as the perpetrators.

4. Defenses

A person will be excused or not be held responsible for an act that otherwise would have been considered a crime if that person validly

---

2. 38 Ill. Rev. Stat. §9-1.

3. 38 Ill. Rev. Stat. §9-2.

4. 38 Ill. Rev. Stat. §9-3.

5. 38 Ill. Rev. Stat. §§12-1 and 12-2.

6. It is commonly estimated that between 75 and 90 percent of all criminal cases are disposed of through the plea bargaining process rather than by going to trial. In a typical plea bargain the defendant agrees to plead guilty to a lesser charge. The prosecutor is assured of getting a conviction without having to go through the time and expense of a trial or to risk losing the case. The defendant usually comes away with a lighter sentence than he or she would expect to receive if the case had gone to trial.

raises one of several accepted defenses. Perhaps the best known of these is the insanity defense. If the individual is found to be legally insane, it is also assumed that the individual was incapable of having the required *mens rea* to commit the crime.[7] In some jurisdictions and under some circumstances, being intoxicated or being under the influence of drugs is also considered a valid defense. Similarly, it is assumed that children under a certain age are incapable of forming criminal intent, and they are protected from being convicted of a criminal offense.[8]

Entrapment represents another form of defense relating the *mens rea*. It allows a person to escape conviction if it can be established that government agents induced the individual to commit a crime by placing the idea in his or her mind. It is considered acceptable for government agents to provide an opportunity to commit a crime that the person is already contemplating. The key then is whether there was a predisposition to commit the crime before the government agents contacted the person.

Because one of the fundamental principles of the criminal law is that the criminal act must be the result of a voluntary act, the law also recognizes duress and compulsion as legitimate defenses. If a defendant can establish that the criminal act was committed because he or she was forced to carry it out, the individual is not considered to be guilty of a criminal act. In the famous Patty Hearst case, attorney F. Lee Bailey unsuccessfully argued that Hearst had participated in a bank robbery and other crimes under duress from her Symbionese Liberation Army

---

7. States and federal circuits disagree about the definition of *insanity* that should be used when determining whether a person is guilty by reason of insanity, but most jurisdictions have adopted a variation of the *M'Naghten* rule or the American Law Institute test. Under the *M'Naghten* rule, which was developed from the English common law, defendants are not considered responsible for the crime if, at the time of committing the act, they were laboring under such a defect of reason from a disease of the mind that they could not understand the nature of their action or tell the difference between moral rightness or wrongness of their actions. Under the ALI test, a person is not criminally responsible if, at the time that the crime was committed, the act in question was a result of a mental disease or defect that resulted in the lack of a substantial capacity to appreciate the wrongfulness of the conduct or to conform his or her actions to the requirements of the law.

   In a successful insanity defense the person is found to be not guilty of a crime and is not incarcerated or otherwise criminally punished for that act. However, that individual usually is sent to a state mental hospital for treatment. When medical officials determine that the individual is no longer a threat to society, he or she is returned to society. In recent years, several states have adopted a "guilty, but insane" verdict under which the perpetrator is considered criminally responsible and given a prison term. Rather than being sent to prison, however, the individual is sent to a mental hospital for treatment. When medical officials have completed their treatment and are ready to release the individual, the person is sent to the prison system to serve the remainder of the prison sentence (if the time spent in the mental hospital was less than the time allocated for the prison sentence).

8. At common law children under the age of seven are conclusively presumed to be incapable of forming criminal intent, while there is a rebuttable presumption that those between ages seven and fourteen are not capable. Juvenile court legislation provides that some or all criminal conduct of juveniles is to be adjudicated in a special juvenile court system.

kidnappers. The state successfully countered that Hearst had passed up opportunities to flee and call police and therefore must have been a willing participant.

Closely related to the duress concept is that of necessity. Necessity may exonerate otherwise criminal conduct when a person believes that such conduct is necessary to avoid a public or private injury greater than the injury that might reasonably result from his or her own act. An example of this might be when a motorist chooses to crash an automobile into a building in order to avoid hitting a child who runs into the street.

Another important defense in the criminal law is the concept of justified use of force (including self-defense). A person is allowed to use force against another when and to the extent that it can reasonably be believed that such conduct is necessary to defend that person or another against this imminent use of unlawful force. The key here is determining when someone reasonable believes that such conduct was necessary. States differ on the extent to which a person is expected to retreat or flee from an approaching danger or can stay and defend oneself. They also differ on the circumstances under which one is allowed to use force to defend one's property. The rules of self-defense also depend on the nature of the force being used to resist the act. The use of force likely to cause death or great bodily harm is more carefully limited than other forms of resistance, and law enforcement officers receive special protections when executing their lawful duties.

5. Application of the Exclusionary Rule

One of the most controversial areas of the criminal law involves the application of the exclusionary rule. Under the terms of this judicially imposed rule, evidence that has been obtained in violation of an individual's constitutional rights cannot be used against that individual in a criminal trial. Furthermore, the "fruit of the poisonous tree" doctrine holds that evidence that is spawned by or directly derived from an illegal search or illegal interrogation is inadmissible against the defendant by virtue of being tainted by the original illegality.

It should be emphasized that application of this rule does not invalidate the arrest or prevent the defendant from being convicted on the basis of independent evidence. In recent years, the United States Supreme Court has created several important exceptions to the application of the exclusionary rule, and some members of the court would like to abolish it altogether.

B. TORTS

Whereas a crime is defined as a public wrong for which the state seeks a fine or imprisonment, a tort is a private wrong (other than a

breach of contract) for which the law provides a remedy in the form of an action for damages. A tort occurs when a person (or a person's property) is harmed as a result of another's failure to carry out a legal duty.[9] A crime is prosecuted by the state using criminal procedures, but a tort must be prosecuted by the injured party through civil procedures.

1. Negligence

The most common types of tort actions involve negligence. Negligence is a failure to act as a reasonably prudent and careful person is expected to act in a similar circumstance. It is a careless or accidental inflicting of an injury as opposed to an intentional one and can result from an omission or failure to act as well as a specific action. Negligence actions include actions arising from a slip on a wet spot on a supermarket floor as well as allegations of medical malpractice.

a. Elements

The four basic elements in a negligence case are duty, breach of duty, causation, and damages. The law imposes a duty to act with "due care." This due care standard is defined in terms of how a "reasonably prudent man" would operate in the same situation. If the person has some specialized type of training, such as a medical degree, then that individual is expected to act not just as a reasonable person would but as a reasonable person with medical training would act. Furthermore, the greater the inherent danger in a particular situation, the more cautious the individual is expected to be. This duty is owed by all persons within the society to a degree that is consistent with their age, physical and mental conditions, and so forth. Jurisdictions differ, however, as to whom it is owed. Most states take the position that this duty to act with due care is owed to anyone who suffers injuries as a proximate or direct result of the person's actions. Other states say the duty applies only to those persons for whom there was a foreseeable risk.

Causation is another difficult legal concept. In a tort action the defendant's actions must be the proximate cause of the plaintiff's injuries.[10] To be considered the proximate cause, a natural and continuous sequence must be shown that is unbroken by any efficient intervening cause. In deciding cases in which determining the proximate cause is a key issue, the courts frequently wrestle with unforeseeable consequences and intervening forces. Under one commonly used test (referred to as the "but for" standard) it is necessary to establish that if the defendant had not acted in that manner, the plaintiff would not have been injured.

---

9. Legal duties are defined in the common law and consist of affirmative obligations to take actions to protect others and to refrain from taking actions that inflict harm on others.

10. The plaintiff is the party who initiates a civil law suit, while the defendant is the party who is being sued.

Under the "substantial factor" test, liability is imposed if the defendant's action is shown to be a substantial factor in having caused the plaintiff's injuries. The courts often are faced with chain reaction situations in which a person's actions lead to an event that in turn leads to several other events that eventually affect other people.

b. Defenses

In representing the defendant in a negligence case, the attorney usually attempts to rebut the plaintiff's evidence on as many of the above four elements as possible. In other words, the defense tries to show that no duty was owed to the plaintiff or that the defendant's action was not the cause of the plaintiff's injuries. Another approach to defending such cases involves raising an affirmative defense in which it is admitted that negligence was established but it is argued that the defendant should not be held liable because of actions taken by the plaintiff.

The doctrine of contributory negligence — a major type of affirmative defense — asserts that the plaintiff contributed to his or her own injuries or otherwise failed to protect himself or herself from risks that were foreseeable. In other words, it was the plaintiff's breach of a duty to protect oneself that was the proximate cause of the injuries. Therefore, the defendant is relieved of any liability connected with his or her original action.

Another affirmative defense involves the concept of assumption of risk. According to this doctrine a plaintiff may not recover for an injury received as a result of voluntarily subjecting oneself to a known danger. Successful use of this defense requires the defendant to establish that the plaintiff knew about the dangerous nature of the situation before voluntarily exposing himself or herself to that danger. It is argued, for example, that when people choose to attend a baseball game, they assume the risk of being hit by a foul ball.

Both contributory negligence and assumption of risk prevent a plaintiff from being compensated for very serious injuries even when the injuries resulted from rather minor breaches when compared to the extreme negligence of the defendant. In response to the perceived unfairness of this situation some jurisdictions have developed the doctrine of "last clear chance." Applied mainly in automobile accident cases, this doctrine states that the negligence of the plaintiff does not preclude a recovery for the negligence of the defendant where it appears that the defendant, by exercising reasonable care and prudence, might still have been able to avoid the accident or at least reduce some of the plaintiff's injuries. For example, if the defendant were speeding in the right lane of a four-lane roadway, and the plaintiff failed to make a complete stop at a crossroad before making a right turn into the right lane, the defendant could have avoided the accident if he had switched to the left lane.

Another approach has involved the adoption of comparative negli-

gence through statutes and court decisions. Under this comparative negligence concept, negligence is measured in terms of percentages, and
damages then are distributed proportionately. There are three main
categories of comparative negligence: (1) Recovery is allowed in situations where plaintiff's negligence was slight but is barred when it was
gross; (2) under a "pure" comparative negligence statute, a plaintiff
recovers an amount that is determined to be the actual damages less a
percentage of the amount of negligence attributable to the plaintiff; and
(3) modified comparative negligence involves reducing the plaintiff's
recovery by the percentage of his or her own negligence if the defendant's negligence is greater than that of the plaintiff and barring the
plaintiff from recovering anything if the plaintiff's negligence is greater
than the defendant's.

2. Intentional Torts

Negligence involves careless or unthinking behavior. No conscious
decision is made to seek to injure another party. When people intention-
ally seek to violate a duty toward others, their purposeful conduct is
classified as an intentional tort and the tortfeasor[11] is subject to a greater
range of damages.

a. Types

While many intentional torts have direct parallels in the criminal
law, they are separate and distinct civil actions. These torts include battery (a harmful or offensive contact with another's person when the act is
done without consent and for the purpose of causing contact or fear of
contact that is not otherwise allowed); assault (an incomplete battery —
an intention to inflict a harmful or offensive contact or to make the
person apprehensive that one will be inflicted); infliction of mental distress (an act of extreme or outrageous conduct intended to cause mental
anguish or distress); trespass to land (physical invasion of another's right
to exclusive possession of land); trespass to chattels (wrongful detention
of someone's personal property); and conversion (permanent deprivation of someone's personal property).

False arrest, false imprisonment, malicious prosecution, and abuse
of process are all intentional torts that are designed to provide some
protection from misuse of the legal system. False arrest occurs when a
person is arrested (by either a law officer or a citizen) without probable
cause and when not covered by special privilege.[12] False imprisonment
involves illegal detention of an individual by either physical actions or

---

11. The tortfeasor, or wrongdoer, is the one who commits the tort.
12. See discussion of defenses on page 129.

threats. Malicious prosecution and abuse of process both involve malicious and improper use of the courts or other forms of legal proceedings. Note that the plaintiff must prove that the behavior was malicious (that is, that the person proceeded even though the charges were known to be invalid) and not just a mistake.

Perhaps the best known of the intentional torts are libel and slander. Libel is defamation directed at the eye (usually in print), while slander is defamation directed at the ear (verbal statements). To be considered defamatory the material must tend to injure a person's reputation, to hold a person up to ridicule, or to excite adverse, derogatory, or unpleasant feelings or opinions about someone.

The tort of invasion of privacy covers appropriation (the unauthorized exploitive use of one's personality, name, or picture for the defendant's benefit), disclosure (the publicizing of embarrassing private affairs, even when they may be true), intrusion (the unjustified intrusion in one's private activities through eavesdropping or when a photographer hounds a movie star everywhere that person goes), and false light (use of a picture or some other means to infer a connection between the person and an idea or statement for which the individual is not responsible).

Finally, there are intentional torts related to business dealings. The tort of deceit prohibits one from making false and misleading statements about important facts, and the tort of interference with a contract prohibits one from inducing a party to breach a contract or interfering with the performance of a contract.

b. Defenses

The primary defenses available in intentional tort cases are consent, self-defense, defense of third parties, and various types of privilege. Consent to a tortious act can sometimes be implied from the nature of the plaintiff's conduct. When one goes to a barber or hair stylist, there is an implied consent for that person to touch and cut the customer's hair. Some types of consent are implied by law. Self-defense and the defense of third parties are self-explanatory. Self-defense, for example, could be used as a valid defense against a battery charge if the plaintiff had started the fight.

In situations involving the torts of trespass, false arrest, and false imprisonment a defendant can cite special privileges to avoid liability. The law enforcement privilege gives police and other law enforcement personnel the right to use deadly force in situations where others cannot. It also prohibits plaintiffs from recovering damages for intentional torts unless they can prove the action was malicious. In other words, police are allowed to make "an honest mistake" as long as it is made in connection with their official duties as law enforcement officers. Other privileges include the right to defend one's property, the right to recover posses-

sions wrongfully held, and the right to invade another's land as a public necessity (such as to put out a fire, or to catch a fleeing felon).

There are four major defenses that apply to defamation. Perhaps the most important is the truth of the statements being challenged. If the defendant can establish the truth of contested material, the plaintiff's case must fail. As with other torts, consent can also be an effective defense. The other two defenses involve the assertions of absolute or qualified privilege. Judges, attorneys, jurors, and other court personnel are protected against being held liable for comments made when performing their judicial function. Many legislators and executive officials also have an absolute privilege for comments that are made as part of their official duties.[13] In situations where the plaintiff is a "public figure," the plaintiff must prove not only that the comments were false and defamatory but also that they were made with "actual malice" as well.[14]

In cases involving invasion of privacy, truth is not considered to be a valid defense. As with other torts, however, consent does remain a viable defense. A second defense is that of newsworthiness. If publication of the material is of legitimate public interest, it is considered to be privileged unless it was done with malice. That is why it is so difficult for movie stars to prove this tort against tabloids and gossip columnists.

3. Sovereign Immunity

The doctrine of sovereign immunity prohibits suits against the government without the government's consent. It can be traced back to the concept of the divine right of kings and the idea that the king could do no wrong. In modern times federal and state governments have passed legislation that modifies this concept. Some states have judicially imposed modifications of the doctrine.[15]

In circumstances where one is prohibited from suing the government directly (or where the conditions attached to such suits are unfavorable), plaintiffs often sue government officials. Although these suits are often successful, limitations apply here as well. Judicial and legislative officials have an absolute privilege against being held liable for any actions performed as part of their official duties. The United States Supreme Court has even held a state judge immune from liability for having indemnified a doctor for a sterilization operation even though nothing in the state's laws authorized the doctor to take such an action.[16]

---

13. See discussion of sovereign immunity below.
14. In this context actual malice arises from the publication of something that was known to be false or from actions that demonstrated a reckless disregard for the truth of the material in question.
15. See, for example, the case of Holytz v. City of Milwaukee, 17 Wis. 2d 26, 115 N.W.2d 618 (1962), used as an illustration in Chapter 3 on page 108.
16. Stump v. Sparkman, 435 U.S. 349 (1978).

While the president has absolute immunity, cabinet members, presidential advisors, governors, and other administrative personnel receive only a qualified immunity. In order to recover damages under the terms of this qualified immunity, the plaintiff must prove that the defendant knew or reasonably should have known that the actions taken would violate a person's rights or that the actions were taken with a malicious intent to cause a deprivation of rights.

4. Strict Liability

As has been demonstrated in the previous sections, both negligence and intentional torts impose liability as a punishment for improper behavior. In the former the injury was caused by carelessness, and in the latter it was intentional. In both cases the tortfeasor has acted in an unreasonable manner and has violated an established standard of care. When the concept of strict liability is applied, however, a person is held responsible for injuries that resulted from actions that were not necessarily unreasonable and did not violate a standard of due care. In other words, it imposes liability in the absence of blame.

The doctrine of strict liability assumes that when persons engage in activities that are inherently dangerous, they should be responsible for any injuries that result, even though the activities may have been carried out in the safest and most prudent way possible. Examples of areas in which strict liability has been imposed through the common law include the use of explosives, the building of dams, and the keeping of non-domesticated animals. In recent years, for example, the doctrine of strict liability has been widely applied in product liability cases in which the manufacturer, rather than the seller, is held liable for defects that occur in the product. This is true even in the absence of evidence of any specific wrongdoing on the manufacturer's part.

A product is considered to be defective if it is unreasonably dangerous to use in the ordinary manner. The manufacturer, however, can assert the affirmative defense of product misuse. To do so, the manufacturer must prove that the product was not being used for its intended purpose or was being used in a dangerous manner that could not reasonably have been foreseen by the manufacturer.

5. Damages

After determining that the defendant is liable for the plaintiff's injuries, the court must assess damages. Damages are sums of money that must be paid by the tortfeasor to the injured parties. These damages can be either compensatory, punitive, or nominal.

Compensatory damages (sometimes also referred to as actual damages) are designed to compensate the injured party for the injury sustained. They are strictly an attempt to replace the value of what was lost.

They can be divided into general damages and special damages. General damages are those resulting from the immediate, direct, or proximate result of the defendant's conduct. They include the cost of repairing or replacing the damaged property and any medical bills, replacement of income lost while unable to work, and compensation for the pain and suffering associated with the injuries. Special damages apply to indirect injuries that were legitimately related but not a necessary result of the injury. An example is a business that claims a loss in profit due to the absence of an accident victim from a job during his recovery period.

Punitive damages (also called exemplary damages) are designed to punish the tortfeasor for his or her wrongdoing and to serve as a deterrent to others. They are awarded when the wrong done was aggravated by circumstances of violence, oppression, malice, fraud, or other particularly grievous conduct.

Nominal damages are awarded in situations where a right has been violated but no compensable injury has occurred or where the amount of the injury has not been proven. An award of nominal damages usually amounts to one dollar. The plaintiff thus ends up with nothing more than a moral victory.

C. CONTRACTS

Contracts are involved in almost every aspect of our lives from day-to-day commercial transactions to corporate mergers — from purchasing and financing a home to insuring that house, our automobile, our life, or our health. A contract is simply a promise that is enforceable in a court of law. Contract law is a combination of statutory and common law. The Uniform Commercial Code (UCC)[17] specifies the conditions that must be met in order to have a valid contract. It also establishes rules for interpreting contracts and for what should be done when one is violated.

1. Elements of a Contract

A contract can be either oral or written, but in order to be considered valid all of its key elements must be present: An offer must be made; an acceptance must be made among two or more parties who are legally capable of incurring contractual duties; and something of value must be exchanged by both parties.

The parties to a contract can be either people or corporations. However, an individual is considered incapable of contracting if that person is a child, is mentally retarded or mentally ill, or is under the

---

17. The UCC applies to contracts for the sale of goods as opposed to the sale of personal services. See the discussion of the UCC on page 139.

influence of drugs or alcohol. Under the common law one had to be at least age twenty-one in order to enter into binding contracts, but today many states have established a lower age limit. In some instances a contract with a minor is considered voidable rather than invalid. That means the terms of the contract are enforceable against the adult party in the contract but not against the minor party.

In order for a valid contract to be formed there must be mutual agreement to create a legally binding relationship. In determining whether this mutual assent took place, courts look for evidence of an offer and an acceptance. An offer is a promise to do something (usually to sell a product or render a service) that is conditioned on the other party's promising to do something in return (usually to pay money or provide some other type of goods or services). However, it may be difficut to determine whether a supposed offer was merely an expression of an intention to enter into further negotiations. In some circumstances parties have argued that the alleged offer was intended as a joke rather than as a serious offer.

Once an offer is made, it is up to the other party to accept, reject, or propose a counteroffer. Frequently the offer includes a specific time frame within which the other party must reach a decision about accepting or rejecting the offer. If the other party has not accepted it by that date, it is automatically withdrawn. If no specific time limit is established, it is assumed to be valid for a reasonable period of time. The reasonableness of the time period is judged on the basis of the nature of the offer itself and the context in which it took place. Finally, an open-ended offer can be revoked at any time prior to its acceptance as long as that revocation is properly communicated to the other party. In some cases this notice of revocation can be indirect (such as by selling the item to a third party).

An offer can be accepted either by sending notification of such acceptance or by performing an act that constitutes an agreed on part of the contractual relationship. So, for example, if A offered to pay B $10 to cut his grass, B's acceptance could take the form of sending a note or making a telephone call stating that she would cut B's grass for that price or by going ahead and cutting the grass.

In addition to an offer and an acceptance, consideration must be present to constitute a valid contract. This means that each party must give something of value as part of the bargain. It can be some right, interest, profit, or benefit, or it can be an avoidance of some loss, responsibility, or detriment. The key is that something of real value has to be exchanged by both parties. In other words, a contract must be distinguished from a gift. When a person promises to give something without expecting to receive anything in return, that promise does not constitute an enforceable contract.

2. Remedies for Breach

When one party fails to live up to the terms of a contract, a variety of different remedies may be available to the other party. These actions include rescission (where one party cancels the contract due to the other's being in default), release (where one party releases the other from any further obligations under the terms of the contract), or novation (substitution of a new contract to replace the old). All these solutions can be arrived at without the court's involvement.

Alternatively, the offended party can go to court to seek monetary damages or specific performance. Specific performance is used in situations where there is no alternative comparable product available (such as a particular parcel of land or a rare piece of art). Under this remedy, the injured party obtains a court order requiring the other party to fulfill the terms of the agreement. Failure to carry out such a court order constitutes contempt of court and is punishable by fine or incarceration. In a situation where one party breaches the agreement after some of the contracted work already was done, the party who did the work is entitled to be paid a fair price for the amount of work that was done prior to the breach.

3. Defenses

As was the case with torts, a variety of affirmative defenses are available. One defense, already alluded to above, is that one party lacked the legal capacity to form a contract because of age or mental condition. Somewhat related are the defenses of fraud and duress. In order to prove fraud it must be demonstrated that the other party made intentional misrepresentations or intentional nondisclosures of material facts during the course of the negotiations. A contract is also not valid if it was agreed to under duress rather than as a result of a truly voluntary action.

Contracts can be declared unenforceable if they are found to be either illegal or unconscionable. Therefore, if the contract involves behavior that is a violation of the criminal law (such as robbery or prostitution), constitutes a violation of antitrust laws, or violates state usury laws, then it is not valid.[18] A somewhat related but much more difficult concept is that of unconscionability. A contract is considered unconscionable if, in the context of general commercial practices and under the specific circumstances in which the contract was made, it is so one-sided as to be oppressive and grossly unfair. An example would be if in a sale to a low-income family that speaks little English, a contract drawn up by the seller included a clause that disclaimed all warranties that traditionally go with such a transaction.

---

18. A usury law regulates interest rates. A loan that imposes an interest charge that exceeds the legal limit is said to be usurious.

Finally, a party can assert the defense of impossibility of contractual performance. This occurs when one party either dies or becomes too sick to carry through with the contractual responsibilities. It also could occur where the object to be sold was destroyed by fire or was stolen before the agreed on transfer was to take place.

4. Rights of Third Parties

There are two ways in which a person or corporation that was not a party to the contract can have a legal interest in enforcing part of the terms of that agreement. The most common of these is through the process of assignment. An assignment occurs when one of the original parties to the contract transfers part or all of his or her interest to the third party. In assigning a right or benefit under the contract, a person may also assign a duty (as long as it is not a personal duty). For example, a consumer might sign a sales contract with a furniture store in which that individual agrees to make certain monthly payments. The furniture store might then assign the rights to receive those payments to a finance company in return for which the finance company gave the furniture store ready cash. The finance company now has a legal interest in receiving the monthly payments that the consumer agreed to pay to the store.

Alternatively the contract itself could contain a provision in which one of the parties agrees to provide some direct benefit to a third party. For example, in purchasing a house, the buyer might agree to assume the seller's current mortgage. In this case the mortgage lender is a third party that has been given a specific benefit under the terms of the contract. In this situation the lending institution is considered to be a creditor beneficiary. In a situation in which a father contracts with a bank to administer a trust fund for his children, those children would be considered donee beneficiaries. In both cases they are directly affected and can use the courts to ensure that their rights are protected.

5. Parol Evidence Rule

Contractual disputes arise not just about whether a valid contract exists but also about what the terms of the contract actually require. Deciding these disputes is particularly difficult when the agreement was verbal rather than set down in writing. When the dispute is reduced to one person's word against the other's, the courts find it difficult to determine who is telling the truth. Even though oral contracts are legally enforceable, it is always wiser to have them put in writing.

A written agreement usually contains an integration clause that merges all previous oral agreements into the new written document. Under the parol evidence rule, a written contract cannot be modified or changed by prior oral or verbal agreements.

D. PROPERTY

In its broadest sense the legal concept of property refers to any valuable right or interest that belongs to a person. Although property usually is thought of in terms of real estate and tangible personal property, forms of property include contractual rights, promissory notes, admission tickets to concerts or sporting events, reputations, and jobs.

1. Real Estate

Real property, or real estate, consists of land and whatever is growing on or built on that land.[19] It includes the rights to gas and minerals under the land and to the air space above it.[20] The nature of one's rights over real property depend on whether that individual owns or leases the land.

a. Ownership

A freehold estate is a right of title to land or other real property that extends for life or some other indeterminate period of time. The most common form of ownership is what is called a fee simple estate. This is ownership that is free from any conditions or restrictions and can be passed on to the owner's heirs as part of that person's estate.[21] There are three other much more specialized ownership patterns. In a fee tail estate, ownership is passed on to the eldest son. In a conditional fee simple estate, the property stays in the hands of the current owner only as long as certain conditions are met (such as the property is used for religious or educational purposes). If that condition ceases to be met, the title then reverts back to the original owner. Finally, a life estate terminates when the current owner dies, and title then reverts back to the original owner or the heirs of the original owner's estate.

Ownership of property can also be shared. A joint tenancy occurs when a single estate of land is acquired by two or more persons who have equal rights in the use of that property during their respective lives. A tenancy in common is very similar in that it also involves two or more people who share ownership of the property. However, the ownership shares do not have to be equal, nor do they have to have been acquired at the same time. In addition, on death, the ownership interest of a tenant in common passes to his or her estate, while with a joint tenancy it passes to

---

19. Items that are attached to the house on a permanent basis are also considered real property and become part of the sale of the land unless special exceptions to the contrary are specified in the sales transaction. Examples include plumbing fixtures, a furnace, and even the drapes in a house.
20. The common law has been modified to limit the air space concept so that it does not interfere with airplane traffic.
21. When a person dies, the total property (both real and personal) owned by that individual at the time of death is considered to constitute that person's estate.

the co-owner(s). A tenancy by the entirety is a special type of joint tenancy applicable only to married couples.[22] In some condominium arrangements the individual living units are individually owned or owned in joint tenancy, and the common halls, walks, parking lots, and garden areas are a form of tenancy in common.

Even a sole owner's rights to use a piece of real estate can be limited by the existence of either a restrictive covenant or an easement. The former is a provision in a deed that prohibits specified uses of the property and commonly is added at the time a developer subdivides and improves the property before it is marketed for housing. Common provisions include requirements relating to minimum square footage, setback, and architectural styles.[23] These covenants are recorded in the county land records and become part of the title for all subsequent owners' title. An easement, on the other hand, is the right to use property owned by another for a limited purpose. Utility companies acquire easements that allow them to install and maintain electrical cables and gas pipes. Another common type of easement allows a neighbor to drive over a small section of a lot in order to gain access to that neighbor's own land.

b. Sales

In the typical real estate sale the potential buyer begins by making an offer to purchase the property in question. Real estate agents usually carry standardized fill-in-the-blank offer forms. The agent then helps the buyer fill in the information regarding the description of the property, the amount of money being offered, a listing of the fixtures and appliances that are to be included, and the date of possession. The offer sheet also usually contains a number of contingency clauses that make the offer contingent on the buyer's being able to obtain financing (often at a specified interest rate), the building's being able to pass a termite inspection, and so forth. The buyer then turns over a specified sum of money to the real estate agent as earnest money.[24] The seller in turn either accepts the offer (by signing the appropriate line on the offer sheet), rejects it, or proposes a counteroffer (usually with a price that is somewhere between the buyer's offer and the original asking price).

---

22. A tenancy by entirety is essentially a joint tenancy modified by the common law theory that husband and wife are one person. On the death of either spouse, the other takes whole title to the exclusion of any other heirs.

23. Restrictive covenants also were used historically to exclude racial minorities from living in certain areas. In Shelly v. Kraemer, 344 U.S. 1 (1948), however, the United States Supreme Court ruled that such racially restrictive covenants could not be judicially enforced, and in Jones v. Alfred H. Mayer Co., 392 U.S. 409 (1968), the Court interpreted the federal Civil Rights Act of 1866 as prohibiting racial discrimination in the purchasing and leasing of property. In addition, the federal Civil Rights Act of 1968 and many state and local open housing ordinances now prohibit such discrimination.

24. This money normally is applied to the purchase price and may be forfeited if the buyer defaults.

While the offer and acceptance (or the acceptance of a counter-offer) create a binding contract, one of the conditions of the offer sheet is frequently a requirement that a more formal contract be drawn up within a specified time. In a typical residential sale, this is the stage at which lawyers first become directly involved in the transaction. Real estate brokers and bar associations disagree about how much legal assistance real estate professionals should provide and how much of the work should be done by attorneys. Local practices differ based on the nature of the accommodations that have been worked out between the two groups.

While the buyer arranges for financing, the seller guarantees that he or she holds valid title to the property (covenant of seisin), that there are no encumbrances on the title,[25] and that the seller will protect the buyer against alleged claims of a superior title. The buyer verifies these guarantees either by obtaining an up-to-date abstract (a condensed history of the title that includes the chain of ownership and a record of all liens, taxes, or other encumbrances that may impair the title) or by purchasing title insurance. The buyer's attorney reviews the title and advises his or her client of any defects. If the seller is unwilling or unable to correct these defects, the buyer can refuse to complete the transaction.

The legal title passes from the seller to the buyer when the deed (a formal legal document conveying title to the new owner) is signed and delivered at the closing. At this time the buyer also signs the mortgage documents, and the seller receives his or her proceeds of the sale. A closing statement is prepared to itemize and allocate all costs and monies exchanged among the various parties (including financial institutions and real estate brokers). The taxes are prorated, and credits are given to adjust for the respective liabilities of the buyer and the seller.[26] If the actual possession of the property does not correspond to the closing date, credits are given to reflect the rent being paid by the former owners to the new owners or by the new owners to the old.

c. Rental

A lease is an agreement in which the property owner (the lessor) gives someone else (the lessee) the right to use that property for a designated period of time. A leasehold is a parcel of real estate held under a lease and is classified as either a tenancy for a term, a periodic tenancy, or

---

25. An encumbrance is a lien or other type of security interest that signifies that some other party has a legitimate claim to the property as a means of satisfying debts that the owner owes to them. Examples include mortgages, mechanics liens, and liens for unpaid taxes.
26. In many states property taxes assessed for one year are not collected until the next year so that the new owner is responsible for paying taxes that were incurred by the previous owner. Alternatively, if the former owner has paid the taxes for the current year, then the new owner must give a credit for the remaining portion of the current year.

a tenancy at will. A tenancy at sufferance denotes a situation in which the person in possession of the land has no legal right to be there.

With a tenancy for a term, the lease establishes a set period of time during which the lessee will have control and after which all rights revert back to the lessor. Under a periodic tenancy the rental periods are set up on a week-to-week, month-to-month, or year-to-year basis. At the end of each rental period the lease can be terminated with proper notice. However, if neither party gives such notice, the lease automatically continues. When no time period is specified, it is called a tenancy at will, and either the lessee can leave or the lessor can reclaim the land at any time.[27]

When real estate is leased, a landlord/tenant relationship is created between the lessor and the lessee. State statutes and the common law establish various rights and duties on the part of both landlords and tenants. The common law clearly favored the landlords. The tenant had to take the property in the condition it was in at the time that the lease was entered into[28] and had to repair any damage resulting from natural disasters or the acts of other people, the tenant, or the tenant's family. The landlord's only obligation was not to interfere with the tenant's "quiet enjoyment" of the premises.[29] Over the years, many state legislatures have enacted statutes that provide more protection for tenants and establish set procedures for evictions. The terms of the lease, however, may add to or otherwise alter the distribution of some of these rights and duties. While statutory or common law rights generally can be waived in the lease agreement, in some cases the statute imposes rights and duties that cannot be waived.

2. Chattel

Chattel is another term for personal property. All property other than real estate is classified as chattel. The selling and leasing of personal property is covered by the general principles of contract law and the Uniform Commercial Code.

a. The Uniform Commercial Code

The Uniform Commercial Code (UCC) is a series of model statutory provisions drawn up by prominent legal scholars. It was developed to encourage states to voluntarily incorporate these provisions into their

---

27. The law in many states requires that the owner give thirty days' notice before reclaiming possession. Thus is becomes the same as a month-to-month periodic tenancy.

28. If the premises contained any defects (for example, if the furnace did not work) that the tenant had not discovered before signing the lease, the tenant still was obligated to the terms of the lease.

29. Quiet enjoyment meant that the landlord could not interfere with the activities of the tenant by prohibiting the tenant from growing crops on the land or by inviting friends over for a party. The landlord was not responsible for disturbances caused by others.

own statutes to provide a uniform set of legal principles that would facilitate commercial transactions among persons in different states. The UCC has subsequently been adopted with minor variations by forty-nine states (all except Louisiana), the District of Columbia, and the Virgin Islands.

The UCC is divided into ten sections:

Article 1.   General Provisions
Article 2.   Sales
Article 3.   Commercial Paper
Article 4.   Bank Deposits and Collections
Article 5.   Letters of Credit
Article 6.   Bulk Transfers
Article 7.   Warehouse Receipts, Bills of Lading, and Other Documents of Title
Article 8.   Investment Securities
Article 9.   Secured Transactions; Sales of Accounts, Contract Rights, and Chattel Paper
Article 10. Effective Date and Repealer

While it is clearly beyond the scope of this text to discuss these provisions in any detail, a few basic concepts merit attention at this time. It must be emphasized that the UCC does not apply to real estate, insurance, bankruptcy, or service contracts.

b. Formation of a Contract

The article dealing with sales is the most important part of the UCC. It alters the common law right to revoke any offer prior to its acceptance and allows the offeree to accept an offer in any reasonable manner regardless of the manner in which the offer was communicated. Therefore, a contract may be formed if a seller's goods are accepted by the buyer, even though those goods did not conform to the order or the offer to buy.[30]

Article 2 also contains its own statute of frauds that applies to the sale of goods.[31] It requires something in writing if the price of the goods is $500 or more. While the quantity of items involved must be in writing, the price and delivery arrangements need not be. It also allows parol evidence under specified conditions.

c. Warranties

Among the most frequently contested issues is the nature of the warranties involved in commercial transactions. In this context, a war-

---

30. UCC §§2-205, 206.
31. Id. §2-201.

ranty is a statement of representation made by the seller, as part of the contract of sale, regarding the character, quality, or title of the goods being sold. The statement must be made by the seller to induce the sale and must be relied on by the buyer. If such warranted facts later prove to be untrue, the seller has an obligation to compensate the buyer for any losses incurred as a result of the misrepresentation.

Under the terms of the UCC any contract of sale automatically includes a warranty of title (an implied promise that the seller owns the goods being offered for sale and that they will be delivered free from any security interest, lien, or encumbrance).[32] There is also an implied warranty of merchantability that the goods being sold will be usable for the purpose for which they were sold.[33] This is a warranty regarding the fitness of the goods for the ordinary purpose for which these types of goods are used. Where a more specialized use of the goods is communicated to the seller during the course of negotiations, an implied warranty of fitness is also created.[34] This is a warranty regarding the fitness of the goods for that special purpose.

In addition to these implied warranties a contract can also create express warranties.[35] The term *warranty* or *guarantee* does not have to be used in order for a warranty to be created. When express warranties are part of the basis of the bargain, they can be created by an affirmation of fact or a promise made by the seller, a description of the goods being sold (including technical specifications and blueprints), or a sample or model provided. A mere expression of opinion as to the value of an item is considered "puffing" and does not constitute a warranty.

d. Unconscionability

While the UCC holds that terms of a contract that are unconscionable cannot be enforced, it does not attempt to define the term unconscionable.[36] One must rely on court cases for applications of the doctrine in specific cases. The courts are more responsive to unsophisticated consumers raising this defense than they are to its use by merchants dealing with other merchants.

e. Remedies for Breach of Contract

If a seller breaches any of the express or implied terms of the contract, the buyer has a right to reject the goods within a reasonable time and with a reasonable notice to the seller. If the goods cannot be returned without their perishing, they must be sold in order to minimize the seller's losses. If substandard goods are accepted and retained, the

---

32. Id. §2-312. See also page 137, note 23.
33. Id. §2-314.
34. Id. §2-315.
35. Id. §2-313.
36. Id. §2-302.

buyer can seek damages that amount to the difference between the value of the goods promised and the value of the goods received.[37]

If, of the other hand, the buyer breaches the contract, the seller may stop delivery of promised goods or reclaim goods from the buyer on appropriate notice to that effect. The seller can also sue for damages (usually calculated as the difference between the market price at the time of performance and the unpaid contract price plus incidental expenses incurred).[38]

f. Commercial Paper

Another important aspect of the UCC is Article 3's discussion of commercial paper. *Commercial paper* is a general term covering a variety of promissory notes, drafts, and other negotiable instruments used for the payment of money. A draft is a three-party instrument in which the drawer instructs the drawee (usually a bank) to pay money to the payee. A check is a specialized form of a draft in which a bank depositor names a specific payee to whom funds are to be paid from the drawer's account. (Checks are covered in Article 4.) A note is also a promise to pay money but involves only two parties. The maker who signs the instrument promises to provide money to the payee. These notes can be collectable either at a specific date in the future (time notes) or at any time the payee wishes to collect (demand notes). Installment notes establish a series of dates on which portions of the money are to be paid. Some notes are secured by a pledge of something of value (such as a house, automobile, or stock certificate) that the payee can seize and sell if the maker is not able to fulfill the obligation to pay. A certificate of deposit is a promissory note signed by a financial institution that is made payable to the order of the depositor or a third party.

If a note, check, or draft meets the requirements of negotiability as they are spelled out in Article 3, the "holder in due course" of that instrument obtains a right to enforce the agreement that is exempt from some of the defenses that could have been asserted against the original payee.[39] Under the provisions of the UCC a party becomes a holder in due course only if it receives the notes through a negotiation process rather than a mere transfer. Article 3 identifies the specific requirements for qualifying as a holder in due course.[40]

---

37. Id. §§2-601 to 2-616.
38. Id. §§2-701 to 2-710.
39. A holder in due course is someone who in good faith and without notice that it is overdue or has been dishonored takes an instrument of value. An example would be a situation in which a finance company purchases a retail installment contract from a furniture store. The finance company becomes the holder in due course and can enforce its rights in court against the consumer who signed the contract with the furniture store. Whereas the consumer might have been able to raise a defense of fraud or breach of warranty against the furniture store, the holder in due course doctrine may prevent it from raising those defenses against the finance company.
40. UCC §3-302.

3. Estates and Trusts

In the context that the term is used here, an estate is the total property of whatever kind (both real and personal) that a person owns at the time of his or her death. This property is then distributed on the basis of the person's will and the probate laws of that state. A person who dies without a valid will is said to have died intestate, and in that situation, the person's property is distributed on the basis of guidelines laid down by the legislature. Although these laws usually favor the spouse and the children, they may not correspond to how the deceased wanted to dispose of the estate. An up-to-date will helps the executor carry out the deceased's wishes and helps reduce the amount of taxation on the estate.

In addition to clauses identifying the party making the will (the testator), clauses making specific legacies and bequests, and signature clauses (for the testator and witnesses), the typical will also includes provisions for payment of taxes and expenses, funeral arrangements, appointment of executors and guardians, and a simultaneous death clause. An executor is a person appointed by the testator to carry out the directions and requests in the will. A guardian is one who is given the duty and responsibility of managing the affairs of a person who is incapable of administering his or her own affairs. In this context, a guardian would be appointed to care for the decedent's minor children. A simultaneous death clause states that if a person named as a beneficiary in the will dies within a set time period (such as 120 hours or 30 days) of when the decedent dies, it will be assumed for purposes of the will that the person in question failed to survive the decedent.

Probate refers to the process of proving that a will is genuine and then distributing the deceased's property according to the will and the various tax laws. Generally, a petition, along with the will and a death certificate, must be filed with the appropriate division of the courts. After payment of required fees, letters of testamentary are issued to give the executor (or a court-appointed administrator if no executor was named in the will) the power to take control of the deceased's assets, pay the bills, and distribute the proceeds of the estate. Various inventories and other reports have to be filed with the court at several stages of this process. Some states exempt very small estates from this formal process and provide a simplified probate administration for intermediate-size estates.

In order to avoid some aspects of probate and to minimize tax liabilities, modern estate planning often includes the creation of specialized trusts. A trust is a legal relationship in which one party holds property for the benefit of another. In this context the property is transferred to a trust fund, where it is to be used for the benefit of a designated person or persons rather than passing directly to them as part of the

probate process. The person who creates the trust is called the donor, grantor, or settlor. The person appointed to administer the trust is the trustee, and the person who receives the benefits of the trust is the beneficiary.

E.   CORPORATE LAW

1. Business Organizations

American businesses are organized in a variety of different types of patterns. In assessing these different organizations, it is important to distinguish between their legal and managerial structures. The number of vice-presidents they have or their degree of decentralization are examples of managerial structure. These variations affect the efficiency and profitability of the business. The legal structure, on the other hand, refers to the relationship among the owners and the legal liabilities that each incurs. This section focuses briefly on those legal considerations.

a. Sole Proprietorships

The most elementary form of business organization is the sole proprietorship. This is a business that is owned by one person; it may have hundreds or even thousands of employees, but it only has one owner. The business is a legal extension of the individual, and all the business's profits and losses are treated as personal profits and losses. Profits are taxed as ordinary personal income, and the owner's personal assets (regardless of whether they are related to the operation of the business) are available to satisfy business-incurred debts. For a variety of reasons, sole proprietorships are usually limited to rather small business operations.

b. Partnerships

A partnership is a form of organization in which two or more persons share ownership in the business. As with a sole proprietorship the business probably has a separate public identity, but from a legal perspective it is just an aggregation of individuals.

While partnerships usually are based on a written partnership agreement, it is possible for a partnership to be based on a verbal agreement or even to evolve out of past practices of sharing control, profits, and losses of a business. While a partnership itself pays no taxes, it must file an informational report that indicates how the profits and losses were divided among the partners. Each partner's share is then taxed as part of personal income. Each partner is an agent for the partnership,[41] and each assumes liability for the others' actions in conducting the business

---

41. See discussion page 146.

of the partnership. One partner is not liable for another's actions when those actions are not related to the business of the partnership. State statutes usually specify certain acts that do not bind the entire partnership unless the acts have been authorized by all of the partners. If a suit is against the partnership alone, a judgment can be satisfied only out of the assets of the partnership, but if a partner is sued individually and found to be personally liable, then the judgment is enforceable against that partner's individual property. The loss of any of the partners (through death or withdrawal from the partnership) results in the dissolution of the partnership, though the business entity often continues under a new restructured partnership agreement.

Some partnerships have both general and limited partners. The general partners have all the rights and liabilities described above. The limited partners, on the other hand, are only investors and do not actively participate in the management of the business. Such a person's liability is limited to the extent of the investment in the partnership.

c. Corporations

The corporation has become the predominant form of business organization in the modern capitalistic economy. A corporation is an artificial legal entity that can sue, be sued, own property, and make contracts. Unlike a partnership, it has a continuing life of its own that is not affected by the death of a stockholder or the exchange of shares of stock. Furthermore, the investors have the advantage of being owners without having to assume any liability beyond the cost of their individual shares.

A corporation is formed when specified legal documents are properly filed with the office of the state's secretary of state. The articles of incorporation must include the legal name of the corporation (not always the same as the merchandising name of a business), the purpose of the corporation, a list of the incorporators and directors, the name and address of a registered agent,[42] and the share structure. Once a certificate of incorporation has been issued, the corporation must maintain certain types of records and file periodic reports to the appropriate state and federal agencies.

Most corporate capital comes from the sale of shares of stock. Purchasers of this stock have voting rights in the selection of the board of directors and receive a share of the corporation's profits when the board chooses to distribute some of those profits through dividends on its stock. The corporation can also borrow money when it needs capital.

The board of directors is responsible for the management of the corporation. It typically makes major policy and investment decisions. The officers of the corporation are elected by the board and are respon-

---

42. The registered agent is a person designated to receive service of legal documents.

sible for executing the board's policies. They are also expected to provide leadership for the corporation. However, in a large corporation the day-to-day operation of the business is delegated to professional managers who are employees of the corporation. As directors, the individuals who assume these positions have a fiduciary responsibility to act in the best interests of the corporation and its stockholders.[43] The directors can be held liable for their actions if they fail to live up to this obligation.

Some corporations are relatively small operations in which one person or members of a family may own all the stock.[44] Most larger corporations, however, are publicly held corporations whose stock is openly traded on the New York and American Stock Exchanges. State and federal blue sky laws regulate the sale of such stock transactions. Among other things, the companies are required to make certain types of financial information available to the public in connection with the public offering of their stocks and bonds. Article 8 of the UCC covers the exchange of stock certificates.

2. Agency Law

The duties, responsibilities, and liabilities of stockholders, directors, officers, and employees are all part of an area of the law referred to as agency. Agency law focuses on the relationships between people in situations where one person acts for or represents another by virtue of some authorization from that other party.

a. Principal and Agent

The stockholder/director relationship is an example of the principal and agent category of agency law. A principal is a person who has permitted or directed another person to act for his or her benefit while being subject to the principal's direction and control. Other examples include a partner negotiating a contract for the partnership or a real estate agent negotiating the purchase of a piece of land. In order for a relationship to be legally recognized as a principal/agent relationship, the agent must have authority to contractually bind the principal with a third party. If a principal knowingly allows his or her agent to appear to have more authority than was actually delegated, the third party may be able to hold the principal responsible for actions of the agent that reflected that apparent authority.

In the principal/agent relationship, the agent owes fiduciary responsibilities to the principal. The agent must not place himself or herself in a conflict-of-interest situation and must exercise reasonable care, skill, and diligence in carrying out the principal's instructions. An agent

---

43. A fiduciary duty is a legally imposed obligation to act in the best interests of the party to whom this duty is owed.
44. Such corporations are referred to as close corporations or closely held corporations.

who fails to fulfill these duties is liable for damages that result from this failure. The principal in turn must take steps to reasonably protect the agent and to compensate for losses incurred in the course of discharging the assigned duties. The principal must also pay the agreed-on fee for the agent's services.

b. Employer and Employee

The employer/employee relationship follows common law principles that grew out of the master/servant relationship. Under the doctrine of *respondeat superior*,[45] a corporation may be sued for the negligent acts of one of its employees. The plaintiffs in these cases choose to sue the company because it can afford to pay larger amounts in damages.[46] In order to hold the employer liable, a plaintiff must prove that a true employer/employee relationship exists and that the employee responsible for the injury was at that time engaged in work of the type he or she was hired to perform. An employer can also be held responsible by the company's own employees if they are injured as a result of the employer's negligence or the negligence of a fellow employee.[47]

c. Employer and Independent Contractor

An independent contractor is an individual who contracts to perform a specific service for a set fee. The contractor is usually expected to supply his or her own equipment. The contractor is not placed on the payroll as a regular salaried employee but receives payments that correspond to the progress of the job he or she was contracted to do. The employer does not withhold taxes or make contributions for retirement funds or health insurance. The legal relationship between the employer and the independent contractor is very similar to the principal/agent relationship discussed above, except that the contractor has no power to bind the employer in a contractual relationship with a third party. The employer, therefore, has the least exposure to liability when an independent contractor is involved.

F. CONSTITUTIONAL LAW

Constitutional law involves the interpretation and application of provisions of state and federal constitutions. Because constitutions focus on what governments and government officials can and cannot do rather than the behavior of the general population, most paralegals have rela-

---

45. A Latin term translated as "Let the master answer."
46. This practice is often referred to as "going after the deep pocket."
47. In some states this liability has been modified through the application of workers' compensation laws.

tively little contact with this area of the law. The most frequent applications of constitutional law principles occur in the areas of administrative
law, civil rights, and criminal law.

1. Federalism

Federalism is a form of government in which the sovereignty[48] is
divided between a central government and regional units of government. In the United States, the Constitution divides the power to govern
between a central government that usually is referred to as the "federal
government" and regional units that constitute the state governments.

The United States Constitution allocates powers on the basis of
three types of categories: delegated powers, prohibited powers, and reserved powers. In the delegated powers category it specifies that some
powers (such as the power to declare war, to make treaties, and to coin
money) are to be exercised exclusively by the federal government, while
others (such as levying of taxes and regulating many types of business
activities) are given to both the federal and the state governments to be
exercised concurrently. In addition to delegating specific powers to these
different governmental units, the Constitution also prohibits them from
undertaking specified activities. For example, both the federal and the
state governments are specifically prohibited from passing bills of attainder[49] and *ex post facto* laws[50] or granting titles of nobility. Some of the
prohibitions are specifically applied to only one of the governments (for
example, the federal government is expressly prohibited from levying
direct taxes, while the state governments are expressly prohibited from
laying any imposts or duties on imports or exports).[51] Since the federal
government is supposed to possess only those powers that are delegated
to it by the Constitution, it is by implication prohibited from exercising
any powers that are not related to those specific delegations.[52] On the
other hand, the state governments are presumed to possess inherent,
reserved powers that did not have to be listed in the Constitution. Thus,
the states can do whatever is necessary to promote the health, welfare,

---

48. Sovereignty is the power or legitimacy behind a government. It is the supreme political
power. In ancient monarchies kings and queens were the sovereign rulers and as such
possessed unlimited power to rule as they saw fit. The U.S. governmental system
presumes that sovereignty rests with the people and that through the adoption of the
Constitution the people delegated limited powers to their chosen leaders to govern
according to the will of the people.
49. A bill of attainder is a legislative act imposing punishment on a specific individual.
50. An *ex post facto* law is a law that is passed after the commission of an act and that
retrospectively makes that action a crime.
51. Except what may be absolutely necessary for executing its inspection laws.
52. Although not specifically stated in the Constitution itself until the adoption of the
tenth amendment, this position was a basic operating assumption on the part of the
framers.

safety, and morals of the people, as long is their action is not specifically prohibited or does not conflict with other constitutional provisions.[53]

These principles of federalism become relevant when one wishes to challenge the constitutionality of a particular law or the jurisdiction of a particular court system. Some of the most difficult legal questions arise in situations where the federal and state governments have concurrent powers. If there is a direct conflict between an act of a state government and one of the federal government, the doctrine of national supremacy dictates that the federal law take precedence over the state's. However, many times the conflict is not direct, or it is not clear from the legislative history whether Congress sought to preempt the field or to allow room for supplementary state actions.

2. Separation of Powers

Not only does the Constitution divide power between the federal government and the states, it also divides the federal government's powers among the legislative, executive, and judicial branches. The so-called checks and balances system then gives each of these branches devices they can use to check or limit actions of the other branches. Thus the legislature makes the laws, but the executive can veto them or modify their effect by the way it chooses to enforce those laws. The judiciary has the final say as to how these laws should be interpreted and can invalidate them completely if it finds them to be unconstitutional. Major presidential appointments must be approved by the Senate, and executive departments must stay within budgets that are passed by Congress. While judges serve for life, they are appointed by the president with the consent of the Senate. They are limited to issues that are brought before them in the proper case and controversy format,[54] and they must rely on the executive branch to enforce their rulings.

Separation of powers issues are most likely to arise in administrative law cases or in appeals that focus on the nature and extent of judicial review. A party who is adversely affected by a particular statute or administrative regulation can argue that the statute or regulation is unconstitutional because it was formulated or enforced in a manner that violates the principle of separation of powers.

3. Due Process

Both the fifth and the fourteenth amendments to the U.S. Constitution contain due process clauses that prohibit the government from

---

53. For example, a state cannot use its powers to violate an individual's constitutional right to free speech or to be free from unreasonable searches and seizures.

54. The matter must be brought in the form of a real controversy involving parties that have adversarial interests and will be personally affected by the outcome of the court's decision.

depriving any person of life, liberty, or property. The fifth amendment
imposes this restriction on the federal government, while the fourteenth
makes it applicable to states and local governments. These clauses cover
not only legislative acts but also those of administrative agencies, sanitary
districts, public schools, and all other governmental units. They cover
not only the official acts of the agency itself but also the job-related
actions of government employees. For example, the actions of an individual policeman are considered to be the actions of the government
itself as long as that policeman was acting as a policeman.

The first question that must be answered in a due process analysis is
whether the clause applies to the situation in question. The due process
clause applies when the government is seeking to deprive a person of
"life, liberty, or property." It is clearly a violation of one's liberty to be
placed in jail, but is it also a violation to be denied the opportunity to
publish a newspaper or to bus children across town rather than allow
them to attend a neighborhood school? Is it a deprivation of property
when a court garnishes a person's wages because that person owes someone money? Is the welfare department's action in reducing a person's
level of benefits a denial of a property right? Each of these questions
must be answered by the courts on a case-by-case basis.

After determining that the due process clause does apply, the
courts then decide what the government must do to meet the standards
of fairness and reasonableness. Here again the answer varies according
to the situation. Procedural due process focuses on the method used to
determine whether the deprivation should take place. Substantive due
process focuses on the government's right to make the deprivation
rather than the way in which it takes place.

The paralegal is most likely to be involved in controversies over the
applicability of various due process procedures. In the administrative
context, there is much variation in procedures at hearings and even in
the decision to hold a hearing.

Listed below are the elements associated with procedural due process. The paralegal must become familiar with all of them. With the
exception of 6c all have been held to be applicable to felony trials. In
other types of trials, however, the government may legitimately decide
not to include certain elements. For example, the Supreme Court has
ruled that juvenile proceedings need not entail the right to a trial by a
jury.[55]

1. Adequate notice
   a. Sufficiently clear to be able to understand the true nature of the
      complaint;

---

55. McKiever v. Pennsylvania, 403 U.S. 528 (1971).

   b. Received long enough in advance of hearing to allow adequate time for preparation.
2. Speedy justice
   a. Trial or hearing held without undue delay.
3. Discovery
   a. Right to see prior to the start of the trial or hearing physical and documentary evidence to be presented by the other side;
   b. Right to be informed of the identity of the witnesses to be used by the other side;
   c. Right to take depositions and/or interrogatories of witnesses;
   d. Right to subpoena relevant information prior to the start of the hearing or trial.
4. Opportunity to be heard
   a. Right to appear in person;
   b. Right to present arguments;
   c. Right to present physical and documentary evidence;
   d. Right to have witnesses testify.
5. Compulsory process
   a. Right to require persons to come forth with evidence or to testify.
6. Representation
   a. Right to retained counsel (lawyer can speak on client's behalf);
   b. Right to appointed counsel (lawyer paid for by the government when the person cannot obtain one on his or her own);
   c. Right to nonattorney representative (paralegal or other non-lawyer can speak for participant);
   d. Self-representation (right to serve as one's own counsel).
7. Confrontation
   a. Participant has the right to be present when evidence is presented.
8. Cross-examination
   a. Participant or proper representative can question adversarial witnesses.
9. Nature of the evidence
   a. Evidence presented under oath;
   b. Only relevant evidence considered;
   c. "Strict" rules of evidence used (as they apply in regular court cases);
   d. Verbatim transcript made of the proceedings.
10. Participation by the public
   a. Hearing or trial is open for the public to observe what takes place;
   b. Right to a jury (the public actually has a role in deciding the case).

11. Nature and basis of the decision
    a. ~~Decision maker must be impartial;~~
    b. Decision must be based on evidence in the record;
    c. Application of the appropriate standard of proof (either pre-
       ponderance of evidence or beyond a reasonable doubt);
    d. Decision must be in writing;
    e. Decision maker must give reasons for the decision.
12. Right to appeal to a higher authority

Some administrative hearings must include adequate notice, personal appearance, representation by retained counsel (or representation
by nonlawyer or self), right to present witnesses, confrontation and
cross-examination, an impartial decision maker, a decision based on evidence at the hearings, and a statement of the reasons for the decision.[56]
On the other hand, the courts have also upheld a procedure in which the
accused had only the rights to notice and to present arguments personally.[57]

Substantive due process prohibits the government or its agents
from acting in an arbitrary or capricious manner. The government must
demonstrate that the action in question was a reasonable means of ad-
vancing a legitimate government interest. At one time this doctrine was
successfully utilized to attack various types of business regulations. Today it is used primarily in abortion and privacy cases.

The due process clause of the fourteenth amendment has also been
used to apply various provisions of the Bill of Rights to the states.[58] It
therefore is considered to be a violation of the due process clause for a
state or local government to restrict the freedom of the press, to conduct
an unreasonable search, or to impose a cruel and unusual form of
punishment.

Finally, it should be noted that the U.S. Supreme Court has used
the fifth amendment due process clause to apply the principles of the
fourteenth amendment's equal protection clause to the federal government.

4. Equal Protection

The equal protection clause is found beside the due process clause
in the fourteenth amendment. It prohibits the states from denying to
any person within its jurisdiction the equal protection of the laws. As was
true of the due process clause the equal protection clause applies to
various local governments and to government officials as well. Furthermore, as mentioned above, the concept of equal protection has been

---

56. Goldberg v. Kelly, 397 U.S. 254 (1970).
57. Goss v. Lopez, 419 U.S. 565 (1975).
58. The Bill of Rights consists of the first ten amendments to the U.S. Constitution.

Table 4.1 Equal Protection Tests

Type of Test Used	Nature of Governmental Purpose	Relationship of Means and Ends
Rational basis (basic test used when others do not apply)	Must be legitimate	Means must be reasonably related
Heightened scrutiny (used primarily in gender discrimination cases)	Must be important	Means must be substantially related
Strict scrutiny (used primarily in race discrimination cases)	Must be compelling	Means can be used only when no reasonable alternative exists

applied to the federal government through the fifth amendment's due process clause. It does not protect persons from discrimination by private individuals or corporations.[59]

The equal protection clause does not require that everyone be treated the same. Rather, it has been interpreted to mean that the government cannot treat people differently unless it has an acceptable reason for doing so. It is the function of the courts to review these reasons and determine if they are acceptable.

Over the years the U.S. Supreme Court has developed a complex series of tests for judging the validity of equal protection claims. In applying these tests the courts must weigh the importance of the benefit being denied with the character of the class affected and the nature of the state interest asserted.

The first phase of the process involves deciding which of three levels of analysis to apply. If the case involves a suspect class (such as a racial minority group) or a fundamental right (such as the right to free speech), the courts will apply the strict scrutiny or compelling interest test. If, on the other hand, the case involves sex discrimination, the courts will apply the heightened scrutiny test. In all other types of equal protection cases, the court utilizes the reasonableness test.

The three tests differ in regard to the nature of the government's purpose behind the discriminatory action and the relationship of the means to the ends. See Table 4.1. Under the strict scrutiny or compelling interest test the government has the burden of proving that there is no reasonable alternative but to treat the group in question differently in

---

59. Although the equal protection clause does not prevent a private individual from discriminating, it does prevent the government from enforcing or otherwise supporting that action. Furthermore, Congress has passed several major civil rights statutes that do prohibit discrimination based on race, sex, religion, and so forth in areas like housing, employment, and public accommodations.

order for it to achieve a compelling government interest. In order to be valid under the heightened scrutiny standard the government's action must be substantially related to important government objectives. Finally, when applying the reasonableness test the party that is discriminated against has the burden of establishing that the government's action is not reasonably related to any legitimate government objective. Under this test the government does not have to select the best method for achieving its objectives; it can select any of several alternatives as long as its action is not irrational.

G.   ADMINISTRATIVE LAW

Sometimes, as in Chapter 2 of this book, the term *administrative law* is defined as the rules and regulations that are promulgated by administrative agencies. When it is defined in this manner, it is being used to classify on the basis of its source and should be distinguished from constitutional law, statutory law, and common law. In this sense all regulations are administrative law regardless of whether they deal with environmental protection, antitrust, or social security benefits.

The term is more commonly used, however, to identify a specialized area of the law that focuses on (1) the structure and authority of administrative agencies; (2) the procedures that administrative agencies must use in both making and enforcing their regulations; and (3) the extent to which the courts exercise control over the agencies through judicial review. It is in this latter context that the term is used in this chapter.

A paralegal's involvement with administrative law is likely to come at two different levels: advocacy on behalf of a client at the agency level and preparation for judicial review of an agency's action. Since many agencies allow direct representation by paralegals,[60] administrative law is an important area of paralegal specialization. The remaining portion of this chapter focuses on basic principles that provide a basis for understanding the powers and procedures of specific administrative agencies. Chapter 5 includes an overview of the actual administrative hearings process.

1. Delegation of Authority

As our society has grown more complex, Congress has generally limited itself to developing general outlines of national policy and then delegated the formulation of specific rules to specialized administrative agencies. Congress has neither the time, the energy, nor the expertise to

---

60. See discussion in Chapter 11, page 480.

develop specific criteria for such areas as licensing radio stations or setting rates for interstate truckers. It certainly does not have the time to be constantly updating these types of rules every time the economy changes or there is a new technological development. The wording of a statute can differ markedly from that of an administrative regulation on the same subject. Note below how a regulation provides operational definitions for terms used in the statute:

Statutes
42 U.S.C. 423(d)(1)(A) defines *disability* as "inability to engage in any substantial gainful activity by reason of any medically determinable impairment which . . . has lasted or can be expected to last for a continuous period of not less than twelve months."

42 U.S.C. 423(d)(3) declares that a "physical or mental impairment" is an impairment that results from anatomical, physiological, or psychological abnormalities demonstrable by medically acceptable clinical and laboratory techniques.

Administrative Regulations
20 C.F.R. 1506(a)(1) lists specific impairments recognized by the agency as being "sufficient to preclude an individual from engaging in any gainful activity." Examples include (1) "Amputation of lower extremity (at or above the tarsal region)" and (2) "Inability to use prosthesis effectively, without other assistive devices, due to stump complications, persisting or expected to persist, for at least twelve months from the onset of disability."

Because the United States Constitution specifically assigns the power to legislate to the Congress, it has been argued that the delegation of legislative power to the executive branch violates the principle of separation of powers. In 1935 the United States Supreme Court invalidated two acts of Congress on such a theory.[61] Those two cases were aberrations, however, and the Court has not struck down a statute on delegation grounds since then.

In upholding delegations to administrative agencies, the courts have traditionally discussed filling in details, or delegation consistent with legislatively determined standards.[62] In reality the delegations have involved much more than filling in details, and the standards provided have often been rather ambiguous.[63]

---

61. Panama Refining Co. v. Ryan, 293 U.S. 388 (1935), and Schechter Poultry Co. v. United States, 295 U.S. 495 (1935).
62. See, for example, United States v. Grimaud, 220 U.S. 506, 521 (1911), and United States v. Chicago, M. & St. P. R.R., 282 U.S. 311, 324 (1931).
63. The courts have held that terms such as "just and reasonable," "unfair methods of competition," and "in the public interest" supply sufficient standards. Amalgamated Meat Cutters v. Connally, 337 F. Supp. 737 (D.C. 1971), provides a particularly good

According to Kenneth Culp Davis, preeminent scholar in the administrative law field:

> The non-delegation doctrine in the federal courts has failed. It has not prevented the delegation of power, and it has not accomplished the later purpose of assuring meaningful standards. Delegation without meaningful standards is a necessity in any modern government.[64]

The state courts face delegation questions similar to those of the federal courts, and Davis reports that state courts still occasionally invalidate statutes on nondelegation grounds.[65]

Recognizing the insufficiency of statutory standards, some courts appear to be requiring the promulgation of administrative standards to control the use of discretion in individual cases.[66] In other words, when an agency official makes decisions involving specific parties, those decisions must be based on general standards announced by the agency prior to their application to specific situations.

In handling administrative law cases, the paralegal should be aware of the delegation question and thoroughly investigate the nature of the legislative and administrative standards that supposedly control the agency's exercise of discretion. The agency must, of course, follow those standards. The vagueness or the lack of such standards might be used as a basis for a court challenge to an unfavorable action.

2. Rulemaking

Administrative agencies make rules and issue orders. When they promulgate rules, they exercise a legislative function that parallels the passing of a statute by the legislature. The rule will apply only to acts that take place after its official enactment. On the other hand, orders are issued as part of an adjudicative process that parallels decisions issued by the courts. The orders are based on the agency's judgment that a person or organization's conduct did not comply with an agency rule or statute. Ratemaking by an agency like the Interstate Commerce Commission is considered to be a form of rulemaking because of its prospective application.

Section 553 of the Administrative Procedure Act[67] requires that many federal agencies follow a rulemaking process that involves publishing proposed new rules in the Federal Register. Following this publica-

---

example of the extent that the courts are willing to stretch the concept of congressional standards when they do not appear on the face of the legislation.

64. K. C. Davis, Administrative Law Text 51 (3d ed. 1972).
65. Id. at 51.
66. See K. C. Davis, Administrative Law in the Seventies (1976).
67. 5 U.S.C. §553.

tion the agency must give interested persons an opportunity to submit written data and arguments related to the proposal. (In some cases the opportunity for oral presentations also may exist.) The agency then must consider these comments in formulating the rule. The final rules must be published again at least thirty days before they are to become effective and include a concise general statement of their basis and purpose. This statement, in conjunction with other agency communications, should demonstrate that there was reasonable basis for rejecting suggestions that were not followed.[68]

There are various exceptions to these procedures. When the rules involve the setting of rates, for example, the agencies are often required to hold formal hearings. The Occupational Safety and Health Act calls for public hearings on proposed rules. The paralegal will need to consult both the statute creating and defining the agency in question and §553 to determine the procedures to be used. Wherever state agencies are involved, the paralegal must consult the state statutes.

One important exception to the requirements of §553 involves interpretative rules, general statements of policy, or rules of agency organization, procedure, or practice. Interpretative rules are the agency's announcements of how it interprets the meaning of statutes it must enforce. Where the legislative rules discussed in previous paragraphs presumably add to the legislative framework of regulation, interpretative rules merely clarify what the legislature included in the statute.

When the courts review such statutes, they consider such interpretative rules to be "a body of experience and informed judgment to which the courts and litigants may properly resort for guidance."[69] However,

> The weight of such a judgment in a particular case will depend upon the thoroughness evident in its consideration, the validity of its reasoning, its consistency with earlier and later pronouncements, and all those factors which give it power to persuade.[70]

In General Electric Co. v. Gilbert, for example, the United States Supreme Court pointedly rejected the Equal Employment Opportunity Commission's (EEOC) interpretative rules on disabilities related to pregnancy.[71] The EEOC had issued an interpretative ruling stating that Title VII of the Civil Rights Act of 1964 requires that disabilities due to pregnancy or childbirth be treated the same as other temporary disabilities in employers' disability insurance plans. After rejecting EEOC's authority to have promulgated the regulations in the first place, the opinion of the

---

68. See Automotive Parts & Accessories Assn. v. Boyd, 407 F.2d 330 (D.C. 1968).
69. Skidmore v. Swift & Co., 323 U.S. 134, 140 (1944).
70. Id.
71. 429 U.S. 125 (1976).

court said the rule in question contradicted an earlier interpretation by the commission. It further indicated that yet another federal agency (the Wage and Hour Administration) had adopted the opposite point of view.

When legislative rules are involved, the courts must ask whether the agency had statutory power to adopt rules on that subject, whether the agency used proper procedures in promulgating those rules, and, sometimes, whether the statute under which the rules were established is constitutional.

3. Adjudication

In addition to promulgating rules and regulations, agencies also adjudicate disputes over the application of their rules. When a person applies for social security disability benefits, a radio station seeks to have its license renewed by the Federal Communications Commission, or an employer contests an alleged violation of National Labor Relations Board regulations, administrative agencies assume quasi-judicial functions.

Adjudicatory hearings vary according to the agency and the type of problem. The procedures at a hearing may be almost identical to those used in a nonjury civil trial, or a party may merely tell his or her story in a very informal manner in an administrator's office. The exact nature of the hearing depends on statutory requirements and how the courts have interpreted the requirements of the due process clause.[72]

In deciding which elements of due process apply to a given administrative situation, the courts appear to have balanced the relative importance of several different factors. In Mathews v. Eldridge the United States Supreme Court emphasized the following three considerations:

> First, the private interest that will be affected by the official action; second, the risk of an erroneous deprivation of such interest through the procedures used, and the probable value, if any, of additional or substitute procedural safeguards; and finally, the Government's interest, including the function involved and the fiscal and administrative burdens that the additional or substitute procedural requisites would entail.[73]

4. Judicial Review

Judicial review is part of the concept of checks and balances that was referred to in the separation of powers section on constitutional law.[74] It is designed to ensure that civil service and appointed bureaucrats are held accountable to the will of Congress and the dictates of the Constitution.

---

72. See the discussion of due process at page 149.
73. 424 U.S. 319, 335 (1976).
74. See discussion at page 149.

The federal Administrative Procedure Act provides that

A person suffering legal wrong because of agency action, or adversely affected or aggrieved by agency action within the meaning of a relevant statute, is entitled to judicial review thereof.[75]

Note that in order to receive this judicial review, the client must have suffered a legal wrong or otherwise be adversely affected by the agency's action. This provision thus is related to the general concept of standing. To be recognized as a legitimate party in a litigation, one must show that one is personally affected by the actions forming the basis of the lawsuit.

In addition to standing, the paralegal must consider the application of the concepts of ripeness, exhaustion, and reviewability. Ripeness requires that the facts have been sufficiently established and clarified by the agency to adequately define the legal issues. If they have not, the court may require further administrative actions before it will consider taking any actions on the merits of the claims. Exhaustion of remedies requires that all available administrative remedies be used prior to taking the matter to the courts. Finally, the litigant must also demonstrate that statutes and court decisions have provided for judicial remedies in that particular type of case. Some types of issues are considered to be totally committed to agency discretion and simply not reviewable by the courts.[76]

If review is possible, it may take place in several different forums:

The form of proceeding for judicial review is the special statutory review proceeding relevant to the subject matter in a court specified by statute or, in the absence or inadequacy thereof, any applicable form of legal action, including actions for declaratory judgments or writs of prohibitory or mandatory injunction or habeas corpus, in a court of competent jurisdiction. Except to the extent that prior, adequate, and exclusive opportunity for judicial review is provided by law, agency action is subject to judicial review in civil or criminal proceedings for judicial enforcement.[77]

In some cases the courts may delay the agency's action until they can review it.[78]

In reviewing agency decisions the courts can set aside agency actions, findings, and conclusions only in circumstances where they have been found to be

(A) Arbitrary, capricious, an abuse of discretion, or otherwise not in accordance with law;

75. 5 U.S.C. §702.
76. 5 U.S.C. §701.
77. 5 U.S.C. §703.
78. 5 U.S.C. §705.

(B) Contrary to constitutional right, power, privilege, or immunity;
(C) In excess of statutory jurisdiction, authority, or limitations, or short of statutory right;
(D) Without observance of procedure required by law;
(E) Unsupported by substantial evidence . . .; or
(F) Unwarranted by the facts to the extent that the facts are subject to trial de novo (a new hearing) by the reviewing court.[79]

Note that conditions B, C, and D are legal. They question the proper interpretation of constitutional and statutory provisions. Conditions A, E, and F draw the court into a review of the facts of the particular dispute. In subsection E, the term "unsupported by substantial evidence" has been interpreted as being "such relevant evidence as a reasonable mind might accept as adequate to support a conclusion."[80] Thus the courts will review factual determinations, but they will seek to minimize situations in which they substitute their own judgment for that of the agency decision maker and instead will give the agency the benefit of any reasonable doubt.

In addition to the substantial evidence rule, reviewing courts have at various times applied other similar formulations to determine the scope of review over factual determinations. These alternatives have included the "clearly erroneous" test, the "no basis in fact" standard, "in the absence of substantial evidence to the contrary," and the requirement that there be a "total lack of evidence."[81] However, one should not place too much importance on the specific test. For as Davis so aptly puts it:

> Formulas about scope of review do not always control judicial action; the formulas can be bent in any direction, in accordance with what the reviewing court deems to be the needs of justice or the public welfare.[82]

H. SUMMARY

This chapter's very condensed introduction to the basic concepts in modern American law is designed to build vocabulary rather than competence. It provides paralegals with a basic legal literacy to be able to understand the substance of major areas of law and to know where to begin their research when faced with common legal problems.

Criminal law is divided into felonies and misdemeanors. Quasi-criminal proceedings involve juveniles, traffic offenses, and ordinance

---

79. 5 U.S.C. §706(2).
80. Consolidated Edison Co. v. NLRB, 305 U.S. 197, 229 (1938).
81. See K. C. Davis, Administrative Law Text 528, 535 (3d ed. 1972).
82. Id. at 529.

enforcement actions. The four basic elements that comprise every crime are *mens rea, actus rea,* causation, and harm. A defendant can escape criminal responsibility for his or her action through one of several recognized defenses, including insanity, infancy, entrapment, duress, necessity, and self-defense.

Whereas crimes are public wrongs, a tort is a private wrong. The most common type of tort actions involve allegations of negligence. The four basic elements of negligence are duty, breach of duty, causation, and damages. Other types of torts include battery, assault, trespass, false arrest and false imprisonment, malicious prosecution and abuse of process, libel, slander, and invasion of privacy. Defenses to tort actions can include consent, contributory negligence, assumption of risk, and privilege. In situations where the doctrine of strict liability has been applied, people and corporations can be held responsible for injuries even though they resulted from actions that were not unreasonable and did not violate a standard of due care. When damages are awarded, they can be either compensatory, punitive, or nominal.

A contract can be in either verbal or written form, but to be enforceable as a legal contract there must be an offer, an acceptance, and a mutual exchange of something of value among parties who are considered legally capable of incurring contractual duties. Remedies for a breach of the terms of a contract include rescission, release, novation, specific performance, and damages. The primary defenses are incapacity of one of the contracting parties, illegality, unconscionability, and impossibility. Third parties can acquire contractual rights through assignment or designation as a beneficiary in the contract itself.

Ownership of real property can take several forms depending on whether it is individually or jointly owned and depending on what happens at the death of one of the owners. Covenants and easements can limit the way in which an owner uses the property. When a person rents someone else's real estate, it can take the form of a tenancy for a term, a periodic tenancy, a tenancy at will, or a tenancy at sufferance. The lease establishes the basic rights and duties of both the landlord and the tenant, but state statutes and the common law impose certain limitations on leases and establish the rights of the parties in the absence of a lease.

The selling and leasing of personal property is covered by the general principles of contract law and the Uniform Commercial Code. Article 2 of the UCC covers sales, warranties, unconscionability, and the remedies for breach of contract. Article 3 states the requirements for the handling of promissory notes, drafts, and other negotiable instruments.

The property that a person owns at the time of death becomes part of that person's estate and is distributed on the basis of the person's will (if a valid will exists) and the probate laws of the state. *Probate* refers to the process of proving that a will is genuine and then distributing the deceased's property. An executor or an administrator is appointed to

carry out this process. Trusts are often established as a means of reducing the taxes, time, and other costs associated with the probate process.

The legal status of a business organization is a function of the relationship among the owners and the nature of the liabilities assumed by each. A sole proprietorship is an extension of its owner, a partnership is an aggregation of individuals, and a corporation is a separate legal entity. Personal liability is greatest in the sole proprietorship form of organization and is least in the corporate form. Directors of a corporation, however, assume personal liability for a fiduciary duty to act in the best interests of the corporation and its stockholders. Blue sky laws regulate the issuance of stocks and bonds to the public.

Agency is an area of the law that applies to people who are authorized to act on behalf of or otherwise represent the interests of others. The three major relationships covered by agency law are principal/agent, employer/employee, and employer/independent contractor.

In addition to its use in criminal cases and civil rights actions, constitutional law is used primarily to attack statutes and regulations that have a negative effect on a lawyer's client. The major concepts covered in this brief presentation were federalism, separation of powers, due process, and equal protection. It is particularly important that paralegals understand the full range of applications of the due process clause.

Finally, administrative law is an area of the law covering the structure and authority of administrative agencies, the procedures for making and enforcing regulations, and the extent to which the courts exercise judicial review. Key concepts involve the delegation of authority, the role of rulemaking and adjudication, and judicial review of agency actions.

KEY TERMS

abstract
actual malice
actus rea
adjudication
administrator of an estate
administrative law
agency
agent
ALI insanity test
assignment
assumption of risk
beneficiary
blue sky laws

certificate of deposit
chattel
check
commercial paper
comparative negligence
compelling interest test
compensatory damages
conditional fee simple estate
constitutional law
contract
contributory negligence
corporation
crime

defamatory
demand note
director of a corporation
due care
duress
easement
employee
employer
encumbrance
equal protection
estate
exclusionary rule
executor
exhaustion of remedies
express warranty
federalism
fee simple estate
felony
fiduciary duty
freehold estate
fruit of the poisonous tree
fundamental right
general damages
general partner
guardian
heightened scrutiny
holder in due course
implied warranty
independent contractor
installment note
intentional tort
invasion of privacy
joint tenancy
judicial review
last clear chance doctrine
law enforcement privilege
lease
lessee

lessor
libel
life estate
limited partner
mens rea
misdemeanor
mootness
M'Naghten rule
necessity defense
negligence
nominal damages
novation
officer of a corporation
parole evidence
partnership
periodic tenancy
personal property
principal (in agency law)
probate
procedural due process
promissory note
punitive damages
quiet enjoyment
rational basis test
real estate
real property
rescission
respondeat superior
restrictive covenant
ripeness
rulemaking
self-defense
separation of powers
slander
sole proprietorship
sovereign immunity
special damages
specific performance

standing   trust
strict liability   testator
strict scrutiny   trustee
substantive due process   UCC
suspect class   unconscionable
tenancy at sufferance   usury
tenancy at will   warranty
tenancy for a term   warranty of fitness
testator   warranty of merchantability
title insurance   warranty of title
tort

REVIEW QUESTIONS

1. What is the relationship between common law crimes and statutory ones?

2. What are the elements of a crime?

3. Why can the same act constitute several different crimes?

4. How does a court determine what a person's *mens rea* was at the time an act was committed?

5. What defenses are available to a defendant in a criminal case?

6. What tests are commonly used to determine causation in negligence cases?

7. What defenses are available in tort cases?

8. What types of torts are classified as intentional torts?

9. Under what circumstances can you sue the government or a government official be sued?

10. What is the difference between a promise and a contract?

11. What remedies are available in a breach of contract situation?

12. What defenses are available in contract cases?

13. What are the different forms of ownership of real property?

14. What is the role of a lease, and what types of tenancies can a lease create?

15. What types of transactions are covered by the UCC?

16. What types of remedies for breach of contract are provided for in the UCC?

17. What types of clauses are usually found in a will?

18. What is the executor's role in probating an estate? What is the judge's role?

19. What are the differences among the three basic forms of business organizations?

20. What are the three types of relationships dealt with in agency law? Which type carries the greatest amount of liability for the employer? The least?

21. What do federalism and separation of powers have in common?

22. What is the difference between the fifth amendment due process clause and the fourteenth amendment due process clause?

23. What are the three levels of equal protection analysis, and on what basis does a court choose one to apply in a given case?

24. What types of limitations have the courts imposed on the delegation of legislative power to administrative agencies?

25. When does an administrative agency engage in rulemaking as opposed to enforcement or adjudication?

26. What conditions must be met before a court can review the actions of an administrative agency?

DISCUSSION QUESTIONS

1. Under what circumstances do you think people should be excused of criminal responsibility for an action committed while they were under the influence of drugs? Under the influence of a mental disorder?

2. Where should the line be drawn in entrapment cases? What's wrong with the government participating in the commission of a crime? To what extent is it fair to tempt someone to commit a crime?

3. What are the advantages and disadvantages of the exclusionary rule? To what extent should it be modified?

4. What are the advantages and disadvantages of comparative negligence? What form of comparative negligence do you think is most desirable?

5. What is the rationale behind the law enforcement privilege in tort cases? What, if any, changes do you think should be made in the application of this doctrine?

6. Libel laws are designed to strike a balance between the public's right to know and an individual's right to privacy. Do you agree with the manner in which the courts have drawn this line? In what way would you like to see the balance altered?

7. What is the rationale for the doctrine of sovereign immunity? When and under what circumstances should governments or their officials be immune from liability for their actions?

8. Under what circumstances should the doctrine of strict liability be applied?

9. What are the pros and cons of allowing restrictive covenants on real estate titles?

10. Where should one draw the line between "puffing" and fraud? To what extent should a seller be allowed to disclaim implied warranties?

11. What are the pros and cons of the holder in due course doctrine? Is it fair to the debtor? To the assignee?

12. To what extent does the equal protection clause protect women? What was the purpose of the proposed equal rights amendment and how would it have differed from the equal protection clause?

13. Many agency decisions involve highly technical areas in which the agency personnel are presumably specialists. To what extent should their decisions be reviewed by judges? Are judges qualified to make technical decisions on such questions as the safe level of radiation or emissions from an automobile? What standard of review should be applied to such technical decisions? How much deference should the courts show to the expertise of the agencies?

PROJECTS

1. Use your state criminal code to determine how it treats the insanity defense. Under what circumstances is a person considered to be not guilty by reason of insanity in your state?

2. Is your state a comparative negligence state? If so, which variation of comparative negligence does it use?

3. Is your state among those that have adopted the Uniform Commercial Code, the Uniform Partnership Act, the Uniform Limited Partnership Act, or the Model Business Corporation Act?

4. How are residential real estate sales handled in your community? How does local practice differ from the process described in this chapter?

5. Locate your state's administrative procedure act and determine the nature and extent of judicial review in your state.

Chapter 5
Litigation and
Adjudication

LITIGATION IS A DISPUTE that has been turned into a formal lawsuit. In other words, someone has begun the process required to have the dispute settled in the courts. Although the specific stages in the process and the specific court documents that must be completed differ in civil and criminal cases, they also have much in common. This chapter presents an overview of how both types of cases are handled in the judicial system. It also covers some of the basic procedures used in administrative adjudication.[1]

There will, of course, be some variation in procedures from one state to another, so one must always consult the statutes and court rules for the particular tribunal. Local federal district court rules are available in pamphlets from the district court office. Federal court rules are also found in the annotated codes and Supreme Court digests as well as some specialized loose-leaf services. Complete texts of the court decisions that construe the federal rules of civil and criminal procedure are in Federal Rules Service and Federal Rules Decisions.[2]

At the state level jurisdictional requirements of the courts are also made clear in constitutions and in state statutes. Paralegals should become thoroughly familiar with the civil practice act of the state in which they are employed. The rules established by the courts themselves are

---

1. In this chapter the term *adjudication* is used to refer to the general process by which individual disputes are settled by courts and administrative agencies. Adjudication involves a hearing in which evidence is presented and arguments are made. A neutral decision maker (or a panel of judges) then decides the outcome of the dispute on the basis of the evidence presented. The reader should be aware, however, that the term *adjudication* also may be used to refer to the entry of an official decree or judgment in a specific case.
2. The jurisdiction of the federal courts is dealt with in 18 U.S.C. §1332 and 28 U.S.C. §§1331-1346. Federal Rules Service is published by Callaghan and Co. It contains a single loose-leaf volume of the rules currently in force as well as other volumes reporting the court decisions that intepret these rules. West Publishing Co. produces Federal Rules Decisions as a unit of its National Reporter System. It reports district court decisions involving the rules of procedure that are not published in the Federal Supplement. West also publishes a multivolume treatise by C. Wright and A. Miller entitled Federal Practice and Procedure.

usually available in pamphlets from the courts involved. In addition, ~~rules of the state's appellate courts are usually published in either the~~ annotated statutes, the case reporters, or specialized publications on court rules.

A. CIVIL PROCEDURE

Before reading further, it may be useful to review the discussion in Chapter 2 regarding the differences between civil law and criminal law. The reader should also scan Figure 5.1 for an overview of the basic stages in the process and frequently refer back to this figure as the textual material is presented. Finally, this chapter uses frequent references to an actual court case involving alleged malpractice to illustrate the process. This case involved a transfusion of what was alleged to be Rh positive blood to a patient who was Rh negative. The state supreme court's decision in this case was reported as Renslow v. Mennonite Hospital,[3] and readers may find it helpful to read that decision in conjunction with this section of the chapter.

1. Filing the Suit

The attorney decides if and when litigation is to begin. The decision to litigate involves not only a determination of who will be sued and the legal grounds for that suit but also in which court the suit will be brought. The paralegal can make an important contribution to this decision by researching some of the available options, tracing corporate ownerships, or finding the location of parties to the suit.

a. Parties to the Suit

The first step in filing a lawsuit is deciding who is going to be sued. The party who allegedly has been wronged sues the party who allegedly is responsible for that wrong. However, the party one might assume to be the logical defendant may not be worth suing (the party may not have money to pay the damages that a court might award).[4] Often there is more than one possible defendant, and the plaintiff will want to make sure the one with the "deepest pocket" is included. In other words, the plaintiff goes after the defendant with the most assets. Therefore, a defendant's employer is often brought into the suit on the basis of agency law and the doctrine of *respondeat superior*.[5] In an automobile accident case the plaintiff may sue the manufacturer of the auto or the governmental unit responsible for maintaining the roadway.

---

3. 67 Ill. 2d 348, 367 N.E.2d 1250 (1977).
4. This is referred to as being "judgment proof."
5. See Chapter 4, page 147.

Figure 5.1 Civil Procedure

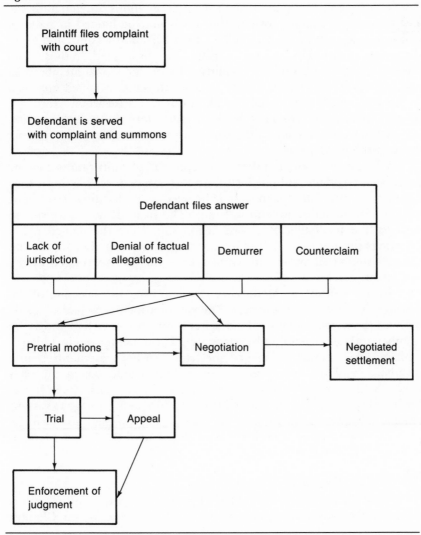

One must also be certain that the named parties of a lawsuit are legally capable of suing and being sued. Corporations can generally sue and be sued, but their access to the courts may be limited in states in which they are not incorporated. In some states, partnerships and unincorporated associations lack the capacity to sue or be sued. In those cases the suit must be brought by or against all of its individual members. In many states a minor must sue or be sued through a named guardian or "next friend."[6] Additional complications can arise when executors, trustees, bailees, or assignees are involved.[7] Here the question is simply whether they can sue in their own name or whether they must act through the legal owner.

When compulsory joinder rules apply, the plaintiff cannot sue one potential defendant without including the others as well. Where such rules do not apply, the plaintiff may be selective in deciding who will be included in the suit and who will not.[8] The plaintiff may also wish to consider the possibility of a class action suit. Here the named plaintiff brings the suit on behalf of a large class of additional plaintiffs who are in a similar situation with respect to having been wronged by the defendant.

In the Renslow v. Mennonite Hospital case, the selection of the parties was fairly straightforward. The young woman who had allegedly received the wrong blood sued individually on her own behalf and as the "mother and next friend" of her daughter. The daughter was included as a plaintiff because it was alleged she had been born prematurely in a jaundiced condition and suffered from hyperbilirubinemia because her mother's blood had been sensitized by the faulty transfusion. It was further alleged that the daughter suffered permanent damage to various organs, the brain, and the nervous system. The hospital at which the transfusion took place and the doctor who headed the hospital laboratory were named as parties in the suit.

b. Selection of the Court

Once the parties of the suit have been decided, the plaintiff's attorney must decide where the case should be filed. As discussed in Chapter

---

6. A guardian is a person who has the legal right and duty to take care of another's property where that person is a child or is otherwise incompetent. A next friend may not be the legal guardian but is a responsible party that the court recognizes as being a legitimate representative of the party's interests. See F. James and G. Hazard, Civil Procedure §10.7 (1985) for a more complete discussion of the competency to sue.

7. An executor is a person appointed to handle the property of a deceased person. A trustee holds money or property for the benefit of someone else through a trust arrangement. A bailee is one who has responsibility for the property someone else has loaned to them (such as when a person leaves his car with a mechanic). An assignee is one to whom certain property or other rights have been transferred by the legal owner (such as when a business assigns a promissory note to a bank or a collection agency).

8. A defendant may later file a third party action to bring in the omitted defendant.

2, specific courts have limited authority to hear only particular types of cases. The plaintiff therefore must take the litigation to a court with the proper jurisdiction.

Sometimes both the federal and state courts have concurrent jurisdiction. In such cases the plaintiff can search for the best available forum. In deciding which court to choose, an attorney will usually consider such matters as filing requirements, deadline dates, the current backlog of cases, discovery procedures, the rules of evidence, and the personalities of the judges. The convenience of the physical location of the court may also be a factor.

In the *Renslow* case both the plaintiffs and the defendants were residents of Illinois, and the allegedly negligent acts took place in Illinois. Thus, in this situation, the plaintiff's attorney had little choice but to file in the circuit courts of Illinois.

c. Notice

Before a court will hear a lawsuit it must be convinced that the defendants have received proper notice that the suit has been filed against them. Proper notice usually requires that the local sheriff (or a United States marshal in federal cases) personally deliver a summons to the defendants. There are occasions where proper notice can be satisfied by mailing the summons to the defendant's last known address, publishing copies of the summons in newspapers of general circulation, or delivering it to an authorized agent. Once again the paralegal must consult the state's civil practice act on the type of service required in the case. Local court rules indicate proper format.

Proper notice should include the names of the parties to the suit, the court in which suit has been filed, statement of the plaintiff's claim, and the number of days within which the defendant must respond. In most jurisdictions a copy of the complaint is delivered along with the summons as a means of notifying the defendant of the nature of the claim. The summons then provides the party with information relating to the required response. Form 5.1 shows the style of a typical summons. The caption for our model malpractice case is

EMMA M. RENSLOW, individually
and as mother and next friend of
LEAH ANN RENSLOW, a minor,
                            Plaintiffs,

        v.

MENNONITE HOSPITAL, a corporation, and HANS STROINK, M.D.,
                            Defendants.

[Page one of the sample summons is presented below.]

In the Circuit Court   No. _____
of the 11th Judicial Circuit
McLean County, Illinois

[Official caption of case goes here]

SUMMONS

To each defendant:

You are summoned and required to file an answer in this case, or otherwise file your appearance, in the office of the clerk of this court within thirty days after service of this summons, not counting the day of service. IF YOU FAIL TO DO SO, A JUDGMENT OR DE-CREE BY DEFAULT MAY BE TAKEN AGAINST YOU FOR THE RELIEF ASKED IN THE COMPLAINT.

To the officer:

This summons must be returned by the officer or other person to whom it was given for service, with indorsement of service and fees, if any, immediately after service. If service cannot be made, this summons shall be returned so indorsed.

This summons may not be served later than thirty days after its date.

Plaintiff's Attorney _____   Witness _____, 19_____

Address _____

City _____   Clerk of Court

Telephone _____   (Seal of Court)

To: _____   Date of Service _____, 19_
(To be inserted by officer on copy left with defendant or other person.)

[Page two of the sample summons, to be filled in by the Sheriff and court, is presented below.]

SHERIFF'S FEES

Service and return .... $_____
Miles .... _____
    Total .... $_____

_____

Sheriff of _____ County

I certify that I served this summons on defendant as follows:

(a) (Individual defendants — personal):
By leaving a copy and a copy of the complaint with each individual defendant personally, as follows:
    Name of Defendant   Date of Service

(b) (Individual defendants — abode):
By leaving a copy and a copy of the complaint at the usual place of abode of each individual defendant with a person of his family, of the age of ten years or upwards, informing that person of the contents of the summons, and also by sending a copy of the summons and of the complaint in a sealed envelope with postage fully prepaid, addressed to each individual defendant at his usual place of abode, as follows:
    Name of Defendant   Person with Whom Left
    Date of Service   Date of Mailing

(c) (Corporation defendants):
By leaving a copy and a copy of the complaint with the registered agent, officer, or agent of each defendant corporation, as follows:
    Defendant Corporation
    Registered Agent, Officer, or Agent
    Date of Service

(d) (Other service):

_____
Sheriff of _____ County
By _____, Deputy

2. The Pleadings

Pleadings are formal written statements filed with the court at the beginning of a lawsuit. They may include the complaint, the answer, the cross-complaint, and the demurrer and are designed to narrow and focus the issues involved.

a. The Complaint

The complaint states the allegations that form the basis of the plaintiff's case. Exhibit 5.1 presents the first three counts of the medical malpractice suit under discussion. It lists the facts that the plaintiff claims entitles her to more than $500,000 in damages.

Complaints must begin with a caption section that identifies the parties, the court, and the docket number. Emma and Leah Renslow are identified as the plaintiffs, and Mennonite Hospital and Dr. Stroink are the defendants. The suit was filed in McLean County in the Circuit Court of the Eleventh Judicial District of Illinois. At the time it was filed, the clerk of the courts assigned the docket number of 75-L-8. The number in this case means that the suit was the eighth case to be filed in the law division during 1975.

The body of the complaint consists of the allegation of facts that constitute a cause of action.[9] In most states the facts being pleaded must be ultimate facts as opposed to conclusions of law or mere evidentiary matter. It is often difficult to make the distinction between these three concepts, and the paralegal drafting complaints will probably need to consult with the attorney at this point.

The federal rules allow for notice pleading. Here the complaint must simply identify the transaction from which the plaintiff's claim arises. The distinction between ultimate facts, conclusions of law, and evidentiary material loses its importance, and the discovery process is used to provide more complete information about the facts.

The *Renslow* complaint was divided into several different counts, each count presenting a separate legal claim and able to stand by itself. For purposes of illustration, only the first three counts of the complaint have been reproduced. The first six paragraphs in Count I identify the individuals and the basic events leading to the transfusion of the blood. Paragraph 7 asserts that these actions were the direct and proximate cause of the plaintiff's injuries. Numbers 8 and 9 describe the nature of plaintiff's injuries and the manner in which they were discovered. Then paragraphs 10 through 13 attempt to fix the blame firmly on the defendants' negligence.

Paragraph 14 sets the stage for the requested relief. It does so by

---

9. In order to present a cause of action, the facts must present a situation for which the law provides a remedy.

Exhibit 5.1 Sample Complaint

Caption

IN THE CIRCUIT COURT
OF THE ELEVENTH JUDICIAL CIRCUIT OF ILLINOIS
McLEAN COUNTY

EMMA M. RENSLOW, individually
and as mother and next friend of
LEAH ANN RENSLOW, a minor,
Plaintiffs,

v.

AT LAW
NO. 75-L-8

MENNONITE HOSPITAL, a corporation, and HANS STROINK, M.D.,
Defendants.

COMPLAINT

COUNT I

Allegations

EMMA M. RENSLOW, by her attorneys, LAW OF-
FICES OF STRODEL & KINGERY, ASSOC., for
cause of action against MENNONITE HOSPITAL, a
corporation, states that:

1. On or about October 8, 1965, Defendant hospital owned, operated, managed and maintained and
controlled a certain hospital, located in the city of
Bloomington, County of McLean, and State of Illinois, wherein it treated persons suffering from various ailments, and provided rooms, laboratories,
drugs, and various medical devices and services for
patients admitted to said hospital for medical care
and treatment in said hospital.

2. On or about October 8, 1965, through and including October 14, 1965, DR. HANS STROINK, Defendant herein, was an agent or employee of said
hospital, and was in fact the Director of Laboratories for said hospital, and had under his supervision
and control various laboratory technicians who,
among other duties, were charged from time to
time, and including the period mentioned herein,
with the typing of blood for use in transfusion of patients in said hospital.

3. On or about October 8, 1965, the Plaintiff,
EMMA M. RENSLOW, then known as EMMA MUR-
PHY, a minor age 13, and born April 16, 1952, was
admitted as a patient in said hospital by Dr. Seymour R. Goldberg, a duly licensed physician and
surgeon in the State of Illinois, and member of the
medical staff of said Defendant hospital.

Exhibit 5.1 (*Continued*)

4. At all times mentioned herein the Plaintiff was in the exercise of all due care and caution for her own personal well being commensurate with her age and experience.

5. On October 8, 1965, pursuant to the order of Dr. Seymour Goldberg, said minor Plaintiff was infused with 500 c.c. of whole blood as part of the care and treatment for her condition of ill-being. Additionally, on or about October 9, 1965, by order of Dr. Seymour Goldberg, an additional 500 c.c. of whole blood was infused in said minor Plaintiff as part of the treatment for her condition of physical ill-being. On both said dates of blood infusion, the Plaintiff was and still is blood type A Rh negative, and the blood infused aforesaid was in fact type A Rh positive.

6. On October 8, 1965, and October 9, 1965, said Defendant hospital, acting through its agent or employee, DR. HANS STROINK, as Director of Laboratories, and acting through its agents, certain laboratory technicians, the exact names of whom are not presently known, selected the blood units to be transfused into the Plaintiff, exercised blood typing techniques, and went through procedures to compare the Plaintiff's blood type with the blood types about to be transfused into the Plaintiff, said acts all occurring in the course of care and treatment of the Plaintiff while a patient in Defendant hospital and in the course of the professional supervision and responsibility of the said DR. HANS STROINK and the laboratory technicians aforesaid, all of said persons being agents or employees of Defendant hospital.

7. As a direct and proximate result of the foregoing the mis-typed blood was in fact transfused into the Plaintiff, permanently injuring her by sensitizing her blood.

8. At the time of the transfusions aforesaid up through and including November 15, 1973, the Plaintiff had no adverse reactions known by her to said blood transfusions, had no knowledge whatsoever of the medical consequences of being transfused with the wrong blood and first became aware of her blood sensitization from said transfusions in December 1973, as a result of routine antibody screening of her blood during the course of prenatal visitation with Dr. A. K. Patel, a duly licensed

physician and surgeon in the State of Illinois specializing in obstetrics and gynecology, who attended the Plaintiff for and during a state of pregnancy at said time.

9. Subsequently, during the course of her pregnancy, the Plaintiff developed increasing medical and blood chemistry signs of sensitization to such an extent that definite jeopardy to her unborn child was diagnosed by the said Dr. A. K. Patel, resulting in the Plaintiff being hospitalized at Brokaw Hospital, Normal, Illinois, on or about March 25, 1974, where labor was induced leading to the live birth of a premature infant female child, now known as LEAH ANN RENSLOW, a minor, who was in fact jaundiced and required an immediate and complete exchange transfusion of her blood at said Brokaw Hospital and subsequent transfer to St. Francis Hospital, Peoria, Illinois, to the premature facility located therein for additional care and treatment as a premature infant, and a second complete exchange transfusion of her blood.

Allegations
10. The selection, transfusion, and management of the infusion of blood in the Plaintiff at MENNONITE HOSPITAL in October of 1965 as aforesaid was exclusively and solely within the control, direction, management, and maintenance of said Defendant hospital and its agents or employees, DR. HANS STROINK, and various laboratory technicians as aforesaid.

11. During the selection and typing of the blood aforesaid and the transfusing of same the Plaintiff exercised no control, direction, or management whatsoever over the entire process aforedescribed.

12. During the transfusion of blood aforesaid in October 1965, the entire process of selection of the blood, typing, comparing, and transfusing was exclusively managed and maintained and controlled by Defendant hospital and its agents or employees aforesaid at the time of the injury thereby committed on the Plaintiff.

13. The occurrence speaks for itself; that is, the occurrence would not have taken place in the ordinary course of things if Defendant hospital acting through its agents or employees aforesaid had not negligently failed to use proper care in the selection, typing, comparing, transfusing and other techniques of the blood infused into the Plaintiff aforesaid; and the control, management, and maintenance of said transfusion process and blood

Exhibit 5.1 *(Continued)*

Allegations

selection and typing process was at all times under the exclusive control, direction, and management of the Defendant hospital, DR. HANS STROINK, as Director of its Laboratories, and the various laboratory technicians involved in the procedure aforesaid.

14. As a direct and proximate result of the aforesaid negligence by Defendant hospital, acting by and through its agent or employee, Defendant DR. HANS STROINK, and the laboratory technicians aforesaid, the Plaintiff sustained severe and permanent personal injuries by virtue of her blood being sensitized, resulting in the premature birth of her child, LEAH ANN RENSLOW, and will in the future incur difficult and abnormal pregnancies and medical problems with the birth of any subsequent children, arising from any and all subsequent pregnancies.

AND FURTHER, the Plaintiff had expended or become obligated to expend large sums of money for hospital care and treatment, medical bills and drug bills, endeavoring to be cared for as a result of her pregnancy and the premature birth of her child aforesaid, and will in the future incur additional unusual and extra expenses for any medical care and attention and hospitalization from any future pregnancies or birth of any future child borne by the Plaintiff.

AND FURTHER, the Plaintiff has suffered great mental anguish following her diagnosis as a blood sensitized person; and throughout the pregnancy and delivery of her child aforesaid, she suffered great mental anguish for her own well being and for the well being of her child. Additionally, she will in the future suffer great fear for her physical well-being and the physical well being of any child in gestation as a result of future pregnancies.

15. At all times mentioned herein, at and subsequent to November 1973, the Plaintiff is and was the duly married spouse of Steven Renslow, and the child born aforesaid, LEAH ANN RENSLOW, is a product of the marriage of Steven Renslow to the Plaintiff.

Prayer

WHEREFORE, the Plaintiff, EMMA M. RENSLOW, prays judgment against MENNONITE HOSPITAL, a corporation, in the sum of FIVE HUNDRED THOUSAND DOLLARS ($500,000) plus costs of this suit.

Plaintiff demands trial of this Count by Jury.

COUNT II

EMMA M. RENSLOW, by her attorneys, LAW OF-
FICES OF STRODEL & KINGERY, ASSOC., for additional cause of action against Defendant hospital,
states that:

1-12. The Plaintiff repeats and realleges the allegations contained in paragraphs (1)-(12) of Count I
as and for paragraphs (1)-(12) of this Count.

13. On October 8, 1965, and October 9, 1965, the
Defendant, MENNONITE HOSPITAL, acting by and
through its agents or employees, DR. HANS
STROINK and various laboratory technicians as
aforesaid, was then and there guilty of one or more
or all of the following negligent and careless acts or
omissions:

Allegations

(a) The Defendant hospital negligently and
carelessly failed to properly select the proper
blood to be transfused into the Plaintiff.

(b) The Defendant hospital negligently and
carelessly mis-typed the blood selected by it to be
infused into the Plaintiff.

(c) The Defendant hospital negligently and
carelessly improperly compared the blood type of
the blood to be transfused into the Plaintiff with
the Plaintiff's blood type.

(d) The Defendant hospital negligently and
carelessly caused the wrong blood to be infused
into the Plaintiff.

14-15. Plaintiff repeats and realleges the allegations contained in paragraphs (14) and (15) of Count
I as and for paragraphs (14) and (15) of this Count.

Prayer

WHEREFORE, the Plaintiff, EMMA M. RENSLOW,
prays judgment against MENNONITE HOSPITAL, a
corporation, in the sum of FIVE HUNDRED
THOUSAND DOLLARS ($500,000) plus costs of this
suit.

Jury
Demand Plaintiff demands trial of this Count by Jury.

COUNT III

Allegations

EMMA M. RENSLOW, by her attorneys, LAW OF-
FICES OF STRODEL & KINGERY, ASSOC., for additional cause of action against MENNONITE

Exhibit 5.1 (*Continued*)

HOSPITAL, a corporation, and HANS STROINK, M.D., states that:

1-15. Plaintiff repeats and realleges the allegations of paragraphs (1) through (15) of Count II as and for paragraphs (1) through (15) of this Count.

Allegations

16. Subsequent to the transfusing of the wrong type blood into the Plaintiff as aforesaid, Defendant hospital, by and through its Director of Laboratories, HANS STROINK, M.D., discovered that the wrong type blood had in fact been administered to the Plaintiff, but, notwithstanding such discovery, at no time subsequent to said transfusion did said hospital or said HANS STROINK, M.D., in any way or manner advise the minor Plaintiff or her family that she in fact had been infused with the wrong typed blood or the future consequences of such infusion of the wrong typed blood into the Plaintiff as she matured, married, and became subject to pregnancy.

17. The aforesaid failure of said hospital and its said Director of Laboratories, HANS STROINK, M.D., in deliberately failing to advise the Plaintiff or her family of the infusion of the wrong typed blood aforesaid, was in fact a willful and wanton and reckless act of misconduct on the part of said hospital and said HANS STROINK, M.D.

Prayer

WHEREFORE, Plaintiff prays judgment against MENNONITE HOSPITAL, a corporation, and HANS STROINK, M.D., jointly and severally, in the sum of FIVE HUNDRED THOUSAND DOLLARS ($500,000) as compensatory damages and the sum of FIVE HUNDRED THOUSAND DOLLARS ($500,000) in punitive damages, plus costs of this suit.

Jury Demand

Plaintiff demands trial of this Count by jury.

elaborating on the consequences of her injuries (physical, financial, and mental). Paragraph 15 relates to a side issue. It happened that Leah Renslow had been conceived before her mother had married her father. This final paragraph establishes that Emma was married to Leah's father prior to her birth.

The allegations section is followed by the prayer for relief. Here the plaintiff indicates what action it wants the court to take. While the relief is usually in monetary damages, it can be a restraining order or some other equitable action. In Count I the plaintiff requests $500,000 plus costs of the suit. Note that the complaint also makes a demand for a jury trial.

This same pattern is then repeated with regard to the remaining counts. Count II essentially repeats Count I except that paragraph 13 alleges four specific instances in which the defendant acted negligently and carelessly. Count III, on the other hand, introduces the additional charges that the defendants committed a willful and wanton and reckless act of misconduct by not informing Emma Renslow of her condition after they had discovered their error. On this count the plaintiff requests $500,000 as compensatory damages and another $500,000 as punitive damages.[10]

While that section is not reproduced here the complaint ends with a signature section that in some cases must be verified (that is, accompanied by an affidavit that the plaintiff has read the complaint and that its contents are correct).

It should also be noted that a single complaint can allege more than one cause of action. Each cause of action, however, must be alleged in a separate section or count. Furthermore, separate counts can allege contradictory facts. (This is known as pleading in the alternative.) Thus, if the plaintiff were not sure which of two passengers had been driving an automobile involved in an accident, the first count of the complaint might allege that one person was driving, and the second count might allege that the other person had been driving.

b. The Defendant's Response

There are five basic options available to a defendant in a civil lawsuit: (1) deny the facts that the plaintiff says took place; (2) admit the facts but assert that those facts do not provide the plaintiff with a legal remedy; (3) assert that there are procedural defects in the complaint; (4) assert a claim of his or her own against either the plaintiff or another defendant; or (5) simply not respond at all. With the exception of not responding at all, these options are generally not considered mutually

---

10. Compensatory damages compensate the victim for actual losses. Punitive damages punish or make an example of the person who was responsible. Sometimes called exemplary damages, punitive damages are reserved for cases in which the defendant acted in a malicious or willful manner.

exclusive. Specific techniques to assert these options differ from one state to the next.

Failure to take any action, however, is viewed as an admission of the allegations contained in the complaint and creates a situation in which the plaintiff can seek a default judgment. While a judgment for the plaintiff is not automatic in such cases (plaintiff must still convince a judge that the claim is legitimate), the defendant has no right either to challenge the evidence presented or to present contrary evidence.[11]

The first line of defense usually involves a technical challenge to the wording of the complaint. In some jurisdictions this takes the form of a demurrer. The modern trend, however, involves instituting a technical challenge through a motion to dismiss. A general demurrer asserts that even if the alleged facts were true, no cause of action would exist. It is considered a special demurrer when the defendant challenges the complaint on the basis of such circumstances as a failure to join an indispensable third party, lack of jurisdiction, the plaintiff's legal capacity to sue, or existence of another suit involving the same matter. Note in Exhibit 5.2 the multitude of procedural attacks being made on the complaint shown in Exhibit 5.1.

If a general demurrer is rejected, in many jurisdictions the defendant must take a default judgment before the decision can be appealed. It is considered a waiving of the demurrer if the defendant goes ahead and answers the complaint after an unfavorable ruling by the trial judge. In the federal system, on the other hand, the defendant is not precluded from raising the issue again both at the trial and on appeal, even though an answer was filed. If the demurrer (or motion to dismiss) is accepted, the plaintiff is usually allowed to amend the complaint so that it will be acceptable to the court.

In the *Renslow* case the trial court judge accepted the assertion contained in paragraph 3 of the defendant's motion and dismissed the portion of the complaint that sought damages for the daughter. It did so on the basis of a conclusion that the law did not provide that a child who had not been conceived at the time could sue for negligent acts committed against the mother. The plaintiff then appealed the case on this narrow issue. Action on the mother's case was suspended until the appellate courts resolved the issue of the daughter's right to sue. Then after the Illinois Supreme Court declared that the daughter could sue, the action returned to the trial court, and the suit advanced normally.

Where the complaint has been found to be technically sound, the defendant must choose to admit or deny the facts that have been alleged in the complaint. Note that in Exhibit 5.3 Mennonite Hospital's answer

11. In a default judgment the judge awards the judgment against a party who failed to appear in court to contest the matter. Although it is possible to have a default judgment set aside, it is a very difficult task — especially if more than thirty days have elapsed.

Exhibit 5.2 Sample Motion to Dismiss

IN THE CIRCUIT COURT.
OF THE ELEVENTH JUDICIAL CIRCUIT OF ILLINOIS
McLEAN COUNTY
TRIAL DIVISION

EMMA M. RENSLOW, individually
and as mother and next friend of
LEAH ANN RENSLOW, a minor,
Plaintiffs,

v. ⎯ AT LAW NO. 75-L-8

MENNONITE HOSPITAL, a corporation, and HANS STROINK, M.D.,
Defendants.

MOTION TO DISMISS

NOW COMES the defendant MENNONITE HOSPITAL and files this its Motion to Dismiss the Complaint of the plaintiff and states:

1. That the Complaint fails to state a cause of action against this defendant.

2. That the Complaint was not filed within the time limited by law.

3. That the plaintiff has no standing to sue in behalf of the plaintiff, LEAH ANN RENSLOW, a minor, for the reason that said minor was not a person contemplating or in being at the time of the allegedly injurious occurrences and thus is not one of the persons who might be entitled to sue for damages allegedly incurred.

4. That the plaintiff attempts to assert several different types of causes of action within a single count in some of the counts respecting this hospital, and thus fails to comply with the Illinois Practice Act, and particularly Section 33 thereof, by failing to state her alleged causes of action in separate counts and in separate paragraphs.

5. That there are no facts alleged that are sufficient to show an employer/employee relationship between Dr. Hans Stroink and this hospital, and the court may take judicial notice that doctors are not ordinarily employees of hospitals in the absence of some peculiar relationship or the allegation sufficient to show the same.

6. That there are no facts alleged sufficient to bring this plaintiff within any exceptions to the Statute of Limitations requiring that plaintiff file her claimed cause of action within two years next following the actions complained about.

7. That there is no cause of action in the plaintiff for the alleged mental anguish and no right to recover for the same.

8. That the allegations of the Complaint are insufficient in law to

Exhibit 5.2 *(Continued)*

sustain a charge of willful and wanton misconduct or a claim for punitive damages.

9. That there are no facts alleged that are sufficient to show that the alleged injury could have taken place only through negligence on the part of this defendant or any other defendant, and thus the doctrine of *res ipsa loquitur* has no application to the allegations of the Complaint.

10. That the alleged damages complained about are too speculative and conjectural to be such as to accord plaintiff a right to sue for the same.

11. That the allegations of Count II are conclusionary in nature and do not allege actionable misconduct on the part of this hospital or any of its agents and servants.

12. That the charge that the hospital caused "wrong blood" to be infused into the plaintiff is a sheer conclusion, unsupported by any factual allegations and ought to be stricken, as should all charges respecting the same.

13. That there are no facts alleged that are sufficient to sustain the allegations in Count III to the effect that this hospital "discovered that the wrong typed blood had been administered."

14. That the allegations that the hospital or its agents failed to "properly select" the "proper blood" constitute nothing other than conclusions and are insufficient to sustain charges of negligence.

15. That the Complaint in this cause is barred in its entirety by the provisions of Chapter 91, Sections 181 et seq. of the Illinois Revised Statutes, it being the public policy of Illinois to promote the health and welfare of the people by limiting the legal liability arising out of such procedures as the transfusing of whole blood.

WHEREFORE, for want of a sufficient Complaint, this defendant prays judgment that the Complaint of the plaintiff may be dismissed at plaintiff's cost.

TRIAL BY JURY IS DEMANDED.

HEYL, ROYSTER, VOELKER & ALLEN

By: _____
Attorneys for Defendant
MENNONITE HOSPITAL,
a Corporation

_____

_____

HEYL, ROYSTER, VOELKER & ALLEN
Suite 300 The Central Building
Peoria, Illinois 61602
Phone: (309) 676-6184

Exhibit 5.3 Sample Answer to a Complaint

IN THE CIRCUIT COURT
OF THE ELEVENTH JUDICIAL CIRCUIT OF ILLINOIS
McLEAN COUNTY
TRIAL DIVISION

EMMA M. RENSLOW, individually
and as mother and next friend of
LEAH ANN RENSLOW, a minor,
                    Plaintiffs,

v.   AT LAW NO. 75-L-8

MENNONITE HOSPITAL, a corporation,
                    Defendant.

ANSWER TO COMPLAINT

NOW COMES the defendant, MENNONITE HOSPITAL, a corporation, and its Answer to the Complaint of the plaintiff states:

COUNT I

1. This defendant denies each and all of the allegations of
Paragraph 1.
2. This defendant denies each and all of the allegations of
Paragraph 2.
3. This defendant admits the allegations of Paragraph 3.
4. This defendant denies each and all of the allegations of
Paragraph 4.
5. This defendant denies each and all of the allegations of
Paragraph 5.
6. This defendant denies each and all of the allegations of
Paragraph 6.
7. This defendant denies each and all of the allegations of
Paragraph 7.
8. This defendant denies each and all of the allegations of
Paragraph 8.
9. This defendant denies each and all of the allegations of
Paragraph 9.
10. This defendant denies each and all of the allegations of
Paragraph 10.
11. This defendant denies each and all of the allegations of
Paragraph 11.
12. This defendant denies each and all of the allegations of
Paragraph 12.
13. This defendant denies each and all of the allegations of
Paragraph 13.

14. This defendant denies each and all of the allegations of
Paragraph 14.

15. This defendant has no knowledge sufficient to form a belief
with respect to the truth of the allegations of Paragraph 15 and
therefore denies the same.

WHEREFORE, this defendant prays judgment that the plaintiff
take nothing by her complaint and that this defendant may recover
its costs.

TRIAL BY JURY IS DEMANDED.

COUNT II

admits that Emma Renslow was admitted as the hospital's patient on
October 8, 1965, but denies all the rest. When the facts are denied, the
conflicting versions must eventually be settled by the trial process.

In some cases the defendant may admit the facts as they have been
alleged but go on to assert additional facts that would lead to a decision
in the defendant's favor even if all the plaintiff's allegations were correct.
Such affirmative defenses might include assumption of risk, contributory
negligence, estoppel (a legal concept that prevents a person from proving something in court because of an action taken at an earlier date),
consent, fraud, or the running of the statute of limitations.

In addition to denying facts and asserting defenses, the defendant
can either counterclaim or file a cross-complaint. In a counterclaim the
defendant asserts a cause of action against the plaintiff, and in a cross-
claim (or third party action, as it is often called) one defendant asserts a
cause of action against another defendant.

c. Additional Responses

When the defendant raises an affirmative defense,[12] presents a demurrer, or files a counterclaim, the plaintiff has the opportunity to respond to those arguments. After the court has ruled on demurrers and
motions to strike or dismiss, the parties are usually permitted to amend
their pleadings. Through this give-and-take of the pleadings the case is
either thrown out or the issues are narrowed and sharpened for trial.

---

12. In an affirmative defense the defendant asserts additional facts that provide a legally
acceptable justification for the actions that form the basis of the complaint. If a valid
affirmative defense is established, the defendant can admit to the plaintiff's allegations
and still win the lawsuit. Examples of an affirmative defense include assumption of risk
and contributory negligence.

3. Discovery

Once the defendant's answer has been filed, both sides frequently begin using various discovery devices to find out more about the strength of the other side's case. They seek to discover information about the identification of witnesses, the nature of the testimony that such witnesses can be expected to provide, and knowledge of the contents of relevant contracts, medical reports, and so forth. Such information is acquired through the use of interrogatories, depositions, requests for admissions, motions to produce documents, and motions for physical and mental exams.

a. Interrogatories

Interrogatories are written questions sent to one of the other parties in the lawsuit to obtain written answers in return. They are usually used by both parties after the complaint and initial responses have been filed. Exhibit 5.4 shows the first page of the interrogatories that the defendants sent to Emma Renslow. In addition to locating potential witnesses, interrogatories are used to establish dates, determine a person's medical or financial condition, and inquire about the existence of documentary evidence.

When a law office receives interrogatories directed at its client, the client usually is instructed to write out the answers as fully as possible. A paralegal may then edit these answers and prepare the formal responses that will be returned to the other party's attorney. The following illustration shows the typical format and content of answers to interrogatories:

14. State whether you have made any statement or statements in any form to any person regarding any of the events or happenings referred to in your complaint. If so, state
    a. The names and addresses of the person or persons to whom such statements were made;
    b. The date such statements were made;
    c. The form of the statement, whether written, oral, by recording device, or to a stenographer;
    d. Whether such statements, if written, were signed;
    e. The names and addresses of the persons presently having custody of such statements.

ANSWER: No statements have been made other than to my attorneys.

15. State the full name and last known address, giving the street, street number, city and state, of every witness known to you or to your attorneys who claims to have seen or heard the defendant make any statement or statements pertaining to any of the events or happenings alleged in your complaint.

ANSWER: Attorney Robert C. Strodel, 900 First National Bank Building, Peoria, Illinois, had a telephone conversation with Hans Stroink, M.D., on December 26, 1974, in which Dr. Stroink admitted that the blood transfused was mistyped by the laboratory technicians and stated that he (Dr. Stroink) learned of the

Exhibit 5.4 Sample Page from Interrogatories

IN THE CIRCUIT COURT
OF THE ELEVENTH JUDICIAL CIRCUIT OF ILLINOIS
McLEAN COUNTY
TRIAL DIVISION

EMMA M. RENSLOW, individually
and as mother and next friend of
LEAH ANN RENSLOW, a minor,
                    Plaintiffs,

v.   AT LAW NO. 75-L-8

MENNONITE HOSPITAL, a corporation, and Hans Stroink, M.D.,
                    Defendants.

INTERROGATORIES

The Plaintiff, EMMA M. RENSLOW, individually and as mother
and next friend of LEAH ANN RENSLOW, a minor, is hereby
notified to answer the following interrogatories separately and fully
in writing, under oath and within twenty-eight (28) days after service of these interrogatories, all in accordance with Supreme Court
Rule 213(c); these interrogatories may be answered on these interrogatories in the space provided and, if necessary, the reverse side
hereof:

1. State your full name, age, and place of birth.
2. Have you ever been known by any other name? If so, give the
other name or names and state where and when you used such
names.
3. State your present residence address and the period during
which you have resided at said address.
4. Are you married at the present time? If so, state: (a) Your
spouse's full name.

---

error sometime later. Also in the possession of Mr. Strodel is a
signed note from Dr. Stroink stating that the two technologists
were employees of Mennonite Hospital. The note is undated,
but was written in response to an inquiry of Mr. Strodel dated
December 28, 1974.

16. Supply the following information with respect to each individual
whose name you have given in the answer to the preceding
interrogatory:
   a. The location or locations where the defendant made any such
   statement or statements;
   b. The name and address of the person or persons in whose
   presence the defendant made any such statement or
   statements;
   c. The time and date when the defendant made any such statement or statements;

     d. The full name and address of any other person who was present at the time and place the defendant made such statement or statements;

     e. Whether you or anyone acting on your behalf obtained statements in any form from any persons who claim to be able to testify to the statement or statements made by the defendant.

ANSWER: See answer to question 15 above.

17. If the answer to paragraph e above is in the affirmative, then state

     a. The names and addresses of the persons from whom any such statements were taken;

     b. The date on which said statements were taken;

     c. The names and addresses of the employers of the persons who took such statements;

     d. The names and addresses of the persons having custody of such statements;

     e. Whether such statements were written, oral, by recording device, by court reporter, or by stenographer.

ANSWER: See answer to question 15 above.

18. State whether you, your attorney, your insurance carrier, or anyone acting on your or their behalf obtained statements in any form from any persons regarding any of the events or happenings that occurred at the scene of the incident referred to in the complaint immediately before, at the time of, or immediately after said incident. If so, state

     a. The name and address of the person from whom any such statements were taken;

     b. The dates when such statements were taken;

     c. The names and addresses of the persons and employers of such persons who took such statements;

     d. The names and addresses of the persons having custody of such statements;

     e. Whether such statements were written, by recording device, by court reporter, or by stenographer.

ANSWER: Other than the information provided in answer to question 15, no such statements have been obtained.

19. State the names and addresses of any and all proposed expert witnesses, and the technical field in which you claim they are an expert.

ANSWER: Unknown at this time; information will be provided on determination.

20. Do you intend to rely on any medical text in your cross-examination of this Defendant's medical experts? If so, state

     a. The exact title of each medical text on which you intend to rely;

     b. The name and address of the publisher of each such medical text;

     c. The date when each such medical text was published;

     d. The name of the author of each such medical text.

ANSWER: Unknown at this time; information will be provided on determination.

Note that for ease of reading the questions are repeated verbatim as they were in the defendant's document. These responses are accom-

Exhibit 5.5 Sample Sworn Statement That Accompanies Interrogatory

---

STATE OF ILLINOIS ⎤
                  ⎥ SS
COUNTY OF McLEAN ⎦

EMMA MURPHY RENSLOW, having first been duly sworn, de-
poses and states that she has read the foregoing Answers to Interrogatories by her subscribed, both individually and on behalf of the
minor Plaintiff, LEAH ANN RENSLOW, and that the answers contained herein are true and correct to the best of her information,
knowledge, and belief.

_____

EMMA MURPHY RENSLOW, in-
dividually and as mother and
next friend of LEAH ANN REN-
SLOW, a minor

Subscribed and sworn to before me this _____ day of May,
1975.

_____

Notary Public

ROBERT C. STRODEL
LAW OFFICES OF STRODEL & KINGERY, ASSOC.
900 First National Bank Building
Peoria, Illinois 61602
Phone: (309) 676-3612

---

panied by a sworn statement that the answers provided are true and
correct to the best of the provider's information, knowledge, and belief
(see Exhibit 5.5). When answers to a firm's interrogatories are received
from the other party, the paralegal may help in analyzing and organizing
them.

b. Depositions

Depositions are witness statements taken under oath prior to the
trial itself. They generally are in the same format as a courtroom testimony where one attorney questions the witness and the opposition has
an opportunity to cross-examine. The judge is not present, but a court
reporter administers the oath and records testimony.

Although interrogatories can be directed only at other parties to

the suit, any witness can be deposed. Depositions are used primarily to preserve the testimony of a witness who may not be available for the trial (as in the case of a physician) or when the attorney wants to ensure that the deposing individual's story cannot be changed. Since a person can be subpoenaed to be deposed, a statement may be obtained from a witness unwilling to give another form of statement to the attorney or to an investigator.

The attorney will ask the questions, but the paralegal may be involved in drafting them and analyzing and organizing the answers.

c. Requests for Admissions

Requests for admissions can be directed only at other parties to the suit and are used primarily to establish the genuineness of documents and to eliminate the necessity of proving more routine matters. Aside from preparing a routine request and organizing the answers, the paralegal usually is not involved with requests for admissions.

d. Motions on Documents and Physical Examinations

The motion to produce documents provides access to relevant documentary evidence so that the party requesting the material can inspect and copy the documents. Whereas this procedure is limited to the obtaining of documents in the possession of one of the other parties to the suit, other documents can be obtained through a subpoena *duces tecum* issued at the time of a deposition. The motion for a physical examination is usually used in personal injury cases or other situations where the health of one of the parties is at issue.

e. Enforcing Discovery Rights

Parties in a suit have an obligation to respond to interrogatories and requests for admissions, attend depositions, undergo physical examinations, and produce documents. On the other hand, there are limits to the materials that must be supplied. If the judge can be convinced that discovery attempts have gone beyond the bounds of reasonableness and amount to an undue burden or harassment, a protective order can be issued to allow the party to refuse to comply with certain types of discovery actions.

If one party refuses to respond to certain questions or to supply certain documents, an attorney can seek a court order for compliance. A plaintiff's failure to follow such a court order can be sanctioned by a prohibition against using certain evidence, dismissal of some counts, and on rare occasions a dismissal "with prejudice" of the entire case.[13]

---

13. *Dismissal with prejudice* means that the case cannot be refiled.

4. Pretrial Motions

During the discovery process, both sides are likely to make a variety of motions. The motion to dismiss in Exhibit 5.2 is just one example. If a count of the complaint is dismissed, the plaintiff probably will move to amend the complaint. A motion to quash the summons provides a method for contesting a court's jurisdiction. The defense may also move to require the plaintiff to make its complaint more specific. A motion for judgment on the pleadings is similar to a demurrer because it asserts that even if the facts alleged in the complaint were true, there would be no cause of action present. A motion for summary judgment, on the other hand, asserts that since there are no material facts in dispute, the judge should decide the case without holding a trial.

Other pretrial motions are designed to affect how the trial will be conducted. For example, Renslow's attorney filed a motion *in limine*[14] (Exhibit 5.6) to prevent the defendants' attorneys from disclosing that Leah Ann had been conceived before her parents were married and to disallow anyone other than Dr. Stroink from presenting medical testimony for the defendants. The plaintiff's attorney also filed the motion shown in Exhibit 5.7 requesting that the judge inquire and permit the attorneys to inquire into certain areas during the *voir dire*.[15]

5. Negotiation and Pretrial Conferences

Pretrial conferences are informal sessions in which the opposing attorneys meet (usually in the presence of the judge) to discuss the case before it goes to trial. Such conferences focus on the issues to be presented at the trial and encourage the parties to stipulate to matters that are not being contested. Such conferences make the trial more efficient and encourage out-of-court settlements.

As both sides learn more about the strengths and weaknesses of the case, they are more likely to agree on the probable outcome of a trial and therefore reach a mutually agreeable accommodation. Such accommodations are encouraged because they serve the public interest by easing the pressure on an overburdened court system.

6. The Trial

Trials are the focus of most of the public attention given to the legal system. This is the part of the process that most captures the public's imagination, and climatic courtroom drama has become a staple of motion pictures and television. A trial provides a setting in which charis-

---

14. A motion *in limine* is a motion seeking to prevent reference to specific information in the presence of the jury.

15. The *voir dire* is the portion of the trial during which potential jurors are questioned to determine if they are fit to serve on a case.

Exhibit 5.6 Sample Motion *in Limine*

IN THE CIRCUIT COURT
OF THE ELEVENTH JUDICIAL CIRCUIT OF ILLINOIS
McLEAN COUNTY
TRIAL DIVISION

EMMA M. RENSLOW, individually
and as mother and next friend of
LEAH ANN RENSLOW, a minor,
               Plaintiffs,

v.   AT LAW NO. 75-L-8

MENNONITE HOSPITAL, a corporation,
               Defendant.

MOTION IN LIMINE

Plaintiffs in the above cause, by their attorneys, LAW OFFICES OF STRODEL & KINGERY, ASSOC., move this court to enter a protective order prior to the trial of the above cause as follows:

1. Forbidding the Defendant and/or its counsel from in any manner questioning, commenting, or otherwise disclosing that EMMA MURPHY, now known as EMMA MURPHY RENSLOW, was, in fact, pregnant with LEAH ANN RENSLOW prior to the time of her marriage to STEVEN RENSLOW.

2. Forbidding the Defendant and/or its counsel from offering the expert testimony of any persons other than HANS STROINK, M.D., by virtue of the answer of Defendant's counsel in the attached letter of May 15, 1978, that the only professional person to be called as a witness would be DR. STROINK.

3. Directing Defendant and/or Defendant's counsel to refrain from asking any questions of any witness at the trial of this cause pertaining to possible Rh blood factor sensitization of EMMA MURPHY RENSLOW, other than the infusion of Rh-positive blood, unless such questioning is, in fact, supported by competent medical testimony that such Rh sensitization could or might occur to a reasonable degree of medical certainty other than by the blood infusion claimed to have been given the Plaintiff by Defendant Hospital in October 1965.

                                 EMMA M. RENSLOW, individu-
                                 ally and as mother and next
                                 friend of LEAH ANN RENSLOW,
                                 a minor,

                                             Plaintiffs,

                           By: _____
                                 One of Their Attorneys

ROBERT C. STRODEL
LAW OFFICES OF STRODEL & KINGERY, ASSOC.
900 First National Bank Building
Peoria, Illinois 61602
Phone: (309) 676-3612

Exhibit 5.7 Sample Motion Regarding Jury Selection

IN THE CIRCUIT COURT
OF THE ELEVENTH JUDICIAL CIRCUIT OF ILLINOIS
McLEAN COUNTY
TRIAL DIVISION

EMMA M. RENSLOW, individually
and as mother and next friend of
LEAH ANN RENSLOW, a minor,
Plaintiffs,

v. ———— AT LAW NO. 75-L-8

MENNONITE HOSPITAL, a corporation,
Defendant.

MOTION REGARDING JURY *VOIR DIRE*

The Plaintiffs in the above cause, by their attorneys, LAW OF-
FICES OF STRODEL & KINGERY, ASSOC., state to the Court that:

1. There has been extensive newspaper, newsmagazine, radio
news reporting, television news reporting and special events programming, legislative debate, together with public forum discussion of what has generally been termed to be a "malpractice crisis"
in the United States and expressly including Illinois.

2. Extensive paid advertising in news media by the American
Medical Association and its state subsidiaries, expressly including
Illinois, has steadfastly concentrated a campaign well calculated to
mold public opinion against holding physicians, hospitals, and
other health-care providers to the same standards of accountability
in tort as other segments of society.

(a) Extensive legislative lobbying in all fifty (50) states, including Illinois, has sought limitations on recovery, attempts to make
new public policy regarding attorneys' fees, and other matters
germane to medical negligence litigation.

3. Because of the enormity of public issue emphasis of problems
relevant to medical malpractice, it is paramount within the framework of the concept of a "fair trial" that both Court and counsel
inquire in depth of prospective jurors beyond the normal course of
inquiry in existing tort litigation.

4. With the advent of Supreme Court Rule 234, broad discretion
is placed in a trial judge to determine and limit the extent to which
attorneys will be allowed *voir dire* examination, in addition to such
examination as may be initiated by the Court. Unless such examination in malpractice litigation is extensive and probing by both
Court and counsel, it becomes increasingly improbable that a
plaintiff in a malpractice case can, in fact, obtain a fair trial by an
impartial jury. Accordingly, *Plaintiff requests this court to inquire*

on its own motion under Rule 234, and to permit counsel for both parties extensive supplemental inquiry relevant to the following specific questions:

(a) Are any prospective jurors, their relatives, close friends, or business associates *employed*

(1) By a physician, chiropractor, osteopathic physician, dentist, or other practitioner of the healing arts?

(2) By any hospital in any capacity whether medical, paramedical, or administrative?

(3) By any nursing home or similar care facility in any capacity whether medical or administrative?

(4) As a nurse, nurse's aid, licensed practical nurse, or orderly by any hospital, clinic, physician's office, dental office, or any other practitioner of the healing arts?

(5) As a medical technician, laboratory technician, blood bank technician, therapist, x-ray technician, or any other paramedical occupation allied with the healing arts?

(b) Do any prospective jurors, members of their families, close friends, or business associates suffer from any chronic or disabling illness that requires regular or periodic medical care, examination, treatment, or therapy of any kind?

---

matic attorneys can display their eloquence and cunning. It also is an ordeal that is suppose to uncover the truth and produce just results.

Although a majority of the suits filed never reach the trial stage, the results of those that are tried influence the results of future settlements in similar cases. In personal injury cases, for example, companies compile and publish reports of recently decided cases in different areas of the country. Knowledge of the amount of damages being awarded in various types of cases strongly influences the terms for which parties are willing to settle out of court.

a. The Right to a Jury Trial

The use of juries in our legal system is a product of our English common law heritage. The system originated as a means of limiting the powers of the English monarchy and safeguarding citizens against corrupt or biased judges and prosecutors. Use of the jury system is most strongly entrenched in criminal cases, but it continues to play an important role in civil cases as well.

The seventh amendment to the U.S. Constitution states that the right to a trial by jury shall be preserved in suits at common law where the value in the controversy exceeds $20. Although a literal reading of the amendment (emphasizing the word *preserve*) limits the constitutional right to a jury trial to actions that were tried by a jury in 1791, in conjunction with the Federal Rules and precedent cases the right to a

jury trial now extends to most types of federal civil cases.[16] Exceptions include admiralty and maritime cases, certain types of immigration and naturalization cases, suits under some workers' compensation acts, and suits to enforce claims against the United States. Because there is no federal right to a jury in civil cases tried in state courts, each state has defined for itself the extent to which juries are to be available at that level. Although usually not available in divorce and probate cases, jury trials usually are provided for, by either statute or constitution, in contractual and tort matters exceeding some dollar limit.

The basic function of the jury is to resolve the factual (as opposed to the legal) questions raised in the case. Generally this comes down to deciding how much credibility to give to the often conflicting testimony of various witnesses. When damage awards are called for, the jury must make the subjective determination of how to measure pain and suffering in terms of dollars and cents.

In cases where the use of a jury is not provided for, or where it has been waived by all parties, the judge takes over the jury's function in addition to his or her normal duties of presiding over the trial and resolving the legal questions raised.

Finally, a word about the number of people on a jury. Under the common law a jury consisted of twelve people. However, the courts have ruled that there is nothing that is constitutionally significant about that number, and six-person juries have been used in civil cases at both the federal and the state levels. Furthermore, it is not unusual to select one or two extra jurors as alternates (especially where the trial is expected to last for more than a few days). These alternatives sit in the jury box with their colleagues throughout the entire trial and are used as substitutes if one of the regular jurors is unable to continue for some reason. They do not participate in the deliberations, however, unless they have replaced one of the original jurors.

b. Jury Selection

If a jury is being used, the first formal step in the trial process is the selection of the individual jurors to be used in that case. This *voir dire* process marks the start of the trial, but jury selection usually started many months before that date when a computer randomly selected names off a list of registered voters.[17] Once these names have been selected, the individuals chosen are screened by a jury commission to determine whether they are eligible to serve as jurors. Most states have statutory exemptions for various occupational groups such as government officials, attorneys, physicians, clergymen, police, firefighters, and

---

16. See 28R U.S.C. Rule 2 and Ross v. Bernhard, 396 U.S. 531 (1970).
17. The manner in which jury pools are selected varies, but the description given here is representative of the most commonly used procedures.

others. Although local practice varies widely, people may be excused from jury service if they are in bad health, if service creates a hardship for their employer, or if they have small children. Those who pass this screening process then have their names placed on a list of people eligible to be called for jury service.

Judges schedule their jury trials during an agreed on time period (usually referred to as a jury calendar) so that the jury commission officials can plan to have a pool of qualified jurors available at that time. An appropriate number of eligible jurors then are subpoenaed to report to the courthouse on a particular day or every day during a particular week.

When they arrive at the courthouse, the jurors usually assemble in a special lounge area from which they are then directed to specific courtrooms as they are needed. A random drawing usually is used to determine which jurors are to be assigned to which cases.

The *voir dire* itself consists of the questioning of potential jurors to determine whether they are fit to serve on the jury for that specific case. Although the person has been cleared by the jury commission as being capable of serving on a jury, there may be something about a particular person that disqualifies him or her from serving on a specific case. For example, a potential juror would be disqualified if he or she had some personal relationship with one of the parties in the case or with one of the attorneys involved. If the person was an executive in a big automobile insurance company, that individual would be qualified to sit on a criminal jury but probably would not be allowed to serve on a jury involving a tort claim involving an automobile accident. Individuals also may be disqualified if they had been exposed to a great deal of prejudicial publicity about the trial or have been involved in a similar law suit themselves.

The specific process used in *voir dire* varies from state to state and even from judge to judge. The judge usually begins by asking general questions about the person's occupation, family, and possible relationship to anyone involved in the case. When pretrial publicity has been extensive, the judge may question the jurors about what they remember from the media accounts and most important whether they think they can lay aside any opinions they may have formed and be able to decide the case solely on the merits of what is presented in the courtroom. In some jurisdictions the lawyers are given a chance to ask their own questions after the judge is finished, while in others they are limited to submitting questions for the judge to ask. Most attorneys prefer to be able to question the jurors personally because they see it as an opportunity to begin to establish a rapport with them and to indoctrinate them to their view of the case.

Attorneys use two types of challenges when seeking to prevent specific individuals from serving on the jury in their case. The first line of

attack is usually the use of a challenge for cause. To exercise this challenge the attorney must convince the judge that something about the juror's background or the answers that were given demonstrates that the person has some sort of a bias. If the judge agrees, the person will not be seated. There is no limit on the number of such challenges that can be raised or granted. In some well-publicized and highly controversial cases, attorneys have gone through hundreds of jurors before being able to arrive at the final twelve.

Attorneys can also exercise peremptory challenges. These allow an attorney to have a potential juror removed without giving a reason for the dismissal. Such peremptory challenges are automatic but limited in number. In deciding whether one of these valuable peremptory challenges should be used on a questionable juror, attorneys must weigh the risk of having to accept a worse juror later because their limited supply of challenges was exhausted.

If a potential juror is excused as either the result of a challenge for cause or a peremptory challenge, that individual is usually returned to the jury lounge for reassignment on another case. The jurors who were found to be acceptable are then seated in the jury box and are officially sworn in.

c. Opening Statements

Each attorney is given an opportunity to address the jury in an opening statement. These presentations are designed to present the plaintiff's and the defendant's respective theories of their cases. In other words, the attorney states what is alleged to have taken place and what various witnesses are expected to testify to. The jury is thus presented with a framework for viewing the upcoming testimony.

The plaintiff's side speaks first. In some cases the defense's opening statement will follow immediately, and at other times it is postponed until the plaintiff's lawyer has finished presenting his or her case and the defense is about to represent its witnesses.

d. Presentation of Evidence

After the opening statements, the plaintiff's evidence is presented. The rules of evidence determine what can be admitted for legitimate consideration and the manner in which witnesses can be questioned.

Evidence, in the general sense, is information. It can be in the form of testimony, documents, or physical objects. When a judge rules that something is admissible evidence, he or she is permitting that piece of evidence to be presented as proof of some fact involved in the lawsuit. The judge's decision to admit or not admit evidence involves the application of various established legal principles. The conditions that must be met in order to introduce something into evidence depend to some extent on the particular type of evidence involved, but all types of evidence must be relevant and material.

Relevancy refers to the probative value of the evidence: Does the presentation of this evidence lead one to logically conclude that an asserted fact is either more probable or less probable? Materiality is usually thought of as either a subcategory of relevancy or simply an equivalent. It relates to whether the evidence is part of the specific issues being tried in the case at hand. For example, the fact that a plaintiff suffered an injury in a previous automobile accident would be relevant and material only if the injury had been to the same part of the body injured in the case at hand.[18] Relevancy alone does not ensure admissibility. Thus a gruesome photograph of the condition of the victim of a multilation murder may be relevant yet excluded because of the probability that it would inflame the jury.[19]

In addition to being relevant the evidence must be competent. With respect to oral testimony from witnesses, it must be established that the witness is:

1. *Capable of expressing himself* so as to be understood by the jury (either directly or through an interpreter); and
2. *Capable of understanding the duty to tell the truth;* and
3. *Has personal knowledge and recollection* regarding the particular matter upon which he is called to testify (except where opinion testimony is permissible).[20]

The first two factors usually involve the age or mental condition of the witness. The third involves the meaning of hearsay evidence.

In nontechnical terms, hearsay is in effect rumor or secondhand information. It is "information that has been told to a witness by someone else."[21] For example, imagine a situation in which Doris tells Sue that she saw Bill, the defendant in a divorce suit, check into a motel with his secretary. Sue would not be allowed to testify about what her friend Doris has told her. Sue has no personal knowledge about Bill's roommates. She did not see Bill and his secretary herself.

Under some circumstances hearsay evidence is admitted. These exceptions to the hearsay rule include dying declarations, spontaneous utterances, former testimony, depositions, confessions and admissions, and business records.[22] In all cases, there are three conditions that must be met:

1. Generally, the original declarant must be unavailable to testify;
2. The declaration must be one which sheds some light upon the establishment of the true facts of the case and the information cannot be presented through any other source;

---

18. W. Rutter, Evidence 12 (8th ed. 1973).
19. Id. at 25.
20. Id. at 68.
21. G. Stuckey, Evidence for the Law Enforcement Officer 128 (2d ed. 1974).
22. See id. at 130-149 for brief description of each category.

3. There must be some test of the trustworthiness of the statement in
   lieu of the oath and the right of cross-examination.[23]

It is also essential to always be aware of the differences between
facts and opinions. When a witness testifies that he saw the defendant's
automobile strike the plaintiff's car broadside, he is testifying about a
fact he observed. But when that same witness states that the defendant
was driving too fast for the icy condition of the road, he is stating an
opinion. Sometimes opinion evidence is admissible, and other times it is
not. So-called expert witnesses can give opinion evidence in situations
where lay witnesses cannot.

Lay witnesses (regular witnesses who have not been shown to have
any special expertise) can give opinions on such subjects as the speed of
moving vehicles, the similarity of a person's voice or handwriting to that
of someone's voice or handwriting with which they are familiar, and
whether or not a person is angry or intoxicated. In order to be allowed to
venture such opinions, the trial judge must be satisfied that:

1. The witness personally observed or perceived that upon which he
   renders an opinion;
2. The matter must be one about which normal persons regularly
   form opinions (speed, size, sound, color, etc.); and
3. Giving an opinion is the best way of getting the matter to the jury
   . . . i.e., the facts upon which the opinion rests are not as meaningful as the opinion itself.[24]

An expert witness is "a person who possesses skill and knowledge in
some art, trade, science, or profession that is beyond and above that of
the *average* man."[25] While jurors are usually impressed by the amount of
formal education a witness has and are especially impressed when the
witness has authored books or articles on the subject, formal education
itself is not a requirement for being an expert witness.[26] There has been
at least one occasion when a burglar was taken from the penitentiary to
act in court as an expert witness on techniques for breaking and entering. The expert witness can testify as to his or her opinion, however, only
when it falls within the area of the witness's established expertise and
goes beyond the knowledge of the common man or woman. If the expert
witness has personal knowledge of the facts on which the opinion is
based (as in the case of a physician who has treated an injury personally),
he or she can testify about that opinion directly. If the expert has no such
personal knowledge (as in the case of a physician who did not treat an
injury personally but is called to give an expert opinion on this injury's

23. Id. at 129.
24. Rutter, Evidence, at 72.
25. A. Golec, Techniques of Legal Investigation 53 (1976).
26. F. Bailey and H. Rothblatt, Fundamentals of Criminal Advocacy 123 (1974).

ramifications), the attorneys must present the witness with a series of hypothetical questions. These hypotheticals ask the witness to express an opinion on the basis of the information provided by the attorney during the questioning.

With testimonial evidence the judge or jury must rely on the descriptions and reports given by other people. In the case of real evidence (also referred to as physical or demonstrative evidence) the judge or jury is presented with tangible objects that speak for themselves. These tangible objects may be clothes, weapons, photographs, tape recordings, maps, and so forth. In a personal injury suit brought because the plaintiff has been paralyzed, for example, the plaintiff's lawyer may show a "one day in the life of . . . " type of movie in order to make the jury more aware of the full implications of the plaintiff's injuries.

Before such real evidence can be admitted, it must be shown to be relevant and to be properly authenticated. For example, it is necessary to establish that the victim bled before the bloodstained clothes found in the defendant's apartment can be introduced into evidence. It is also necessary to establish that the bloodstained clothes being presented were in fact the same ones that were found in the defendant's apartment and that they are in the same condition as when they were found.[27]

In order to properly authenticate such physical evidence the investigator should (1) keep the object in his or her exclusive personal control from the time it is found until the time it is presented in court, (2) maintain a complete record of everyone involved in the chain-of-possession (that is, everyone who handled it from the time it was found to the time it was presented in court), or (3) mark the object in a way that will make it easily distinguishable at a later time.[28]

The rules governing the authentication of photographs differ from one jurisdiction to the next. Most courts simply require that a witness who is familiar with an object or scene in the photograph testify that it is an accurate representation of that object or scene as it appeared at the time of the incident. On the other hand, a few courts require that the person who actually took the photograph testify about the type of camera and the settings used. Some require testimony relating to the developing process and the chain-of-possession.[29]

Written documents must also be relevant and authentic. According to the best evidence rule the original document itself usually must be produced at the trial. Proper testimony must establish that the document

---

27. The record of who had possession of the evidence prior to the trial is referred to as the "chain of custody." Under some circumstances the evidence can be admitted even when its condition has changed. For example, if some of the blood is removed for purposes of laboratory analysis, the bloodstained clothes still can be introduced if evidence is given as to what changed and why.
28. Stuckey, Evidence for the Law Enforcement Officer, at 210.
29. Rutter, Evidence, at 25.

presented is in fact what it is purported to be. Under some circumstances, however, a copy may be considered admissible. Public records (official governmental documents as well as private deeds and mortgages that are officially recorded with the government) can be presented through the use of certified copies. In addition to presenting a copy showing an official seal and signature, an affidavit from the record's custodian usually is presented explaining what the record shows and attesting that it is an accurate copy of the one on file.[30] Copies of private papers may be allowed when the original has been lost or destroyed, is in the hands of an adverse party who has refused to produce it, or in the hands of a third party who is outside the jurisdiction of the court's subpoena power.[31] In cases where the original is so voluminous that it is impractical to produce it in its entirety, the litigant is allowed to produce a summary.[32]

Before physical and documentary evidence can be introduced, witnesses must be called to lay a proper foundation. In other words, they must give testimony to establish the relevancy and materiality of the evidence as well as to properly identify and authenticate it.

In posing questions to witnesses called on the plaintiff's behalf, the plaintiff's attorney generally is prohibited from asking leading questions. Questions cannot be phrased in such a way as to suggest a desired answer (such as, "Wouldn't you say the defendant appeared to be very angry at that point in time?").

Once the plaintiff's attorney has completed questioning a witness, the defense attorney is given an opportunity to cross-examine that same witness. The cross-examination clarifies any potentially misleading statements or half truths and attacks the credibility of the witness. Therefore, the defense attorney attempts to bring out possible biases or questions the ability of witnesses to see what they claim to have seen. On cross-examination a lawyer is allowed to ask leading questions.

The defendant's cross-examination is then followed by re-direct, where the plaintiff's attorney has the opportunity to ask additional questions of the witness. These re-direct questions are designed to rehabilitate the witness after the defense's attack on the witness's credibility. These questions cannot be used to raise new subjects or to explore topics that were not covered as part of the cross-examination. The re-direct is then followed by an opportunity for a re-cross by the defendant's attorney, but that must in turn be limited to topics raised during the re-direct. At that point the witness is finally excused, and the plaintiff's attorney then procedes to call the next witness.

After all the plaintiff's witnesses have been called and the physical

---

30. Golec, Techniques of Legal Investigation, at 260.
31. Rutter, Evidence, at 115.
32. Id. at 116; Stuckey, Evidence for the Law Enforcement Officer, at 259.

and documentary evidence presented, the defense has the opportunity to present its case. Before this occurs, it is not unusual for the defense attorney to move for a directed verdict. This motion requests that the judge end the trial at that point and find in favor of the defendant on the basis that the plaintiff's side failed to meet its obligation of presenting a *prima facie* case supporting its position. A directed verdict will be entered if the judge concludes that the evidence presented by the plaintiff is so weak that even considered in its most favorable light (without considering any rebuttal evidence from the defendant) it is not sufficient as a matter of law to merit a verdict in the plaintiff's favor.

It is very unusual for a motion for a directed verdict to be accepted at this point in the trial. Typically the motion is denied, and the defense attorney goes on to present his or her witnesses. The same process of direct, cross, re-direct, and re-cross is used, with the defendant's lawyer now prohibited from asking leading questions on direct examination. The defense strategy involves presenting evidence that contradicts evidence presented by the plaintiff and possibly attempting to use one of the legally accepted defenses available for that particular type of case.[33]

Once the defendant's case is complete, the plaintiff can ask for a directed verdict on the basis that even if the defendant's evidence is taken in its most favorable light, it would be insufficient to rebut the plaintiff's case. If, as is usually the case, this motion is also denied, the plaintiff then has an opportunity to present witnesses who will attempt to rebut testimony and evidence presented by the defense. After that, either side can once again move for a directed verdict.

e. Closing Arguments

Perhaps the most dramatic part of any trial is the closing arguments. Here the attorneys are given the opportunity to review and interpret the evidence in its most favorable light and develop emotional appeals. It represents their final chance to persuade the jury. Although both the plaintiff and the defendant receive equal time, the plaintiff has the advantage of being able to split the time and speak both first and last. The plaintiff is given this supposed advantage because the plaintiff also has the burden of proof to overcome.

f. Jury Instructions

Before sending the jury members out to deliberate, it is the judge's responsibility to see that they are properly instructed about the nature of their duties and the requirements of the law. The jury's duty is to determine the facts and then apply the requirements of the law to those facts. However, the jury is composed of a group of lay persons who do not

---

33. See the discussion on tort and contract defenses on pages 127, 129, 134.

know what the law requires. Therefore, it becomes the duty of the judge
to explain the law in terms that the jury will be able to understand.

Rather than start from scratch and risk reversal for failure to include some key element or to explain some concept in a misleading way,
judges tend to rely on pattern jury instructions. These are collections of
instructions that have already been tested on appeal in other cases. Furthermore, the attorneys in the case have the opportunity to submit instructions they would like to see included. The judge then reviews their
submissions and often discusses the issues with the attorneys in chambers
before deciding which instructions to give at the trial.

g. Jury Deliberations, Verdict, and Judgment

Once they have been properly instructed, the jurors retire to a
special room where they are kept isolated while they deliberate over their
verdict. Their first task is always to select one of their number to act as
the foreman. The person selected becomes the official spokesperson for
the jury and the one who sends messages to the judge and delivers the
verdict.

The actual deliberations take place in secrecy. No one, other than
the jurors themselves, is allowed in the room. Not even the bailiffs who
are responsible for looking after the jury are allowed to be present during the actual deliberations. By a series of discussions and votes, the
deliberations go on until either a verdict has been reached or the judge
declares a mistrial. In most cases the jurors must come to unanimous
agreement regarding the verdict, although some states have provisions
for less than unanimous verdicts in certain types of cases.

If the case involves a possible damage award, the jury must then
consider the proper amount to award as either compensatory or punitive
damages.[34] In most cases evidence is presented at the trial regarding
both the question of liability and damages. In those cases the jurors
consider the amount of damages as soon as they decide that damages are
in fact owed. In some cases, however, a bifurcated trial is held. Testimony regarding liability is allowed during the first phase of the trial,
and the jury is sent out to deliberate on that issue alone. If the defendant
is found guilty, the trial enters a second stage where evidence is given
about the nature of the damages, followed in turn by another jury delib-
eration session focused on the damage issue.

After the deliberations are complete, the jury files back into the
courtroom and the foreman either reads the verdicts aloud or hands a
piece of paper to the clerk for the judge or the clerk to read aloud. The
judge then checks with the other jurors to ensure that the verdict read
was indeed what they had agreed to.

In bench trials (cases without a jury) the judge usually recesses and

---

34. See the discussion on damages at page 131.

announces the verdict at a later date rather then giving it immediately. This happens when the case is relatively complex and the judge wishes to review some of the evidence and some interpretations of the law.

The judgment is the court's official statement regarding the rights and obligations of the parties involved in the case. A formal judgment must be entered into the record by the clerk in order for the plaintiff to use the power of the state to enforce those rights. For example, if the defendant fails to pay damages that were part of the judgment, the plaintiff can get a writ of execution that instructs the sheriff to seize the defendant's property, sell it at public auction, and then use the proceeds to pay the plaintiff. Such a writ also would authorize garnishing the defendant's wages or attaching his or her bank accounts. The judgment usually is entered in such a way that it becomes effective automatically if no appeal is taken within a specified period of time. If appeals are taken, the judgment is stayed until the appeals are exhausted.

h. Posttrial Motions

After the verdict has been announced, the losing party has a certain time period within which to file posttrial motions. The most common of these motions are a motion for judgment notwithstanding the verdict and a motion for a new trial. The motion for a judgment notwithstanding the verdict (also known as judgment *non obstante veredicto* and judgment N.O.V.) is a request to the judge to reverse the jury's decision on the basis that the evidence was legally insufficient to support its verdict.

The motion for a new trial is usually based on the assertion that some procedural error has tainted the outcome. For example, it might be argued that some piece of evidence was admitted that should not have been admitted or that someone made improper contacts with a juror on the case.

Both motions are frequently made but seldom granted. Nevertheless, they are important because they may be necessary to preserve the client's right to appeal to a higher court. The doctrine of exhaustion requires that the trial court be given every possible opportunity to correct its own errors before the appellate courts intervene.

7. Appeals

"I'll take my case all the way to the Supreme Court" is a battle cry that has been echoed by many concerned litigants. It recognizes the possibility that an initial decision might not be satisfactory and represents a commitment to take the cause to a higher authority. Attorneys do not like to lose a case, and the appeal represents a possible vindication for them. There are few attorneys who have not dreamed of arguing a case before the United States Supreme Court.

On the other hand, appeals consume time and money. The client's

initial desire for appeal often pales because of costs. Additionally, the
option to appeal may either be very limited or even nonexistent. Although almost everyone has the right to one appeal, the nature of the
issues considered in that appeal may be narrow in scope and subsequent
appeals are usually at the discretion of the reviewing court.

a. The Timing of the Appeal

A case cannot be appealed until posttrial motions have been acted
on and the final judgment has been entered. This gives the trial court a
chance to correct its own errors and possibly avoid the need for an
appeal. The party wishing to have the case reviewed by the appellate
courts must file a notice of appeal within a specified time period after the
final judgment is entered. In the federal court system this notice must be
filed within thirty days.[35] Although federal rules do allow for a thirty-
day extension on a showing of excusable neglect, these time limits are
strictly followed.[36] If the notice is not filed within the proper time limits
in a civil case, the federal appellate courts will refuse to hear it.[37] Most
states are equally strict about the enforcement of their time limits.

These practices may appear to be arbitrary or overly restrictive, but
they are necessary for the orderly administration of justice. To allow for
the execution of the judgment, the issue of the finality of the decision
must be determined as soon as possible. It is also important that the
appeal take place while the record is readily available. Since a transcript
of the proceedings is not ordinarily made until the appeal is filed, delay
could result in loss of the reporter's notes or problems in translating
them. In a few situations the appellate courts will review a specific action
of a trial court before an actual trial even takes place — for example,
when a temporary injunction[38] or an order quashing a subpoena[39] was
being appealed.

b. The Scope of the Review

When an appellate court considers a case, it does not conduct a new
trial. It simply reviews the official record of the proceedings at the trial
court. Moreover, it limits its review to specific appealable issues. To meet
the requirements of an appealable issue the party appealing the case
must have laid a proper foundation at the trial level.

---

35. A party has sixty days to file the notice of appeal when the United States government is
    one of the parties. See section 4 of the Federal Rules of Appellate Procedure.
36. Federal Rules of Appellate Practice 4(a).
37. Pittsburgh Towing Co. v. Mississippi Valley Barge Line Co., 385 U.S. 32 (1966);
    Dyotherm Corp. v. Turbo Machine Co., 434 F.2d 65 (3d Cir. 1970).
38. A temporary injunction — or temporary restraining order, as it also is called — is an
    emergency remedy of brief duration that is in effect only until the court has time to
    hear evidence and reach a decision on the merits of the case.
39. The decision of a court to vacate or overturn a subpoena would mean, for example,
    that someone originally ordered to appear as a witness or to produce some evidence
    does not have to do so.

In addition to generally refusing to consider a case until after the final judgment has been entered, appellate courts usually require that the attorney have raised the appropriate objections at the proper point in the trial. In other words, the attorney cannot complain later to the appellate judges about something that was not complained about at the proper time to the trial judge.

This requirement for a proper foundation places additional pressures on the trial attorney. A careless or incompetent attorney can destroy the client's chances for a successful appeal and at the same time destroy the client's chance to win at the trial level. Attorneys will make objections for the record even when they do not expect the trial judge to accept them. This is sometimes called protecting the record, or making a record for appeal.

In reviewing a case appellate courts are supposed to consider only legal issues. (Legal issues involve interpretation and application of the law; factual issues involve the determination of whether a given event took place in a particular way.) In practice, however, the fact/law distinction tends to break down, and the resolution of a legal issue sometimes can require the court to review the facts.

Cases in which the appellate court must review a trial judge's interpretation of a statute or legal document such as a will or a lease offer examples of legal issues. Similarly, questions about the nature of the jury instructions or a decision on admissibility of evidence also present legal issues. Take, however, a party's appeal on the trial judge's decision to deny a motion for a directed verdict. In effect the appellant[40] is arguing that the evidence was so one-sided that it could support only one conclusion. Therefore, it is argued that the trial judge should have directed the jury to return a given verdict rather than given them the choice of deliberating on several alternatives. Since it is a ruling on a motion, it is a legal question, but to reach a decision the appellate court must make a judgment about the strength of the evidence itself.

The appellate court can be drawn into similar evaluations of the facts in circumstances involving motions for judgment notwithstanding the verdict and motions for a new trial. It should be noted, however, that when the appellate courts review the facts, they do so on a limited basis. Conflicts in the testimony and questions of credibility of the witnesses will be resolved in favor of the trial judge's position. Only where there is a lack of admissible evidence or where the trial judge's decision was clearly erroneous will the appellate courts reverse.

If the appellate court decides that the trial judge made a legal error, it must determine whether that error was prejudicial or merely harmless. Errors are defined as prejudicial when they likely affected the results. Harmless errors are classed as so minor and peripheral that they have no

---

40. The appellant is the party appealing the decision from the lower court. The party defending the lower court's decision is the appellee.

significant effect on the outcome. Only prejudicial errors are considered
to be reversible errors.

Errors in the pleadings are usually considered to be harmless because the true facts can be emphasized at the trial. Errors in jury instructions are considered reversible only when there is reason to believe that
the jury may have been misled by them. It is also generally assumed that
a judge presiding at a bench trial is less likely to be affected by incompetent evidence than a jury exposed to the same incompetent evidence.

In another aspect of the reversible error, the attorney who appeals
cannot be responsible for the error that is being appealed. In other
words, the appellant cannot complain about the admission of inflamma-
tory evidence if the appellant's attorney was the one who introduced it.[41]

c. Filing the Appeal

Exhibit 5.8 presents an example of a notice of appeal. The notice
must be written and must contain specific information, but no special
format is required. It is filed in the trial court that rendered the decision
being appealed.

As soon as the notice of appeal has been filed, paralegals or other
personnel from the office of the appellant's attorney must contact the
court reporter and the court clerk to order appropriate portions of the
official record. The court reporter is then instructed to prepare a written
transcript of either the entire trial or selected portions of the trial,[42] and
the court clerk is asked to prepare copies of various official court records
relating to the case. This request is often referred to as a *praecipe*[43] for
record. Exhibit 5.9 shows a commonly used format for this request. The
specific records ordered will depend on the nature of the case and the
specific rules of the appellate court.

Either the paralegal or some other representative of the firm must,
on behalf of the client, pay a filing fee with the appellate court and quite
possibly file one or more bonds. In the federal courts, for example, the
appellant must post a bond to secure payment of the costs on appeal. If
the appellant wants to stay the judgment pending the outcome of the
appeal, a *supersedeas* bond must be filed in the trial court.[44]

---

41. An exception to this principle could occur in a criminal case where a different attorney is handling the appeal and is charging that the trial attorney's performance was
incompetent.

42. Federal rules provide that "Unless the entire transcript is to be included, the appellant
shall within the time above provided, file and serve upon the appellee a description of
the parts of the transcript which he intends to include in the record and a statement of
the issues he intends to present on the appeal." Federal Rules of Appellate Procedure
10(b). The appellee can then order additional sections.

43. A *praecipe* is a formal request that the clerk take some action. Unlike a motion, it does
not require a judge's approval.

44. When the court stays a judgment, it permits the party who owed the judgment to
withhold paying it until the appellate court has had an opportunity to review it. The
bond provides a guarantee to the person to whom the judgment is owed that the
money (plus interest) will be paid if either the appeal is dismissed or the judgment is
affirmed.

Exhibit 5.8 Sample Notice of Appeal

APPEAL TO THE APPELLATE COURT OF ILLINOIS
FOURTH DISTRICT
From the Circuit Court of the Eleventh Judicial Circuit,
McLean County

EMMA M. RENSLOW, individually and as mother
and next friend of LEAH ANN
RENSLOW, a minor,

Plaintiffs,

v.

MENNONITE HOSPITAL, a corporation, and HANS STROINK, M.D.,

Defendants.

AT LAW NO.
75-L-8

NOTICE OF APPEAL

EMMA M. RENSLOW, as mother and next friend of LEAH ANN
RENSLOW, a minor, hereby appeals to the Appellate Court of Illinois, Fourth District, from the Order of the Trial Court entered in
this cause on June 4, 1975, supplementing a previous Order of said
Court dated May 5, 1975, dismissing Counts VI through X of the
original Complaint filed herein, and requests the Appellate Court to
reverse the decision of the Trial Court and direct the Trial Court to
sustain the Complaint as to Counts VI through X, and overrule or
deny the Motion of the Defendants to Dismiss the original Complaint, Counts VI through X.

EMMA M. RENSLOW, in-
dividually and as mother
and next friend of LEAH
ANN RENSLOW, a minor,
Plaintiffs

By: _____
One of Their Attorneys

ROBERT C. STRODEL
LAW OFFICES OF STRODEL & KINGERY, ASSOC.
900 First National Bank Building
Peoria, Illinois 61602
Phone: (309) 676-3612

APPEAL TO THE APPELLATE COURT OF ILLINOIS
FOURTH DISTRICT
From the Circuit Court of the Eleventh Judicial Circuit,
McLean County

EMMA M. RENSLOW, individually and as mother
and next friend of LEAH ANN
RENSLOW, a minor,

Plaintiffs,

v.

MENNONITE HOSPITAL, a corporation, and HANS STROINK, M.D.,

Defendants.

AT LAW NO.
75-L-8

PRAECIPE FOR RECORD

TO: The Circuit Clerk of McLean County, Illinois
McLean County Court House
Bloomington, Illinois

You are hereby requested to prepare and make up a complete transcript of the record in your court in the above-entitled cause as to Counts VI through X inclusive to be used on Appeal to the Appellate Court of Illinois, Fourth District, including a *placita* for each term of court, all pleadings, all Orders, all papers of record, the Notice of Appeal and Proof of Service thereof, this *Praecipe* and Proof of Service thereof, and all Motions, Orders, and stipulations that may have been made relative to the preparation of said record, together with your certificate that the same is a complete transcript of all proceedings had in your court in said cause.

DATED this first day of July, 1975.

LAW OFFICES OF STRODEL &
KINGERY, ASSOC.

By: _____
ROBERT C. STRODEL

ROBERT C. STRODEL
LAW OFFICES OF STRODEL & KINGERY, ASSOC.
900 First National Bank Building
Peoria, Illinois 61602
Phone: (309) 676-3612

Within a specified time period from the filing of the notice of appeal, the appellant must file a brief. The brief explains the facts of the case, lists the relevant statutes and court cases, and then presents legal arguments that support overturning the lower court's decision.[45]

Within another specified time period the other side must file a brief that presents the appellee's version of the facts, relevant statutes and cases, and legal arguments that favor upholding the lower court decision. It is interesting to note that the lower court judge who made the decision plays no part in this appeal process and cannot present his or her own brief in defense of the contested decision.

After the appellee's brief has been filed, the appellant can file a reply brief that attempts to respond to the appellee's argument and to any new authorities that may have been introduced. The appellee can file a reply brief only in situations where a cross-appeal is involved.[46]

d. Oral Arguments

Depending once again on the rules of the particular court and sometimes at the discretion of the appellate judges, the court may hear oral arguments on appeal. When oral arguments are held, each side's attorneys have an opportunity to make a verbal presentation of their side's position. During these presentations, the judges will usually interrupt with their own questions. These questions probe weak points in the argument and explore the implications of particular lines of reasoning.

e. The Decision and Its Publication

With or without the benefit of oral argument, the judges study the matter for an indefinite period of time until they reach a decision by majority vote. The case then usually is assigned to one of the judges in the majority to prepare the official opinion of the court. The judge's law clerks check the authorities cited in the briefs and sometimes find additional cases that apply. The clerks typically prepare rough drafts of the opinions for the judges to edit and polish. Other judges on the court have the right to prepare either dissenting or concurring opinions if they want the record to reflect their differences.[47] These opinions are then published in the appropriate reporters.[48]

The decision usually involves either affirming the lower court's action or returning (remanding) the case to the lower court for reconsideration. If the nature of the case is such that a new trial is not required to

---

45. See pages 379-397 in Chapter 9 for an explanation of the content and format of appellate briefs.
46. A cross-appeal occurs when both sides are appealing different aspects of the lower court's decision.
47. In a concurring opinion the writer agrees with the outcome but disagrees with part of the reasoning in the opinion of the court. In a dissenting opinion the writer disagrees with both the outcome and the reasoning.
48. See discussion on reporters in Chapter 3 at page 63.

supplement the factual record, the judges may simply enter a final judg-
~~ment on the basis of the existing record.~~

f. Further Appeals

Depending on the court structure and the nature of the case, the
party that loses at the appellate level (regardless of which party lost at the
trial court level) often has the option of appealing to yet a higher level
appellate court. Frequently such higher appeals are discretionary rather
than a matter of right: The judges on the appellate court choose to hear
only the cases that they believe to have the greatest judicial significance.
If the appeal to the higher court is accepted, new briefs are filed, and the
process described above begins all over again.

B. CRIMINAL PROCEDURE

Figure 5.2 presents the major stages in a criminal prosecution.
Although the details of criminal procedure vary among jurisdictions, this
diagram should help the reader understand how the various stages discussed in this section are related.

1. Investigation and Arrest

The criminal process usually begins when a law enforcement
officer (such as police officer, sheriff, FBI agent, or state trooper) learns
that a crime has been committed. Either the officer personally observes
the crime being committed, or the officer is sent to investigate a crime
that either the victim or a witness has reported.

When the officer actually observes the crime being committed (for
example, finding a burglar in a warehouse or operating a speed trap),
the officer can arrest the wrongdoer on the spot based on personal
knowledge of evidence that is sufficient to establish the probable cause
needed for an arrest.[49] Even where the police do not personally see a
crime take place, they can still make an arrest if, on the basis of information given them by witnesses or other police, they have probable cause to
believe that the person they are arresting committed a crime.

Alternatively, but much less frequently, police will take their information to prosecutors, who in turn may take the matter to a grand jury
or to a judge. The operation of the grand jury is discussed in more detail
later in this chapter. At this point it is sufficient to point out that if the
grand jury believes there is probable cause to believe that a specific

---

49. Probable cause is usually interpreted to mean that the available knowledge about the
    facts and circumstances should lead a reasonable person to conclude that the suspect
    probably committed the crime.

Figure 5.2 Criminal Procedure

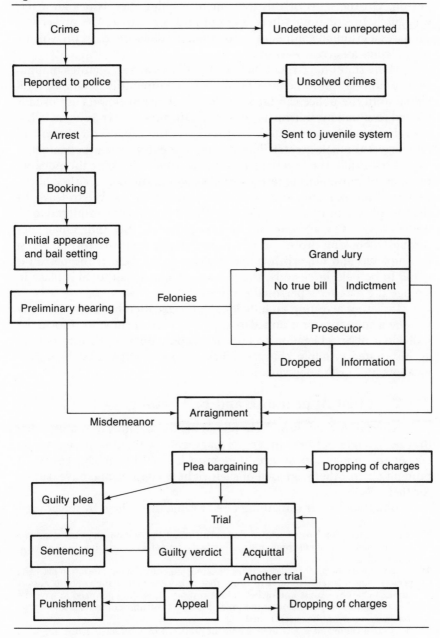

individual has committed a crime, it returns an indictment[50] against that person. On the basis of this indictment a judge then issues an arrest warrant.[51] In situations where a grand jury is not used, the prosecutor prepares a criminal complaint[52] that then becomes the basis on which a judge issues an arrest warrant.

Many states have retail theft and "citizen's arrest" statutes that authorize non–law enforcement personnel to temporarily detain an individual until the police can take custody. Such arrest powers are usually limited to situations in which the person effecting the arrest actually has seen the crime be committed. Furthermore, the liability for the tort of false arrest is much greater than it is for law enforcement personnel.[53]

Technically the arrest takes place at whatever point the person's freedom of movement is restrained. As soon as the police either physically restrain someone, announce that he or she is not free to leave, or that the person must come with them, that individual is considered to be under arrest. On arriving at the police station, the individual goes through a booking process in which the actual paperwork for the arrest is completed and fingerprints and a picture are taken. If the person is going to be held in custody, the police will also inventory and place in storage the arrestee's personal property.

In lieu of arresting an individual, officials often have the authority to issue a summons or a notice to appear. These documents inform the individual of an obligation to appear in court on a set date to defend against stated criminal charges. They are most often used in misdemeanors and ordinance violations.

2. Initial Appearance and Bail Setting

After individuals have been placed in custody, the law requires that they be brought before a judge (or magistrate) without unnecessary delay. At this initial appearance, they must be told of the charges being brought against them, advised of their right to counsel, and have bail set for them.[54]

Bail is money or something else of value that is held by the govern-

---

50. An indictment is a formal written document issued by a grand jury that accuses a person named therein of committing a specified criminal act or acts. It is also known as a true bill.

51. An arrest warrant is a formal document directing law enforcement officials to place the person named in custody and to bring that individual before the court to answer criminal charges against him or her. The arresting officer does not need to have the document itself in possession at the time of arrest. It is sufficient to have knowledge that such a warrant has been issued.

52. A criminal complaint is a written statement prepared by a prosecutor that accuses a person named therein of committing a specified criminal act or acts. It serves essentially the same function as an indictment. In felonies the criminal complaint may be referred to as an information.

53. See the discussion of tort defenses on page 129.

54. In some states the amount of the bail is preset for minor offenses, and the accused can bail out at the police station prior to this initial court appearance.

ment as a means of ensuring the appearance of the defendant in court. The bail is set in terms of a cash amount, and in order to be released the defendant must either come up with that amount of money or something else of comparable value that the court is willing to accept. These alternatives may be securities, equity in real property, or a bond from a recognized bail bondsman. As long as the defendants show up for all of the required court appearances, they will have their bail returned at the completion of their case. However, if they should attempt to skip town, the bail is forfeited to the government.

Over the years major criticisms have been made of the manner in which the bail system operates. Among them have been the charges that the system keeps innocent people in jail simply because they are too poor to come up with the bail money and that it places people's freedom in the hands of professional bondsmen.[55] In response to these arguments many states have attempted various types of bail reforms including greater use of personal recognizance bonds[56] and the reduction of the actual cash requirements for bail. In Illinois, for example, the defendant is required to come up with the cash equivalent of 10 percent of the total amount set for bail. People are still liable for the entire amount if they do not show, but they have to produce only 10 percent in order to be released. In many states one's driver's license is accepted in lieu of a cash bail for most traffic offenses.

At this initial appearance a defendant who cannot afford the services of a private attorney will usually have either a public defender or a member of the private bar appointed to provide representation.[57] Most courts have developed local guidelines that take into consideration the income and assets of the defendant as well as the nature of the offense. The United States Supreme Court has ruled that attorneys do not have to be provided in all misdemeanor cases but that indigent defendants cannot be given jail sentences unless they either were provided with counsel at the trial[58] or waived their right to such representation.

3. Preliminary Hearings and Grand Juries

A defendant in a felony case cannot be put through the ordeal of a trial solely on the authority of the prosecutor. The evidence must be

---

55. It has been alleged that some bondsmen are tied to organized crime and that they give credit to career criminals who then commit more crimes in order to pay the bondsman's fee.
56. A person released on a personal recognizance bond is released prior to the trial date on the basis of a personal promise to appear in court when instructed to do so. The person is indebted to pay a specified amount if he or she fails to carry out the conditions of the bond.
57. A public defender is an attorney who is employed by the government on either a full- or part-time basis for the purpose of representing indigent defendants in criminal cases. An assigned counsel is a private attorney who is paid on a contractual basis to defend a specific individual.
58. Scott v. Illinois, 440 U.S. 367 (1979).

tested independently to determine whether sufficient probable cause exists to justify placing the individual on trial. This independent testing of the evidence occurs through the conducting of preliminary hearings and the use of the grand jury.

The fifth amendment to the U.S. Constitution requires that "no person shall be held to answer for a capital or otherwise infamous crime, unless on a presentment or indictment of a grand jury." Although this applies only to federal cases, some states require the use of a grand jury. Other states allow the prosecutor the option of using a grand jury or not using it, and some do not use grand juries at all. The federal government and most states that do use grand juries follow the common law format of having twenty-three persons serve during a term and requiring at least twelve votes for an indictment or presentment.[59]

One of the basic functions of the grand jury is to review the government's case to determine whether there is enough evidence to justify holding the defendant for trial. Critics have charged that because the prosecutor suggests who the witnesses should be and also interprets the meaning of the criminal statutes, the lay persons who serve on the grand jury do little more than rubber stamp the prosecutor's decisions and do not act as an effective check on the prosecutor's use of discretionary powers.

The grand jury also can serve as an investigative arm of the government and can be especially useful when it comes to organized crime or corruption in the government's own bureaucracy. The Watergate grand jury is probably the most famous example of a grand jury used for such investigations. The ability to subpoena and give immunity to key witnesses makes the grand jury an effective weapon in the hands of a well-trained prosecutor. When the grand jury takes on this type of investigative role, its investigations frequently include people who are not yet under arrest. If the grand jury decides that those people should be brought to trial, an arrest warrant is issued on the basis of the grand jury's indictment. A defendant arrested in this manner goes directly from the initial appearance stage to the arraignment.

Because grand juries do not always meet on a frequent and regular basis, the law usually requires that a judge test the credibility of the government's case even before it goes to the grand jury. Therefore, at the preliminary hearing stage the judge must determine whether there is enough evidence to justify holding the person for the grand jury.

In cases where the grand jury is not used, the preliminary hearing takes on added significance because it is then the only check on prosecu-

---

59. Both an indictment and a presentment are formal written documents accusing the named individual of specific criminal acts. The technical difference is that an indictment is returned in response to evidence presented by the prosecutor, and a presentment is the result of the grand jury's own initiative.

torial discretion. When the grand jury is not being used, the preliminary hearing can also serve as a good way to get a key witness's testimony on the record.

4. The Arraignment

At the arraignment the defendant is informed of the charges contained in the indictment (or the information) and makes his or her formal plea to those charges. The judge must speak with the defendant to be sure that he or she understands the nature of the charge, the minimum and maximum sentences prescribed by law, and that by entering a guilty plea the defendant waives the right to a trial and to confront and cross-examine witnesses. If the defendant still wants to plead guilty, the judge must determine that the plea is voluntary.[60]

If a guilty plea is accepted, the judge may either pronounce the sentence at that time or set a specific time for a sentencing hearing at some later date. If the defendant enters a not guilty plea, a tentative date is set for the trial based on whether the defendant requests a jury trial or a bench trial.

5. Discovery and Pretrial Motions

As is the case in civil proceedings, the parties in a criminal case also have an opportunity to use various discovery devices to learn more about the nature of the other side's case prior to the start of the trial. Although the particulars vary from one jurisdiction to another, the defense generally has a right to such things as the names, addresses, and statements of persons that the prosecution intends to call as witnesses; minutes of the grand jury proceedings; documentary and physical evidence to be used at the trial; and transcripts of any electronic surveillance to be used. The prosecution in turn has a right to have the defendant appear in line-ups, give handwriting samples and so forth, provide names and addresses of people who will be called as defense witnesses, and provide results of laboratory and medical reports to be used.

During this pretrial period the defense files motions to exclude certain types of evidence that have been identified through the discovery process. Such motions to exclude often are based on allegedly unconstitutional police practices that led to the acquisition of the evidence in question.[61] Motions for a continuance are also common.

6. Plea Bargaining

As is the case in civil trials, the majority of criminal cases never reach the trial stage. In the criminal context the process of reaching a

---

60. See the discussion on plea bargaining below.
61. See the discussion on the exclusionary rule in Chapter 4 at page 125.

negotiated settlement is called plea bargaining. The defendant agrees to plead guilty to a criminal charge in return for some type of benefit given by the prosecutor to induce the plea. The incentives offered by the government can include reducing the severity of the charge (for example, settling for a guilty plea on a robbery charge where the original charge was for the more serious offense of armed robbery), dropping related counts (for example, an original indictment may include three counts of burglary, but the prosecutor may agree to drop two of them in return for a guilty plea to the third), or recommending the minimum sentence or even a suspended sentence rather than going for the maximum authorized by the law.

The prosecutor is willing to make these types of bargains for a variety of reasons. Because most prosecutors' offices are understaffed and overworked, plea bargaining provides a way to both reduce their workload and produce a high conviction rate. Many prosecutors are willing to trade an uncertain conviction with longer jail time for an assurance that the defendant will end up with a conviction on the record and at least do some jail time.

Plea bargaining has been firmly entrenched in the legal system for many years, and yet some states continue the charade of having defendants who have accepted plea bargains declare in open court that their plea is not based on any threats or promises. Other states have sought to bring plea bargaining into the open and to fully acknowledge in open court that a plea agreement has been struck. The United States Supreme Court has sought to encourage plea bargaining by recognizing its existence and insisting that the terms of the bargain be enforced in situations where the state may seek to abandon its commitment after the defendant enters the plea.[62]

7. The Trial

There are few (and relatively minor) differences between the conduct of civil and criminal trials. This section will briefly highlight these differences. Where nothing is mentioned to the contrary, the reader can assume that the criminal trial proceeds in the same manner as described in the first part of this chapter.

a. The Right to a Jury Trial

The sixth amendment to the United States Constitution creates a right to a speedy and public trial by an impartial jury in federal criminal cases. The United States Supreme Court has ruled that the due process clause of the fourteenth amendment applies the right to a trial by jury to

---

62. Santobello v. New York, 404 U.S. 257 (1971).

defendants in state criminal actions who face possible incarceration of six months or more.[63]

The U.S. Constitution requires that criminal juries at the federal level consist of twelve members and that their verdicts be unanimous. At the state level, the U.S. Constitution allows for the use of six-member juries with unanimous verdicts or twelve-person juries with less than unanimous verdicts, as well as for traditional twelve-person unanimous juries.[64] The states themselves select which of these options they wish to use. As is the practice in civil jury trials, the court sometimes selects alternate jurors who sit through the trial but do not participate in the deliberations unless they are formally substituted for a juror who is unable to continue.

One of the most frequently misunderstood aspects of the jury system is the concept of being tried before a jury of one's peers. A jury of one's peers need not consist of a group of people who are similar to the defendant. The jury simply must be broadly representative of the community in which the trial takes place. The focus is not on the twelve people on the final jury but rather on the nature of the general pool from which those twelve were selected.

b. Trial Procedures

Criminal trials follow the procedural steps discussed in the civil section of this chapter. The prosecutor addresses the jury or presents evidence in a criminal case at the same point as the plaintiff's attorney does in a civil case. The defendant's lawyer in the criminal case operates in the same manner as the defendant's lawyer in the civil case.

The major difference is that the prosecutor must bear the burden of a higher standard of proof (beyond a reasonable doubt as opposed to preponderance of the evidence). The motion for a directed verdict is often referred to as a motion for acquittal.

Following the announcement of a guilty verdict, the defendant usually files a motion for a judgment notwithstanding the verdict and one for a new trial. Exhibit 5.10 presents an example of a combined motion.

8. Sentencing

Except in capital punishment cases, the jury usually has no role to play in the sentencing process. Once the jury has found the defendant guilty of a specified crime, it becomes the sole responsibility of the judge to determine the sentence. The judge must act within the limitations set down by the statutes, but those statutes frequently leave a broad range of

---

63. Duncan v. Louisiana, 391 U.S. 145 (1968); Baldwin v. New York, 399 U.S. 66 (1970).
64. Williams v. Florida, 399 U.S. 78 (1970); Apodaca v. Oregon, 406 U.S. 404 (1972).

STATE OF ILLINOIS
In the Circuit Court of the Eleventh Judicial Circuit
County of McLean

THE PEOPLE OF THE
STATE OF ILLINOIS,
                Plaintiff,

v.

JOHN DOE,   NO. 85-CF-248
                Defendant.

MOTION FOR NEW TRIAL OR
FOR JUDGMENT NOTWITHSTANDING THE VERDICT

NOW COMES the Defendant, John Doe, by his attorneys, Reynard & Robb, and moves this Court to enter an order granting the Defendant a new trial, or in the alternative, to enter judgment of acquittal notwithstanding the findings of the Court, and in support hereof the Defendant states:

1. The Defendant was not proved guilty beyond a reasonable doubt.

2. The guilty finding of the Court is against the manifest weight of the evidence.

3. The Court erred by denying the Defendant's Motion for Directed Verdict at the close of the State's evidence-in-chief.

4. The Court erred by admitting over objection evidence of the supposed prior activities and evidence of other crimes of the Defendant and Gale White.

5. The Court erred by striking over objection that portion of the testimony of Dan Black describing the declarations against interest and declarations against penal interests made by Gale White at and shortly after the time of his arrest.

6. The Court erred by disregarding the testimony of Shannon Green.

7. The Court erred by overruling Defendant's scope and relevancy objections to the State's cross-examination of the Defendant.

8. The Court erred by admitting over objection the September 15, 1985, written statement of Gale White as supposedly reliable hearsay.

9. The Court erred by sustaining the State's objection to the admission of Dan Black's testimony as to the declarations against interest and declarations against penal interest of Gale White as tending to support the declarant's previous statements to Shannon Green.

WHEREFORE, Defendant prays this Court enter an Order granting a new trial of this cause, or, in the alternative, granting judgment of acquittal notwithstanding the finding of the Court.

JOHN DOE, Defendant

By: _____
His Attorney

---

discretion between a minimum and a maximum sentence for the crime
in question. Furthermore, judges often have the power to suspend the
sentence altogether. Most capital punishment statutes, on the other
hand, allow the defendant to have a decision regarding the imposition of
the death penalty included as part of the jury's deliberations.

After the guilty verdict, the judge usually holds a special sentencing
hearing in which evidence can be presented "in aggravation and mitigation." At such a hearing both the prosecution and the defense have an
opportunity to present evidence that was not relevant to whether the
defendant committed the crime but is relevant to the nature of the
punishment that is to be imposed. The judge also receives a presentence
report that reviews the defendant's criminal record, work record, family
background, and other factors considered relevant in determining the
appropriate punishment.

9. Appeals

As with civil appeals, a defendant who wishes to appeal a conviction must make the appropriate posttrial motions and then file a notice
of appeal within the specified time period. Although the fifth amendment protection against double jeopardy prevents the government from
appealing an acquittal, it does not prevent a prosecutor from appealing the dismissal of a case on technical grounds. Nor does the double
jeopardy clause prevent the prosecutor from appealing the decision of a
lower-level appellate court to a higher-level one.

In addition to the standard appeal route, a convicted person also
can use the writ of *habeas corpus* to gain a review of his or her conviction
after the deadline for a normal appeal has expired. This writ is a court
order to someone who detains or has custody of another individual, and
it requires that person to "produce the body" of the detainee before the
court so that the judge can conduct an inquiry into the legality of the
detention. In criminal cases, the prisoner claims that the detention is
illegal because a constitutional error in the trial invalidates the verdict on
which he or she was imprisoned. Some states have developed a petition

for postconviction review that serves the same function as the writ of
habeas corpus approach.

C. ADMINISTRATIVE PROCEDURE

Administrative adjudication is designed to relieve the courts of the
burden of resolving certain types of disputes. This section presents some
of the similarities and differences between litigation and administrative
adjudication.

Just as court procedures vary somewhat among states or between
the federal and a particular state, so too do administrative procedures.
Furthermore, procedures vary among agencies within the same unit of
government. The federal and state Administrative Procedures Acts
specify certain types of procedures that must be used in all adjudicatory
hearings, but the agencies use their rulemaking powers to specify additional procedures that apply only to their own agency's hearings.

1. Commencing the Action

Individuals or businesses usually become involved in administrative
adjudication when either they seek review of a bureaucratic decision that
they disagree with or when the agency charges them with some violation
of its regulations. For example, review might be sought by someone who
applied for but was denied social security disability benefits, or a state
agency might seek to revoke a real estate broker's license or to charge an
employer with unfair labor practices. Parties therefore can become involved in such hearings by either initiating the action themselves or
having another party institute an action against them.

2. Pleadings and Service

Pleadings are important in civil litigation but relatively unimpor-
tant in administrative adjudication. They serve solely to notify the parties
that a hearing will be held. Service can be made through certified mail.
In a social security disability case, for example, one need file only the
request for hearing form shown in Form 5.2.

Section 554 of the federal Administrative Procedure Act states that
notice should consist of:

1. The time, place, and nature of the hearing;
2. The legal authority and jurisdiction under which the hearing is
   being held; and
3. The matters of fact and law asserted.[65]

---

65. 5 U.S.C. §554(b).

Form 5.2 Request for Hearing

DEPARTMENT OF HEALTH, EDUCATION, AND WELFARE
SOCIAL SECURITY ADMINISTRATION
BUREAU OF HEARINGS AND APPEALS

REQUEST FOR HEARING

Take or mail original and all copies to your local Social Security Office.

CLAIMANT'S NAME	CLAIM FOR
	(Check one or more boxes) (Circle type of claim)
WAGE EARNER'S NAME (Leave blank if same as above)	☐ Entitlement to Disability Benefits DIB DWB CDB
SOCIAL SECURITY NUMBER	☐ Continuance of Disability Benefits DIB DWB CDB
	☐ Other (Specify) _____
SPOUSE'S NAME AND SOCIAL SECURITY NUMBER (Complete ONLY in Supplemental Security Income Case)	☐ Supplemental Security Income Aged Blind Disabled
	☐ Continuance of Supplemental Aged Blind Disabled Security Income

I disagree with the determination made on the above claim and request a hearing. My reasons for disagreement are:

_____

_____

Check one of the following:

☐ I have additional evidence to submit.
(Attach such evidence to this form or forward to the Social Security Office within 10 days.)

☐ I have no additional evidence to submit.

Check ONLY ONE of the statements below:

☐ I wish to appear in person.

☐ I waive my right to appear and give evidence, and hereby request a decision on the evidence on file.

Signed by: (Either the claimant or representative should sign. Enter addresses for both. If claimant's representative is not an attorney, complete Form SSA-1696.)

SIGNATURE OR NAME OF CLAIMANT'S REPRESENTATIVE	CLAIMANT'S SIGNATURE
☐ ATTORNEY ☐ NON ATTORNEY	
ADDRESS	ADDRESS
CITY, STATE, AND ZIP CODE	CITY, STATE, AND ZIP CODE
TELEPHONE NUMBER DATE:	TELEPHONE NUMBER

(Claimant should not fill in below this line)

TO BE COMPLETED BY SOCIAL SECURITY ADMINISTRATION

Is this request timely filed?   ☐ Yes   ☐ No
If "No" is checked: (1) Attach claimant's explanation for delay, (2) Attach any pertinent letter, material, or information in the Social Security Office.

ACKNOWLEDGMENT OF REQUEST FOR HEARING

Your request for a hearing was filed on _____ at _____
The Administrative Law Judge or the Hearing Examiner, SSI, will notify you of the time and place of the hearing at least 10 days prior to the date which will be set for the hearing.

	TO:	For the Social Security Administration
HEARING OFFICE COPY	☐ Hearing Office _____ (Location) ☐ _____ (Location) (Claims Involving SSI or combined SSI-RSDI) ☐ Supplemental Security Income File Attached	By: _____ (Signature) _____ (Title)
CLAIMS FILE COPY	TO: ☐ Hearing Office ☐ Claim File(s) Requested by Teletype to _____ (Location) ☐ ACB (BDP)	(Street Address) _____ (City) _____ (State) _____ (Zip Code)

Interpreter Needed _____ (Language) _____ Servicing Social Security Office Code _____

Form HA-501
(3/74)

HEARING OFFICE COPY

3. Discovery

Most agency procedures provide a limited role for discovery techniques. Lists of exhibits to be presented and witnesses who will appear are usually available from the agency. Subpoenas can usually be issued on a showing of "general relevance and reasonable scope of the evidence sought."[66] Depositions can be taken "when the ends of justice would be served."[67]

In some cases the paralegal may be able to obtain very helpful information under the Freedom of Information Act.[68] The act declares in part that an agency shall

> upon request by an individual to gain access to his record or to any information pertaining to him which is contained in the system, permit him and upon his request, a person of his own choosing to accompany him, to review the record and have a copy made of all or any portion thereof in a form comprehensible to him, except that the agency may require the individual to furnish a written statement authorizing discussion of that individual's record in the accompanying person's presence.[69]

In preparing for the hearing, the paralegal should carefully examine the statements of policy and interpretative rules of the agency. Some of these are published in the Federal Register, but others must be specifically requested under the provisions of §552(a)(2):

> Each agency, in accordance with published rules, shall make available for public inspection and copying —
>
> (A) final opinions, including concurring and dissenting opinions, as well as orders, made in the adjudication of cases;
> (B) those statements of policy and interpretations which have been adopted by the agency and are not published in the Federal Register; and
> (C) administrative staff manuals and instructions to staff that affect a member of the public; unless the materials are promptly published and copies offered for sale.

Administrative staff manuals and other instructions to field staff are particularly useful because they give explicit and detailed information on how factors are measured and evaluated. The presentation at the hearing can then be geared to meeting these criteria.

---

66. 5 U.S.C. §555(d).
67. 5 U.S.C. §556(e)(4).
68. See 5 U.S.C. §§552, 552a, and 552b.
69. 5 U.S.C. §552a(d)(1).

4. Hearings

In the administrative context, an adjudicatory hearing is a mechanism through which parties to a dispute can present arguments and evidence about their case to an administrative decision maker. (Rulemaking hearings, on the other hand, resemble legislative hearings in which interested parties present evidence and arguments about what the general law should be in the future.) While hearings are usually presided over by the individual who has been given at least the initial responsibility for rendering a decision, on some occasions the hearing officer is there solely to record what will be reviewed by the actual decision makers.

a. The Participants

The hearing officer directs the actions of the parties involved in a hearing in much the same way that a judge does during a trial. Because hearings are usually less structured than trials, the hearing officer has more flexibility in organizing the hearing and influencing the atmosphere.

Section 3105 of the Administrative Procedure Act provides that hearing examiners be appointed by the various agencies and assigned to cases on a rotating basis. In order to help ensure their impartiality, Congress has given the Office of Personnel Management (rather than the agency itself) control over the hearing officers' wages.[70] Similarly, the hearing officers can be removed from office only by independent procedures conducted by the commission.[71]

The hearing officers, or administrative law judges, as they have been officially designated by the Civil Service Commission,[72] have the power to

1. Administer oaths and affirmations;
2. Issue subpoenas authorized by law;
3. Rule on offers of proof and receive relevant evidence;
4. Take depositions or have depositions taken when the ends of justice would be served;
5. Regulate the course of the hearing;
6. Hold conferences for the settlement or simplification of the issues by consent of the parties;
7. Dispose of procedural requests or similar matters;
8. Make or recommend decisions in accordance with §557 of this title; and

---

70. 5 U.S.C. §5362. The Office of Personnel Management is the successor to the Civil Service Commission.
71. 5 U.S.C. §7521.
72. 5 C.F.R. §930.203a.

9. Take other action authorized by agency rule consistent with this subchapter.[73]

Most states also attempt to ensure the independence of their hearing officers and give them similar types of powers.

In addition to the hearing officer a court reporter or a hearing assistant is present to record the proceedings. A hearing assistant is an agency employee who serves the function of court reporter and clerk. Tape recorders are used more frequently than the special shorthand machines used by most court reporters.

Depending on the agency, there may or may not be a lawyer present to represent the government's position. In cases where an advocate for the agency is not present, the hearing officer is expected to take an active role in the questioning and to ensure that the government's positions and concerns are adequately reflected in the final record. The individual claimant or defendant has a right to be represented by counsel, and in some agencies this representation can be provided by paralegals, but there is no constitutional right to have an attorney appointed at government expense. Although legal aid agencies often provide legal assistance to those who meet their low-income guidelines, many people represent themselves at such hearings. When this occurs, the hearing officer has the additional responsibility of ensuring that the final record adequately reflects that individual's position as well.

In addition to the above-named participants, various witnesses also may be called to give testimony at the hearing. As with the regular courts, some of these witnesses may fall into the expert witness category.[74]

b. The Hearing Room

Administrative hearings are held in a variety of locations. Some agencies have impressive wood-paneled hearing rooms in which the hearing officer sits at a desk that has been placed perpendicular to and raised above the level of a long table where the other participants in the hearing sit. (See Figure 5.3 for a diagram of a typical hearing room arrangement.) However, hearings also can be held with all of the participants sitting around a table in a conference room or a library.

c. Hearing Procedures

The hearing itself usually begins with the hearing officer reading the case name and number into the record, identifying for the record who is present at the hearing, and briefly explaining the purpose of the

---

73. 5 U.S.C. §556(c).
74. See the discussion on expert witnesses at page 200.

Figure 5.3 Typical Seating Arrangement at Social Security Administration Disability Hearings

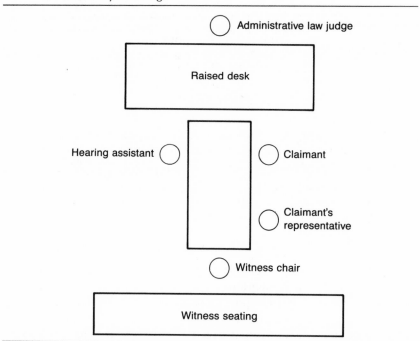

hearing to the people involved. Opening statements by attorneys are rare.

Before taking testimony from witnesses the hearing officer usually determines what documentary evidence is to be admitted. It is not necessary to have witnesses testify to lay a foundation for the documentary evidence before it can be accepted. After all the participants have had an opportunity to examine the documents, the hearing officer gives those involved a chance to raise objections, and then decides what shall be admitted into the official record.

Testimonial evidence is taken in much the same way as during a trial, except that the hearing officer takes a much more active role in the questioning. Frequently the hearing officer questions the witness before giving the attorneys an opportunity to do so.

In dealing with both testimonial and documentary evidence the hearing officers need not follow the strict rules of evidence used in trials. The trend is to admit unreliable or hearsay evidence but then give it little or no weight in reaching a final decision.

Closing arguments, if used at all, are usually submitted to the hearing officer as a written memorandum rather than given as an oral statement at the hearing itself.

d. The Form of the Decision

The hearing officer then takes the matter under consideration, reviews the testimony and the files, and renders a written decision. In most agencies this decision is reviewed by a staff attorney or a special review panel before it is released.

The format of the hearing officer's decision will vary from one agency or governmental unit to another. Section 557(c) of the federal Administrative Procedures Act requires that

> The record shall show the ruling on each finding, conclusion, or exception presented. All decisions, including initial, recommended, and tentative decisions, are a part of the record and shall include a statement of (A) findings and conclusions, and the reasons or basis therefor, on all the material issues of fact, law, or discretion presented on the record; and (B) the appropriate rule, order, sanction, relief, or denial thereof.

The released decision usually begins by listing the date and location of the hearing and who attended. It then identifies the issues, cites the relevant statutes and regulations, and offers summaries of witnesses' testimony. The three most important sections are (1) an evaluation of the evidence (the relative weight or credibility given to different testimony and documents); (2) the findings section in which the hearing officer states his or her opinion of the facts; and (3) the decision section in which the hearing officer clearly states the legal effect of the decision (that is, the party will or will not receive disability benefits).

5. Appeals

Many agencies provide a format for an appeal to a special appeals unit, but the appeal procedure usually is limited to submission of written documents — and the grounds for appeal are often quite narrow. Ordinarily the appealing party must allege either availability of new evidence, existence of an error on the face of the record, misapplication of the law, or gross abuse of discretion. A specific request for review form is ordinarily supplied by the agency. This document is often accompanied by an appeal brief.

After all administrative appeals have been exhausted, it may be possible to have the matter reviewed in the courts as well. State and federal statutes specify the circumstances under which administrative actions are subject to such judicial review.[75]

---

75. See the discussion of judicial review at page 158.

D. SUMMARY

Although specific rules of civil and criminal procedure are complex and vary from one jurisdiction to the next, the basic stages in the processes are similar. Civil litigation begins when the plaintiff files a complaint and serves the defendant with a summons. The defendant's response can involve a variety of pretrial motions and counterclaims.

Between the time that the defendant's answer has been filed and the date of the trial itself, motions are heard, pretrial conferences and negotiations take place, and each side uses various discovery mechanisms to find out more about the other side's case. Frequently these negotiations result in an out-of-court settlement.

If the jury is being used, the trial begins with the *voir dire* selection process in which jurors are questioned and the lawyers can raise challenges for cause and exercise their peremptory challenges. Opening statements are followed by the presentation of the plaintiff's evidence. The defense counsel has an opportunity to cross-examine the plaintiff's witnesses as they are presented. The cross-examination is followed by re-direct, which can be followed by a re-cross. After the plaintiff's case is completed, the defense presents its case in the same manner with the plaintiff now having the opportunity to cross-examine. Following the presentation of rebuttal witnesses, attorneys make their closing arguments to the jury, and the judge instructs them in the meaning of the law.

Appeals must be timely and must be based on legal issues for which a proper foundation was laid at the trial level. After giving proper notification of the intent to appeal, the appellant must arrange to have the necessary transcripts prepared and file a legal brief with the appellate court. The appellee must then prepare a brief defending the action of the lower court. If oral arguments are involved, the attorneys also have an opportunity to make verbal presentations to the court.

Criminal cases begin with an arrest and then proceed through a variety of stages that can include: booking, bail setting, a preliminary hearing, grand jury action, an arraignment, and plea bargaining. Once the case reaches the trial stage, the procedures used closely resemble those used in civil cases, except that the prosecutor takes the place of the plaintiff. With the exception of capital punishment cases, the jury does not participate in the determination of the punishment in a criminal case.

Although double jeopardy prevents the prosecution from appealing an acquittal, the prosecution can appeal an unfavorable appellate court decision to a higher-level appellate court. Once again the procedures parallel those used in civil cases.

Adjudicatory hearings tend to follow the general outlines of a civil

trial, but they are less formal and do not involve as many due process protections. To meet requirements of the due process clause, an agency's procedures must be fair and reasonable. The courts have decided that the fair and reasonable procedures required in some agency hearings are not necessary in others.

The hearing is presided over by a hearing officer (officially designated as an administrative law judge), who acts much as a judge would. An assistant usually records the proceedings and takes notes. Although it is relatively easy to get evidence admitted into the record, the decision makers have great discretion over the weight assigned to that evidence.

When the law provides for appeal within the agency itself, the party is usually required to pursue this appeal before the courts will agree to intervene. The agency's decision must include a summary of what that agency determined as facts as well as a clear statement of the reasons for its decision. The administrative appeal is usually handled through submission of written documents with no room for oral advocacy.

KEY TERMS

adjudication

administrative law judge

admissible evidence

affirm

appealable issue

appellant

appellee

arraignment

arrest

bail

cause of action

challenge for cause

class action suit

competent evidence

compulsory joinder

count

counterclaim

cross-claim

default judgment

demonstrative evidence

demurrer

deposition

discovery

dismissal with prejudice

documentary evidence

expert witness

grand jury

harmless error

hearing officer

hearsay evidence

indictment

information

initial appearance

interrogatories

judgment

judgment N.O.V.

judgment proof

lay witness

litigation

material evidence

motion for a new trial

motion for acquittal

motion for directed verdict

motion *in limine*

notice

notice pleadings

peremptory challenge

personal recognizance bond

physical evidence

plea bargaining

prejudicial error

preliminary hearing

presentment

real evidence

relevant evidence

remand

request for admissions

reversible error

sentencing hearing

subpoena *duces tecum*

summons

testimonial evidence

voir dire

writ of execution

writ of *habeas corpus*

REVIEW QUESTIONS

1. What decisions must be made before a civil complaint is filed?

2. What are the essential elements in a civil complaint?

3. What alternatives are available to a defendant who has a civil suit filed against him or her?

4. What is the purpose of discovery? What techniques are used to achieve this purpose?

5. What is the difference between a jury trial and a bench trial?

6. How are jurors selected?

7. Under what circumstances is hearsay evidence admissible?

8. What must be done to properly authenticate real evidence?

9. Identify the major posttrial motions and explain their functions.

10. Under what circumstances can a person be arrested?

11. What determines whether a grand jury is used in a criminal case?

12. What types of bargains are usually struck when the prosecutor and the defense plea bargain?

13. How does a sentencing hearing differ from a trial?

14. Under what circumstances can the government appeal to a higher court in a criminal case?

15. What conditions must be satisfied before an appellate court will agree to hear an appeal?

16. What constitutes laying a proper foundation for an appeal?

17. Why are errors in the pleadings usually considered to be harmless errors?

18.   How does the role of a hearing officer in an administrative hearing differ from that of a judge in a civil or criminal trial?

19.   How does one appeal an unfavorable decision from an administrative hearing?

DISCUSSION QUESTIONS

1.   Is there too much use of plea bargaining? What are the advantages and disadvantages of plea bargaining?

2.   Many people complain that our society has become too litigious — that is, that too many people sue others and take controversies to the courts that should be settled elsewhere. Do you agree? What could be done to reduce this problem?

3.   Which type of evidence (testimonial, documentary, or physical) is most reliable? Which is least reliable? What are the potential advantages and disadvantages of each?

4.   Why do appellate courts generally insist that a final judgment be entered before they will review the matter? When, if ever, should the courts deviate from this rule?

5.   Why do the appellate courts generally limit their review to situations in which the attorney raised the appropriate objection at the trial? Is it fair to punish the client for the attorney's mistake?

6.   To what extent should the appellate courts review the factual determinations of a judge or jury? Should greater deference be shown to judges than to juries?

7.   Which elements of due process should be required in an administrative hearing? If you believe that there should be a variable standard, what should be the maximum and minimum? In which types of hearings should the maximum and minimum apply?

PROJECTS

1.   Consult your state's civil practice act to determine the requirements for serving a summons. List the various methods available and the conditions under which each can be used.

2.   Under what circumstances does your state court have jurisdiction over a party who is not a resident of your state and who is not physically in the state?

3.   Locate the rules for appellate practice in your state. Now answer the following questions on the basis of those rules: (a) Is a *praecipe* for the record required, and if so, when should it be filed? (b) What

should be done if there is no verbatim transcript of the trial available? (c) Who must pay the cost of having the record produced? (d) Are there limitations on the number of pages included in a brief? (e) What are the time limits for filing of briefs? (f) Under what circumstances is oral argument available?

4.   Read Richardson v. Perales, 402 U.S. 390 (1971). The application of what aspect of due process is involved in this case? Why do the dissenters disagree with the majority position in this case? With which position do you agree, and why?

Chapter 6
Organization and Management of Law Offices

THE PRACTICE OF LAW IS carried out through a variety of organizational structures and involves a variety of different types of support personnel. Paralegals may be employed in small, one-attorney law offices or large manufacturing corporations. Furthermore, they routinely work with attorneys and paralegals from law offices that may be quite different from their own. This chapter discusses the variety of ways that law offices are structured, the type of personnel that they employ, and some of the basic procedures that they use. In addition it discusses the role of office automation and applications of computer technology.

A. ORGANIZATIONAL STRUCTURES

1. Private Practice Arrangements

Most people involved in the delivery of legal services are employed in some variation of private practice. They are self-employed or employed by other attorneys rather than employed by a financial institution, an insurance company, a manufacturing corporation, a trade association, or a governmental agency. There are four main types of private practice.

a. Partnerships and Professional Corporations
Most lawyers belong to either a partnership or a professional corporation. In both arrangements, several lawyers pool their resources in a joint effort. In traditional partnership arrangements, attorneys work cooperatively on cases that are taken by the firm, and the partners share proportionately in the profits of those joint endeavors.

Lawyers who work in a partnership are designated as either associates or partners. Associates are employees of the firm and receive a set salary for their efforts.[1] Partners, on the other hand, receive a share

---

1. However, in some firms associates may be given bonuses based on new business they have generated for the firm or the firm's profitability for that year.

of the firm's profits rather than a set salary.[2] The percentage of the profits received and the extent to which each partner participates in the decision making for the firm depend on a variety of factors including the amount of business they bring into the firm, the amount of fees generated by the cases they work on, the contribution they make to the management of the firm, their longevity with the firm, and so forth. Generally speaking, the associate category is used for training and evaluating young attorneys. After approximately five to eight years the associate is either offered a partnership or expected to leave the firm.[3] Some firms also distinguish between junior partners and senior partners.[4] The differences relate to a combination of the amount of capital they contribute, the degree to which they participate in decision making, and the proportion of the profits they receive. The term "of counsel" is usually used to designate the status of a semi-retired former partner or an attorney who is affiliated with the firm on a part-time basis.

In small partnerships, most decisions are made by a "committee of the whole" comprised of the partners, who meet and discuss the matter together. As firms grow larger, however, partners are usually delegated to specialized committees in areas like fee setting and finance, recruitment of associates, lay personnel, office equipment and space utilization, and the library. The managing partner takes responsibility for seeing that the policies decided on are properly implemented.

Most professional corporations operate much as partnerships do. They form a corporation, rather than a partnership, in order to limit their individual financial liability and receive certain tax advantages. Individual attorneys contribute capital to the corporation much like they would to a partnership. The corporation pays salaries to all the attorneys who work for it but pays dividends only to the attorneys who are shareholders in the corporation. Attorneys who are designated as directors have a voice in controlling the corporation, and the officers are responsible for managing it.

b. Sole Proprietor and Office Sharing Arrangements

Several lawyers share in the profits of a partnership or corporation, but in a sole proprietorship one lawyer owns all the assets of the business

---

2. Since it would be impractical for most attorneys to wait until the end of the year before receiving their share of the profits, partners establish a monthly draw that provides a set amount of compensation to meet their routine living expenses.

3. Figures compiled by the National Association for Law Placement, Inc. indicate that the average length of time required before associates are considered for partnership status is 6.7 years in firms of twenty-five or more lawyers. Years Required to Make Partner, Natl. L.J., Nov. 26, 1984, at 8.

4. Other names commonly used to designate junior partners include income partners, nonequity partners, nonpercentage partners, and contract partners. See Stille, Turning to 2-tiered Partnerships, Natl. L.J., Oct. 22, 1984, at 1.

and receives all the profits (or absorbs the losses). This form of practice usually involves a single lawyer assisted by paralegals and clerical staff. However, it also can consist of an arrangement in which the solo practitioner employs other attorneys on a regular salaried basis. Those employees are strictly employees, however, and do not have any rights to share in the firm's profits or participate in the management of the firm.

Some lawyers develop various office sharing arrangements that may appear to outsiders to be partnerships or professional corporations but are technically still sole proprietorships. Typically, two or more attorneys share office space, a telephone system, and a receptionist. Sometimes they share a common secretarial pool and paralegals. Each attorney is responsible for paying his or her share of these common expenses, but the fees earned by each attorney are not pooled or shared.

Another variation of office sharing among sole practitioners occurs when one attorney gives another attorney (usually a young attorney trying to start his or her own practice) office space, library use, and sometimes secretarial help in return for help on some cases. The attorney receiving these office benefits is expected to do some legal research, to answer some court calls, appear at real estate closings, and otherwise cover for the first attorney when he or she has schedule conflicts, takes a day off, or goes on vacation.

2. Other Forms of Practice

In the private practice forms discussed above, some lawyers share directly in the capital formation and the profits or losses of the firm, while others may be straight salaried employees. In each case, however, their actual employer is either an attorney or a legal entity owned and operated by attorneys. In the alternative forms of practice discussed below, attorneys are employees of either the government or some entity that is not owned and operated solely by attorneys. These types of positions usually provide more predictable hours and compensation, greater security, and relief from the pressure to generate new clients for the firm.

a. Legal Department of a Business Corporation

All businesses need legal advice from time to time, legal assistance in filing various forms with governmental agencies, or legal representation when they are involved in litigation. They can obtain this legal assistance by either contracting for the services of a law firm or hiring lawyers as their own employees. Depending on the nature and size of the business, there are advantages and disadvantages to each approach, but since internal legal departments frequently offer greater economy, more responsive service, and greater integration with management, most large corporations hire lawyers as regular salaried employees.

The top legal position in most companies is that of general counsel, and the position is usually placed at the vice-presidential level. This office has responsibility for advising corporate officials on how to minimize legal risks and how to respond to legal difficulties. The general counsel's office monitors proposed regulations and legislation that might affect the company's operations and then organizes appropriate lobbying efforts supporting or opposing the proposed changes.

In centralized legal departments all staff attorneys report to the general counsel and usually are located in the corporate headquarters building. In decentralized systems staff lawyers are organized into smaller units and located in operating divisions and regional offices. They may report to the vice-president of finance or the vice-president for research and development rather than the general counsel.

When companies are involved in litigation, they frequently retain the services of a law firm to represent them in court even if they have their own staff attorneys. The outside firm may have special expertise in that area of litigation, may have attorneys who are familiar with local judges, or may be licensed to practice in a particular state. When such outside firms are used, the company's legal department is responsible for selecting the attorneys to be used, negotiating the fees that will be paid, and approving any settlement offers. Depending on the number and expertise of the company's lawyers, they also may draft pleadings, memos, and interrogatories; respond to discovery requests from opposing parties; and digest depositions. In some instances they participate in the trial itself with the attorneys from the outside firm.

b. Legal Departments in Governmental Agencies

Government agencies — from local park districts to the Federal Trade Commission — also need legal assistance. If their needs are very limited, they usually retain a private law firm on a limited basis, but if their workload justifies it, they also hire lawyers as full-time employees just as business corporations do. These in-house law firms closely parallel those of the private sector: They advise agency officials on the requirements of the law, keep them informed regarding proposed legislation and regulations that might affect the agency, and manage any litigation of which the agency is a party. The lawyers in their agencies frequently enjoy civil service protections.

In some cases an entire governmental agency is formed for the specific purpose of providing legal services. The federal Justice Department and a local district attorney's or public defender's office provide examples of agencies designed solely for such a purpose. These types of agencies also employ attorneys on a salaried basis, but they function very like private law offices.

c. Other Variations

In addition to the forms of practice discussed above, attorneys may be employed in the legal departments of private nonbusiness organizations such as labor unions, trade associations, consumer groups, and charities. Although the parent organization may have varying goals the function and operation of the legal department parallel those of a business corporation or a governmental agency.

The terms *legal clinic* and *legal services office* are frequently used incorrectly and interchangeably. Legal clinics provide low-cost legal services on routine matters by stressing low overhead and high volume. They frequently operate out of store-front offices and make extensive use of paralegals. The attorneys who operate the clinic, however, are usually organized as either a partnership or a professional corporation. Legal services offices usually are legal aid services designed to help poor people and are affiliated with the federal government's Legal Services Corporation. The attorneys who work in such offices are salaried employees of a not-for-profit corporation that receives both public funds and private donations to provide free legal services to the poor. They hold positions similar to attorneys working for a public defender's office, except that they handle civil rather than criminal cases.

B.   SUPPORT PERSONNEL

The personnel who provide support services for attorneys are part of the legal team and have important contributions to make to the process of providing quality legal services.

1. Paralegals

An explanation of the paralegal's role in the legal system is presented in Chapter 1. Parts 3 and 4 of this book describe in greater detail some of the specific functions performed by paralegals and how they relate to the work of attorneys. At this point the reader is reminded that the paralegal is a key member of the legal team.

2. Law Clerks, Investigators, and Librarians

Law clerks, investigators, and librarians are specialized positions that are sometimes found in law offices. Although their formal training differs from that of a paralegal, they perform tasks that frequently overlap work done by paralegals.

A law clerk usually is a law school student who works for the firm part time during the school year or full time during the summer, but may be a recent law school graduate who has not yet passed the bar

exam. Most of the clerk's time is typically spent doing legal research. Investigators are often ex–law enforcement officers who locate and interview witnesses, take photographs of accident scenes, and gather documentary evidence. Librarians are responsible for updating and maintaining the firm's law library. In large firms the librarian may have a degree in library science and sometimes joint library and J.D. degrees. In smaller firms the library may be one of several other responsibilities assigned to either a paralegal or a secretary.

3. Clerical Personnel

No law office can function efficiently without skilled clerical personnel. In addition to typing correspondence and legal documents, the clerical staff answers the telephone, greets visitors, sets up appointments, distributes and posts mail, finds and files internal office records, files documents in the courthouse, and processes billing records.

In smaller offices one or two legal secretaries will perform all of the above functions. In larger offices the clerical staff will be more hierarchical and have specialized jobs, such as receptionist, file clerk, legal stenographer, and bookkeeper, as well as legal secretary.

As is discussed in Chapter 1, some experienced legal secretaries perform some paralegal duties. The key distinction is that where clerical personnel take dictation and transcribe material produced by lawyers or paralegals, the paralegal composes the content of the letters, memoranda, and legal documents being typed.

In many instances the relationships between legal secretaries and paralegals have been stressful. This is likely to happen when a firm introduces paralegals into its operation without having developed clear job descriptions and without having properly prepared the clerical staff for their arrival. Do the secretaries type for the paralegals? If so, whose work takes priority — the paralegals' work or the attorneys'? Should paralegals have to operate the copy machine, or should they be able to delegate that task to someone on the clerical staff? Do experienced secretaries resent that they were not selected for the new positions? Time and experience usually help to reduce but not eliminate tensions between paralegals and secretaries. As a contributing editor of a prominent magazine for paralegals observed: "Legal assistants have everything to gain from building peace with legal secretaries, whose secretarial skills are crucial to the smooth functioning of the entire legal team."[5] The key to building such a peace, she suggests, consists of "healthy doses of the three R's — respect, recognition, and realism."[6]

---

5. McGowan, How to Wage Peace, 2 Legal Assistant Today 22 (1985).
6. Id. at 23.

4. Administrators

The titles and job descriptions of administrative positions differ widely from one law office to another. In some cases there is a professional legal administrator whose responsibilities may extend to assigning legal work among the firm's attorneys. More commonly the administrator supervises only the business aspects of the firm. These duties typically include hiring and training the support staff, maintaining personnel records, procuring and maintaining office equipment, overseeing billing operations and bank accounts, and preparing budgets and financial statements.

Administrative positions also exist within departments or units of larger law offices. Thus there may be an office manager in charge of the secretarial pool or word processing unit, a business manager in charge of the bookkeeping department, or a paralegal manager who supervises other paralegals.

Growth in the use of specialized legal administrators is illustrated by the fact that the Association of Legal Administrators is one of the fastest-growing professional associations in the country. Furthermore, 40 percent of its 4,500 members come from firms with fewer than twenty attorneys, which demonstrates that their use is not limited to large firms. A variety of career paths can lead to these positions: Twenty-four percent of the ALA's membership comes from a general management background, 23 percent rose from secretarial ranks, 15 percent were accountants, 4 percent were in finance, and 3 percent in personnel.[7]

5. Outside Contractors

Law firms will frequently contract for various support services rather than use their own employees. Cleaning services and office machinery repair are common examples. Some very large firms even contract with food services to operate employee cafeterias.

Law firms also use outside contractors for performing real estate title searches, preparing income tax returns, searching for corporate names and filing incorporation documents, researching legal issues, and preparing briefs. Other services offered by outside contractors include tracing the whereabouts of heirs, debtors, and witnesses and providing information about the size of settlements and judgments in cases with similar facts so that attorneys can predict what a case should be worth. Still others specialize in providing litigation support services that include processing and retrieving computerized documents and supplying expert witnesses. As is mentioned in Chapter 1, some freelance paralegals contract with law firms to provide specific services for individual cases.

---

7. Murry, The Association of Legal Administrators: On the Move, 2 Legal Assistant Today 28, 29 (1985).

C.   FEE STRUCTURE

Lawyers use various systems for determining what they will charge for their legal services. Paralegals should be familiar with these systems and their implications for paralegals.

1. Fixed Fees

Consumers generally pay a set fee for a particular product or service. A physician typically charges a set amount for a routine office call or a specific surgical procedure. Some lawyers also price some of their services in this manner. This is especially true of routine tasks such as drawing a simple will, incorporating a small business, or handling an uncontested divorce. In many areas real estate closing fees are also billed in this manner.

When fixed fees are used, it is to the firm's advantage to delegate as much work as possible to paralegals because they typically cost the firm less than attorneys do. The decreased overhead that results from such delegation to paralegals should result in higher profits and/or a reduction in the established fee. A fee reduction not only benefits consumers of legal services but also improves the firm's competitive position in the marketplace.

2. Contingency and Percentage Fees

Contingency fees are calculated as a set percentage of what the client gains as a result of the law firm's work. However, the fee is contingent on the client's collecting some sort of award or settlement. The plaintiff's attorney in a personal injury suit is typically hired on this basis. If the defendant refuses to settle the matter out of court and the court then finds for the defendant, neither the plaintiff nor the plaintiff's attorney receives any money. On the other hand, if either the defendant settles out of court, or the court awards damages to the plaintiff, his or her lawyer will receive a set percentage of the money received. It is common for the law firm to receive 33 percent if it is settled before it goes to trial, 40 percent if it goes to trial, and 50 percent if the case is appealed. Percentage fees are also common in collections work, where the attorney gets a percentage of whatever is eventually collected. Although percentage fees used to be common in real estate and probate work, the trend in those areas has been to use fixed fees and time charges respectively.

As with fixed fees, it is economically advantageous for a law firm to delegate as much as possible to paralegals because it reduces costs without affecting the fees received from the case.

3. Time Charges

Many legal fees are based on hourly rates rather than on percentages or fixed charges. This is particularly true for litigation defense and corporate work. Hourly charges vary depending on whether the work is done by a paralegal, an associate, or a senior partner. The client's best interests are served by having less complex matters delegated to paralegals and paying top dollar only for the matters that require the expertise and experience of a senior partner.

The hourly fees established by the firm reflect the firm's overhead costs, the income expectations of its partners, and the competition. Part of the amount collected for an hour of paralegal time pays the paralegal's salary, but part pays for office space and secretarial services, and part is the firm's profit.

4. Retainers and Advances

Two other important elements of legal fees are retainers and case advances. A retainer is a fee given to an attorney to engage his or her services on a particular matter or for matters that might come up during a set period of time. Retaining the attorney's services also means that the attorney is prohibited by professional ethics from acting on behalf of any adverse parties.

Sometimes a retainer is a nonreturnable fee that is collected before the attorney begins work on the case. This is particularly common in criminal defense and divorce work. A retainer can also consist of a set monthly fee paid to a firm for specified continuing legal services. Thus a small business or a school board might pay a monthly fee for advice on routine legal matters.

A case advance is money that is collected from the client before work is begun. Rather than an advance on the attorney's fees, it is an advance on other costs (filing fees, witness fees, and so forth) that will be incurred as part of the litigation. Advances for costs may be deposited in a special client's trust fund and must be carefully accounted for. All unused funds must then be returned to the client at the conclusion of the case.

5. Prepaid Legal Services

Group legal services plans offer still another way to pay for legal services. In some forms of closed panel plans, an existing organization (such as a labor union, professional group, or student government association) hires or contracts with one or more attorneys to provide specified legal services for its members. Some services may be free, and others may be offered at reduced rates. The organization either uses general dues money or special assessments to fund its payments to the attorneys.

In open panel programs participants can choose any attorney they wish rather than be limited to those specifically designated by the sponsoring organization. These programs more closely resemble standard medical insurance. Participants contribute a monthly amount to an insurance pool that then provides reimbursements for specified legal services.

D. STANDARD OPERATING PROCEDURES

Although every firm has its own variations, many administrative practices are common to most law offices. This section examines common administrative practices in traditional law offices. Section E discusses some of the changes brought about by office automation and computerization.

1. Office Procedures Manual

Most large offices maintain a loose-leaf manual containing written copies of their basic policies and procedures. The manual usually explains personnel policies on such things as holidays, sick leave, vacation time, and breaks. It also describes how the filing system operates, what kinds of records must be kept, and how supplies are obtained. Some manuals include a glossary of acceptable abbreviations and checklists for handling certain types of matters.

2. Client Files

A law office must maintain complete files on every case in which it is involved. The type and number of file folders used may vary, but most legal files consist of the following materials: a client information sheet (including names and addresses of all parties involved and billing arrangements); correspondence between the firm and either the client or other outside parties connected to the case; internal office memoranda including research memos prepared in connection with the case; copies of all pleadings related to the case; copies of relevant contracts, leases, medical reports, laboratory reports, and so forth; and notes by attorneys and paralegals working on the case. These materials usually are placed in separate folders that are treated as subfiles. Within each subfile the materials are arranged in chronological order with the most recent item placed on the top or at the front of the subfile.

Most firms store their client files in a central location and assign a specific individual to set up and maintain these files. When a new file is opened, the names of the adverse parties must be cross-referenced with other law firm records to avoid possible conflict of interest problems. (Memos are frequently circulated within the firm to inform other attor-

neys of the firm's new clients.) The files are usually arranged in alphabetical order in smaller firms and in numerical order in larger firms. In a numerical system, cases are given consecutive numbers based on when the file was first opened. A separate alphabetical card file is then kept to cross-reference the client's name with the file number. When lawyers or paralegals wish to use one of these files, they formally check it out so that someone else wishing to use the same file will know where to locate it.

After the firm's involvement in a matter is completed, a file clerk or secretary officially closes the file. Some materials in the file are returned to the client, some are discarded, and some remain as part of a permanent file. Closed files are frequently stored in a separate, more remote area and eventually may be microfilmed in order to cut down on storage costs.

3. Work Product Files

Legal research can be time consuming, and there is nothing to be gained from duplicating work that already has been done. Rather than beginning from scratch, an attorney or a paralegal reviews the work that someone else has done on a similar topic or problem. The previous research may not be exactly on point and in any event must be updated to see what changes may have taken place since it first was done, but it provides a convenient and time-saving starting point.

In order to facilitate the sharing of previous research, many offices maintain special work product files to be used when drafting memos and legal documents. When a legal memorandum is produced, a complaint is drafted, or an appellate brief is prepared, a copy of the document is evaluated as to its future usefulness, and if it is determined to be of future value, the document is placed in the firm's work product files. Separate files are usually kept for federal and state pleadings. They are typically stored in loose-leaf binders in the library.

4. Tickler Systems

Every law office needs a reliable way to keep track of and give advance warnings of important dates. If a lawsuit is not filed within the time limits established by the statute of limitations, clients may not be able to receive a remedy for their wrong and the law firm may in turn be sued for malpractice. Once a defendant has been served with a summons, there is a set period of time within which to respond. Every time a motion is filed or an answer is received, another time period begins and another deadline approaches. If any of these deadlines is missed, the process may have to be started all over again, or a default judgment may be rendered against the client, or a statute of limitations may run out. Because these deadline dates are very important, lawyers develop docket

control systems to monitor important dates. Such systems are frequently referred to as tickler systems.

Although a tickler system can be as simple as writing important dates on a desk calendar, most law firms use more complex and more reliable methods. One method involves setting up a system of 3 × 5 index cards filed in a set of dividers tabbed to reflect day, month, and year. Every time a deadline is established, a separate index card is completed indicating the client's name, file number, and what needs to be done on that date. These cards are then placed behind the proper divider card along with any other cards that also apply to that date. Another variation involves preparing reminder memos that are then filed in file folders marked with a specific day, month, and year.

The key to the success of a tickler system is that at periodic intevals someone must check these files and notify the proper attorneys or paralegals of what must be done with enough advance notice for them to get the task completed by the deadline date. In some firms secretaries prepare weekly memos that are then circulated to all concerned parties. The tickler file often has one entry three months in advance of the actual due date, another entry one month in advance, and still another a week in advance.

5. Timekeeping and Billing

Depending on the nature of the practice, many law offices keep detailed records of the amount of time each attorney and paralegal spends on individual cases. If the firm charges at an hourly rate for its services, it must maintain adequate records to document those charges. In cases where a court may order the payment of attorneys' fees, a specific accounting must be made of the time actually spent on the case by different legal personnel. When a firm handles the case for a flat fee or on a contingency fee basis, the time records are not necessary to bill the client, but information about time spent on the case is used in setting future fees for similar kinds of work, for evaluating the productivity of employees, and for dividing the firm's profits.

Several different systems are used for recording how the time is spent. The diary system is probably the simplest. The attorney or paralegal keeps a calendar book that divides the day into time blocks. Hours of the day are typically subdivided into five-, six-, ten-, or fifteen-minute segments.[8] A clerk then copies the information from the diary onto ledger sheets that are maintained for each client. A variation of the

---

8. Although a six-minute segment may seem like an awkward number to work with, it represents one-tenth of an hour and thus simplifies calculation of bills by allowing the use of a decimal system.

diary system involves the use of daily or weekly timesheets that are kept in a loose-leaf form rather than permanently bound together. This makes it easy for a billing clerk to transfer the information to client ledgers. The diary system creates a permanent record of how each person spent the day, and reviewing this record may help that person to become more efficient.

In order to eliminate the need to transfer the information from the attorney's or paralegal's time records to the client ledger sheets, some firms have personnel record time directly onto the ledger sheets. However, this method becomes very time consuming and inefficient if a large number of cases is involved and if the attorneys and paralegals must constantly shuffle through ledger sheets to find the sheet that they need. The benefit of having a comprehensive record of how an individual's day is spent also is lost with this method.

Still another variation of timekeeping uses special time slips. Each time slip has a space to indicate the name of the client, a description of the nature of the work performed, and the time spent on the project. These slips are then sorted and placed in the appropriate client's files. The most sophisticated forms are constructed in such a way that after the form is completed, a top part can be peeled off and placed in the client's file, and a permanent daily log is left behind.

6. Practice Systems

Some firms use highly developed office systems for handling various types of cases. Kline Strong is frequently credited with being the major designer of these integrated packages of checklists and forms.[9] With the assistance of fellow law school professors and 4,050 hours of law student labor, Strong developed systems for divorce, probate, and corporate law in 1971. The following year he developed law office systems for bankruptcy, collections, real estate transactions, and the administration of intestate estates. Those were followed in succeeding years by systems in estate planning and public securities issues.[10]

Strong's systems and others that have followed are based on the development of a master information list. The paralegal usually gathers all the information called for on the master form. This master information form then is correlated to a set of standardized practice forms so that the blanks on the forms are numbered to correspond to specific items on the master information list. A checklist is used to remind the paralegal of the various tasks that have to be accomplished and when they should be done.

---

9. Gullickson, Lawyering Systems, 4 U. Tol. L. Rev. 399 (1973).
10. Id.

E. OFFICE AUTOMATION AND COMPUTERIZATION

Just as the computer has revolutionized many other aspects of modern life, it has also had a major effect on how law offices are run today. At first large firms contracted with specialized firms that provided computerized billing services. Then as computer prices dropped, law firms purchased their own systems. Word processors so increased the efficiency of the secretarial staff that even small firms could not afford not to purchase them. Today the reduced cost and increased power of desktop computers have made labor-saving features available at prices that almost every office can afford. Furthermore, the increased availability of user-friendly legal software packages makes it possible for lawyers, paralegals, and legal secretaries to use their computers without any special training in computer programming.

1. Computer Equipment and Terminology

This section provides an elementary and nontechnical introduction to some of the computer equipment and terminology used in modern law offices. Learning to use a computer is much like learning to use a television. You do not have to know how the television actually generates the picture on the screen or how to replace a resistor in the set; you only need to learn which switches to use in order to get the set to display the channel that you want to watch. So it is with computers. You do not have to know how computers are engineered, and you do not even need to know common programming languages such as BASIC, PASCAL, COBOL, or FORTRAN. With relatively little instruction about the particular system being used, one can soon begin to make productive use of a variety of software packages.

Just as good stereo systems are often sold as separate components (a receiver, an amplifier, a tape deck, a turntable, and speakers), computer systems are composed of several components that are connected into an operating system. Computer hardware consists of various kinds of input devices, a central processing unit, auxiliary storage units, and output devices.

The input device is usually a keyboard on which the operator types instructions and enters data. Keyboards can be supplemented by optical character readers (devices that convert printed characters on paper directly into a form that the machine can read) or modems (devices that can receive computer information transferred over telephone lines from other computers). The CPU (central processing unit) is the brain of the computer. It is here that arithmetic and logical operations take place. The control unit of the CPU monitors and supervises the actual data manipulations. The ROM (read only memory) contains permanent in-

structions about how the computer is to function. The RAM (random access memory) provides temporary storage for information while it is being processed. After the required data manipulations have been completed, the result is sent to an output device. The most common output devices are video monitors and printers. It can also be sent over telephone lines to other computers through the use of a modem.

Because the information contained in the RAM portion of the computer is lost when the computer is turned off or when it must be cleared to make room for new data, computer systems also use auxiliary devices to store information on a more permanent basis. The most common type of storage device is the disk drive, which stores and retrieves large amounts of information on either floppy or hard disks. The disks resemble phonograph records and are able to store electronic signals. The rigid hard disks have much greater storage capacity than the flexible floppy disks. Magnetic tapes also can be used for storage.

Whereas once only large firms were able to afford to hire outside specialists to program their computers for them, today approximately fifty companies market legal software, and almost any size firm can afford to purchase standard software packages designed for the most popular types of personal desktop computers.[11] Software consists of instructions on how the computer should operate. User-friendly software packages translate simple English instructions into the computer languages that are necessary to run that particular computer system. These software packages program the computer to be used for such things as word processing, file storage and retrieval, billing, and preparation of management reports. It is important to note, however, that a software package is specifically designed for a particular computer. Software developers must take into account both the memory capacity and the type of operating system used in its CPU.

2. Word Processing

Perhaps the most common application of computer technology in the average law office involves the use of word processing equipment. Such equipment allows secretaries to edit a document before it is printed and make minor changes on previously used documents without having to retype the entire document. Sophisticated word processing programs allow the operator to move sentences and paragraphs at will and to automatically adjust the margins to conform to specific requirements. Many packages even correct misspelled words and generate their own indexes.

In the 1970s many firms purchased specialized word processing typewriters or dedicated word processors, as they are known technically.

---

11. See Buyer's Guide, Natl. L.J., Dec. 17, 1984, at 17.

These DWPs are actually small computers that are programmed solely to do word processing. However, as the cost of personal computers decreased and the quality of word processing software and printers increased, many firms saw the advantages of investing in PCs rather than DWPs.

A number of legal publishers now market legal forms on disks as well as in the traditional bound book format. The disks allow the attorney or paralegal to load the form on the word processor, personalize it for the needs of the client, and then have it printed without having a secretary retype it from the book. Similarly, if the firm has placed its work product files on disks, the attorney or paralegal can call forth old letters, pleadings, and contracts, make the appropriate editorial changes, and then have the document printed without a secretary laboriously retyping the standardized materials.

3. File Indexing and Retrieval

Any information that can be typed on a piece of paper and stored in a file cabinet also can be typed into a computer and stored on a disk. The big advantage to computerized files is the speed and ease with which that file information can be retrieved. Rather than walking to the file room and searching through file drawers to locate the precise document required, the paralegal or attorney types identification information, and the computer either displays the requested document on the monitor or produces a written copy on the printer. One software manufacturer claims that its program will retrieve any document in less than a minute and usually within thirty seconds.[12]

Computerized document retrieval is fast because computers index and sort the contents of their files so rapidly. Thus, a computer can produce a specific file by being supplied with a name or an identification number for that file, or it can produce all files that refer to a specific individual or all files that deal with a specific legal concept.

The computer therefore can provide a quick and efficient cross-check of clients and adversaries in order to determine whether a new case presents any conflict of interest problems. It is very useful in maintaining docket control and office tickler systems because it sorts out and lists by attorney or paralegal all types associated with any particular day or week. It is particularly useful for indexing depositions, interrogatories, and other discovery documents. In the federal government's antitrust case against IBM, for example, 37 million documents were involved.[13] Without the use of computers it would be impossible for any group of attorneys and paralegals to organize that many materials into a usable format.

---

12. Syntrex Electronic File Room advertisement, in 2 Legal Assistant Today 7 (1985).
13. Middleton, Getting Support, Natl. L.J., June 4, 1985, at 1, 28.

The programs used for these types of applications are commonly referred to as data base management systems (DBMS). They have been called the fourth generation of programming languages because they are so much easier to use than traditional programming languages. They allow law offices to set up computerized filing systems that are tailored to each office's specialized needs.

4. Number Crunching

Computers are also very good at performing mathematical tasks with great speed and accuracy. Computers therefore have been used widely in timekeeping and billing. Once the information from the attorneys' and paralegals' timesheets are fed into the system, the computer can post those figures to the appropriate client's account, multiply them by the appropriate rate, total the entire account, and then prepare an itemized bill. Similarly the computer can prepare staff paychecks and calculate various partners' contributions to the income of the firm. A number of software packages handle the monthly billing process and also produce comprehensive financial reports on receipts, expenses, status of bank accounts, and so forth.

Computers have also proved very useful in the area of tax preparation. Software packages allow office personnel to enter a client's financial information in response to prompts provided by the computer. Then the computer prints out the appropriate entries on the proper federal or state tax form. Similar packages exist for preparing probate, real estate, and securities documents. In a real estate closing, for example, a last-minute change in the price or in the date of sale may require a great deal of recalculation. The computer handles it quickly and accurately.

So-called electronic spreadsheet programs are especially useful in advising clients about the tax implications of potential personal or business decisions and in estate planning work. These programs give fast and accurate answers to a series of "what if" questions. How much income would a trust produce each year if the interest rates were at one level versus another level? How much would one's taxes be reduced by investing a certain amount of money in an oil drilling operation? Such programs are also useful for a law firm's own long-range financial planning.

As with the DBMS, an electronic spreadsheet requires some limited programming in order to structure spreadsheets to fit a particular situation. However, for those who do not want to attempt these relatively simple programming operations, a growing number of spreadsheets come already programmed to handle common legal applications.

5. Communications

With a communications software package and a modem, one computer can communicate with other computers. The modem is an elec-

tronic device that changes a computer's digital signals into analog signals so that they can be transmitted along standard telephone lines. Modems can use regular telephone lines, but major data base services like LEXIS, WESTLAW, and DIALOG use special private lines to ensure clear transmission at high speeds.[14]

One advantage of being able to communicate with other computers is the so-called electronic mail function. A computer can send a written message or a copy of a document more rapidly than the United States Postal Service or private couriers can. The sender dials the appropriate phone number, gives the required password to gain access to the system, designates the receiver of the message, and then leaves the message. The receiver dials the appropriate phone number, gives the password, and then instructs the computer to print out the messages that the receiver has been designated to receive. ABA/NET is an example of one such computer bulletin board that was established specifically for lawyers. Such bulletin boards help to avoid "telephone tag" — where busy people exchange a series of telephone messages because the parties are not available to talk at the same time.

Probably the most important advantage of communications packages is that they allow the user to search through and transfer information from large external data banks. LEXIS and WESTLAW provide extensive legal research materials that will be discussed in Chapter 8. DIALOG, NEXIS, ORBIT, and VU/TEXT provide access to a variety of nonlegal data bases including the texts of major newspapers, credit and financial information, and airline flight schedules.

6. Future Developments

As the technology continues to advance, paralegals can look forward to even more widespread use of computers. Speech recognition systems will allow people to dictate directly into a word processor, and laser technology will vastly increase the speed with which optical scanners can read printed documents and printers can reproduce them. In the courtroom of the future, judges, lawyers, clerks, and court reporters will probably have computer terminals at their desks to provide access to evidence, pleadings, and other court records. Paralegals should learn as much as they can about them and use such knowledge to open new opportunities within the law office.

F.   SUMMARY

Paralegals may be employed in a variety of organizational settings, including sole practitioners, large partnerships engaged in private prac-

---

14. M. Mason, An Introduction to Using Computers in the Law 25 (1984).

tice, and legal departments within corporations and governmental units. Although the status and treatment of attorneys may differ significantly among organizations, the status of the paralegal within the organization is usually pretty much the same regardless of the form of practice. The type of legal organization that one is dealing with often provides clues regarding the resources and perspectives of the people that are associated with it.

In addition to attorneys and paralegals a number of other people serve as part of the legal team. Although law clerks, investigators, and librarians do many things that we define here as paralegal work, these positions are associated with a distinct set of duties usually assigned to a person with a distinctive type of background. Secretaries, file clerks, receptionists, word processing operators, and other clerical personnel provide a variety of necessary clerical services. No law office can function effectively without someone to answer the phone, make appointments, and type and file documents. Legal administrators reduce some of the attorneys' administrative burdens so that attorneys can concentrate on the practice of law. Finally, law firms may also engage specialized contractors for both legal and nonlegal support services.

Lawyers use a variety of different pricing systems in establishing their professional fees. Paralegals must be familiar with how these systems work and the types of cases that are associated with each format. They also must understand the basic procedures used in most law offices, including the filing system, the timekeeping and billing system, and the tickler system. Because the computer has changed many of these procedures, paralegals must be aware of the manner in which the computer is used in law offices today. Computerization has greatly reduced the number of clerical personnel needed to operate a law office and has opened new opportunities for paralegals to increase their effectiveness.

KEY TERMS

associate	employee
case advance	fee advance
central processing unit (CPU)	file clerk
client file	fixed fee
computer hardware	floppy disk
computer software	general counsel
contingency fee	group legal services
dedicated word processor (DWP)	hard disk
director of a corporation	investigator
electronic mail	junior partner
electronic spreadsheet	law clerk

law librarian

legal administrator

legal clinic

modem

monthly draw

of counsel

office sharing arrangement

officers of a corporation

partnership

practice system

prepaid legal services

private practice

professional corporation

random access memory (RAM)

read only memory (ROM)

retainer

salary

senior partner

sole proprietor

tickler system

time charge

time slip

user friendly

word processing

work product files

REVIEW QUESTIONS

1. What is the difference between a partnership and a professional corporation? Between a sole proprietorship and an office sharing arrangement?

2. What are the major alternatives to a private practice?

3. What different job titles and duties are assigned to clerical personnel within a law office?

4. What types of services are provided by outside contractors?

5. When is a lawyer most likely to use a fixed fee, a contingency fee, and an hourly fee?

6. What factors are considered when setting a fixed fee or an hourly rate?

7. What are the major sections of a client file, and where are these materials usually stored?

8. Briefly describe how a tickler system operates.

9. What are the most common ways in which a law office uses communications software packages?

DISCUSSION QUESTIONS

1. From an attorney's perspective, what are the advantages and disadvantages of the various forms of practice?

2. Job titles and duties are not always well defined in many law offices. Discuss the extent to which the work of various support personnel

frequently overlaps that of attorneys as well as that of those in other positions within the office.

3.   What are the advantages and disadvantages of a law firm's using outside contractors for legal services?

4.   From the perspective of the client, what are the advantages and disadvantages of using a contingency fee structure?

5.   Why do smaller firms usually use alphabetical filing systems but larger ones usually use numerical ones?

6.   Why are most law offices greatly increasing their use of computers? In what ways are computers better than people?

PROJECTS

1.   Using the Martindale-Hubbell Law Directory or some other directory of local attorneys, identify (1) the total number of attorneys listed in your area, (2) the number of attorneys who work in firms of ten or more attorneys, (3) the number of attorneys listed that appear to work at firms of more than one attorney but less than ten, and (4) the number of attorneys who appear to be in solo practice.

2.   Examine a recent survey of salaries of legal personnel. (Consult your instructor for information about where to find such surveys.) What type of relationship exists between type of practice and average earnings? Among the salaries of the various support personnel?

PART III
Paralegal Skills

PARTS I AND II PRESENTED a general introduction to the American legal system and the paralegal's role within that system. This section of the text focuses on building basic paralegal skills. Although the specific duties performed by paralegals differ among specialty areas, these duties all involve applying a common core of basic skills. Part III builds the basic skills that paralegals use to find and analyze facts, find and analyze the law, draft legal documents, and advocate a client's position.

Chapter 7 discusses how facts are gathered and analyzed. It begins with the initial client interview in the law office and covers such topics as taking statements from witnesses, taking photographs, and collecting documentary and physical evidence. Chapter 8 presents strategies and techniques for doing legal research. Both chapters include references to the availability and use of computer data bases. Chapter 9 covers how to draft legal documents — from contracts and pleadings to research memoranda and appellate briefs. Chapter 10 focuses on the advocacy skills required to assist attorneys in trials and to represent clients in administrative hearings.

Chapter 7
Interviewing and
Investigation

RESOLVING A LEGAL CONFLICT involves applying general principles of law to a specific set of facts. Before attorneys can advise a course of action for a client to take, they need to know the factual details of the client's situation. When attorneys file a lawsuit, the initial complaint specifies a great deal about the facts. Good trial attorneys never proceed to trial without a firm expectation of what the various witnesses are likely to say. Getting the facts straight is thus central to the practice of law. It is an area in which paralegals can make major contributions.

A. THE CLIENT INTERVIEW

The attorney can obtain important knowledge of the factual details of a client's situation from documentary evidence (such as police reports, medical reports, contracts, and photographs) and personal observation (such as visiting the scene of an accident or examining the condition of an apartment). However, knowledge of many of the most important facts is usually gained by interviewing clients and witnesses. It is therefore essential that attorneys and their paralegals develop considerable interviewing skills.

Depending on the procedures established in the office in which they work, paralegals may be involved in several types of interview situations. These situations can include the initial client interview, follow-up interviews with the client (either in the office or in the field), and field interviews with both friendly and hostile witnesses.

In many legal aid and some group legal services programs, the client is interviewed by a paralegal prior to meeting with an attorney. In most legal aid programs the first order of business is determining whether the client meets the program's financial eligibility standards, which requires obtaining information about the client's income, assets, debts, and number of dependents. (In soliciting such personal financial information it is very important that the interviewer explain why such information is necessary.) This information may then need to be verified

in some fashion and examined in light of the agency's eligibility standards.

Once it has been determined that the client is financially eligible for the program's services, paralegals gather information about the nature of the client's problems. Here the paralegal must gather enough factual information to separate the legal problems from the nonlegal ones and to be able to provide the agency's attorneys with the type of information they need to begin solving the legal problems. The paralegal also should be able to help these clients obtain assistance from appropriate social service agencies for their nonlegal concerns.

In some law offices the attorneys prefer to have paralegals collect a considerable amount of information about their clients' problems before they meet with them personally, but in others the attorneys prefer to handle the initial interview and then have paralegals obtain follow-up information. In most private law firms the attorneys conduct the initial interviews themselves. This is usually related to their desire to impress the client, to reserve the right to make an immediate decision as to whether to accept the case, and to negotiate the fee arrangement.[1] Once the attorney/client relationship has been established, the attorney may bring the paralegal into the interview or completely turn the client over to the paralegal to gather further information about the client's case.

No matter how productive the initial interview is, it often is necessary to gather additional facts from the client. This can be done by having the client come to the office, by going to the client's home or office, or by using the telephone. The paralegal may have to inteview other persons who have knowledge of the facts of the dispute, and these interviews may take place in a variety of settings.

1. Principles of Good Communication

The authors of a book on communication problems report having seen the following sign in a lawyer's office:

> I know you believe you understand what you think I said, but I am
> not sure you realize that what you heard is not what I meant.[2]

It would probably be worthwhile if every law office prominently displayed such a sign because it points out a common communication problem — the listener is not getting the message that the speaker has intended to convey.

The communications process begins with the speaker's desire to

---

1. In legal aid, group legal services, and legal clinics the types of cases accepted are usually determined by established policies, and the fees are either nonexistent, prepaid, or standardized.
2. G. Nierenberg and H. Calero, Meta-Talk 16 (1975).

send a message to another party. Before a message can be sent, however, the speaker must decide what combination of words, gestures, and facial expressions to use. Then he or she must transmit the message using these symbols. The listener, on the other hand, must first be alert enough to accurately perceive which symbols the speaker is using. Then the listener must in turn decide what meaning should be attached to these symbols. It is quite possible for two people to receive different messages from the same set of words and gestures. We are constantly faced with the possibility that our listeners do not comprehend the meaning that we intend to convey and that in turn we do not accurately perceive the messages they send to us.

Good listening skills are essential to understand what the person being interviewed is really saying. As Alfred Benjamin has written in an excellent book on interviewing skills,

> Listening requires, first of all, that we not be preoccupied, for if we are we cannot fully attend. Secondly, listening involves hearing the way things are being said, the tone used, the expressions and gestures employed. In addition, listening includes the effort to hear what is not being said, what is only hinted at, what is perhaps being held back, what lies beneath or beyond the surface. We hear with our ears, but we listen with our eyes and mind and heart and skin and guts as well.[3]

Good listening involves recognizing not only what the interviewee perceives to be the facts but how he or she feels about those facts as well. As Thomas Shaffer stresses in his discussion on legal interviewing, "Feelings are facts." Even though statements that begin with "I think" or "I feel" are ordinarily inadmissible in a court of law, it is important that the attorney knows that a person thinks or feels that way.[4]

The interviewer learns about these feelings not only from statements in which the interviewee says that he feels angry or that she resents the action of someone else but from a variety of gestures and expressions. As Makay and Gaw explain,

> While we are engaged in conversations with another, we are being continuously bombarded with messages from the other's face or hands or posture, the sound of his or her voice, the distance that separates us, the amount of time we spend together and spend looking at each other, and so on. We can't escape from nonverbal communication.[5]

---

3. A. Benjamin, The Helping Interview 44 (2d ed. 1974).
4. T. Shaffer, Legal Interviewing and Counseling 65 (1976).
5. J. Makay and B. Gaw, Personal and Interpersonal Communication: Dialogue with the Self and with Others 58 (1975).

These nonverbal messages can be either conscious or unconscious and either intentional or unintentional. A smile is both intentional and conscious. A quivering voice is usually conscious yet unintentional.[6]

The interviewer must work at being a good listener. It is especially important to avoid the trap of allowing previous experiences to color perception of the case at hand. After a paralegal has interviewed dozens of clients with landlord/tenant disputes, he or she may begin to think in terms of stereotyped categories. One then begins to assume that simply because something happened one way in a similar case, it happened the same way in the case at hand. Having once categorized the current case, the interviewer may fail to hear what the interviewee really says. The danger is greater when the interviewer has undergone a similar experience.

Communication is a two-way street, and the interviewer also has an obligation to make sure that the person being interviewed understands what the interviewer is saying. Although interviewers cannot give clients lessons on good listening, they should be very conscious of the words, expressions, and gestures used as well as the reactions they evoke. To as great a degree as possible, the interviewer's vocabulary should be modified to fit the interviewee's educational and cultural background.[7] Great efforts should be made to keep legal jargon out of the conversation. Above all, the interviewer needs to be alert for signals that the other person does not understand what is being said. In those cases, the interviewer must go back and restate the message in different terms.

2. Putting the Subject at Ease

Communication between the interviewer and the interviewee can be improved by having the interview take place in a comfortable and quiet location in which there will be privacy and few interruptions. Such facilities help to establish good rapport. Avoiding interruptions from telephone calls and secretaries shows respect for the interviewee and helps to build trust.

Communication can be facilitated or impeded by a circumstance as simple as where the parties sit during the interview. In the traditional arrangement either the lawyer or the paralegal sits behind a large imposing desk, which reinforces the authority image. The client sits across the desk — usually in a chair that is lower than that of the interviewer. Such a seating arrangement intimidates clients and does not put them at ease.

Figure 7.1 shows the basic seating arrangements available in most offices. Arrangements A, B, and C use a desk and side chairs, and ar-

---

6. Id. at 67.
7. This does not mean that a middle-age, middle-class white should attempt to talk like a young ghetto black. The interviewer should use key words that the interviewee will understand.

Figure 7.1 Alternative Seating Arrangements for Interviews

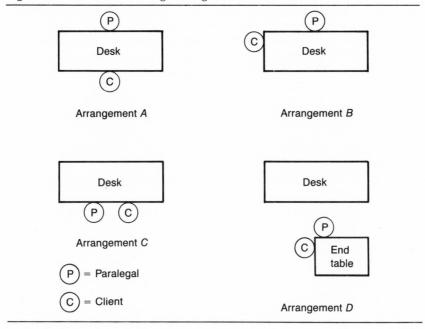

rangement *D* gets away from the desk and uses chairs placed around a low table of some sort. The behavioral science literature strongly suggests that *D* is the arrangement most conducive to good communication. It places the interviewer and the interviewee on an equal level at a distance that facilitates personal communication.[8] It also has the advantage of providing comfortable eye contact; it allows the two parties either to look directly at each other or to easily glance away at a 90° angle. About the only disadvantage is that it is more difficult for the interviewer to take notes. In effect, the interviewer now has to balance a legal pad on a knee.

In smaller offices where such end table arrangements may not be available, the paralegal should use arrangement *B*. This positioning of client and paralegal offers the same advantages of distance and eye contact. It also provides the interviewer with a large surface on which to take notes.

Although note taking can be distracting, it is essential in most legal interviewing situations. The paralegal has to understand the facts and

---

8. Although the parties should be close, they should not be so close that they invade each other's private sphere. The social sphere, which is considered the optimal space for this type of communication, is found to be approximately two to four feet from the other person.

cannot afford to rely on memory until the interview can be written up. Indeed, as Benjamin suggests,

> In our culture, when note taking is discriminately handled, it is not resented. On the contrary, its absence may be looked upon as negligence or lack of interest.[9]

Seeing the types of notes that are taken (which is possible from positions *B* and *D*) is thought to strengthen the trusting aspect of the relationship.

In addition to the factors discussed above, the general conduct of the interviewer can put the client at ease. Allen Ivey identifies three aspects of what he calls "attending behavior."[10] To begin with, the interviewer needs to be comfortable and relaxed. Ivey advises interviewers to

> Relax physically; feel the presence of the chair as you are sitting on it. Let your posture be comfortable and your movements natural; for example, if you usually move and gesture a good deal, feel free to do so at this time.[11]

The interviewer's sense of relaxation can go a long way toward placing the interviewee at ease.

Second, Ivey stresses the importance of initiating and maintaining eye contact. He warns, however, that such eye contact can be overdone:

> A varied use of eye contact is most effective, as staring fixedly or with undue intensity usually makes the client uneasy. If you are going to listen to someone, look at them.[12]

The final element in attending behavior is verbal following:

> the interviewer's use of comments which follow directly from what the interviewee is saying. By directing one's comments and questions to the topics provided by the client, one not only helps him develop an area of discussion, but reinforces the client's free expression, resulting in more spontaneity and animation in the client's talking.[13]

3. Starting the Interview

The handling of the initial contact between client and paralegal can contribute greatly to establishing a meaningful rapport. If the attorney begins the interview while the paralegal is present or calls in the paralegal at some point during the course of the client's visit, the attor-

---

9. Benjamin, supra note 3, at 58.
10. A. Ivey, Microcounseling: Innovations in Interviewing Training 35, 149 (1971).
11. Id. at 150.
12. Id. at 149.
13. Id.

ney introduces and explains the paralegal's presence. On the other hand, if the paralegal meets the interviewee without a previous introduction, the paralegal should enter the reception room, greet with an introduction, and personally accompany the client to the office. The traditional handshake is an effective gesture to show interest in and respect for the person to whom one is being introduced.

As part of the introduction process, the paralegal should give a brief explanation of the paralegal's role. The person being interviewed has a right to know who the interviewer is and that the interviewer is not a lawyer. On the other hand, there is no need to launch into a five-minute description of everything that a paralegal can or cannot do. The paralegal's role should be described in relatively simple positive terms. For example: "I am a paralegal — not an attorney. My job involves gathering the basic facts for (attorney's name). I will be working with him/her on your case." If the paralegal handles administrative hearings, the type of representation given can be explained and the amount of experience summarized.

On an initial visit to the law office, the client should be allowed to introduce the problem in the manner and at the pace most comfortable for him or her. The interviewer should be willing to engage in some small talk about the weather or about the parking situation until the client feels relaxed enough to move on to the nature of the problem. If after some awkward periods of silence, the client seems to have trouble discussing the specific situation, the paralegal can initiate the conversation with an inquiry such as, "Well, Mr./Mrs. . . . what is it that brings you in to see us?"

It is very important that the paralegal have clients describe the problem independently and not in response to specific questions from the interviewer. As Benjamin warns,

> If we begin the helping interview by asking questions and getting answers, asking more questions and getting more answers, we are setting up a pattern from which neither we nor surely the interviewee will be able to extricate himself. By offering him no alternative we shall be teaching him that in this situation it is up to us to ask the questions and up to him to answer them. What is worse, having already become accustomed to this pattern from previous experience, he may readily adapt himself to it. Here again, he will perceive himself as an object, an object who answers when asked and otherwise keeps his mouth closed — and undoubtedly his mind and heart as well.[14]

The net result is that communication is reduced and valuable information may not be volunteered. A further danger is that the interviewer will

---

14. Benjamin, supra note 3, at 66.

concentrate on framing the next question and will fail to listen to what the client really says.

4. Keeping the Interview Going

Although the interviewer needs to avoid a straight question-and-answer format, carefully selected questions are an important part of most interview situations. When properly used, questions can clarify areas of ambiguity and assist the interviewee in telling the story. In successful interviewing the questions are asked in the proper form and at the proper time.

A question can take many forms. Consider, for instance, the difference between open and closed questions. Open questions such as "How did the accident take place?" focus the interview without greatly limiting the freedom of the respondent. On the other hand, closed questions are by their nature very specific and usually demand very short answers: "What color was the car that hit you?" "How far in advance did you see it coming?" "Was the sun shining in your face at the time?" Note that if the interviewee, in responding to the general open question, fails to discuss the point at which the other car was first seen, the interviewer can always follow it up with a more specific closed question. However, if the interviewer, in asking a closed question, fails to ask about the condition of the roadway, the information is unlikely to be volunteered by the interviewee.

Earlier in this chapter, we emphasized that "feelings are facts." The emotional state of the client in relating the incident, as well as the emotional state of the various parties at the time of the incident, also are important. Responses to open questions are likely to reveal these emotional factors. Compare the information given below by the client in response to the different forms of questions from the paralegal:

> *INTERVIEW NO. 1*
> *Paralegal:* Did you receive a written eviction notice?
> *Client:* Yes.
>
> *INTERVIEW NO. 2*
> *Paralegal:* How did you find out that you were going to be evicted?
> *Client:* The landlord came up to me around 7 o'clock in the evening while I was sitting on the front porch with some other residents. He yelled something about my being a no-good troublemaker because I was always complaining to the city inspections department. Then he stuck this eviction notice in my hand and stomped off.

Better information usually is obtained from open questions. The closed variety should be reserved for pulling together potentially important details that the interviewee may have overlooked.

Once the client has begun to expound on one of these open questions, the interviewer should attempt to keep the conversation going through the use of minimal encourages to talk, paraphrasing, and reflection of feelings. The *minimal encourages* to talk, as Ivey labels it, are single words or very short phrases that communicate that the interviewer hears what is being said and that the interviewee should continue with his or her narrative. Examples of these minimal encourages include the following:

> "Then?" "And?" "So?"
> Repetition of a key word or two.
> "Could you tell me more?"
> "How do you feel about that?"
> "Could you give me an example?"
> "What does that mean to you?"
> "Um-hm."[15]

Minimal encourages also include head nods and various other gestures.[16]

Paraphrasing is simply the process of repeating, in a shortened form, what the interviewee has just finished saying. It serves three basic functions:

1. To convey to the client that you are with him, that you are trying to understand what he is saying;
2. To crystallize a client's comments by repeating what he has said in a more concise manner; and
3. To check the interviewer's own perceptions to make sure he really does understand what the client is describing.[17]

For example, if a client relates a rather involved conversation with a bill collector, the interviewer might respond: "So the bill collector threatened to get you fired if you didn't pay by Tuesday. Is that right?"

In addition to using paraphrasing to reflect the interviewer's perception of the facts, the paralegal should use it to acknowledge the client's emotions. It demonstrates that the interviewer has been listening closely and understands the feelings that have been expressed.[18] The goal is to communicate an understanding of how the client feels — a sense of empathy. It is not necessary to show acceptance for the person's feelings — just that those feelings are respected. As Benjamin puts it,

> acceptance means treating the interviewee as an equal and regarding his thoughts and feelings with sincere respect. It does not mean agreeing; it does not mean thinking or feeling the way he does; it

---

15. Ivey, supra note 10, at 152.
16. Id. at 56.
17. Id. at 156.
18. Id. at 154.

> does not mean valuing what he values. It is, rather, the attitude that
> the interviewee has as much right to his ideas, feelings, and values as
> I have to mine and that I want to do my utmost to understand his life
> space in terms of his ideas, feelings, and values rather than in terms
> of my own.[19]

After listening to a client describe an incident in which her husband
made derogatory remarks about her at a party, the interviewer might
comment, "You must have felt pretty angry about being embarrassed in
front of your friends."

When using either the paraphrasing or the reflection of feeling
technique, the interviewer should deliver the feedback in a tentative tone
of voice. This offers the interviewee a chance to respond by either (1)
affirming that the stated understanding is correct, (2) correcting what
was a false understanding on the interviewer's part, (3) elaborating further on the topic, or (4) using some combination of the first three. These
techniques show the interviewee that the interviewer is listening and
force clarification of the presentation.

Nonverbal behavior also plays an important role in the feedback
process. Just as the client sends nonverbal cues to the interviewer, so too
the interviewer sends nonverbal cues to the client. The paralegal therefore must remain conscious of nonverbal behavior and the effect it has
on the client.

A good interviewer also tries to avoid using "why" questions because they have come to connote disapproval and displeasure.[20] They
put the interviewee on the defensive and erode the relationship of trust
that the interviewer is supposed to be building. While there are occasions
when these why questions can legitimately be used (such as, "Why did
you move out of your apartment?"), they especially should be avoided
where matters of values and judgment are involved.[21]

Bear in mind that the paralegal has an obligation to seek out all
relevant information — including information that may be damaging to
the client's case. It is necessary to explain to the client that the attorney
needs to know about any damaging evidence to be prepared to deal with
it. The client needs to be reminded that there may be cross-examination
during the trial and that the opposing side is likely to bring up any
damaging evidence at that time. The client also can be told that what
may appear to be damaging may in fact turn out to be beneficial.
Whenever possible the paralegal should avoid situations in which the
client may feel compelled to lie to either the lawyer or the paralegal.
Before you ask a client whether he or she was speeding at the time of the

---

19. Benjamin, supra note 3, at 39.
20. Id. at 80.
21. Id. at 85.

accident, gently warn the client that the police report probably will show a speed that has been estimated on the basis of skid marks.[22]

5. Ending the Interview

As mentioned previously, the interviewer should let the client begin the interview on his or her own terms. General open questions are used along with minimal encourages, paraphrasing, and reflections of feeling. Closed questions are used for following up and clarifying details in the later stages of the interview. Near the end of the interview the paralegal should summarize his or her understanding of the client's problem in order to ensure accuracy and to give the client a chance to add any additional information that may have been overlooked.

Once these steps have been completed, the paralegal should collect, or make arrangements to collect, copies of all relevant legal documents. These documents should be photocopied and returned to the client as soon as possible. If authorization forms are to be signed, the client should sign them at the same time.

The client should also be told what to expect next from the office — whether to expect to see the attorney soon and just what the nature of the next contact with the attorney's office might be. In the case of legal aid work it may be appropriate to refer the client to various social service agencies that can assist in other ways.

It is also important at this stage that paralegals remember the ethical prohibitions that apply to their role. Clients often attempt to elicit advice and opinions about their cases from the paralegal, but paralegals are not allowed to give legal advice, and the clients should not be given false expectations about the outcomes of their cases. Likewise, the paralegal must remember to respect the client's rights to confidentiality.

As soon as possible after the interview the paralegal should review and polish the notes on the case while the matter is still fresh. These notes, along with the copies that were made of relevant documents, should then be placed in the appropriate office file.

B.   THE INVESTIGATION

After completing the initial client interview, the attorney and the paralegal will have a fair idea of the nature of the case. The client, however, seldom knows all of the relevant facts, such as why the traffic signal was not operating, why the brakes failed, why the welfare worker denied your client's requested benefits, and whether the condition of the apartment violates any provision of the housing codes.

---

22. R. Gordon, Interviewing Strategy, Techniques, and Tactics 16 (1975).

Even when the client can provide an answer, it will be necessary to confirm the client's perceptions of those facts. The client's perception is sometimes biased and inaccurate and needs to be verified through the examination of other witnesses as well as physical and documentary evidence.

Attorneys may do much of this investigative work on their own, hire an outside investigator, or use a paralegal on their own staff. If the attorney does the actual investigative work, it may be awkward in court when it comes to laying the proper foundation for photographs or impeaching the testimony of a witness. It is much better if the attorney is able to call somebody else to the witness stand to give this type of testimony.

Above all else the investigator must conduct an unbiased search for the truth. In order to protect the client's interests the attorney must be aware of the unfavorable as well as favorable factors in the case. If there is a witness or a document that contradicts the client's story, the attorney needs to know about it. Good attorneys seek to avoid surprises, and they rely on sound investigation to accomplish that end.

The nature of the investigation varies considerably with the area of law involved, as well as with the particular facts of the case at hand. Negligence cases require a great deal of investigative work. Damaged cars, broken machines, and injured persons all have to be examined. Witnesses have to be interviewed at length in order to determine the existence of negligence on the part of one or more parties to the accident. In workers' compensation cases the issue is not negligence but the extent of damage. The extent to which an injury was work related also becomes an important aspect of the investigation. In probate an investigation may involve locating missing heirs or attempting to determine what the mental state of the deceased was at the time a will was written.

The skills exercised in all areas are basically the same. Whether a witness is being sought to testify about an automobile accident or an armed robbery, the problems of locating that witness or of gaining cooperation are often the same. Investigators must be resourceful and persistent without being obnoxious. Persons are not usually located on the first try, and investigators must be able to cope with the prospect of frequently ending up on dead-end roads. Investigators must also be patient, for they spend many hours waiting for people. The hours are irregular, and they often have to work while others play. Yet the area of investigation is one of the most challenging and rewarding activities in which a paralegal can participate.

1. Getting Started

Generally speaking, the legal system is a slow-moving process in which delays and continuances are common. It is not uncommon for a

period of four to five years to pass between the time of an accident and the eventual courtroom resolution of the negligence and damages issues that arose from the accident. For the investigator time is of the essence. Accident scenes change. Witnesses' memories fade. Witnesses move. Broken parts are repaired or discarded. Injuries heal. It is therefore essential that the investigator take certain actions as soon as possible.

Before the investigator rushes into the field, careful thought must be given to identifying just what is being sought. Many investigators find it useful to begin by listing chronologically the events that the client described. The investigator then attempts to identify evidence that either substantiates or contradicts the description of each event provided by the client. This analysis provides a basis for identifying additional information that the investigator will have to gather. For each event on the list, the investigator identifies witnesses who may have observed it or documents that might substantiate it.

The investigator also identifies areas in which gaps appear within this sequence of events. Is it possible that something else could have taken place at that same time? Are there key details that the client cannot remember? Is there something that you would expect to have happen that did not? What was the mental state of the people involved? Who was responsible for creating the conditions that may have contributed to the events that took place? For each gap found, the investigator must identify possible sources of information that could help complete the picture.

In developing these lists, it is important that the investigator discuss the theory of the case with the supervising attorney. The investigator must thoroughly understand the types of evidence that the law requires to be introduced before the court will recognize something as being a fact. It is necessary to know, for example, what the elements of a particular crime are or what must be proven in order to establish a cause of action in a negligence case. In discussing the theory of the case, it is also important to remember that there may be several alternative theories of the case. The attorney and the investigator must discuss their primary theory of the case and also alternative theories that they might pursue and the theories that the opposition may pursue. Evidence must be gathered that will be relevant to all these alternatives.

The investigator also must be aware of how the evidence must be collected and preserved in order to be considered admissible in court. Taking time to mark a piece of evidence or excluding a remark from a statement can mean the difference between being able to use the item in court or not being able to use it. However, the investigator should provide the attorney with all the facts possible, irrespective of whether they are admissible. Inadmissible evidence often can be used as the basis for obtaining evidence that is admissible. It also can be important in negotiating settlements. A resourceful attorney may be able to use one of the numerous exceptions in the rules to admit something that the paralegal thought would not be admissible.

2. Physical and Photographic Evidence

The investigator usually begins by personally visiting the scene at which the events in question took place. In a situation involving an automobile accident, for example, the investigator should take a variety of photographs of both the damage to the vehicles involved and the condition of the roadway. Pictures should include any tire marks present and the condition of tires on the vehicles involved in the accident. If there is any suspicion that a faulty part may have been responsible, a series of close-up photographs should be taken of that part. Pictures of the scene should show the existence of all road signs and traffic control signals as well as any obstructions to the driver's vision. Wherever appropriate, the photographer should take pictures that show the nature of the injuries suffered.

Since dirt and debris usually fall off a car at the moment of impact, the investigator should look very carefully for this type of physical evidence. Spilled oil or antifreeze will often mark the point on the road at which the impact took place. The nature of damage to the headlights can indicate whether or not the lights were on at the time of the accident.[23]

When taking photographs of this type, the investigator should strive to reproduce as faithfully as possible what ordinary human beings see. Artistic urges and fancy camera angles must be subordinated to straightforward shots that show the proper depth perception. While some courts still prefer black and white pictures over colored ones, most find both types equally acceptable.[24] Identification can be aided by placing a marker (such as a small chalkboard or, for close-ups, a business card) in the area to be photographed.[25] This helps establish the authenticity of the photo and helps viewers place the objects pictured in proper perspective.[26]

In addition to taking photographs, the investigator should prepare detailed diagrams wherever they are appropriate. Such diagrams must, in order to be admissible, be drawn to scale. At the accident scene, for example, the investigator should carefully measure everything from the width of the street to the location of various traffic signs. This information should then be converted into one or more detailed diagrams. The diagrams can be useful aids in interviewing witnesses and at the trial itself.

---

23. If the ends of the bulb broke cleanly and there are no signs of oxidation present, the lights were not on at the time of the impact.
24. A. Golec, Techniques of Legal Investigation 92 (1976), and G. Stuckey, Evidence for the Law Enforcement Officer 296 (2d ed. 1974).
25. Stuckey, supra note 24, at 288.
26. On rare occasions a trial court will object to the marker on the basis that it has changed the scene. The investigator should therefore routinely take two photographs: one with the marker and one without. The second photo can be introduced if an objection to the marker is made.

3. Locating Witnesses

The investigator should locate and interview witnesses as soon after the incident as possible. The longer the delay, the more difficult it will be to find them, and the less they will accurately remember.

During the initial interview the client should be asked to supply as much information as possible about both the identity and possible location of relevant witnesses. Depending on the type of event involved, police reports or newspaper articles should be checked for information about possible witnesses. (Form 7.1 provides an example of a typical police report.) Whenever there is a chance that someone who lives or works nearby may have seen or heard something related to the event in question, the investigator should check with the occupants of all nearby buildings. If the event took place at a particular intersection at a particular time, one should observe and record the license numbers of automobiles that go through that intersection at approximately the same time every day. There is a good chance that the drivers of some of those vehicles may have seen at least something relevant to the event in question. Sometimes the search for witnesses may also involve posting a notice in the area or even taking out a display advertisement in a local newspaper.

Occasionally an investigator will have a witness's name but will be unable to locate that witness either because the address is missing or incorrect. When this occurs, there are a number of steps a resourceful investigator can take. The telephone book and the city directory are good starting points. If the person has moved, landlords, utility companies, neighbors, and relatives often know where the person moved. If the investigator knows where the person is employed, the witness can either be contacted there or the home address can be obtained through the employer. If the individual being sought has school-age children, it may be possible to find out through the school system where their transcripts were forwarded. If the person is a member of a trade union or professional association, the national headquarters may be able to provide a current address. For a nominal fee the post office will provide address correction information. Still another method of search involves sending a certified letter marked for the addressee only and with a return receipt requested. If the witness has an unlisted telephone number, the local telephone company office may be willing to relay a message that an attorney is trying to reach someone in that household.[27]

In addition to locating lay witnesses, the investigator may also need to contact expert witnesses for a court appearance. The expert witnesses should be contacted early so that they can advise the investigator on the types of factual material that should be gathered (see Exhibit 7.1).

---

27. F. Bailey and H. Rothblatt, Fundamentals of Criminal Advocacy 56 (1974).

Form 7.1 Traffic Accident Report

POLICE

TRAFFIC ACCIDENT REPORT

POLICE ACCIDENT NO	A78-944
INCIDENT NUMBER	

ON Number or Name of Highway or Street
1. Linden Street

COUNTY McLean
TOWNSHIP OR CITY Normal

At Intersection With Virginia Avenue

1 (Number or Name of Intersecting Highway or Street)

2 If not at Intersection — Feet — or — Miles — N E S W of _____ (Circle 1)
(Nearest Highway Street Bridge or other Landmark)

I.D.O.T. USE ONLY

Sheet 1 of 1 Sheets

DATE OF ACCIDENT
MO 02 / DAY 02 / YR 78
TIME OF ACCIDENT 6:54 A.M. / P.M.
TOTAL UNITS INVOLVED 2

DAY OF THE WEEK
M T (W) T F S S

TYPE OF REPORT
CIRCLE ONE OR MORE: Conventional
CIRCLE ONE OR MORE:
1. Fatal
2. Injury
3. Property Damage
4. Arrest
5. Interstate/Expressway
6. Supplementary

UNIT 1 / DR

DRIVER'S NAME: Last Hart, First Thomas, M.I. L.	DATE OF BIRTH MO 10 / DAY 24 / YR 56	SEX: (1 MALE) 2 FEMALE
DRIVER'S ADDRESS 1700 North School, Apt. 27		
CITY/STATE/ZIP Normal, Ill. 61761	PHONE 438-8638	INJ. CODE 0
DRIVER'S LICENSE NO H620-8295-8308	STATE Ill.	CLASSIFICATION A & M	RESTRICTIONS None	Total Occ Unit 1 Including Driver 1
COLOR Whi	YEAR 66	MAKE Pontiac	MODEL Tempest 4 dr	VEHICLE TYPE Passenger	
VEHICLE REGIST. NO TKL 177	STATE Ill.	YEAR 78	CITY	VEHICLE IDENTIFICATION NO. 23369P268458	STATE Il
VEHICLE OWNER same as driver			1 DRIVEN AWAY 2 TOWED AWAY
OWNER'S ADDRESS same			
VEHICLE REMOVED BY driver	VEHICLE REMOVED TO driven		

UNIT 2 / DR

DRIVER'S NAME Last Hooper, First James, M.I. B.	DATE OF BIRTH MO 02 / DAY 25 / YR 07	SEX: (1 MALE) 2 FEMALE
PEDESTRIAN		
DRIVER'S ADDRESS 1306 South Linden		
CITY/STATE/ZIP Normal, Ill. 61761	PHONE 436-6709	INJ. CODE 0
DRIVER'S LICENSE NO H260-2199-7058	STATE Ill.	CLASSIFICATION B	RESTRICTIONS 1-0-0	Total Occ Unit 2 Including Driver 3
COLOR Grn	YEAR 73	MAKE Dodge	MODEL Polara 4 dr	VEHICLE TYPE Passenger	
VEHICLE REGIST. NO CJ1316	STATE Ill.	YEAR 78	CITY	VEHICLE IDENTIFICATION NO DM41K3F271053	STATE Il
VEHICLE OWNER same as driver			1 DRIVEN AWAY 2 TOWED AWAY
OWNER'S ADDRESS same			
VEHICLE REMOVED BY driver	VEHICLE REMOVED TO driver		

DAMAGE TO PROPERTY OTHER THAN VEHICLES

NAME OF OWNER OF PROPERTY None
ADDRESS OF OWNER
NATURE OF DAMAGE
APPROX. COST OF REPAIR OR REPLACE $

TIME NOTIFIED OF ACCIDENT 6:54 A.M. P.M.	DATE NOTIFIED OF ACCIDENT MONTH 02 / DAY 02 / YEAR 79	DATE REPORT COMPLETED MONTH 02 / DAY 02 / YEAR 79	
ARREST (NAME) Last Hart, First Thomas, M.I. L.	SECTION NUMBER 11-904	TICKET NUMBER 12884	5235937
ARREST (NAME) Last First M.I. one issued	SECTION NUMBER	TICKET NUMBER	
SIGNATURE OF INVESTIGATING OFFICER X D. Cowsebi	ID NUMBER 602	DISTRICT OF ASSIGNMENT NPO #3	COURT DATE 03/05/79	REVIEWING OFF

CIRCLE POINT OF CONTACT (Unit 1)
APPROX. COST TO REPAIR OR REPLACE $ 250.00
SEATING IN VEHICLE
1 2 3
4 5 6
7 8 9

CIRCLE POINT OF CONTACT (Unit 2) STATION WAGON
APPROX. COST TO REPAIR OR REPLACE $ Under 250.00
CODE FOR INJURY
Use only most serious one on each space for injury
K-Dead Before Report Made
O-No Indication of Injury
A-Bleeding Wound, Distorted Member, Carried From Scene
B-Other Visible Injury as Bruises, Abrasions, Swelling, Limping, etc.
C-No Visible Injury But Momentary Unconsciousness or Complaint of Pain

List Additional Passenger or Witness Information on Separate Sheets Attached Sheet

PASSENGERS AND/OR WITNESSES

NAME Last Hooper, First Mrs. James, M.I.	
ADDRESS 1306 S. Linden	
CITY Normal	STATE Ill.
AGE M / 2-F 69	TAKEN TO not	UNIT NO 2 SEAT POS 2	TAKEN BY: not	INJ. CODE 0
NAME Last Williams, First Ann, M.I.	
ADDRESS 1306 South Linden	
CITY Normal	STATE Ill.
AGE M 91 / 2-F	TAKEN TO St. Joseph's Hospital	UNIT NO 2 SEAT POS 3	TAKEN BY: AAA Ambulance	INJ. CODE B
NAME Last DNA First M.I.	
ADDRESS	
CITY	STATE
AGE 1-M / 2-F	TAKEN TO	UNIT NO SEAT POS TAKEN BY:	INJ. CODE
NAME Last DNA First M.I.	
ADDRESS	
CITY	STATE
AGE 1-M / 2-F	TAKEN TO	UNIT NO SEAT POS TAKEN BY:	INJ. CODE

(SR1733-300M - Rev. 3-78)

274

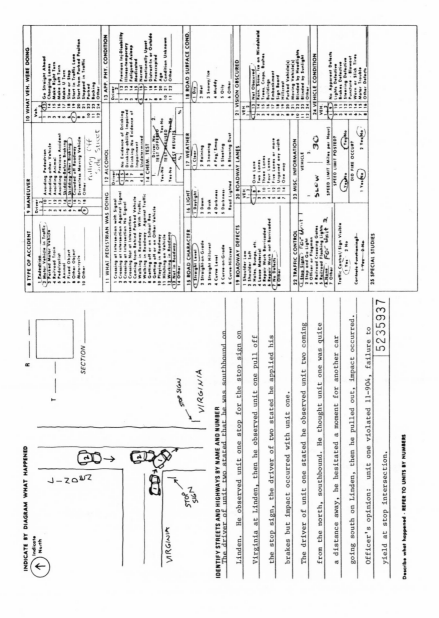

INDICATE BY DIAGRAM WHAT HAPPENED

Indicate North ←

R

T ——

SECTION

LINDEN

VIRGINIA

STOP SIGN — VIRGINIA

STOP SIGN

IDENTIFY STREETS AND HIGHWAYS BY NAME AND NUMBER

Describe what happened · REFER TO UNITS BY NUMBERS

The driver of unit two stated that he was southbound on Linden. He observed unit one stop for the stop sign on Virginia at Linden, then he observed unit one pull off the stop sign, the driver of two stated he applied his brakes but impact occurred with unit one.

The driver of unit one stated he observed unit two coming from the north, southbound. He thought unit one was quite a distance away, he hesitated a moment for another car going south on Linden, then he pulled out, impact occurred.

Officer's opinion: unit one violated 11-904, failure to yield at stop intersection.

5235937

---

8 TYPE OF ACCIDENT
1 Pedestrian
2 Motor Vehicle in Traffic
3 Parked Motor Vehicle
4 Railroad Train
5 Pedalcyclist
6 Animal
7 Fixed Object
8 Other Object
9 Motorcycle
10 Other

9 MANEUVER (Driver)
1 /10 Avoiding Pedestrian
2 /11 Avoiding other Vehicle
3 /12 Avoiding Animal
4 /13 Avoiding Previous Accident
5 /14 Skidding Before Braking
6 /15 Coming from Behind Parked Vehicle
7 /16 Other
/17
/18

Pulling off Side Street

10 WHAT VEH. WERE DOING (Veh.)
1 /13 Go Straight Ahead
2 /14 Changing Lanes
3 /15 Make Right Turn
4 /16 Make Left Turn
5 /17 Make U Turn
6 /18 Slow or Stop
7 /19 Start in Traffic Lane
8 /20 Start from Parked Position
9 /21 Stopped in Traffic
10 /22 Parked
11 /23 Backing
12 /24 Other

11 WHAT PEDESTRIAN WAS DOING
1 Crossing at intersection with Signal
2 Crossing at intersection Against Signal
3 Crossing at intersection No Signal
4 Crossing Not at intersection
5 Coming from Behind Parked Vehicle
6 Walking in Roadway With Traffic
7 Walking in Roadway - Against Traffic
8 Getting off or on School Bus
9 Getting off or on Other Vehicle
10 Playing in Roadway
11 Hitching on Vehicle
12 Working in Roadway
13 Not in Roadway
14 Other

12 ALCOHOL (Driver)
5 No Evidence of Drinking
6 Drinking ability impaired
7 Drinking No Evidence of Impairment
8 Undetermined

14 CHEM. TEST
Driver No. 1 / Driver No. 2
TEST OFFERED Yes-No
TEST USED
TEST RESULTS %

13 APP. PHY. CONDITION (Driver)
1 /12 Previous Inj-Disability
2 /13 Illness-Temporary
3 /14 Fatigued-Asleep
4 /15 Medicated
5 /16 Normal
6 /17 Emotionally Upset
7 /18 Distraction or Outside
8 /19
9 /20 Age
10 /21 Condition Unknown
11 /22 Other

15 ROAD CHARACTER
1 Straight Level
2 Straight-on-Grade
3 Straight Hillcrest
4 Curve Level
5 Curve-on-Grade
6 Curve-Hillcrest

16 LIGHT
1 Daylight
2 Dawn
3 Dusk
4 Darkness
5 Darkness Road Lighted

17 WEATHER
1 Clear
2 Raining
3 Snowing
4 Fog/Smog
5 Blowing Dust

18 ROAD SURFACE COND.
1 Dry
2 Wet
3 Snowy/Ice
4 Muddy
5 Oily
6 Other

19 ROADWAY DEFECTS
1 Shoulder Low
2 Shoulder Soft
3 Holes, Bumps, etc.
4 Loose Material
5 Repair Work Barricaded
6 Repair Work not Barricaded
7 No Defects
8 Other

20 ROADWAY LANES (VEH 1-2)
8 One Lane
9 Two Lanes
10 Three Lanes
11 Four Lanes
12 Five Lanes or more
13 Unpaved any width
14 One way

21 VISION OBSCURED (VEH 1-2)
13 Not Obscured
14 Rain, Snow, Ice on Windshield
15 Trees, Crops, Bushes
16 Buildings
17 Embankment
18 Sign Board
19 Hillcrest
20 Parked Vehicle(s)
21 Moving Vehicle(s)
22 Blinded by Headlights
23 Blinded by Sunlight
24 Other

22 TRAFFIC CONTROL
1 Stop Sign — For Unit 1
2 Stop and Go Light
3 Officer or Flagman
4 None — For Unit 2
5 Railroad Crossing Gates
6 Railroad Flashing Lights
7 Other

Traffic Control/Sign Visible 1 Yes 2 No

23 MISC. INFORMATION
VEHICLE 1 - 2
SPEED LIMIT (Miles per Hour): Slow 30
DID FIRE OCCUR? 1 Yes/No 2 Yes/No
Controls Functioning? 1 Yes 2 No

24 VEHICLE CONDITION (VEH 1-2)
9 No Apparent Defects
10 Lights Defective
11 Brakes Defective
12 Steering Defective
13 Puncture - Blowout
14 Worn or Slick Tires
15 Motor Trouble
16 Other Defects

25 SPECIAL STUDIES

Exhibit 7.1 Sample Letter to a Prospective Expert Witness

MINT & WALLER   **Robert Mint**
Trial Lawyers   **Bruce Waller**

500 First National Bank Bldg.
Bloomington, Illinois 61761   September 12, 1978

Prof. George Grain
Department of Agriculture
Rock State University
Rock, Iowa

Dear Prof. Grain:

This office represents a client who was injured while painting
the roof of a metal grain bin. I am trying to locate an expert
witness for consultation regarding design safety and possibly
some court testimony, and thought you may be able to give me some
help.

The grain bin was a cylindrical structure about twenty feet high
with a cone-shaped metal roof on top of the cylinder at approximately 45 degrees pitch. The client slipped, lost his footing,
and slid off the roof onto the ground.

A product liability suit has been filed in McLean County, Illinois. The complaint alleges that at the time the bin left the
control of the defendant, it was not reasonably safe in that:

1. There was no railing, bar, or other device at the edge of
    the roof to prevent a person on the roof from sliding off;
2. There was no warning to persons who were climbing to the
    roof or on the roof of the danger of standing on the roof.

I would greatly appreciate it if you could send me any suggestions on possible expert witnesses. If you are interested in
serving in this capacity, please send me your resumé and fee
schedule. I would appreciate hearing from you even if you do not
have any suggestions.

                        Sincerely yours,

                        Suzanne Little

                        Suzanne Little
                        Legal Assistant

Although most expert witnesses may be used in almost any type of case, they are most likely to be found in various types of negligence cases. In product liability and professional malpractice cases, an expert is usually needed to testify about the generally accepted practices and standards of that industry or profession. For example, in product liability cases the plaintiff must show that there was a defect in the design or manufacture of the product. As Anthony Golec states,

> To qualify as an expert in a products liability case, the engineer must demonstrate sufficient technical familiarity with the general type or class of product or equipment under consideration. He must also be able to describe a state-of-the-art knowledge at or before the date of manufacture of the product and often must have conducted appropriate tests with the product in question.[28]

Several useful directories list experienced expert witnesses and their fields of expertise. Two of the most widely used are H. Philo, D. Robb, and R. Goodman, Lawyers' Desk Reference: Technical Sources for Conducting a Personal Injury Action,[29] and the Directory of Expert Witnesses in Technology, both of which are updated periodically.

It is usually a little harder to find expert witnesses in the medical area — especially when an allegation of malpractice is involved. Golec writes that

> One of the formidable obstacles is the difficulty in obtaining the technical help of experts, namely other doctors, in a medical malpractice investigation and subsequent trial. The medical profession has historically been extremely reluctant to testify against its own, yet has also been extremely lax in policing itself and weeding out bad practitioners.[30]

Medical school faculty members or doctors on the staffs of veterans' hospitals are one of the best sources for locating doctors who will testify in court.[31] Doctors usually are willing to serve as expert witnesses in an area such as workers' compensation, where the focus is on the nature of the employee's injury rather than the negligence of another professional.

4. Interviewing Witnesses

When conducting interviews the investigator generally should make advance arrangements to ensure that the time available is adequate

---

28. Golec, supra note 24, at 191.
29. This handy reference also has information about relevant industry standards and various other background sources.
30. Golec, supra note 24, at 211.
31. Id. at 216.

and convenient for the witness.[32] The investigator must rely on the cooperation of the witness and should therefore make every effort to accom-
modate the witness's needs. The interview can take place in the law
office, in the witness's home, or even at the witness's place of work. The
most important consideration is that it take place in a relatively peaceful
setting where interruptions can be minimized. If at all possible, the interview should take place out of the presence of friends, family, or co-
workers.[33]

In general, telephone interviews should be avoided because rapport is difficult to establish and appearance and demeanor cannot be
observed. Nevertheless, the advantages of convenience and expense may
sometimes outweigh these disadvantages, especially if the person has
already been interviewed in person or if the nature of the information to
be provided is routine and unlikely to be contested.

As in the case of the client interview, the witness interview should
begin on an open-ended basis. The witness should not be confronted
with a series of yes or no questions. The witness may be approached as if
the investigator has only a general knowledge of the situation and needs
the witness to fill in the details. The same types of feedback mechanisms
discussed earlier in this chapter should be used (minimal encourages,
paraphrasing, and reflection of feelings). As the interview progresses,
the investigator can use closed questions to extract the essential details.

When a witness evaluates some person or event, the interviewer
should probe to find the specific observations on which that evaluation is
based. Exactly what the witness said or heard personally must be distinguished from what was heard secondhand.

As the investigator conducts the interview, he or she should carefully evaluate the person's strength as a witness in the courtroom: How
convincing will the witness be on the witness stand? Will the witness be
able to follow the questions easily or become confused easily? If the
interviewee was an eyewitness to something or overheard something, the
investigator should subtly test the witness's eyesight and/or hearing. If a
person wears eyeglasses, it is wise to determine the type of prescription
and whether the eyeglasses were worn at the time of the incident being
testified about.

Generally speaking, the investigator should attempt to interview
adverse witnesses first. Time is of the essence, and it is important to get

---

32. On occasion it is best to appear at the witness's doorstep without advance notice. This is
particularly true when there is reason to believe that the person might rehearse a story
with someone else. See below and page 279 for a more complete discussion of the
problems of adverse witnesses.
33. One exception to this rule is when a young child is being interviewed because having a
parent present may help put the child at ease. It is always possible, however, that
children may be willing to tell the interviewer something that they would not tell their
parents. Another exception is the situation in which an interpreter is needed because
the witness cannot speak English.

these witnesses on record before they have time to establish various defenses. If they have consulted with a lawyer, they have probably been told not to say anything to an investigator. (If it is determined that a witness has retained an attorney, that witness should be approached only through that attorney.) If the investigator makes contact soon enough, the adverse party may not yet have talked to an attorney or have carefully developed all aspects of the story. Statements from such adverse witnesses can indicate problem areas that the paralegal's attorney may have and can provide clues for the type of information needed to impeach that testimony.

In approaching a hostile witness it is sometimes better to interview without making an appointment in advance. Such a strategy reduces the chances that the witness carefully will rehearse a story before the investigator's arrival.[34] Interviewers must be prepared for any eventuality, for they probably will have only one opportunity to talk to the hostile witness.

When witnesses appear to be reluctant to cooperate, the investigator should attempt to determine the cause for this reluctance: Are they friends of the other party or the victim? Do they fear some sort of retaliation? Are they simply afraid of being called to testify at the trial stage? The investigator can point out that by giving a statement now the person may avoid being subpoenaed to testify at a trial.

When interviewing friendly witnesses, the investigator must be especially careful not to use leading questions and to guard against the witness who embellishes the truth to win approval or help a friend.

5. Taking Formal Statements

After engaging the witness in conversation long enough to establish rapport and develop some idea about what the person witnessed, most investigators attempt to take some type of formal statement.[35] This statement cannot be used as direct evidence at the trial, but it can be used to refresh the witness's memory or to impeach a hostile witness's testimony. If a witness's testimony is detrimental to the investigator's side of the case, the judge or jury may be shown that the witness is not credible, perhaps by demonstrating that the testimony given in court is inconsistent with statements that the witness made in an earlier statement out of court.

---

34. Golec, supra note 24, at 58.
35. It should be pointed out that opinions differ about how formal statements should be taken. Because such statements are discoverable by the opposing side, some attorneys prefer not to take them. They simply rely on the investigative notes. If the witness changes the story, the attorney has the investigator testify about what the witness told the investigator earlier. Such testimony is not likely to carry as much weight as a formal statement would. Where the attorney really wants to pin down a witness for the record, a deposition can be taken. (See discussion at page 190.)

There are three main types of statements taken by investigators. The most common and widely recognized is the narrative type, in which the investigator records in his or her own handwriting what the witness says (see Exhibit 7.2). The investigator simply takes out a pad of legal paper and starts writing. If the witness asks about the procedure, simply explain that pertinent facts are being recorded before they fade from memory. Although the witness's words are not taken down verbatim, an attempt should be made to use his or her own phrases and descriptions as much as possible.

A typical narrative statement is organized according to the following outline:

1. *Identity of the witness*
   Name
   Age, sex, and marital status
   Occupation and employer
   Residence and business address, phone numbers
   Organizational affiliations and other items that will help locate the
      person in the future
2. *Identification of the accident*
   Date, day of the week, time
   Location of the accident
   Type of accident
   Identification of parties involved (drivers, passengers, etc.)
   Were parties traveling as part of their job?
   Description of vehicles involved (owner, make, model, color, year,
      license number, serial number)
   Identification of potential witnesses
3. *Detailed description of the scene of the accident*
   Description of streets and highways
      Direction
      Width
      Number of lanes
      Grade
      Speed limit
      Traffic controls
      Type and condition of surface
   Weather conditions
   Buildings and other objects that could obstruct one's view
4. *Detailed description of the accident*
   Direction and speed of vehicles, pedestrians
   Status of traffic signals
   Evasive action
   Point of impact (on roadway and on each vehicle)
   Final resting place of vehicles

Skid marks and debris
Statements made
Location of witnesses
5. *Bodily injuries (for each person injured)*
Part of body injured
Extent of injury
Nature of treatment (ambulance, hospital, doctor)
Nature of disability
Occupation and salary
Preexisting medical problems
6. *Property damage*
To vehicles
To buildings, etc.
7. *Attestation clause*
Pages numbered
Corrections initialed
Signed by witness

The first section of the narrative statement should supply as much information as possible about the witness. In addition to such items as name, address, and phone number, it should include information about employer, relatives, professional group memberships, social clubs, and even hobbies. Most of this information is simply for the purpose of making it possible to locate the witness in case of a move prior to the trial. This first section also should include the date when and location where the statement is being given. If witnesses are present, that too should be mentioned.

The heart of the statement is the description of whatever it is that the witness observed. Usually the events are presented in chronological order. In addition to describing the events themselves, it is important to have the witness carefully describe the environment in which those events took place. Thus in an automobile accident case, the witness would be asked to describe such matters as the weather and the existence of any temporary obstructions to a driver's view.

Slang or improper English should be included just as the witness used it. If, however, it is not clear what is intended by a phrase, the witness should be asked to clarify it. If the witness makes a value judgment, a request should be made for the basis for that judgment.[36] However, if a friendly witness makes some sort of racial slur or refers to hearsay evidence, the remark should not be included. The inclusion of such material could either make the statement inadmissible or allow the statement to later damage the witness's position. On the other hand, if

---

36. Golec, *supra* note 24, at 81.

Exhibit 7.2 Sample Narrative Statement

I am Carl Jones. I am 27 years old and am married to Helen Jones. We have two children, Bobby and Lois. We live at 908 South Oak St., Atlanta, Illinois. My phone number is 663-1708. I am employed by Cotter-Hyde Co. on Route #130 in Lincoln, Illinois. I am a Drill press operator and earn $7.83 per hour also a representative each I work 40 to 48 hours. I am a member of the Drill Press Operators Union, the Elks, and the V.F.W. My parents are Thomas #39, Theodore Jones, Lois live at Route #39, Houston, Illinois. Arkansas. Both of my parents are retired.

On March 17, 1979, at 10:30 p.m. while driving my 1974 Olds 98 Delta Royale, I was involved in an accident with Oscar Lee who was driving a 1977 Mercury Marquis. My car is a route. and the Mercury is first green. It is my understanding Oscar Houston is the owner of the 1977 Mercury. My car license number is CJ-309 and the license on the Mercury was C H 9231. The accident occurred at the intersection of Oakland Avenue and Regency Drive in Bloomington, Illinois. The occupants in my car were my wife Helen who was sitting in the right front seat, my son Bobby who was sitting in the left rear seat, and my daughter Lois who was sitting up in the right

rear seat. There was just the driver in the Mercury. My wife and children and I had been to the Oak House for our evening meal. We had been shopping at the Oakland Mall until about 8:30 and had gone directly to the Oak House from the Mall. I would suggest it is a five minute drive from the Mall to the Oak House. We intended to eat at the Oak House and then go home to Atlanta. We left the restaurant at about 10:15.

The weather conditions were clear and the roads were dry. Oakland Avenue is a black top street running generally east and west. It is four lanes wide with two wide, given the lanes to it. 18 ft wide. Regency Drive is four lanes wide and generally runs north and south. It dead ends at Oakland Avenue. Both streets are relatively level at this point. I'm not sure what the speed limits are in this area. I am most likely were what my speed was and his and I were driving at an approximate. I would guess it was about 25 mph. This is a semi-commercial area. On the southwest side of Oakland is a big insurance company office and some small real estate offices. There is a building on the northwest corner of the intersection that I think they call the N.R. building. On the northeast corner is a Sunoco service station. There is a overpass over the traffic

CJ

headed west on Legacy located on the north-west corner. The lighting conditions were average in my opinion, as I could see cars coming toward me and turning in front of me.

I did just before the accident happened. There are two ways to leave. One way is to get onto Legacy and head west. The other way is to drive past the east side of the Sunoco station and then right onto Oakland. I would judge the drive on the east side of the Sunoco station is 110 feet from the curb line of Legacy. I had pulled up to Oakland and I could see a car on Oakland headed west. It was about 125 feet east of the drive I was away to exit. I made a whip right turn onto the turn lane to the curb lane west on Oakland. I had what you might call a running start in that I didn't stop before entering Oakland. There is no sign at the drive so I felt if I could beat the car approaching my left lane west I would have it made. I was kind of upset because I just think I was saying as I left the upper thing I saw the 1977 Mercury pulling onto Oakland from Legacy. The Mercury was headed west whereas I was driving the west curb lane of Oakland when we collided. I don't think the Mercury driver ever saw me and I'm sure he was not stop. I would judge his speed at 30 to 35 MPH

CJ

when I saw him. I was only 10 feet away from him when I first saw him. I put on my brakes and had all but stopped when he hit me. He hit my passenger part of the Mercury hit the entire front end of my car. After the impact I would say about 10 feet past Legacy still in the west curb lane of Oakland Avenue.

The Mercury was angled toward the northeast and was sitting in the inside westbound lane on Oakland. The the westbound curb lane I noticed about 15 feet of debris marks which I'd to be made by my car. I told Officer that he would not be where in the hill he was going. I pointed out the wrong way to him. He said I never saw you at all. He claimed that I didn't have my lights on. I told him I saw them off after the impact and when I stopped. About that time the police came and others. Everyone there. The officers and I think were safety and theory.

When we hit, my arm hit the steering wheel and sometimes a compound fracture of the right arm. The injury was to the upper part of my arm and grief for stitches for the the right day or so that it was firing injuries. I think had a cut on his lip by broken. I think it hit the ashtray in my car. I to had to have 34 stitches running from his left

CJ

Exhibit 7.2 (continued)

have driven faster, his order. He did not have any further injuries. Our children were not injured in the accident. They did not miss any time from school, are staying well, and are playing just like the neighbor kids every day. My wife Sheila is not employed now nor has she been since our marriage in 1967. We were taken to Catholic Hospital by AAA Ambulance Service. The emergency room doctor was Dr. Elmer Wells. Our family doctor is a Bloomington doctor and his is Dr. Carl Smith. He treated me while in the hospital and continues to treat us at this time. It is his opinion at this time that I will be out of work for 6 to 8 weeks. I can't run a drill press but am able to do a lot of things around the house. I am light-headed, and while I am getting well I have been missing a spending respect in my own.

My car appears to be a total loss. The estimate of damage is $838.73. The damage is pretty much confined to the front end. There is some damage to the top and quarter panel and the rear body panel.

I can think of nothing further to add concerning this accident.

I have read these 3 pages and they are true.

Carl Jones   May 12, 1979

such items occur in the statement of a hostile witness, they should be left in.[37]

The final stage of the statement is the verification phase. At the end of the statement the investigator should have the witness write: "I have read these ―― pages and they are true." Golec suggests adding the phrase, "This is all I know about this matter and all I can say about it," in order to protect against additional adverse material being brought forth at a later date.[38]

In writing up the statement the investigator should keep the margins even on all four sides and carefully number each page. It is best to use lined paper and to use every available line. These guidelines are designed to protect against possible charges that the statement was altered at some later date. The bottom line of each page should be skipped to leave room for the witness's initials.

When the statement has been completed, the investigator should hand it to the witness and ask that it be read to make sure that the investigator recorded everything correctly. If any errors are pointed out, the investigator should make the changes and then ask the witness to initial the change. Finally, the witness should be asked to both sign the statement's verification clause at the end and to initial it at the bottom of each page.

If the witness cannot read, the investigator should have a neighbor or some neutral third party read the statement to the witness. If there are corrections, both the neighbor and the witness should initial them. The neighbor should then write something like: "I have read the above statement of ―― pages to ――― and he has said they are correct to the best of his knowledge." The neighbor then also signs. The witness also signs (or makes his mark) and initials in the regular manner. Since some people are too embarrassed to admit that they cannot read, the investigator should watch the person's eyes when he or she is asked to read over the statement. If the eyes stay fixed on one spot, it is probable that the witness is not really reading it.[39] The investigator must then probe the witness to determine illiteracy. A signed statement in and of itself is not worth much in court if it is later determined the witness could not read it.

A second type of statement is one that is mechanically recorded. Usually, a plastic belt (dictaphone type) is used rather than magnetic tape because the belt is more difficult to alter.[40] At the beginning of the recorded statement the investigator should identify himself or herself; state the date, time, and location of the interview; and describe the make and model of the recording equipment being used.[41] The statement then

37. Bailey and Rothblatt, supra note 27, at 99.
38. Golec, supra note 24, at 71.
39. Id. at 84.
40. Id. at 76.
41. Bailey and Rothblatt, supra note 27, at 99.

consists of the investigator's questions and the witness's answers. The same general format should be followed as for developing a written statement. At the end of each belt of tape the investigator should state that it is the end of the belt, name the belt number, and ask the witness if the statements have been true and complete up to that point. At the end the entire interview should be played back for the witness. The recorder should then be turned on again and the witness asked if the tape has been played back and if it is true and complete. If there are any corrections, the witness should make those corrections at that time.[42]

A third type of statement is similar to the question and answer format discussed above, but a verbatim record is made by someone taking shorthand. The person who has taken the shorthand then prepares a written transcript and attests to the accuracy of its contents.

Each method has advantages and disadvantages. The verbatim records are often best used with witnesses who are very old, very young, or hostile. In these cases it is preferable because it can help protect the investigator against charges that he or she manipulated the witnesses or otherwise took unfair advantage of them. The recorded statement may also be helpful when the witness is unwilling to sign any written documents. As F. Lee Bailey and Henry Rothblatt remark,

> Many witnesses are sensitive about signing anything that looks like a document, but will permit the recording of their voices, perhaps not fully realizing that a properly recorded statement is as effective and legally binding as a written statement.[43]

When used with simple telephone interviews, the mechanically recorded statements can be big time-savers. However, as the statement becomes more complex or involved, it becomes increasingly more difficult to have people carry through with the elaborate authentication process suggested above. Another problem with both the mechanically recorded and the shorthand methods is that the interviews often tend to ramble, and thus the answers appear to be very disorganized.

Whatever the method used, the investigator should try to get some type of statement from each known witness. Even when a witness claims to know nothing about the event, it is wise to obtain a formal statement to that effect in order to protect oneself from a situation in which the witness has a change of mind and later becomes a star witness for the opposition. If the witness will not even make a negative statement, the investigator should carefully record the dates and circumstances under which those refusals came.[44]

---

42. Id. at 100.
43. Id. at 105.
44. Golec, supra note 24, at 61.

6. Obtaining Documentary Evidence

Depending on the nature of the case at hand, various kinds of documentary evidence may be needed. In any type of case involving a personal injury, for example, the injured party's medical records become an important factor. In a product liability suit, information about safety records and industry standards are usually vital to its outcome. Likewise, information about a company's financial position can be a key element in many types of cases.

When reviewing medical records, the investigator's focus is usually on determining the diagnosis (that is, the nature and extent of the illness or injuries), the treatment (the drugs, surgery, and so forth used to control or alleviate the condition), and the prognosis (the long-term effect of the condition, including the need for further treatment). The patient's medical history, his or her symptoms, and the types of diagnostic tests given also may prove to be important.

If the patient has been hospitalized, the hospital itself will usually be the best source for information about the medical condition. In order to be accredited by the Joint Commission on Accreditation of Hospitals,[45] the institution must maintain a complete set of patient records that conform to the commission's specific standards. Private physicians, on the other hand, often keep little more than a record of a patient's charges and payments. When records are requested for a lawsuit, many physicians simply dictate a letter based on their rough notes. Exhibit 7.3 shows a typical response.

Hospital records usually begin with an admissions form that gives personal data, including birth date and place of birth, marital status, occupation, religion, former names, relatives, insurance carrier, and a medical history. The admissions order shows the doctor's analysis of the reason for admission. The examination that is conducted at the time of admission[46] and the daily observations of temperature, blood pressure, pulse rate, skin condition, and so on are recorded as part of the hospital record. The order sheets show the various laboratory tests and medications administered. Lab reports and consultation reports of other doctors also are present in the record. Exhibit 7.4 provides an example of what the history and physical sections look like.

If an operation was performed, a physician's report is included that describes the type of surgical procedure used and what was observed about the patient's condition during the operation. The discharge sum-

---

45. The Joint Commission on Accreditation of Hospitals is the major accrediting group in the United States and is jointly sponsored by the American Medical Association, the American College of Surgeons, the American College of Physicians, and the American Hospital Association.

46. Although hospital policies vary, the examination usually must be done between five days before admission and the first day after admission.

mary reviews the patient's condition on admission, progress while in the hospital, results of diagnostic procedures used, and condition of the patient on release and lists any medication that was prescribed for the patient to be taken at home. See Exhibit 7.5.

Some states provide a statutory right for the patient (or the authorized agent) to review and copy these hospital records. Some states also provide the defendant access to a plaintiff's hospital records when that plaintiff alleges to have sustained injuries as a result of defendant's actions. In still other states no such rights to access exist, and each hospital establishes its own policies.

Where access to hospital records is allowed (either by law or by decision of the hospital), the patient usually is required to sign a specific authorization form. In all states, however, the hospital must turn over patient records when a proper *subpoena duces tecum* has been issued by the courts.[47]

These various medical reports contain a great deal of technical terminology that is difficult to understand without a medical background. A good medical dictionary is therefore required, as well as a handbook on prescription drugs and an anatomy book that identifies the parts of the body, refers to the functions of these parts, and discusses the ramifications of injuries to them.

Depending on the nature of the case, the investigator can make great use of various types of governmental documents. City building departments have information on building construction plans and safety inspections. Coroners' offices have autopsy and inquest reports.[48] County recorders' offices have information on mortgages, bankruptcies, trusts, and judgments. License bureaus have all sorts of background information on license holders. The secretary of state's office and the federal Securities and Exchange Commission have extensive data about the structure and financial position of corporations.

While the law differs from one state to the next, the general rule is that the public has a right to inspect public records during reasonable business hours. The right to inspect such documents carries with it the right to make copies. In order to both facilitate the process and protect the documents, most offices will provide a member of the public with photocopies of the document for a nominal service fee. At the federal level, the Freedom of Information Act requires each agency to make various records available to the public.[49] Exemptions are allowed, however, for such matters as defense and foreign policy secrets, trade secrets,

---

47. See the discussion of subpoena on page 191.
48. While the inquest results are generally not admissible as to the cause of death, the reports can still be used as an investigative tool. Testimony at an inquest could be used to impeach a witness's testimony at the trial if it were inconsistent with that given at the inquest.
49. 5 U.S.C.A. §552 (1900).

confidential commercial or financial information, personnel and medical files, and investigatory files compiled for law enforcement purposes.

In product liability cases, the investigator will need to obtain copies of relevant industry standards established by both governmental agencies and voluntary associations. While the courts of different states vary with regard to their treatment of the admissibility of such codes, the modern trend seems to favor their use. The National Safety Council, the American Standards Institute, and the American Society of Safety Engineers are some of the most common sources of such standards. The Lawyers' Desk Reference: Technical Sources for Conducting a Personal Injury Action is a handy source for locating relevant organizations.[50] The American National Standards Institute and the Underwriters Laboratories publish catalogs that list the availability of published standards.

There will be times when important documentary evidence cannot be obtained from the sources mentioned above. Occasionally an investigator can obtain information from businesses, private individuals, and even governmental agencies despite the fact that there is no legal right to receive it. Approaching the correct people in a suitable manner can often gain voluntary cooperation. Where such cooperation is not forthcoming, the investigator will have to confer with the attorney about using the subpoena power of the court.

---

50. H. Philo, D. Robb, and R. Goodman, Lawyer's Desk Reference: Technical Sources for Conducting a Personal Injury Action (updated periodically).

Exhibit 7.3 Sample Physician's Response to Request for Medical Records

(Date)

To: (Law Firm)

Re: (Patient's Name)

Dear Sir:

I have received your request and authorization for release of medical information.

This will confirm that Mr. _____ was hospitalized on (date), at _____ Hospital, for repair of a right recurrent inguinal hernia. His recovery from the surgery was satisfactory.

I did confirm severe arthritis, involving the back, neck, arms, and shoulders. In addition, he has had discogenic disease of the cervical spine treated surgically in the past.

It was my impression that he is totally disabled from employment and that this does appear to be permanent and progressive in character.

Very truly yours,

(Physician's name), M.D.

(Name of Hospital)   (Physician's Name)

(Patient's Name)

Admitted: (Date)

Room: _____

History and Physical

This fifty-four-year-old white male was brought to the emergency room after being injured in an automobile accident. The patient states that he was turning the corner and after turning the corner he became somewhat lightheaded and then everything went black and he hit a parked car. He was brought to the emergency room. He was complaining of some numbness of the lips. He was hyperventilating at the time and complaining of some low backache and pain over various parts of the body. X rays were taken of the skull, cervical spine, lumbosacral spine, pelvis, and left shoulder and all the X rays failed to reveal any evidence of fracture. There was considerable degenerative disc disease of the cervical and lumbar spine. He had a slight spondylolisthesis of L4 and L5. There was narrowing of the disc space of L4, L5, and marked degenerative changes of C5 and C6. The patient in the past has had a gallbladder removed. He has had a tonsillectomy. He has had a double hernia repaired and he has had a ruptured disc removed from his back. The patient has been under a lot of nervous tension recently. Recently he had been complaining of various arthritic pains. He has been taking Valium and Motrin at home. He has been complaining of some vague headaches with lightheadedness. The patient was first seen in his hospital bed the evening of admission at which time he was complaining of pain in the back and some pain in his hip. BP 130/90. Pulse 84. Respiration 16.

Head: Negative.

Eyes: Pupils are equal size and shape. React to light and accommodation.

Chest: Symmetrical.

Lungs: Clear to percussion and auscultation.

Heart: Borders within normal limits. Regular rate and rhythm. No murmurs. No extrasystoles.

Abdomen: Scaphoid. Liver, kidney, and spleen are not palpated. There are no masses or tenderness.

External genitalia: Normal.

Admission diagnosis: Syncope, multiple contusions, degenerative arthritis, anxiety reaction.

D: ____ T: ____   _____, M.D.

Exhibit 7.5 Sample Discharge Summary Section of Hospital Records

(Name of Hospital)

Hospital no. ————————

Room no. ———————————

Date of admission: —————————

Date of discharge: —————————

Discharge Summary

Patient was admitted to the hospital after an automobile accident. He was seen then by the physician on call. During this hospitalization, he complains of multiple aches and pains over the entire body. His urinalysis reveals some hematuria, he was seen by (Physician's Name) who cystoscoped the patient. He had a normal brain scan, a normal EEG. He was discharged from the hospital, condition improved. Will be followed as an outpatient.

Final Diagnosis:
1. Syncope, etiology unknown
2. Osteoarthritis
3. Degenerative disc disease of the cervical and lumbar spine
4. Spondylodesis of L4 and L5, narrowing of the interval tubal disc space of L4, L5
5. Microscopic hematuria
6. Chronic prostatitis
7. Urethritis
8. Benign prostatic hypertrophy with secondary early lower urinary tract obstruction
9. Multiple contusions

7. Using Computer Data Bases

In the process of investigating for a specific case, certain types of public information may be helpful. It might be important to know what the weather conditions were like at the time of an automobile accident. Although a witness might be able to estimate the temperature or the amount of snowfall, the weather bureau's records would be more precise and more reliable. In different contexts, it might be useful to know the price that a share of company's stock sold for on a particular day, the latest medical treatment techniques, or the side effects of specific drugs.

Long hours used to be spent in libraries to acquire such information, but today many commercial services make this kind of information available through computerized data bases. These data bases usually store references to, or summaries of, articles in periodicals and journals, books, news stories, scientific and technical reports, and so forth. By

using a communications software package and a modem, these data bases can be accessed with the types of computers that are now common in many law offices.[51]

LEXIS and WESTLAW, the two most prominent legal data bases, are covered in the discussion of legal research in Chapter 8. Some of the common nonlegal data bases are listed below:

Accounting Information Library: includes annual reports of corporations listed on the New York and American Stock Exchanges as well as corporations quoted over the counter;

APOLIT: provides current information on political candidates and issues at both the state and national levels;

BNA: includes reports prepared by the Bureau of National Affairs, Inc. in the areas of antitrust and trade regulations, taxes, federal contracts, patents, trademarks and copyrights, pensions, government employee relations, environment, energy, and securities regulation;

BRS: includes an index of biomedical literature, abstracts from pharmaceutical journals, and an index of social science journals;

DIALOG: provides more than 175 separate data bases including citations and abstracts for patents in various engineering fields, information on corporate acquisitions and mergers, forecasts of sales and profits for major companies, indexes and abstracts of journals in the fields of medicine, engineering, and social science, and a daily index of news stories from over 1,400 of the most important newspapers and periodicals;

Dow Jones News Retrieval Service: includes complete text of articles from the Wall Street Journal, financial analysis of companies from Barron's;

EXCHANGE: provides SEC information and analysts' reports from leading investment banking, brokerage, and research firms on more than 3,000 companies and 100 industries;

INFOBANK: includes news summaries and abstracts in the marketing and advertising fields;

LEXPAT: offers full text of all utility, plant, and design patents issued from 1975 to date;

NAARS: provides over 8,000 annual reports, proxy materials, SEC, and other financial and accounting information;

NEXIS: offers full text of over 100 publications including the New York Times Information Service, the Washington Post, U.S. News and World Report, Newsweek, Business Week, the Economist, the Federal Register, the Congressional Quarterly Weekly, and the Associated Press and United Press International wire services;

---

51. See the discussion of computers at pages 248-249, 251-252.

The Source: includes a variety of stock market information and schedules of congressional committees and regulatory agency hearings;
VU/Text: provides full text of the Washington Post, Chicago Tribune,
Boston Globe, and Philadelphia Inquirer, as well as other newspapers and wire services.

These data base retrieval systems search for a key word and then
reproduce on the screen entries that contain that key word. Fees for the
service are based on the time used. A service like DIALOG actually
contains many individually owned data bases, and the hourly rate
charged depends on which specific data base is being accessed.

8. The Investigative Report

The investigator's work will be of little use if it is not communicated
effectively to the attorney. The format used to relay this information
depends on the needs of the parties involved. Usually the investigator
prepares a formal report to describe what was done and to provide an
analysis of the results. Statements, diagrams, or photographs that have
been taken are then usually attached as appendexes to the report. There
may be one comprehensive report or, in longer, more complex matters,
a series of interim reports.

In the report's analysis section the investigator should isolate each
factual question about which there is some dispute. For each one the
investigator should then compare and contrast all aspects of the evidence
(testimonial, physical, and documentary) that relate to that specific issue.
At this point the investigator also should draw attention to various factors that may affect a witness's credibility. For instance, if a given witness
is hard of hearing or has a surly manner, that information should also be
included.

Although the investigator should work hard to present this information in a concise manner, it is important that it be complete. An item
might appear to be insignificant at the time the report is being prepared
but may become extremely important at some later date.

C.   SUMMARY

In both civil and criminal suits, there is usually more of a dispute
over what actually took place (the facts) than there is about the meaning
of the law. Although on occasion both sides may stipulate[52] to a particular description of the facts, the major part of the attorney's energy goes
toward convincing the court to adopt the client's view of the facts rather

---

52. A stipulation in this context involves an agreement by the attorneys for both sides that
   a particular description of the facts should be placed on the record.

than the opponent's contrary view. A good paralegal therefore should be a skilled fact-finder.

The attorney's initial view of the facts ordinarily comes directly from the client at the time of the initial interview. In many legal aid programs, a paralegal conducts these initial fact-finding interviews. In other situations, the paralegal may be assigned to conduct an in-depth fact-gathering session with the client after the attorney has talked with the client on more general terms.

Whenever possible these interviews should take place in a comfortable and quiet location in which there will be privacy and a lack of interruptions. The seating arrangement should be one that facilitates personal communication rather than one that intimidates the person being interviewed. The interviewer should put the client at ease and should be conscious of the nonverbal as well as the verbal aspects of communication.

The paralegal should begin the interview by explaining the paralegal's role in terms that the client will understand. The client should then be given the opportunity to describe the problem in his or her own terms and not merely to respond to the interviewer's questions. The interviewer should ask direct questions in order to clarify areas of ambiguity and to assist the interviewee who becomes bogged down or forgets a train of thought. Minimal encourages to talk, paraphrasing, and reflections of feelings are useful techniques for keeping the interview moving ahead constructively.

In bringing the interview to an end it is wise to summarize one's understanding of what the client has said in order to ensure accuracy and to give the client a chance to add information that might have been overlooked. The paralegal should collect copies of all relevant documents and have the client sign appropriate authorization forms. Immediately afterward, notes from the interview should be reviewed and polished while the matter is still fresh in the interviewer's mind.

Since one cannot rely solely on the client's perception of the facts, the paralegal must be prepared to interview other witnesses as well as examine the physical and documentary evidence that is available. The attorney must be made aware of the unfavorable as well as the supportive evidence.

To as great an extent as possible, the paralegal should strive to collect information in a form that is admissible in a court of law. Developing a basic understanding of the rules of evidence and what constitutes relevant and competent evidence prepares the investigator to properly authenticate real evidence. Nevertheless, inadmissible evidence can be useful and should be collected even if it cannot be admitted in court.

Since physical surroundings change, witnesses' memories fade, and injuries heal, it is important that the paralegal begin the investigation as

soon after the incident as possible. Time is particularly important when one is investigating an automobile accident or similar event in which the physical evidence is likely to change or disappear. A good investigator attempts to preserve the scene in photographs and prepares scale diagrams that will help others to see what happened.

In cases that lend themselves to the use of expert witnesses, the paralegal should identify appropriate individuals and enlist their support. These experts then can be used as resources for the investigation as well as for witnesses at the trial.

The strategy used in approaching a witness depends on whether the witness is perceived as being friendly or adverse. Whenever possible the investigator should take a formal statement from both types of witnesses. The most common type of statement involves having the interviewer transpose the witness's answers into a simple narrative account and then obtain the witness's signature to indicate that the account is accurate. Mechanically recorded statements make up a second type of statement, and typing a verbatim transcript constitutes the third. There are advantages and disadvantages to each strategy, and the paralegal should use the one that best fits the particular situation at hand.

Medical records as well as various government documents are often very useful. The paralegal should become familiar with both the content of such documents and the procedures for obtaining copies of them.

Situations also arise in which the investigator must locate medical, scientific, or financial information from newspapers, periodicals, and other specialized reporting services. Computerized data bases make such searches much easier and more efficient.

Finally, the investigator should communicate all this information to the attorney through reports that effectively summarize and integrate the results of the investigation.

KEY TERMS

attending behavior	narrative statement
attestation clause	open questions
closed questions	paraphrasing
computerized data base	prognosis
diagnosis	recorded statement
expert witness	reflection of feelings
hospital admission form	transcribed statement
hospital discharge summary	treatment
lay witness	verbal following
minimal encourages to talk	

REVIEW QUESTIONS

1. What factors contribute to poor communication?

2. What are the advantages and disadvantages of closed versus open questions?

3. Why should the interviewer avoid the use of "why" questions?

4. How should an investigator organize the investigation?

5. What must be done to properly authenticate real evidence?

6. What are the most common means of locating both lay and expert witnesses?

7. What are the primary elements that should be included in a standard narrative statement?

8. What type of information usually appears in hospital records?

DISCUSSION QUESTIONS

1. What are the advantages and disadvantages of having a paralegal rather than the attorney conduct the initial interview with a client? What are the advantages and disadvantages of having a paralegal rather than the attorney interview other witnesses?

2. Do you agree with how the author suggests that paralegals should explain their roles to the client? How might you improve on this description?

3. In attempting to locate witnesses, where does one draw the line between ethical and unethical behavior? What techniques would not be ethical?

PROJECTS

1. In reading medical reports, it is likely that you will face some unfamiliar terminology. Go to your library and familiarize yourself with medical reference works. You should find some that are specifically directed at lawyers. Now use several of these references to assist you in writing out a short explanation of each of the following medical terms: (1) pneumothorax, (2) hypertrophic changes, (3) spondylolisthesis, and (4) sciatica. Which references did you find most useful and why?

2. Locate a recent copy of National Safety News (try the library again). Carefully examine this publication of the National Safety Council and then write up a brief (one-page) summary of the nature of its

contents. In what ways could this publication be useful to some paralegals?

3. Pair off with a classmate or friend and practice conducting an interview with a new client. After the interview has been completed, analyze how it could have been improved.

4. Pair off with someone else as in 3 above. This time have the other person play the role of a witness to an automobile accident. Develop a narrative statement on the basis of this interview.

Chapter 8
Legal Research

CHAPTER 3 COVERED THE manner in which constitutions, statutes, administrative regulations, and court decisions are published, and how one goes about interpreting them. It explained how a paralegal can locate these materials by their legal citations. But what if one does not know the proper citation, or does not even know if there is a relevant statute or a case on point? How does one know if a helpful case has been reversed by a higher court, or had its precedent value negated by subsequent decisions of other courts? This chapter seeks to answer those and other questions about legal research. It builds on the material presented in Chapter 3 to develop basic legal research skills.

A. ANALYZING THE PROBLEM

Legal research is not conducted in a vacuum. It is undertaken to answer a specific legal problem. Therefore, the first step in the research process is to analyze the problem itself. What specific legal issues are involved? Are any statutes known to be involved? Is the problem primarily a matter of local or state law or of federal law? What general substantive areas of the law are involved — contract, torts, criminal?

Let us suppose, for example, that a paralegal working for a legal aid agency in Peoria, Illinois, is brought into the following landlord/tenant problem. A client arrives at the office with a written notice from her landlord stating that if she does not paid the $250 that she owes in back rent within five days, she will be evicted from her apartment. The client explains that the landlord left the notice with her nine-year-old son while she was shopping at the grocery store. Although she is very unhappy with the apartment and wants to move out, she has been unable to find suitable housing that she can afford. She wants to move because the place is infested with cockroaches and the apartment's temperature during the winter never rises above 60°F. The client does not have a lease and makes monthly rent payments to the building manager. The attorney handling the case instructs the paralegal to write a memorandum analyzing the client's options.

Recognizing the legal issues in this situation strongly depends on knowing landlord/tenant law. If the paralegal is generally familiar with this type of law, it immediately is apparent that the research should focus on the implied warranty of habitability, the tenant's right to repair and offset, the procedural requirements for eviction, and the right to raise affirmative defenses in various types of eviction actions. The paralegal also knows that the research will involve state statutes, local ordinances, and the common law.

If the researcher is not familiar with the law in this area, he or she must learn some of the basic principles of landlord/tenant law to decide where to direct the research.

Since the paralegal's knowledge differs from topic to topic, this chapter begins with a research strategy that assumes that the researcher knows very little about the particular area involved. A paralegal who comes to a legal problem with a more complete background can eliminate some of the earlier stages in the research process.

B.   LIBRARY RESEARCH

Paralegals are fortunate to be dealing with a highly organized and well indexed set of knowledge. In most situations at least two alternative methods can be followed in seeking the same piece of information. The materials are widely cross-indexed so that one piece of information usually leads to several other relevant sources. However, all this information and all these indexing tools are expensive and take up a great deal of space. Some large law firms and corporations may have large, expansive libraries, but many sole practitioners and small firms can afford to maintain only very limited libraries consisting of the most commonly used state references. Paralegals and attorneys who have limited libraries in their own firms usually have access to large libraries maintained by county bar associations, the courts, or law schools.

1. Discovering Basic Principles

General overviews of various areas of the law are found in encyclopedias, treatises, articles in periodicals, and annotations. (Sample pages from these research volumes, labeled Exhibit 8.1 through Exhibit 8.17, appear at the end of this section at pages 307-325.) Since treatises, periodical articles, and annotations are usually more specialized and less comprehensive, it is wise to begin with an encyclopedia. An encyclopedia can introduce the basic language and principles and provide a frame of reference for further research.

a. American Jurisprudence 2d

American Jurisprudence 2d or simply Am. Jur. 2d, as it is formally cited and usually referred to, is one of two general encyclopedias that summarize the entire body of American case law as well as significant federal and common state statutory laws. The encyclopedia is divided into 443 separate topics, ranging from abandoned property to zoning and planning. The treatment of each these topics takes up fifty-eight volumes of textual materials. Each topic is broken down into numerous subtopics, and each of the subtopics contains a narrative description of the general rules that have emerged from various court decisions. Wherever conflicting decisions are found, the authors point out the conflict and briefly explain both positions. Exhibit 8.1 shows the manner in which the authors discuss the habitability of an apartment.

In addition to this type of general narrative discussion, Am. Jur. 2d also provides various types of cross-references with the citations to specific court cases, annotations in American Law Reports, Annotated,[1] selected law review articles, other sections of Am. Jur. 2d, and parallel sections of American Jurisprudence. American Jurisprudence (Am. Jur.) is an earlier version of Am. Jur. 2d that has been gradually replaced by the newer volumes. Am. Jur. 2d volumes supersede the corresponding Am. Jur. books.[2]

Like most secondary legal reference books, Am. Jur. 2d is kept current with the publication of pocket part supplements. New material is organized to correspond with the numbering system used in the bound volume and then inserted in a special pocket at the back of that volume. Exhibit 8.2 shows the pocket part materials that supplement the material discussed in the main text in Exhibit 8.1. When these pocket supplements get too thick and unwieldy, the publisher issues a replacement volume.

There are two primary methods for locating the appropriate sections to research. The paralegal's ability to find the most relevant sections of the textual material will depend on prior knowledge of the law in that particular area.

The person who is totally unfamiliar with a particular area should start with the subject analysis method. Each general topic in Am. Jur. 2d begins with a short narrative description of what will be discussed in that section as well as a review of related topics that are covered elsewhere. (See Exhibit 8.3.) This is followed by an outline of the major topics covered in that section and a detailed outline of each subtopic. Exhibit 8.4 shows the amount of detail contained in the outlines of the subtopics.

---

1. This set is abbreviated as A.L.R. and is discussed in greater detail at pages 304-305.
2. A table of parallel references between Am. Jur. and Am. Jur. 2d can be found at the beginning of each Am. Jur. 2d volume.

A careful review of the entire outline for the landlord and tenant area will help the researcher locate all potentially relevant sections.

An alternative method of finding the relevant sections of Am. Jur. 2d involves using the indexes in separate volumes at the end of the series and those at the back of each substantive volume. The procedure is similar to that used in reading any normal index. The key is to determine the correct words to locate. Exhibit 8.5 demonstrates that once the researcher has looked up "uninhabitability" several sections appear to be quite promising. But how does the researcher know that one should look up "uninhabitability"? There is no secret formula. The researcher should compile a list of potential key words to be researched. If the words cannot be located in an index, the researcher should attempt to identify several synonyms and then try to find them in an index. If none of these efforts work, the subject analysis method described previously would probably be the best approach.

b. Corpus Juris Secundum

Corpus Juris Secundum is the other general encyclopedia. It too is usually referred to by its standard abbreviation — C.J.S. It is acclaimed as "the most exhaustive and comprehensive legal encyclopedia ever written" and "a complete restatement of the entire body of American law based upon all reported cases from 1658 to date."[3] C.J.S. is divided into 433 topics spread over 101 textual volumes. These topics are in turn subdivided into many specific subtopics.

Exhibit 8.6 demonstrates the similarity in approach between Am. Jur. 2d and C.J.S. Both summarize the sometimes contradictory decisions of various state and federal courts and include citations to these cases and to law review articles. Although Am. Jur. 2d includes cross-references to Am. Jur. and to A.L.R., C.J.S. includes cross-references to Corpus Juris (an earlier version of C.J.S.) and to the key number system used in West's digests.[4] C.J.S. also uses pocket supplements to update the material as shown in Exhibit 8.7 and issues replacement volumes when the supplements become too unwieldy. On the other hand, C.J.S. begins each subtopic with a summary statement in boldface type but Am. Jur. 2d does not.

As with Am. Jur. 2d the researcher can use either the subject analysis or the index methods to locate relevant textual materials in Corpus Juris Secundum. Exhibits 8.8, 8.9, and 8.10 show the similarities in makeup of the subject analysis and index sections in Am. Jur. 2d and C.J.S. Both individual volume indexes and a multivolume general index at the end of the set are included in C.J.S. Note that in Am. Jur. 2d information about the implied warranty of habitability was found under

---

3. West's Law Finder 34 (1978).
4. See pages 335-337 for an explanation of key numbers and the digest system.

the index heading of "uninhabitability." However, the C.J.S. index has no such heading. In the C.J.S. index the heading is "habitable condition." The general index contains a law chart designed to help select the current topic areas, as shown in Exhibit 8.11. It divides all of the more than 400 topics into subcategories under the general areas of persons, property, contracts, torts, crimes, remedies, and government.

c. Local Reference Encyclopedias

American Jurisprudence 2d and Corpus Juris Secundum cover cases from all fifty states. Sometimes it helps to compare and contrast the differences between laws of various states. At other times only the laws of one particular state will be relevant. In these cases one should use a local encyclopedia specifically geared to the laws of that state. (Unfortunately, such local encyclopedias are not published in all states.)

These local encyclopedias carry names such as California Jurisprudence 2d, Michigan Law and Practice, and Pennsylvania Law Encyclopedia. They are usually arranged by topics that parallel those in the national encyclopedias. They have subject analysis sections, indexes, and supplements that also closely resemble those in Am. Jur. 2d and C.J.S. Exhibits 8.12 and 8.13 show the manner in which Illinois Law and Practice handles the implied warranty of the habitability question.

d. Special Subject Encyclopedias, Treatises, and Restatements

In addition to the types of encyclopedias discussed above, there are encyclopedias that focus on a single broad topic such as contracts or evidence. They bear names like Fletcher's Cyclopedia of the Law of Private Corporations. Such encyclopedias closely resemble multivolume treatises — Corbin on Contracts and Wigmore on Evidence, for example.

There are differences between an encyclopedia and a treatise — an encyclopedia simply summarizes the law, but a treatise summarizes, interprets, and evaluates the law. Although some treatises are published as multivolume sets, most look just like a standard library book. In addition to the standard table of contents, text, and index, legal treatises usually also contain a table of cases, and many are also supplemented with pocket parts. They are given regular library call numbers and can be found in the standard library card catalog.

Restatements represent still another source of general background information. In 1923 a group of prominent law professors, judges, and lawyers founded the American Law Institute and began a series of books to summarize the basic principles of the common law in several major areas. Recognizing that there was disagreement among some courts on the meaning of some of these principles, the Institute sought to present what its experts thought were the best rules. These are printed in bold-face type as relatively short statements. Each principle is then followed

by an explanation of the situations in which it should be applied. Restatements have been published in the areas of agency, conflict of laws, foreign relations, torts, and trusts.

e. Legal Periodicals

Law reviews and other types of legal periodicals represent still another source on the meaning of the law. Law reviews contain a wealth of thoroughly researched information about a specific area of the law. The lead articles are usually expansive pieces, often written by law professors. The comments or notes section contains contributions of the student editors. Because the law review staffs are traditionally made up of the brightest students, their work has earned a high reputation. Other periodicals are often more specialized and practitioner oriented and also can contain articles of great value.

The most efficient way to locate relevant periodical articles is to use one of the various indexes that are available. These publications usually contain both a subject index and a separate title and author index. The Index to Legal Periodicals covers publications from 1908 to the present, and the Current Legal Index begins in 1980. The Index to Periodical Articles Related to Law covers law-related articles in such popular magazines as Time and Newsweek. Index sets are also available for foreign, specialized, and very old periodicals. A sample page from the Index to Legal Periodicals is shown in Exhibit 8.14.

f. American Law Reports, Annotated

The American Law Reports, Annotated is published in four groups of volumes: A.L.R., A.L.R.2d, A.L.R.3d, and A.L.R.Fed. All four reprint important court cases, summarize the briefs of counsel, and give cross-references to Am. Jur. 2d, Proof of Facts, and the A.L.R. Digest. In addition, they provide an encyclopedia-type essay of one or more of the key issues raised by the reported case and include a discussion of related cases and an analysis of any trends that appear to be developing. If one can find a pertinent A.L.R. annotation, one will obtain a fairly accurate overview of the law in that given area.

Exhibit 8.15 shows how the annotation is organized. Note that both an outline of the topics covered and an extensive index are included at the beginning of the annotation. A table of the jurisdictions represented shows the state courts cited. After listing the content of related annotations, citations are included for relevant periodical articles. Exhibit 8.16 provides an example of the text of the annotation and demonstrates a more detailed discussion of individual cases than would be found in encyclopedias.

The A.L.R.3d and A.L.R.Fed. are supplemented with pocket parts in the same manner as the other publications mentioned previously. The

A.L.R. and A.L.R.2d, on the other hand, are supplemented through the Blue Book and Later Case Service respectively. The A.L.R. Blue Book of Supplemental Decisions consists of three volumes that list related annotations appearing in later volumes as well as new cases. This supplements the A.L.R. The A.L.R. Later Case Service consists of volumes of similar content that supplement the A.L.R.2d. These permanent volumes are in turn supplemented by pamphlet supplements.

Many other publications contain cross-references to one of the A.L.R. series. If, however, the paralegal does not have such a reference, research should begin with the A.L.R. Quick Index. This convenient reference provides citations to annotations in both A.L.R.2d and A.L.R.3d. Exhibit 8.17 shows that the Quick Index identifies two annotations related to the habitability question. Annotations in A.L.R. and A.L.R.2d also can be found by consulting the A.L.R. Word Index to Annotations and the A.L.R.2d Word Index to Annotations.

g. Citations for Secondary Sources

The proper formats for the citation of cases and statutory materials are discussed in Chapters 5 and 6. The paralegal also should become familiar with citations for the secondary sources discussed in this chapter.

Encyclopedias are usually cited by both the volume number and topic. For example, the section on habitability, which is presented in Exhibit 8.1, would be cited as

49 Am. Jur. 2d Landlord and Tenant §769 (1970)

The material covered in Exhibits 8.6 and 8.12 would be cited as

51C C.J.S. Landlord and Tenant §305 (1968)
24 I.L.P. Landlord and Tenant §237 (1956)

The year is included in parentheses to avoid confusion that might result after replacement volumes have been issued.

Treatises are cited by author, title, page, and year of publication, and restatements are simply cited by the section and the year. Examples of these would be

J. Nowak, R. Rotunda, and J. Young, Constitutional Law 419 (1978)
Restatement of Contracts §287 (1932)

Periodical citations include the author's last name, title of the article, volume number, abbreviation for the periodical, page number on which

the article begins, and the date. If a specific page within the article is
~~cited, the reference follows the page on which the article begins.~~

 Brickman, Expansion of Lawyering Process through a New Delivery
   System, 71 Colum. L. Rev. 1, 21 (1971)

 References to annotations in American Law Reports are cited in a
format that parallels a case citation. For example, one would find Exhibit
8.16 cited either as

 Lemle v. Breeden, 40 A.L.R.3d 637 (1969)

or simply

 Annot., 40 A.L.R.3d 646, 653

Exhibit 8.1 Sample Am. Jur. 2d Page Regarding Habitability of Dwelling or Apartment

accordingly been held that a letting of premises equipped as a motion-picture theater carries with it an implied warranty that they are fit for immediate occupation and use as a theater, which is broken where the heating apparatus proves inadequate to heat the theater during the winter months.[18]

§ 769. Habitability of dwelling or apartment.

Although there are a few decisions to the contrary,[19] the general rule supported by nearly all the authorities on the subject is that in the absence of statute, there is no warranty, covenant, or condition implied in the letting of an unfurnished house or tenement that it is reasonably fit for habitation, and uninhabitability does not warrant abandonment or constitute a constructive eviction,[20] unless there are some special terms in the lease which will raise an implied covenant or condition that the premises shall be fit for occupancy as a dwelling.[1] Nor is there any implied warranty that premises habitable at the time of the demise will continue habitable during the term.[2] These rules apply equally to the case of the letting of several rooms in a tenement or apartment house, if they pass out of the control of the landlord into the exclusive possession of the tenant.[3]

Responsibility of the landlord for the habitable condition may rest upon an express provision in the lease, but a warranty that a house is habitable is not a warranty that it will continue to be habitable.[4] While a recital in a lease that the premises are in good condition has been held in some cases to have the effect of a warranty of habitability,[5] in other cases such a recital has not been deemed to have that effect.[6] Representations as to

---

18. Davey v Christoff, 36 **Ont** L 123, 28 DLR 447.

As to furnished houses, see § 770, infra.

19. Leonard v Armstrong, 73 **Mich** 577, 41 NW 695. See also Buckner v Azulai, 251 **Cal** App 2d Supp 1013, 59 Cal Rptr 806, 27 ALR3d 920, discussed infra this section, at note 15.

Annotation: 27 ALR3d 924, 931, § 3 (vermin infestation); 4 ALR 1453, s. 13 ALR 818, 29 ALR 52, 34 ALR 711.

20. Doyle v Union P. R. Co. 147 **US** 413, 37 L Ed 223, 13 S Ct 333; Webel v Yale University, 125 **Conn** 515, 7 A2d 215, 123 ALR 863; Purcell v English, 86 **Ind** 34; Young v Povich, 121 **Me** 141, 116 A 26, 29 ALR 48; Hopkins v Murphy, 233 **Mass** 476, 124 NE 252, 13 ALR 816; York v Steward, 21 **Mont** 515, 55 P 29; Faber v Creswick, 31 NJ 234, 156 A2d 252, 78 ALR2d 1230; Daly v Wise, 132 **NY** 306, 30 NE 837; Franklin v Brown, 118 **NY** 110, 23 NE 126; Moore v Weber, 71 **Pa** 429; Pines v Perssion, 14 **Wis** 2d 590, 111 NW2d 409 (recognizing rule).

Annotation: 27 ALR3d 924, 931 et seq., §§ 4, 6, 8 (vermin infestation); 4 ALR 1453, 1454, s. 13 ALR 818, 29 ALR 52, 34 ALR 711.

The reason for the fact that in the absence of statute there is no warranty that leased property is habitable, as stated by Baron Parke in Hart v Windsor, 12 Mees & W 68, 152 **Eng** Reprint 1114, is that "there would be no limit to the inconvenience which would

ensue. It is much better to leave the parties in every case to protect their interests themselves by proper stipulations, and if they really mean a lease to be void by reason of any unfitness in the subject for the purpose intended, they should express that meaning."

1. Wolfe v Arrott, 109 **Pa** 473, 1 A 333.
Annotation: 4 ALR 1453, 1455, s. 13 ALR 818, 29 ALR 52, 34 ALR 711.

2. York v Steward, 21 **Mont** 515, 55 P 29; Blake v Dick, 15 **Mont** 236, 38 P 1072; Moore v Weber, 71 **Pa** 429.
Annotation: 4 ALR 1453, 1455, s. 13 ALR 818, 29 ALR 52, 34 ALR 711.

3. St. George Mansions v Hetherington, 42 Ont L 10, 4 ALR 1450, 41 DLR 614.
Annotation: 4 ALR 1453, 1455, s. 13 ALR 818, 29 ALR 52, 34 ALR 711.

4. Wolfe v Arrott, 109 **Pa** 473, 1 A 333.
Annotation: 4 ALR 1453, 1455, 1459, s. 13 ALR 818, 29 ALR 52, 34 ALR 711.

5. Curran v Cushing, 197 **Ill** App 371 (abstract); Tyler v Disbrow, 40 **Mich** 415.
Annotation: 4 ALR 1453, 1459, 1460, s. 13 ALR 818, 29 ALR 52, 34 ALR 711.

6. Foster v Peyser, 9 Cush (**Mass**) 242, holding that where a lease of a dwelling house provided that the lessor should not be called upon to make any repairs during the term, "the house being now in perfect order," the latter provision related to the state of

Exhibit 8.2 Sample Am. Jur. 2d Pocket Part Supplement Page

liability for injury or death of tenant or third person caused by dangerous condition of premises. 64 ALR3d 339.

Love, Landlord's Liability for Defective Premises: Caveat Lessee, Negligence, or Strict Liability? 1975 Wisconsin L Rev 19.

Additional case authorities for section:
Covenant of habitability is implied in residential but not business leases. Van Ness Ind., Inc. v Claremont Plainting & Decorating Co., NJ Super 507, 324 A2d 102.

p 706, n 6—
See, however, Marini v Ireland, 56 NJ 130, 265 A2d 526, 40 ALR3d 1356, holding that a covenant is implied, at least in residential letting, that there are no latent defects, at inception of lease, in facilities vital to use of premises for residential purposes, and that these facilities will remain in usable condition during entire term of lease.

To the same effect, see Mease v Fox, — Iowa —, 200 NW2d 791.

Doctrine of implied warranty of habitability did not apply to corporate tenant taking premises "as is" under commercial lease. Coulston v Teliscope Productions, Ltd (Sup App T) 378 NYS2d 553.

Court will not reject common law doctrine of caveat emptor in landlord-tenant relationships; no implied warranty of habitability arises from residential lease. Blackwell v Del Bosco (Colo) 558 P2d 563 (court noted that implied warranty theory involves social and economic complexities better suited to legislative research, and explained that embracing the theory might cause landlords to raise rents significantly or abandon run-down premises, leaving the poor without any place to live.

§ 769. Habitability of dwelling or apartment

Practice Aids: Modern status of landlord's tort liability for injury or death of tenant or third person caused by dangerous condition of premises. 64 ALR3d 339.

Line, Implied Warranties of Habitability and Fitness for Intended Use in Urban Residential Leases. 26 Baylor L Rev 161, Spring 1974.

Moskovitz, The Implied Warranty of Habitability: A New Doctrine Raising New Issues. 62 California L Rev 1444, December 1974.

Meyers, The Covenant of Habitability and the American Law Institute. 27 Stanf L Rev 879, Feb., 1975.

p 708, n 19—Lemle v Breeden, 51 Hawaii 426, 478, 462 P2d 470, 40 ALR3d 637.
Mease v Fox, — Iowa —, 200 NW2d 791.
Marini v Ireland, 56 NJ 130, 265 A2d 526, 40 ALR3d 1356.

Annotation: 40 ALR3d 646, 652, 653, §§ 4[b], 5[a].

p 708, n 2—
See, however, Javins v First Nat. Realty Corp.

138 App DC 369, 428 F2d 1071, cert den 400 US 925, 27 L Ed 2d 185, 91 S Ct 186, in which under the Housing Regulations for the District of Columbia a warranty to maintain the leased premises in habitable condition was held implied by operation of law into leases of urban dwelling units covered by the Regulations; Marini v Ireland, 56 NJ 130, 265 A2d 526, 40 ALR3d 1356, stating that even though lease of apartment did not include specific covenant to repair, landlord should, in residential letting, be held to implied covenant against latent defects, whether designated as covenant "to repair" or as covenant "of habitability and livability fitness," which is a covenant that at inception of lease there are no latent defects in facilities vital to use of premises for residential purposes as well as a covenant that these facilities will remain in usable condition during entire term of lease, in performance of which covenant the landlord is required to maintain those facilities in condition that renders premises livable.

p 709, n 13—
Annotation: Landlord and tenant: Constructive eviction based on flooding, dampness, or the like. 33 ALR3d 1356.

Uniform Laws:
A landlord is required to make all repairs and do whatever is necessary to put and keep the premises in a fit and habitable condition. Uniform Residential Landlord and Tenant Act § 2.104(a)(2).

Hirsch, Hirsch & Margolis, Regression Analysis of the Effects of Habitability Laws Upon Rent: An Empirical Observation on the Ackerman-Komesar Debate. 63 Cal L Rev 1098, Sept. 1975.

In the light of the implied warranty of habitability in an apartment lease agreement, it was error to refuse the tenant's application for a judicial declaration that she was obliged to make rental payments only after the landlord complied with his duty to substantially obey the housing codes and make the premises habitable where the court found that the premises developed defects, not caused by the tenant, during her occupancy which constituted substantial violations of the governing municipal housing code. Hinson v Delis, 26 Cal App 3d 62, 102 Cal Rptr 661.

In general, there is no implied warranty of habitability given to a tenant, but rather, he takes the premises as he finds them and bears the risk of any defective conditions which are within the area under his exclusive possession and control. Thomas v Roper, 162 Conn 343, 294 A2d 321 (no finding that alleged defect existed at the beginning of the tenancy).

p 709, n 15—
See Lemle v Breeden, 51 Hawaii, 426, 478, 462, P2d 470, 40 ALR3d 367, in applying an implied warranty of habitability and fitness for use in the lease of a dwelling and observing that the application of such a warranty in leases of rented dwellings recognizes changes in the

Exhibit 8.3 Sample Am. Jur. 2d Topic Analysis Page

⅃MERICAN JURISPRUDENCE

SECOND EDITION

Volume 49

LANDLORD AND TENANT

Scope of Topic: This article discusses the principles and rules of law applicable to and governing the relation of landlord and tenant. In general, it embraces the creation and existence of the relation through a formal lease, or otherwise, and the rights, duties, and liabilities arising out of the relationship, including the rights and liabilities of third persons such as assignees of the leasehold, subtenants, and transferees of the landlord's reversion, and including the liability of the landlord and tenant for injuries sustained on, or as a result of the use of, the demised premises. The article also includes ground rents and permanent leaseholds.

Treated elsewhere are the following: the responsibility as between landlord and tenant for injuries to persons upon highways, streets, or sidewalks adjacent to the leased premises (see 39 Am Jur 2d, HIGHWAYS, STREETS, AND BRIDGES §§ 369, 370, 499, 502, 521, 522, 537, 544); the liability of a landlord or tenant for injuries sustained in the use of elevators on the leased premises (see 26 Am Jur 2d, ELEVATORS AND ESCALATORS §§ 18–20, 28, 29, 40, 49); the taking of leased property in eminent domain, compensation and damages therefor, and apportionment thereof between landlord and tenant (see 26, 27 Am Jur 2d, EMINENT DOMAIN §§ 79, 177, 250, 352 et seq.); a property owner's duty and liability to a prospective tenant (see NEGLIGENCE); the status and rights of cotenants (see 20 Am Jur 2d, COTENANCY AND JOINT OWNERSHIP); estates and tenancies generally, including estates for life created by leases with reservation of rent, and estates less than freehold (see 28 Am Jur 2d, ESTATES §§ 9 et seq., 56 et seq., 130, 131); the power of corporations to lease their realty (see 19 Am Jur 2d, CORPORATIONS §§ 1023, 1024); leases involving persons of a particular status or in a particular relationship or under disability (see 3 Am Jur 2d, ALIENS AND CITIZENS § 23; 31 Am Jur 2d, EXECUTORS AND ADMINISTRATORS §§ 249, 250; 39 Am Jur 2d, GUARDIAN AND WARD §§ 113–117; 41 Am Jur 2d, HUSBAND AND WIFE §§ 154, 164 et seq.; 42 Am Jur 2d, INFANTS §§ 69, 75, 111; LIFE TENANTS AND REMAINDERMEN; MORTGAGES; MUNICIPAL CORPORATIONS, COUNTIES AND OTHER POLITICAL SUBDIVISIONS; PARTNERSHIP; TRUSTS); leases of particular kinds of property or for particular purposes (see 38 Am Jur 2d, GARAGES, AND FILLING AND PARKING STATIONS §§ 153 et seq.; 38 Am Jur 2d, GAS AND OIL §§ 54 et seq., 103 et seq., 164 et seq.; LOGS AND TIMBER; MINES AND MINERALS; RAILROADS; SCHOOLS); leases of personal property (see 8 Am Jur 2d, BAILMENTS §§ 28 et seq., 91, 96 et seq., 149 et seq., 225, 251) or

1

Exhibit 8.4 Sample Am. Jur. 2d Subject Analysis Outline

28

Exhibit 8.5 Sample Am. Jur. 2d Index Page for Landlord and Tenant Volume

INDEX

Exhibit 8.6 Sample C.J.S. Text Page

not excuse the lessor from his obligation to deliver the building in a sound condition as to structural parts,[61] or exclude the lessor's warranty against essential defects.[62] Under a statute requiring the lessor to maintain a thing in condition such as to serve for the use for which it was hired, where a room is rented for the storage of goods, the lessor is liable for damages to the goods due to the condition of the room.[63]

Compliance with ordinances. The general rule of no implied warranty of suitability of property for the purpose for which it was leased has been applied where property cannot be used for the purpose for which it was leased because such use would consti-

§ 305. ——— Dwellings

    a. In general
    b. Furnished dwellings

a. In General

Ordinarily there is no implied covenant or warranty on the part of a landlord that property leased for dwelling purposes is habitable or fit for habitation, or that it is free from vermin; but such a covenant or warranty may be implied where the lease is of an apartment in a multiple dwelling.

Library References

Landlord and Tenant ⊜125.

It is generally recognized that there is no implied warranty or covenant on the part of a landlord

that property leased for dwelling purposes is habitable or fit for habitation,[69.50] or that it is safe, tenantable, or fit for the purposes of the lease,[70] at least where the dwelling is unfurnished.[71] The rule applies equally to the case of the letting of several rooms in a tenement house if they pass out of the control of the landlord into the exclusive possession of the tenant.[72]

Some authorities hold that, in the absence of fraud,[73] there is no implied covenant or representation by the landlord that a house or apartment is free from vermin or disease germs;[74] while other authorities are to the effect that, unless there is a provision to the contrary in the lease of an apartment in a multiple dwelling, the landlord impliedly covenants that the premises will be habitable,[75] free from vermin,[76] and suitable for the dwelling

purposes for which they are leased,[77] and that the landlord is under a duty to maintain a leased apartment in a reasonably safe condition.[78]

A fraudulent concealment of defects or conditions making the premises unfit for residence may justify an abandonment thereof,[79] or may be waived by the tenant.[80] A mere expression of opinion on the part of the landlord does not amount to a warranty that a dwelling is fit for habitation.[81] In any event, the scope of a warranty does not extend beyond the terms of the representation.[82]

An express covenant that the lease of a dwelling is subject to the landlord obtaining a certificate of occupancy may be waived by the tenant where he takes possession and remains for a substantial period of time although the landlord has not obtained the required certificate.[82.5]

69.50 U.S.—State of Md., for Use of Pumphrey v. Manor Real Estate & Trust Co., C.A.Md., 176 F.2d 414.
Ill.—Ciskoski v. Michalsen, 152 N.E. 2d 479, 19 Ill.App.2d 327.
Pa.—De Raczynski v. Mack, Com.Pl., 25 Monroe L.R. 15.

Safe for habitation
Normally, there is no implied covenant that leased premises are safe for habitation and use or that they will remain in that condition.
Del.—Brandt v. Yeager, Super., 199 A.2d 768.

Implication
Although no covenant of habitability shall be implied from a landlord-tenant relationship, such a covenant may be implied from the terms of a lease.
N.Y.—Heissenbuttel v. Comnas, 177 N.Y.S.2d 850, 14 Misc.2d 509.

Abandonment for uninhabitability
Tenant should inspect premises before taking them, or he should secure an express warranty, and he is not entitled to abandon premises before taking them, there being no such express covenant.
N.Y.—Mulligan v. Fioravera, 239 N.Y. S. 438, 228 App.Div. 270, affirmed 175 N.E. 304, 255 N.Y. 539.
Shea v. Dyas, 12 N.Y.S.2d 951.

Under oral lease of apartment in multiple dwelling, landlord does not impliedly warrant that demised premises are in a reasonably safe condition.
Conn.—Bentley v. Dynarski, 186 A.2d 791, 150 Conn. 147—Torre v. De Renzo, 122 A.2d 25, 143 Conn. 302.

71. Del.—**Corpus Juris cited in** Leech v. Husbands, 152 A. 729, 731, 4 W.W.Harr. 362.
36 C.J. p 47 note 8.
Furnished dwellings see infra subdivision b of this section.

72. Mass.—McKeon v. Cutter, 31 N. E. 389, 156 Mass. 296.
36 C.J. p 47 note 9.

73. Del.—Leech v. Husbands, 152 A. 729, 4 W.W.Harr. 362.

74. U.S.—**Corpus Juris cited in**

76. Cal.—Buckner v. Azulai, supra.
Minn.—Delamater v. Foreman, 239 N. W. 148, 184 Minn. 428.

77. Cal.—Buckner v. Azulai, Super., 59 Cal.Rptr. 806.
Ill.—Allmon v. Davis, 248 Ill.App. 350.

Heat
Landlord leasing modern apartment containing apparently modern heating system impliedly warrants it will maintain reasonably comfortable temperature.
La.—Purnell v. Dugue, 129 So. 178, 14 La.App. 137.

Lack of plumbing and sewage system
Where leased house did not contain proper plumbing and sewage disposal system as required by state and parish law, mere showing that no application or plans for sewage system had been submitted, without further proof that premises were in fact unsanitary and uninhabitable, did not render lease void ab initio.
La.—Hancock v. Sliman, App., 175 So. 2d 437.

Exhibit 8.7 Sample C.J.S. Page of Updated Material from Pocket Supplement

Pages 771–777

27.5 Del.—Brown v. Robyn Realty Co., Super., 367 A.2d 183.
D.C.—Kanelos v. Kettler, C.A., 406 F.2d 951, 132 U.S.App.D.C. 133.

Statute not retroactive
N.Y.—Kaplan v. Coulston, 381 N.Y.S.2d 634, 85 Misc.2d 745.

Implied warranty of habitability
Iowa—Duke v. Clark, 267 N.W.2d 63.
Tex.—Johnson v. Highland Hills Drive Apartments, 568 S.W.2d 661.

page 772

27.10 La.—Reed v. Classified Parking System, App., 232 So.2d 103, writ den. 234 So.2d 194, 255 La. 1097, writ ref. 234 So.2d 194, 255 La. 1098.
29. Ill.—Longenecker v. Hardin, 264 N. E.2d 878, 130 Ill.App.2d 468.
La.—McCrory Corp. v. Latter, App., 331 So.2d 577, writ den. 334 So.2d 229.
N.Y.—Houston Realty Corp. v. Castro, 404 N.Y.S.2d 796, 94 Misc.2d 115.
Ohio—Glyco v. Schultz, 289 N.E.2d 919, 35 Ohio Misc. 25.

Statute held inapplicable to business property
N.J.—Van Ness Industries, Inc. v. Claremont Painting & Decorating Co., 324 A.2d 102, 129 N.J.Super. 507.

Untenantable conditions not found
Conn.—Thomas v. Roper, 294 A.2d 321, 162 Conn. 343.
N.J.—Park Hill Terrace Associates v. Glennon, 369 A.2d 938, 146 N.J.Super. 271.

Statutory provision breached
N.Y.—Kekllas v. Saddy, 389 N.Y.S.2d 756, 88 Misc.2d 1042.
35. Mo.—Henderson v. W. C. Haas Realty Management, Inc., App., 561 S.W. 2d 382.

§ 304. Suitability of Premises for Purpose for Which They Were Leased

page 773

43. U.S.—Pointer v. American Oil Co., D.C.Ind., 295 F.Supp. 573.
Ala.—Martin v. Springdale Stores, Inc., Civ., 354 So.2d 1144, cert. den. Ex parte Martin, 354 So.2d 1146.
N.J.—Conroy v. 10 Brewster Ave. Corp., 234 A.2d 415, 97 N.J.Super. 75—Coleman v. Steinberg, 253 A.2d 167, 54 N.J. 58.
Academy Spires, Inc. v. Jones, 261 A.2d 413, 108 N.J.Super. 395.
N.Y.—Refrigeration for Science, Inc. v. Deacon Realty Corp., 334 N.Y.S.2d 418, 70 Misc.2d 500, affd. 344 N.Y.S. 2d 1018, 42 A.D.2d 691.
Tex.—Cameron v. Calhoun-Smith Distributing Co., Civ.App., 442 S.W.2d 815.

page 774

44. Kan.—Service Oil Co., Inc. v. White, 542 P.2d 652, 218 Kan. 87.
47. **Suitability assured**
Ga.—Warner v. Arnold, 210 S.E.2d 350, 133 Ga.App. 174.
48.10 Minn.—Vermes v. American Dist. Tel. Co., 251 N.W.2d 101.
N.J.—Academy Spires, Inc. v. Jones, 261 A.2d 413, 108 N.J.Super. 395.

page 775

49. Kan.—Service Oil Co., Inc. v. White, 542 P.2d 652, 218 Kan. 87.
N.J.—Reste Realty Corp. v. Cooper, 251 A.2d 268, 53 N.J. 444, 33 A.L.R.3d 1341.
51. Kan.—Service Oil Co., Inc. v. White, 542 P.2d 652, 218 Kan. 87.
52.5 N.H.—Goglia v. Rand, 319 A.2d 281, 114 N.H. 252.

Lessee's knowledge of difficulties immaterial
N.Y.—Benderson Development Co., Inc. v. Commenco Corp., 355 N.Y.S.2d 859, 44 A.D.2d 889, affd 337 N.E.2d 130, 37 N.Y.2d 728, 374 N.Y.S.2d 618.
53. La.—Evans v. Does, App., 283 So.2d 804.

Intended as protection for lessee
N.Y.—Benderson Development Co., Inc. v. Commenco Corp., 355 N.Y.S.2d 859, 44 A.D.2d 889, affd. 337 N.E.2d 130, 37 N.Y.2d 728, 374 N.Y.S.2d 618.
54. **Language not ambiguous**
Ga.—Gilreath v. Argo, 219 S.E.2d 461, 135 Ga.App. 849.
55. Iowa—C.J.S. quoted in Osterling v. Sturgeon, 156 N.W.2d 344, 348, 261 Iowa 836.

page 776

58. Del.—Brown v. Robyn Realty Co., Super., 367 A.2d 183.
60.10 La.—Add Chemical Co. v. Gulf-Marine Fabricators, Inc., App., 345 So.2d 216, writ den., Sup., 347 So.2d 263.

§ 305. —— Dwellings

page 777

69.50 Colo.—Blackwell v. Del Bosco, 536 P.2d 838, 35 Colo.App. 399, affd. Sup., 558 P.2d 563.
N.Y.—Graham v. Wisenburn, 334 N.Y. S.2d 81, 39 A.D.2d 334.
Or.—Cook v. Salishan Properties, Inc., 569 P.2d 1033, 279 Or. 333.

Statutory tenants no action based on contract
N.Y.—Committee For Preservation of Fresh Meadows, Inc. v. Fresh Meadows Associates, 403 N.Y.S.2d 839, 62 A.D.2d 529.

70. **Would not be implied under circumstances**
Colo.—Blackwell v. Del Bosco, 536 P.2d 838, 35 Colo.App. 399, affd. Sup., 558 P.2d 563.

There is other authority that in a lease of a dwelling house there is an implied warranty of habitability and fitness for use intended,[72.5] which exists in unfurnished as well as furnished dwellings.[72.10] In determining whether there exists a breach of this implied warranty each case must depend on its own facts and circumstances.[72.15]

72.5 Cal.—Hinson v. Delis, 102 Cal.Rptr. 661, 26 C.A.3d 62.
Hawaii—Lemle v. Breeden, 462 P.2d 470, 51 Haw. 426, 478, 40 A.L.R.3d 637.
Iowa—Mease v. Fox, 200 N.W.2d 791.
Minn.—Fritz v. Warthen, 213 N.W.2d 339, 298 Minn. 54.
N.J.—Berzito v. Gambino, 308 A.2d 17, 63 N.J. 460.
N.Y.—Tonetti v. Penati, 367 N.Y.S.2d 804, 48 A.D.2d 25.
Hall v. Fraknoi, 330 N.Y.S.2d 637, 69 Misc.2d 470.

Substantial compliance with building code
Ill.—Jack Spring, Inc. v. Little, 280 N. E.2d 208, 50 Ill.2d 351.
Mo.—King v. Moorehead, App., 495 S.W. 2d 65.
N.Y.—Morbeth Realty Corp. v. Velez, 343 N.Y.S.2d 406, 73 Misc.2d 996.

Protection does not coincide with State Sanitary Code
Mass.—Boston Housing Authority v. Hemingway, 293 N.E.2d 831, 363 Mass. 184.

Oral or written lease
Wash.—Foisy v. Wyman, 515 P.2d 160, 83 Wash.2d 22.

Provisions of housing code part of lease
Kan.—Steele v. Latimer, 521 P.2d 304, 214 Kan. 329.

Bare living requirements to be maintained
Cal.—Green v. Superior Court of City and County of San Francisco, 111 Cal.Rptr. 704, 517 P.2d 1168, 10 C. 3d 616.

Implied warranty created by ordinance
N.Y.—401 Boardwalk Corp. v. Gutzwiller, 368 N.Y.S.2d 122, 82 Misc.2d 84.

Object
N.Y.—401 Boardwalk Corp. v. Gutzwiller, 368 N.Y.S.2d 122, 82 Misc.2d 84.

Breach of warranty
N.Y.—Cohen v. Werner, 368 N.Y.S.2d 1005, 82 Misc.2d 295, affd. 378 N.Y.S. 2d 868, 85 Misc.2d 341.

Read into leases
N.Y.—Kipsborough Realty Corp. v. Goldbetter, 367 N.Y.S.2d 916, 81 Misc.2d 1054.

Statute held not retroactive
N.Y.—Francais v. Cusa Bros. Enterprises, Inc., 385 N.Y.S.2d 183, 53 A.D.2d 24.

Applicable to rent control or stabilized buildings
N.Y.—Park West Management Corp. v. Mitchell, 404 N.Y.S.2d 115, 62 A.D. 2d 291.

Statute retroactive
N.Y.—Park West Management Corp. v. Mitchell, 404 N.Y.S.2d 115, 62 A.D. 2d 291.

Same remedies as for breach of express warranty
Pa.—Pugh v. Holmes, 384 A.2d 1234.
72.10 Hawaii—Lund v. MacArthur, 462 P.2d 482, 51 Haw. 473.
72.15 **Relevant factors to be considered**
Cal.—Hinson v. Delis, 102 Cal.Rptr. 661, 26 C.A.3d 62.
Hawaii—Lemle v. Breeden, 462 P.2d 470, 51 Haw. 426, 478, 40 A.L.R.3d 637—Lund v. MacArthur, 462 P.2d 482, 51 Haw. 473.
Iowa—Mease v. Fox, 200 N.W.2d 791.
Mo.—King v. Moorehead, App., 495 S.W. 2d 65.
N.J.—Timber Ridge Town House v. Dietz, 338 A.2d 21, 133 N.J.Super. 577.
Wash.—Foisy v. Wyman, 515 P.2d 160, 83 Wash.2d 22.

Presence of rats in dwelling
Hawaii—Lemle v. Breeden, 462 P.2d 470, 51 Haw. 426, 478, 40 A.L.R.3d 637.

Complaint held to state cause of action
Ill.—Gillette v. Anderson, 282 N.E.2d 149, 4 Ill.App.3d 838.
Mich.—Borman's Inc. v. Lake State Development Co., 230 N.W.2d 363, 60 Mich.App. 175.

Constructive eviction as material breach
Mass.—Boston Housing Authority v. Hemingway, 293 N.E.2d 831, 363 Mass. 184.

Right to negotiate better terms is no defense
N.Y.—Morbeth Realty Corp. v. Velez, 343 N.Y.S.2d 406, 73 Misc.2d 996.

Notice of defects by other tenants is sufficient
Mass.—Boston Housing Authority v. Hemingway, 293 N.E.2d 831, 363 Mass. 184.

Reasonable time for correction of defect
Mo.—King v. Moorehead, App., 495 S.W. 2d 65.

Breach must be of substantial nature
Cal.—Green v. Superior Court of City and County of San Francisco, 111 Cal.Rptr. 704, 517 P.2d 1168, 10 C. 3d 616.
Iowa—Mease v. Fox, 200 N.W.2d 791.
Mass.—McKenna v. Begin, App., 362 N. E.2d 548.

Abandonment not essential element of cause of action
N.Y.—401 Boardwalk Corp. v. Gutzwiller, 368 N.Y.S.2d 122, 82 Misc.2d 84.

Mail delivery
Tex.—Johnson v. Highland Hills Drive Apartments, Civ.App., 552 S.W.2d 493.

Notice of breach
Ill.—Jarrell v. Hartman, 363 N.E.2d 626, 6 Ill.Dec. 812, 48 Ill.App.3d 985.

313

Exhibit 8.8 Sample C.J.S. Topic Summary Page

CORPUS JURIS SECUNDUM

———•———

LANDLORD AND TENANT

This Title includes nature and incidents of estates for years and tenancies from year to year, at will, or at sufferance; leases and agreements for the occupation of real property in general, the relation between the parties thereto, and their rights and liabilities as between themselves and as to others incident to such relation; and remedies relating thereto.

Excluded are leases of property of particular classes of persons (Infants; Insane Persons; Corporations; and other specific titles); leases of particular species of property (Railroads; Mines and Minerals; Waters; and other specific titles); rent charges and ground rents (Ground Rents); and implied liabilities for use and occupation of real property (Use and Occupation).

Analysis

See also descriptive word index in volume containing end of this Title

Exhibit 8.9 Sample C.J.S. Topic Outline Page

LANDLORD & TENANT

See also descriptive word index in volume containing end of this Title

12

315

Exhibit 8.10 Sample C.J.S. Index Page for Landlord and Tenant Volume

LANDLORD & TENANT

316

Exhibit 8.11 Sample C.J.S. General Index Page

THE LAW CHART

A Practical Working Index of the Standard Law
Titles Under the Seven Grand Divisions:

1. PERSONS
2. PROPERTY
3. CONTRACTS
4. TORTS
5. CRIMES
6. REMEDIES
7. GOVERNMENT

ALL RELATED TITLES ARE HERE GROUPED
Enabling Comparison and Discrimination in the Selection of the Right One.

DIRECTIONS

FIRST: Select the Grand Division that Covers Your Question.
SECOND: Select its Pertinent Subhead.
THIRD: Under the Subhead Select the Most Specific Title.

1. PERSONS

INCLUDING ASSOCIATIONS, PARTNERSHIPS, AND
CORPORATIONS

Classes of Natural Persons in General

Absentees
Adjoining Landowners
Aliens
Ambassadors and Consuls
Amicus Curiæ
Bastards
Citizens
Convicts
Drunkards
Indians
Infants
Innkeepers
Insane Persons
Paupers
Principal and Surety
Slaves
Spendthrifts

Family and Domestic Relations

Adoption of Children
Apprentices
Divorce
Guardian and Ward
Husband and Wife
Marriage
Master and Servant
Parent and Child

Fiduciary and Representative Relations

Agency
Attorney and Client
Brokers
Depositaries
Executors and Administrators
Factors

Exhibit 8.12 Sample Illinois Law and Practice Page

§ 237. Tenantable Condition and Suitability for Purposes of Lease

While it has been stated that there is no implied covenant on the part of a landlord that the premises are, or will remain, in a tenantable condition fit for the purposes for which rented, it has also been stated that there is a legal duty resting on the landlord in the first instance to have the premises in such condition.

It has been stated that in the absence of express agreement the tenant takes the premises as he finds them without implied covenants that they are fit for habitation or in any particular condition of repair,[36] and that there is no implied contract on the part of the landlord that the leased premises are tenantable or that they will continue so during the term.[37] It has also been stated that ordinarily there is no implied covenant that the premises demised are reasonably fit for the purposes for which they are rented.[38]

However, in the case of Allmon v. Davis, 1928, which was an action involving liability for rent, it was said that it is the duty of the landlord to furnish to the tenant premises which may be used for the purpose for which they are leased, since otherwise the object for which the contract is made entirely fails.[39]

36. Farmer v. Alton Building & Loan Ass'n, 1938, 13 N.E.2d 652, 294 Ill. App. 206.

Express covenant as excluding implied covenant

Where the lease contains an express covenant by the landlord to put the house on the leased premises in habitable condition, this excludes any implied covenant on the same matter.—Rubens v. Hill, 1904, 72 N.E. 1127, 213 Ill. 523.

Prior inspection

There is no implied covenant on part of landlord that premises at time of letting are in tenantable condition or that physical condition of premises shall remain unchanged during the term, and especially so when tenant inspects them before executing lease, except in case of fraudulent concealment of hidden defects.—Russell v. Clark, 1912, 173 Ill.App. 461.

37. Carpenter v. Stone, 1904, 112 Ill. App. 155.

Watson v. Moulton, 1901, 100 Ill.App. 560.

McCoull v. Herzberg, 1889, 33 Ill.App. 542.

Blake v. Ranous, 1887, 25 Ill.App. 486.

38. Long v. Joseph Schlitz Brewing Co., 1919, 214 Ill.App. 517.

Cohen v. Plumtree, 1912, 170 Ill.App. 311.

Rubens v. Hill, 1904, 115 Ill.App. 565, affirmed 72 N.E. 1127, 213 Ill. 523.

Lazarus & Cohen v. Parmly, 1904, 113 Ill.App. 624.

39. Allmon v. Davis, 1928, 248 Ill. App. 350 (adequate supply of water is necessary in order to make premises used as dwelling tenantable and habitable).

Exhibit 8.13 Sample Illinois Law and Practice Page from Pocket Part

LANDLORD AND TENANT § 252

§ 237. Tenantable Condition and Suitability for Purposes of Lease

Library References

C.J.S. Landlord and Tenant §§ 303–305. Landlord and Tenant ⚖125 (1, 2).

Modern Legal Forms ch. 42, Leases.

36. Ciskoski v. Michalsen, 1958, 152 N.E.2d 479, 19 Ill.App.2d 327.

Contract law and the form lease. See 71 N.W.L.Rev. 204 (1976).

Leaseholds and warranty of habitability, see 47 Chicago-Kent L.Rev. 53 (1970).

Caveat vendor—a trend in the law of real property see 5 De Paul L.Rev. 263 (1956).

A tort remedy for slum tenant see 58 Ill.Bar. J. 204 (1969).

37. Dapkunas v. Cagle, 1976, 356 N.E. 2d 575, 1 Ill.Dec. 387, 42 Ill.App.3d 644 (tenant could not recover against landlord for injuries sustained in fall from back steps of single unit dwelling under theory of implied warranty of habitability and fitness for intended purpose).

The Supreme Court in a 1972 case has held that an implied warranty of habitability is deemed included in contracts, oral and written, governing tenancies in multiple dwellings,[37.5] which is fullfilled by substantial compliance with the provisions of the applicable building code.[37.10]

37.5 Jack Spring, Inc. v. Little, 1972, 280 N.E.2d 208, 50 Ill.2d 351.

Jarrell v. Hartman, 1977, 363 N.E.2d 626, 6 Ill.Dec. 812, 48 Ill.App.3d 985.

Gillette v. Anderson, 1972, 282 N.E.2d 149, 4 Ill.App.3d 838 (complaint by tenant against former landlord alleging that defendant failed to provide bathtub or shower in violation of city ordinances stated cause of action based on theory of implied warranty of habitability).

Implied warranty of habitability see 20 De Paul L.Rev. 955 (1971); 66 N.W.L.Rev. 790 (1972).

37.10 Jack Spring, Inc. v. Little, 1972, 280 N.E.2d 208, 50 Ill.2d 351.

38. Hendricks v. Socony Mobil Oil Co., 1963, 195 N.E.2d 1, 45 Ill.App.2d 44

(use to which lessee may intend to put premises).

Violations of ordinance

In absence of showing that lessors knew of existence of violations of ordinance when lease was executed and failed to disclose such knowledge to lessees who were ignorant of violations or showing as to whether violations occurred during period when lessees were in occupancy or were prior thereto, lessees were not entitled to recover from lessors on ground that lessees had expended sums to correct violations and lost rentals because city prohibited use of certain portions of property.

Eskin v. Freedman, 1964, 203 N.E.2d 24, 53 Ill.App.2d 144.

B. POSSESSION, ENJOYMENT, AND USE

§ 251. In General

2. People v. Goduto, 1961, 174 N.E.2d 385, 21 Ill.2d 605, cert. den. 82 S.Ct. 361, 368 U.S. 927, 7 L.Ed.2d 190 (lessee of property used as parking lot for lessee's customers and employees had right to demand that union organizers, who were not employees or prospective customers, but who were on parking lot for sole purpose of distributing leaflets, leave premises).

People v. DeFilippis, 1964, 203 N.E.2d 627, 54 Ill.App.2d 137, revd. on oth. grds. 214 N.E.2d 897, 34 Ill.2d 129.

3. People v. DeFilippis, 1964, 203 N.E. 2d 627, 54 Ill.App.2d 137, revd. on oth. grds. 214 N.E.2d 897, 34 Ill.2d 129.

Possessory ownership

At common law, tenant becomes possessory owner of an estate for a period of time during which term primary indicia of ownership passes to him.

People v. May, 1970, 262 N.E.2d 908, 46 Ill.2d 120.

§ 252. Delivery of Possession

Exhibit 8.14 Sample Index to Legal Periodicals Page

SUBJECT AND AUTHOR INDEX 279

LANDAU, Jack C.
Due process (F)
Freedom of the press (F)

LANDAU, Norman J.
Ind diseases (D)

LANDERS, Jonathan M.
Consumer protect (D, S, T)
Credit (D, S, T)
Loans (T)
Mortgages (T)

LANDERS, Joseph W., Jr
Adm agencies—Fla (R)
Environ law (R)

LANDES, William M.
Courts (I)
Economics (E, L)
Judicial stat (L)
Pol sci (E)
Precedents (L)

LANDLORD and tenant
Adjusting the economic relationship of landlord and tenant—rent alteration remedies. Urban L Ann 11:155-85 '76
Application of the principle of mitigation of damages to landlord-tenant law. A. J. Bradbrook. Sydney L Rev 8:15-30 Ja '77
Balancing act: strengthening South Dakota's landlord-tenant law. M. A. Wolff. SD L Rev 22:15-40 Wint '77
Can distraint stand up as a landlord's remedy? Real Estate L J 5:242-59 Wint '77
Civil remedies available to residential tenants in Ontario: the case for assertive action. Osgoode Hall L J 14:65-91 Je '76
Constitutional law—action under color of state law—legislative authorization of private action resembling public function constitutes action under color of state law. Vand L Rev 29:851-9 Ap '76
Contract law and the form lease: can contract law provide the answer? D. V. Kirby. Nw U L Rev 71:204-37 My-Je '76
Contracting out of the landlord and tenant act. R. A. Weidberg. Modern L Rev 39:337-42 My '76
Distributive impact, allocative efficiency, and overall desirability of ideal housing codes: some theoretical clarifications. R. S. Markovits. Harv L Rev 89:1815-46 Je '76
Droits et recours des parties à un contrat de bail devant la Commission des loyers. L. Robert. McGill L J 22:380-414 Fall '76
"Equal justice under the law": the evolution of a national commitment to legal services for the poor and a study of its impact on New Jersey landlord-tenant law. J. B. Ventantonio. Seton Hall L Rev 7:233-97 Wint '76
Examination of some of the recent amendments to the Ontario landlord and tenant act. M. Gorsky. Dalhousie L J 3:663-705 Ja '77
Kentucky uniform residential landlord and tenant act: tenants' new lease on life? J Family L 14:597-624 '75-'76
Landlord and tenant—landlord may be liable for theft after suitable notice of defective lock. Seton Hall L Rev 7:683-702 Spr '76
Landlord and tenant—prohibition of retaliatory eviction in landlord-tenant relations. a study of practice and proposals. NC L Rev 54:861-84 Je '76
Landlord control of tenant behavior: an instance of private environmental legislation. J. A. Humbach. Fordham L Rev 45:223-334 N '76
Landlord-tenant—caveat emptor—implied warranty of habitability in residential leases. NY L F 21:613-33 Spr '76
Landlord-tenant—commercial landlord's liability for criminal acts of third party. Wayne L Rev 22:1483-91 S '76
Landlord-tenant—due process—tenant of federally subsidized housing may not be evicted upon expiration of lease absent a showing of good cause. Md L Rev 36:255-69 '76
Landlord-tenant: proving motive in retaliatory eviction—Minnesota's solution. Minn L Rev 61:523-41 F '77
Landlord-tenant—repairs—landlord could be liable under covenant to repair for injuries to tenant's invitees caused by breach of such agreement. Fordham Urban L J 5:165-73 Fall '76
Landlord-tenant: the medieval concepts of feudal property law are alive and well in leases of commercial property in Illinois. John Marshal J 10:338-58 Wint '77
Landlords' notices to quit. D. C. S. Phillips. Sol J 120:596-8 S 3 '76
Lessor's bankruptcy: the draftsman's response to the tenant's plight. L. H. Jacobson. Real Estate L J 1:152-62 Fall '72
Neither seen nor heard: keeping children out of Arizona's adult communities under Arizona revised statutes section 33-1317(B) Ariz St L J 1975:813-40 '75
New act is a step toward landlord-tenant equality in Georgia. Mercer L Rev 28:351-70 Fall '76
New look at law of landlord and tenant. G. C. Hawkins. Ala Law 38:71-80 Ja '77
Overview of the Tennessee residential landlord and tenant act. Memphis St U L Rev 7:109-28 Fall '76
Reassessment of the laws relating to the determination of tenancies. A. J. Bradbrook. Adelaide L Rev 5:357-81 N '76
Repair obligations of landlords and tenants: a plea for reform. A. J. Bradbrook. UWAL Rev 12:437-66 D '76
Residential tenant's security deposit—a protected interest worth litigating. St Mary's L J 8:829-52 '77
Responsibility of landlords for conditions of habitability. J. G. Rose. Real Estate L J 1: 53-80 Summ '72
Retaliatory eviction in California—a common law defense or a semantical exercise? T. G. Treece. Orange County B J 3:237-42 Fall '76
Role of the judiciary in reforming landlord and tenant law. A. J. Bradbrook. M U L R 10: 459-80 S '76
State housing commissions and their tenants: the need for legislative control. A. J. Bradbrook. M U L R 10:409-41 Je '76
Texas landlord-tenant law and the deceptive trade practices act—affirmative remedies for the tenant. St Mary's L J 8:807-28 '77
Uniform residential landlord and tenant act and its potential effects upon Maryland landlord-tenant law. S. G. Davison. U Balt L Rev 5: 247-98 Spr '76
See also
Eviction
Fixtures
Leases
Notice
Possession
Rents and rent control

Cases

Anastasia v. Cosmopolitan Natl Bank, 527 F 2d 150
U Cin L Rev 45:301-4 '76
Liverpool City Council v. Irwin [1976] Q B 619
Camb L J 36:15-17 Ap '77
Putnam v. Stout (NY) 345 N E 2d 319
Brooklyn L Rev 43:206-8 Summ '76

LANDO, Ole
Compar law (S)
Conflict of laws: contracts (S)

LANDRETH, Duane P.
City planning (F)
Grants-in-aid (F)
Housing (F)
Regional planning (F)

LANDRIEU, Moon
Mun corps (U)

LANDRUM, Charles, Jr
Biog (Lively)
Judges (F)

LANDRY, James E.
Air law (I)
US: CAB (I)

LANDS. See Public lands

LANDY, Craig A.
Commerce clause (T)
Corp: consol and merger (T)
Fed preemption (T)
Securities: state reg (T)

LANDYNSKI, Jacob W.
Biog (Black)
Search and seizure (I)

LANE, Bruce S.
Bonds (N)
Inc tax: exemptions—US (N)
Interest (N)

LANE, Horace C.
Automob insur (A)

LANG, Jonathan
Collective bargaining (T)
Due process (T)
Unions (T)

LANGBEIN, John H.
Banks and banking (M)
Investments (M)
Stocks (M)
Trusts and trustees (M)

Exhibit 8.15 Sample A.L.R.3d Pages Showing the Scope of an Annotation

ANNOTATION

MODERN STATUS OF RULES AS TO EXISTENCE OF IMPLIED WARRANTY OF HABITABILITY OR FIT-NESS FOR USE OF LEASED PREMISES

by

Jonathan M. Purver, LL.B.

INDEX

TOTAL CLIENT-SERVICE LIBRARY® REFERENCES

49 Am Jur 2d, Landlord and Tenant §§ 309, 768–772

22 Am Jur Proof of Facts 17, Eviction of Tenant

ALR Digests, Landlord and Tenant §§ 41, 44, 45

ALR Quick Index, Landlord and Tenant

Consult POCKET PART in this volume for later case service

Exhibit 8.15 (continued)

TABLE OF JURISDICTIONS REPRESENTED
Consult POCKET PART in this volume for later case service

---

§ 1. Introduction

[a] Scope

This annotation[1] discusses those decisions which have expressly recognized that there exists, in today's modern leasing transactions, an implied warranty of habitability or fitness for use of the premises which are the subject matter of

---

1. Attempting merely to show the modern status of the rules, this annotation does not purport exhaustively to collect all of the cases within its scope.

the lease. Also included, as appearing to reflect a transitional stage in the common law of leasing arrangements, is a representative selection of decisions creating some limited exceptions to the heretofore nearly universal doctrine of no implied warranty, or caveat emptor.[2]

Excluded are cases wherein a statutory provision was relied upon as giving rise to an implied warranty of habitability or fitness for use, the thrust of the collection of cases herein being to show how some courts have judicially carved and remolded the old common law pertaining to landlord and tenant in regard to warranties, in an attempt to bring the common law into line with the economic realities of modern leasing law.

Treated elsewhere is the queston as to the tenant's remedies where his premises are untenantable or unfit for the purposes for which they were leased as a result of the landlord's breach of an express covenant, or lease provision, to repair the leased premises.[3]

[b] Related matters

Tenant's right, where landlord fails to make repairs, to have them made and set off cost against rent. 40 ALR3d 1369.

Validity and construction of statute or ordinance authorizing withholding or payment into escrow of rent for period during which premises are not properly maintained by landlord. 40 ALR3d 821.

Retaliatory eviction of tenant for reporting landlord's violation of law. 40 ALR3d 753.

Landlord and tenant: constructive eviction based on flooding, dampness, or the like. 33 ALR3d 1356.

Infestation of leased dwelling or apartment with vermin as entitling tenant to abandon premises or as constructive eviction by landlord, in absence of express covenant of habitability. 27 ALR3d 924.

Who, as between landlord and tenant, must make, or bear expense of, alterations, improvements, or repairs ordered by public authorities. 22 ALR3d 521.

Implied covenant or obligation of lessor to furnish water or water supply for business needs of the lessee. 65 ALR2d 1313.

Rights and remedies of tenant upon landlord's breach of covenant to repair. 28 ALR2d 446.

Breach of covenant to furnish heat for building or room other than dwelling or apartment as an eviction. 69 ALR 1093.

Liability of landlord for damage to tenant because of infection from contagious or infectious disease. 26 ALR 1265.

Effect of nonhabitability of leased dwelling or apartment. 4 ALR 1453, 13 ALR 818, 29 ALR 52, 34 ALR 711.

✦

Skillern, Implied Warranties in Leases: The Need For Change. 44 Denver LJ 387 (1967).

Quinn & Phillips, The Law of Landlord-Tenant: A Critical Evaluation of the Past With Guidelines For the Future. 38 Fordham L Rev 225 (1969).

Schoshinski, Remedies of the Indigent Tenant: Proposal for Change. 54 Georgetown LJ 519 (1966).

Recent decision, landlord and tenant —application of implied warranty. 45 Marquette L Rev 630 (1962).

Sax & Hiestand, Slumlordism as a Tort. 65 Mich L Rev 869 (1967).

Lesar, Landlord and Tenant Reform. 35 NYU L Rev 1279 (1960).

---

2. Not discussed are cases wherein there existed an express warranty by a lessor to provide particular services, equipment, or facilities, and the question before the court was whether, based upon the express undertaking, there necessarily followed the implied warranty or understanding that the service or facility promised would be reasonably adequate to meet the expressly stated needs.

3. 49 Am Jur 2d, Landlord and Tenant § 616. As to rights and remedies of tenant upon landlord's breach of covenant to repair, see 28 ALR2d 446.

Exhibit 8.16 Sample A.L.R.3d Annotation Page

Pointing out that herein it clearly appeared that the parties contemplated the use of a building for a furniture store, the court said that since there was no showing that the construction had progressed to such an extent as to afford the lessee an opportunity to judge the suitableness of the building, it could not be said that he took the building at his peril. Accordingly, it was recognized that the lessee in such circumstance would not be liable for the rent of a building which when constructed was leaky and failed completely to keep rainwater from entering the store.

§ 5. Rejection of doctrine of caveat emptor

[a] Recognition of implied warranty of habitability or fitness for use

In the past 10 years some courts, instead of creating exceptions to the rule, have proceeded to expressly reject the doctrine of caveat emptor with respect to modern leasing agreements, and have recognized the existence of an implied warranty of habitability or fitness for use of leased premises.

Hence, in Javins v First Nat. Realty Corp. (1970) 138 App DC 369, 428 F2d 1071, cert den 400 US 925, 27 L Ed 2d 185, 91 S Ct 186, an action by a landlord for nonpayment of rent, wherein the tenants alleged numerous violations of the District of Columbia housing regulations, the court held that the common law itself "must recognize the landlord's obligation to keep his premises in a habitable condition." Saying that the housing code must be read into housing contracts, the court explained that under contract principles (which are to be applied), the tenant's obligation to pay the rent is dependent upon the landlord's performance of his obligations, and that in order to determine whether any rent is owed therein, the tenant must be given an opportunity to prove the alleged housing code violations as a breach of the landlord's warranty. At trial, said the court, the finder of fact must make two findings: (1) whether the alleged violations existed during the period for which past-due rent is claimed, and (2) what portion, if any or if all, of the tenant's obligation to pay rent was suspended by the landlord's breach. The court did state, however, that the jury should be instructed that one or two minor violations standing alone which do not affect habitability are de minimis and would not entitle the tenant to a reduction in rent.

In Lemle v Breeden (1969) 51 Hawaii 426, 478, 462 P2d 470, 40 ALR3d 637, the court affirmed a judgment in favor of a lessee who sued to recover the deposit and rent payment for a leased home upon discovering severe rat infestation, and upheld the trial judge's grounds for recovery that there was a material breach of an implied warranty of habitability and fitness for the use intended which justified the lessee's rescinding the rental agreement and vacating the premises. Significantly stating that it need not consider the ruling of the trial court that the plaintiff was constructively evicted in light of the holding that there was an implied warranty of habitability in the case, the court pointed out that the doctrine of constructive eviction, "as an admitted judicial fiction designed to operate as though there were a substantial breach of a material covenant in a bilateral contract," no longer serves its purpose when the more flexible concept of implied warranty of habitability is legally available. Saying that it was a decided advantage of the implied warranty doctrine that there were a number of remedies available, the court pointed out that under the constructive eviction analysis the lessee must always abandon the premises at the risk of establishing sufficient facts to constitute constructive eviction or he will be liable for breach of the rental

Exhibit 8.17 Sample A.L.R. Quick Index Page

Sanity: existence of other remedy as affecting habeas corpus on ground of restoration to sanity of one confined as an incompetent other than in connection with crime, 21 ALR2d 1004

§ 2. Grounds for relief and matters reviewable.

Absence of counsel for accused at time of sentence as requiring vacation thereof or other relief, 20 ALR2d 1240

Anticipatory relief in federal courts against state criminal prosecutions growing out of civil rights activities, 8 ALR3d 301

Appeal, habeas corpus on ground of deprivation of right to, 19 ALR2d 789

Charge: determination whether crime is charged, 40 ALR2d 1151

Child support: court's power in habeas corpus proceedings relating to custody of child to adjudicate questions as to child's support, 17 ALR3d 764

Court martial: review by habeas corpus of court-martial convictions, 15 ALR2d 387

Custody of child
- illegitimate child, proceedings to obtain custody of, 98 ALR2d 421
- modification: child custody provisions of divorce or separation decree as subject to modification on habeas corpus, 4 ALR3d 1277
- nonresidence as affecting one's right to custody of child in habeas corpus proceedings, 15 ALR2d 432
- support: court's power in habeas corpus proceedings relating to custody of child to adjudicate questions as to child's support, 17 ALR3d 764

Identity: right of prisoner held under extradition warrant to raise question of identity in habeas corpus proceeding, 93 ALR2d 916

Insanity of accused at time of commission of offense [not raised at trial] as ground for habeas corpus after conviction, 29 ALR2d 703

Parolee's right to habeas corpus, 92 ALR2d 682

Race as factor in custody proceeding, 57 ALR2d 678

Sanity: habeas corpus on ground of restoration to sanity of one confined as an incompetent other than in connection with crime, 21 ALR2d 1004

Service of process: attack, by petition for writ of habeas corpus, on personal service as

having been obtained by fraud or trickery, 98 ALR2d 600

Sexual psychopaths, habeas corpus to test validity of confinement under statutes relating to, 24 ALR2d 376

Speedy trial: waiver or loss of accused's right to speedy trial as affecting right to habeas corpus, 57 ALR2d 339

Subsequent proceedings: discharge on habeas corpus of one held in extradition proceedings as precluding subsequent extradition proceedings, 33 ALR3d 1443

Suppression of evidence by prosecution in criminal case as ground for habeas corpus, 33 ALR2d 1421

HABENDUM CLAUSE

Conflict between granting and habendum clauses as to estate conveyed, 58 ALR2d 1374

What amounts to development or operation for oil or gas within terms of habendum clause extending primary term while the premises are being "developed or operated", 96 ALR2d 322

HABITABILITY

Implied warranty: modern status of rules as to existence of implied warranty of habitability or fitness for use of leased premises, 40 ALR3d 646

Infestation of leased dwelling or apartment with vermin as entitling tenant to abandon premises or as constructive eviction by landlord, in absence of express covenant of habitability, 27 ALR3d 924

HABITS

Custom and Usage (this index)

HABITUAL CRIMINALS

Chronological or procedural sequence of former convictions as affecting enhancement of penalty for subsequent offense under habitual criminal statutes, 24 ALR2d 1247

Felony: determination of character of former crime as a felony, so as to warrant punishment of an accused as a second offender, 19 ALR2d 227

Form and sufficiency of allegations as to time, place, or court of prior offenses or convictions, under habitual criminal act or statute enhancing punishment for repeated offenses, 80 ALR2d 1196

Identity: evidence of identity for purposes of

2. Finding Statutes and Regulations

Once there is a general understanding of the applicable legal principles in a problem, an effort should be made to determine if any relevant statutes or administrative regulations are in force. (Sample pages from these research volumes, labeled Exhibit 8.18 through Exhibit 8.23, appear at the end of this section at pages 329-334.) This may involve federal, state, and/or local legislation. There will be times when the researcher already knows about pertinent legislation and may even have obtained the citation through the general reading discussed above. For a thorough search, however, one should begin with a subject index.

a. Subject Index Technique

A paralegal should begin a search of the federal statutes with one of the subject indexes in the United States Code (U.S.C.), the United States Code Annotated (U.S.C.A.), the Federal Code Annotated (F.C.A.), or the United States Code Service (U.S.C.S.).[5] These indexes provide relatively easy access to both the Constitution and federal laws of a general and permanent nature that are currently in force. (See Exhibit 8.18.) General laws no longer in force can be located by using the subject indexes in each volume of the Statutes at Large. State codifications also have subject indexes. When looking for local legislation the researcher can simply scan the table of contents in the front of the volume.

b. Using Popular-Name Tables

Many pieces of legislation are commonly referred to by the names of the sponsors (the Taft-Hartley Act) or a descriptive title (the Truth in Lending Act). U.S.C., U.S.C.A., and U.S.C.S. all contain popular-name tables that give the formal citations for these acts. In addition, Shepard's Acts and Cases by Popular Names, Federal and State provides a convenient source for both federal and state legislation. The U.S. Supreme Court Reports Digest also contains a popular-name table.

c. Checking for Subsequent Legislative or Judicial Action

Once the applicable statutes have been located, the researcher needs to verify that they have not been repealed or amended into other forms. One can do this by consulting the pocket part or the separate

---

5. The United States Code Service replaces the Federal Code Annotated. It comes in both an F.C.A. Edition and a Lawyers' Edition. The Lawyers' Edition contains a research aids section that includes references to Am. Jur., Am. Jur. Trials, Am. Jur. Proof of Facts, A.L.R., and law reviews.

paperbound supplemental volumes that accompany the codifications. Exhibit 8.19 indicates the type of entry found in such a supplement.[6]

One can also locate amendments by using Shepard's Citations. Shepard's puts out both statute and case editions that relate to both federal and state law. At the federal level, the statute and department reports edition of Shepard's United States Citations contains material on the United States Constitution and federal statutes as well as various decisions of federal regulatory agencies and specialized courts such as the court of customs and patent appeals. It reports legislative changes and cites court cases that have interpreted the statutes. The type of format used in these volumes is shown in Exhibit 8.20. An explanation of the abbreviations used in Shepard's is found in the beginning of each volume.

State legislation and constitutions are included in the Shepard's volumes published separately for each state. These state volumes also include local charters and ordinances. Citations to state cases which interpret federal statutes are also included in the United States Citations.

Court interpretations of statutes can also be found through the statutes construed tables in volumes of the National Reporter System[7] or the table of laws cited and construed in the Digest of the United States Supreme Court Reports.[8]

d. Locating the Legislative History

The annotated codes usually contain some basic information about the law's legislative history. A sample page from the U.S.C.A. is shown in Exhibit 8.21. Note that in addition to printing the text of section 1292 of Chapter 15 of the code, it also provides its public law numbers and dates of passage for both the original 1961 act and a 1966 amendment. It then briefly identifies the nature of that 1966 amendment and gives cross-references to the United States Code Congressional and Administrative News. This historical note is then followed by brief summaries of two federal court cases that interpreted this section. Exhibit 8.22 demonstrates a similar approach taken in the annotated code of one of the states. It is of special interest because it contains a quotation from the committee that drafted the legislation.

At the federal level the United States Code Congressional and Administrative News provides an excellent source for more complete infor-

---

6. Here, as in several other figures used later in the chapter, the substantive area of the law involved in the illustration is not related to the landlord/tenant problem described at the chapter's beginning. In this case it is done because there are no materials in U.S.C.A. relevant to the landlord problem. In other cases, it may be done to illustrate a feature of the research tool that could not be illustrated as easily with landlord/tenant materials.

7. See the discussion of the National Reporter System at page 63 and Table 3.2.

8. See pages 335-337 for a further discussion of the use of digests.

mation on legislative history. In addition to the verbatim text of the act a committee report from either the House or the Senate is included. Several very useful tables provide dates for certain actions. These dates allow the researcher to trace floor debates and committee testimony through the Congressional Record and published hearings. The Commerce Clearing House Congressional Index provides yet another excellent method for cross-referencing bills and identifying key dates in the legislative process.

e. Administrative Actions

Once the researcher has analyzed a statute, an effort should be made to identify how it has been interpreted and applied by administrative agencies. The Code of Federal Regulations contains a table of all those sections of C.F.R. that have been promulgated under the authority of a particular statute. (One can also go from the C.F.R. citation back to the statutes by looking for the authority section found in the textual discussion of the regulation itself.) Other tables in C.F.R. allow the paralegal to relate statutes to presidential proclamations and executive orders.

The paralegal can trace back the historical development of administrative regulations using a table in C.F.R.'s list of sections affected. Research can begin with the subject index, in the same way the subject index of a statutory code would be used. Exhibit 8.23 presents a sample of the actual text of the Code of Federal Regulations. In order to be as up to date as possible, one should also check the latest issues of the Federal Register.

Unfortunately there is no clear pattern for the publication of agency rulings. The American Digest System covers court decisions on administrative law questions but not the agency decisions themselves. As is the case with state administrative regulation questions, the paralegal is advised to consult directly with the agency on the most convenient source for this type of information. Some loose-leaf services provide administrative regulations and rulings in such special interest areas as taxation and commerce. When available, they are a particularly useful source.

Exhibit 8.18 Sample U.S.C.A. Subject Index Page

Exhibit 8.19 Sample U.S.C.A. Pocket Part Supplement Page

21 § 823   FOOD AND DRUGS

(A) security of stocks of narcotic drugs for such treatment, and (B) the maintenance of records (in accordance with section 827 of this title) on such drugs; and

(3) if the Secretary determines that the applicant will comply with standards established by the Secretary (after consultation with the Attorney General) respecting the quantities of narcotic drugs which may be provided for unsupervised use by individuals in such treatment.

As amended Pub.L. 93–281, § 3, May 14, 1974, 88 Stat. 124; Pub.L. 95–633, Title I, § 109, Nov. 10, 1978, 92 Stat. 3773.

1978 Amendment. Subsec. (f). Pub.L. 95–633 added provision relating to the construction of the Convention on Psychotropic Substances.

1974 Amendment. Subsec. (g). Pub.L. 93–281 added subsec. (g).

Effective Date of 1978 Amendment. Amendment by Pub.L. 95–633 effective on the date the Convention on Psychotropic Substances enters into force in the United States, see section 112 of Pub.L. 95–633, set out as a note under section 801a of this title.

Legislative History. For legislative history and purpose of Pub.L. 93–281, see 1974 U.S.Code Cong. and Adm.News, p. 3029. See, also, Pub.L. 95–633, 1978 U.S. Code Cong. and Adm.News, p. 9496.

Code of Federal Regulations

Registration provisions, see 21 CFR 1301.01 et seq.

§ 824. Denial, revocation, or suspension of registration—Grounds

(a) A registration pursuant to section 823 of this title to manufacture, distribute, or dispense a controlled substance may be suspended or revoked by the Attorney General upon a finding that the registrant—

(1) has materially falsified any application filed pursuant to or required by this subchapter or subchapter II of this chapter;

(2) has been convicted of a felony under this subchapter or subchapter II of this chapter or any other law of the United States, or of any State, relating to any substance defined in this subchapter as a controlled substance; or

(3) has had his State license or registration suspended, revoked, or denied by competent State authority and is no longer authorized by State law to engage in the manufacturing, distribution, or dispensing of controlled substances.

A registration pursuant to section 823(g) of this title to dispense a narcotic drug for maintenance treatment or detoxification treatment may be suspended or revoked by the Attorney General upon a finding that the registrant has failed to comply with any standard referred to in section 823(g) of this title.

[See main volume for text of (b) and (c)]

Suspension of registration in cases of imminent danger

(d) The Attorney General may, in his discretion, suspend any registration simultaneously with the institution of proceedings under this section, in cases where he finds that there is an imminent danger to the public health or safety. A failure to comply with a standard referred to in section 823(g) of this title may be treated under this subsection as grounds for immediate suspension of a registration granted under such section. A suspension under this subsection shall continue in effect until the conclusion of such proceedings, including judicial review thereof, unless sooner withdrawn by the Attorney General or dissolved by a court of competent jurisdiction.

[See main volume for text of (e) and (f)]

As amended Pub.L. 93–281, § 4, May 14, 1974, 88 Stat. 125.

1974 Amendment. Subsec. (a). Pub.L. 93–281, § 4(a), provided for revocation or suspension of a registration pursuant to section 823(g) of this title for failure of a registrant to comply with standards referred to in such section 823(g).

Subsec. (d). Pub.L. 93–281, § 4(b), substituted in second sentence "A suspension under this subsection" for "Such suspension".

Legislative History. For legislative history and purpose of Pub.L. 93–281, see

22

Exhibit 8.20 Sample Shepard's United States Citations Page

§§ 702 to **705**
538F2d938

§§ 702 to **704**
519F2d682
551F2d1056
391FS12
396FS281
428FS1103
436FS854

§ 702
L88St1978
[§321
A90St2721
412US685
418US177
421US560
422US690
425US829
426US38
41LE681
44LE379
45LE483
48LE409
48LE460
51LE196
53LE522
94SC2947
95SC1852
95SC2599
96SC1924
96SC1962
97SC982
97SC2423
485F2d180
485F2d738
485F2d782
489F2d1212
490F2d719
490F2d886
490F2d1360
491F2d856
492F2d413
492F2d489
492F2d539
494F2d1324
495F2d274
497F2d430
498F2d386
498F2d1211
498F2d1303
498F2d1352
501F2d757
502F2d80
504F2d156
504F2d259
504F2d268
505F2d499
506F2d234
507F2d768
507F2d1107
507F2d1169
508F2d493
508F2d1040
509F2d243
509F2d247
509F2d1080
510F2d351
510F2d703
511F2d1271
512F2d573
512F2d775
512F2d889
512F2d1190
512F2d1354
513F2d1143
514F2d812
514F2d1165
515F2d368
515F2d398
515F2d468
516F2d1009
519F2d936
519F2d1161
520F2d54
520F2d457
521F2d1151
523F2d730
523F2d1346
524F2d9
524F2d242
524F2d407
525F2d145
525F2d269
526F2d231
527F2d721
527F2d786
527F2d1302
528F2d46
528F2d1140
528F2d1296
529F2d191
529F2d537
530F2d1087
530F2d1223
531F2d687
533F2d416
533F2d478
534F2d1138
535F2d216
537F2d29
537F2d289
537F2d578
537F2d946
538F2d1149
539F2d837
539F2d1015
539F2d1075
540F2d866
541F2d151
541F2d250
542F2d1264
543F2d529
547F2d47
547F2d184
547F2d311
648F2d102
549F2d1115
551F2d16
551F2d322
551F2d448
552F2d824
554F2d462
554F2d885
554F2d1212
555F2d970
556F2d358
556F2d451
556F2d903
557F2d286
558F2d1153
559F2d730
559F2d1016
561F2d402
561F2d632
363FS1053
364FS227
364FS424
364FS750
364FS1013
365FS478
366FS58
366FS261
366FS607
366FS1233
367FS1377
368FS721
369FS741
369FS1040
370FS325
370FS946
370FS1195
371FS734
371FS1141
373FS589
373FS591
374FS162
374FS450
374FS759
374FS874
374FS1286
375FS199
375FS437
376FS249
376FS328
376FS615
376FS889
377FS257
377FS531
377FS832
377FS1226
377FS1285
378FS212
378FS243
378FS286
378FS1288
379FS1170
380FS206
380FS365
380FS744
381FS295
381FS305
381FS1147
382FS323
382FS363
383FS1249
384FS188
384FS219
384FS626
384FS1295
384FS1355
385FS435
386FS573
386FS668
386FS945
386FS1347
387FS292
387FS673
387FS948
387FS977
387FS1086
388FS381
388FS494
389FS87
389FS287
389FS690
389FS1152
390FS357
390FS928
391FS710
392FS74
392FS133
392FS1247
393FS367
393FS601
393FS1116
393FS1369
394FS653
394FS767
394FS900
394FS980
394FS1224
395FS516
395FS923
396FS637
396FS1108
397FS41
397FS1018
397FS1050
398FS3
398FS187
399FS58
399FS340
400FS706
400FS851
400FS1050
401FS524
401FS943
401FS1078
401FS1383
402FS582
402FS988
402FS1067
402FS1204
403FS633
403FS1005
403FS1206
404FS221
404FS365
404FS894
404FS927
405FS512
405FS1227
406FS1025
406FS1258
407FS794
408FS142
408FS280
408FS893
408FS1325
408FS1358
409FS28
409FS1192
410FS68
411FS5
411FS1364
412FS171
413FS186
413FS827
414FS186
414FS217
414FS299
414FS985
414FS1106
415FS653
415FS1237
416FS288
416FS811
416FS865
417FS136
417FS299
418FS183
418FS890
418FS1243
419FS223
419FS683
419FS810
419FS859
420FS1221
420FS1302
421FS80
421FS385
421FS848
422FS355
423FS407
423FS1065
424FS108
425FS72
425FS332
426FS990
426FS1025
427FS226
427FS1370
428FS118
428FS389
428FS711
428FS938
429FS143
429FS415
429FS691
429FS1140
430FS426
430FS701
430FS856
431FS106
431FS469
431FS487
431FS722
432FS564
433FS838
433FS1326
61FRD175
64FRD565
73FRD620
74FRD387
10ARF802s
17ARF33s
17ARF116n
23ARF303n
30ARF358n
30ARF718n
31ARF797n
32ARF380n
33ARF63n
33ARF91n

§ 703 et seq.
555F2d1114

§ 703
A90St2721
51LE196
97SC982
485F2d738
485F2d766
485F2d782
490F2d886
490F2d1369
491F2d1143
493F2d141
501F2d1369
507F2d768
507F2d1110
510F2d798
515F2d659
519F2d936
527F2d593
528F2d1051
531F2d1398
538F2d513
539F2d788
543F2d707
544F2d333
547F2d243
548F2d1142
551F2d1280
554F2d1212
559F2d730
364FS1013
366FS1241
367FS893
370FS325
372FS539
374FS759
374FS1286
375FS305
375FS437
376FS249
376FS1100
377FS244
377FS776
384FS219
385FS1217
386FS668
387FS299
390FS216
390FS928
392FS74
393FS1116
397FS1126
401FS1001
403FS633
405FS512
406FS1258
407FS1201
409FS28
420FS27
423FS1065
426FS1001
426FS1027
429FS683
429FS837
18ARF620n

§§ 704 to **706**
518F2d306
528F2d125

§ 704
421US560
422US690
426US52
44LE379
45LE466
45LE483
48LE468
51LE196
53LE522
95SC1852
95SC2599
95SC2615
96SC1931
97SC982
97SC2423
485F2d697
485F2d738
487F2d1302
488F2d909
489F2d618
492F2d998
495F2d274
495F2d789
498F2d455
498F2d1303
501F2d757
502F2d84
502F2d443
504F2d452
505F2d1161
508F2d493
509F2d243
512F2d580
512F2d1190
514F2d817
514F2d1168
515F2d368
515F2d664
516F2d1009
519F2d84
519F2d376
519F2d692
520F2d54
520F2d1042
521F2d130
522F2d304
522F2d1170
523F2d730
524F2d631
526F2d1369
528F2d46
530F2d625
530F2d1223
532F2d282
534F2d1138
534F2d1141
538F2d967
538F2d1021
538F2d1149
542F2d1366
543F2d707
545F2d1242
547F2d47
547F2d241
548F2d1079
550F2d543
363FS670
364FS1013
365FS478
365FS902
369FS413
370FS362
371FS734
371FS1374
374FS162
374FS450
374FS759
375FS203
375FS437
376FS249
376FS1102
377FS832
380FS369
380FS744
382FS323
385FS435
386FS685
388FS651
388FS830
389FS87
389FS292
389FS690
389FS1152
390FS357
390FS532
391FS847
392FS1246
393FS1116
393FS1335
394FS980
396FS1108
397FS360
398FS3
400FS892
400FS1050
401FS1072
402FS1067
403FS1207
404FS365
404FS1091
405FS507
405FS1227
407FS1201
408FS281
410FS68
411FS1222
412FS283
414FS186
414FS935
414FS976
415FS212
415FS800
415FS1086
415FS1237
416FS865
416FS1144
417FS366
417FS876
417FS1070
417FS1365
418FS92
419FS223
421FS80
421FS848
423FS1085
425FS332
427FS327
428FS118
428FS711
429FS691

Continued

See note on first page of this division. See 1968 and 1968-1974 Bound Volumes, Statute Edition for earlier citations

Exhibit 8.21 Sample U.S.C.A. Page

Cross References

Federal Trade Commission Act, definition of antitrust acts, see section 44 of this title.

§ 1292.   Area telecasting restriction limitation

Section 1291 of this title shall not apply to any joint agreement described in the first sentence in such section which prohibits any person to whom such rights are sold or transferred from televising any games within any area, except within the home territory of a member club of the league on a day when such club is playing a game at home.

Pub.L. 87–331, § 2, Sept. 30, 1961, 75 Stat. 732; Pub.L. 89–800, § 6(b)(2), Nov. 8, 1966, 80 Stat. 1515.

Historical Note

1966 Amendment. Pub.L. 89–800 substituted "described in the first sentence of such section" for "described in such section".

Legislative History. For legislative history and purpose of Pub.L. 87–331, see 1961 U.S.Code Cong. and Adm.News, p. 3042. See, also, Pub.L. 89–800, 1966 U.S. Code Cong. and Adm.News, p. 4327.

Notes of Decisions

Championship games 1
Injunctions 2

-----

1. Championship games

This chapter, which authorized a league composed of professional sports teams to sell to broadcasting companies package deals for exclusive televising of games of its various teams and to restrict area televising of a game within home territory of a team on a day when such club was playing at home, applied not only to regularly scheduled season at-home games but also to championship games, and plaintiffs were not entitled to an injunction restraining professional football league from blacking out the televising of championship football game within home territory of one of teams participating in championship game. Blaich v. National Football League, D.C. N.Y.1962, 212 F.Supp. 319.

2. Injunctions

Plaintiffs, who resided in area which was blacked out for televising of championship football game of professional football league, did not suffer irreparable injury which would entitle them to an injunction which in effect would require televising of the game. Blaich v. National Football League, D.C.N.Y.1962, 212 F. Supp. 319.

§ 1293.   Intercollegiate and interscholastic football contest limitations

The first sentence of section 1291 of this title shall not apply to any joint agreement described in such section which permits the telecasting of all or a substantial part of any professional football game on any Friday after six o'clock postmeridian or on any Saturday during the period beginning on the second Friday in September and ending on the second Saturday in December in any year from any telecasting station located within seventy-five miles of the game site of any intercollegiate or interscholastic football contest scheduled to be played on such a date if—

Exhibit 8.22 Sample Smith-Hurd Annotated Page — An Annotated Version of the Illinois Revised Statutes

§ 7–8. Force Likely to Cause Death or Great Bodily Harm

(a) Force which is likely to cause death or great bodily harm, within the meaning of Sections 7–5 and 7–6 includes:

(1) The firing of a firearm in the direction of the person to be arrested, even though no intent exists to kill or inflict great bodily harm; and

(2) The firing of a firearm at a vehicle in which the person to be arrested is riding.

Laws 1961, p. 1983, § 7–8, eff. Jan. 1, 1962.

Committee Comments—1961

Revised by Charles H. Bowman

This section is intended to make clear the status of a rather common police practice of firing in the direction of a person fleeing from arrest, either on foot or in a vehicle, although the circumstances are not such that the officer is authorized to use deadly force to prevent defeat of the arrest. While firing into the air, without endangering the offender's safety, undoubtedly is permissible, firing so close to him that his safety is endangered is the use of deadly force, which can be justified only in the circumstances in which the officer is authorized to use deadly force, as stated in sections 7–5 and 7–6. (See Perkins, "The Law of Arrest," 25 Iowa L.Rev. 201 at 270, 288, 289 (1940); Note, "Use of Deadly Force in Preventing Escape of Fleeing Minor Felon," 34 N.Car.L.Rev. 122 (1955).)

Several Illinois cases illustrate this point; and the Supreme Court has approved a trial court's refusal to admit evidence that the defendant's firing at a car in which an offender was riding, was in accordance with a common police practice: "Such a custom has never been approved and cannot be too severely condemned." (People v. Klein, 305 Ill. 141 at 149, 137 N.E. 145 (1922). See also People v. Cash, 326 Ill. 104, 157 N.E. 76 (1927); and Miller v. People, 216 Ill. 309, 74 N.E. 743 (1905)—a "horse and buggy" case.)

Cross References

Method of arrest, use of force, see section 107–5 of this chapter.

Law Review Commentaries

Force in making arrest. Marvin E. Aspen. 1966 Law Forum 247.

Library References

Arrest ⟲68.
Assault and Battery ⟲64.
Homicide ⟲105.
C.J.S. Arrest § 11 et seq.
C.J.S. Assault and Battery § 97.
C.J.S. Homicide §§ 102, 137.

I.L.P. Arrest § 5.
I.L.P. Assault and Battery § 44.
I.L.P. Homicide § 51.
Illinois Pattern Jury Instructions —
IPI Criminal, 24.15.

Notes of Decisions

See, also, Notes of Decisions relative to Deadly Force following section 7–1 of this chapter.

1. In general

In prosecution for murder, defended on ground that defendant police officer was

426

in type of the same style and not less than half of the point size of that used for the words "peanut butter." This statement shall immediately precede or follow the words "peanut butter," without intervening written, printed, or graphic matter.

(e) The label of peanut butter shall name, by their common names, the optional ingredients used, as provided in paragraph (c) of this section. If hydrogenated vegetable oil is used, the label statement of optional ingredients shall include the words "Hydrogenated ———— oil" or "Hardened ———— oil", the blank being filled in either with the names of the vegetable sources of the oil or, alternatively, with the word "vegetable"; for example, "Hydrogenated peanut oil" or "Hardened peanut and cottonseed oils" or "Hydrogenated vegetable oil".

PART 165—NONALCOHOLIC BEVERAGES

Subpart A—[Reserved]

Subpart B—Requirements for Specific Standardized Nonalcoholic Beverages

§ 165.175   Soda water.

(a) *Description.* Soda water is the class of beverages made by absorbing carbon dioxide in potable water. The amount of carbon dioxide used is not less than that which will be absorbed by the beverage at a pressure of one atmosphere and at a temperature of 60° F. It either contains no alcohol or only such alcohol, not in excess of 0.5 percent by weight of the finished beverage, as is contributed by the flavoring ingredient used. Soda water designated by any name which includes the word "cola" or "pepper" shall contain caffeine from kola nut extract and/or other natural caffeine-containing extracts. Caffeine may also be added to any soda water. The total caffeine content in the finished food shall not exceed 0.02 percent by weight. Soda water may contain any safe and suitable optional ingredient, except that vitamins, minerals, and proteins added for nutritional purposes and artificial

sweeteners are not suitable for food encompassed by this standard.

(b) *Nomenclature.* (1) The name of the beverage for which a definition and standard of identity is established by this section, which is neither flavored nor sweetened, is soda water, club soda, or plain soda.

(2) The name of each beverage containing flavoring and sweetening ingredients shall appear as "———— soda" or "———— water" or "———— carbonated beverage", the blank to contain the word or words that designate the characterizing flavor of the soda water as prescribed in § 101.22 of this chapter.

(3) If the soda water is one generally designated by a particular common name; for example, ginger ale, root beer, or sparkling water, that name may be used in lieu of the name prescribed in paragraph (b) (1) and (2) of this section. For the purposes of this section, a proprietary name that is commonly used by the public as the designation of a particular kind of soda water may be used in lieu of the name prescribed in paragraph (b) (1) and (2) of this section.

(c) *Label declaration.* Each of the optional ingredients used shall be declared on the label as required by the applicable sections of Part 101 of this chapter.

(Secs. 401, 701, 52 Stat. 1046 as amended, 1055-1056 as amended by 70 Stat. 919 and 72 Stat. 948 (21 U.S.C. 341, 371))

[42 FR 14477, Mar. 15, 1977]

PART 166—MARGARINE

Subpart A—General Provisions

Sec.
166.40   Labeling of margarine.

Subpart B—Requirements for Specific Standardized Margarine

166.110   Margarine.

Subpart A—General Provisions

§ 166.40   Labeling of margarine.

The Federal Food, Drug, and Cosmetic Act was amended by Pub. L. 459, 81st Congress (64 Stat. 20) on colored

3. Finding Court Decisions

Whether dealing with the common law or with statutes, the researcher must identify all relevant court decisions. Under normal circumstances a review of encyclopedias, treatises, annotations, and the like produces several significant case citations. Similarly, the annotated statutes also contain citations to court decisions. The researcher should locate these decisions in the reporters discussed in Chapter 3 and study them carefully. However, one cannot rely on these citations alone. The researcher must use the methods described here to ensure an exhaustive search. (Sample pages from these research volumes, labeled Exhibit 8.24 through 8.28, appear at the end of this section at pages 339-344.)

a. Digests

Court decisions frequently consider several points of law. (Chapter 3 indicated how one must determine the different issues raised in the case.) When court decisions are published in reporters, the editors of the reporter usually provide their own analysis that identifies and summarizes these points of law. Exhibit 8.24 presents the type of introductory material contained in one of the West reporters. The syllabus (a narrative summary or abstract of the case) is followed by several key number designations and short summaries of the court's holdings on those particular points of law.

The West Publishing Company has divided the entire body of American law into a uniform classification system based on what they call key numbers. These key numbers consist of a topic title (for example, Appeal and Error) followed by the key number symbol (⚬) and the proper numerical designation. Cases printed in West reporters always contain this listing of key numbers involved. The numbers are aids for understanding the nature of the case and link the case with the West digest system.

A digest is an index tool with short summaries of the points of law decided in different cases. These digest statements are arranged so that all cases on the same point of law are grouped together. If a given case involves five different points of law, it will be listed in five different parts of the digest. In West digests cases are arranged on the basis of the key numbers. In other digests they are arranged under similar classification schemes. Exhibit 8.25 demonstrates how entry 10 from the preliminary analysis of the *Jack Spring* case (see Exhibit 8.24) appears verbatim in the digest listing for Illinois cases under Landlord and Tenant ⚬125(1).

The American Digest System covers both federal and state court decisions from 1658 to the present time. Cases decided between 1658 and 1896 are covered in the fifty-volume Century Digest. The cases decided between 1897 and 1976 are divided into ten-year periods and published as part of the Decennial series. The First Decennial covers

1897 to 1906, the Second Decennial covers 1907 to 1916, and so forth up to the Eighth Decennial for 1967 to 1976. When complete the Ninth Decennial eventually will cover 1977 to 1986, and the Tenth Decennial 1987 to 1996. Cases that are decided before a Decennial is published appear in volumes of the General Digest. As each Decennial is issued, it replaces the issues of the General Digest that covered those same years.

The Century Digest covers 238 years and groups in one volume all reported cases that relate to the same key number in the multivolume series. Likewise, with each of the first eight Decennials, all reported cases from the ten years that relate to the same key number and that are covered by that Decennial are grouped together in one volume. However, beginning with the Ninth Decennial, West has divided the series into a Part I covering the first five years together and a Part II for the second five years. In the General Digest, however, each volume is a self-contained unit covering all the key numbers for a period of less than one year. In working with the Decennials all the cases on a given key number can be found in one volume, but when working with the General Digest the researcher must check each individual volume in the series.

In addition to the inclusive digest system described above, West publishes a series of specialized digests that correspond to the regional reporters, state reporters, and federal reporters. Thus a paralegal looking only for California cases can go to either the California Digest or the Pacific Digest to avoid searching the entire American Digest System. The U.S. Supreme Court Digest covers only Supreme Court decisions, and the Modern Federal Practice Digest covers all federal cases reported since 1939. Lawyers' Co-operative Publishing Company also publishes a digest covering the United States Supreme Court — the U.S. Supreme Court Reports Digest.

If the researcher has already found one or more cases relevant to the problem, those cases can be looked up in a West reporter to find the appropriate key number and a summary of what that key number involves (as in Exhibit 8.24). One also can find the proper key number by using the table of cases that identifies the key numbers in each indexed case.

Alternatively, one can use the descriptive-word index to locate appropriate key numbers. Exhibit 8.26 shows a page from one of these descriptive-word indexes. In using it, the researcher should look up key words associated with the case. These words can relate to the parties in the suit, the place where the action occurred, the type of action it is (such as negligence, defamation, and so on), the relief being sought (such as damages, injunction, and so on), and the defense being relied on (such as assumption of risk or act of God).

The appropriate key number also can be found through the topic-analysis sections at the beginning of each major topic. One can simply turn to the beginning of the landlord and tenant section of the digest and

scan the list until the appropriate subtopic is found. Exhibit 8.27 presents an example of part of the subject analysis section for landlord and tenant.

b. Shepard's Citations

Shepard's can be used to determine whether a statutory provision is still in force and whether a case has been overruled by subsequent judicial action. Little is more embarrassing to a lawyer than to rely on a case for authority only to find that it has been reversed by a higher court. Shepard's also provides the researcher with citations to other cases in which the case being cited was formally mentioned by another court. These types of references can be useful means of locating additional cases from the same or other jurisdictions.

Shepard's United States Citations covers decisions from United States Reports, United States Supreme Court Reports, Lawyers' Edition, and the Supreme Court Reporter. Each set has its own section with cases geared to its citation. Federal Reporter Citations covers the courts of appeals and district courts as well as such specialized material as decisions of the commissioner of patents. In addition to these sets, Shepard's also publishes sets that correspond to each of the regional reporters and to the state reporters. They carry names such as Shepard's Atlantic Reporter Citations and Shepard's Michigan Citations.

Citations for Jack Spring, Inc. v. Little, 280 N.E.2d 208 (Ill. 1972) (see Exhibit 8.24) are presented in Exhibit 8.28. To locate the proper citation, the researcher must find the page or pages that cover the relevant volume. The volume numbers located in the top corners of the pages help speed this process. Once the correct page is found, one must read up and down the columns until the volume number is found within the column (in this case near the bottom of the first column). The boldface numbers that follow reflect the page numbers on which the case begins. Thus the researcher looks up and down the columns until the number 208 is found near the top of the fifth column. The actual citation information is located under number 208 in that column.

The citation information will ordinarily begin by listing any parallel cites for the same case in parentheses. Thus it can be seen that *Jack Spring* was also published at 50 Ill. 2d 351. In this case the decision was not reviewed by a higher court. If it had been, there would also be a citation for that same case at the higher court level. (The designation in the citations for 280 N.E.2d 205 reports that the U.S. Supreme Court denied *certiorari* at 409 U.S. 948.) After reviewing any actions on the same case by other courts, Shepard's lists other cases in which the judges formally cited *Jack Spring* in their opinions. These citations are grouped together by the states in which they were decided. The small letters *f, j, d,* and *e* stand for followed, dissenting opinion, distinguished, and explained. Other commonly used abbreviations are explained in the front

of each Shepard's volume. The small superior numbers appearing after the reporter abbreviation (for example, the 10 in 282NE¹⁰151) corresponds to the point of law that was listed as number 10 in the syllabus analysis in *Jack Spring* (in this case, the issue of implied warranty of habitability). In addition to citing cases, Shepard's may also include citations to law review articles and American Law Reports, Annotated. See, for example, the A.L.R.3d citation under 280 N.E.2d 300 in Exhibit 8.28.

Exhibit 8.24 Sample North Eastern Reporter, Second Series Syllabus and Key Number Analysis

him. None of these matters are privileged because the privilege applies only to communications made by Miss Walker to defendant. It cannot be determined from the record and briefs whether there were in fact privileged matters communicated to the defendant, and if so, in whose presence, and for what purpose, nor can it be determined whether Miss Walker testified to any such communications. Whether a series of questions might have covered matters, some privileged and some not, is pure conjecture. Under the circumstances, in refusing to answer the question in the form in which it was propounded, we are unable to say defendant was in contempt.

For the reasons herein set forth the petition for a writ of *habeas corpus* is denied. The judgment of the circuit court of Cook County adjudging the defendant guilty of contempt for refusal to answer questions 1 and 3 is affirmed, and as to question 2 is reversed and remanded for further proceedings.

Affirmed in part, and reversed in part and remanded, and writ quashed.

50 Ill.2d 351

JACK SPRING, INC., Appellee,

v.

Emma LITTLE, Appellant.

SUTTON & PETERSON, INC., Appellee,

v.

Zeleta PRICE, Appellant.

Nos. 41730, 41739.

Supreme Court of Illinois.

Jan. 28, 1972.

Separate actions by landlords against tenants seeking to recover possession of rented premises for nonpayment of rent. The Circuit Court, Cook County, Robert C. Buckley, J., entered judgments for plaintiffs, and defendants' appeals were consolidated. The Supreme Court, Goldenhersh, J., held that insofar as section of Forcible Entry and Detainer Act required furnishing of bond as prerequisite to prosecuting appeal, it was violative of Fourteenth Amendment of the United States Constitution and of articles of State Constitution containing due process and equal protection clauses and governing appellate court jurisdiction. The Court further held that included in oral and written contracts governing tenancies of tenants in multiple unit dwellings occupied by them was implied warranty of habitability which would be fulfilled by substantial compliance with pertinent provisions of city building code, and that affirmative defenses alleging breach of implied warranty of habitability were germane to question whether defendants were indebted to plaintiffs for rent and thus should not have been struck.

Reversed and remanded.

Kluczynski, J., dissented and filed opinion in which Underwood, C. J., joined.

Ryan, J., dissented and filed opinion.

1. **Appeal and Error** ⬯373(1)

Having created right of appeal, statutes adopted and rules promulgated in implementation of such right may not serve to discriminate against appellants by reason of inability to furnish an appeal bond.

2. **Constitutional Law** ⬯249, 316
Forcible Entry and Detainer ⬯2

Insofar as section of Forcible Entry and Detainer Act required furnishing of bond as prerequisite to prosecuting appeal, it was violative of Fourteenth Amendment of the United States Constitution and of articles of State Constitution containing due process and equal protection clauses and governing appellate court jurisdiction. S.H.A.Const.1970, art. 1, § 2; art. 6, § 6; U.S.C.A.Const. Amend. 14; S.H.A. ch. 57, § 19.

Exhibit 8.24 *(continued)*

3. Forcible Entry and Detainer ⬅43(4)

In view of invalidation of Forcible Entry and Detainer Act section requiring furnishing of bond as prerequisite to prosecuting appeal, Supreme Court rule purporting to embody such section for time and method of appeal in forcible entry and detainer cases is no longer operative. S.H.A. ch. 57, § 19; Supreme Court Rules, rule 303(b), S.H.A. ch. 110A, § 303(b).

4. Forcible Entry and Detainer ⬅45

Stay of judgment pending appeal is governed by Supreme Court rule, and its provisions supersede those contained in Forcible Entry and Detainer Act section governing conditions of defendant's appeal bond. S.H.A. ch. 57, § 20 ; Supreme Court Rules, rule 305, S.H.A. ch. 110A, § 305.

5. Forcible Entry and Detainer ⬅45

Right to an appeal is matter separate and apart from right to supersedeas during pendency of the appeal, and in being required to furnish a bond as condition to staying judgment, appellant in an action in forcible entry and detainer is in no different situation than an appellant who seeks a stay of judgment in any other type of appeal. S.H.A. ch. 57, § 20; Supreme Court Rules, rule 305, S.H.A. ch. 110A, § 305.

6. Landlord and Tenant ⬅285(7)

Supersedeas conditioned upon payment by appealing tenants of rental installments as they became due was within contemplation of Supreme Court rule governing stay of judgments pending appeal. S.H.A. ch. 57, § 20; Supreme Court Rules, rule 305, S.H.A. ch. 110A, § 305.

7. Landlord and Tenant ⬅196

Liability for rent continues so long as tenant is in possession.

8. Landlord and Tenant ⬅48(1), 223(2)

Tenant may bring action against landlord for breach of a covenant or may recoup for damages in an action brought to recover rent.

280 N.E.2d—14

9. Landlord and Tenant ⬅284(2)

Tenants' affirmative defenses, in landlords' actions to recover possession of rented premises because of nonpayment of rent, alleging breach of express covenants to repair were germane to issue whether tenants were indebted to landlords for rent and thus should not have been struck.

10. Landlord and Tenant ⬅125(1)

Included in oral and written contracts governing tenancies of tenants in multiple unit dwellings occupied by them was implied warranty of habitability which would be fulfilled by substantial compliance with pertinent provisions of city building code.

11. Landlord and Tenant ⬅284(2)

Tenants' affirmative defenses, in separate actions by landlords to recover possession of rented premises for nonpayment of rent, alleging breach of implied warranty of habitability were germane to question whether tenants were indebted to landlords for rent and thus should not have been struck.

12. Landlord and Tenant ⬅284(2)

Tenant's affirmative defense, in action by landlord to recover possession of rented premises for nonpayment of rent, insofar as it presented issue of whether lease provision governing examination and acceptance by tenant of condition of premises precluded implied warranty of habitability and proof of breach of alleged express agreements to repair premises was germane to issue whether rent was due and owing and thus should not have been struck.

———◆———

Kleiman, Cornfield & Feldman, Chicago (Gilbert A. Cornfield and Barb J. Hillman, Chicago, of counsel), for appellants.

Irving Goodman and Nathan Einhorn, Chicago, for appellee Sutton and Peterson, Inc.

Stephen J. Epstein, Chicago, for appellee Jack Spring, Inc.

Exhibit 8.25 Sample Eighth Decennial Digest Page

ing condition at inception of lease, tenant was not relieved of generally imposed burden of bearing risk of any defect in conditions within area under his exclusive possession and control by exception rendering general rule inapplicable to defects which are result of faulty design or disrepair and which existed at beginning of tenancy, were not discoverable by tenant on reasonable inspection, and were known, either actually or constructively, to the landlord.—Id.

D.C.App. 1968. In absence of statute or express covenant in lease, landlord does not impliedly covenant or warrant that leased premises are in habitable condition.—Saunders v. First Nat. Realty Corp., 245 A.2d 836.

Hawaii 1969. Implied warranty of habitability exists in unfurnished as well as furnished dwellings.—Lund v. MacArthur, 462 P.2d 482, 51 Haw. 473.

Seriousness of defects in rented dwelling and length of time during which they persist are both relevant factors to be considered in determining materiality of breach of implied warranty of habitability.—Id.

Hawaii 1969. Application of implied warranty of habitability and fitness in leases of dwellings recognizes changes in history of leasing transactions and takes into account contemporary housing realities.—Lemle v. Breeden, 462 P.2d 470, 51 Haw. 426, 478, 40 A.L.R.3d 637.

A "lease" is in essence as well as a transfer of estate in land and is, more importantly, a contractual relationship from which warranty of habitability and fitness is a just and necessary implication.—Id.

In lease of dwelling house, there is an implied warranty of habitability and fitness for use intended.—Id.

Where plaintiff leased dwelling from defendant for immediate occupation and after taking possession was forced with his family to sleep in living room rather than proper quarters because of presence of rats in dwelling, there was breach of implied warranty of habitability and fitness for use in lease.—Id.

Doctrine of constructive eviction, as an admitted judicial fiction designed to operate as though there were a substantial breach of material covenant in bilateral contract, no longer serves its purpose when more flexible concept of implied warranty of habitability is available.—Id.

Under doctrine of implied warranty of habitability and fitness in every lease of dwelling, there are a number of remedies available for breach in contrast to doctrine of constructive eviction which requires that tenant abandon premises within reasonable time after giving notice that premises are uninhabitable or unfit for his purposes.—Id.

Under doctrine that a lease is essentially a contractual relationship with an implied warranty of habitability and fitness, available remedies for breach of warranty include damages, reformation and rescission.—Id.

Under doctrine of implied warranty of habitability and fitness in leases of dwellings, seriousness of claimed defect and length of time it persists are relevant factors in considering materiality of the alleged breach.—Id.

In determining whether there exists a breach of implied warranty of habitability and fitness in lease of dwelling, each case must turn on its own facts.—Id.

Ill. 1972. Included in oral and written contracts governing tenancies of tenants in multiple unit dwellings occupied by them was implied warranty of habitability which would be fulfilled by substantial compliance with pertinent provisions of city building code.—Jack

Spring, Inc. v. Little, 280 N.E.2d 208, 50 Ill.2d 351.

Ill.App. 1970. Assertion of tenants, sued by landlord for past due rent under written lease, that premises violated city of Chicago housing code presented a valid affirmative defense to action since violations of the code would invalidate lease, and tenants were entitled to present evidence that the premises were in substantial violation of code.—Longenecker v. Hardin, 264 N.E.2d 878, 130 Ill. App.2d 468.

Ind.App. 1976. Apartment residential lease is essentially contractual in nature and carries with it mutually dependent covenants including implied warranty of habitability and full range of remedies for breach of contract. (Per Buchanan, P. J., with one Judge specially concurring.)—Old Town Development Co. v. Langford, 349 N.E.2d 744.

Prior notice, either actual or constructive, and opportunity to repair are prerequisites to landlord's breach of implied warranty of habitability. (Per Buchanan, P. J., with one Judge specially concurring.)—Id.

Iowa 1972. Question of whether landlord's breach of implied warranty of habitability is of such substantial nature as to render premises unsafe or unsanitary and, thus, unfit for habitation will usually be fact question to be determined by circumstances of each case. I.C.A. §§ 413.1 et seq., 413.9, 413.106.—Mease v. Fox, 200 N.W.2d 791.

When tenant vacates premises because of landlord's breach of implied warranty of habitability, condition of premises loses relevance in determining tenant's damage; measure of tenant's damages after vacation of premises is difference between fair rental value of premises if they had been as warranted and the promised rent computed for balance of term. I.C.A. §§ 413.1 et seq., 413.9, 413.106, 554.-2715.—Id.

Tenant is under obligation to give landlord notice of deficiency or defect not known to landlord.—Id.

Iowa 1967. Generally, subject to express contractual provisions and some fairly well defined exceptions, a tenant takes the demised premises as he finds them; the rule of caveat emptor ordinarily applies as between lessor and lessee.—Fetters v. City of Des Moines, 149 N.W.2d 815.

Kan. 1974. Provisions of city housing code relating to minimum housing standards were, by implication, read into and became part of rental agreement.—Steele v. Latimer, 521 P.2d 304.

Provisions of municipal housing code prescribing minimum housing standards are deemed by implication to become a part of a lease of urban residential property, giving rise to an implied warranty that the premises are habitable and safe for human occupancy in compliance with the pertinent code provisions and will remain so for the duration of the tenancy.—Id.

Where a breach of an implied warranty of habitability has occurred, traditional remedies for breach of contract are available to the tenant, including the recovery of damages.—Id.

La.App. 1976. Lease provision, whereby landlord agreed to make all repairs on premises due to leaks from plumbing or utility lines within or without leased premises, constituted covenant to repair; however, additional lease provision, whereby landlord agreed to at all times keep basement of leased premises waterproof, was not mere covenant to repair, but was instead obligation to keep basement

waterproof.—McCrory Corp. v. Latter, 331 So.2d 577.

La.App. 1973. Tenant's complaint, which alleged that landlord leased property to her which was unfit for purpose for which it was let, stated a cause of action for damages for emotional discomfort, loss of convenience, humiliation, etc.—Evans v. Does, 283 So.2d 804.

La.App. 1970. Sublessee accepting demised premises in condition in which they are is still entitled to warranty protection afforded him by statute. LSA–C.C. arts. 2692, 2695.—Reed v. Classified Parking System, 232 So.2d 103, writ denied 234 So.2d 194, 255 La. 1097, writ refused 234 So.2d 194, 255 La. 1098.

La.App. 1968. A tenant seeking damages under statute providing that lessor guarantees the lessee against all the vices and defects of the thing, which may prevent its being used, even in case it should appear he knew nothing of the existence of such vices and defects, must establish his claim by fair preponderance of the evidence. LSA–C.C. art. 2695.—Long v. McMichael, 219 So.2d 810.

Negligence on part of owner or lessor is not an indispensable prerequisite to recovery by tenant for a loss under statute providing that lessor guarantees the lessee against all the vices and defects of the thing, which may prevent its being used, even in case it should appear he knew nothing of the existence of such vices and defects, at time the lease was made. LSA–C.C. art. 2695.—Id.

Knowledge on part of lessor of existence of defect is not required for tenant's recovery for loss under statute providing that lessor guarantees lessee against all the vices and defects of thing, which may prevent its being used even in case it should appear he knew nothing of the existence of such vices and defects, at time lease was made, for it suffices if the defect exists and it is established as the cause of the loss, damage or injury. LSA–C.C. art. 2695.—Id.

The preponderance of evidence exacted of the tenant or lessee under statute providing lessor guarantees lessee against all vices and defects of the thing, which may prevent its being used even in case it should appear the knew nothing of the existence of such vices and defects at time lease was made, does not mean proof beyond a reasonable doubt but contemplates evidence sufficient to establish tenant's claim to reasonable certainty and beyond the realm of mere possibility, speculation or conjecture. LSA–C.C. art. 2695.—Id.

Md.App. 1974. Implied warranty of merchantability is inapplicable to leases, as title does not pass in such transactions. Code 1957, art. 95³, §§ 2–105(1), 2–314.—Sheeskin v. Giant Food, Inc., 318 A.2d 874, 20 Md.App. 611.

Mass. 1973. In rental of any premises for dwelling purposes, under a written or oral lease, for a specified time or at will, there is an implied warranty of habitability, that is, that the premises are fit for human occupation; such warranty means that at inception of rental there are no latent or patent defects in facilities vital to use of premises for residential purposes and that such facilities will remain during the entire term in a condition which makes the property livable; such warranty, insofar as it is based on the State Sanitary Code and local health regulations, cannot be waived by any provision of the lease or rental agreement. M.G.L.A. c. 111 § 5.—Boston Housing Authority v. Hemingway, 293 N.E.2d 831.

Since tenant's covenant to pay rent is dependent on the landlord's implied warranty of

For references to other topics, see Descriptive-Word Index

Exhibit 8.26 Sample General Digest Descriptive-Word Index Page

LANDLORD & TENANT

LANDLORD & TENANT

VI. TENANCIES AT WILL AND AT SUFFERANCE.—Cont'd

119. Creation of tenancy at sufferance.
    (1). In general.
    (2). Tenant holding over after expiration of term.

120. Termination.
    (1). In general.
    (2). Necessity and sufficiency of notice to quit in general.
    (3). Waiver by tenant of right to notice.
    (4). Surrender and abandonment.

VII. PREMISES, AND ENJOYMENT AND USE THEREOF.

(A) DESCRIPTION, EXTENT, AND CONDITION.

⭢121. Sufficiency of description.
122. Extent of premises.
123. Property included in general.
124. Appurtenances.
    (1). In general.
    (2). Means of entrance or exit.
    (3). Power and light.
125. Tenantable condition of premises.
    (1). In general.
    (2). Suitability of premises for the purpose for which they were leased.

(B) POSSESSION, ENJOYMENT, AND USE.

⭢126. Duty of tenant to take possession.
127. Right of entry and possession of tenant.
128. Delivery of possession.
    (1). In general.
    (2). Waiver of failure to deliver possession.
129. Actions for failure to deliver possession.
    (1). In general.
    (2). Pleading.
    (3). Evidence.
    (4). Damages.
    (5). Questions for jury.
130. Covenants for quiet enjoyment.
    (1). Implied covenant.
    (2). What constitutes breach of covenant.
    (3). Actions for breach of covenant in general.
    (4). Damages.
131. Disturbance of possession of tenant.
132. —— By landlord.
    (1). In general.
    (2). Actions in general.
    (3). Damages.
133. —— By third persons.
    (1). In general.
    (2). Liability of landlord.
    (3). Actions.
134. Mode and purposes of use of premises in general.
    (1). Mode of use in general.
    (2). Restrictions in lease as to mode of use.
    (3). Purpose for which premises may be used.
    (4). Rights, duties, and liabilities of sub-lessees or assignees.
    (5). Interference with use by landlord or others.
    (6). Actions by landlord.
135. Cultivation of land under farm leases.
136. —— Rights and duties of tenant in general.
137. —— Timber.
138. —— Manure.
139. —— Crops.

    (1). Right or title to crops in general.
    (2). Right to way-going crop.
    (3). Tenant of land subject to judgment lien.
    (4). Injury to crop.
    (5). Action to recover value.
140. Injuries to premises.
141. —— By landlord.
142. —— By third persons.
    (1). In general.
    (2). Injuries to grass and crops.
    (3). Obstruction of light.
    (4). Obstruction of way.
    (5). Liability of landlord.
    (6). Actions in general.
    (7). Damages.
    (8). Right of tenant to abate nuisance.
144. Duty of tenant to surrender on termination of lease.

(C) INCUMBRANCES, TAXES, AND ASSESSMENTS.

⭢145. Incumbrances on leasehold in general.
146. Covenants against incumbrances.
147. Duty to remove or discharge incumbrances.
148. Covenants and agreements as to taxes and assessments.
    (1). In general.
    (2). What taxes or assessments are within the covenant.
    (3). Liability of assignees.
    (4). Actions for breach of covenant.
149. Liabilities for taxes and assessments.

(D) REPAIRS, INSURANCE, AND IMPROVEMENTS.

⭢150. Right and duty to make repairs in general.
    (1). In general.
    (2). Duty to rebuild on destruction of property.
    (3). Landlord's right of entry to make repairs.
    (4). Rights of subtenants.
    (5). Right of tenant to repair at landlord's cost.
151. Statutory provisions.
152. Covenants and agreements as to repairs and alterations.
    (1). In general.
    (2). Consideration for agreement.
    (3). Construction and operation of covenants in general.
    (4). Nature of repairs included in covenant or agreement.
    (5). Duty to rebuild on destruction of property.
    (6). Right of landlord to notice that repairs are necessary.
    (7). Agreement by landlord to pay for repairs.
    (8). Rights and liabilities of assignees and subtenants.

Exhibit 8.28 Sample Shepard's Northeastern Reporter Citations Page

– 878 –
(29❾S99)·
(58❾p194)
s269NE⁵53
15A2.1428s

– 884 –
(29❾S135)
(58❾p323)

– 886 –
(29❾S123)
(58❾p317)

– 889 –
(29❾A189)
(58❾p328)

– 892 –
(29❾A187)
(58❾p327)

– 894 –
(31M34)
(58❾p188)
288NE²3307

– 901 –
287NE⁴461
287NE⁵461

– 902 –
279NE343
279NE¹909
297NE²519

– 906 –
279NE343
f279NE⁵905
280NE¹679
280NE²679
280NE³679
280NE⁴679

– 915 –
281NE¹573
282NE⁴380
282NE⁴480
296NE¹202
Ill
287NE¹29
DC
302A2d754
Me
294A2d689

Vol. 280

– 1 –
(31IA1063)
290NE⁴418

– 3 –
(41IA497)

– 4 –
(31IA1059)

– 7 –
(31IA1055)

– 10 –
(31IA1050)
281NE⁴426
304NE¹16

– 13 –
(31IA1078)

– 14 –
(41IA23)

– 16 –
(41IA90)

– 17 –
(31IA1047)
285NE²252
292NE42
e301NE²302

– 19 –
(41IA391)
305NE¹638

– 23 –
(31IA1065)
299NE²42

– 29 –
Case 1
(41IA85)

– 29 –
Case 2
(41IA6)
cc280NE42
279NE¹732

– 42 –
(41IA4)
cc280NE29

– 43 –
(31IA1085)

– 46 –
(31IA1074)

– 49 –
(41IA65)
284NE474
302NE³432

– 52 –
(41IA369)

– 57 –
j280NE¹316
281NE¹802
282NE¹862
j282NE¹869
d285NE¹683
294NE¹821
301NE¹238

– 59 –
284NE⁴91

– 64 –
297NE⁵440

– 69 –
s285NE830

– 81 –
283NE⁴387
283NE³388
283NE⁵389
e285NE⁴827
291NE¹902
291NE²902
291NE⁵902

– 88 –
s198NE233
282NE⁶553
282NE⁷553
283NE⁸585
285NE841
286NE⁷851
287NE⁶366
287NE⁶574
287NE⁵900
289NE⁵300
289NE¹²333
291NE⁵578
298NE²332
301NE⁶206

– 95 –
Case 1
(29NY930)
(329S2d321)
s313S2d189
337S2d338

– 95 –
Case 2
(29NY931)
(329S2d322)
s321S2d200
344S2d58

– 96 –
(29NY933)
(329S2d323)

– 97 –
Case 1
(29NY934)
(329S2d323)

– 97 –
Case 2
(29NY935)
(329S2d324)
s291S2d829
286NE¹732
304NE¹366
335S2d¹296
349S2d¹669

– 98 –
(29NY937)
(329S2d325)
s323S2d1
286NE¹716
j286NE²735
294NE¹206
331S2d337
335S2d¹273
j335S2d²300
340S2d240
341S2d¹619

– 99 –
(29NY938)
(329S2d326)
s326S2d191

– 100 –
(29NY939)
(329S2d327)
s324S2d426

– 101 –
(29M190)

– 106 –
(29M190)
(57❾p361)

– 110 –
(29M190)
(58❾p129)

– 129 –
cc141NE269
cc233NE730
cc293NE260
cc393US5
cc21LE5
cc89SC35
297NE501
NH
293A2d767

– 144 –
285NE⁹784

– 149 –
NY
349S2d562

– 152 –
23A2.932s

– 155 –
284NE⁶926
291NE424
296NE¹475
296NE²475
296NE³475

– 166 –
296NE⁴495
f296NE⁶501
298NE²156
298NE⁷159

– 171 –
cc225NE921

– 174 –
289NE886
294NE382

– 183 –
287NE⁷463
303NE⁶738

– 187 –
289NE886
294NE382

– 199 –
282NE86

– 201 –
(51Il2d14)
s397US95
s25LE78
s90SC818
cc263NE833

– 203 –
(51Il2d35)
f284NE²431
302NE³217
302NE⁴217

– 205 –
(51Il2d46)
US cert den
in409US948

– 208 –
(50Il2d351)
282NE¹⁰151
290NE⁵590
f298NE⁸175
f298NE⁹175
j298NE¹¹176
j298NE¹²176
d301NE¹²11
j301NE⁸12
j301NE¹²13
e302NE¹⁰209
e302NE¹⁰211
467F2d1273
468F2d²798
Mass
293NE⁶841
293NE¹²841
j293NE¹⁰850
j293NE¹²850
Calif
517P2d1169
Iowa
200NW796
Mo
495SW71
NJ
291A2d582
308A2d22
Wash
515P2d163

– 224 –
(50Il2d379)
j278NE249
e303NE6

– 230 –
(50Il2d390)
279NE¹⁵531
289NE23
295NE¹⁵552
298NE³220
301NE⁶274

– 234 –
(31IA1034)
r294NE267
s298NE7
L305NE¹584

– 236 –
(41IA34)

– 239 –
(41IA45)
s305NE308
288NE¹535
292NE¹754
293NE¹629
293NE²734
293NE²766
d297NE²362

– 240 –
(41IA55)

– 242 –
(41IA48)
303NE¹504

– 244 –
(41IA38)

– 249 –
(41IA118)

– 253 –
(41IA51)
d294NE²63
301NE²341

– 256 –
(41IA113)
289NE⁶117

– 260 –
(41IA46)

– 262 –
Case 1
(41IA112)

– 262 –
Case 2
(41IA59)

– 264 –
(41IA123)
f288NE³632

– 266 –
(41IA881)

– 268 –
(41IA60)

– 269 –
(41IA494)
298NE²415
d299NE¹103

– 276 –
(41IA90)

– 281 –
(41IA89)

– 283 –
(41IA86)

– 286 –
(31IA1090)
296NE¹91
304NE518
d304NE¹519

– 288 –
(41IA26)

– 291 –
(41IA29)

– 294 –
(41IA106)
s295NE266

– 297 –
(41IA111)

– 298 –
(41IA109)

– 300 –
s270NE764
288NE²²184
j288NE³567
NC
189SE756
RI
298A2d531
25A2.383s

– 307 –
f283NE⁵804
285NE⁷683
286NE⁵704
286NE⁶704
286NE⁷704
286NE⁵843
286NE⁶843
286NE⁷843
f288NE⁷553
289NE³320
292NE595
292NE⁷615
296NE¹664
298NE⁴464
298NE³508
300NE¹136
301NE¹180
301NE²180
301NE⁵190
301NE¹521

– 313 –
j281NE¹803
j282NE837
282NE³860
285NE³683
286NE³669
300NE372
301NE³238
301NE³670
303NE297
303NE¹683

– 327 –
299NE219
304NE⁶829

– 336 –
289NE¹⁰177
289NE303

– 359 –
(29NY457)
(329S2d569)
s282NE625
s321S2d132
s331S2d672

– 362 –
(29NY939)
(329S2d574)
s312S2d35

– 364 –
Case 1
(29NY942)
(329S2d576)

– 364 –
Case 2
(29NY944)
(329S2d577)
s320S2d943

– 365 –
Case 1
(29NY946)
(329S2d578)
s318S2d670

– 365 –
Case 2
(29NY947)
s304S2d147
s316S2d393

– 366 –
Case 1
(29NY949)
(329S2d579)
s316S2d238
338S2d970
347S2d418
348S2d621

– 366 –
Case 2
(29NY950)
(329S2d580)
s323S2d527
s331S2d780
329S2d82
338S2d401
344S2d994

– 367 –
Case 1
(29NY952)
(329S2d581)
s314S2d137

– 367 –
Case 2
(29NY952)
(329S2d582)
s315S2d768
s336S2d781

– 368 –
Case 1
(29NY953)
(329S2d583)
s305S2d434

– 368 –
Case 2
(29NY954)
(329S2d584)
s322S2d849
337S2d843

– 371 –
(29❾S139)
(58❾p342)
s285NE763

– 374 –
(29❾S144)
(58❾p344)

°Illinois Appellate Court Cases when Certiorari or Appeal Denied or Dismissed   1583

C.   COMPUTER-ASSISTED RESEARCH

Two great advantages of computers are their ability to store large amounts of information and their ability to rapidly sort through and retrieve information.[9] These characteristics make computers valuable tools for legal researchers. When connected to an on-line legal data base, a small microcomputer or a video display terminal can provide instant access to legal information that goes far beyond what the normal law firm can maintain in its library.

1. Contents of the Data Bases

a. LEXIS

LEXIS is one of the two major commercial legal data bases. It is a product of the Mead Corporation and has been marketed to lawyers since the early 1970s. Its data base includes the full text of court cases, statutes, administrative regulations, and various specialized legal publications.

At the federal level it contains decisions of the United States Supreme Court, the Court of Appeals, the District Courts, and the Court of Claims. It includes all cases from the 1960s until present, but its coverage of the older cases varies. It also contains the U.S. Code, the Code of Federal Regulations, and the Federal Register from 1980 on. The federal materials also include a variety of administrative law materials such as FCC Reports, NLRB Reports, and IRS regulations; patent, trademark, and copyright cases; and trade regulation decisions.

At the state level, LEXIS contains the full text of cases from the appellate courts of all fifty states. All new cases are included, but the coverage of older cases varies a great deal from one state to the next. Generally, they go back to at least the 1960s. With the exception of Kansas, Missouri, and New York, the system does not contain state statutes. At the international level it includes cases and statutes from the United Kingdom and France.

The inclusion of Shepard's Citations and AUTO-CITE are other features of LEXIS that make it particularly useful to a researcher. Shepard's provides the same information that can be obtained from its printed volumes. In other words, one can find parallel citations, the subsequent history of the same case, and a listing of manner in which it was cited by other courts in later cases. AUTO-CITE, on the other hand, is used primarily for checking the accuracy of case citations and locating cases that directly affect the cases's validity as a precedent.

---

9. See the discussion on computers in the law office at pages 248-252.

b. WESTLAW

WESTLAW is the other commercial legal data base. Developed and
marketed by the West Publishing Company in the late 1970s WESTLAW
covers the same types of materials contained in the LEXIS data base.
Perhaps the most significant difference is that in addition to the full text
of appellate court cases, WESTLAW also contains the headnotes and key
numbers that appear in West's National Reporter System. This feature
can simplify the search process for some users and makes it easier to
coordinate the results with materials gathered from West's regular publications.

At the federal level WESTLAW contains decisions of the United
States Supreme Court, the Court of Appeals, the District Courts, and
the Court of Claims. U.S. Supreme Court cases go back to 1925, and
most of the other decisions go back to the 1940s or 1950s. It also contains
the U.S. Code, the Code of Federal Regulations, and the Federal Register from 1980 on. Specialized sublibraries include cases and administrative reports in the fields of tax, securities, antitrust, communications,
labor, energy, admiralty, patents, copyrights, bankruptcy, and military
justice.

At the state level, WESTLAW also contains the full text of cases
from the appellate courts of all fifty states. Their coverage generally
begins in the 1950s or 1960s. It does not include state statutes. At the
international level WESTLAW provides access to Common Market, English, and Scottish legal materials.

To handle citations, WESTLAW also includes Shepard's citations
as well as a service called INSTA-CITE. INSTA-CITE is similar to
AUTO-CITE in that it provides a case history and parallel citations as
well as verifying citations.

c. Other Data Bases

In addition to LEXIS and WESTLAW several other computerized
legal data bases are maintained in the United States. They are operated
as specialized services for governmental agencies and are not available to
the general legal profession on a commercial basis.

JURIS is operated by the United States Department of Justice and
is available to U.S. attorneys' offices and to programs affiliated with the
Legal Services Corporation. Its data base focuses on the U.S. Code and
federal case law. FLITE provides access to the same materials as JURIS
plus Court Martial Reports and other military justice materials, labor
law, and tax materials. It is operated by the Department of Defense for
the benefit of the military services, although other federal agencies can
also arrange to have access to it. Finally, RIRA is an Internal Revenue
Service data base that is maintained exclusively for internal use.

2. Operation of the Systems

With the exception of FLITE, all of the above-mentioned data bases are interactive systems, which means that the researcher can sit down at a remote terminal or a microcomputer connected through a telephone modem and communicate directly with the computer that contains the data base. In the FLITE system, by contrast, the researcher sends in a request to the agency and then must wait to receive a printed copy of the results of the search at a later date. With the interactive system, the researcher receives almost instantaneous feedback and can alter his or her requests on the basis of that feedback. Once the researcher learns the basic skills involved, the interactive system is a much more efficient way of proceeding.

The most difficult part of computerized research is learning how to define and limit the nature of the search. Traditional legal research is not begun by going to the law library and then simply paging through the books in the order that they appear on the shelf. The researcher usually comes to the library with a list of relevant cases and/or key terms that can be looked up in the appropriate legal indexes. When the researcher approaches the computer terminal, he or she also must have carefully thought out the nature of the issues and have identified key words or cases that will become the basis of the computer search. The computer is very quick, but computerized research is still expensive. Because the cost of computer research is based on the amount of computer time used, there is a clear incentive to be as prepared as possible before the meter starts running.

The first step in communicating with the computer that holds the legal data base usually involves dialing into the computer and supplying the appropriate passwords and account numbers. Throughout the entire research process, the user-friendly computer provides a series of prompts on the screen to guide the researcher through the various stages of the search. The most critical step in the process is entering key words and phrases that tell the computer what it is to search for. The researcher also must instruct the computer as to which types of libraries (that is, which sets of court decisions or statutes) are to be searched.

Both LEXIS and WESTLAW have internal indexes that record where specific words appear in all of the documents contained in its computerized files.[10] The computer then searches this index to identify the documents that contain the key terms that were identified by the researcher. Once the search is complete, the computer will display abbreviated information about the results of the search (such as the num-

---

10. Common linking words such as *an, and, but, or,* and *the* are not included, but otherwise this index, or *concordance* as it is sometimes called, is complete.

ber or the titles of cases found). The researcher must then instruct the
computer as to whether the documents found should be displayed
(either on the screen or through an attached printer) or whether a new,
more limited search should be conducted. The researcher can also preview materials on the screen and then print specific pages of the documents.

Although the specific commands used in formulating the searches
for these key words differ from one system to the other, the same concept is used in both LEXIS and WESTLAW. If the computer is instructed to search for a single key word, the result frequently is an
overwhelming number of cases, and many of them are not relevant to
the legal issue at hand. For example, a list of all cases that include a term
as general as *negligence* or *contract* is not helpful. However, in addition to
being able to substitute more narrow terms, the systems also allow one to
search for combinations of terms appearing together within a specifically
defined space (such as *assumption* and *risk* appearing together, or *store,
wet, floor,* and *negligent* all appearing within the same paragraph). In
order to avoid missing reference to a word that is used in its plural form
or as an adjective, it is possible to have the computer identify the location
of any word with a specifically identified root (such as *contract, contracts,*
and *contractual*).

In addition to searching for legal terms, searches can be conducted
on the basis of the court, the title, the citation, the judge, and the attorneys involved in the case. With WESTLAW, one can search for West key
numbers. In using Shepard's, AUTO-CITE, and INSTA-CITE the researcher simply enters the citation and then instructs the computer as to
which of several types of information it wishes to receive. In using
Shepard's, for example, the retrieval can be limited to cases that reverse
the original case or to cases that deal with a specific issue within the case.

As previously mentioned, both LEXIS and WESTLAW are user
friendly and come with instruction books containing the specific codes
and formats used for communicating with the system. Both companies
also offer special training programs for new users. Software packages for
personal computers have been developed that assist the operator in setting up search parameters before going on line. The real skill is not in
learning how to talk with the computer; it is in figuring out what you
want to tell the computer to do. The paralegal defines what is being
searched for and then interprets it after it has been located and retrieved.

D. SUMMARY

Legal research is one of the most important tasks that a paralegal
can perform because the findings form the basis for advising the client

and preparing the case. Research involves skills developed through experience, imagination, ingenuity, patience, and perseverance.

Although there is no single correct way to approach a legal research problem, all the alternatives begin with a careful examination of the nature of the legal issues involved. If the paralegal's substantive background is not developed well enough to recognize the key words and basic principles involved, general background reading in a legal encyclopedia should be undertaken. The subject analysis section provides a quick overview of the subtopics to help locate relevant sections. The encyclopedia provides knowledge on key terms that should be indexed in other sources and cross-references to specific cases, law review articles, and annotations. The treatises, restatements, legal periodicals, and annotations also offer the general background usually needed before focusing on a specific problem.

The search for relevant legislation usually begins with the subject index of the codes. Popular-name tables also can be very helpful. Once a specific statute has been located, the researcher must check to be sure that it has not been repealed or amended. This check is usually made through the use of pocket supplements in the code volumes and Shepard's Citations.

Valuable information about an act's legislative history can be located in the annotated codes. The United States Code Congressional and Administrative News is an even better source for such information because it allows the researcher to easily locate appropriate floor debates and committee testimony.

After the relevant statutes have been analyzed, the researcher should check on any administrative regulations or decisions interpreting those statutes. At the federal level, consult the Code of Federal Regulations and the Federal Register. There is a wide variation in reporting this information at the state level.

Relevant case citations can be located in several ways. Usually the background reading in encyclopedias, law reviews, and so forth yields references to promising cases. By reading and then Shepardizing those cases the paralegal will find additional cases. However, the researcher cannot rely exclusively on this cross-reference technique. The digests should be used to systematically identify relevant cases. Either the descriptive word index or the subject analysis sections of a digest will indicate the appropriate key numbers for the principles of law involved. These key numbers lead to the sections of the digest with short summaries of what each case decided about that particular principle of law.

Computerized legal data bases provide quick access to court cases and other legal materials. LEXIS and WESTLAW — the two major commercial systems available today — are interactive systems that allow the researcher to instruct the computer as to the nature of the search desired; receive feedback from the computer regarding the number of

documents found; alter the nature of the search; preview the documents on the screen; and receive printed copies of designated documents. Both systems also contain options that allow for fast, accurate checking on citations and for determining the manner in which the original case has been treated in other, more recent, cases.

There is no single correct way to approach a legal research problem. Indeed, the availability of alternatives is one of the major features of legal research. The same topic usually can be approached under several different index headings. If the explanation offered in C.J.S. seems confusing, turn to Am. Jur. 2d for a slightly different approach to the same topic. If digests are not available, use citators. Each researcher should develop a personal style.

After locating and analyzing the relevant statutes, administrative regulations, and cases, the researcher may wish to return again to (or perhaps read for the first time) the general reference works (encyclopedias, annotations, law review articles, and so forth) to better understand the effect of those statutes and cases. When the proper resource materials are available, legal research can be both challenging and rewarding.

KEY TERMS

American Jurisprudence 2d	legal encyclopedia
American Law Reports	LEXIS
AUTO-CITE	pocket part
Corpus Juris Secundum	popular-name table
digest	restatements
index method	Shepard's Citations
Index to Legal Periodicals	subject analysis method
INSTA-CITE	treatise
key number system	WESTLAW
law review	

REVIEW QUESTIONS

1. What methods are used to keep legal reference books up to date?
2. What are the differences between Am. Jur. 2d and C.J.S.?
3. What is the difference between an encyclopedia, a treatise, and an annotation?
4. What does each of the following digests cover: Century Digest, Decennial Digest, General Digest, and a state digest?
5. What are the differences between LEXIS and WESTLAW?

DISCUSSION QUESTIONS

1. What are the advantages and disadvantages of the West key number system?

2. What are the advantages and disadvantages of using computerized data bases for legal research?

3. Why is it better to use a variety of approaches to legal research rather than rely on a single method?

PROJECTS

1. Under what circumstances can a used car dealer be held liable for injury caused by a defective vehicle he sold? Find the answer in both Am. Jur. 2d and C.J.S. What is the answer? Now compare the features of each and indicate which encyclopedia you prefer. Why?

2. Use the U.S. Code and Administraive News to find answers to the following questions about the legislative history of the Speedy Trial Act of 1974.

   a. What was the act's official public law number?
   b. When was it passed in each chamber?
   c. What was the purpose for the act?
   d. What is the relationship of this act to the sixth amendment?

   Use a legislative history table to find the

   e. the number assigned to the bill when it was first introduced in the Senate;
   f. the house committee to which the bill was assigned;
   g. the proper citation in Statutes at Large.

3. Use Shepard's to find a U.S. Supreme Court case interpreting Title 8, section 1423, of the U.S. Code. What is the citation for that case? Use Shepard's to find out what happened to 306 F. Supp. 1255 in both the Court of Appeals and the Supreme Court. What are the citations for these cases, and what was the outcome of each case?

4. Use the descriptive-word index of the West digest system to find the key number relating to the immunity of school officials from liability for damages under the federal Civil Rights Act. What is the key number? Cite a 1975 Supreme Court case dealing with this issue.

5. Use the Index to Legal Periodicals to find a citation for a 1975 article dealing with defenses in drunk driving cases. What is the citation for this article?

Chapter 9
Legal Writing

GOOD LEGAL WRITING IS ONE of the most important skills that a paralegal can possess. The results of the factual investigations and legal research performed by a paralegal usually are reported in written form. In addition, paralegals are frequently expected to prepare drafts of letters, contracts, wills, and various court documents. Because writing is such an important part of the job, it is essential that paralegals develop and refine their writing skills. This chapter covers the various types of legal writing in which paralegals are likely to be involved. Different formats and approaches are used for specialized documents, but certain fundamental principles apply to all types of legal writing.

Above all else, good legal writing must communicate substantive information as clearly and efficiently as possible. Contrary to what you may have been led to think, verbosity and complex Latin phrases are not a sign of good legal writing. Sentences should be tightly constructed to eliminate excess verbiage, and common, easily understood words should be substituted for archaic legalese. Long compound sentences and strings of alliterative adjectives and adverbs may sound pleasing to the ear and draw forth memories of an English literature class, but they are not part of good legal writing. The writer should use familiar, commonly understood words in simple, straightforward sentences.

A. INTERNAL RESEARCH MEMORANDA

1. Purpose

An internal legal memorandum carefully analyzes a specific legal problem. This involves identifying and summarizing the relevant cases, statutes, and other sources of law; analyzing the probable application of these legal principles to the facts presented in a given situation; and evaluating the strengths and weaknesses of alternative courses of action.

The memorandum is used not only to inform the person to whom it is addressed (usually an attorney or a paralegal supervisor) as to what the writer has discovered but also to create a concise permanent record

that can be used at a later date by the party it was addressed to, by the writer, or by someone else working on the same or a similar project at some future date.[1] Because it is for internal use only and may later be used by someone representing a client on the other side of a similar issue, the memo must be objective rather than an advocacy document.

2. Format and Content

The degree of detail and the precise headings of a legal memorandum may vary from one law office to another (or even from one lawyer within an office to another), but it usually consists of a heading, a statement of the facts, a listing of the issues raised, a discussion of the law, and the conclusions. An example of how a research memorandum may be organized follows at the end of this section.

The heading section should identify the client's name and office file number, the person who prepared it, and the date on which the memo was prepared. It also may include the name of the person to whom it is addressed and identify the subject area involved.

The facts should be summarized in the style used for preparing a case brief[2] except that the writer should discuss the case in greater detail. The writer also should differentiate between facts that have been independently confirmed and those that are based solely on the client's statements. Adjectives must be chosen as precisely as possible. Rather than just saying that a car was new or a day was cold, the writer should give the car's model year or the day's actual temperature.

The issue identification process is also similar to that used in case briefs. This issue identification should take place before the research begins. In writing the memorandum, the analysis section is organized around these issues. A concise statement of the issues helps the reader focus attention on the case's most relevant points.

The discussion section forms the real body of the memo. It identifies and analyzes the constitutional provisions, the statutes, the regulations, and the court cases that apply to each issue. The analysis proceeds on an issue-by-issue basis, with careful attention given to the applicability of each of the laws and cases being cited. Statutes and regulations should be directly quoted rather than paraphrased. Wherever possible, reference to the legislative intent should be included with definitions of key statutory terms. When discussing court cases, the writer should highlight both the similarities and the differences between the facts of the case being cited and the client's situation. Finally, the writer must be sure to report the extent to which any statutes or cases

---

1. Such memoranda are usually placed in a permanent file so that at some future date when attorneys and paralegals research similar cases they can take advantage of the work that has already been done and avoid needless duplication of their efforts.
2. See the discussion at pages 97-99, 103.

have been modified or limited by intervening court cases. All references should include their proper legal citations.[3]

The final section of the memo should provide a brief and concise summary that points out the strengths and weaknesses of the client's position. It also may include the writer's recommendations for further action, including additional factual investigation and further legal research on specific points.

Format for a Research Memorandum

Heading: Use a traditional To:, From:, Re: format to identify the client's name and office file number, the person who prepared the memo, the date on which the memo was prepared, and the subject area involved.

Facts: State the relevant facts of the legal problem being researched beginning with a short summary of the general nature of the case and continuing with a review of the key events in chronological order. Important facts should be precisely stated, but unnecessary detail should be avoided.

Issue: State the legal issue that is being researched.

Conclusion: Give a brief answer to the issue that was raised. If more than one issue is being researched within one memorandum, separate issue and conclusion sections should be written for both.

Discussion: Analyze relevant constitutional provisions, statutes, administrative regulations, and court cases. Quote from the key provisions of statutory materials. With cases state the holdings of relevant cases and discuss the similarities and differences between the facts of the case being cited and the facts involved in the problem being researched. All references to legal authorities should include proper citations. In assessing the strengths and the weaknesses of the client's case be as objective as possible. Specify which courses of action appear most promising, and when relevant also identify facts that need to be clarified or additional legal materials that need to be examined.

Summary: Brief review of the most significant conclusions and suggestions for appropriate actions.

---

3. See the discussion at pages 60-68, 305-306.

3. Application of the Format

Some of the research techniques discussed in Chapter 8 were illustrated with a hypothetical landlord/tenant problem. Some sample sections from a legal memorandum regarding that same research are presented at the end of this section. The memo begins with a simple statement of the facts as they have been reported to the paralegal. Although the facts may be incomplete, they provide a basis for research on the status of the law. Some of the client's assertions will have to be confirmed by independent evidence, and legal research may reveal areas in which additional facts will be needed before the client's position can be completely evaluated.

There is no magic formula for determining the issues in a case; it takes experience and some knowledge of the law. The paralegal usually consults with the attorney regarding the issues before beginning the research but also may see new issues as he or she gets further into the research.

In the discussion section, the writer should repeat the issue being discussed and then review both statutory and case materials relevant to that issue.

The researcher often finds citations to relevant cases while doing the general background reading in encyclopedias, annotations, and other general reference works. In this case the researcher could have come across the citation for *Jack Spring* in the pocket supplement for C.J.S. (Exhibit 8.7) or the pocket supplement for Illinois Law and Practice (Exhibit 8.13). If the researcher had not taken note of the citation in the general readings, the citation would have been found in the Eighth Decennial Digest (Exhibit 8.25).

After reading the case, the researcher summarizes the holding relevant to the issue (not the holdings that relate to such subjects as the bond requirement under the Forcible Entry and Detainer Act). Note that in comparing the facts of the cited case with the facts of the situation being researched, one often finds that more knowledge is needed about the client's situation. These gaps in the facts should be carefully noted in the memorandum.

Although other cases are related to Issue 1 and would be discussed in the same manner that the *Jack Spring* case was, this sample legal memorandum then skips ahead to show part of the treatment given to Issue 2.

The *Jack Spring* case is discussed again because it also is related to the resolution of Issue 2. Note that the holding and relevant facts differ from the holding and facts discussed in relationship to the first issue. Fredman v. Clore shows how courts can use what may seem to be a very insignificant difference in the facts as basis for reaching an opposite

conclusion. It also shows how the basis for a holding can shift from one level of appellate court to another.

Sample Research Memorandum

To: William Smith, Staff Attorney
From: Mary Jones, Paralegal
Re: Sarah Thompson, #85-342
         Landlord/tenant (implied warranty of habitability and eviction procedures)

Facts

Our client rents an apartment in Peoria, Illinois, on a month-to-month basis without a lease. She has received a written notice that she owes $250 in back rent and that if this back rent is not paid within five days, she will be evicted. The notice was left with her nine-year-old son while she was out. The client claims that the apartment has had a problem with cockroaches and is never heated above 60° Fahrenheit in the winter. The client has been unable to find alternative housing at a price she can afford.

Issues

Issue 1:   Does the poor condition of the apartment relieve the client of her obligation to pay the rent?
Conclusion: Yes, if it can be established that the conditions violated the implied warranty of habitability.

Issue 2:   Can the client use the implied warranty of habitability as a defense against the threatened eviction?
Conclusion: Yes, if the landlord's forcible entry and detainer action is based on section 8; no, if the action is based on section 6.

Issue 3:   Did delivery of the notice to her nine-year-old son constitute adequate notice of her delinquency?
Conclusion: No, the son was too young under the terms specified by the statute.

Issue 4:   What additional procedures must the landlord undertake in order to retake possession of the apartment?
Conclusion: The landlord will have to serve proper notice by delivering a written or printed copy of notice to the client personally, by sending it by certified mail with return receipt requested, or by leaving it with someone else residing in the

client's apartment who is over age ten. Then the landlord
will have to take the client to court under the Forcible
Entry and Detainer Act.

Discussion

Issue 1: Does the poor condition of the apartment relieve the client
of her obligation to pay the rent?

There are no applicable provisions of federal or state constitutions,
statutes, or regulations.

Chapter 10, section 8, of the local ordinances provide as part of the
building code that either all dwelling units must be equipped with a
heating system that is capable of maintaining a minimum temperature of
68° Fahrenheit in the unit or the landlord must provide through a central heating system enough heat to maintain a minimum temperature of
68° Fahrenheit in each unit.

The client's landlord seems to be in violation of this provision. The
ordinances do not say anything about cockroaches.

Jack Spring, Inc. v. Little, 50 Ill. 2d 351, 280 N.E.2d 208 (1972),
held that there was an implied warranty of habitability that must be filled
by substantially complying with the provisions of the building code. If
this warranty is not fulfilled, the tenant is relieved of the obligation to
pay rent.

This case is similar to our client's case in that it involves a tenant
who had not paid all of her rent, there was no written lease involved, the
rental unit was an apartment in a large complex, the apartment was not
in compliance with the local building code, and the tenant had sought
but been unable to obtain suitable alternative housing. On the other
hand, in this case, the city had already filed a formal complaint. . . .

Issue 2: Can the client use the implied warranty of habitability as a
defense against the threatened eviction?

There are no applicable provisions of the federal Constitution or
statutes.

Chapter 80, section 8, of the Illinois Revised Statutes authorizes a
landlord to take action for possession of the owned apartment under the
procedures of the Forcible Entry and Detainer Act if a tenant fails to pay
back rent after being notified in writing that the lease will be terminated
if the rent is not received in five days.

Chapter 80, section 6, authorizes a landlord to terminate a month-
to-month tenancy with thirty days' written notice and then maintain an
action for forcible detainer and ejectment after that thirty days.

These two provisions establish the basis for a landlord's taking

possession after having given the appropriate written notice. The notice received by the client would appear to meet the requirements of section 8.

Jack Spring, Inc. v. Little, 50 Ill. 2d 351, 280 N.E.2d 208 (1972), held that a tenant could assert an affirmative defense based on an implied warranty of habitability in an action by a landlord for possession of rented premises because of nonpayment of rent.

In this case, the landlord's complaint alleged that rent for the premises for a period of two months was due and owing and that plaintiff claimed possession of the property and for damages equal to the amount of rent owed. While the client's landlord has not yet filed a complaint, it is likely that this too would be for possession based on nonpayment of rent.

If this case is followed, it will allow the client to use the violation of the building code as a defense against the landlord's probable forcible entry and detainer action.

Fredman v. Clore, 13 Ill. App. 3d 903, 301 N.E.2d 7 (1973), held that tenants could not raise a defense based on implied warranty of habitability where the landlord brought action for possession only after having given notice under Chapter 80, section 6.

In this case, the landlord simply gave the tenant one month's notice that the month-to-month tenancy was to end and that he intended to take possession when it ended. Our client's landlord's notice indicates that he is acting under section 8 rather than section 6.

If the landlord sues for possession based on overdue rent, then this case would not apply. If he were to switch tactics and give the notice called for in section 6, this case would definitely work against our client's position.

Clore v. Fredman, 59 Ill. 2d 20, 319 N.E.2d 18 (1974), held that tenants could raise a defense of retaliatory eviction under a forcible entry and detainer action based on notice given under Chapter 80, section 6.

When the Illinois Supreme Court reviewed the appellate court decision discussed above, it did allow the tenants to introduce a defense based on retaliatory eviction. The tenants in this case had reported building code violations to the city inspections department and had begun making their rent payments to an escrow account rather than to the landlord. As far as we know, our client has not made any complaint to a public official about the potential violation existing in her apartment.

While this case allows the tenant to raise a retaliatory eviction defense that ultimately comes back to the implied warranty of habitability, it is doubtful that our client could use such a defense if she had not in fact made a formal complaint with the city. . . .

Summary

Our client appears to be in a pretty good position. Since the lack of heat is in violation of the building code, she can assert an implied warranty of habitability. This implied warranty can be used to defeat a forcible entry and detainer action by the landlord for possession based on overdue rent.

On the other hand, if the landlord were to simply give our client a month's notice that her tenancy was being terminated, he would be able to retake possession under a forcible entry and detainer action without her being able to assert the implied warranty defense. If our client reports the violation to city officials, however, she may then be able to assert a defense based on retaliatory action.

Since the notice was delivered to someone under age ten, it is not considered a valid notice. Thus our client could also defend against an eviction action on the basis that the notice was defective.

If the landlord is to retake possession of the apartment, he will have to serve proper notice by delivering a written or printed copy to the client personally, sending it by certified mail with return receipt requested, or leaving it with someone else residing in the client's apartment who is over age ten. Then he will have to take the client to court under the Forcible Entry and Detainer Act.

Additional Research

Several factual questions need to be answered before our client's case can be completely evaluated. The most important questions are:

1. Has there been any inspection of the apartment's heating system by the city inspections department?
2. What kind of evidence is there as to the actual temperature in the apartment?
3. Do other apartments in the building have the same problem?
4. Is the landlord aware of the problem, and has he made any attempt to resolve it?
5. How extensive have been our client's efforts to locate alternative housing?

Additional research should also be done with respect to the infestation by cockroaches. If it could be established that they permeated the entire building, only the landlord would be in a position to correct it. There are some cases that hold that such infestation is grounds for constructive eviction. This aspect thus deserves further research.

B. LETTERS

1. Purpose

Business letters are frequently used to exchange information, seek some action, or simply create a record. In some cases a paralegal may be asked to draft a letter to be sent under the attorney's signature, and in others the paralegal may be responsible for writing and signing the letter.

2. Format and Content

The letter may follow any one of several major business letter styles. Most offices have a stylebook that specifies the precise format that they wish to have followed. The letter should be cordial and polite but avoid flowery introductions and lengthy acknowledgments.

The keys to good letter writing are organization and clarity. Sentences should be kept short, and legal jargon should be avoided. Be sure to identify who you are and who you represent, the person or event you are writing about, what you want the addressee to do, and in many cases, what the consequences will be if the addressee does not do what you have requested.

C. INSTRUMENTS

1. Purpose

While many people seek out the assistance of a lawyer because they want to sue, others seek legal advise because either they wish to avoid having to go to court or because they want to ensure that they are in the best position to win any future court challenges. Documents such as contracts, wills, deeds, leases, and bank notes are classified as legal instruments. They are sometimes also referred to as forms of agreement because they represent attempts to preserve the terms of an agreement in written form.

The difficult part about drafting wills and contracts is that one must consider the effect of future events. The same is true of drafting corporate bylaws, statutes, and administrative regulations. The writer must consider what would happen "if" and then include instructions to handle such a situation. What is suppose to happen to the agreement if someone dies, gets a divorce, or becomes disabled?

2. Format and Content

Other than suggesting that one include a definitions section in which all key terms are explicitly defined in the agreement itself, it is

beyond the scope of this text to discuss desirable formats and the necessary content for a wide variety of legal agreements.

It should be pointed out, however, that when paralegals become involved in such drafting work it is usually a matter of adapting standardized forms and old agreements rather than starting from scratch. As was mentioned in Chapter 6, most law firms maintain files of model forms.

In addition, commercial publishers have developed a wide selection of specialized formbooks. These publications contain standardized clauses that have withstood judicial scrutiny, as well as discussions of when and how to use these clauses. Exhibit 9.1 illustrates the types of topics covered in the wills section of Nichols Cyclopedia of Legal Forms Annotated. Exhibit 9.2 illustrates the variety of forms and clauses presented, and Exhibit 9.3 provides a sample of one of the forms provided. Exhibit 9.4 illustrates part of a form for a short-term business or residential lease. By using these boilerplate phrases, one reduces the risks of being misunderstood or misinterpreted at a later date. Examples of some of the other major sets of agreement forms include Am. Jur. Legal Forms, West's Modern Legal Forms, Rabkin and Johnson's Current Legal Forms, Warren's Forms of Agreement, and Gordon's Modern Annotated Forms of Agreements. Legal software packages are also available to help draft a wide variety of corporate and contractual documents.

Exhibit 9.1 Sample Nichols Cyclopedia of Legal Forms Annotated Page

WILLS

I. SUGGESTIONS

A. IN GENERAL

B. BEFORE DRAFTING

C. DRAFTING WILL

1

Exhibit 9.2 Sample Nichols Cyclopedia of Legal Forms Annotated Page

WILLS

9.3501   — Instructions and information for executor.

IV. FORMS

A. SHORT FORMS OF WILLS

9.3511   A skeleton form.
9.3512   — Another form.
9.3513   Short will signed by mark.
9.3514   Will giving all property to one person.
9.3515   — To spouse.
9.3516   Will merely appointing executor.
9.3517   — Disposing of property as if owner died intestate.
9.3518   Will merely revoking prior will.
9.3519   Will of husband and father.
9.3520   — Authorizing carrying on of business by executor.
9.3521   Will of husband who has no children.
9.3522   Will of widower.
9.3523   Will of bachelor.
9.3524   Will of wife and mother.
9.3525   Will of wife who has no children.
9.3526   Will of unmarried woman.
9.3527   Will of married woman in exercise of power of appointment.
9.3528   Will of widow.

B. COMPLETE FORMS

9.3536   Simple will—Generally.
9.3537   — Husband's simple will.
9.3538   — Wife's simple will.
9.3539   Community property—Will disposing of entire community.
9.3540   — Another form.
9.3541   — Husband's share of community property with no marital deduction.
9.3542   Pour-over will with alternative provisions.
9.3543   — Husband's pour-over will.
9.3544   — — Another form.
9.3545   — Wife's pour-over will.
9.3546   — — Another form.
9.3547   Wife's will leaving all property to husband or trusts he established.
9.3548   Will with contingent trust for minor children.
9.3549   Will with residuary trust for descendants.
9.3550   Trust under will with alternative provisions.
9.3551   Will with marital and nonmarital trusts.
9.3552   — Another form.
9.3553   Qualified terminable interest will.
9.3554   Residuary estate to prior trust.

C. JOINT, MUTUAL, AND JOINT AND MUTUAL WILLS

1. General Forms

9.3566   Joint will.
9.3567   Separate mutual wills.
9.3568   Joint and mutual will.
9.3569   — Of husband and wife.

7

Exhibit 9.3 Sample Will from Nichols Cyclopedia of Legal Forms Annotated

WILLS 9.3511

(e) Tax claims and deficiencies.

    (1) History.
    (2) Amounts.
    (3) Tax years audited.
    (4) Latest return filed.
    (5) Questionable tax items.

(f) Powers of attorney outstanding.

    (1) Name.
    (2) Date.
    (3) Purpose.
    (4) Duration.
    (5) Terms.

IV. FORMS

A. SHORT FORMS OF WILLS

9.3511 A skeleton form.[1]

Last Will and Testament of ———

I, ———, of [residing in] the city [county] of ———, state of ———, do make, publish and declare[2] this my last will and testament, and I do hereby revoke all other and former wills and codicils to wills made by me.

First. I direct my executor hereinafter named to pay all my just debts and obligations, including the expenses of my last illness as soon after my decease as is practicable.[3]

Second. I make the following gifts of specific sums of money or specific personal property:

1. To ——— I give [bequeath] the sum of ——— dollars.
2. To ——— I give [bequeath] my ——— automobile.
[Etc.]

Third. I made the following gifts of specific real property:

1. To ——— I give [devise] my real estate at ——— in the county of ———, state of ———, more particularly described as follows: ——— [legal description].

Fourth. I hereby nominate and appoint ——— of ——— to be executor of this my last will and testament and direct that he [it] be [not] required to furnish a bond as required by law and directed by the court [or: to furnish a bond in the amount of ——— dollars]; and, in event ——— for any reason does not qualify for, or ceases to be, executor of this, my last

161

LEASES (REAL PROPERTY)[*]   **5.4315**

(c) Witnesses.
(d) Acknowledgments.

IV. FORMS

A. SHORT-TERM LEASES

1. In General

5.4315 Comprehensive lease adaptable for business or residential purposes.

This lease made in ——, state of ——, ——, 19—, [1] between ——, of ——, hereinafter referred to as lessor,[2] and ——, of ——, hereinafter referred to as lessee,[3] witnesseth:

Lessor, for and in consideration[4] of the agreements of lessee hereafter mentioned, hereby leases to lessee, and lessee hereby leases from lessor, the premises [or as the case may be] located at ——, state of——, described as follows: ——,[5] excepting and reserving to lessor ——, including the right to ——.[6]

This lease is for the term of —— years [or as the case may be], beginning ——, 19—, and ending ——, 19—, unless sooner terminated as hereafter provided.[7]

A. Agreements of Lessee

Lessee, in consideration of said leasing, agrees:

1. To pay as rent for premises the sum of —— dollars per month [or as the case may be], payable on the —— day of each month [or as the case may be] during the term of this lease, at ——.[8]

2. To pay all charges for light, heat, fuel, power and water furnished or supplied to or on any part of premises.[9]

3. To pay all taxes and assessments, ordinary and extraordinary, general and specific, including the same for 19—, which may be levied or assessed on premises.[10]

4. To pay all reasonable costs, attorneys' fees and expenses that shall be made and incurred by lessor in enforcing the agreements of this lease.[11]

5. To use and occupy the premises for —— purposes only, and for no other object or purpose without written consent of lessor, and to not use premises for any unlawful purpose or purpose deemed extra hazardous.[12]

181

D.   PLEADINGS AND MOTIONS

1. Purpose

As was explained in Chapter 5, pleadings are written statements that are filed with the court at the beginning of a lawsuit. They include the complaint, the answer, the cross-complaint, and the demurrer. Their purpose is to inform the court and the other parties about the facts and the issues involved in the litigation. A motion is a request to a court or judge to make a specific ruling or to issue a specific order in a case. It would be a good idea to review Form 5.1 and Exhibits 5.1, 5.2, and 5.3 before proceeding to the next section.

2. Format and Content

The format for pleadings is closely regulated by the court in which the case is to be filed. All documents must show the proper case name and docket number. In cases involving matters such as divorce or adoption, the court is usually very explicit about both the form and the content.

Rules 3 through 25 of the Federal Rules of Civil Procedure for the United States district courts spell out the specific content and format requirements for the various pleadings documents in federal courts. Rule 8, for example, covers the type of information that must be included in the claim for relief and various defenses that might be raised. Section (a) of Rule 8 reads as follows:

> (a) *Claims for Relief.* A pleading which sets forth a claim for relief, whether an original claim, counterclaim, cross-claim, or third-party claim, shall contain (1) a short and plain statement of the grounds upon which the court's jurisdiction depends, unless the court already has jurisdiction and the claim needs no new grounds of jurisdiction to support it, (2) a short and plain statement of the claim showing that the pleader is entitled to relief, and (3) a demand for judgment for the relief to which he deems himself entitled. Relief in the alternative or of several different types may be demanded.

Rule 10, on the other hand, provides an example of a Rule that specifies the format to be used:

> (a) *Caption; Names of Parties.* Every pleading shall contain a caption setting forth the name of the court, the title of the action, the file number, and a designation as in Rule 7(a). In the complaint the title of the action shall include the names of all the parties, but in other pleadings it is sufficient to state the name of the first party on each side with an appropriate indication of other parties.
> (b) *Paragraphs; Separate Statements.* All averments of claim or defense shall be made in numbered paragraphs, the contents of each of

Form 1.

SUMMONS

UNITED STATES DISTRICT COURT FOR THE
SOUTHERN DISTRICT OF NEW YORK

Civil Action, File Number _____

A. B., Plaintiff

    v.   ⌐ Summons

C. D., Defendant

To the above-named Defendant:

You are hereby summoned and required to serve upon _____, plaintiff's attorney, whose address is _____, an answer to the complaint which is herewith served upon you, within 20[1] days after service of this summons upon you, exclusive of the day of service. If you fail to do so, judgment by default will be taken against you for the relief demanded in the complaint.

_____,

Clerk of Court.

[Seal of the U.S. District Court]

Dated _____

---

[1] If the United States or an officer or agency thereof is a defendant, the time to be inserted as to it is sixty days.

---

which shall be limited as far as practicable to a statement of a single set of circumstances; and a paragraph may be referred to by number in all succeeding pleadings. Each claim founded upon a separate transaction or occurrence and each defense other than denials shall be stated in a separate count or defense whenever a separation facilitates the clear presentation of the matters set forth.

(c) *Adoption by Reference; Exhibits.* Statements in a pleading may be adopted by reference in a different part of the same pleading or in another pleading or in any motion. A copy of any written instrument which is an exhibit to a pleading is a part thereof for all purposes.

Rule 84 provides for an Appendix of Forms to illustrate the requirements spelled out in the other rules. Forms 9.1 and 9.2 present

Form 9.2 Complaint from Federal Rules Appendix of Forms

Form 14.

COMPLAINT FOR NEGLIGENCE UNDER FEDERAL EMPLOYERS' LIABILITY ACT

1. Allegation of jurisdiction.

2. During all the times herein mentioned defendant owned and operated in interstate commerce a railroad which passed through a tunnel located at _____ and known as Tunnel No. _____.

3. On or about June 1, 1936, defendant was repairing and enlarging the tunnel in order to protect interstate trains and passengers and freight from injury and in order to make the tunnel more conveniently usable for interstate commerce.

4. In the course of thus repairing and enlarging the tunnel on said day defendant employed plaintiff as one of the workmen, and negligently put plaintiff to work in a portion of the tunnel which defendant had left unprotected and unsupported.

5. By reason of defendant's negligence in thus putting plaintiff to work in that portion of the tunnel, plaintiff was, while so working pursuant to defendant's orders, struck and crushed by a rock, which fell from the unsupported portion of the tunnel, and was (here describe plaintiff's injuries).

6. Prior to these injuries, plaintiff was a strong, able-bodied man, capable of earning and actually earning _____ dollars per day. By these injuries he has been made incapable of any gainful activity, has suffered great physical and mental pain, and has incurred expense in the amount of _____ dollars for medicine, medical attendance, and hospitalization.

Wherefore plaintiff demands judgment against defendant in the sum of _____ dollars and costs.

---

examples of forms contained in this appendix. In addition to sample forms adopted by the courts, several commercial publishers have marketed books of sample pleadings. At the federal level the major series of formbooks are: Am. Jur. Forms 2d, Bender's Federal Practice Forms, Nichols Cyclopedia of Federal Procedure Forms, and West's Federal Forms. In addition to commercial formbooks for specific states, the continuing legal education divisions of state bar associations often produce instructional materials that include model pleadings. Form 9.3 shows a sample page from a typical formbook.

Legal software packages have been developed that integrate materials from office files with either standardized or customized forms.

NEGLIGENCE   § 151.02

concise statement of defendant's defense or defenses,[29] and (3) set up any counterclaim or counterclaims that he may have.[30] If new matter by way of defense is pleaded in the answer, the plaintiff should file a reply [31] admitting or denying each allegation of such new matter.[32]

II. FORMS

A. Complaints

§ 151.02. General form.[33]

[Caption as in § 2.02.]

Plaintiff ———, by his [or, her] attorney ———, complaining of defendant ——— [, a corporation], alleges as follows:

1. At the time of the occurrence [or, accident] hereinafter complained of [or, described], and prior thereto, defendant ——— was, and still is, a resident of [or, a corporation organized and existing under the laws of the state of Illinois and having its principal office and place of business in] ———, ——— county, Illinois; and said defendant then and there owned or possessed and controlled, and [, by his (or, its) agents and employees,] was operating ——— [state what defendant owned, etc.] [or, said defendant (, by his [or, its] agents and employees,) was then and there ——— (state what defendant was doing)].

2. [Allege duty of defendant as in § 151.04.]

3. [Allege exercise of due care by plaintiff as in § 151.05.]

4. On or about ———, 19—, at approximately ——— —.m., in [or, near] ———, ——— county, Illinois, disregarding his [or, its] aforementioned duty, defendant [, by his (or, its) said agents and employees,] negligently ——— [state what defendant did or omitted to do in violation of his or its duty, and, if breach of a statutory duty is alleged, cite the statute]; and, as a direct and

[29] Ill Rev Stats c 110, § 33, subd (1).

[30] Ill Rev Stats c 110, § 38.

Law governing answers and counterclaims in automobile accident cases, see §§ 56.03, 56.04.

[31] Ill Rev Stats c 110, § 32.

[32] Ill Rev Stats c 110, § 40, subd (1).

Law governing replies in automobile accident cases, see § 56.05.

[33] Composite complaint in automobile accident case, see § 56.07.

Allegations as to damages in personal injury actions, see §§ 30.64–30.172.

Allegations as to property damage, see §§ 30.173–30.191.

297

proximate result thereof, ——— [describe occurrence or accident] ; whereby plaintiff then and there sustained injuries to his [or, her] person [and/or, plaintiff's aforementioned property was then and there damaged] as hereinafter alleged.

5. [Allege damages as in § 151.12.]

Wherefore, plaintiff demands judgment against defendant for the sum of ——— dollars ($———) and his [or, her] costs of suit.

———, Plaintiff's attorney

[Name, address and telephone
of plaintiff's attorney.]

§ 151.03.   Golfer struck by other player's ball.[34]

[Caption and commencement as in § 151.02.]

1. At the time of the occurrence hereinafter mentioned, and prior thereto, defendant ——— was engaged in playing golf upon a certain golf course commonly known as "———" and located adjacent to ——— street, near the intersection thereof with ——— avenue, in [or, near] the city [or, village] of ———, ——— county, Illinois.

2. As defendant then and there well knew, or in exercise of ordinary care would have known, various other players and persons were then lawfully present upon and about said course; wherefore it became, and was, the duty of defendant to exercise ordinary care, in conducting himself and playing upon said course, to guard against injury to such other players and persons, including plaintiff.

3. At said time, and immediately prior thereto, plaintiff was lawfully present and playing golf upon said course, and was in the exercise of due care for the safety of his [or, her] own person.

4. On or about ———, 19—, at approximately ——— —.m., defendant negligently drove his golf ball, as hereinafter specified, and, as a direct and proximate result thereof, said ball struck plaintiff with great force and violence, and greatly injured him [or, her] as hereinafter alleged.

[34] Adapted from Hampson v. Simon, 345 Ill App 582, 104 NE2d 112. Allegations as to damages in personal injury actions, see §§ 30.64–30.172.

298

E.   INTERROGATORIES AND OTHER DISCOVERY REQUESTS

1. Purpose

As was discussed in Chapter 5, interrogatories are written questions that are sent to another party in a lawsuit to obtain important information regarding the case. The party to whom they are directed then supplies written answers to these questions. Interrogatories often are used to identify and then locate documents and witnesses. They are also useful for learning about the organization and procedures of a business. Their main focus, however, is usually on ascertaining the details of one person's account of the events involved in the suit.

In addition to interrogatories, a party to a lawsuit can request that various types of documents be produced or that a litigant submit to a physical or mental examination. If the requests for any information, including responses to specific questions, are not forthcoming from the other party, the attorney can file a motion requesting the court to order that the item be produced or that the person submit to the requested examination.

2. Format and Content

The Federal Rules of Civil Procedure say very little about the actual content and format of interrogatories. The applicable section of Rule 33 states the following:

> (a) *Availability: Procedures for Use.* Any party may serve upon any other party written interrogatories to be answered by the party served or, if the party served is a public or private corporation or a partnership or association or governmental agency, by an officer or agent, who shall furnish such information as is available to the party. Interrogatories may, without leave of court, be served upon the plaintiff after commencement of the action and upon any other party with or after service of the summons and complaint upon that party.
>
> Each interrogatory shall be answered separately and fully in writing under oath, unless it is objected to, in which event the reasons for objections shall be stated in lieu of an answer. The answers are to be signed by the person making them, and the objections signed by the attorney making them. The party upon whom the interrogatories have been served shall serve a copy of the answers, and objections if any, within 30 days after the service of the interrogatories, except that a defendant may serve answers or objections within 45 days after service of the summons and complaint upon that defendant. The court may allow a shorter or longer time. The party submitting the interrogatories may move for an order under Rule 37(a) with respect to any objection to or other failure to answer an interrogatory.

Form 9.4 Request for Production of Documents from Federal Appendix of Forms

Form 24.

REQUEST FOR PRODUCTION OF DOCUMENTS, ETC., UNDER RULE 34

Plaintiff A. B. requests defendant C. D. to respond within _____ days to the following requests:

(1) That defendant produce and permit plaintiff to inspect and to copy each of the following documents:

(Here list the documents either individually or by category and describe each of them.)

(Here state the time, place, and manner of making the inspection and performance of any related acts.)

(2) That defendant produce and permit plaintiff to inspect and to copy, test, or sample each of the following objects:

(Here list the objects either individually or by category and describe each of them.)

(Here state the time, place, and manner of making the inspection and performance of any related acts.)

(3) That defendant permit plaintiff to enter (here describe property to be entered) and to inspect and to photograph, test or sample (here describe the portion of the real property and the objects to be inspected).

(Here state the time, place, and manner of making the inspection and performance of any related acts.)

Signed: _____

Attorney for Plaintiff

Address: _____

Form 25.

REQUEST FOR ADMISSION UNDER RULE 36

Plaintiff A. B. requests defendant C. D. within _____ days after service of this request to make the following admissions for the purpose of this action only and subject to all pertinent objections to admissibility which may be interposed at the trial:

1. That each of the following documents, exhibited with this request, is genuine.
(Here list the documents and describe each document.)
2. That each of the following statements is true.
(Here list the statements.)

Signed: _____
                                    Attorney for Plaintiff

Address: _____

The Appendix of Forms contains a Request for Production of Documents (see Form 9.4) and a Request for Admissions (Form 9.5), but it does not contain any sample interrogatories. Therefore, the paralegal should consult office files on previous cases as well as a variety of specialized trial practice books when drafting interrogatories. American Jurisprudence Trials, for example, is a multivolume series published by Lawyers' Co-operative Publishing Company that contains essays on preparation for trials involving different types of legal problems. These discussions often include ideas for interrogatories (see Exhibit 9.5).

In drafting the questions to be included in an interrogatory, the writer must be both as explicit and as inclusive as possible. Any ambiguity over key terminology will provide an excuse for the other side to evade giving the information that is actually being sought. For example,

MEDICAL MALPRACTICE   § 32

names and respective duties of all persons making entries on such records.[4]

All autopsy reports should be examined with particular attention to the dates of the reports and the cause of death stated. The persons who made the reports should be questioned to determine to what extent they relied upon information given to them by the doctor or hospital personnel.[5] Depositions should be taken of hospital personnel who have since left the employ of the defendant hospital. These persons may give information more freely than if they were still employed there.

§ 32. INTERROGATORIES TO PARTIES[6]

Interrogatories should be used to discover each defendant's part in the mishap, and to determine relationships of agency, employment, or partnership. All interrogatories should request that the party produce whatever records or reports he may have in his possession.

The following are suggested lines of inquiry to be pursued in interrogatories to particular defendants. The list of queries is not necessarily exhaustive.

Referring Physician
1. Explain the purpose of the history that was taken of the patient.
2. State what complaints the patient had and what symptoms you discovered.
3. Explain in detail your diagnosis of the patient's symptoms.
4. State what treatments or medications you prescribed.
5. State what recommendations you made about surgery, anesthesia, or a particular surgeon or hospital.
6. State to what extent you informed the surgeon, obstetrician, or hospital personnel of the plaintiff's history, treatment, and medication.

---

4. How to Handle an Anesthesia Injury Case, by Albert Averbach. Clev-Mar L Rev vol 15 no 3 p 404 (Sept 1966).

5. How to Handle an Anesthesia Injury Case, by Albert Averbach. Clev-Mar L Rev vol 15 no 3 p 403 (Sept 1966).

6. See, generally, 4 AM JUR TRIALS, DISCOVERY—WRITTEN INTERROGATORIES, p. 1.

Exhibit 9.5 *(continued)*

§ 32   12 AM JUR TRIALS

7. Did you inform the surgeon or hospital personnel as to the patient's known allergies, or any other contraindications to the use of spinal anesthesia?

8. State any partnership arrangements you have with any other medical practitioner.

Surgeon or Obstetrician

9. State in detail what preanesthetic history was taken of the patient.

10. State any information you have as to who prescribed saddle block anesthesia to be given.

11. Describe in detail the scope of your responsibilities to the patient.

12. Describe in detail what control you exercised over the anesthetist or other attendants.

13. State who furnished the anesthetist, the anesthetic agents, and anesthetic apparatus for this particular patient.

14. In the course of the operation, did you assist at all in the administration of anesthesia or did you make any recommendations? Describe.

15. Describe in detail the events that took place from the start of the operation until the patient left your supervision.

16. State any partnership arrangements you have with any other individual in the practice of medicine.

Anesthetist

17. Explain in detail the taking of the preanesthetic history of the patient.

18. State who determines the type of anesthesia to be used and how this decision is made known to the anesthetist.

19. What anesthetic agent or agents were used on the patient?

20. Describe in detail how you administered anesthesia to this patient.

21. Describe the events from the time you first began administration of anesthesia.

22. Give a chronological history of the patient's vital signs during this time.

23. Describe employment or other arrangements resulting in your engagement to administer anesthesia to this patient.

288

the respondents might withhold reference to a letter because the interrogatory asked only for memoranda. In order to avoid this, it is wise to be as inclusive as possible, and draft an interrogatory that seeks letters, memoranda, reports, interim reports, financial records, or any other written documents relating to the specific subject. Rather than repeating long inclusive lists in each of a series of questions, the drafter may wish to include a definitions section in which a term like *document* is defined in an inclusive manner. Then each question can refer to documents, but such references will include all of the specified alternatives.

Opportunities must be minimized for the opposition to interpret questions in a way that allows a claim that the interrogatories did not really ask for certain information. In addition, it is important to force a complete response for the information they do supply. Exhibits 5.4 and 5.5 and the sample interrogatories with responses on pages 187-189 were used in the Renslow v. Mennonite Hospital case discussed in Chapter 5. Writing in their book on investigation, David Binder and Paul Bergman suggest that the following general instructions be added to interrogatories in order to elicit as much information as possible.

D. Binder and P. Berman, Sample Interrogatory Instructions
Fact Investigation from Hypothesis to Proof 344 (1984)

A. Whenever you are requested to identify or state the identity of any "person," state the following with respect to such person:
  1. The full name of the person;
  2. The last known business and residence address of the person;
  3. The last known business and residence telephone number of the person;
  4. Occupation of the person.
B. Whenever you are requested to identify any document, state the following with respect to such document:
  1. A description of the document in sufficient detail so that it may be readily identified by its custodian;
  2. The date appearing on the document;
  3. The name of any person signing the document;
  4. The present location of the original of the document;
  5. The names and addresses of the person or persons having custody or control of the original, and any and/or all copies of the document;
  6. Whether you will make it available to counsel for _____ without the necessity of a Motion to Produce.
C. Whenever you are requested to identify any fact state the following with respect to each such fact:

1. The full name and business and residence address and telephone number of each person having knowledge of such fact;
2. The date and location of the occurrence of such fact;
3. The identity of each document or electronic recording which
   evidences, pertains to, refers to and/or records such fact.

3. Responding to Interrogatories

When a law firm's client receives an interrogatory, a paralegal may
be assigned to assist the client in responding to the document. Many
clients panic when they receive such a document and need help to
understand what they are being asked to do. Some clients have trouble
writing. The paralegal can help to interpret the document and write
down the answers.

The answers to the questions must be truthful and complete, but
they should be drafted in a way that makes them as limited as possible. In
other words, the answers should not volunteer additional information
that was not specifically requested. Furthermore, where appropriate, the
responses should be prefaced with qualifiers such as "to the best of my
knowledge" or "as far as I know." These types of responses help to
protect the client if contradictory information arises at a later time.

The format used in responding to an interrogatory is illustrated on
pages 187-189. The question is repeated as it was given and then followed by the client's response.

F.   EXTERNAL MEMORANDA OF LAW

1. Purpose

The memorandum referred to in this section is a document addressed to a judge or an administrative hearing officer that presents legal
arguments and supporting documentation. The research memorandum
discussed at the beginning of this chapter is an internal document designed to objectively present the results of one's research; this type of
memorandum, however, is an advocacy document designed to convince
the reader to take a specific legal action. Within the context of litigation,
these memoranda are sometimes called trial memoranda and are submitted in support of a motion relating to discovery requests or the manner in which the trial will be conducted. They also are used to support
posttrial motions. In the administrative context this memo is sometimes
referred to as a hearing memorandum and is submitted to the hearing
officer or the agency in support of positions being taken by the someone
who seeks some action from the agency or is involved in adjudication
before the agency.

2. Format and Content

In drafting an external memorandum, the heading should follow the same requirements as those required in pleadings. The name of the parties, the name of the court or agency, and the docket or file number is displayed in the caption format that is specified by that particular court or agency. The format for the rest of the memorandum is usually left to the discretion of the attorney filing it. Since it is an advocacy document, it tends to follow the style of presentation used in appellate briefs. Like a brief, it contains a statement of the facts, a statement of the issues, and a discussion of relevant cases and statutes, but it probably will not have a formal table of contents, a table of authorities, or an appendix.

G.   APPELLATE BRIEFS

1. Purpose

An appellate brief is an advocacy document that is submitted to an appellate court for the purpose of providing legal justifications for either sustaining or reversing a specific action by a lower court.[4] The appellant (the party who appeals a case from one court or jurisdiction to another) obviously wishes to have the decision of the lower court overturned, and the appellee (the party against whom the appeal is being taken) argues to have it sustained. In their respective briefs the attorneys have the opportunity to present the facts, the issues, and the relevant legal authority in the manner that is most favorable to their clients' positions. Although oral argument also may play a role, the briefs remain the primary means of influencing the court's decision.

2. Format and Content of the Appellant's Brief

The specific format requirements for both the appellant's and the appellee's briefs are spelled out in the applicable court rules. Rules 28 through 32 of the Federal Rules of Appellate Procedure apply to appeals in the federal Court of Appeals, and Rules 33 through 36 of the Rules of the Supreme Court of the United States apply to appeals before the nation's highest court.

There are some variations among states regarding the order in which parts are presented and the number of pages allowed, but the basic components of a brief are fairly standard. Compare and contrast, for example, the brief requirements for the Federal Rules of Appellate Procedure and a similar overview of the requirements for an appellate

---

4. A case brief, which is a summary analysis of a specific case, is discussed at pages 103-105.

brief in the Illinois courts. Each component of the brief (such as cover page, table of authorities cited, statement of issues presented, arguments presented, and so forth) should be started on a separate page.

Composition of Appellate Briefs: Federal Format
adapted from Federal Rules of Appellate Procedure 28 and 30

Appellant's Brief

Cover page. In addition to identifying the document as the appellant's brief, this section usually includes the name of the appellate court, the names of the parties, the docket number, the name of the court from which the appeal is coming, and the name and address of the lawyer submitting the brief.

Table of contents. This section lists the other sections of the brief and the page numbers on which these sections begin.

Table of authorities cited. This section lists alphabetically the various statutes and cases cited in the brief and the page number on which these references can be found.

Statement of issues presented. A series of concise statements is made about the legal issues raised in the context of the case being appealed.

Statement of the case. This section contains a brief summary of the nature of the case, the course of proceedings, and its disposition in the court below. This is then followed by a more detailed statement of the facts that are relevant to the issues presented for review. This discussion of the facts should contain appropriate references to the record so that the reader can easily locate the material in an appendix or the original transcript.

Arguments presented. This section weaves an interpretation of the facts and the law together to show why the appellant's position is correct. (If the argument is complex, this section frequently begins with a brief summary and then is divided into several parts.)

Conclusions. This section concisely summarizes the nature of the errors that were made by the lower court and requests that the appellate court take some specific action to change the lower court's decision.

Appendix. The appendix begins with a list of the parts of the record that it contains, in the order in which the parts are set out therein and with references to the pages of the record at which each part begins. The relevant docket entries are listed after the list of contents, followed by other parts of the record set out in chronological order. The page of the transcript at which the matter may be found is indicated in brackets immediately before the matter that is set out. Exhibits designated for inclusion in the appendix may be contained in a separate volume, or volumes, suitably indexed. (The court of appeals may by rule dispense

with the requirement for an appendix and permit appeals to be heard on the original record.)

Appellee's Brief

The brief format used is the same as that used in an appellant's brief except that the statement of the issues, the jurisdictional statement, and the statement of the facts need not be made unless the appellee is dissatisfied with the statements made by the appellant.

Reply Briefs

The appellant can file a reply brief to attempt to rebut arguments made in the appellee's brief. The appellee can file a reply brief only if a cross-appeal is made. Reply briefs usually consist only of a cover sheet and an argument section.

Composition of Appellate Briefs: A State Format
adapted from Illinois Supreme Court Rules 341 and 342

Appellant's Brief

Cover page. In addition to the names of the parties, it contains the number of the case in the reviewing court and the name of that court, the name of the court from which the case was brought, and the name of the case as it appeared in the trial court. The status of each party in the reviewing court also is indicated (such as plaintiff-appellant). The name of the trial judge entering the judgment to be reviewed and the individual names and addresses of the attorneys filing the brief (and if desired, of their law firm) also are stated. The cover page is color coded to reflect that it is an appellant's brief.

Points and authorities. This section contains summary statements of the points argued and the authorities cited in the argument. Headings of points and subpoints should correspond to those used in the argument section. The cases under each point or subpoint should be cited in order of their importance.

Nature of the case. An introductory paragraph stating (i) the nature of the action and of the judgment appealed from and whether the judgment is based on the verdict of a jury and (ii) whether any question is raised on the pleadings and, if so, the nature of the question.

Statement of issues presented for review. A series of concise statements is presented on the legal issues that are raised in the context of the case being appealed. It does not include citations of authorities.

Jurisdiction statement. In cases that are appealed to the Supreme Court directly from the trial court or as a matter of right from the

appellate court, a brief statement of the jurisdictional grounds for the appeal must be included.

Statutes involved. If the case involves the construction or validity of a statute, constitutional provision, treaty, ordinance, or regulation, the pertinent parts of the provision should be quoted verbatim. (If the section is very long, it is cited and then quoted in an appendix.)

Statement of the facts. This section contains a summary of the facts that are considered necessary to an understanding of the case. Exhibits may be cited by reference to pages of the abstract or of the record on appeal or by exhibit number followed by the page number within the exhibit.

Arguments. This section weaves together an interpretation of the facts and the law to show why the appellant's position is correct. (If the argument is complex, it frequently begins with a brief summary and then is divided into several parts.) Citations are given to legal authorities and to pages in the record.

Conclusions. This section states the precise relief sought, followed by the names of counsel as they appear on the cover.

Appendix. This section includes a copy of the judgment appealed from, any opinion, memorandum, or findings of fact filed or entered by the trial judge, the notice of appeal, and a complete table of contents.

Table of contents. This table includes page references of the record on appeal and states (1) the nature of each document, (2) the date of filing or entry for pleadings, motions, notices, and so forth, and (3) the names of all witnesses and the pages on which their direct, cross-, and redirect examinations begin.

Abstract. An abstract of the record should be filed only when the reviewing court requests it. It should refer to the pages of the record by numerals in the margin, be preceded by a table of contents, be condensed in narrative form, and be limited to those parts of the record that are necessary for an understanding of the issues being presented.

Appellee's Brief

The format used is the same as that used in an appellant's brief except that (1) the cover page is coded a different color and (2) sections such as the statement of the facts and the statutes involved can be excluded if the appellee does not wish to challenge the content of the corresponding sections of the appellant's brief.

Reply Briefs

This brief is limited to replying to arguments presented in the brief of the appellee and need contain only a color-coded cover page and an argument section.

a. Digesting or Abstracting the Record

Because the appeal is based on the record of the case, it is essential that both the attorney and the paralegal be thoroughly familiar with all aspects of the pleadings and motions as well as the transcript of the trial. This is best achieved by having the paralegal digest or abstract the record.[5]

The digesting process involves compiling summaries of key parts of the record and indexing where in the record they appear. Digesting familiarizes the paralegal with contents of the documents and facilitates quick reference to original sources.

Several techniques can be used in preparing this type of digest. The most thorough one involves recording a summary for each distinct item on separate note cards. These cards can be arranged so that all allegations or testimony about a single fact can be catalogued together regardless of where the pleadings or testimony appear.[6] The following sample entries from a digest of the record come from a criminal trial in which Black and four other defendants were charged with obstructing a peace officer by not obeying his order to disperse during a demonstration at a county jail:

Testimony Related to Defendant Black's Alleged Failure to Hear
Sgt. Leary's Dispersal Order
Sgt. Leary, in a "loud voice," gave an order for the demonstrators to
  leave the area. Leary's Direct R-6
Sgt. Leary was not over twenty feet away from the demonstrators
  when he gave the order. Leary's Direct R-10
Black did not hear Leary's dispersal order. Black's Direct R-356
Lynn Allen, who was standing next to Black, did not hear Leary's, or
  anyone else's dispersal order. Allen's Direct R-310
Suzanne Little, who was near Black, did not hear Sgt. Leary's dis-
  persal order. S. Little's Direct R-258

Testimony Related to Defendant Black's Arrest
Sgt. Little and several county officers tried to "move Black along."
  Black was holding onto a telephone pole. Sgt. Little's Direct R-105
The county police were already restraining Black when Sgt. Little
  arrived. Sgt. Little's Cross R-113 and 114
Sgt. Little did not give Black a dispersal order. Sgt. Little's Cross R-
  122
Black was not given a chance to move on while Sgt. Little was there.
  Sgt. Little's Cross R-114
Black was approached by a group of officers who ordered him to get
  off the street and move onto the sidewalk. Black's Direct R-370;
  Allen's Direct R-314

---

5. An abstract of the record is a summary of its contents. The paralegal takes each section in order of appearance and summarizes the essential material. A digest not only summarizes the material but classifies and rearranges it.
6. See M. Pittoni, Brief Writing and Argumentation ch. 5 (1967).

Following the order to get off the street, an officer told Black to
~~"move on." When Black asked where he was supposed to move to,~~
he was grabbed by two officers. Black's Direct R-370; Allen's Direct R-328 and 329

b. Identifying the Issues

Prior to deciding to go ahead with the appeal, the attorney carefully
considers the issues that form the basis of the appeal. Carefully analyzing
the digested record sharpens the focus of those issues and may lead to
the discovery of additional issues.

The issues presented must relate to legitimately debatable points.
Frivolous issues that have no reasonable basis for support weaken the
brief's credibility.

On the other hand, it is a good policy to raise issues involved in
fallback positions. In other words, a brief can raise secondary issues for
the court to consider if the court rules against the primary issue. For
example, one issue can assert that a supposed contract was not valid
because there was a lack of adequate consideration. The next issue can
then assert that the contract should be interpreted in such a way as to
favor one's client's position. Also, one issue might assert a right of recovery based on a breach of contract theory, and the next issue might be
based on negligence.

Once the paralegal has a clear understanding of the issues that the
attorney intends to raise, the statement of the issues presented and the
statement of the facts can be drafted. Examples of the issue statements
from two different cases follow. People v. Black is the criminal case that
was used in the sample entries from a digest of the record in section a
above. The appeal is designed to reverse the convictions of defendants
Robert Reyes and Peter Black.

People v. Black
1. Whether the evidence failed, as a matter of law, to establish that
   the Defendant, Robert Reyes, knowingly resisted or obstructed
   Sergeant Leary's order to disperse.
2. Whether the evidence failed, as a matter of law, to establish that
   the Defendant, Peter Black, knowingly resisted or obstructed
   Sergeant Leary's order to disperse.

Astor v. Curry is an appeal from a summary judgment in a civil case. Tim
and Kassandra Astor had signed an agreement to purchase a mobile
home through monthly installments. The home was located in a mobile
home park operated by the seller. The trial judge had ruled that a key
paragraph in the contract was properly interpreted as a month-to-month
lease.

Astor v. Curry
Whether the Court erred in interpreting the agreement as a matter of law and granting summary judgment on that interpretation.

Note that the issues are phrased in terms of the factual situations involved in each case. The paralegal should present the issues so that they
persuasively suggest the answer that favors the client's position.

c. Presenting the Facts

The facts of the case can be divided into two categories. The first
relates to the events that created the original dispute, and the second
reports the nature of the legal action taken and its outcome in the lower
courts. Many brief formats start (after the cover page, table of contents,
and so on) with a concise summary of the legal history of the case. This
type of summary is sometimes called the jurisdictional statement because
it establishes that the case falls within the jurisdiction of the appellate
court where it was filed. Sample nature of the case or jurisdictional
statements follow:

JURISDICTIONAL STATEMENT FOR PEOPLE v. BLACK

This is an appeal from a jury verdict finding the defendants,
Robert Reyes, Peter R. Black, and Harry Brent DeLand, guilty of a
violation of Chapter 38, section 31-1, of the Illinois Revised Statutes.
In the same trial, Robert Sutherland and David Nelson were found
not guilty by the jury. No question is raised on the pleadings.

JURISDICTIONAL STATEMENT FOR ASTOR v. CURRY

This is an appeal from trial court's order granting defendant-
appellee's motion for summary judgment as to Count I of plaintiff-
appellant's amended complaint. The trial court found as a matter of
law that the only reasonable interpretation was that paragraph 5 of
the written agreement was a lease from month to month and defeated plaintiff's claim. The court found no just reason to delay
enforcement or appeal.

This cause involves an action brought by plaintiff-appellant TIM
and KASSANDRA ASTOR, to recover from the defendant DAVID
CURRY, money paid by the plaintiff to the defendant. The money
represents the amortized amount of a contract for the purchase of a
mobile home plus the amount expended for improvements to that
mobile home. The case involves the interpretation and construction
of a clause of the contract.

The defendant has not denied plaintiff's amended verified complaint nor submitted any affidavits to contradict any of the terms
of plaintiff's complaint nor attacked the substance of plaintiff's
complaint. The trial court granted summary judgment for defendant-appellee holding that clause 5 of the contract constituted a
month-to-month lease as a matter of law and could be terminated
prior to the termination of the contract. The trial court entered
judgment for the defendant-appellee and against the plaintiff-
appellant as to Count I of plaintiff's amended complaint.

Unlike the summary of the legal history, which usually is quite
straightforward and relatively easy to prepare, preparing the statement

of facts involves much more skill. This section seeks to summarize the various factual contentions involved in the legal action. The facts should be portrayed in a manner most favorable to the client's position. Although the writer should not ignore central facts unfavorable to the client, the amount of emphasis given to them and the nature of supporting materials can be persuasive. An excerpt from the statement of facts in the People v. Black case follows:

STATEMENT OF FACTS FOR PEOPLE v. BLACK

On Sunday afternoon November 3, 1974, a group of people gathered in the vicinity of the McLean County Jail for a demonstration and protest against McLean County Sheriff John King. A large contingent of police from Bloomington, Normal, and the McLean County Sheriff's office were present to maintain order during the demonstration.

Sergeant Michael Leary of the Bloomington Police Department was in charge of a thirty-man police squad that was originally held in reserve at a secluded spot until approximately 2:45 P.M. (R-4) Responding to requests from his superiors, Sergeant Leary moved his squad to the county jail to prevent the demonstration from "getting out of hand." (R-4) When Sergeant Leary and his squad arrived at the McLean County Jail, he observed a group of about 100 persons, some of whom were "more or less jeering and harassing" the police officers who were in position around the jail. (R-5) Police officer Bobby Friga, who had been stationed in the alley beside the jail for at least two hours prior to the arrival of Sergeant Leary, estimated the number of demonstrators as "approximately forty-five." (R-76) Officer Bob Little, who was also present at the scene, estimated the group at "eighty, maybe one hundred people" and agreed that there was a lot of shouting and jeering. (R-103)

At this point, Sergeant Leary testified that he ordered his police officers to form a line. (R-6) In a "loud voice" he then ordered the demonstrators to disperse and leave the area. (R-6) Although later orders given to the demonstrators by Sergeant Leary were given over a bullhorn, Sergeant Leary admits that this first order was not given over the bullhorn. (R-10) Sergeant Leary testified that the demonstrators were not over twenty feet away from him when he gave the order. (R-6)

Without any further orders to the demonstrators, Sergeant Leary ordered his police line to move forward. (R-7) As the police line started to move forward, Sergeant Leary stated that some of the demonstrators fell down. (R-7) Members of Sergeant Leary's police squad tried to get the fallen demonstrators up and "move them along." (R-8) Right in the area where some of the demonstrators had fallen, "one subject turned and came back toward the line." (R-7) Sergeant Leary testified that the subject came back toward the police line to "counter the officer" but no further testimony was forthcoming from Sergeant Leary to describe any actions or conduct of the subject. (R-8) Sergeant Leary next testified that he grabbed the subject and told other officers to take him to the paddy wagon. (R-8) This subject was the Defendant Robert Reyes.

The actual officer making the arrest of Robert Reyes was Bloomington Police Officer Bobby Friga. Officer Friga testified that Sergeant Leary "more or less pointed to a subject [Robert Reyes]" and told him to "arrest this guy." (R-79) While Officer Friga testified that Robert Reyes was arrested because he refused to leave the area, he admitted during cross-examination that he personally did not observe Robert Reyes do anything that would cause him to be selected by Sergeant Leary for arrest. (R-86)

Although the facts usually are presented in chronological sequence, the writer may present the most favorable materials first to capture the reader's initial sympathies. In developing this section, careful attention should be given to the selection of descriptive words. Confusion is avoided if the parties are referred to by their proper names (such as Mr. Smith and Ms. Jones) or by a descriptive noun (such as the driver, the real estate agent, or the banker) rather than by the terms *appellant* and *appellee,* or even *plaintiff* and *defendant.* Colorful adjectives can convey added meaning and also invoke a particular type of emotional response.

Presentation of these facts should refer to the page number of the record that shows when the fact in question was presented in court. This documentation is provided by including the appropriate page numbers from the record in parentheses at the end of the sentence, as shown in the excerpt from the statement of facts presented above. When the facts are in dispute, the summary should reflect their disputed status.

Although it may at times be appropriate to include an exact quotation from someone's testimony or from some portion of a document, quoting should be done sparingly. It is better to paraphrase the item and let the judges read it directly from the record.

d. Developing the Argument

The argument section interprets both the meaning of the law and the extent to which that law is applicable to the facts of the case. A good argument skillfully combines analysis of the facts in the record with an intepretation of relevant statutes, cases, and constitutional provisions. While digesting the record the paralegal learns the facts, and while doing the legal research and analysis discussed in Chapters 3 and 8 the paralegal gains a basis for interpreting the law.

The argument section of the brief should be divided into subsections that correspond to the subsections in the issues section. Each of these subsections should begin with a single-sentence summary of the main point. It should restate the issue involved in the form of a statement rather than question. The statement should be phrased to favor the client's position and typed in capital letters. Moreover, it is usually wise to further subdivide these issue arguments with similar capitalized lead sentences. This subdivision scheme makes the argument easier to follow and increases its impact. Because these capitalized headings are so

important, the writer should spend time revising and tightening them for maximum impact.

When the interpretation of the record is involved, the writer should highlight those sections that favor the client's position. This type of argument is directed at persuading the appellate court to accept the reasonableness of a particular interpretation. The following example of an argument centering on interpretation of the facts shows how this approach was used in Black's brief.

THE EVIDENCE FAILED, AS A MATTER OF LAW, TO ESTAB-LISH THAT THE DEFENDANT PETER BLACK KNOWINGLY RESISTED OR OBSTRUCTED SERGEANT LEARY'S ORDER TO DISPERSE . . .

The entire evidence put forward by the State against Peter Black consists of the testimony of Officer Bobbie Little. On direct examination, Officer Little stated that as Sergeant Leary's police line moved northward on Roosevelt Street, "we came in contact with a gentleman that refused to leave the area." (R-105) The following dialogue between the Assistant State's Attorney and Officer Little represents his description of the "contact" and the arrest. . . .

[At this point the brief quotes verbatim from a section of Officer Little's testimony.]

Cross-examination of Officer Little probed the circumstances of the arrest in more detail. Officer Little admitted that when he came up to Peter Black, "Mr. Black was already being confronted by two or three county policemen at this time." (R-113) Officer Little also admitted that the county policemen already had their hands on Peter Black, preventing him from any movement. (R-114) Officer Little further testified that he had no conversation with the Defendant other than telling him that he was under arrest. (R-122)

The "county policemen" were not called as witnesses to testify against Peter Black or identified by name. Yet, these county police officers are crucial to the sufficiency of the State's burden of proving that Peter Black was guilty of obstructing the orders of Sergeant Leary. . . .

All three defense witnesses who testified regarding the arrest of Peter Black explain the incident in similar terms. Peter Black testified that he did not hear any order to disperse. (R-356) He also testified that he did not hear any police officer giving orders over a bullhorn. (R-355) In this respect, Peter's testimony is entirely consistent with Sergeant Leary, who admitted that he did not use a bullhorn to give the initial order to disperse. The Defendant further testified that he was approached by a group of officers who told him to move. (R-357) In response, the Defendant asked them where he was supposed to move. (R-357) One of the police officers also told Peter to get off the street. (R-357) Peter stated that he moved off the street (Roosevelt Street) onto the sidewalk on the grassy area between the curb and the sidewalk. (R-369) He was then told by another police officer to move. (R-369) Peter Black then testified that he again asked "move where?" (R-370) He further stated that the verbal exchange between the group of police officers, presumably the "county policemen" re-

ferred to by Officer Little, lasted "ten or fifteen seconds at the most."
(R-359)

The testimony of Lynn Allen, who was standing with Peter Black,
is consistent. She testified that she did not hear any order to disperse.
(R-310) She also testified that a group of police officers came up to
them and told them to get on the sidewalk. (R-314) She and Peter
Black asked the police officers what they were supposed to do. (R-
328) Lynn also testified that the police officers pushed them with
their clubs shortly before the police officers grabbed Peter Black. (R-
328) Lynn further testified that after the police officers grabbed
Peter Black he held onto the telephone pole. (R-316)

The testimony of Suzanne Little, who was standing with Peter
Black and Lynn Allen, is consistent in all material aspects to the other
defense testimony. Suzanne testified that the police officers who approached them told them to get off the street and move on. (R-292)
She further testified that Peter Black was talking to the police officers
and asked them why they had to move since they were on public
property. (R-292)

It is important to note that the testimony presented by the defense
witnesses indicates that Peter Black questioned the police officers
and asked them why and where he should move. The Supreme
Court has stated that mere argument with a policeman about the
validity of an arrest or other police action does not constitute resist-
ing or obstructing within the proscription of the statute. People v.
Roby, 49 Ill. 2d 392, 240 N.E.2d 595, *cert. denied,* 393 U.S. 1083
(1968). Officer Little testified that Peter Black was "unwilling to
move" and "refused to leave the area." However, he admits that
other police officers had already detained Peter when he arrived. He
also admits that he had no conversation with the Defendant other
than to tell him he was under arrest. None of the other police officers
testified against Peter.

In summary, the evidence against Peter Black taken in its totality
does not prove that the Defendant knowingly resisted or obstructed
Sergeant Leary's order to disperse.

At other times, the argument focuses on interpretation of a particular case, statute, or constitutional provision. In these cases the paralegal
must use the techniques discussed in Chapter 3. If a statute or constitutional provision is involved, one should use the plain meaning, legislative
history, and contextual analysis approaches to build as strong an argument as possible. If case law is involved, one should emphasize the extent
to which factual situations involved in favorable cases are analogous to
facts of the case being appealed. When cases are unfavorable, one should
emphasize the extent to which the situations are not analogous. One
must remember also the difference between mandatory authority and
persuasive authority.

In the case of Falco v. Bates the police had been holding a friend of
Bates (named Wallraven) and had threatened to arrest this friend if he
failed to pay a motel bill he owed to the Falco corporation. Bates had
written a check to the motel on the basis of the friend's promise to repay

him the next morning, and the police had then released the friend.
When Wallraven did not pay him the money, Bates stopped payment.
The corporation then sued Bates. The trial court found in Falco's favor
and Bates appealed. The following examples of arguments center on
interpreting precedent cases.

Interpreting a Favorable Precedent

A VALID CONSIDERATION OR AN ESTOPPEL CANNOT
BE FOUNDED UPON CIRCUMSTANCES THAT SHOW
THE USE OF CRIMINAL PROCESSES TO COLLECT A
PRIVATE INDEBTEDNESS.

Clearly, the plaintiff initiated the actions which resulted in the
apprehension of Wallraven and his request for help. The record
shows that the defendant, Bates, was the second party who gave a
check to Wallraven while he was in the custody of a police officer.
The law is quite clear on the use of the criminal process in obtaining
payment of private indebtedness. The principle is examined in
Shenk v. Phelps, 6 Ill. App. 612 (1880). Shenk v. Phelps presents a
case with a fact situation similar to the case at bar. The appellant's
son had obtained credit through false statements. A warrant for the
arrest of Mr. Shenk's son was procured and the arrest was made by a
deputized detective working for the creditor. The accused was not
taken before the justice of the peace who issued the warrant, but held
at the office of the detective agency. He was released upon Shenk's
promise to pay the funds fraudulently obtained by his son. Shenk
was sued on the note when he refused to pay. The court reversed a
decision for the creditor, ruling that the consideration for the note
constituted compounding a crime and was therefore void.

The Shenk court's ruling that the plaintiff's instructions to the
jury were improper is instructive. The creditor offered the following
instruction:

If the jury finds from the evidence that the defendant executed
the note in question, knowing at the time of the execution of
the same that he was executing a note, and for the amount,
and payable as shown by the same, that he voluntarily assumed
the debt or debts of his son, and understood the effect of what
he was doing, and if the jury finds from the evidence, that the
consideration for said note, as between the plaintiffs and defendant, was the assignment to said defendant of the accounts
against his son, and they were so assigned, and that at the time
of the giving of said note, the defendant had notes due the said
son in his possession or control, then the assigning of said
accounts was a good and valid consideration, and the jury
should find for the defendants.

The court continued:

All that is said in this instruction may have been true and still
the plaintiffs would not be entitled to recover if the jury further believed from the evidence that the defendant was induced to execute the note by an illegal use of the criminal
process. Shenk v. Phelps, 6 Ill. App. 618 (1880).

The court addressed directly the issue of equitable estoppel:

> The court (below) seems to have worked the principle of an equitable estoppel in order to give effect to a contract tainted with illegality. It was, in effect, saying the plaintiff has procured the execution of a contract by illegal means, and through an abuse of the criminal process of the State: but because the defendant has not returned so much of the consideration as he actually received, the plaintiff shall have a verdict. The cases are numerous to the effect that where a contract is void on the ground of public policy or against a statute, any attempt to enforce it will fail whenever the illegality appears — and the circumstances that one party has failed to perform his part of the agreement cannot operate as a waiver of such illegality. Shenk v. Phelps, 6 Ill. App. 619 (1880).

Distinguishing an Unfavorable Precedent

THE AFFIRMATIVE DEFENSE OF COMPOUNDING A CRIME DOES NOT HAVE TO BE PROVED BEYOND A REASONABLE DOUBT IN ALL CASES.

The contention that when a defense of compounding a crime is tendered the crime of compounding must be proven beyond a reasonable doubt must be dealt with. Zimmerman Ford, Inc. v. Cheney, 132 Ill. App. 2d 871, 271 N.E.2d 686 (1971); Rudolph Stecher Brewing Co. v. Carr, 194 Ill. App. 32 (1915); Germania Fire Ins. Co. v. Klewer, 129 Ill. 612 (1889); Grimes v. Hilliary, 150 Ill. 141 (1894).

In Zimmerman Ford, Inc. v. Cheney, a grandmother of a youthful purchaser of an automobile claimed lack of consideration for her co-signature because she thought her signing would prevent prosecution of the buyer. Her grandson had forged her original signature in order to purchase the automobile. She signed a replacement contract. Indicating that there was a sufficient consideration in the forbearance in repossessing the automobile to support the action on the grandmother's signature, the court stated:

> Plaintiff was solely interested in recovering its loss and bargained for that purpose. She only thought it would prevent prosecution which is distinguishable in legal effect from finding that a creditor has promised to forbear from prosecuting a crime. . . .
>
> Moreover, proof has to be beyond a reasonable doubt: Rudolph Stecher Brewing Co. v. Carr, 194 Ill. App. 32, 37 (1915).

In the *Stecher* case the defendant, Carr, had endorsed a check that his client, Sarafin, presented to his creditor at the preliminary court proceeding against Sarafin, who had received $502 in goods from the creditor through a so-called confidence scheme. Sarafin was then admitted to personal recognizance bond and proceeded to stop payment on the check. Carr was sued as the endorser and tendered the defense of compounding of a crime. The suit was on the common counts alleging the delivery of goods. Noting the emphatic denial of

the defendant's charge by the plaintiff and corroboration of the plaintiff's testimony the court stated this rule:

> We think that the law is well settled in this state that where the defense of compounding a crime is relied upon to defeat the plaintiff's action that then the burden is upon the defendant to prove the criminal offense alleged beyond a reasonable doubt, and that it is not sufficient that it be proven by a preponderance of the evidence. Germania Fire Ins. Co. v. Klewer, 129 Ill. 599; Grimes v. Hilliary, 150 Ill. 146; Rudolph Stecher Brewing Co. v. Carr, 194 Ill. 34. . . .

It is important to note that the criminal act alleged in *Germania,* relied upon by the *Stecher* court, is quite different from the compounding of a crime. In *Germania* the act of burning down a building was alleged to defeat a claim on an insurance policy. That seems to be a more substantive crime, and the allegation and proof of it of greater consequence, than an agreement between two parties to a suit to drop a criminal prosecution. Proof of the crime defeats the entire contractual obligation. In the present case, the defense of compounding a crime does not defeat the underlying obligation. Wallraven still owes Falco. Clearly, when one party emphatically denies the compounding agreement, very likely a secretive affair, the extraordinary burden of proof would be impossible to achieve, making the defense practically useless. Illinois law has, in fact, despite the above cases, not followed this rule; most such cases, as the one at bar, are distinguishable from the harsh rule of *Zimmerman* and *Stecher.* It will be found that the cases requiring proof beyond a reasonable doubt of the crime offered as defense to a contractual action have these things in common:

1. There is a clear contractual liability which but for the criminal act would be owing.
2. The wrong-doer himself is a party to the note or security in issue.
3. There is an alternative consideration upon which to base recovery.
4. There is no other public policy reason for denying recovery.

Applying these distinguishing characteristics to the *Zimmerman* case, for example, it can be seen:

1. That there was clearly an outstanding debt owing on the automobile sold by plaintiff to the defendant's grandson;
2. That the grandmother became a co-signer for the grandson after she ratified her forged signature;
3. That consideration existed in the plaintiff's forbearing to repossess the automobile;
4. That no public policy issue was raised aside from the sole issue of compounding. . . .

Thus is appears that there are more basic equitable and public policy reasons for the court to grant or deny recovery in the compounding cases and that the plaintiff cannot find much refuge in the few cases stating that proof beyond a reasonable doubt is required before a defense of compounding a crime can be sustained.

The brief should provide adequate, but not excessive, documentation of its assertion of legal principles. When widely accepted general legal principles are stated, two or three case citations are adequate. If they are widely recognized, they are unlikely to be contested and need no further documentation. When the principle is more likely to be contested, the brief should emphasize recent cases and those that are mandatory authority. Where persuasive authority is involved, it is better to cite cases from several different jurisdictions than to include only a long list of cases from the same jurisdiction.

When a citation follows the statement of a legal principle, it is assumed that the holding of that case supports the principle stated. If the principle being referred to or the quotation being used represents dictum[7] or comes from a concurring or dissenting opinion, it should be identified as such in parentheses following the citation. For example,

> National League of Cities v. Usery, 426 U.S. 833, 860 (1976) (Brennan, J., dissenting),

means that the quotation or principle appears on page 860 of Mr. Justice Brennan's dissenting opinion.

> Moose Lodge No. 107 v. Irvis, 407 U.S. 163, 169 (1972) (dictum),

means that the principle enunciated on that page was a form of dictum. If the holding of a case is not clear, the word *semble* should be placed in parentheses after the cite. If the holding of the case being cited is contrary to the principle being presented, its citation should be introduced by the *contra* or *but see*. The term *cf.* means that while it is not a direct holding, the case is somewhat analogous and that it does offer some support for the principle being cited.

The brief also should emphasize the consequences of the court's decision. If a decision against the client will affect a larger group of people, that effect should be emphasized in the brief. Where possible the brief should argue that justice and fairness require a decision supporting the client and that such a decision is consistent with the general public interest. It is much easier to win a judge's support for your legal arguments if the judge can be convinced that justice and fairness will be best served by the result. The following example from the appellant's brief in the mobile home case illustrates an argument centering on a sense of equity and general concerns of public policy.

> A further policy consideration must be made. The defendant was not only the seller of the mobile home but the lessor. If the lessor is

---

7. It is a comment not essential to the decision of the case at hand.

permitted to represent to purchasers that they can live at the mobile
home court until the agreement is paid in full, but later evicts them,
the purchaser may be forced to not only remove himself, but be
faced with the costly removal of a mobile home. Worse yet, the
purchaser may be required to move his person without being allowed
to remove the mobile home, resulting in a forfeiture of his rights
under the purchase agreement. In the instant case, the seller violated
a health statute requiring adequate supplies of water and constructively evicted prior to the actual eviction. Should the seller-lessor
be allowed to profit from his wrongdoing? The seller could gain both
the payments and the mobile home by simply evicting the purchaser,
forcing the purchaser to find a new site for the mobile home and
paying transportation costs, a burden that the purchaser may not be
able to pay.

In the instant case, the purchaser paid all sums when due and was
not in default under provisions of the agreement. The case might be
different if the purchaser were in default under the lease or the
principal payments. In this case, the seller-landlord received all payments, rents, and the mobile home. Seller-landlord has coun-
terclaimed for the balance of the purchase price.

A decision in favor of defendant-appellee would work a serious
hardship on purchasers of mobile homes. Since many of these homes
are located in mobile home parks, and it is believed that seller-
landlord relationships as in this case are not uncommon, purchasers
will be left to the mercy of landlord-sellers who may control the
environment in such a manner as to constructively evict contract
purchasers, thus reselling the same chattel. If the vendees are unable
to recover the amortization and improvements on the chattel a seller-
landlord may be able to unjustly enrich himself at the cost of the
innocent purchasers.

The situation becomes acute with the lack of legal remedies available in this relatively new area of single family dwelling. If the plaintiff had purchased a house without the land, choosing to rent the
land, and the seller committed acts that interfered with vendee's
rights as a tenant and in fact evicted the tenant and told him to
remove (or not remove) the house, would the vendee have any remedy? This situation could easily arise in a commercial setting where
complex tax laws favor leasing of nondepreciable assets (such as a
building). There is no evidence that a "mobile " home is any more or
less mobile than a small building, and, indeed, an older mobile home
may be more difficult to move than a well-constructed building.

e. Summing It Up

After the argument has been drafted, revised, tightened, and still
further revised, the paralegal should begin work on the conclusion section. This section consists of a concise summary of the nature of the
errors that were made by the lower court and a request that the appellate
court take some specific action to change the lower court's decision.
Examples of conclusion sections follow:

People v. Black
The evidence against both Defendants was insufficient as a matter
of law to prove that the Defendants were guilty of a violation of

Chapter 38, section 31-1 of the Illinois Revised Statutes. The convictions should therefore be reversed. At the least, judgment should be reversed and the Defendants granted a new trial.

Falco v. Bates

The plaintiff claims that the defendant must pay the motel bill of a former customer because it accepted a check from the defendant in payment of that debt and in reliance thereon allowed the customer to leave its premises. All the testimony showed that the debtor was brought to plaintiff's premises by an officer of the local police department. In asserting that consideration for the check was the release of the debtor the plaintiff admits use of the criminal process in securing payment of a private indebtedness that violates the clear public policy of the State of Illinois. Having tendered no evidence of an alternative consideration or justification of the method of obtaining custody over its debtor, the plaintiff's action against the defendant must fail for voidness of the consideration and the decision of the lower court granting recovery to the plaintiff be reversed.

f. Table of Authorities

Most appellate courts require some type of summary of the legal authorities cited in the brief. One common format lists all constitutional provisions, statutes, cases, and other types of authorities under generalized categories. In this system all the citations to federal constitutional provisions are grouped together. Federal statutes are cited in one group while state statutes are cited in another section. Municipal ordinances are grouped in still another category. Similarly, Supreme Court cases are separated from Circuit Court of Appeals decisions, and state cases are grouped by state. References to law review articles, encyclopedias, and other sources are grouped under a miscellaneous references section.

Within each category the provisions of the constitutions and statutes are arranged according to the order in which they appear in the constitution itself or in the code. Court opinions, on the other hand, are usually arranged within each subcategory by alphabetical order. The citations should be accurate and complete. While United States Supreme Court cases are only cited to the official United States Reports, state decisions should include reference to the unofficial and official citations.[8] This table of authorities should then provide cross-references back to the pages of the brief on which each citation appears. This allows the reader to turn directly to all discussions of any particular case or statute.

As an alternative to the table just described, some appellate courts require that the citations be arranged on the basis of subpoints of the argument that they support. This approach was used in the following excerpts from the points and authorities section of the appellant's brief in Falco v. Bates.

---

8. This occurs because official reporters are usually not readily available to persons in other states. The judges and other attorneys are most likely to be consulting West's regional reporters.

THE AFFIRMATIVE DEFENSE OF COMPOUNDING A CRIME
~~DOES NOT HAVE TO BE PROVED BEYOND A REASONABLE~~
DOUBT IN ALL CASES.

Zimmerman Ford, Inc. v. Cheney, 132 Ill. App. 2d 871, 271 N.E.2d
    682 (1971)
Rudolph Stecher Brewing Co. v. Carr, 194 Ill. App. 32 (1915)
Germania Fire Ins. Co. v. Klewer, 129 Ill. 612 (1889)
Grimes v. Hilliary, 150 Ill. 141 (1894)
Good Hope State Bank v. Kline, 303 Ill. App. 381, 25 N.E.2d 425
    (1940)
Shenk v. Phelps, 6 Ill. App. 612 (1880)
Williamsen v. Jernberg, 99 Ill. App. 3d 37, 240 N.E.2d 758 (1968)

IN ASSERTING THE AFFIRMATIVE DEFENSE OF COM-
POUNDING A CRIME IT IS NOT NECESSARY TO SHOW AN
ACTUAL WRITTEN CHARGE IN THE PROSECUTION
WHICH WAS DISMISSED.

Good Hope State Bank v. Kline, 303 Ill. App. 381, 25 N.E.2d 425
    (1940)

AN EQUITABLE ESTOPPEL CANNOT BE APPLIED WHERE
THE FACTS SHOW THE PARTY ASSERTING THE ESTOPPEL
OBTAINED HIS ADVANTAGE BY ILLEGAL MEANS.

Mills v. Susanka, 394 Ill. 439, 68 N.E.2d 904 (1946)
Ptaszek v. Konczal, 7 Ill. 2d 145, 130 N.E.2d 257 (1955)

POLICE CANNOT OBTAIN LAWFUL CUSTODY OF A PER-
SON EXCEPT AS PRESCRIBED BY STATUTE.

Ill. Rev. Stat., ch. 38, Sec. 107-2
Ill. Rev. Stat., ch. 38, Sec. 107-6
Ill. Rev. Stat., ch. 38, Sec. 107-14

When statutes or provisions of a constitution are involved, some
courts also require that the brief reproduce the text of the specific provisions in question. When such statutes sections are required, they are
usually located at the front, near the authorities section.

g. Assembling Appendexes, Table of Contents

The appellant's brief usually includes several appendexes of various supporting documents. Typically included are parts of the pleadings, sections of the trial transcript, exhibits introduced as evidence, and
jury instructions. These materials should be arranged in a logical order
and then given consecutive numbers that tie in with the brief itself.

Depending on the court involved, the paralegal may also be asked
to prepare a table of contents. Such a table provides an overview of the
entire document and easy reference to specific parts. It should include
references to the pages on which the main sections begin (such as issues
presented, statement of facts) and the subdivisions of the argument sec-

tion. This will provide the judges with a good overview of the structure of the argument itself (much as a table of points and authorities does).

h. Preparation of the Cover Sheet

The one remaining section of an appellate brief is the cover page. Here again, the brief must be carefully prepared to meet the standards of each particular appellate court. In general, the cover page includes the name of the appellate court, the names of the parties, the docket number, the name of the court from which the appeal is coming, and the name and address of the lawyer submitting the brief. It should also contain a clear designation as to whether it is the appellant's or the appellee's brief and whether it is an initial brief or a reply brief. In designating the parties, it is also wise to indicate not only which one is bringing the appeal but which one was the plaintiff or defendant at the trial court level. In some jurisdictions a request for oral argument also appears on the cover sheet. The following cover sheet is typical for a brief filed in an Illinois appellate court:

Exhibit 9.6 Sample Cover Sheet for an Illinois Appellate Court

---

NO. 13444

IN THE APPELLATE COURT
OF THE STATE OF ILLINOIS
FOURTH DISTRICT

TIM and KASSANDRA ASTOR,
        Plaintiff-Appellants,
 	
v.
 	
DAVID CURRY,
        Defendant-Appellee.
	Appeal from the Circuit Court
	of the Eleventh Judicial Circuit
	McLean County, Illinois
	NO. 77-LM-403
	Honorable James A. Knecht
	Judge Presiding

BRIEF AND ARGUMENTS OF PLAINTIFF-APPELLANTS

John J. Pavlou
STUDENTS' LEGAL SERVICES
Illinois State University
225 North University, Suite 200
Normal, Illinois 61761
Attorney for Plaintiff-Appellants

JOHN J. TIELSCH
Of Counsel

ORAL ARGUMENT REQUESTED

---

3. Format and Contents of Appellee's Brief

Although the appellee's brief generally follows the same format as the appellant's, it need not define the issues or characterize the facts in the same way that the appellant did. The appellee's argument section should respond to each of the points raised by the appellant, but those points do not have to be treated in the same sequential order. Instead, the appellee should arrange the points and authorities in the order that gives them their maximum persuasive impact. As with the appellant's brief, each segment of the brief should be started on a separate page.

In the sample appellee's brief that follows (Exhibit 9.7), note that the author of the brief did not include a statement of the facts because he did not disagree with the way they had been stated in the appellant's brief. Defendant Dennis Hale was charged with the offense of aggravated battery in violation of section 12-4(b)(6) of the Illinois criminal code. The trial court judge dismissed the charges on the basis that the information[9] failed to allege either the offense of aggravated battery or simple battery. The information in question specifically charged that Hale had "willfully, unlawfully and knowingly without legal justification, made physical contact of an insulting and provoking nature with Elijah Rusk, by striking him with his fist, knowing said Elijah Rusk to be a peace officer engaged in the execution of his official duties." The state then appealed this trial judge's decision.[10]

---

9. In Illinois a defendant can be formally charged with a felony through indictment returned by a grand jury or an information returned by the prosecuting attorney.

10. Although the double jeopardy clause prevents a state from appealing a not guilty verdict in a criminal trial, it does not prevent the state from appealing a judge's decision to invalidate an indictment or information.

Exhibit 9.7 Sample Brief for Appellee

NO. 14579

IN THE APPELLATE COURT
OF THE STATE OF ILLINOIS
FOURTH DISTRICT

PEOPLE OF THE STATE OF ILLINOIS,
 	
      Plaintiff-Appellant,
 	
v.
 	
DENNIS HALE,
      Defendant-Appellee.
	Appeal from the Circuit Court of the Eleventh Judicial Circuit McLean County, Illinois No. 77-CF-147
	Honorable Wayne C. Townley, Jr. Judge Presiding

BRIEF AND ARGUMENT OF DEFENDANT-APPELLEE

Fred B. Moore
LIVINGSTON, BARGER,
BRANDT, SLATER &
SCHROEDER
204 Unity Building
Bloomington, Illinois 61701
Telephone: (309) 828-5281

ORAL ARGUMENT REQUESTED

[BEGIN NEW PAGE]

POINTS AND AUTHORITIES

A.

A DIFFERENT STANDARD IS APPLIED FOR REVIEWING THE SUFFICIENCY OF AN INFORMATION OR INDICTMENT IN THE AP-PELLATE COURT FROM THE STANDARDS FOR REVIEWING THE INFORMATION OR INDICTMENT WHEN THE ISSUE IS RAISED IN THE TRIAL COURT.

People v. Pujoue, 61 Ill. App. 2d 335, 335 N.E.2d 437 (1975)

People v. Haltom, 37 Ill. App. 3d 1059, 347 N.E.2d 502 (1st Dist. 1976)

People v. Pfeiffer, 354 N.E.2d 678 (3d Dist. 1976)

DISCUSSION OF AN ISSUE NOT NECESSARY FOR THE DECI-SION OF AN APPELLATE COURT IS NOT BINDING ON THAT AP-PELLATE COURT OR INFERIOR COURTS.

People *ex rel.* Scott v. Chicago Park District, 66 Ill. 2d 65 (1976)

Exhibit 9.7 *(continued)*

B.

THE DOCTRINE OF STARE DECISIS DOES NOT PRECLUDE REEXAMINATION OF A QUESTION PREVIOUSLY DECIDED BY THE APPELLATE COURT.

Nudd v. Matsoukas, 7 Ill. 2d 608, 131 N.E.2d 525 (1956)

Bradley v. Fox, 7 Ill. 2d 106, 129 N.E.2d 699 (1955)

A STATUTE SHOULD NOT BE SO CONSTRUED TO RENDER ANY WORDS, CLAUSE OR SENTENCE SUPERFLUOUS OR MEANINGLESS AND IN ASCERTAINING THE LEGISLATIVE INTENT OF A STATUTE THE COURT MUST GIVE MEANING AND EFFECT TO ALL OF ITS PROVISIONS.

Peacock v. Judge's Retirement System of Illinois, 10 Ill. 2d 498, 140 N.E.2d 684, 686 (1957)

Sternberg Dredging Co. v. Estate of Sternberg, 10 Ill. 2d 328, 140 N.E. 2d 125, 128-129 (1957)

INSULTING AND PROVOKING CONDUCT OR CONTACT DIRECTED TOWARDS A POLICE OFFICER IS NOT A BASIS FOR THE CHARGE OF AGGRAVATED BATTERY, ABSENT SOME ALLEGATION OF HARM.

People v. Nance, 26 Ill. App. 3d 182, 324 N.E.2d 652 (5th Dist. 1975)

People v. Crane, 3 Ill. App. 3d 716, 279 N.E.2d 134 (5th Dist. 1971)

People v. Benhoff, 51 Ill. App. 3d 651 (5th Dist. 1977)

People v. Haltom, 37 Ill. App. 3d 1059, 347 N.E.2d 502 (1st Dist. 1976)

THE VARIOUS PROVISIONS OF CHAPTER 38, SECTION 12-4 WERE INTENDED TO REMEDY VARIOUS SPECIFIC SITUATIONS.

People v. Cole, 47 Ill. App. 3d 775, 362 N.E.2d 432 (4th Dist. 1977)

Smith-Hurd Annotated Statute, Chapter 38, Section 12-4, Committee Comments 1961 and Historical Notes

[BEGIN NEW PAGE]

ARGUMENT

A.

The State's argument seems to consist of two parts. The first is that the decision in People v. Meints, 41 Ill. App. 3d 215, 355

N.E.2d 125 (4th Dist. 1976), should have controlled the Trial Court's decision in this case and that the Trial Court is obligated to follow that decision, since it does come from the Fourth District.

This Court in the *Meints* decision did spend a substantial amount of time discussing whether or not an allegation that a party who was battered was harmed, would be necessary to state a charge of aggravated battery. This Court expressed a view in that decision that is contrary to opinions expressed by the First and Fifth District Appellate Courts in other cases. People v. Nance, 26 III. App. 3d 182, 324 N.E.2d 652 (5th Dist. 1975); People v. Crane, 3 III. App. 3d 716, 279 N.E.2d 134 (5th Dist. 1971); People v. Benhoff, 51 III. App. 3d 651 (5th Dist. 1977); People v. Haltom, 37 III. App. 3d 1059, 347 N.E.2d 502 (1st Dist. 1976).

It is the Defendant's position that the question of whether or not an allegation of harm is necessary for a charge of aggravated battery, as opposed to an allegation of contact of an insulting or provoking nature, was not necessary for the decision in the *Meints* case. This Court correctly set forth the standard that was necessary to uphold the indictment in the *Meints* case. This Court concluded that "the indictment was sufficient to fully apprise Defendant of the offense charged, enabled him to prepare a defense, and will protect him from future prosecution for the same conduct." 355 N.E.2d 125 at 129.

This Court was not required to decide whether or not the charge, as it was made against the Defendant in *Meints,* set forth the nature and elements of the offense charged. Where the issue of the correctness of the charge is first raised on appeal, the standard used in *Meints* is correct. Since the issue is raised in the Trial Court in this case, the *Meints* decision is inappropriate so far as being authority on the point. The discussion of whether or not the allegation of bodily harm was needed was not necessary to the decision in *Meints* and, therefore, amounted to dicta. This is what the trial judge in the present case referred to as an "aberration" in the *Meints* decision. He was not referring to the fact that this Court's opinion was inconsistent with other opinions. Instead he indicated that this Court's opinion was "an aberration which was a result of the fact that the Defendant . . . pleaded guilty." (R. Vol. II, 18) In other words, the Trial Court correctly recognized, as it must be assumed this Court recognized, that when a party raises the issue for the first time on appeal, the standard for reviewing the information or indictment differs from the standard used when the issue is raised in the Trial Court.

The Supreme Court of this State and other Appellate Courts have held that a more strict standard, requiring the information or indictment to set forth the nature and elements of the offense charged, is the standard to be applied where, as in the instant case, the information is challenged in the Trial Court. People v. Pujoue, 61 III. App. 2d 335, 335 N.E.2d 437 (1975); People v. Haltom,

Exhibit 9.7 *(continued)*

37 Ill. App. 3d 1059, 347 N.E.2d 502 (1st Dist. 1976); People v. Pfeiffer, 354 N.E.2d 678 (3d Dist. 1976).

Any portion of the *Meints* decision which discussed whether a statement of "harm" in the charge of aggravated battery was required should be treated as dicta, or at least inapplicable to the charge against Dennis Hale. In this case we are not determining whether or not the information was sufficient to fully apprise him of the offense charged, enabling him to prepare a defense to protect him from future prosecution for the same conduct. Here we are concerned with whether or not the nature and elements of the offense charged have been properly set forth. Discussion in *Meints* of matters that are not necessary for the decision is neither binding on this Appellate Court or upon the Trial Court. People *ex rel.* Scott v. Chicago Park District, 66 Ill. 2d 65 (1976).

B.

The second part of the State's argument is that the charge in this case properly sets for the nature and elements of the offense of aggravated battery. Even if this Court feels the *Meints* decision has answered the question, they are not precluded by the doctrine of stare decisis from reexamining the question and reaching a conclusion contrary to the conclusions reached in the discussion in *Meints.* Nudd v. Matsoukas, 7 Ill. 2d 608, 131 N.E.2d 525 (1956); and Bradley v. Fox, 7 Ill. 2d 106, 129 N.E.2d 699 (1955).

In determining the meaning of the term "harm" as it is used in Chapter 38, Section 12-4(b)(6), rules of statutory construction have been established by the Supreme Court of this State. Those rules include the rule of construction that "a statute should be so construed, if possible, that no word, clause or sentence is rendered superfluous or meaningless. . . ." Peacock v. Judge's Retirement System of Illinois, 10 Ill. 2d 498, 140 N.E.2d 684, 686 (1957), and that "in ascertaining the legislative intent of a statute, this Court is bound to give meaning and effect to all of its provisions, and they must be construed together." Sternberg Dredging Co. v. Estate of Sternberg, 10 Ill. 2d 328, 140 N.E.2d 125, 128-129 (1957). If those standards are seriously applied with any thought, it seems almost impossible to say that "harm" is synonymous with "battered." Those two terms are used in Sections 12-4(b)(6) and 12-4(b)(8) and in applying the rules of construction some separate meaning must be given to each. The guidance of the Supreme Court is being ignored if those are treated as being synonymous.

The State argues that in order to carry out the intent of the legislature, their intepretation of the statute must be followed. However, that assumes that the legislature intended to mean the same thing in each subsection of the statute in question but did not use the same language. This Court has recognized in other cases that the various provisions of Chapter 38, Section 12-4 have been intended

to remedy various specific situations. People v. Cole, 47 Ill. App. 3d 775, 362 N.E.2d 432 (4th Dist. 1977). The various subsections were not adopted at the same time and they were not intended to correct the same condition. Obviously, there is no unanimous underlying legislative purpose for the entire statute. Smith-Hurd Annotated, SHA Chapter 38, Section 12-4, Committee Comments-1961 and Historical Notes. There is no basis for saying that the legislature intended the same meaning should be applied to terms that are on their face different. It is quite plausible and believable that the legislature felt that contact causing harm of a physical type to a police officer or peace officer is a much more serious matter than contact that does not cause harm but is merely provocative or insulting. Nor is it proper for this Court to say that contact that is insulting or provoking to a peace officer engaged in his official duties is more serious or less serious than the same contact or conduct directed toward a private citizen but made in a public place or on a public way.

If the legislature had intended that insulting or provocative physical contact with a peace officer should amount to a felony of aggravated battery rather than a misdemeanor of simple battery, they could have so stated. However, the terms actually employed by the legislature may not be glossed over only because it is felt by this Court or this State that acts of harassment or interference directed against persons in positions of authority constitute a greater social evil than similar acts directed in public places against private citizens. People v. Benhoff, 51 Ill. App. 3d 651 (5th Dist. 1977). The decision of what is to become a felony and what is to be a misdemeanor is one that is left for the legislature and not for the Appellate Courts.

The Supreme Court of this State has not ruled on the question raised in this appeal. It is apparent that decisions from the First and Fifth Districts in the *Nance, Crane, Benhoff,* and *Haltom* cases held that a charge such as that placed against Dennis Hale is not sufficient when objection is raised in the Trial Court. As has been mentioned before, the *Meints* case involved objection that was raised in the Appellate Court for the first time. The same is true of other cases cited by the State in its brief. The two other Fourth District decisions cited by the State, People v. Lutz, 10 Ill. Dec. 587, 367 N.E.2d 1353 (4th Dist. 1977); and People v. Hurlbert, 41 Ill. App. 3d 300, 354 N.E.2d 652 (4th Dist. 1976), this Court decided the cases without the necessity of determining whether or not the nature and elements of the offense were properly set forth. Again in those cases there was discussion that is in agreement with the decision in *Meints,* but the cases were decided on other grounds.

The Defendant urges this Court to follow the lead of the First and Fifth Appellate Court Districts in following the rules of construction set forth above. This Court should either treat the present case as one of first impression in the Fourth District and affirm the ruling of the Trial Court dismissing the charge of aggravated battery or

Exhibit 9.7 (continued)

reconsider its discussion in *Meints* and the subsequent cases in light of the directions set forth by the Supreme Court and the decisions of other Appellate Courts of this State.

[BEGIN NEW PAGE]
CONCLUSION

Wherefore the Defendant, Dennis Hale, respectfully requests that this Court affirm the ruling of the Trial Court dismissing the information.

Respectfully submitted,
Dennis Hale, Defendant-Appellee

By: Fred B. Moore
LIVINGSTON, BARGER,
   BRANDT, SLATER &
   SCHROEDER
204 Unity Building
Bloomington, Illinois 61701
Telephone: (309) 828-5281

Counsel for Defendant-Appellee

4. Format and Contents of Reply Briefs

After the appellee's brief has been filed, the appellant can file a reply brief that attempts to respond to the appellee's line of argument and any new authorities that may have been introduced. Only the cover sheet and argument section are usually contained in this reply brief. One must be sure, however, to concentrate the argument on rebutting the points presented by the adversary and not simply restating what already has been said in the original brief. The appellee can file a reply brief only in situations where there has been a cross-appeal.[11]

5. Briefs for Administrative Appeals

When appealing an unfavorable administrative decision to an administrative review panel, briefs are also prepared to convey the facts and arguments in the case. These briefs closely resemble those used in the appellate courts. The following example illustrates this type of brief.

---

11. A cross-appeal is brought by the appellee when one party is appealing one part of the lower court's decision and the other party is appealing a different part of the decision in the same case.

Exhibit 9.8 Sample Appeal to Social Security Administration for Benefits

UNITED STATES OF AMERICA
BEFORE THE DEPARTMENT OF HEALTH,
EDUCATION AND WELFARE
SOCIAL SECURITY ADMINISTRATION

In the matter of the
application of Ms. Elizabeth
Nelson for Disability
Insurance Benefits and ——No. 652-29-3186
Supplemental Security
Income

MEMORANDUM OF FACTS, LAW, AND AUTHORITY IN SUPPORT
OF CLAIMANT'S REQUEST FOR REMAND TO PRESIDING
OFFICER FOR THE TAKING OF ADDITIONAL EVIDENCE

This memorandum is submitted pursuant to 20 C.F.R. §404.948(b)
and appellant's written request of May 9, 1978. That the record be
left open for the submission of this memorandum and additional
medical information.

STATEMENT OF FACTS

Ms. Nelson is a forty-year-old widow, D.O.B. (10-20-37), with a
10th grade education.[1] She has worked primarily in bars and supper clubs as a waitress and bartender.[2] She does have some limited experience as a clerical worker.[3] She quit her last job on
October 13, 1977, because of a pain in her side, back, and leg.[4]
She suffered a seizure on October 15, 1977, and again on November 5, 1977. She was admitted to a hospital via the emergency
room for a diagnostic workup.[5] A peculiar brain scan was noted,
and she was sent for a C.I.T. scan at St. James Hospital in
Springfield, Illinois.[6] This scan indicated a meningioma in the left
parietal region.[7] Surgery to remove the tumor was performed on
November 22, 1977, by Dr. Lloyd Kissenger. It appeared successful
and he told Ms. Nelson to return in a year.[8]

Since her operation, she has been treated by Dr. Herman Greenburg. His notes indicate that on January 13, 1978, she could not

1. S.S.A. Form 16, Exhibit no. 1.
2. S.S.A. Form 401, Exhibit no. 13.
3. S.S.A. Form 401, Exhibit no. 13.
4. S.S.A. Form 401, Exhibit no. 12, and Dr. Greenburg's case notes of September
27, 1977, and October 11, 1977.
5. Dr. Greenburg's Admittance Notes, November 6, 1977.
6. Dr. Greenburg's Discharge Notes, November 8, 1977.
7. November 8, 1977, C.I.T. scan. Dr. James Andrews, St. James Hospital.
8. Exhibit no. 18, Dr. Kissenger's report.

Exhibit 9.8 *(continued)*

work.[9] On February 13, 1978, she was having seizures, had been weak, and unable to work.[10] On May 3rd, he notes that she was suffering from headaches, dizziness, and had a seizure approximately ten days before. He also notes that she was nervous and jittery. He increased both her prescriptions.[11] Since that time, Ms. Nelson has been unable to work. Her right arm is still so uncoordinated that she cannot use an ashtray. She cannot lift her arm above her head, nor hold pots and pans with her right hand. She has severe headaches from above the right eye to the temple area, and is so heavily medicated that she must sleep for three to four hours after she takes her medication.[12]

Dr. Greenburg's report of July 25, 1978, indicates that he is unsure of the causes of Ms. Nelson's epilepsy, and whether it is related to the meningioma. He found her to be severely nervous; with a "flattened and aggressive personality, and near paranoia."[13] He felt she could return to work, but suggested that "an examination by a neurologist would probably be in order."[14] When asked on July 25, 1978, whether a psychiatric consultation would be in order, Dr. Greenburg replied, "It would certainly help in evaluation."[15]

That these facts indicate the need for a remand by the appeals council to the presiding officer for the taking of additional evidence will be established in the paragraphs that follow.

PROCEDURAL HISTORY OF THE CASE

Ms. Nelson applied for O.A.S.D.I. benefits on November 10, 1977, prior to her first surgery.[16] She alleges an onset date of November 5, 1977, when she was hospitalized after a seizure, during which the tumor was discovered.[17] The application was denied on December 20, 1977, although no notice of denial was ever made part of the record. She appealed this decision, and was again denied benefits although no notice of reconsideration is part of the record.[18] The "D.D.T." of January 25, 1978, states that the denial of benefits was based on Dr. Greenburg's report of January 13, 1978, and a telephone contact of January 23, 1978.[19] No copies of that phone contact was now part of the record, nor were they at the

---

9. Exhibit no. 23, Dr. Greenburg.
10. Dr. Greenburg's case notes, February 13, 1978.
11. Dr. Greenburg's case notes, May 3, 1978.
12. Ms. Nelson's affidavit of August 7, 1978.
13. Dr. Greenburg's report of July 25, 1978.
14. Dr. Greenburg's report of July 25, 1978.
15. Smith-Greenburg letter of July 25, 1978.
16. Exhibit no. 1.
17. Exhibit no. 2.
18. Decision of March 20, 1978, "jurisdiction" section.
19. Exhibit no. 6.

time of Administrative Law Judge, A.L.J. Hanrahan's decision.[20] She requested a hearing on February 14, 1978, and waived her right to a hearing.[21] She was afraid to appear without an attorney, could not afford one, and was not advised of the availability of free legal services in the community by employees of the Social Security Administration.[22]

A.L.J. Richard Hanrahan made a decision on the record on March 20, 1978. Although the last piece of medical evidence he had from the claimant's treating physician stated Ms. Nelson was unable to work, A.L.J. Hanrahan determined that Ms. Nelson had not established that her impairment would last the required twelve months.[23]

The appellant requested review by the appeals council on May 5, 1978. An accompanying letter of May 9, 1978, outlined several reasons for requesting review, and requested an opportunity to submit additional evidence. With this memorandum are five pieces of additional evidence: two letters and a copy of case notes from her treating physician, and two affidavits.

It is the appellant's contention that the additional evidence is new and material, and indicates the need for consultative examinations by a psychiatrist and a neurologist. That the remand of the instant case to a presiding officer is appropriate will be established in the paragraphs which follow.

STATEMENT OF THE LAW

A. Jurisdiction

The regulations which pertain to the granting of a review by the appeals council (20 C.F.R. §404.947(a)(b)) read in part:

> (b) Where new and material evidence is submitted with the request for review, the entire record will be evaluated and review will be granted where the appeals council finds the presiding officer's action, finding, or conclusion is contrary to the weight of evidence currently of record.

The previous section contains two other criteria which allow review by the appeals council that apply to this case:

(1) There is an abuse of discretion by the presiding officer.

(2) There is an error of law.

B. Admissibility of New Evidence

New evidence may be admitted "where it appears to the appeals council that such evidence is relevant and material to an issue before it, thus may affect its decision." (20 C.F.R. §404.949(a))

---

20. Decision of March 20, 1978, exhibit list.
21. Decision of March 20, 1978.
22. Ms. Nelson's affidavit of August 3, 1978.
23. Decision of March 20, 1978, page 6.

Exhibit 9.8 *(continued)*

If the appeals council finds that additional evidence is necessary for a sound decision "it will remand the case to a presiding officer for the receipt of additional evidence, further proceedings, and a new decision. . . ." (20 C.F.R. §404.949(b))

C. The Taking of Additional Evidence on Remand to the Presiding Officer

> The appeals council may remand to the presiding officer for rehearing, receipt of evidence, and decision any case which it decides to review provided in 20 C.F.R. §404.947, and §404.947a . . . the presiding officer shall initiate such additional proceedings and take such action . . . as directed . . . and may take any additional action not inconsistent with the order of remand. (20 C.F.R. §404.950)

ARGUMENT

That the appeals council should remand the instant case for the taking of additional evidence will be established in the following paragraphs.

A. THE EVIDENCE SUBMITTED SUBSEQUENT TO THE REQUEST FOR REVIEW IS RELEVANT AND MATERIAL.

> A.L.J. Hanrahan stated in his decision of March 20, 1978, that: This decision should not be interpreted as to preclude a further consideration of a new claim . . . if it is substantiated by appropriate medical evidence *with* respect . . . to a continuance of disabling severity, actually or prospectively.[24]

The evidence submitted with this memorandum describes two types of problems. The first is that Ms. Nelson has not returned to work, has severe headaches, epileptic seizures which occur even with medication, continues to be uncoordinated and weak in her right arm, and is so heavily medicated that she sleeps a great deal.[25] Dr. Greenburg has suggested that a neurological examination "would probably be in order."[26]

The second and a new problem which surfaces in the new evidence is the question about Ms. Nelson's mental health. Dr. Greenburg stated that she was "nervous and jittery," and suffered from severe nervousness, "a tremendously flattened and aggressive personality, and near paranoia."[27]

24. Decision of March 20, 1978, page 6.
25. Dr. Greenburg's report of July 25, 1978; Ms. Nelson's affidavit of August 7, 1978.
26. Dr. Greenburg's report of July 25, 1978.
27. Dr. Greenburg's report of July 25, 1978.

408

The claimant's representative has also noted the problem. In his affidavit, it is noted that the claimant is depressed, cries during interviews, and believes her doctor is lying about her.[28] Dr. Greenburg, in his note of July 25th, notes that a psychiatric examination "would certainly help in evaluation."[29] The claimant also notes in her affidavit that she has been nervous and depressed.[30]

The new evidence is apparently contradictory. Dr. Greenburg states that Ms. Nelson could return to work. But, in the same letter, states she is having severe emotional problems,[31] and later he stated that she should be examined by a psychiatrist.[32] Ms. Nelson has not returned to work.[33]

Numerous cases have discussed the question of whether a remand is appropriate when new evidence is presented. The standard outlined in United States v. Dorgan, 522 F.2d 969 (9th Cir. 1975), was initially set out in Wray v. Folson, 166 F. Supp. 390 (W.D. Ark. 1958), wherein the court stated:

> In these circumstances, courts must not require such technical and cogent showing of good cause as would justify the granting of a new trial, but where no party will be prejudiced by the acceptance of additional evidence and the evidence offered bears directly and substantially on the matter in dispute.

When the issue becomes one where a psychiatric impairment is a possible disability which has never adequately been examined, the courts have routinely remanded cases to the secretary for a consultative psychiatric examination. McGee v. Weinberger, 518 F.2d 330 (5th Cir. 1975), Dodsworth v. Celebrezze, 349 F.2d 312 (5th Cir. 1965), Hassler v. Weinberger, 502 F.2d 172 (7th Cir. 1974).

B. THE ADMINISTRATIVE LAW JUDGE FAILED TO MAKE FULL INQUIRY INTO THE FACTS AND THERE ARE ERRORS OF LAW IN THE RECORD.

On January 13, 1978, Ms. Nelson presented Social Security with a note from her doctor which said she was unable to work.[34] The state agency responsible for making the determination contacted Dr. Greenburg by telephone on or about January 23, 1978. As a result the state agency determined that Ms. Nelson was not disabled because her impairment was not expected to last twelve months.[35] No copy of, notes of, or transcription from that call is currently available to the appellant nor was it available to A.L.J. Hanrahan

28. T. Smith's affidavit of August 7, 1978.
29. Smith-Greenburg letter of July 25, 1978.
30. Ms. Nelson's affidavit of August 7, 1978.
31. Dr. Greenburg's report of July 25, 1978.
32. Smith-Greenburg letter dated July 25, 1978.
33. Affidavit of Ms. Nelson, August 7, 1978.
34. Dr. Greenburg's statement, exhibit no. 22.
35. Exhibit no. 6.

Exhibit 9.8 *(continued)*

when he made his decision.[36] The appellant contends this deprives her of her due process right to cross-examine guaranteed by the courts, in that it assumes that a conversation did in fact take place between someone at the state agency and Dr. Greenburg, and that Dr. Greenburg did in fact state that Ms. Nelson would not be disabled for a period of twelve months or longer. As Chief Justice Hughes once wrote in Consolidated Edison Co. v. N.L.R.B., 305 U.S. at 230, "mere uncorroborated hearsay or rumor does not constitute substantial evidence." The Supreme Court distinguished that standard in the case of Richardson v. Perales, 409 U.S. 389 (1971). In that case involving the right of Social Security claimants to cross-examine reporting physicians, the court ruled at 397 that the procedural integrity and fundamental fairness of the administrative process was maintained *when the reporting physician's reports admitted into evidence* were based on *actual* examinations of the claimant, based on *personal consultation* and *personal examination.*

The process by which Dr. Greenburg's opinion on the duration of Ms. Nelson's disability was sought does not even begin to comport to the standard outlined in *Perales* (supra). Indeed, it is "material without a basis on evidence having rational probative force," which is inadmissible in administrative hearings. *Perales* 407 & 408. Yet, it was upon just such questionable evidence A.L.J. Hanrahan based his conclusion. In Rios v. Hackney, 294 F. Supp. 885 (N.D. Tex. 1974), the court held that this type of process violated the appellant's due process rights to cross-examination.

Confronted with the lack of actual evidence regarding the length of time Ms. Nelson would be unable to work, the A.L.J. had the "affirmative duty to inquire into all the facts at issue." Coulter v. Weinberger, 527 F.2d 224 (3d Cir. 1975). Social Security regulations state that: "[t]he Administrative Law Judge shall inquire fully into the matters at issue." 20 C.F.R. §404.927. "[A] duty devolves on the hearing examiner to scrupulously and conscientiously probe into, inquire of, and explore for all the relevant facts surrounding the alleged claim." Henning v. Gardner, 276 F. Supp. 662, 624-625 (N.D. Tex. 1967). The failure on the part of the A.L.J. to ask Doctor Greenburg for a statement regarding the severity and longevity of Ms. Nelson's impairment and to admit that statement into evidence does not comply with the standards outlined above, and is therefore an abuse of discretion, and an error in law.

THE APPELLANT'S CLAIM SHOULD BE REMANDED TO A PRESIDING OFFICER FOR TAKING OF ADDITIONAL EVIDENCE.

20 C.F.R. §404.949(a) states that where the appeals council has determined that additional evidence is needed to reach a sound

---

36. Exhibit list attached to decision.

decision, it will remand the case to a presiding officer . . . except where the appeals council can obtain the evidence more expediently. . . .

The issue before the administration is whether Ms. Nelson is currently disabled. Ms. Nelson does not believe she can return to work.[37] Her treating physician believes a consultative psychiatric and neurological examination would be appropriate.[38]

Therefore, there are questions as to whether this is a single or multiple impairment. It is important, therefore, that Ms. Nelson be given the right to a hearing in which she be able to present evidence as to the extent of her impairments.

Respectfully submitted,

Prairie State Legal Services, Inc.
219 North Main Street — Suite 500
Bloomington, Illinois 61701
TEL: (309) 827-5021

By: Thomas E. Smith
      Legal Assistant

37. Ms. Nelson's affidavit of August 7, 1978.
38. Dr. Greenburg's report of July 25, 1978.

H. SUMMARY

Paralegals must use good writing skills in a variety of different formats and must communicate substantive information in a clear and efficient manner.

Internal research memoranda are used to inform other members of the law firm's team of the results of legal research. Although the format may vary from one law office to another, the basic elements usually include identification and summary of relevant cases, statutes, and other sources of law; analysis of the probable application of these legal principles to specific facts of the case at hand; and evaluation of the strengths and weaknesses of several alternative courses of action.

Business letters may be used to exchange information, to seek a particular action, or simply to create a record for a case. Most offices include a specified format in their office manuals. As is the case with other specialized types of legal writing, organization and clarity are the keys to writing a good letter.

Documents such as contracts, wills, leases, and notes are called legal instruments. They represent attempts to preserve in written form the terms of an agreement. They are difficult to draft because the parties

must attempt to anticipate future events. When participating in the drafting of these types of documents, paralegals frequently use customized office forms or standardized forms published in handbooks and specialized formbooks.

The formats required for various types of pleadings are determined by the courts, and the paralegal must consult the appropriate court rules to be sure that the established requirements are being met. Formbooks provide examples of substantive wording of different types of complaints and motions. In drafting interrogatories, it is especially important to prepare questions that are sufficiently inclusive without being too vague.

External memoranda of law are similar to appellate briefs in that they are advocacy documents designed to convince a judge to rule a particular way on a legal issue. They are submitted to a trial judge or an administrative law judge in support of a motion or a point of law involved in the trial or hearing. It focuses primarily on the argument section and does not require such things as a table of contents or an appendix. The organization and pagination are also much less formal.

Before drafting the appellate brief, the paralegal usually begins by preparing a digest or abstract of the record. Such a document then becomes the basis for identifying the appealable issues and writing the fact section of the brief. Legal research must be undertaken to test the strength of potential issues and to ultimately provide the authorities to be cited in the brief.

The brief should be a persuasive document. Although it cannot alter or ignore important facts, the brief can present an interpretation of those facts most supportive of the client's position. The issues should be phrased to suggest the answer that favors the client's position. The argument section should weave an analysis of the facts together with an interpretation of the law. The argument should emphasize precedent cases that support the client's position and attempt to distinguish those that do not. The writer should use whichever method of statutory or constitutional analysis (plain meaning, legislative history, or contextual analysis) that best supports the position being advocated.

When completed, the appellant's brief should consist of a cover page, table of contents, table of authorities cited, jurisdictional statement, statement of the issues presented, list of statutes involved, statements of the facts, the arguments, conclusion, and appendixes (relevant excerpts from the record). The appellee's brief follows the same general format, though it need not define the issues in the same way. Although the argument section attempts to refute the arguments of the appellant, it need not address those arguments in the same sequential order. The reply brief consists solely of a cover sheet and the argument section.

The paralegal's role in preparing the brief depends on that

paralegal's understanding of the issues involved and his or her writing ability. The paralegal will almost certainly be involved in digesting the record and doing some of the legal research. The extent of direct participation in drafting the brief itself will depend on the paralegal's legal sophistication and writing skills. Writing styles are personal, however, and the attorney may choose to revise part of a brief for stylistic reasons.

KEY TERMS

abstract of the record

appellant's brief

appellee's brief

but see

cf.

contra

cover page

digest of the record

formbook

instruments of agreement

jurisdictional statement

memorandum of law

points and authorities

praecipe

reply brief

research memorandum

semble

statement of the issues presented

table of authorities cited

REVIEW QUESTIONS

1. What are the primary differences between an internal research memorandum and an external memorandum of law?

2. What are the key elements of a good letter?

3. What are the differences between forms of agreement and pleadings?

4. Name some of the most common formbooks. Under what circumstances are these books usually used?

5. What is the most difficult aspect of drafting interrogatories?

6. What are the differences between an external memorandum at law and an appellate brief?

7. What is the difference between the statement of the facts and the jurisdictional statement?

8. What form of notation should be used to indicate that one is quoting from a concurring opinion rather than the opinion of the court?

9. What are the primary differences between the appellant's brief and the appellee's brief? How does a reply brief differ from either of the above?

DISCUSSION QUESTIONS

1. To what extent should a paralegal author of an internal research memorandum include his or her own conclusions about the meaning of the law and recommend actions that should be taken?

2. What differentiates a letter sent by an attorney or a paralegal from a general business letter?

3. What types of letters, if any, should be sent out under the paralegal's own signature?

4. What are the pros and cons of relying on formbooks?

5. What are the advantages of digesting a record as opposed to simply abstracting it?

6. What is the best way to organize the argument section of a brief?

PROJECTS

1. Using the facts of the hypothetical landlord/tenant problem discussed in the internal memorandum section of this chapter, research the law of your state and city, and then write an internal memorandum regarding the client's situation as if it occurred in your city.

2. Using the landlord/tenant situation involved in project 1, draft a letter for your supervising attorney to sign in which you notify the landlord as to your client's reasons for not having paid the rent and her demands for improved living conditions within the apartment.

3. Using Am. Jur. Forms, Modern Legal Forms, or a similar set of formbooks, draft a simple will in which, on his death, a man's estate will be divided in such a way that his wife will get two-thirds and his surviving children will divide the remaining one-third equally. If his wife dies at the same time or before him, then the children should receive the entire amount to divide equally among them.

4. Draft a complaint on behalf of a client who was injured in a traffic accident. Assume that the plaintiff was a passenger in an automobile operated by the defendant and that while traveling at a speed of 65 M.P.H. the auto went through a stop sign on a country road and collided with another. Plaintiff suffered a cerebral concussion in the accident and later developed a seizure disorder that made it difficult for him to maintain a job. Assume that both parties are residents of your state and that the accident occurred in your state.

5. Assume that you worked for a law firm representing the defendant

in the situation described in project 4 above. Draft a set of interrogatories to be sent to the plaintiff.

6. Use the memorandum you wrote for project 1 as the basis for an
    appellant's brief. Assume that the trial court ruled against your
    client's defenses and ordered her to surrender possession of the
    apartment.

7. Now write a brief for the appellee in the case in project 6.

Chapter 10
Trials and Hearings

PARALEGALS PERFORM A variety of important tasks at various stages in the legal process. Except in a few jurisdictions in which paralegals are allowed to answer court calls or present purely procedural motions, however, persons who are not licensed attorneys are not allowed to represent clients in a court of law. Nevertheless, paralegals can serve a number of useful courtroom functions as part of a legal team and can provide direct representation before many administrative agencies.

A. PREPARATIONS FOR TRIAL

Good lawyers never just wing it in the courtroom. They come prepared for every imaginable circumstance. They have carefully thought out not only the evidence that they must present and how they will introduce it, but also what the opposition will try to present and what must be done to counter the effect of their evidence. Paralegals can be of great assistance in helping attorneys prepare for trials.

1. Assembling a Trial Notebook

Most lawyers come to court with some type of a trial notebook. It may be a three-ring loose-leaf binder divided into sections or a series of file folders. Regardless of its physical form, the content generally will be the same. The order in which the materials are organized and the extent of the detail will depend on the personal preferences of the attorney who is trying the case.

a. Outline of the Case
The outline of the case is the master plan of how the case will be developed. It lists the order in which witnesses will be called and what each is expected to establish through his or her testimony. In both civil and criminal cases the plaintiff or the prosecutor must prove various facts in court in order to win the case. Failure to establish one of these key elements can lose the case before the defendant's evidence is even

presented. (When an affirmative defense is being offered, the burden of either proving certain elements or of presenting certain types of evidence shifts to the defendant.) This type of case outline can ensure that the attorney does not overlook one of these key elements in the presentation of the case.

A paralegal can provide assistance by researching American Jurisprudence, Proof of Facts,[1] or some other specialized practice aid to find the elements that need to be proved. An example of the type of material found in such practice aids is found in Exhibit 10.1. Paralegals can also assist by providing cross-references to the witness file, the exhibits file, pleadings, and so forth.

b. Identification Lists

This section contains a listing of those associated with the case, including adverse parties, lay and expert witnesses, attorneys, and anyone whose name may arise in testimony or documents during the course of the trial. Each person should be identified in terms of their relationship to the case as well as by address, occupation, and so forth. The paralegal assembles this list by going through the pleadings and discovery documents and cross-references the list back to those documents.

c. Witness Section

This section is usually divided into subfiles for each witness. In addition to background information about the witnesses, the files contain statements that the witnesses made in the past and comments on what they are expected to testify to at the trial. The identity of opposing witnesses and what they are expected to say can be gathered from discovery documents. Because the rules of evidence require that certain foundations be laid before particular questions can be asked, and because the rules of evidence are very particular about the precise form of the question, it is wise for the attorney to have prepared in advance a list of specific questions for each witness. Such a list helps the attorney to proceed in an orderly fashion and ensures that nothing of importance will be missed.

Although the attorney selects the questions, the paralegal can again provide assistance by researching practice aids to locate sample questions (see Exhibit 10.1). If the testimony will be technical, the paralegal can prepare a glossary of terms that helps the attorney understand what will be said. The paralegal also should prepare a conflicts list that notes any inconsistencies that have been identified through the discovery process.

---

1. This multivolume series is published by Lawyers' Co-operative Publishing Company and specifies the elements needed to prove various types of lawsuits. It also provides questions that the attorney can ask witnesses to elicit the proper information.

Exhibit 10.1 Sample American Jurisprudence, Proof of Facts Proof

PROOF NO. 6

STANDARD OF CARE—TESTIMONY OF EXPERT

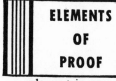

Proof by an expert witness that the defendant-physician's conduct has not conformed to the standard fixed by law is an essential element in any medical malpractice case in which the question of the defendant's negligence is not a matter of common knowledge or the subject of a presumption or inference arising out of the doctrine of res ipsa loquitur. Proof of the following facts and circumstances tends to establish that defendant-physician has breached the duty of care owed to the plaintiff:

— Witness and defendant belong to same school of medicine

— Witness and defendant practice same specialty

— Witness and defendant practice in same locality

— Familiarity of witness with skill and knowledge of average practitioner in locality

— Familiarity of witness with amount of care exercised by average practitioner in locality

— Basis of witness' familiarity with skill, knowledge, and care of average practitioner in locality

    — length of time witness has practiced in locality

    — discussion with others

    — association with others

    — local medical literature

— Opinion of witness as to whether defendant-physician's conduct conformed to standard

— Opinion of witness as to how practitioner in same locality possessing average skill and knowledge and exercising an average amount of care would have treated patient

---

School of medical thought. A defendant-doctor is entitled to be judged according to the tenets of the school he holds himself out as following. It has consequently been held that

595

419

Exhibit 10.1 *(continued)*

Proof 6   MALPRACTICE

the conduct of naturopaths, homeopaths, chiropractors, and osteopaths among others is to be measured by the standards of their own school and not those of licensed medical doctors. The particular school followed, however, must be a recognized one of definite principles, as distinguished from a cult or quackery. Regardless of the school defendant belongs to, where he holds himself out as capable of treating a bodily ill he will be held to certain minimum requirements of skill and knowledge. Where defendant professes a skill he does not in fact have, he will nevertheless be held to the standards of those possessing such skill. In this . proof it has been established that defendant held himself out as a medical doctor.

Q. What kind of a doctor are you?

A. A medical doctor.

Q. What degree do you hold in this regard?

A. That of doctor of medicine.

Locality in which defendant practices. Historically the conduct of the physician has been judged according to the norm in his particular community. Many courts today have broadened the geographical area in the belief that such a limitation is unrealistic in an age of mass communication and rapid transportation. Some courts accordingly make only a general urban-rural distinction. Other courts have made the state the pertinent locality.

Q. Where is your office?

A. On . . . . Street in the Town of . . . ., State of . . . .

Q. Is your practice confined to this town?

A. Yes.

Particular medical specialty. The defendant-physician holding himself out as a specialist is held to the standards of that specialty. It has already been established in this case that defendant is a general practitioner.

Q. Do you practice a particular medical specialty?

596

All entries contained in this section should be cross-referenced to discovery documents, pleadings, and so forth.

d. Exhibits File

This file contains a listing of all documents and other pieces of evidence introduced by either side. It is updated during the trial as the court rules on requests from both sides. The log should contain a brief description of the exhibit, the purpose for its use, and the nature of the testimony needed to lay the foundation.

The paralegal often assembles all the documents, models, and so forth that are to be introduced and keeps them in the proper order and ready to be introduced.

e. Pleadings File

The pleadings file contains copies of the original and amended complaints, answers, demurrers, motions to dismiss, and similar documents. In addition to assembling these documents, the paralegal should prepare a cover sheet that summarizes the complaint and the responses and then cross-reference these summaries to the original documents.

f. Motions File

The motions file contains copies of motions that the attorney might wish to make during the course of the trial as well as a listing of authorities to support those motions. The attorney can then cite these authorities to the judge if his or her position is challenged during the trial. It is also good to have authorities lined up with which to contest motions that the opposing side might be expected to make.

g. Jury File

If the trial is going to be conducted before a jury, a special folder should be prepared to aid in the jury selection process. This folder should contain as much information as possible about the individuals who will be on jury duty at the time the case is filed. In large important cases a firm may use the services of organizations that specialize in obtaining information about potential jurors. Some of these firms interview neighbors and co-workers to obtain information about life styles and attitudes.

Regardless of how much information has been obtained in advance, the file should contain a list of questions the attorney would like to see asked on *voir dire*. In some jurisdictions the attorneys are allowed to ask their own questions, and in others they must be content with submitting requests to the judge.

A jury folder also should contain a list of the instructions that the attorney would like the judge to read to the jury at the end of the trial. The early organization of these instructions can assist the attorney in

preparing a case by highlighting the type of evidence that must be presented. Sample instructions can usually be found in books that specialize in printing varieties of jury instructions. In many states the courts have approved specific sets of instructions that must be followed when applicable. An example of jury instructions follows:

> To sustain the charge of home invasion occurring on January 8, 1984, the state must prove the following propositions:
> First: That the defendant was not a police officer acting in the line of duty; and
> Second: That he knowingly and without authority entered the dwelling place of another; and
> Third: That when he entered the dwelling place he knew or had reason to know that one or more persons was present; and
> Fourth: That he intentionally caused an injury to Jane Doe, a person within the dwelling place.
> If you find from your consideration of all the evidence that each one of these propositions has been proved beyond a reasonable doubt, you should find the defendant guilty.
> If you find from your consideration of all the evidence that any one of these propositions has not been proved beyond a reasonable doubt, you should find the defendant not guilty.
>
> People's Tendered Instruction No. _____
> IPI-Criminal No. 11.22

h. Computerized Litigation Support

Modern litigation support software packages can assist the paralegal in organizing and cross-referencing the above-mentioned files. Such programs also make the task of retrieval much easier.[2]

2. Coordinating and Preparing Witnesses

As the time for trial approaches, it is usually possible to estimate within a few days the date on which the various witnesses will be needed to testify. Because it is unreasonable to keep a person just waiting around the courthouse for days at a time, the witness frequently is instructed to simply be available on short notice, and a paralegal then is responsible for keeping the witness updated as to when they must actually appear. If a witness is coming from another town, the paralegal's duties may include arranging for transportation and lodging.

In addition to coordinating the scheduling of witnesses, paralegals also may help them to prepare for their testimony. Because people are often nervous about testifying in court, the paralegal can calm their fears somewhat by describing the procedures that are used for examining witnesses. At a substantive level, the paralegal may review the types of questions that the witness will be asked and how the testimony will fit into

---

2. See the discussion at pages 250-251.

the case. It is also useful to review key documents, the person's answers to interrogatories, and the transcript of any depositions in which they were involved.

Witnesses should be told to be sure that they understand each question before attempting to answer it and to ask to have it repeated or rephrased if necessary. They always should pause long enough to see if an objection is raised and to wait for the judge to make a ruling if there is an objection. In giving the answer they should be directed to speak calmly and forcefully. Although they should be careful to answer the question completely, witnesses should not go on to volunteer any additional information that was not specifically requested. If a mistake is made, or if the opposing attorney confronts them with conflicting statements, they should answer truthfully, admit the prior mistake, and, if possible, give an explanation for the earlier mistake. The witnesses should be cautioned against losing their tempers. Finally, they should be instructed how to respond to the "Have you discussed your testimony with anyone?" question that attorneys like to ask as part of their cross-examinations.

B.   ASSISTANCE DURING THE TRIAL

During the actual trial, attorneys are frequently assisted by a secretary, a paralegal, or another attorney. Sometimes someone must be sent out of the courtroom to call a key witness or to find some key document. In the courtroom itself, the attorney can work more efficiently if someone else has taken the responsibility of keeping the exhibits in order and locating key documents that are being referred to by the other side. This assistant must be able to anticipate the attorney's needs and to have the required documents ready at the proper time. If an attorney's questioning appears to elicit responses that conflict with discovery documents, the assistant must point this out and provide the attorney with a copy of the document that establishes this contradiction.

Finally, when an attorney is questioning a witness, he or she does not have time to take notes on the responses to their questions or to watch the jury's reaction to the witness. It is good for attorneys to use a paralegal's notes to refresh their memories and to be able to have someone who can critique their own performances.

In most situations a paralegal is better prepared to serve these "second chair" functions than either a secretary or another attorney. They are more useful than secretaries because they have more legal knowledge and because they are usually more familiar with the facts and the issues of the case. Because they probably have participated in abstracting and indexing the pleadings and discovery documents, they are in a better position to spot contradictions and to locate both appropriate

documents and specific quotations within those documents. Another attorney would have greater legal knowledge and would be able to address the court or question witnesses, but that attorney's usefulness is directly related to the extent to which the attorney has been working with the case in earlier stages and is familiar with the exhibits and the discovery documents. Furthermore, using a paralegal is more cost-effective than using an attorney.

C. ADJUDICATORY HEARINGS

In administrative agencies that allow lay representation, paralegals can perform the same advocacy functions as attorneys. Although administrative hearings are more informal than trials and do follow more flexible rules of evidence, the paralegal advocate must exercise the same basic skills exercised by attorneys in trials.

1. Preparation for the Hearing

The key to successful advocacy is preparation. The paralegal must be thoroughly familiar with all of the details of the case, as well as with the procedures of the agency in question. Chapter 5 presents an overview of adminisistrative procedures, but each agency has its own particular rules, and the paralegal must study them carefully.

The paralegal should prepare a "trial notebook" like those discussed in section A1 of this chapter. It should contain an outline of the case, a witness file, an exhibits file, and so forth. The major difference in the paralegal's participation in the preparation of this trial notebook is that the paralegal has greater responsibility for preparing the outline of the case and the questions to be asked of the witnesses.

No matter how carefully one has prepared, the unexpected will occur. Preparation helps maintain one's train of thought and self-confidence.

2. Conduct of the Hearing

Depending, of course, on the rules of the agency, the paralegal advocate may or may not be expected to make some sort of opening statement. If such a statement is appropriate, the paralegal should keep it simple and informative. Emotionalism is not appropriate.

Documentary evidence is frequently entered into the record at the beginning of the hearing and does not require testimony to lay a proper foundation. The paralegal, however, must be familiar with the documents being introduced by the other side and must register any objections at this point.

The direct examination of a witness should begin with questions

designed to identify and elicit relevant background information about the witness. The questions should then go on to establish the witness's connection to the case and the substance of what he or she has to contribute. Let the witness tell the story in his or her own words and interrupt only when the person is getting off the track. Try to anticipate and cover points that the other side is expected to bring out.

The purpose of the cross-examination is to bring out additional information that may be more favorable to the client's position and/or challenge the credibility of unfavorable information the witness has brought out during the other side's direct examination. In order to do the former, the paralegal must ask specific questions that will require the witness to respond with the information being withheld. The credibility of the person's testimony can be challenged by pointing out internal inconsistencies within the story or showing that it is contrary to common experience or past events. Another tack is to challenge the credibility of the source of the testimony. This involves pointing out a lack of expertise, some bias, or some physical or mental impairment.

Cross-examination can also be used to reemphasize favorable aspects of your client's case. This can be done by asking "Isn't it true that . . ." questions that force the adverse witness to provide favorable information. Bear in mind, however, that you never should ask a question of an adverse witness for which you do not know the answer.

The following selections (Exhibit 10.2) are taken from a transcript of an administrative hearing conducted before the Iowa Civil Rights Commission. It is an example of a relatively formal type of hearing and is included to provide examples of the manner in which witnesses are questioned and evidence is presented.

Exhibit 10.2 Selections from the Transcript of an Administrative Hearing

BEFORE THE IOWA CIVIL RIGHTS COMMISSION

COMMISSIONER JACK W. PETERS
        Complainant,

v.
        — CP NO. 02-81-7487

RED BARN SUPPER CLUB, LTD.,
        Respondent.

COMMISSIONER EVELYNE VILLINES,
        Complainant,

v.
        — CP NO. 05-81-7686

RED BARN SUPPER CLUB, LTD.,
and BRUCE RUSSELL,
        Respondents.

COMMISSIONER JACK W. PETERS,
        Complainant,

v.
        — CP NO. 11-81-8290

RED BARN SUPPER CLUB, LTD.,
and BRUCE RUSSELL,
        Respondents.

Conference Room, Third Floor
Lucas State Office Building
Des Moines, Iowa
Wednesday, May 5, 1982

EDIE SPRIGGS DANIELS — CERTIFIED SHORTHAND REPORTER

PETERSEN COURT REPORTERS
Certified Shorthand Reporters
606 United Central Bank Building
Des Moines, Iowa
(515) 243-6596

PROCEEDINGS

THE HEARING OFFICER: Why don't we go ahead and go on the record, then, and I will make my opening remarks.

My name is Mark Wheeler, and I will be your Hearing Officer today, and this is an administrative hearing conducted under Sec-

tion 601A of the Code of Iowa. It is before the Iowa Civil Rights Commission, and there has been a motion and a ruling that there was a consolidation of three complaints, those being CP No. 02-81-7487, which is Commissioner Jack W. Peters versus Red Barn Supper Club, Ltd., and there has been a prehearing summary judgment in favor of the Complainant on this particular complaint, and it will not be addressed during the subject matter of this hearing.

The other two complaints that remain to be heard during this hearing are CP No. 05-81-7686, which is Commissioner Evelyne Villines against Red Barn Supper Club, Ltd., and Bruce Russell; and CP No. 11-81-8290, which is Commissioner Jack W. Peters versus the Red Barn Supper Club, Ltd., and Bruce Russell.

The alleged violations involved in these two complaints are of Section 601A.7(b) of the Code of Iowa; in particular, actions or indications by the Respondent that customers of a particular national origin were not welcome at a public accommodation establishment, particularly Iranians in this case.

The hearing is taking place at the Lucas State Office Building, 3rd floor conference room, at approximately five minutes after 10, on May the 6th, 1982.

Just a couple more opening remarks on my part. Now, I am going to be rather liberal in allowing information and evidence into the record, and in particular I am talking about hearsay evidence, and I will not adhere strictly to the rules of evidence that will be applicable during a judicial proceeding.

One other point, which I am sure I don't even have to be concerned with, but for the record I would like to state that if at any time during this hearing either counsel, parties or any witnesses or any other persons become disruptive of this proceeding, I will im-

Exhibit 10.2 *(continued)*

mediately go off the record and will recess until I am satisfied that we can continue in an orderly fashion.

Let me state that the Complainant will be represented by Mr. Scott Nichols, Assistant Attorney General; and the Respondent is represented by Mr. Steve Jayne, a private attorney.

Before we go into opening statements, is there anything counsel would like to address to the Hearing Officer at this time?

MR. NICHOLS: Yes. Mr. Jayne and myself have entered into a number of stipulations.

We would like to have the record include the Court of Appeals decision in the Iowa Civil Rights Commission versus the Red Barn Supper Club case, also the appendix that was part of the record of that appellate proceeding.

And we have a number of evidentiary stipulations to make for this proceeding.

First of all, the legal description of the land on which the Red Barn Supper Club and Mr. Russell's house is one and the same.

It may be that for purposes of clarification we should say that there are three signs involved here, the first sign being the one on the public accommodation; the second sign being the one in Mr. Russell's yard; and the third one being the sign on Mr. Russell's porch.

The dimensions of the first sign are 8 inches by 10 inches. The dimensions of the second sign and the third sign are 4 feet by 12 feet; four feet wide, 12 feet long.

The second and third signs had red lettering on a white background with blue trim.

Unless I left something out, I think that about covers it.

MR. JAYNE: Yes.

THE HEARING OFFICER: Okay. Those stipulations are accepted and will become part of the record.

If there is nothing further in regard to introductory matters, then we can go ahead.

Does the Complainant have an opening statement he would like to make at this time?

MR. NICHOLS: Yes, Mr. Wheeler, I would.

Bruce Russell is the proprietor of the Red Barn Supper Club, which is a public accommodation. That public accommodation has licenses from several State agencies.

Both Mr. Russell and his supper club are subject to the terms of the Iowa Civil Rights Act, and in particular Section 601A.7(1)b, which prohibits a proprietor from advertising directly or indirectly or in any other manner indicating that people of a particular national origin are unwelcome as patrons.

Now, there are three signs in this matter, the first sign being the sign on the supper club. The second sign was a sign displayed in Mr. Russell's front yard, which is adjacent to the supper club; and the third sign is now being displayed on Mr. Russell's front porch.

The Complainant contends that one of the crucial aspects of this case is the relationship between Mr. Russell's yard and his house with the supper club. We think the evidence today will show that basically the house and the yard is an extension of the supper club for purposes of Section 601A.7(1)b.

The matter of Mr. Russell's intent in displaying the various signs is also going to be a crucial factor in this case. . . .

Now, all three signs that are the subject of complaints say the same thing, "Iranians not welcome here." . . .

Mr. Hearing Officer, we think that when you examine the total-

Exhibit 10.2 *(continued)*

ity of the evidence in this case, you will be led to the conclusion that Mr. Russell clearly intended to give the world a message that Iranians were not welcome in his supper club.

Thank you.

THE HEARING OFFICER: Thank you. The Respondent's attorney.

MR. JAYNE: Mr. Wheeler, Mr. Nichols: Mr. Nichols is accurate in his opening statement; in fact it will be up to the Iowa Civil Rights Commission to sustain the burden of proof to establish that the actions of Mr. Russell were the concurrent action of the proprietorship and not his singular actions protected by the First Amendment to the United States Constitution.

The evidence will set forth certain activities that were engaged in over a period of — actually we are centralizing on April 10, 1981, and the primary objection, to my understanding from the Civil Rights Commission, is the proximity of the sign to the public accommodation.

Visibility issues will also present the fact that it is not only visible to patrons, but it is visible to non-patrons as well, who use the public road that passes by in front of the facility.

The evidence will show that the facility, the public accommodation is clearly separate and distinct from the private residence of Russell.

The Respondent has asserted as an affirmative defense to the subject complaints that there is judicial sanction for the posting of the sign in the front yard and to the front of the house, and this arises out of Judge Smith's order which was issued in late March, 1981, and is a part of the record. . . .

Thank you. I have no further opening statement.

THE HEARING OFFICER: Thank you. Would you like to proceed with the presentation of your evidence at this time?

MR. NICHOLS: Thank you, Mr. Wheeler. Before I call my first witness, may I have access to the photographs that were attached to the motion for summary judgment?

THE HEARING OFFICER: Sure.

MR. NICHOLS: Thank you. The Complainant would like to call as their first witness Mr. Bruce Russell.

THE HEARING OFFICER: If you could come up here please, sir.

BRUCE RUSSELL,

called as a witness by the Complainant, being first duly sworn by the Certified Shorthand Reporter, was examined and testified as follows:

DIRECT EXAMINATION

BY MR. NICHOLS:

Q. Mr. Russell, we know that you have licenses from the Department of Revenue, Agriculture and the Iowa Beer and Liquor Control Department.

Do you have any other licenses from State agencies?

A. A restaurant license from the Department of Agriculture. . . .

Q. Any other licenses from State agencies?

A. Those are basically the ones you need to operate.

Q. And I would imagine you don't have any licenses from local governments in addition?

A. No. You are routinely inspected by health inspectors from the Department of Agriculture. The Department of Environmental Quality monitors our water systems since we are private citizens, but they don't require any licensing; just reports.

Exhibit 10.2 *(continued)*

Q. No other license?

A. Right.

Q. Mr. Russell, let's go back to April 10, 1981. On that date you called a press conference did you not?

A. Yes, we did.

Q. And that press conference was held at the Red Barn Supper Club, is that correct?

A. That's correct.

Q. And it moved over to your yard during the course of it, is that correct?

A. Yes, it did.

Q. Can you tell us who you contacted from the media alerting them to this press conference?

A. I believe that most of the media — I don't remember each one or who called — were notified that we were holding a press conference, and that we were going to comply with Judge Smith's order. . . .

Q. Mr. Russell, I take it you wanted to give this press conference on April 10th, 1981, wide coverage?

A. I wanted them to know that we were going to comply with Judge Smith's order. We did not want to be in any violation of these acts which would endanger our business, which is our livelihood.

Q. Now, during that press conference, you removed the sign from the front window of the supper club, is that correct?

A. We did. We actually had it removed before then.

Q. And that sign, of course, said, "Iranians not welcome here," isn't that true?

A. That is correct.

Q. Mr. Russell, I am going to hand you what has previously been marked as Motion Exhibits 1 and 2, and I would just like to ask you if those photographs accurately portray you removing the sign.

A. Yes, they accurately portray. The photographers asked us if we would do it, even though we had it down at that time, for their accommodation.

MR. NICHOLS: Mr. Wheeler, the Complainant would like to offer into evidence Motion Exhibits 1 and 2.

THE HEARING OFFICER: Any objection?

MR. JAYNE: No objection.

THE HEARING OFFICER: Let it be noted that they will be made a part of the record, and they will be marked as they are marked right now.

(Motion Exhibits Nos. 1 and 2 were received in evidence.)

Q. (BY MR. NICHOLS) Now, Mr. Russell, during the course of this press conference, you and some other people unveiled a second sign that said, "Iranians not welcome here," is that correct?

A. Yes, that's correct.

Q. And that sign stood roughly six feet high, didn't it?

A. Well, the sign itself was 4-by-12.

Q. And it was on posts which elevated it somewhat higher than four feet?

A. Well, yes, they were off the ground. I don't know exactly.

Q. Okay. And can you tell us what the color scheme of your supper club is; red and white, is that basically it?

A. Red, basically, with white trim.

Q. Okay. And this sign matched that color scheme, didn't it?

A. Basically, yes.

Q. Okay. Mr. Russell, I am going to hand you now three pho-

Exhibit 10.2 *(continued)*

tographs which have previously been marked Motion Exhibits 3, 4 and 5, and I would ask you to take a look at those and tell the Hearing Officer whether those accurately depict the sign being unveiled on April 10th, 1981.

A.   Yes, they do. . . .

MR. NICHOLS: Okay. Mr. Wheeler, I am going to offer into the record Motion Exhibits 3, 4 and 5.

THE HEARING OFFICER: Any objection?

MR. JAYNE: No objection.

THE HEARING OFFICER: Let it be noted they are accepted as part of the record, and they will be marked as they are so marked now.

(Motion Exhibits Nos. 3, 4 and 5 were received in evidence.) . . .

Q. (BY MR. NICHOLS)   Mr. Russell, I am going to hand you what has been marked as Motion Exhibit 13, and I would like you to tell us whether that accurately portrays the entrance to the Red Barn's parking lot.

A.   This depicts the entry, the driveway and the basic parking lot.

Q.   And you will notice on that exhibit there is a sign to the left that says, "The Red Barn," and then some other information.

Can you tell us roughly what the dimensions of that sign are?

A.   I think that's about a four-by-four, I imagine, about half a sheet of plywood.

Q.   Okay. And what color is the writing on that sign?

A.   Red, white and black.

Q.   Red, white and black, okay. And has that sign been standing during the period that the second and the third "Iranians not welcome here" signs have been standing?

434

A.   I imagine this — I don't recall the date that we put this sign up which depicts our open hours so that on our day off, when we are closed, people don't have to drive all the way up to the club to see the hours on the door, because we are out in the country. They can notice it from the driveway in their car, and if they want to drive back to another place that's open, they are free to do so; but I think this sign was put up probably in '78 or '79.

Q.   So it has been up during the whole time that the "Iranians not welcome here" signs have been up?

A.   Yes.

Q.   And the four-by-four foot sign is large enough to alert patrons as to what your hours are, if they pass by, so they don't have to get out of their car; they don't have to go into the supper club, right?

A.   Yes. It has lights on it so people can see it, right.

Q.   And that sign is much smaller than the two "Iranians not welcome here" signs which were in your yard and are now on your porch, is that right?

A.   That's true, it is smaller. . . .

Q. (BY MR. NICHOLS)   Obviously the sign that now stands on your front porch is visible to patrons coming to your supper club, isn't it?

A.   Yes, and also to non-patrons.

Q.   And that's the way you want it to be, isn't it?

A.   It is an expression of my personal feelings, yes.

Q.   Okay. So you want your patrons to know that "Iranians are not welcome here"?

A.   I don't quite put it that way.

MR. JAYNE: First of all, I would like to object to the question as vague and confusing. I don't know what Mr. Nichols means by

Exhibit 10.2 (*continued*)

"you" and "here" in the way he phrased the question. Perhaps if he rephrased the question —

THE HEARING OFFICER: Could you rephrase the question, please, so that the witness could give a clearer answer?

Q. (BY MR. NICHOLS) Would it be unreasonable for a patron or a passerby to interpret the sign "Iranians not welcome here" on your front porch as meaning Iranians are not welcome in the supper club?

MR. JAYNE: I object to the form of the question. It calls for speculation on the part of this witness as to what other people would think. He can only testify as to his intent in putting the sign up.

THE HEARING OFFICER: Any response to the objection?

MR. NICHOLS: No response, Your Honor.

THE HEARING OFFICER: The objection is sustained. . . .

Q. Now that the sign is on your front porch — or I should say ever since the sign has been on your front porch, have patrons in your supper club expressed opinions about the sign?

A. Some do and some don't. It is their own personal belief and what they believe. I am not going to ask them. I am not soliciting opinions on that sign. That's my expression of my belief at that situation that happened over in Iran.

Q. Do they come up to you and say, "Yeah, I really like that sign you have got up there"?

MR. JAYNE: I object to this line of questioning as irrelevant to whether or not a violation of the act has been committed by Russell in his capacity as a proprietor of a public accommodation.

MR. NICHOLS: I would respond to that objection by noting that we are trying to establish what patrons of the supper club per-

ceive, and that's very relevant to whether a discriminatory act has been perpetrated.

MR. JAYNE: I would suggest then that it would require testimony of patrons of the club to testify as to what they understand.

THE HEARING OFFICER: As I said, I am going to be rather liberal in allowing testimony into the record, and I am going to overrule the objection and allow this line of questioning, unless I see that it goes too far out of bounds, and I will give it whatever weight it is due when I make my decision.

MR. NICHOLS: Could you read back the question for us, please?

(Question read by the reporter.)

A. There are some that do and some that don't. Whether they are patrons or not, I don't ask them. Some people see me on the street and voice their opinion pro or con, and I believe they are entitled to that opinion, as long as they don't try to sway mine.

Q. Can you estimate how many customers in your supper club have expressed comments about your sign, one way or another, whether they agree with it or disagree with it?

A. No, I don't have any estimate on that. . . .

MR. NICHOLS: I have no further questions for you at this time, Mr. Russell.

THE HEARING OFFICER: Any cross examination?

MR. JAYNE: Two or three, Your Honor.

CROSS EXAMINATION

BY MR. JAYNE:

Q. Did you ever direct any employee of the Red Barn Supper Club to participate in any of the incidents that we have talked about this morning?

437

Exhibit 10.2 *(continued)*

A. No, I never did.

Q. Isn't it true that they participated, if they were an employee, as a volunteer?

A. Yes, they did. I never gave any orders for anybody to participate in something they didn't believe in. That's the exact same principles we are standing up for here, our freedom of speech and our rights.

MR. JAYNE: I have no further questions of this witness at this time.

THE HEARING OFFICER: Redirect?

MR. NICHOLS: I have no further questions for you, Mr. Russell.

The Complainant will rest at this time.

THE HEARING OFFICER: Okay. You may step down.

(Witness excused.)

THE HEARING OFFICER: You have no further witnesses?

MR. NICHOLS: That's correct, Your Honor.

THE HEARING OFFICER: Respondent, would you like to have any witnesses?

MR. JAYNE: Well, yes. The Respondent would call Bruce Russell, please.

THE HEARING OFFICER: Just let it be noted you are still under oath.

THE WITNESS: All right.

THE HEARING OFFICER: You may proceed.

MR. JAYNE: Thank you. . . .

For clarity, could you indicate, in your best estimate, the distance between the Red Barn facility and your private residence in feet or yards?

A.   Okay. Between the club and our residence is roughly 700, 800 feet, in that area.

Q.   And is it not true that there is a white rail fence that surrounds the club itself?

A.   There is.

Q.   Is it not true that there are a number of railroad ties that are laid down in the lot?

A.   This is true, so the cars cannot roll into the fence.

Q.   And what is the reason for having the fence around the club?

A.   For the reasons of the liquor license, we have to define the separation of the residence as opposed to the business establishment. According to the liquor law, I have to close the bar, quit serving at 2 A.M. If I had friends over in my house, they could drink over there all night, if they wanted to, but in the club itself, I have to define that away from the residence so we are not in violation of any liquor laws; also for insurance. . . .

Q.   I believe Mr. Nichols went into this in some detail. It was concerning the press conference that was called by yourself, admittedly, on April 10, 1981, I believe. And I believe you testified that the purpose of the press conference was to reflect your disagreement, your personal disagreement with the opinion of Judge Smith, but to comply with the order.

Was there any other reason that you called the press conference?

A.   Well, we felt at this point that the Civil Rights Commission was infringing upon our right to freedom of speech and expression as guaranteed under the First Amendment. We were abiding by the judge's order, but we also felt that because they pressured us, we were not going to buckle under to them for that.

Exhibit 10.2 *(continued)*

I still believe the message that's on the sign I put on my personal residence.

Q. In addition to reflecting your First Amendment feelings, was the purpose of the conference to perhaps attempt to clarify and make it clear that it is not the policy of your club, but rather your own personal feelings, and that was the reason for the press conference as well?

A. Definitely, because there is a clear and distinct separation between the business area there and our residence, and anybody with average intelligence can see that it is clearly defined there and I wanted that distinction to show there because I felt that the Civil Rights Commission was harassing me at taxpayers' expense. . . .

Q. (BY MR. JAYNE) Was the posting of the second sign in your front yard intended to be a personal expression protected by the First Amendment of the United States Constitution, or was it intended to be a reflection of the policy of the Red Barn Supper Club?

A. It was my personal reflection of my personal opinions, as I feel they are guaranteed under the First Amendment. That sign would be in the same spot if the wind had not taken it down. That's the only reason that it went on the house, was to guarantee that my feelings were there. . . .

THE HEARING OFFICER: Do you have any further witnesses?

MR. JAYNE: No, I don't.

THE HEARING OFFICER: That's the end of the evidence presentations, and I would entertain closing statements.

Counsel for the Complainant.

MR. NICHOLS: Mr. Wheeler, I think this testimony today, taken in conjunction with the photographs that are part of the re-

cord in this case, certainly indicates that Mr. Russell, as proprietor of the Red Barn Supper Club, has displayed a sign at three different locations all saying, "Iranians not welcome here." The first sign was on the supper club itself.

No matter what Mr. Russell says about his subjective reasons for putting the sign on the supper club, that sign very clearly and unmistakably advertised and indicated to Iranians and other customers that people of a particular national origin were unwelcome in that supper club.

He took down that sign to conform with the Court order, and erected a much larger sign saying the same thing, "Iranians not welcome here," a sign that was much more visible to patrons of the supper club; a sign that's 16 feet from the parking lot of the supper club.

Again, Mr. Russell tries to tell us that his intent was just to indicate some personal feelings about the tragic seizure of the hostages in Iran, but the message is clearly the same: Iranians are not welcome in the supper club. It is an advertisement. It is an indication, and it is a violation of the Civil Rights Act.

Well, when the sign blew down a few days later, he attached it to his front porch. The front porch of his house is very close to the supper club. It is on the same plot of land. The message is still the same; the color scheme still matches the supper club. . . .

Lastly, Mr. Russell has claimed that Judge Smith in his injunction order sanctioned the display of the "Iranians not welcome here" signs on his house.

Well, as counsel for the Respondent has conceded, there was no evidence in the record before Judge Smith to let him know where Mr. Russell's house stood in relation to the supper club, and when the Hearing Officer reads the injunction order, the spirit and

Exhibit 10.2 *(continued)*

intent of that order are very plain. The "Iranians not welcome here" sign that stood in the front entrance of the supper club irreparably injured human dignity, and if that small cardboard sign irreparably injured human dignity, it doesn't take too much imagination to see whether the second and third signs did.

Thank you, Your Honor.

THE HEARING OFFICER: Respondent, closing statements?

MR. JAYNE: Thank you. Addressing the legal issues, first of all, referring to Judge Smith's order, he states in that order under his findings that, "The Commission finds objectionable primarily the placing of the sign." The Court agrees that that is their objection, apparently. They aren't objecting about the calling of a press conference or the color of the sign. They are concerned with the proximity of the sign.

The Court goes on to state, "Mr. Russell can place the sign on his home and he will not commit an unfair practice."

I fail to see how it is relevant where Russell's home is, if it is 50 miles away from the club or if it is 50 feet away from the club.

We do not have a sign that says, "Iranians not welcome at the Red Barn Supper Club." Whether that sign were posted within 50 feet of the club, in front of Russell's home, or 50 miles away from the club, clearly that would be a violation of the act and not to be condoned by this board, yourself or myself, for that matter; however, we are now in this rather fragile area of the First Amendment protection.

I submit to you that if the Commission's position were to be sustained, it would have a recurring effect on any businessman in this State or in this country.

Just by virtue of the fact that a businessman or a person hap-

pens to be engaged in a business, running a bar, running a restaurant, motel, any form of public accommodation, do they sacrifice their right to express themselves within the protection of the First Amendment to the United States Constitution?

What the Commission is asking for here is to treat Mr. Russell as a second class citizen by virtue of the fact that his home — and I have no statistics, but it is in a relatively rural area still in Iowa, and there are many occasions, I am sure, when you have the mom and pop grocery store, and they live next door. Sometimes they will live above the store.

Going with their argument, if Russell lived three miles away from the facility and people knew that's where Mr. Russell lived, and he puts a sign on his front lawn that says, "Iranians not welcome here," and this sign is red, white and blue, and he calls a press conference to take down the old sign that was on the front of his public accommodation, the same premise applies; therefore, he could not apply — he could not place a sign in his front yard, and it just doesn't make any sense to me. A line has to be drawn.

To me, the Court has already determined that it is his personal expression. The issue is not appealed from that, whether it was his personal expression or not. To me, that is res judicata relative to the initial expression, whether or not it was personal.

The Court has already found that it was personal; just misplaced. A big "just." It was removed and has not been up since April 10, 1981, nor will it be reattached to the front of that facility because it is clearly in violation of the Court order.

It is the burden of proof for the Civil Rights Commission to establish that the posting of the second and third sign was the act of the public accommodation. It must establish that it was not the act of an individual who also happens to be a proprietor of the public

Exhibit 10.2 (*continued*)

accommodation. This cannot be done by — or this burden cannot be sustained by — speculation or innuendo. It must be sustained by obviously the actions of the parties; the statements of the parties made to media, to third persons.

I don't see a single member of the Civil Rights Commission giving any testimony as to what was said during the press conference, or at any time, that would indicate that this was not a personal expression, but was perhaps a concurrent expression of the public accommodation.

You have before you two exhibits, I believe, C and D. The public accommodation has attempted to conciliate these grievances; these complaints.

A condition for conciliation and an absolute condition was the precondition that the second and third signs be removed before anything could be conciliated.

You have previously rendered summary judgment in favor of the Commission on the issue of the first sign. The Respondent alleged in its answer that the issue was moot because the sign has been down since April 10, 1981, and has not been replaced.

Coupling that with Mr. Grove's attitude as representative of the Civil Rights Commission, it does not reflect, to me, a good faith attempt to conciliate these problems. It indicates to me an attempt, as Mr. Russell indicated in his testimony, for the Civil Rights Commission to shove down his throat what they think is right; not what you or I may think is right, but what the Commission thinks is right.

I cannot envision that Mr. Russell should be penalized concerning this first complaint because of the Commission's precondition that, "Before we can conciliate Complaint No. 1, you have to take down the signs pertaining to Complaint No. 2 and Complaint

No. 3," the very signs that are the fighting issue here today and have been the fighting issue in district court in Boone County and before the Court of Appeals of the State of Iowa.

Mr. Russell is not a radical. He abides by the laws of the State of Iowa, the laws of the United States of America.

He has previously indicated, in prior testimony, that he will abide by the lawful orders of the Court and the statutes of this State, but there has to be a line drawn as to when there is a violation.

We have a Constitution that's unique. The First Amendment is very unique, and the protection of the individuals of this country in the application of that particular constitutional protection should be applied carefully and with restraint when it seeks to restrain an expression of one of its citizens; therefore, I would respectfully request that the Commission's complaint be overruled.

Thank you very much.

THE HEARING OFFICER: Thank you. If there is nothing further, then maybe I should bring up the issue of whether or not counsel believe that briefs would be appropriate, and if so — your expression, Mr. Nichols?

MR. NICHOLS: Yes, Mr. Wheeler, I would very much relish the opportunity of filing a brief, and if the Hearing Officer could set a date, let's say 30 days after the transcript is available to the parties, that would be fine.

THE HEARING OFFICER: Mr. Jayne, do you have any response to that?

MR. JAYNE: Certainly. The Respondent would be happy to submit a brief.

THE HEARING OFFICER: Fine. Why don't we go ahead and make that part of the proceedings, and briefs will be due 30 days

Exhibit 10.2 *(continued)*

after the receipt of the transcript of this hearing.

If there is nothing else further to be done, then this hearing is adjourned. Thank you.

(At 11:40 A.M., hearing in the above-entitled matter was concluded.)

D. SUMMARY

Paralegals make important contributions to their employers as a case enters the trial stage. Good lawyers come to court well prepared, and paralegals can be of great assistance in preparing the case for trial. Although the attorney creates the outline of the case and determines the questions to be asked, paralegals can be extremely helpful in locating appropriate references in trial aids and in assembling the trial notebook.

They also can assist in witness preparation and coordination. In addition to keeping witnesses informed regarding the times at which they will be needed, paralegals can help prepare those witnesses for the ordeal of testifying.

Although paralegals do not make opening statements to the jury, cross-examine witnesses, or address the judge during the course of a trial, their importance to the legal team does not end once a trial begins. In addition to coordinating exhibits and taking notes, paralegals also may be called on to serve as emergency messengers. After each day's proceedings they can help the attorney to critique the day's performance.

Finally, in administrative agencies that allow lay representation, paralegals perform the same functions as attorneys. They present arguments to the hearing officer, examine witnesses, and introduce evidence. As was true with attorneys in trials, the key to a paralegal's success in these activities is thorough preparation.

KEY TERMS

Am. Jur. Proof of Facts	pleadings file
exhibits file	practice aid
identification section	second chair
jury file	trial notebook
motions file	witness file
outline of the case	

REVIEW QUESTIONS

1. What is the purpose of a trial notebook?

2. Name each section of a trial notebook and briefly describe the content of each.

3. What tasks are likely to be undertaken by a paralegal who assists an attorney in preparing a trial notebook?

4. What is the nature of the paralegal's contact with witnesses?

5. What types of general advice should a paralegal give to prospective witnesses?

6. What are paralegals expected to do when they "second chair" a trial?

7. How should a paralegal prepare to represent a client at an administrative hearing?

8. What is the purpose of the cross-examination?

DISCUSSION QUESTIONS

1. What is the difference between legitimately preparing a witness and unethically coaching that witness? Give some examples of both the legitimate and the nonlegitimate.

2. What are the advantages and disadvantages of using secretaries, paralegals, and lawyers to assist in the courtroom?

3. What makes a witness credible, and how can an attorney reduce a witness's credibility through cross-examination?

4. Why should you never ask an adverse witness a question for which you don't know the answer?

PROJECTS

1. Use the CFR to locate the rules for conducting adjudicatory hearings for appeals of denials for social security disability claims.

2. Develop an outline of the case for the plaintiff to use in the traffic accident case involved in projects 4 and 5 in Chapter 9.

3. Develop an outline of the case for the defendant to use in the same case discussed in project 2 above.

PART IV
Professional
Responsibilities

PARALEGALS ARE PART OF A profession because their work involves specialized expertise and training and they are subject to highly developed ethical responsibilities that do not apply to other groups in society. Paralegals hold positions of responsibility and trust. Their actions directly and indirectly affect the well-being of their clients.

This final part of the book considers the legal and ethical restrictions that apply to paralegals. Although the topics covered here would logically fit into Part I's discussion of the paralegal profession, they are saved to conclude the book because they can be best understood after the other materials in the book are understood. It also seems appropriate to end on this topic because it has so much to do with the future growth and success of the profession.

Chapter 11
Legal and Ethical
Requirements for
Paralegals

THIS CHAPTER DISCUSSES the statutes, judicial decisions, court rules, and ethical codes that directly or indirectly affect paralegals. It examines what constitutes the unauthorized practice of law and the nature of a paralegal's ethical obligations to both the client and the employer.

A. THE STRUCTURE OF PROFESSIONAL RESPONSIBILITY

The limitations and the obligations discussed here arise out of a combination of statutes, judicial decisions, professional codes of ethics, and advisory opinions concerning those ethical codes. The chapter therefore begins with an analysis of these basic source materials before moving on to examine specific substantive topics.

1. Legal Requirements

Both paralegals and lawyers are, of course, covered by general criminal statutes prohibiting theft, fraud, obstruction of justice, and so forth. Lawyers are additionally bound by requirements that may be included in the state statutes that license attorneys[1] and the state unauthorized practice of law statutes.

As was pointed out in Chapter 3, court decisions play an important role in the interpretation of statutes. Thus, in order to fully understand the application of statutory requirements, one must examine court cases that have interpreted key phrases and have applied the statutes in question to specific activities of lawyers and paralegals. Common law princi-

---

1. If, at some time in the future, states should choose to license paralegals, then those licensing statutes might well place statutory obligations or restrictions on paralegals.

ples of agency and tort liability have some effect on the behavior of lawyers and paralegals.

Court rules are also relevant. In many states the basic rules of admission to the bar and attorney discipline are handled by rules adopted by the state's highest court. Although these rules apply only to attorneys, they indirectly affect paralegals as well. One state — Kentucky — has incorporated specific guidelines on the use of paralegals into its court rules.

Kentucky Paralegal Code, Rule 3.700 Provisions Relating to Paralegals
(1980)

The Paralegal Code (with Commentary) governing lawyer conduct in relation to the use of paralegals became effective January 1, 1980 (SCR 3.700). Kentucky [was] the first state to have a Code for paralegals adopted as a rule of Court.

Preliminary Statement

The availability of legal services to the public at a price it can afford is a goal to which the Bar is committed, and one which finds support in Canons 2 and 8 of the Code of Professional Responsibility. The employment of paralegals furnishes a means by which lawyers may expand the public's opportunity for utilization of their services at a reduced cost.

For purposes of this Rule, a paralegal is a person under the supervision and direction of a licensed lawyer, who may apply knowledge of law and legal procedures in rendering direct assistance to lawyers engaged in legal research; design, develop or plan modifications or new procedures, techniques, services, processes or applications; prepare or interpret legal documents and write detailed procedures for practicing in certain fields of law; select, compile and use technical information from such references as digests, encyclopedias or practice manuals; and analyze and follow procedural problems that involve independent decisions.

Purpose

Rapid growth in the employment of paralegals increases the desirability and necessity of establishing guidelines for the utilization of paralegals by the legal community. This Rule is not intended to stifle the proper development and expansion of paralegal services, but to provide guidance and ensure growth in accordance with the Code of Professional Responsibility, statutes, court rules and decisions, rules and regulations of administrative agencies, and opinions rendered by Committees on Professional Ethics and Unauthorized Practice of Law.

While the responsibility for compliance with standards of professional conduct rests with members of the Bar, a paralegal should understand those standards. It is, therefore, incumbent upon the lawyer employing a paralegal to inform him of the restraints and responsibilities incident to the job and supervise the manner in which the work is completed. However, the paralegal does have an independent obligation to refrain from illegal conduct. Additionally, and notwithstanding the fact that the Code of Professional Responsibility is not binding upon lay persons, the very nature of a paralegal's employment imposes an obligation to refrain from conduct which would involve the lawyer in a violation of the Code.

Sub-Rule 1

A lawyer shall ensure that a paralegal in his employment does not engage in the unauthorized practice of law.

Sub-Rule 2

For purposes of this rule, the unauthorized practice of law shall not include any service rendered involving legal knowledge or legal advice, whether representation, counsel or advocacy, in or out of court, rendered in respect to the acts, duties, obligations, liabilities or business relations of the one requiring services where:

A. The client understands that the paralegal is not a lawyer;
B. The lawyer supervises the paralegal in the performance of his duties; and
C. The lawyer remains fully responsible for such representation, including all actions taken or not taken in connection therewith by the paralegal to the same extent as if such representation had been furnished entirely by the lawyer and all such actions had been taken or not taken directly by the lawyer.

Sub-Rule 3

For purposes of this rule, the unauthorized practice of law shall not include representation before any administrative tribunal or court where such service or representation is rendered pursuant to a court rule or decision, statute, or administrative rule or regulation, which authorizes such practice by nonlawyers.

Sub-Rule 4

A lawyer shall instruct a paralegal employee to preserve the confidences and secrets of a client and shall exercise care that the paralegal does so.

Sub-Rule 5

A lawyer shall not form a partnership with a paralegal if any part of the partnership's activities consists of the practice of law, nor shall a lawyer share on a proportionate basis, legal fees with a paralegal.

Sub-Rule 6

The letterhead of a lawyer may include the name of a paralegal where the paralegal's status is clearly indicated: A lawyer may permit his name to be included in a paralegal's business card, provided that the paralegal's status is clearly indicated.

Sub-Rule 7

A lawyer shall require a paralegal, when dealing with a client, to disclose at the outset that he is not a lawyer. A lawyer shall also require such a disclosure when the paralegal is dealing with a court, administrative agency, attorney or the public, if there is any reason for their believing that the paralegal is a lawyer or is associated with a lawyer.

2. Codes of Ethics

Formal codes of ethics are another source of obligations and restrictions for both lawyers and paralegals. Although the state bar associations' codes of ethics are directed at attorneys and not paralegals, paralegals are indirectly affected and therefore must have a thorough knowledge of several key sections of those codes. Over the years the American Bar Association has taken the lead in developing codes of ethics for attorneys. In 1908 the Association adopted the Canons of Ethics, which in 1969 was replaced by the Code of Professional Responsibility and then in 1983 replaced by the Model Rules of Professional Conduct. Once each of these codes was adopted, the ABA then sought to persuade state bar associations to use their national model as the basis for their own state codes.[2] These state codes, in turn, are frequently incorporated into formal court rules.

The ABA's Code of Professional Responsibility consists of nine canons. These canons are broad statements of general norms. Each of the nine canons is supplemented by various Ethical Considerations and Disciplinary Rules. The Ethical Considerations (E.C.) are aspirational statements concerning the objectives toward which members of the pro-

---

2. During the early 1970s the ABA was very successful in persuading states to adopt its new Code of Professional Responsibility, but the Code generated relatively little controversy about changes made in the old Canons of Ethics. The ABA's adoption of the 1983 Model Rules of Professional Conduct was much more controversial, however, and widespread opposition to some features of the new code may slow the process of state adoption. The president of one state bar predicted that few states would adopt the Model Rules in toto. Flaherty, Ethics Fight: Round 2, Natl. L.J., Jan. 16, 1984, at 1, 8.

fession are supposed to strive — such as, "A lawyer should maintain high standards of professional conduct and should encourage fellow lawyers to do likewise."[3] Disciplinary Rules (D.R.), on the other hand, are mandatory in character. They establish a minimum level of behavior below which no lawyer can fall without being subject to a disciplinary action — such as, "A lawyer shall not form a partnership with a nonlawyer if any of the activities of the partnership consist of the practice of law."[4] The nine canons of the Code are cited below.

American Bar Association, Code of Professional Responsibility
(1969)

Canon 1: A lawyer should assist in maintaining the integrity and competence of the legal profession.

Canon 2: A lawyer should assist the legal profession in fulfilling its duty to make legal counsel available.

Canon 3: A lawyer should assist in preventing the unauthorized practice of law.

Canon 4: A lawyer should preserve the confidences and secrets of a client.

Canon 5: A lawyer should exercise independent professional judgment on behalf of a client.

Canon 6: A lawyer should represent a client completely.

Canon 7: A lawyer should represent a client zealously within the bounds of the law.

Canon 8: A lawyer should assist in improving the legal system.

Canon 9: A lawyer should avoid even the appearance of professional impropriety.

Canon 1 and its accompanying ethical considerations and disciplinary rules state in essence that lawyers should make sure that high requirements are established for entrance into the profession; that those who are in it should follow the rules; and that they should report colleagues who do not.

Through its ethical considerations and disciplinary rules, Canon 2 is primarily concerned with the topics of solicitation and advertising, specialization, and the amount and division of fees.

The material associated with Canon 3 deals with a lawyer's relationships with lay personnel. In addition to discussing delegation to paraleg-

---

3. E.C. 1-5.
4. D.R. 3-103.

als (E.C. 306), it also discusses relationships to banks, collection agencies, insurance companies, and so forth.

Canon 4 discusses the circumstances under which the confidences of a client can be revealed. E.C. 4-2 states in part that "It is a matter of common knowledge that the normal operation of a law office exposes confidential professional information to nonlawyer employees of the office, particularly secretaries and those having access to the files; and this obligates a lawyer to exercise care in selecting and training his employees so that the sanctity of all confidences and secrets of his clients may be preserved."

The material in Canon 5 deals with the proper handling of potential conflicts of interest. According to Canon 6 once the attorney takes on a client, he or she should devote the necessary time and energy to do the job correctly. Canon 7 discusses topics such as the proper and improper ways of communicating with adverse parties, witnesses, judges, and juries. It also covers aspects of trial conduct. Topics discussed in Canon 8 include seeking and holding political office and criticism of judges and other public officials. These E.C.s and D.R.s in Canon 9 are concerned primarily with conditions of employment and the use of clients' funds.

Some rules are presented as imperatives and use terms such as *shall* or *shall not,* and others use the permissive *may* or *should.* Although some rules establish obligations that are to be enforced through disciplinary action, others are merely descriptions of complex relationships. These formal codes of ethics are supplemented by formal opinions (of broad general interest) and informal opinions (of comparatively narrow scope and involving an infrequent problem) issued by the ABA and many state bar associations.[5]

The ABA Model Rules of Professional Conduct are made up of fifty rules grouped under the eight general topics of client/lawyer relationship, counselor, advocate, transactions with persons other than clients, law firms and associates, information about legal services, and maintaining the integrity of the profession. The following summary lists the topics covered by the ABA rules.

Summary of the American Bar Association Model Rules of Professional Conduct
(1983)

Client-Lawyer Relationship
1.1 Competence
1.2 Scope of representation

---

5. The practice of issuing advisory opinions in unauthorized practice of law cases has come under attack as being an anticompetitive device that violates the Sherman Antitrust Act. See Surety Title Ins. Agency v. Virginia State Bar, 431 F. Supp. 298 (1977).

1.3 Diligence
1.4 Communication
1.5 Fees
1.6 Confidentiality of information
1.7 Conflict of interest: general rule
1.8 Conflict of interest: prohibited transactions
1.9 Conflict of interest: former client
1.10 Imputed disqualification: general rule
1.11 Successive government and private employment
1.12 Former judge or arbitrator
1.13 Organization as the client
1.14 Client under a disability
1.15 Safekeeping property
1.16 Declining or terminating representation

Counselor
2.1 Advisor
2.2 Intermediary
2.3 Evaluation for use by third person

Advocate
3.1 Meritorious claims and contentions
3.2 Expediting litigation
3.3 Candor toward the tribunal
3.4 Fairness to opposing party and counsel
3.5 Impartiality and decorum of the tribunal
3.6 Trial publicity
3.7 Lawyer as witness
3.8 Special responsibilities of a prosecutor
3.9 Advocate in nonadjudicative proceedings

Transactions with Persons Other Than Clients
4.1 Truthfulness in statements to others
4.2 Communication with person represented by counsel
4.3 Dealing with unrepresented person
4.4 Respect for rights of third persons

Law Firms and Associations
5.1 Responsibilities of a partner or supervisory lawyer
5.2 Responsibilities of a subordinate lawyer
5.3 Responsibilities regarding nonlawyer assistants
5.4 Professional independence of a firm

Public Service
6.1 Pro bono public service
6.2 Accepting appointments

6.3 Membership in legal service organization
6.4 Law reform activities affecting client interests

Information about Legal Services
7.1 Communications concerning a lawyer's services
7.2 Advertising
7.3 Personal contact with prospective clients
7.4 Communication of fields of practice
7.5 Firm names and letterheads

Maintaining the Integrity of the Profession
8.1 Bar admission and disciplinary matters
8.2 Judicial and legal officials
8.3 Reporting professional misconduct
8.4 Misconduct
8.5 Jurisdiction

As was indicated in Chapter 1, both the National Association of Legal Assistants and the National Federation of Paralegal Associations have adopted codes of ethics for their members to follow. The NALA and NFPA codes follow.

National Association of Legal Assistants, Code of Ethics and Professional Responsibility
(1977)

Canon 1: A legal assistant shall not perform any of the duties that lawyers only may perform nor do things that lawyers themselves may not do.

Canon 2: A legal assistant may perform any task delegated and supervised by a lawyer so long as the lawyer is responsible to the client, maintains a direct relationship with the client, and assumes full professional responsibility for the work product.

Canon 3: A legal assistant shall not engage in the practice of law by giving legal advice, appearing in court, setting fees, or accepting cases.

Canon 4: A legal assistant shall not act in matters involving professional legal judgment as the services of a lawyer are essential in the public interest whenever the exercise of such judgment is required.

Canon 5: A legal assistant must act prudently in determining the extent to which a client may be assisted without the presence of a lawyer.

Canon 6: A legal assistant shall not engage in the unauthorized practice of law and shall assist in preventing the unauthorized practice of law.

Canon 7: A legal assistant must protect the confidences of a client, and it shall be unethical for a legal assistant to violate any statute now in effect or hereafter to be enacted controlling privileged communications.

Canon 8: It is the obligation of the legal assistant to avoid conduct which would cause the lawyer to be unethical or even appear to be unethical, and loyalty to the employer is incumbent upon the legal assistant.

Canon 9: A legal assistant shall work continually to maintain integrity and a high degree of competency throughout the legal profession.

Canon 10: A legal assistant shall strive for perfection through education in order to better assist the legal profession in fulfilling its duty of making legal services available to clients and the public.

Canon 11: A legal assistant shall do all other things incidental, necessary, or expedient for the attainment of the ethics and responsibilities imposed by statute or rule of court.

Canon 12: A legal assistant is governed by the American Bar Association Code of Professional Responsibility.

National Federation of Paralegal Associations, Affirmation of Responsibility
(1977)

Preamble

The paralegal profession is committed to responsibility to the individual citizen and the public interest. In reexamining contemporary institutions and systems and in questioning the relationship of the individual to the law, members of the paralegal profession recognize that a redefinition of the traditional delivery of legal services is essential in order to meet the expressed needs of the general public.

This Affirmation of Responsibility asserts that the principles recognized by the National Federation of Paralegal Associations are essential to the continuing work of the paralegal.

Through this Affirmation of Responsibility, the National Federation of Paralegal Associations recognizes the responsibility placed upon each paralegal and encourages the dedication of the paralegal to the development of the profession.

I. Professional Responsibility

The paralegal is dedicated to the development of the paralegal profession and endeavors to expand the responsibilities and the scope of paralegal work.

Discussion: There is room for a great deal of growth in the paralegal profession and an opportunity to tap human resources to assist an over-

burdened legal system. This Affirmation of Responsibility aims to establish a positive attitude through which the paralegal may perceive the importance, responsibility and potential of the paralegal profession and work toward enhancing its professional status.

II. The Role of the Paralegal and the Unauthorized Practice of Law

The paralegal performs all functions permitted under law which are not in violation of the unauthorized practice of law statutes within the applicable jurisdiction.

Discussion: The increase in the number of paralegals has given rise to much discussion concerning what the paralegal may or may not do. This development has prompted new interpretations as to what constitutes the practice of law, and thus it is unwise to delineate exactly or to restrict the types of tasks which the paralegal may perform.

However, this Affirmation of Responsibility insists on compliance with regulations governing the practice of law as determined by the applicable jurisdiction. It is not within the scope of the Affirmation of Responsibility to change or challenge any of these statutes.

Whenever the paralegal performs tasks related to the delivery of legal services, it is the responsibility of the paralegal to insure that the applicable unauthorized practice of law statutes are not violated and that the best interests of the public are met. To this end, it is the responsibility of the paralegal to be aware of legislation affecting the paralegal profession and the legal welfare of the public.

III. Competence and Education

The paralegal maintains integrity and promotes competence through continuing education.

Discussion: The growth of a profession and the attainment and maintenance of individual competence require an ongoing incorporation of new concepts and techniques. Continuing education enables the paralegal to become aware of new developments in the field of law and provides the opportunity to improve skills used in the delivery of legal services.

The paralegal recognizes the importance of maintaining an interest in the development of continuing paralegal education. Professional competence is each paralegal's responsibility. The exchange of ideas and skills benefits the profession, the legal community, and the general public.

IV. Client Confidences

The paralegal is responsible for maintaining all client confidences.
Discussion: The paralegal is aware of the importance of preserving

all client confidences. Such information is understood to be a vital part of the relationship between the paralegal and the client, facilitating the delivery of legal services. The confidentiality of this information is respected at all times.

V. Protection of the Public Interest

The paralegal upholds the responsibility of protecting public interests by contributing to the delivery of quality legal services and by maintaining a sensitivity to public needs.

Discussion: The paralegal should make every effort to educate the public as to the services and tasks that paralegals may render. Such services may be performed within the setting of a law firm, public agency, governmental agency, business or within a defined program specifically addressing the needs of increased legal services to the public, including *pro bono* work.

The paralegal should inform the public of the scope of duties that the paralegal may perform and should encourage the public to examine issues and to explore innovative means by which an increased availability of modern cost legal services may be obtained. It is also within the responsibility of the paralegal to maintain an interest in the development and continuation of paralegal education programs that address the public interest.

VI. Support of Professional Association

The paralegal recognizes the necessity of membership and participation in the professional association.

Discussion: One of the hallmarks of any profession is its professional association, founded for the purpose, among many others, of determining standards and guidelines for the growth and development of the profession. The paralegal profession is in a dynamic stage of growth. The ability of individual paralegals to determine the direction and quality of that growth depends largely upon the success of the paralegal association in providing effective representation of and communication among members of the profession. Through the professional association, the paralegal is able to promote a cooperative effort with members of the legal community, paralegal educators and the general public to improve the quality of paralegal participation in the delivery of legal services.

The role which the paralegal occupies in the legal system is, to some extent, the result of the cumulative and cooperative efforts of paralegals working through the paralegal association. The continued and increased contribution of paralegals to the delivery of legal services is dependent upon a further delineation of their skills, qualifications and areas of responsibility. It is, therefore, incumbent upon each paralegal to pro-

mote the growth of the profession through support of and participation in the endeavors of the paralegal association.

3. Bar Guidelines on the Use of Paralegals

As a supplement to their codes of ethics, several state bar associations have developed specific guidelines to be used by paralegals.[6] The Kentucky guidelines shown in section A1 above allow paralegals to perform a wide variety of legal tasks and provide explicit rules on such things as the use of a paralegal's name on a law firm's letterhead and methods of compensating the paralegal. It also places affirmative obligations on the paralegal.

In an attempt to influence the content of bar association guidelines, the National Association of Legal Assistants has published a set of model standards (see below) that include definitions of what a legal assistant is and who is eligible to hold such a position, the nature of the supervision that they require, the tasks that they can perform when properly supervised, and a listing of activities that are specifically prohibited.

National Association of Legal Assistants, Model Standards and Guidelines for Utilization of Legal Assistants Annotated
(1985)

Introduction

The purpose of this annotated version of the National Association of Legal Assistants, Inc. (NALA) Model Standards and Guidelines for the Utilization of Legal Assistants is to provide references to the existing case law and other authorities where the underlying issues have been considered. The authorities cited will serve as a basis upon which conduct of a legal assistant may be analyzed as proper or improper.

The Guidelines represent a statement of how the legal assistant may function in the law office. The Guidelines are not intended to be a comprehensive or exhaustive list of the proper duties of a legal assistant. Rather, they are designed as guides to what may or may not be proper conduct for the legal assistant. In formulating the Guidelines, the reasoning and rules of law in many reported decisions of disciplinary cases and unauthorized practice of law cases have been analyzed and considered. In addition, the provisions of the American Bar Association's Model Code of Professional Responsibility and the Model Rules of Professional Conduct, as well as the ethical promulgations of various state

---

6. These states include Illinois, Kentucky, New Hampshire, New York, and South Carolina. Several other states are in the process of developing such guidelines.

courts and bar associations have been considered in development of the Guidelines.

While the Guidelines may not have universal application, they do form a sound basis for the legal assistant and the supervising attorney to follow in the operation of a law office. The Model will serve as a definitive and well-reasoned guide to those considering voluntary standards and guidelines for legal assistants. If regulation is to be imposed in a given jurisdiction the Model may serve as a comprehensive resource document.

I. Preamble

Proper utilization of the services of legal assistants affects the efficient delivery of legal services. Legal assistants and the legal profession should be assured that some measures exist for identifying legal assistants and their role in assisting attorneys in the delivery of legal services. Therefore, the National Association of Legal Assistants, Inc., hereby adopts these Model Standards and Guidelines as an educational document for the benefit of legal assistants and the legal profession.

COMMENT: The three most frequently raised questions concerning legal assistants are (1) How do you define a legal assistant; (2) Who is qualified to be identified as a legal assistant; and (3) What duties may a legal assistant perform? The definition adopted answers the first question insofar as legal assistants serving attorneys are concerned. The Model sets forth minimum education, training, and experience through standards which will assure that one denominated as a legal assistant has the qualifications to be held out to the public in that capacity. The Guidelines identify those acts which the reported cases hold to be proscribed and give examples of services which the legal assistant may perform under the supervision of an attorney.

The three fundamental issues in the preceding paragraph have been raised in various cases for the past fifty years. In Ferris v. Snively, 19 P.2d 942 (Wash. 1933), the Court stated work performed by a law clerk to be proper and not the unauthorized practice of law required supervision by the employing attorney. The Court stated:

> We realize that law clerks have their place in a law office, and we recognize the fact that the nature of their work approaches in a degree that of their employers. The line of demarcation as to where their work begins and where it ends cannot always be drawn with absolute distinction or accuracy. Probably as nearly as it can be fixed, and it is sufficient to say that it is work of a preparatory nature, such as research, investigation of details, the assemblage of data and other

necessary information, and such other work as will assist the employing attorney in carrying the matter to a completed product, either by his personal examination and approval thereof or by additional effort on his part. The work must be such, however, as loses its separate identity and becomes either the product, or else merged in the product, of the attorney himself. (19 P.2d at pp. 945-46.) (See Florida EC3-6, infra at, Section IV.)

The NALA Guidelines constitute a statement relating to services performed by non-lawyer employees as approved by court decisions and other sources of authority. The purpose of the Guidelines is not to place limitations or restrictions on the legal profession. Rather, the Guidelines are intended to outline for the legal profession an acceptable course of conduct. By voluntary recognition and utilization of the Model Standards and Guidelines the legal profession will avoid many problems.

II. Definition

Legal assistants* are a distinguishable group of persons who assist attorneys in the delivery of legal services. Through formal education, training, and experience, legal assistants have knowledge and expertise regarding the legal system and substantive and procedural law which qualify them to do work of a legal nature under the supervision of an attorney.

COMMENT: This definition has been used to foster a distinction between a legal assistant as one working under the direct supervision of an attorney and a broader class of paralegals who perform tasks of a similar nature, but not necessarily under the supervision of an attorney. In applying the standards and guidelines it is important to remember that they in turn were developed to apply to the legal assistant as defined herein.

III. Standards

A legal assistant should meet certain minimum qualifications. The following standards may be used to determine an individual's qualifications as a legal assistant:

1. Successful completion of the Certified Legal Assistant (CLA™) examination of the National Association of Legal Assistants, Inc.;
2. Graduation from an ABA approved program of study for legal assistants;

---

* Within this occupational category some individuals are known as paralegals.

3. Graduation from a course of study for legal assistants which is institutionally accredited but not ABA approved, and which requires not less than the equivalent of 60 semester hours of classroom study;
4. Graduation from a course of study for legal assistants, other than those set forth in (2) and (3) above, plus not less than six months of in-house training as a legal assistant;
5. A baccalaureate degree in any field, plus not less than six months in-house training as a legal assistant;
6. A minimum of three years of law-related experience under the supervision of an attorney, including at least six months of in-house training as a legal assistant; or
7. Two years of in-house training as a legal assistant.

For purpose of these Standards, "in-house training as a legal assistant" means attorney education of the employee concerning legal assistant duties and these Guidelines. In addition to review and analysis of assignments, the legal assistant should receive a reasonable amount of instruction directly related to the duties and obligations of the legal assistant.

COMMENT: The Standards set forth suggested minimum qualifications for a legal assistant. These minimum qualifications as adopted recognize legal related work backgrounds and formal educational backgrounds, both of which should provide the legal assistant with a broad base in exposure to and knowledge of the legal profession. This background is necessary to assure the public and the legal profession that the one being identified as a legal assistant is qualified.

The Certified Legal Assistant (CLA) examination offered by NALA is the only voluntary nationwide certification program for legal assistants. The CLA designation is a statement to the legal profession and the public that the legal assistant has met the high levels of knowledge and professionalism required by NALA's CLA program. Continuing education requirements, which all CLA's must meet, assure that high standards are maintained. Certification through NALA is available to any legal assistant meeting the educational and experience requirements.

IV. Guidelines

These guidelines relating to standards of performance and professional responsibility are intended to aid legal assistants and attorneys. The responsibility rests with an attorney who employs legal assistants to educate them with respect to the duties they are assigned and to supervise the manner in which such duties are accomplished.

COMMENT: In general, a legal assistant is allowed to perform any task, which is *properly* delegated and *supervised* by an attorney, so long as *the attorney is ultimately responsible to the client and assumes complete professional responsibility for the work product.*

The Code of Professional Responsibility of the American Bar Association, EC3-6 states:

> A lawyer often delegates tasks to clerks, secretaries, and other lay persons. Such delegation is proper if the lawyer maintains a direct relationship with his clients, supervises the delegated work, and has complete professional responsibility for the work product. This delegation enables a lawyer to render legal services more economically and efficiently.

The ABA Model Rules of Professional Conduct, Rule 5.3 provides:

> With respect to a nonlawyer employed or retained by or associated with a lawyer, the lawyer:
>
> (a) Shall make reasonable effort to ensure that the person's conduct is compatible with the professional obligations of the lawyer; and
> (b) Is responsible for conduct of such a person that would be a violation of the Rules of Professional Conduct if engaged in by a lawyer if (1) the lawyer orders or ratifies the conduct involved; or (2) the lawyer is a partner in the law firm in which the person is employed, or has supervisory authority over the person, and knows of the conduct at a time when its consequences can be avoided or mitigated but fails to take reasonable remedial action.

The Florida version of EC3-6 provides:

> A lawyer or law firm may employ nonlawyers such as secretaries, law clerks, investigators, researchers, legal assistants, accountants, draftsmen, office administrators, and other lay personnel to assist the lawyer in the delivery of legal services. A lawyer often delegates tasks to such persons. Such delegation is proper if a lawyer retains a direct relationship with his client, supervises the delegated work, and has complete professional responsibility for the work product.
>
> The work which is delegated is such that it will assist the employing attorney in carrying the matter to a completed product either by the lawyer's personal examination and approval thereof or by additional effort on the lawyer's part. The delegated work must be such, however, as loses its separate identity and becomes either the product or else merged in the product of the attorney himself.

The Kentucky Paralegal Code defines a legal assistant as:

> . . . a person under the supervision and direction of a licensed lawyer, who may apply knowlege of law and legal procedures in rendering direct assistance to lawyers engaged in legal research; design; de-

velop or plan modifications or new procedures, techniques, services, processes or applications; prepare or interpret legal documents and write detailed procedures for practicing in certain fields of law; select, compile and use technical information from such references as digests, encyclopedias or practice manuals; and analyze and follow procedural problems that involve independent decisions.

Kentucky became the first state to adopt a Paralegal Code, which sets forth certain exclusions to the unauthorized practice of law:

For purpose of this rule, the unauthorized practice of law shall not include any service rendered involving legal knowledge or advice, whether representation, counsel or advocacy, in or out of court, rendered in respect to the acts, duties, obligations, liabilities or business relations of the one requiring services where:

A. The client understands that the paralegal is not a lawyer;
B. The lawyer supervises the paralegal in the performance of his duties; and
C. The lawyer remains fully responsible for such representation, including all actions taken or not taken in connection therewith by the paralegal to the same extent as if such representation had been furnished entirely by the lawyer and all such actions had been taken or not taken directly by the attorney. Paralegal Code, Ky. S.Ct. R. 3.700, Sub-Rule 2.

While the Kentucky rule is an exception, it does provide a basis for expanding services which may be performed by legal assistants.

There are many interesting and complex issues involving the use of legal assistants. One issue which is not addressed in the Guidelines is whether a legal assistant, as defined herein, may make appearances before administrative agencies. This issue is discussed in Remmert, Representation of Clients Before Administrative Agencies: Authorized or Unauthorized Practice of Law?, 15 Valparaiso Univ. L. Rev. 567 (1981).

In any discussion of the proper role of a legal assistant attention must be directed to what constitutes the practice of law. The proper delegation of work and duties to legal assistants is further complicated and confused by the lack of adequate definition of the practice of law and the unauthorized practice of law.

In Davies v. Unauthorized Practice Committee, 431 S.W.2d 590 (Texas, 1968), the court found that the defendant was properly enjoined from the unauthorized practice of law. The Court, in defining the "practice of law," stated:

According to the generally understood definition of the practice of law, it embraces the preparation of pleadings and other papers incident to actions of special proceedings, and the management of such actions in proceedings on behalf of clients before judges in courts. However, the practice of law is not confined to cases conducted in

court. In fact, the major portion of the practice of any capable lawyer consists of work done outside of the courts. The practice of law involves not only appearance in court in connection with litigation, but also services rendered out of court, and includes the giving of advice or the rendering of any service requiring the use of legal skill or knowledge, such as preparing a will, contract or other instrument, the legal effect of which under the facts and conclusions involved must be carefully determined.

The important distinguishing fact between the defendant in *Davies* and a legal assistant is that the acts of the legal assistant are performed under the supervision of an attorney.

EC3-5 of the Code of Professional Responsibility states:

It is neither necessary nor desirable to attempt the formulation of a single, specific definition of what constitutes the practice of law. Functionally, the practice of law relates to the rendition of services for others that call for the professional judgment of a lawyer. The essence of the professional judgment of the lawyer is his educated ability to relate the general body and philosophy of law to a specific legal problem of a client; and thus, the public interest will be better served if only lawyers are permitted to act in matters involving professional judgment. Where this professional judgment is not involved, non-lawyers, such as court clerks, police officers, abstracters, and many governmental employees, may engage in occupations that require a special knowledge of law in certain areas. But the services of a lawyer are essential in the public interest whenever the exercise of professional legal judgment is required.

There are many cases relating to the unauthorized practice of law, but the most troublesome ones in attempting to define what would or would not form the unauthorized practice of law for acts performed by a legal assistant are those such as Crawford v. State Bar of California, 355 P.2d 490 (Calif. 1960), which states that any act performed in a law office is the practice of law because the clients have sought the attorney to perform the work because of the training and judgment exercised by attorneys.

See also, Annot. "Layman's Assistance to Parties in Divorce Proceedings as Unauthorized Practice of Law," 12 A.L.R.4 656; Annot. "Activities of Law Clerks as Illegal Practice of Law," 13 A.L.R.3 1137; Annot. "Drafting of Will or Other Estate Planning Activities as Illegal Practice of Law," 22 A.L.R.3 1112; Annot. "Sale of Books or Forms Designed to Enable Layman to Achieve Legal Results Without Assistance of Attorney as Unauthorized Practice of Law," 71 A.L.R.3 1000; Annot. "Nature of Legal Services or Law-Related Services Which May Be Performed for Others By Disbarred or Suspended Attorney," 87 A.L.R.3 272. See also, Karen B. Judd, CLA, "Legal Assistants and the Unau-

thorized Practice of Law," Facts & Findings, Vol. VIII, Issue 6, National Association of Legal Assistants, May-June, 1982.

V

Legal assistants should:

1. Disclose their status as legal assistants at the outset of any professional relationship with a client, other attorneys, a court or administrative agency or personnel thereof, or members of the general public;
2. Preserve the confidences and secrets of all clients; and
3. Understand the attorney's Code of Professional Responsibility and these guidelines in order to avoid any action which would involve the attorney in a violation of that Code, or give the appearance of professional impropriety.

COMMENT: Routine early disclosure of the legal assistant's status when dealing with persons outside the attorney's office is necessary to assure that there will be no misunderstanding as to the responsibilities and role of the legal assistant. Disclosure may be made in any way that avoids confusion. If the person dealing with the legal assistant already knows of his or her status, further disclosure is unnecessary. If at any time in written or in oral communication the legal assistant becomes aware that the other person may believe the legal assistant is an attorney, it should be made clear that the legal assistant is not an attorney.

The attorney should exercise care that the legal assistant preserves and refrains from using any confidences or secrets of a client, and should instruct the legal assistant not to disclose or use any such confidences or secrets.

DR 4-101(D), ABA Code of Professional Responsibility, provides in part that:

A lawyer shall exercise reasonable care to prevent his employees, associates, and others whose services are utilized by him from disclosing or using confidences or secrets of a client . . .

This obligation is emphasized in EC4-2:

It is a matter of common knowledge that the normal operation of a law office exposes confidential professional information to non-lawyer employees of the office, particularly secretaries and those having access to the files; and this obligates the lawyer to exercise care in selecting and training his employees so that the sanctity of all confidences and secrets of his clients may be preserved.

While the ultimate responsibility for compliance with approved standards of professional conduct rests with the supervising attorney, a legal assistant should understand what he may or may not do. The burden rests upon the attorney who employs a legal assistant to educate the latter with respect to the duties which may be assigned and then to supervise the manner in which the legal assistant carries out such duties. However, this does not relieve the legal assistant from an independent obligation to refrain from illegal conduct. Additionally, and notwithstanding that the Code is not binding upon non-lawyers, the very nature of a legal assistant's employment imposes an obligation not to engage in conduct which would involve the supervising attorney in a violation of the Code. NALA has adopted the ABA Code as a part of its Code of Ethics.

VI

Legal assistants should not:

1. Establish attorney-client relationships; set legal fees; give legal opinions or advice; or represent a client before a court; nor
2. Engage in, encourage, or contribute to any act which could constitute the unauthorized practice of law.

COMMENT: Reported cases holding which acts can and cannot be performed by a legal assistant are few.

The legal assistant cannot create the attorney-client relationship. DeVaux v. American Home Assur. Co., 444 N.E.2d 355 (Mass., 1983).

The legal assistant cannot make court appearances. The question of what constitutes a court appearance is also somewhat vague. See, for example, People v. Alexander, 53 Ill. App. 2d 299, 202 N.E.2d 841 (1964), where preparation of a court order and transmitting information to court was not the unauthorized practice of law, and People v. Belfor, 611 P.2d 979 (Colo., 1980), where the trial court found that the acts of a disbarred attorney did not constitute an appearance and the Supreme Court of Colorado held that only the Supreme Court could make the determination of what acts constituted an appearance and the unauthorized practice of law.

The following cases have identified certain areas in which an attorney has a duty to act, but it is interesting to note that none of these cases state that it is improper for an attorney to have the initial work performed by a legal assistant. This again points out the importance of adequate supervision by the employing attorney.

Courts have found that attorneys have the duty to check bank statements, preserve a client's property, see and sign all pleadings, insure that all communications are opened and answered, and make inquiry

when items of dictation are not received. Attorney Grievance Commission of Maryland v. Goldberg, 441 A.2d 338, 292 Md. 650 (1982). See also Vaughn v. State Bar of California, 100 Cal. Rptr. 713, 494 P.2d 1257 (1972).

Attorneys have the responsibility to supervise the work of associates and clerical staff. Moore v. State Bar Association, 41 Cal. Rptr. 161, 396 P.2d 577 (1964); Attorney Grievance Committee of Maryland v. Goldberg, supra.

An attorney must exercise sufficient supervision to insure that all monies received are properly deposited and disbursed. Black v. State Bar of California, 103 Cal. Rptr. 288, 499 P.2d 968 (1972); Fitzpatrick v. State Bar of California, 141 Cal. Rptr. 169, 569 P.2d 763 (1977).

The attorney must insure that his staff is competent and effective to perform the work delegated. In Re Reinmiller, 325 P.2d 773 (Oregon, 1958). See also, State of Kansas v. Barrett, 483 P.2d 1106 (Kansas, 1971); Attorney Grievance Committee of Maryland v. Goldberg, supra.

The attorney must make sufficient background investigation of the prior activities and character and integrity of his employees to insure that legal assistants have not previously been involved in unethical, illegal, or other nefarious schemes which demonstrate such person unfit to be associated with the practice of law. See In the Matter of Shaw, 88 N.J. 433, — A.2d 678 (1982), wherein the Court announced that while it had no disciplinary jurisdiction over legal assistants, it directed that disciplinary hearings make specific findings of fact concerning paralegals' collaboration in nefarious schemes in order that the court might properly discipline any attorney establishing an office relationship with one who had been implicated previously in unscrupulous schemes.

VII

Legal assistants may perform services for an attorney in the representation of a client, provided:

1. The services performed by the legal assistant do not require the exercise of independent professional legal judgment;
2. The attorney maintains a direct relationship with the client and maintains control of all client matters;
3. The attorney supervises the legal assistant;
4. The attorney remains professionally responsible for all work on behalf of the client, including any actions taken or not taken by the legal assistant in connection therewith; and
5. The services performed supplement, merge with and become the attorney's work product.

COMMENT: EC3-6, ABA Code of Professional Responsibility, recognizes the value of utilizing the services of legal assistants, but provides certain conditions to such employment:

> A lawyer often delegates tasks to clerks, secretaries, and other lay persons. Such delegation is proper if the lawyer maintains a direct relationship with his client, supervises the delegated work, and has complete professional responsibility for the work product. This delegation enables a lawyer to render legal services more economically and efficiently.

VIII

In the supervision of a legal assistant, consideration should be given to:

1. Designating work assignments that correspond to the legal assistants' abilities, knowledge, training and experience.
2. Educating and training the legal assistant with respect to professional responsibility, local rules and practices, and firm policies;
3. Monitoring the work and professional conduct of the legal assistant to ensure that the work is substantively correct and timely performed;
4. Providing continuing education for the legal assistant in substantive matters through courses, institutes, workshops, seminars and in-house training; and
5. Encouraging and supporting membership and active participation in professional organizations.

COMMENT: Attorneys are responsible for the actions of their employees in both malpractice and disciplinary proceedings. In the vast majority of the cases, the courts have not censured attorneys for the particular act delegated to the legal assistant, but rather, have been critical of and imposed sanctions against attorneys for failure to adequately supervise the legal assistants. See, e.g., Attorney Grievance Commission of Maryland v. Goldberg, supra.

The attorney's responsibility for supervision of legal assistants must be more than a willingness to accept responsibility and liability for the legal assistant's work. The attorney must monitor the work product and conduct of the legal assistant to insure that the work performed is substantively correct and competently performed in a professional manner. This duty includes the responsibility to provide continuing legal education for the legal assistant.

Supervision of legal assistants must be offered in both the procedural and substantive legal areas in the law office.

In Spindell v. State Bar of California, 118 Cal. Rptr. 480, 530 P.2d 168 (1975), the attorney was suspended from practice because of the improper legal advice given by a secretary. The case illustrates that it is important that both attorneys and legal assistants confirm all telephonic advice by letter.

In all instances where the legal assistant relays information to a client in response to an inquiry from the client, the advice relayed telephonically by the legal assistant should be confirmed in writing by the attorney. This will eliminate claims if the client acts contrary to the advice given. It will establish that the legal advice given is in fact that of the attorney, not the legal assistant, and obviate any confusion resulting from transmission of the advice through the legal assistant.

The *Spinell* case is an example of an attorney's failure to supervise and educate his staff. Not only was the secretary uneducated as to the substantive provisions of the law, but more importantly, she was uneducated as to her duty and authority as an employee of the attorney.

IX

Except as otherwise provided by statute, court rule or decision, administrative rule or regulation, or the attorney's Code of Professional Responsibility; and within the preceding parameters and proscriptions, a legal assistant may perform any function delegated by an attorney, including, but not limited to the following:

1. Conduct client interviews and maintain general contact with the client after the establishment of the attorney-client relationship, so long as the client is aware of the status and function of the legal assistant, and the client contact is under the supervision of the attorney.
2. Locate and interview witnesses, so long as the witnesses are aware of the status and function of the legal assistant.
3. Conduct investigations and statistical and documentary research for review of the attorney.
4. Conduct legal research for review by the attorney.
5. Draft legal documents for review by the attorney.
6. Draft correspondence and pleadings for review by and signature of the attorney.
7. Summarize depositions, interrogatories, and testimony for review by the attorney.
8. Attend executions of wills, real estate closings, depositions, court or administrative hearings and trials with the attorney.
9. Author and sign letters provided the legal assistant's status

is clearly indicated and the correspondence does not contain independent legal opinions or legal advice.

COMMENT: Except for the specific proscription contained in Section VI, the reported cases, such as Attorney Grievance Commission of Maryland v. Goldberg, supra, do not limit the duties which may be performed by a legal assistant under the supervision of the attorney.

The Guidelines were developed from generally accepted practices. Each supervising attorney must be aware of the specific rules, decisions and statutes applicable to legal assistants within his jurisdiction.

4. Enforcement

The legal and ethical restrictions mentioned above are enforced through a variety of sanctions. Acts of fraud, bribery, obstruction of justice, and so forth can result in felony convictions and imprisonment. In most states violation of the unauthorized practice of law statutes can result in a misdemeanor conviction. Unauthorized practice of law statutes usually are enforced through injunctions and the threat of contempt charges.

Attorneys who breach ethical requirements can be reprimanded, suspended, or disbarred. A reprimand or censure is an announcement that the attorney's conduct has been found to be in violation of the code of ethics. A suspension means that the attorney is prohibited from practicing law during some fixed time period, and a disbarment constitutes a revocation of the person's license to practice. The specific mechanisms for imposing these sanctions vary from one state to another, but it is ultimately up to the state's judiciary to impose a suspension or a disbarment.

Because paralegals are not licensed, they cannot be suspended or sanctioned as attorneys can. Attorneys can, however, be sanctioned for the misdeeds of their employees because the codes of ethics hold them responsible for adequately supervising their lay employees. This gives attorneys a vested interest in sanctioning their own employees for any breach of their ethical duties and means that such employees will probably lose their jobs and have difficulty finding new ones.

To some extent, professional responsibility can also be enforced through tort liability.[7] In determining whether a professional is guilty of negligence, the courts look to see whether the defendant exercised the skill and knowledge normally possessed by members of that profession.[8] Furthermore, some courts have held that any violation of prescribed standards (such as codes of ethics or licensing statutes) constitutes negli-

---

7. See the discussion on torts at pages 125-132.
8. See Restatement (Second) of Torts §299A (1965).

gence per se.[9] Finally, breach of a confidential or fiduciary relationship constitutes an intentional tort.[10]

After a comprehensive analysis of the application of these principles to paralegals, John Wade concluded that if as a result of something having gone wrong the plaintiff is damaged, then the paralegal will not be judged by the standard of care expected of a lawyer

> as long as he (1) holds himself out only as a paralegal, (2) does not attempt to perform services outside the scope of the customary for paralegal personnel, and (3) conforms to the standard of care, skill, and knowledge normal for the paralegal. On the other hand, if he fails to make clear that he is only acting as a paralegal, or if he undertakes to render legal services outside the scope of his competency, he will be held to the higher standard applicable to the normal attorney.[11]

Lawyers on the other hand, can be held liable for a paralegal employee's negligence through the doctrine of *respondeat superior*.[12] The lawyer can also incur tort liability for improper selection of a paralegal, inappropriate delegation to that paralegal, or inadequate supervision of the person.[13]

B.   UNAUTHORIZED PRACTICE OF LAW

Despite the early distrust of lawyers that was noted in Chapter 1,[14] as American lawyers worked their way into positions of political power and influence, they sought to develop an exclusive franchise for legal business. Although these efforts to create and preserve their monopoly go all the way back to the colonial period, the greatest successes were achieved between 1920 and 1960.[15]

Prior to the twentieth century the bar associations focused on prohibiting unlicensed persons from appearing in court and prohibiting specified public officials like court clerks, bailiffs, and sheriffs from practicing law.[16] Then in the early 1900s more emphasis was placed on limiting potential competition from other professional groups (including

---

9. Id. 286, 288.
10. Id. 874.
11. Wade, Tort Liability of Paralegals and Lawyers Who Utilize Their Services, 24 Vand. L. Rev. 1133, 1140 (1971).
12. See the discussion on agency law at pages 146-147.
13. Wade, supra note 11, at 1145.
14. See page 4.
15. Christensen, The Unauthorized Practice of Law: Do Good Fences Really Make Good Neighbors — or Even Good Sense?, 2 Am. Bar Found. Research J. 159 (1980).
16. Id. at 180.

accountants, banks, collection agencies, insurance adjusters, life insurance agents, and realtors).

Since the 1960s, however, the bar has been in a more defensive position regarding the preservation of their monopoly. The courts have decided several major cases that undercut the bar's traditional position,[17] and in one state the voters approved a constitutional amendment giving real estate brokers and salespersons the right to perform certain legal tasks.[18]

1. Justifications for Restrictions

Although unauthorized practice of law statutes have historically been used to protect lawyers from competition from laypersons seeking to perform similar services for less money,[19] they are defended in public discussion and in the courts on the basis of the "public interest." Under the Model Code of Professional Responsibility, Ethical Consideration 3-1 declares that the prohibition against the practice of law by laypersons is "grounded in the need of the public for integrity and competence of those who undertake to render legal services." Rule 5.5 of the Model Rules of Professional Conduct states that "limiting the practice of law to members of the bar protects the public against the rendition of legal services by unqualified persons." The following statement from West Virginia State Bar v. Earley is typical of the manner in which courts have justified these restrictions:

> The justification for excluding from the practice of law persons who are not admitted to the bar and for limiting and restricting such practice to licensed members of the legal profession is not the protection of the members of the bar from competition or the creation of a monopoly for the members of the legal profession, but is instead the protection of the public from being advised and represented in legal matters by unqualified and undisciplined persons over whom the judicial department of the government could exercise slight or no control.[20]

However, as one author has pointed out:

> Courts have not required any factual showing that unqualified restraints on lay practice are necessary — or even closely related — to

---

17. See Faretta v. California, 422 U.S. 806 (1975); Goldfarb v. Virginia State Bar, 421 U.S. 773 (1975); Johnson v. Avery, 393 U.S. 483 (1969); Brotherhood of R.R. Trainmen v. Virginia *ex rel.* Virginia State Bar, 377 U.S. 1 (1964); Sperry v. State of Florida, 373 U.S. 379 (1963); NAACP v. Button, 371 U.S. 217 (1963); Moreley v. J. Pagel Realty Ins., 27 Ariz. App. 62, 550 P.2d 1104 (1976); Chicago Bar Assn. v. Quinlan Tyson, Inc., 34 Ill. 2d 116, 214 N.E.2d 771 (1966).
18. Ariz. Const. art. 26, 1 (1910, amended 1962).
19. Morgan, The Evolving Concept of Professional Responsibility, 90 Harv. L. Rev. 702, 707 (1977).
20. 109 S.E.2d 420, 435 (1959).

the states' interest in preventing incompetent assistance. Nor have courts inquired whether that interest could be realized through less restrictive means. Existing research in the most active areas of unauthorized practice enforcement suggests that states would have considerable difficulty making either demonstration.[21]

Indeed, one major empirical study found that only 2 percent of the 1,188 matters studied originated from complaints by dissatisfied customers, and few of those involved claims of incompetence.[22]

This appears to make little difference to the courts, though. In State ex rel Johnson v. Childe, for example, the court even concedes that Childe may have been more knowledgeable about the establishing of transportation and service rates for common carriers than most lawyers would be:

> It is urged as a defense that to acquire and possess the knowledge necessary to have reasonable skill and efficiency in the handling of matters relating to the fixing and revision of transportation and service rates and charges of common carriers requires years of intensive and undivided study which few lawyers, if any, have undertaken. This is not a defense. We do not doubt that respondent possesses high qualifications in the transportation rate field. But the fact that he can qualify as an expert in a particular field will not permit his engaging lawfully in the profession of the law without a license to do so.[23]

The court's real concern in the unauthorized practice of law area seems to focus on the ability of the judicial branch to exercise control over those who practice law. As Lloyd Derby has noted, lawyers possess basic legal skills and ethical restraints that their lay competitors do not. Writing in the California Law Review, Derby supports this position with references to those portions of the Code of Professional Responsibility that protect against conflict of interest and impose a strict fiduciary standard for attorney/client relations.[24]

2. Defining the Practice of Law

Although every state has some sort of statutory or judicially imposed restriction against the unauthorized practice of law, few statutes explicitly define the specific acts that constitute practicing law. Those that do attempt definitions speak in broad terms, such as

---

21. Rhode, Policing the Professional Monopoly: A Constitutional and Empirical Analysis of Unauthorized Practice of Law Prohibitions, 34 Stan. L. Rev. 1, 85 (1981).
22. Id.
23. 295 N.W. 381, 382 (1941).
24. A fiduciary relationship is one in which a person acts for another in a position of trust. See Derby, The Unauthorized Practice of Law by Laymen and Lay Associates, 54 Calif. L. Rev. 1331, 1363 (1966).

(1) representing others before judicial or administrative bodies;
(2) preparing legal instruments or documents which affect the legal rights of others; and
(3) advising others on their legal rights and responsibilities.[25]

Canon 3 of the Model Code says only that "A lawyer should assist in preventing the unauthorized practice of law," without making any attempt to specify what constitutes unauthorized practice. Indeed Ethical Consideration 3-5 states that

> It is neither necessary nor desirable to attempt the formulation of a single, specific definition of what constitutes the practice of law. Functionally, the practice of law relates to the rendition of services for others that call for the professional judgment of a lawyer. The essence of the professional judgment of the lawyer is his educated ability to relate the general body and philosophy of law to a specific legal problem of a client; and thus, the public interest will be better served if only lawyers are permitted to act in matters involving professional judgment. Where this professional judgment is not involved, non-lawyers, such as court clerks, police officers, abstracters, and many governmental employees, may engage in occupations that require a special knowledge of law in certain areas. But the services of a lawyer are essential in the public interest whenever the exercise of professional legal judgment is required.

Model Rule 5.5 states that

> A lawyer shall not: (a) practice law in a jurisdiction where doing so violates the regulation of the legal profession in that jurisdiction; or (b) assist a person who is not a member of the bar in performance of activity that constitutes the unauthorized practice of law.

In seeking to apply the concept of unauthorized practice of law to specific situations, the courts have developed several tests that they sometimes seek to apply. The first involves whether the activity in question requires legal skills and knowledge beyond that of the average layperson.[26] The problem with this standard is that accountants, real estate brokers, insurance agents, bankers, and other laypersons often know more about recent legal developments in their specialty than the average lawyer does.

A second approach focuses on whether the activity is one that traditionally has been performed by lawyers or is commonly understood to involve the practice of law.[27] This is obviously a rather vague standard

---

25. ABA/BNA Lawyers' Manual on Professional Conduct 21:8004 (1984).
26. See Baron v. City of Los Angeles, 469 P.2d 353, 86 Cal. Rptr. 673 (1970); Agran v. Shapiro, 127 Cal. App. 2d 807, 273 P.2d 619 (1954).
27. See State Bar Assn. of Arizona v. Arizona Land Title Tr. Co., 90 Ariz. 76, 366 P.2d 1 (1961); State Bar Assn. v. Connecticut Bank & Trust Co., 145 Conn. 222, 236, 140 A.2d 863, 870 (1958).

and subject to local variation. Furthermore, what does one do if the lawyers have traditionally performed a function that does not require special legal expertise? Can others be prohibited from doing a task simply because it traditionally has been performed by lawyers? A variation on this approach is to inquire as to whether the situation is one that is characterized by a personal relationship between lawyer and client.[28]

Still another approach that occasionally has been used by the courts considers whether the activity is frequently performed by laypersons as incidental to another business or transaction.[29] This approach provides some exemptions for accountants, bankers, real estate agents, and so forth but again leads to a great deal of local variation.

3. Applications to Laypersons

a. Courtroom Representation

The application of unauthorized practice statutes is least ambiguous in the area of courtroom representation. With very few exceptions, only licensed attorneys are allowed to present motions and argue cases in court.[30] Only a few minor courts of no record allow laypersons to represent others.[31] Prior to the United States Supreme Court's decision in Faretta v. California,[32] there was even some doubt about one's right to represent oneself in the courtroom. Although the courts have recognized a constitutional right to self-representation, they have rejected interpreting the sixth amendment right to counsel in such a way as to require the courts to allow a defendant who so wishes to be represented by a nonlawyer.[33]

A corporation is considered to be a legal person, but it obviously must be represented by a specific agent when it is involved in legal actions. Most states require the corporation to be represented by a licensed attorney and do not allow lay officers or employees to handle the case *pro se*.[34]

---

28. See New York County Lawyers Assn. v. Dacey, 21 N.Y.2d 694, 287 N.Y.S.2d 422, 234 N.E.2d 459 (1967); Oregon State Bar Assn. v. Gilchrist, 538 P.2d 913 (Ore. 1975).
29. See State Bar Assn. v. Guardian Abstract Title Co., 91 N.M. 434, 575 P.2d 943 (1978); In re New York County Lawyers Assn., 272 A.D. 524, 78 N.Y.S.2d 209, aff'd mem., 299 N.Y. 728, 87 N.E.2d 451 (1949).
30. See, for example, United States v. Stockheimer, 385 F. Supp. 979 (W.D. Wis. 1974), where Judge Doyle held that in the absence of any constitutional or federal statutory provision compelling him to forbid or not forbid the defendant's use of a lay assistant, he would use his discretion to allow it.
31. See, for example, Idaho Code §§3-104, 16-304 (Supp. 1969).
32. 421 U.S. 806 (1975).
33. Turner v. American Bar Assn., 407 F. Supp. 451 (N.D. Tex. 1975), aff'd, 539 F.2d 715 and 542 F.2d 56.
34. See Osborn v. Bank of United States, 9 Wheat. 738 (1824); Simbraw, Inc. v. United States, 367 F.2d 272 (3d Cir. 1966); Ramada Inns, Inc. v. Lane & Bird Advertising, 102 Ariz. 127, 426 P.2d 395 (1967); Briggs v. Schwalge, 341 Ill. App. 268, 93 N.E.2d 87 (1950). But see Prudential Ins. Co. v. Small Claims Court, 76 Cal. App. 2d 379, 173 P.2d 38 (1946); Burgess v. Federated Credit Serv., 148 Colo. 8, 365 P.2d 264 (1961); United Sec. Corp. v. Pantex Pressing Mach., 98 Colo. 79, 53 P.2d 653 (1936).

b. Administrative Representation

At the federal level the Administrative Procedure Act states that

A person compelled to appear in person before an agency or representative thereof is entitled to be accompanied, represented, and advised by counsel or, if permitted by the agency, *by other qualified representatives* (emphasis added).[35]

The Patent Office, the Social Security Administration, and the Department of Immigration and Naturalization have all made provisions for such lay representation.

In Sperry v. State of Florida,[36] the United States Supreme Court upheld the right of the Patent Office to authorize nonlawyers to practice before it. The court ruled that the Patent Office regulations in question were a legitimate exercise of authority that had been properly delegated by Congress. It further ruled that this congressional authorization superseded conflicting provisions of the state of Florida's attorney licensing act. Thus, even though the preparation and prosecution of patent applications for others constituted the practice of law under Florida statutes, these statutes could not be applied to the practices of a federal agency.

At the state level some statutes and administrative regulations also permit lay representation in many agencies. Workers' compensation boards, unemployment compensation boards, and public utility commissions are most apt to have made such allowances. Although the state courts usually have upheld these practices, in some instances they have struck them down as either being in violation of the state's unauthorized practice law or being a usurpation of the judiciary's inherent power to control the practice of law.[37]

c. Preparation of Legal Documents

The preparation of legal documents becomes an area in which it is frequently difficult to draw clear lines regarding what does or does not constitute the unauthorized practice of law. The court cases regarding this type of activity have generally arisen in the areas of real estate, divorce, workers' compensation, and estate planning.

In the real estate area some courts have applied the principle that it is permissible for laypersons to prepare standard business forms when such preparation is incidental to their business.[38] Thus in several states real estate agents and brokers have been allowed to draft sales contracts

---

35. 5 U.S.C.A. 555(b) (1972).
36. 373 U.S. 379 (1963).
37. West Virginia State Bar Assn. v. Earley, 144 W. Va. 504, 109 S.E.2d 420 (1959).
38. See Conway-Bogue Realty Inv. Co. v. Denver Bar Assn., 135 Colo. 398, 312 P.2d 998 (1957); Petitions of Ingham County Bar Assn., 342 Mich. 214, 69 N.W.2d 713 (1955); Hulse v. Criger, 363 Mo. 26, 247 S.W.2d 855 (1952).

and leases. This is especially true when they are merely filling in the blanks on standardized forms drafted by attorneys.[39]

Rosemary Furman attracted a great deal of media attention in her battle with the Florida State Bar Association over her divorce forms preparation service. Furman was a former court stenographer and legal secretary who opened her own secretarial service. For a $50 fee she would provide clients with the court documents they needed to file in order to obtain an uncontested divorce. She also sold kits for adoptions, name changes, power of attorney, wills, and bankruptcies. She is said to have handled as many as twenty divorces a week and serviced over 10,000 clients.[40] She informed her clients orally and in writing that she was not an attorney and did not have any attorneys working in her office.[41]

In 1977 the state bar started legal actions against her for unauthorized practice of law, and in 1979 the Florida Supreme Court held that she could sell preprinted court forms and general instructions on do-it-yourself divorces but she could not advise clients on the various remedies that were available.[42] Although she could type in the blanks with her client's answers, the client had to independently determine what those answers should be, and she was not allowed to modify their responses.[43] Indeed, she could not even correct their spelling errors.

When Furman continued her business after this decision, the bar association again took her to court alleging that she was violating the terms stated in the court's injunction to refrain from doing more than merely selling the forms and typing her client's answers. In April 1984 the Supreme Court of Florida held that she was in contempt of court, sentenced her to 120 days in jail, and ordered her to pay $7,802 in court costs. Ninety days of this sentence would be suspended if she did not violate the injunction during the next two years.[44] The governor (with the unanimous concurrence of his cabinet) suspended her sentence and reduced the court costs owed to $5,000 when she agreed to close her business.[45]

A similar set of rules appears to apply to laypersons who assist people in filing workers' compensation claims. Goodman v. Beall[46] and

39. State Bar Assn. of New Mexico v. Guardian Abstract & Title Co., 90 Ariz. 76, 366 P.2d 1 (1961); Creekmore v. Izard, 367 S.W.2d 419 (Ark. 1963).
40. Murry, Slugging It Out for Justice, 1 Legal Assistant Today 20, 22 (Summer 1984).
41. Id.
42. See section B3d of this chapter for further discussion on giving legal advice.
43. Florida Bar Assn. v. Furman, 376 So. 2d 378 (Fla. 1979). See also Colorado Bar Assn. v. Miles, 192 Colo. 294, 557 P.2d 1202 (1976); Delaware State Bar Assn. v. Alexander, 386 A.2d 652 (Del. 1978); Florida Bar Assn. v. Brumbaugh, 355 So. 2d 1186 (Fla. 1978); Florida Bar Assn. v. American Legal & Bus. Forms, 274 So. 2d 225 (Fla. 1973).
44. Murry, supra note 40, at 23.
45. Pearson, Update, 2 Legal Assistant Today 7 (1985).
46. 130 Ohio St. 427, 200 N.E. 470 (1936).

West Virginia State Bar Association v. Earley[47] both allowed laypersons to assist in the preparation and filing of standardized claim forms supplied by the commission as long as no special legal skill or knowledge was required.

Numerous cases forbid public stenographers, notaries, bank clerks, and insurance agents from assisting people in drafting wills.[48]

d. Giving Legal Advice

As the *Furman* case illustrates, a layperson can type a client's answers onto a standardized legal form but cannot advise the client as to which form should be used or how their answers should be worded. Other cases have reached similar results in the areas of immigration law.[49] It is also unauthorized practice of law for a nonlawyer to advise people as to their rights under workers' compensation laws,[50] their tax liability,[51] or how they should dispose of their property in planning their estates.[52]

Some fine lines have been drawn regarding the activities of insurance adjusters and collection agencies. Regarding the former, laypersons are allowed to estimate the value of a loss and in some cases negotiate a settlement of claims against the insurance company that employs them. However, they are not allowed to give legal advice or make legal recommendations.[53] Several courts have held that a collection agency is engaged in the unauthorized practice of law when it advises or threatens legal proceedings in an effort to collect a claim on behalf of a creditor.[54]

Although a layperson is not allowed to give a particular individual personal legal advice on a specific problem, some court decisions have allowed publications to offer general legal advise. New York County Lawyers Association v. Dacey[55] was one of several cases considering Nor-

---

47. 144 W. Va. 504, 109 S.E.2d 420 (1959).
48. See Biakanja v. Irving, 49 Cal. 2d 647, 320 P.2d 16 (1958); People *ex rel.* Attorney General v. Hanna, 127 Colo. 481, 258 P.2d 492 (1953); Grievance Comm. of Bar Assn. v. Dacey, 154 Conn. 129, 222 A.2d 339 (1966); Grievance Comm. of State Bar Assn. v. Dean, 190 S.W.2d 126 (Tex. Civ. App. 1945).
49. Florida Bar v. Moreno-Santana, 322 So. 2d 13 (Fla. 1975); Texas State Bar Unauthorized Practice Comm. v. Cortex, #C-3380 (Tex. Sup. Ct. 1985).
50. People *ex rel.* Chicago Bar Assn. v. Goodman, 366 Ill. 346, 8 N.E.2d 941 (1937); Hoffmeister v. Tod, 349 S.W.2d 5 (Mo. 1961).
51. In the Matter of New York County Lawyers Assn., 237 A.D. 324, 78 N.Y.S.2d 209, *aff'd mem.,* 299 N.Y. 728, 87 N.E.2d 451 (1949).
52. In re Florida Bar Assn., 215 So. 2d 613 (Fla. 1968); State Bar Assn. v. Osborne, 241 Ind. 375, 172 N.E.2d 434 (1961); People *ex rel.* Illinois State Bar Assn. v. Schafer, 404 Ill. 45, 87 N.E.2d 773 (1949).
53. See Herman v. Prudence Mutual Casualty Co., 41 Ill. 2d 468, 244 N.E.2d 809 (1969); State *ex rel.* Junior Assn. of Milwaukee Bar Assn. v. Rice, 236 Wis. 38, 294 N.W. 550 (1940); Wilkey v. State, 244 Ala. 568, 14 So. 2d 536 (1943).
54. See Berk v. State, 225 Ala. 324, 142 So. 832 (1932); In re Lyon, 301 Mass. 30, 16 N.E.2d 74 (1938); In re Shoe Manufacturers Assn., 295 Mass. 369, 3 N.E.2d 746 (1936); State *ex rel.* McKittrick v. C. S. Dudley & Co., 340 Mo. 852, 102 S.W.2d 895 (1937).
55. 21 N.Y.2d 694, 287 N.Y.S.2d 422, 234 N.E.2d 459 (1967).

man F. Dacey's How to Avoid Probate! The book consisted of about 310 pages of forms for *inter vivos* trusts, wills, and other related documents. It was accompanied by fifty-five pages of textual material with advice as to how the forms should be completed. In rejecting the conclusion that the publication of this book constituted unauthorized practice of law, the New York court concluded that the publication of a text that purports to tell what the law says did not constitute the practice of law because there was no personal contact that involved the establishment of a relationship of confidence and trust. There was no express or implied contract to perform a service. Finally, because every individual has a right to self-representation, the court reasoned that such do-it-yourself material could not be suppressed and the individual who chose to rely on this information had to assume the risks that accompanied a reliance on this type of information.

In contrast to the position taken by New York courts, the Florida Supreme Court issued an injunction against the advertisement, publication, and sale of a divorce kit sold for use in the no-fault dissolution of marriages.[56] In reaching this decision the Florida Supreme Court concluded that the information contained in the publication was so specific that it paralleled what customarily would be given by a lawyer to his or her client. Thus, it was not the sale of the forms per se but their being coupled with the specific instructions that constituted unauthorized practice. On the other hand, New York and Oregon have upheld the sale of such do-it-yourself divorce kits,[57] and California has even instituted a state-approved set of do-it-yourself will and trust agreements.[58]

4. Laypersons Supervised by Attorneys

The cases discussed in the previous section all involved the activities of nonlawyers who were working independently. However, when a layperson works under the proper supervision of a licensed attorney, that individual is allowed to perform various legal tasks that otherwise would be considered the unauthorized practice of law.

As mentioned in Chapter 1, the issuance of the ABA's Formal Ethics Opinion 316 on January 18, 1967, marked a major milestone in the paralegal movement because it clarified the nature of the duties that could be delegated to lay assistants. That opinion stated that

> A lawyer can employ lay secretaries, lay investigators, lay detectives, lay researchers, accountants, lay scriveners, nonlawyer draftsmen, or nonlawyer researchers. In fact, he may employ nonlawyers to do any task for him except counsel clients about law matters, engage directly in the practice of law, appear in court, or appear in formal proceed-

---

56. Florida Bar Assn. v. Stupica, 300 So. 2d 683 (Fla. 1974).
57. State v. Winder, 42 A.D.2d 1039, 348 N.Y.S.2d 270 (1973); Oregon State Bar Assn. v. Gilchrist, 538 P.2d 913 (Ore. 1975).
58. Granelli, Do-It-Yourself Wills Ready in California, Natl. L.J., Nov. 1, 1982, at 7.

ings as part of the judicial process, so long as it is he who takes the
work and vouches for it to the client and becomes responsible to
the client. In other words, we do not limit the kind of assistance the
lawyer can acquire in any way to persons who are admitted to the
Bar, so long as the nonlawyers do not do things that lawyers may not
do or do things that lawyers only may do.

In 1969 the ABA issued Ethical Consideration 3-6 clarifying the
circumstances under which delegation to laypersons was appropriate:

> A lawyer often delegates tasks to clerks, secretaries, and other lay
> persons. Such delegation is proper if the lawyer maintains a direct
> relationship with his client, supervises the delegated work, and has
> complete professional responsibility for the work product. This dele-
> gation enables a lawyer to render legal services more economically
> and efficiently.

The commentary accompanying Rule 5.5(b)[59] of the Model Rules states
that

> Paragraph (b) does not prohibit a lawyer from employing the ser-
> vices of paraprofessionals and delegating functions to them, so long
> as the lawyer supervises the delegated work and retains responsibility
> for their work.

Rule 5.3 further emphasizes the nature of the attorney's responsibility
for lay employees:

> With respect to a nonlawyer employed or retained by or associated
> with a lawyer:
>
> (a) A partner in a law firm shall make reasonable efforts to ensure
>   that the firm has in effect measures giving reasonable assurance
>   that the person's conduct is compatible with the professional
>   obligations of the lawyer;
> (b) A lawyer having direct supervisory authority over the nonlawyer
>   shall make reasonable efforts to ensure that the person's conduct
>   is compatible with the professional obligations of the lawyer; and
> (c) A lawyer shall be responsible for conduct of such a person that
>   would be a violation of the Rules of Professional Conduct if
>   engaged in by a lawyer if:
>   (1) the lawyer orders or, with the knowledge of the specific con-
>   duct, ratifies the conduct involved; or
>   (2) the lawyer is a partner in the law firm in which the person
>   is employed, or has direct supervisory authority over the
>   person, and knows of the conduct at a time when its con-
>   sequences can be avoided or mitigated but fails to take
>   reasonable remedial action.

---

59. A lawyer shall not assist a person who is not a member of the bar in the performance of
activity that constitutes the unauthorized practice of law.

Finally it should be noted that when lawyers use lay assistants, they are not allowed to share fees with them or form a partnership, association, or professional corporation with a nonlawyer if any of the activities of the partnership, association, or corporation involve the practice of law.[60]

a. Contact with Clients and People outside the Office

As long as paralegals clearly identify their lay status, they are able to deal directly with clients, adverse parties, other attorneys, witnesses, and other relevant people. The major limitations are that they cannot commit an attorney to represent them or negotiate fee arrangements for the attorney's services,[61] and they cannot give legal advice.[62] Paralegals can gather and summarize information from clients and can keep clients informed as to developments in the case but can only be conduits or relay devices. They can relay instructions from attorneys to clients but cannot provide their own opinions.

Laypersons may make telephone calls, send out correspondence, and in other ways interact with third parties on behalf of the client as long as they identify their status with the law firm and act only within the bounds of their delegated authority. In most states they are allowed to use business cards that contain the name of the law firm they work for as long as it clearly designates their lay status[63] but are not allowed to have their names listed on the firm's letterhead even though they are clearly designated as nonlawyers.[64]

b. Participation in Legal Proceedings

A layperson working under the supervision of an attorney can, of course, provide direct representation of clients in those situations discussed in sections B3a and B3b above in which lay representation is authorized for some administrative agencies and inferior courts. Thus, legal aid agencies frequently assign paralegals to handle government benefits cases involving administrative hearings.

A few states allow paralegals to answer calendar calls and make

---

60. Model Rule 5.4. Section (a)(3) of this rule does provide that "a lawyer or law firm may include nonlawyer employees in a compensation or retirement plan, even though the plan is based in whole or in part on a profit-sharing arrangement." See Lyons v. Swope, 154 Cal. App. 2d 598, 317 P.2d 121 (1957); Florida Bar Assn. v. Meserve, 372 So. 2d 1373 (Fla. 1979).
61. ABA Informal Opinions 875 (Sept. 23, 1965) and 998 (Aug. 26, 1967). DeVaux v. American Home Assurance Co., 444 N.E.2d 355 (Mass. 1983).
62. Ferris v. Snively, 172 Wash. 167, 19 P.2d 942 (1933).
63. ABA Informal Opinions 909, 1000, and 1185 and numerous state opinions. But see Los Angeles County Bar Assn., Opinions 346 and 332; New Jersey Bar, Opinion 296; Oregon Bar Assn., Opinion 238.
64. ABA Informal Decisions 619 and 845; ABA Informal Opinion 1000; and numerous state opinions. But see Ky. Code, Rule 3.7000; New York State Bar Assn., Opinion 500.

~~purely ministerial motions for such things as uncontested continu~~ances.[65] Although paralegals can apparently attend and observe depositions, they are not allowed to question the deponent on the record.[66]

When working under the supervision of an attorney, a layperson can, of course, perform the various "second chair" duties described in Chapter 10.[67]

c. Drafting Legal Documents

Lay personnel who are working under the supervision of an attorney can draft a wide range of legal documents from contracts to pleadings and briefs. However, the supervising attorney is responsible for approving the final draft. Such documents can be filed only with the approval of the attorney.

C. ETHICAL RESPONSIBILITIES OF PARALEGALS

The preceding sections have specified some of the restrictions that have been placed on the activities that paralegals can undertake. This section focuses on the ethical duties that accompany these roles. In evaluating these ethical duties, the paralegal should be familiar with the ABA standards for lawyers as well as their own paralegal organization's code of ethics.[68] Because supervising attorneys are ultimately held accountable for the actions of their paralegals, those paralegals must be sufficiently familiar with the ethical restrictions placed on attorneys to be certain that their behavior does not violate those standards.

1. Avoiding Unauthorized Practice of Law

The ethics codes of both the National Association of Legal Assistants and the National Federation of Paralegal Associations contain pronouncements against paralegals' undertaking tasks that constitute the unauthorized practice of law. Neither attempts to define what specific activities fall within the prohibited classification. Thus the paralegal must take careful note of the various principles discussed in section B above and be sure to avoid activities that constitute unauthorized practice in the state in which one works.

---

65. People v. Alexander, 53 Ill. App. 2d 299, 202 N.E.2d 841 (1964); New York State Bar Assn., Opinion 44.
66. People v. Miller, No. 238381 (Bakersfield Mun. Ct.). See the discussion of this case in Orlik, The Unauthorized Practice of Law and the Legal Assistant, 2 J. of Paralegal Educ. 120, 126 (1985).
67. See pages 423-424.
68. Canon 12 of the NALA code makes direct reference to legal assistants' being governed by the ABA's ethical code.

2. Maintaining Confidentiality

Section 4 of the Affirmation of Responsibility of the National Federation of Paralegal Associations states simply that

> The paralegal is responsible for maintaining all client confidences.

while Canon 7 of the National Association of Legal Assistant's code states that

> A legal assistant must protect the confidences of a client, and it shall be unethical for a legal assistant to violate any statute now in effect or hereafter to be enacted controlling privileged communications.

The ABA's Canon 4 stated simply that

> A lawyer should preserve the confidences and secrets of his client.

Model Rule 1.6 goes into much greater detail:

> (a) A lawyer shall not reveal information relating to representation of a client unless the client consents after consultation, except for disclosures that are impliedly authorized in order to carry out the representation, and except as stated in paragraph (b).
> (b) A lawyer may reveal such information to the extent the lawyer reasonably believes necessary:
>   (1) to prevent the client from committing a criminal act that the lawyer believes is likely to result in imminent death or substantial bodily harm; or
>   (2) to establish a claim or defense on behalf of the lawyer in a controversy between the lawyer and the client, to establish a defense to a criminal charge or civil claim against the lawyer based upon conduct in which the client was involved, or to respond to allegations in any proceeding concerning the lawyer's representation of the client.

This confidentiality is important because the lawyer cannot effectively serve the client without knowing all of the facts, and without this protection many clients would be reluctant to reveal potentially embarrassing or incriminating information to their attorney.

Model Rules 1.2(d) and 3.3(a)(4) create exceptions to the confidentiality rule in situations where protecting the client's confidentiality would constitute the lawyer's assisting the client in committing a crime or a fraud or in using false evidence. Another exception involves situations in which the attorney has knowledge that the client plans an action that is criminal and probably will result in death or substantial bodily harm to another person. If paralegals become aware of situations involving these exceptions, they must bring them to the attention of the supervising

attorney so that the attorney can determine the proper course of action
to be taken.

Closely related to this ethical obligation to protect confidentiality is
the attorney/client privilege. This is a matter of the rules of evidence and
is narrower than the scope of the ethical obligation. It protects the attorney from being compelled to supply information when called as a
witness, and the attorney's "work product" cannot be subpoened. This
protected work product includes private memoranda, written statements
of witnesses, and mental impressions, conclusions, or legal strategies
related to litigation. It is particularly important to note that this privilege
also covers paralegal employees; the paralegal's notes are also part of the
protected work product, and the paralegal cannot be compelled to reveal
confidential information that an attorney could not be compelled to
reveal.

Model Rule 1.6(a) requires the lawyer to invoke the attorney/client
privilege whenever it is applicable but then to comply with the final
orders of the court. This privilege belongs to the client so that any
decision to waive it rests with the client; the attorney must then act
accordingly.

3. Avoiding Conflict of Interest

Paralegals must also be careful in the way in which they respond to
situations that present possible conflicts of interest. A serious problem
could develop if the law firm for which a paralegal works takes a case that
involves a friend, relative, former employer, former client, or business
interest of the paralegal.

In general an attorney is not supposed to take a case that will
involve advocating against a client that is represented in another matter,
even if the new case has no relationship to the situation for which the
first client is being represented. Model Rule 1.7 spells out these limitations and recognized exceptions:

(a) A lawyer shall not represent a client if the representation of that
    client will be directly adverse to another client, unless:
    (1) the lawyer reasonably believes the representation will not
        adversely affect the relationship with.the other client; and
    (2) each client consents after consultation.
(b) A lawyer shall not represent a client if the representation of that
    client may be materially limited by the lawyer's responsibilities to
    another client or to a third person, or by the lawyer's respon-
    sibilities to another client or to a third person, or by the lawyer's
    own interests, unless:
    (1) the lawyer reasonably believes the representation will not be
        adversely affected; and
    (2) the client consents after consultation. When representation
        of multiple clients in a single matter is undertaken, the con-

> sultation shall include explanation of the implications of the common representation and the advantages and risks involved.

If a conflict will exist, the lawyer should decline to take the second case. If a conflict of interest arises after representation has already been established, the attorney should withdraw from the case according to the provisions of Rule 1.16.

Rule 1.9 states that after a lawyer/client relationship has been terminated, the lawyer should not represent another party with adverse interests in the same matter.

> A lawyer who has formerly represented a client in a matter shall not thereafter:
>
> (a) represent another person in the same or a substantially related matter in which that person's interests are materially adverse to the interests of the former client unless the former client consents after consultation; or
> (b) use information relating to the representation of the disadvantage of the former client except as Rule 1.6 would permit with respect to a client or when the information has become generally known.

Model Rule 1.8 specifies a number of specific transactions that are prohibited on the grounds that they constitute a real or potential conflict of interest. The transactions listed include entering into certain types of business relationships, preparing instruments that give some benefit to the lawyer or a family member of the lawyer, providing financial assistance to a client in connection with pending litigation, accepting compensation from third parties, and in situations where a lawyer is related (parent, child, sibling, spouse) to another lawyer, each is prohibited from representing clients whose interests will conflict with those of a client already represented by the attorney-relative.

Model Rules 1.11 and 1.12 cover conflicts that can arise when an attorney leaves government service to work for clients that were formerly in an adversarial relationship when the attorney worked for the government and in situations in which the attorney had been a judge, arbitrator, or law clerk to a judge.

Finally, Model Rule 1.10 considers conflicts that can arise out of an association with a particular law firm and the problems that can develop when one changes jobs:

> (a) While lawyers are associated in a firm, none of them shall knowingly represent a client when any one of them practicing alone would be prohibited from doing so by Rules 1.7, 1.8(c), 1.9, or 2.2.

(b) When a lawyer becomes associated with a firm, the firm may not knowingly represent a person in the same or a substantially related matter in which that lawyer, or a firm with which the lawyer was associated, had previously represented a client whose interests are materially adverse to that person and about whom the lawyer had acquired information protected by Rules 1.6 and 1.9(b) that is material to the matter.

(c) When a lawyer has terminated an association with a firm, the firm is not prohibited from thereafter representing a person with interests materially adverse to those of a client represented by the formerly associated lawyer unless:

    (1) the matter is the same or substantially related to that in which the formerly associated lawyer represented the client; and

    (2) any lawyer remaining in the firm has information protected by Rules 1.6 and 1.9(b) that is material to the matter.

(d) A disqualification prescribed by this Rule may be waived by the affected client under the conditions stated in Rule 1.7.

The term *firm* includes lawyers employed by the legal department of a corporation or a legal services organization as well as a private law firm. A lawyer who is changing firms has a continuing duty to preserve the confidentiality of information about former clients.

Although there do not appear to be any cases involving paralegals per se, there are cases in which various courts have considered the extent to which law clerks and other nonlawyer personnel must disqualify themselves due to a conflict of interest.[69] These cases are somewhat contradictory, however, and no clear standard for paralegal disqualification currently exists.[70] In a leading article on that topic Ronald Marquardt has proposed a standard that closely resembles the principles expressed in Model Rule 1.10. Paralegals who have worked on a specific client's case cannot work on another client's case in a substantially related matter, but other lawyers and paralegals who did not possess confidential information about the first client could.[71] Marquardt argues that the imputed disqualifications section of 1.10 should be modified in its application to paralegals so that the standard would be

> whether the paralegal gained information about the client which could not be obtained through traditional legal procedures such as depositions, interrogatories, information on file at the Secretary of State's Office, and typical courthouse records.[72]

---

69. See Consolidated Theaters v. Warner Brothers Circuit Management Corp., 216 F.2d 920 (2d Cir. 1954); State of Arkansas v. Dean Foods Products Co., 605 F.2d 380 (8th Cir. 1979); Towns v. Towns, 36 Cal. App. 2d 88, 96 P.2d 971 (1939); Prichec v. Tecon Corp., 139 So. 2d 712 (Fla. Dist. Ct. App. 1962), *cert. denied*, 146 So. 2d 375 (Fla. 1962); Garver v. Early, 58 Cal. App. 725, 209 P. 390 (1922); Pisa v. Commonwealth, 393 N.E.2d 386 (Mass. 1979).

70. Marquardt, Running with the Hares and Chasing with the Hounds: The Emerging Dilemma in Paralegal Mobility, 2 J. Paralegal Educ. 57, 75 (1984).

71. Id. at 78.

72. Id. at 80.

On the other hand, if the paralegal's knowledge was based on confidential information revealed by the client, the imputed disqualification would apply and the firm would be unable to take the case.

Paralegals therefore must always be alert to any possible conflicts. Whenever such conflicts exist, the supervising attorney should be notified immediately, in order that appropriate action can be taken to either disclose the conflict to the client or to withdraw from the case.

4. Avoiding Deception

Model Rules 3.3, 3.4, and 4.1 relate to the candor an attorney owes the court, opposing counsel, and third parties, respectively. All three prohibit the attorney from making statements or presenting evidence known to be false. Because paralegals act as agents for their supervising attorneys, they must live by the same restrictions. They should be especially familiar with the requirements of Rule 3.4 because there are times in which they communicate directly with opposing counsel, clients, and witnesses. It states that

A lawyer shall not:

(a) unlawfully obstruct another party's access to evidence or unlawfully alter, destroy or conceal a document or other material having potential evidentiary value. A lawyer shall not counsel or assist another person to do any such act;

(b) falsify evidence, counsel or assist a witness to testify falsely, or offer an inducement to a witness that is prohibited by law;

(c) knowingly disobey an obligation under the rules of a tribunal except for an open refusal based on an assertion that no valid obligation exists;

(d) in pretrial procedure, make a frivolous discovery request or fail to make a reasonably diligent effort to comply with a legally proper discovery request by an opposing party;

(e) in trial, allude to any matter that the lawyer does not reasonably believe is relevant or that will not be supported by admissible evidence, assert personal knowledge of facts in issue except when testifying as a witness, or state a personal opinion as to the justness of a cause, the credibility of a witness, the culpability of a civil litigant or the guilt or innocence of an accused; or

(f) request a person other than a client to refrain from voluntarily giving relevant information to another party unless:

(1) the person is a relative or an employee or other agent of a client; and

(2) the lawyer reasonably believes that the person's interests will not be adversely affected by refraining from giving such information.

In most cases there is no affirmative duty to inform an opposing party of relevant facts, but misrepresentation can occur if one affirms a statement made by someone else that is known to be false.

Model Rule 4.2 prohibits a lawyer from communicating directly

with the opposing party about a matter in which the lawyer has been retained, if he or she knows that the other party is represented by a lawyer. Therefore, a paralegal cannot interview the opposing party in a civil case or a codefendant in a criminal case without first receiving the permission of that party's attorney.

Model Rule 4.4 is of special importance to paralegals who do investigative or collections work. It states that

> In representing a client, a lawyer shall not use means that have no substantial purpose other than to embarrass, delay, or burden a third person, or use methods of obtaining evidence that violate the legal rights of such a person.

These restrictions mean that paralegals cannot misrepresent their identity or make other false statements in order to gain the confidence of a reluctant witness. Nor can any compensation beyond ordinary witness fees be offered as an inducement to testify.[73]

Another restriction imposed on attorneys and paralegals, but not applicable to police or private investigators, is the requirement that a conversation not be recorded without the consent of all parties.[74]

A person employed by an attorney to collect debts must operate under the same restrictions that apply to attorneys, rather than the less restrictive regulations that apply to independent collection agencies. For example, a lawyer or a paralegal may not tell the debtor that failure to pay may affect one's credit rating or reputation in the community.[75] No threat of criminal prosecution can be used,[76] and in some states debtors cannot be told that their employers will be contacted or their wages garnished.[77] A few states even refuse to allow an attorney or paralegal to threaten a civil law suit.[78]

5. Avoiding Solicitation

Although the new Model Rules specifically allow for attorneys to advertise through telephone directories, newspapers, periodicals, billboards, radio, and television,[79] they still contain prohibitions against certain types of solicitation. Rule 7.3 states that

> A lawyer may not solicit professional employment from a prospective client with whom the lawyer has no family or prior professional

---

73. E.C. 7-28.
74. See ABA Informal Opinions 1008 and 1009 (1967) and United States v. White, 401 U.S. 745 (1971).
75. See ABA Informal Opinion 303.
76. D.R. 7-105.
77. See Haddon, Ethical Considerations for Paralegals and Investigators, 5 Colo. Law. 157, 159 (1976).
78. Id.
79. See Model Rule 7.2.

relationship, by mail, in-person or otherwise, when a significant motive for the lawyer's doing so is the lawyer's pecuniary gain. The term "solicit" includes contact in person, by telephone or telegraph, by letter or other writing, or by other communication directed to a specific recipient, but does not include letters addressed or advertising circulars distributed generally to persons not known to need legal services of the kind provided by the lawyer in a particular matter, but who are so situated that they might in general find such services useful.

Although lawyers are permitted to pay for advertising, they are not allowed to pay another person for sending them clients. Thus, paralegals cannot go out and solicit clients on behalf of their employers.

D. SUMMARY

The practice of law has been limited to individuals who have been admitted to the bar (that is, are licensed to practice) in their respective states. This monopoly has been justified as a legitimate means of protecting the public from those who do not have either the necessary legal knowledge or the ethical responsibilities that admission to the bar is supposed to guarantee. Although persons have a constitutional right to act as their own attorneys, there is no right to be represented by someone else who is not an attorney.

The practice of law is not limited to those activities that take place in a courtroom. It also extends to the giving of legal advice and the preparation of legal documents. It is often difficult, however, to identify when the legitimate business activities of real estate brokers, tax accountants, and others cross over into the forbidden practice of law.

Lay appearances before administrative tribunals are sometimes allowed and at other times prohibited. It depends on whether the legislative branch and the administrative agency have authorized such practices and whether the courts have approved. State courts cannot restrict the rights of a federal agency to allow lay representation in its own tribunals even if the hearings take place in that state.

When paralegals work under the proper supervision of an attorney, they can legitimately perform functions that would otherwise be considered unauthorized practice. They cannot give legal advice or present substantive matters in court, but they can communicate with clients under the protection of the attorney/client privilege, and they can draft legal documents.

As professionals, paralegals have ethical responsibilities to their profession, their employers, and their clients. These responsibilities are spelled out in the codes of ethics of paralegal associations and indirectly through the bar associations' codes of ethics. In addition to avoiding the unauthorized practice of law, paralegals must maintain confidential-

ity, avoid possible conflicts of interest, avoid deception, and avoid solicitation.

KEY TERMS

attorney/client privilege

Code of Professional
  Responsibility

confidentiality

conflict of interest

disbarment

Disciplinary Rule

Ethical Consideration

formal opinion

informal opinion

Model Rules of Professional
  Conduct

privileged communication

professional reprimand

solicitation

suspension

unauthorized practice of law

REVIEW QUESTIONS

1. What are the primary sources of legal restrictions on the activities of paralegals?

2. Under what circumstances is a paralegal subject to tort liability for damages that resulted from the paralegal's errors?

3. What is the judiciary's justification for granting a monopoly to lawyers?

4. What tests have the courts developed for defining what activities constitute unauthorized practice of law?

5. Under what circumstances can a person receive legal representation from a person who has not been admitted to the bar?

6. To what extent can a layperson assist another in completing do-it-yourself divorce forms?

7. What activities are paralegals prohibited from undertaking even when they are operating under the supervision of an attorney?

8. What are the differences between the ethical requirement to maintain confidentiality and the attorney/client privilege? How are these concepts relevant to paralegals?

9. Under what types of circumstances would a paralegal be guilty of conflict of interest? Deception? Solicitation?

DISCUSSION QUESTIONS

1. To what extent is the state justified in giving licensed attorneys a monopoly on the right to practice law? In what ways does it serve

the public interest? Does it artificially inflate the cost of legal services?

2. In Faretta v. California the court emphasized that the government does not have a right to protect the defendant from his own incompetence as an attorney. Do you agree? Should the court have the power to protect persons from knowingly selecting a nonlawyer to represent them?

3. Do you agree with the manner in which courts have generally drawn the limits as to what real estate agents can and cannot do without engaging in the unauthorized practice of law? What about accountants, bankers, and insurance agents?

4. To what extent do you think justice was done in the *Furman* case? What do you think an appropriate resolution would have been?

5. How should paralegals who violate their ethical responsibilities be punished? Who should be responsible for determining if violations have occurred and for determining appropriate sanctions?

PROJECTS

1. Are the attorneys in your state subject to a code of ethics? Has it been adopted by your state's highest court? How does this code differ from the ABA's Code of Professional Responsibility and the Model Rules of Professional Conduct?

2. Investigate and report on the procedures that are used for disciplining attorneys in your state. How many attorneys are disciplined each year and for what types of offenses?

3. Have the bar associations in your state given any consideration to the adoption of official guidelines on paralegal usage? If so, report what actions they have taken to date and any probable actions they may take in the near future.

Table of Cases

(Italics indicate decisions that are partially reproduced in the text.)

497

Index